501

MUST-VISIT WILD PLACES

501

MUST-VISIT WILD PLACES

Bounty
Books

Publisher: Polly Manguel
Project Editor: Emma Beare
Designer: Ron Callow/Design 23
Production Manager: Neil Randles

Chapters Written By:
Canada – *Fid Backhouse and Joe Toussaint*
USA – *Fid Backhouse, Kieran Fogarty and Janet Zoro*
Mexico – *Kieran Fogarty*
Central America – *Kieran Fogarty*
Caribbean – *Jackum Brown and Janet Zoro*
South America – *Roland Matthews and Janet Zoro*
Africa – *Jackum Brown (Benin, Cape Verde, Cote d'Ivoire, Gabon, Gambia, Morocco, Tunisia, Senegal and Sierra Leone), Arthur Findlay (Djibouti, Ethiopia, Kenya, Malawi, Mozambique, Rwanda, Tanzania, Uganda and Zambia), Kieran Fogarty (Botswana, Lesotho, Namibia, South Africa and Swaziland), Joe Toussaint (Cameroon, Chad, Ghana, Mali, Mauritania and Niger), Janet Zoro (Egypt and Libya)*
Europe – *Fid Backhouse (Armenia, Latvia, Lithuania, Ukraine), Jackum Brown (Spain, Portugal and Italy), Arthur Findlay (Netherlands, British Isles and France), Kieran Fogarty (Denmark, Estonia, Finland, Iceland, Norway and Sweden), Roland Matthews (Austria, Czech Republic, Germany, Poland, Russian Federation, Slovakia and Switzerland), Joe Toussaint (Bulgaria, Hungary and Romania), Janet Zoro (Albania, Croatia, Greece, Serbia and Slovenia)*
Eastern Mediterranean – *Jackum Brown and Janet Zoro*
Middle East – *Jackum Brown*
Central Asia – *Kieran Fogarty and Joe Toussaint*
South Asia – *Jackum Brown and Janet Zoro*
South East Asia – *Arthur Findlay, Roland Matthews and Joe Toussaint*
East Asia – *Arthur Findlay and Kieran Fogarty*
Oceania & Antarctic – *Fid Backhouse and Roland Matthews*

First published in Great Britain in 2010 by Bounty Books,
a division of Octopus Publishing Group Limited

This paperback edition published in 2013 by Bounty Books,
a division of Octopus Publishing Group Limited
Endeavour House, 189 Shaftesbury Avenue, London WC2H 8JY
www.octopusbooks.co.uk

An Hachette UK Company
www.hachette.co.uk

Copyright © 2010, 2013 Octopus Publishing Group Limited

A CIP catalogue record is available from the British Library

ISBN: 978-0-753726-01-3

Printed and bound in China

Please note: We now know that political situations arise very quickly and a city or country that was quite safe a short time ago can suddenly become a 'no-go' area. Please check with the relevant authorities before booking tickets and travelling if you think there could be a problem.

The seasons given in this book relate to the relevant hemisphere. Be sure to check that you visit at the correct time.

Contents

Introduction

The dictionary defines the word 'wild' as describing uninhabited and unspoilt regions, and also plants or animals that live independently of humankind. But this evocative word has as many nuances as there are people who use it. For some unapologetic city lovers, a wild place is anywhere more than 30 minutes away from a decent restaurant, warm bath and comfortable bed. At the opposite extreme others feel the 'wildness' of a remote island can be ruined by a distant glimpse of another person. In between are those who simply want to appreciate the breathtaking variety of Nature's bounteous natural wonders. *501 Must-Visit Wild Places* provides an overview of many different types of wild place around the world, with the aim of surprising and satisfying every reader . . . whatever their definition of 'wild'.

Despite today's booming travel industry and easier access to parts of the world our grandparents had barely heard of, it is practically impossible for any individual to see more than a fraction of Planet Earth in a lifetime. And for reasons of climate and politics, there will forever be wilderness areas that are hard to reach. Always check in advance whether a wild place could also be a dangerous one – particularly near borders where there are hostilities or countries where extremists target tourists to try and score crude political points. Take official advice about travel and safety arrangements.

Even when nearer home common sense should prevail when going off the beaten track. Leave information with family or friends about the latest adventure and where you expect to be on certain dates. Take a detailed map, torch, lightweight warm-and-waterproof clothing, water and even a whistle with which to attract attention. More elaborate survival packs may be bought from specialist shops or made up following advice on adventure-travel websites.

It almost seems unfair to single out any of the amazing places featured in this book, but a perfect example of the unexpected is Dasht-e Lut in Iran. One of the hottest places on earth, it is such a hostile environment that no flora or fauna live there. However, it can be seen from settlements in the surrounding hills and is a quite remarkable sight. For most, it is enough just to have seen it from afar. Other extraordinary places are endangered by the number of visitors they attract, putting rare plants, animals and sometimes the landscape itself in jeopardy. It goes without saying (but is still worth repeating) that visitors must behave responsibly to help conserve precious wilderness areas. Observe basic rules such as not lighting fires in tinder-dry forests or digging up plants imagining that just one won't matter. And if advised to stay on tracks do just that. In Jamaica's Cockpit Country, a fascinating region, exploring tempting virgin forest off-trail can lead to disaster. In many places what appears to be solid rock is actually a deceptively thin layer covering deep sinkholes beneath.

Of course, it's not necessary to travel to distant lands to experience the untamed natural world. Some places that appear familiar in daylight – say a local wood – can seem very different in the moonlight when night birds call and badgers, foxes, stoats and weasels go about their business. Nature is full of surprises. A beautiful but sparse hillside in the west of England, grazed by sheep, became an extraordinary wild place in the autumn of 2009 when thousands of poppies in every shade from red to cream appeared spontaneously, having lain dormant throughout living memory. Unusually warm and sunny weather and a local farmer turning over a field to aerate the soil prompted this unexpected reclamation of the land by wild flowers. In a few short weeks they were gone.

Not everyone wants to visit truly wild places, preferring instead to visit the national parks that preserve some of the world's landscapes, animals and plants before returning to civilization for a good night's rest. And some of us have a deep desire to see a specific place or animal during our lifetime. It might be mountain gorillas in Rwanda or Royal Bengal tigers in Nepal, lemurs in Madagascar or the hundreds of thousands of water birds that rest at Lake Ichkeul in Tunisia . . . perhaps simply the sun setting over the Pacific from a lonely palm-fringed beach in the company of a loved one or true friends. Whatever the dream, it may be possible to make it come true. Hatch a firm plan, start saving and go with an enquiring mind and open heart.

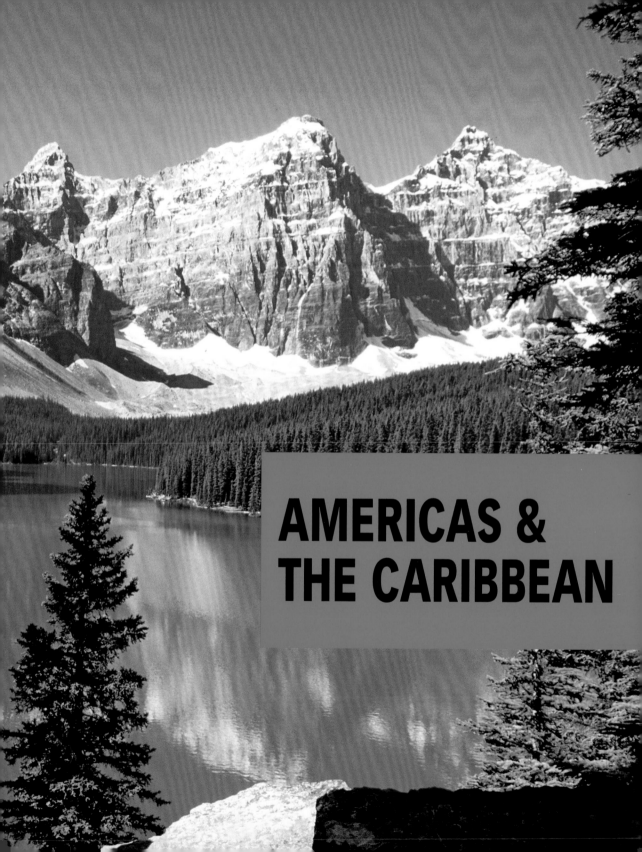

AMERICAS & THE CARIBBEAN

The Yukon

HOW TO GET THERE:
Fly into Erik Nielsen Whitehorse International Airport from various Canadian cities, including Vancouver and Calgary, or long haul from Europe in the summer months.
WHEN TO GO:
Late May to September
DON'T MISS:
Seeing Mount Logan, the second-highest mountain in North America after Mount McKinley in the neighbouring US state of Alaska. Mount Logan is in Yukon's spectacular Kluane National Park and Reserve.
YOU SHOULD KNOW:
The Klondike Gold Rush that began in the late 1890s was sparked by the discovery of a rich gold deposit in Rabbit Creek – which soon became Bonanza Creek in honour of the untold wealth it produced for the lucky ones among tens of thousands who stampeded to the then Yukon Territory from all over the world, seeking the life-changing wealth that could be found in the chill waters of the Klondike River and surrounding creeks. It was not in vain – nearly 400 tonnes of gold have been recovered from the Yukon since 1897.

The Ogilvie Mountains in beautiful Yukon

The Yukon in the far west is the smallest of Canada's three federal territories, and down from a desolate arctic coast in the north is one of the wildest – and loneliest – places on earth. Some 35,000 people occupy an area of 482,400 sq km (186,250 sq mi) and intrepid travellers should be prepared for an adventurous experience. It will start in Whitehorse, where most of the territory's population lives. This thriving city on the Alaska Highway is famed for its beautiful natural setting on the banks of the Yukon River.

However, Whitehorse is but a staging post for those visiting Yukon because they love wild places. The territory largely consists of the Yukon River's watershed, a fabulous landscape dotted with snow-capped mountains and long alpine lakes fed by glaciers, often surrounded by a sporadic growth of stunted trees. Elsewhere, dense pine forests surround crystal-clear meltwater lakes. The Yukon supports a fascinating diversity of animals and birds and the whole place comes alive with a brilliant display of wild flowers in summer. Vast areas are completely undeveloped, and much of the Yukon is strictly protected by National Park or other conservation status.

To the delight of visitors who want to get away from it all, the destructive hand of man has barely touched this pristine wilderness. That can make exploration difficult or even dangerous, but happily the locals are welcoming and many of them make a good living from helping visitors to enjoy individual access to this unique environment. Every settlement has its own airstrip and outfitter, while guides may be found for numerous rewarding activities ranging from simple backcountry trekking through angling, kayaking, skiing, snowboarding, dog sledding, ice climbing and snowmobiling to exceptional opportunities to observe the varied local wildlife.

Tuktoyaktuk and the Pingos

A visit to the atmospheric Pingo National Landmark on the Arctic Ocean shore of Canada's Northwest Territories is an experience to treasure. The protected area contains just eight pingos – hydrolaccoliths to the scientifically minded – but these are representative of 1,350 in the surrounding coastal region, a quarter of the world's pingo inventory. These amazing domed ice hills in areas of permafrost have been formed over time by the slow build-up of ice during the long winters. The landmark extends to 16 sq km (6 sq mi) and in addition to large pingos rising from the watery landscape, it contains fine examples of impressive frozen features like massive ice blocks and wedge ice that forms intricate patterns of interlocking tundra polygons.

An aerial view of snow-covered Tuktoyaktuk

Before accessing the landmark's unique natural wonders, it is necessary to reach Tuktoyaktuk, located on Kugmallit Bay in the far north. This is an Inuvialuit settlement usually referred to simply as Tuk, and many of the local Inuit people still follow a traditional way of life – hunting, fishing, trapping, herding caribou, picking berries and gathering driftwood. But to that may be added thoroughly modern oil and gas industries plus transportation (mainly by tugs and barges). Tuktoyaktuk has around 900 inhabitants, and some of them cater for determined travellers who wish to explore the nearby Pingo National Landmark, just west of town.

This is best done by boat. The National Landmark has no facilities, although plans for a boardwalk and interpretive trail have been mooted. The sensible option is to secure the services of a local guide – there are several specializing in individual pingo tours – although experienced wilderness hikers might prefer to go in on foot. As ever, the unpredictable Arctic weather can at best spell a change of plans and at worse mean real danger.

HOW TO GET THERE:
Only by air from Inuvik (small planes) to Tuktoyaktuk/James Gruben Airport
WHEN TO GO:
Summer (June to August), although in May, September and October the temperature is only just below zero. Adventurous winter visitors can drive the famous Tuktoyaktuk Winter Road along the frozen Mackenzie River's delta channels, as featured in TV's *Ice Truckers*.
DON'T MISS:
Ibyuk Pingo in the National Landmark, at 49 m (160 ft) the largest pingo in Canada and the world's second-biggest example of this rare natural feature.
YOU SHOULD KNOW:
The Pingo National Landmark has unique recognition as Canada's only National Landmark – not as a result of being the country's finest landmark, impressive though the pingos may be, but rather because they were the first area to be awarded such status . . . after which the programme was abandoned.

The majestic beauty of Pangnirtung Fjord on the Cumberland Peninsula

Cumberland Peninsula

Baffin Island in Nunavut is an outpost of Canada's northland and the demanding climate ensures that the population consists of no more than 10,000 hardy souls. This remote place is mostly above the Arctic Circle, so the sun sets in late November and does not rise again until mid January, while night doesn't fall at all during three-and-a-half summer months when eerie twilight is the darkest part of an endless day.

One unusual specialist leisure activity for which Baffin Island is well known is BASE-jumping, thanks to a profusion of high cliffs scattered around the island, but more traditional possibilities still seduce dedicated backcountry adventurers. One ideal destination is the east coast's Cumberland Peninsula, home to Auyuittuq National Park. The latter consists of classic Arctic wilderness, where granite mountains rub jagged shoulders with sweeping glaciers, rugged fjords and polar sea ice. The name means 'land that never melts' in the language of indigenous Inuits, although it remains to be seen whether global warming will eventually call for a rethink.

This opportunity to experience the majestic beauty of the Arctic is not for the unfit, faint-hearted or budget travellers. It's hard enough to reach the access points – Qikiqtarjuaq on Broughton Island or Pangnirtung – and registration is required at either park office. Would-be explorers must then attend an orientation session before proceeding to the park with a local guide by boat, snowmobile or dog sled, depending on the time of year. This is a harsh and dangerous land, and it is essential to go equipped for every eventuality – adjusting to the weather's rhythms and being prepared to sit out a sudden storm or high winds in a tent for days on end. But those prepared to meet the challenges posed by this extraordinary park will enjoy the experience of a lifetime.

HOW TO GET THERE:
The park can be reached only from Qikiqtarjuaq or Pangnirtung, which are served by scheduled or chartered light aircraft from the regional hub of Iqaluit.
WHEN TO GO:
March to May (overland access) or August and September (boat access). The park is inaccessible when the ice is breaking up or new-season ice has not yet formed, and winter conditions are treacherous.
DON'T MISS:
The rare but compelling opportunity to see polar bears in their natural habitat
YOU SHOULD KNOW:
It is almost certain that Baffin Island was the Helluland described in Icelandic sagas and artefacts indicating that the Vikings arrived on the island around AD 1000 have been found, along with mysterious evidence of even earlier European visitors.

Gwaii Haanas National Park

This unspoiled archipelago, consisting of 138 of the southernmost Queen Charlotte Islands, is 130 km (80 mi) off the coast of British Columbia. It is well worth the considerable effort needed to reach this magical destination from the mainland. Gwaii Haanas – or to choose a specific destination Gwaii Haanas National Park Reserve and Haida Heritage Site – is home to Canada's indigenous Haida Nation. These indigenous people have maintained a pristine environment protected by sustainable management practices. With the advent of NMCAR (National Marine Conservation Area Reserve) status, the whole of Gwaii Haanas from mountain top to seabed will be protected forever.

The dramatic landscapes of Gwaii Haanas Park range from rugged mountains to deep fjords, alpine meadows to sub-alpine tundra, wetlands to rushing streams, dense forests to beguiling lakes. Within this unique environment distinct flora and fauna have evolved. The local animals – such as a subspecies of black bear larger than its mainland cousin – have been joined by imported species such as beaver, squirrel, racoon and Sitka black-tailed deer. There are great opportunities for wildlife-watching and in addition to four-footed inhabitants there is a thriving bird population. This includes extensive seabird colonies where nesting can be observed along the shorelines between May and September. Bald eagles are a common sight and many different species stop off as they migrate along the Pacific flyway.

Carefully managed tourism is important to the local economy and for those who like to escape from the madding tourist crowd Gwaii Haanas is a destination to die for – happily, with a little help from knowledgeable local guides, it shouldn't come to that – although many backcountry expeditions are not without a whiff of danger that heightens the senses and intensifies the experience.

HOW TO GET THERE:
By boat (BC Ferries out of Prince Rupert), sea kayak, chartered helicopter or floatplane only (from Moresby Island)

WHEN TO GO:
Summer (spring or autumn for spectacular displays of migrating birds)

DON'T MISS:
Ninstints (officially Sgang Gwaay Llanagaay, which translates as 'Red Cod Island Village') – a UNESCO World Heritage Site on Anthony Island at the southern end of Gwaii Haanas that is a former Haida village site complete with a large collection of totems in their original locations and ruined cedarwood houses.

YOU SHOULD KNOW:
The best way to experience the natural beauty of Gwaii Haanas and its unhurried pace of life is to book an inclusive package that offers transport to the islands, rustic homestead accommodation, home-cooked food and local guides. This is definitely not a place where nature lovers can turn up and expect to explore unaided.

Mosquito Lake and Cumshewa Inlet form part of the dramatic and unspoilt landscape of Gwaii Haanas National Park.

Hotsprings Island

HOW TO GET THERE:
Kayak, boat or floatplane
WHEN TO GO:
May to September for *al fresco* hot
bathing
DON'T MISS:
The opportunity to see a pod of
orcas swimming past the island from
the relaxing vantage point of a
natural hot tub.
YOU SHOULD KNOW:
Camping is not permitted and there
are no facilities for overnight stays
on Hotsprings Island – a policy
policed by watchful guardians from
the Haida Nation.

Within Gwaii Haanas National Park Reserve is Hotsprings Island (also known as Gandla'kin), one of the jewels in the crown of the Queen Charlotte Islands. Located off the east coast of Moresby Island in Swanson Channel, the island's name suggests its principal attraction. There are numerous hot springs in British Columbia, many of which have been developed into popular tourist resorts. But other examples of this impressive natural phenomenon are found only in remote locations where a real effort is required from those who wish to experience the ultimate pleasure of relaxing in warm spa waters amid the spectacular scenery of an unspoilt wilderness.

Hotsprings Island definitely falls into the latter category, and simply getting there calls for a well-planned expedition. It can be independently reached by kayak, or alternatively it's possible to book a trip as part of a select group who will be decanted into kayaks from a mother ship, close to the island. These expeditions often take in more than Hotsprings Island during the day-long outing, offering a more general chance to explore the wondrous Gwaii Haanas Reserve. For those whose wallets are bigger than their muscles, hiring a floatplane from Moresby Camp might be the answer.

Whatever the means of transport, once on Hotsprings Island the first delight is exploring the fascinating shoreline and craggy interior. There are stunning scenic views out over Juan Perez Sound – a kayaker's paradise – and to the San Christoval Mountains back on the west coast of Moresby Island. After that, what could be more relaxing than dabbling in the island's dozen hot springs and seeps, followed by a plunge into one of the spring-fed hot pools carved into the volcanic rock – an experience sure to nourish both body and soul.

Jedediah Island

The phrase 'small but beautifully formed' could have been coined to describe British Columbia's Jedediah, located between the larger islands of Lasqueti and Texada in the Straits of Georgia, off Vancouver Island. Jedediah Island is a tranquil haven that extends to 2.4 sq km (0.9 sq mi). It was privately owned – and occupied – by the Palmer family until 1994, when it became a Marine Provincial Park following an enthusiastic fundraising campaign. In the best Canadian tradition, there are no restrictions on camping, so the place becomes a favourite summer haunt for kayakers, recreational boaters and wilderness campers attracted by the pristine marine environment.

The island has five bays that offer safe harbour, with excellent camping areas around Long Bay and more isolated possibilities along the eastern shore. The coastline has bays, rocky coves, deep anchorages and sandy beaches. The unspoiled interior consists of rocky outcrops surrounded by forest containing a variety of tree species including arbutus and the ubiquitous Douglas fir, plus flat meadow areas that are ideal for pitching camp. Although a campfire ban is sometimes in operation for safety reasons, fires are generally allowed below the high-tide mark. There are a number of established hiking trails that connect the secluded bays, and visitors are asked to keep to these designed paths rather than striking off into the woods (beware – there are sometimes bears on the island!). No formal campsites exist and the only facilities provided on Jedediah Island are four pit toilets, located near the most popular anchorages. Anyone with the get-up-and-go to reach Jedediah will be aware of the 'Leave no Trace' camping ethic, and respect it for the benefit of those yet to visit this enchanting island. The park is open all year round.

HOW TO GET THERE:
By kayak or boat from Lasqueti Island (itself served by passenger-only ferry from French Creek near Parksville on Vancouver Island)

WHEN TO GO:
The island gets quite busy at the height of the summer kayak-touring season (July and August), so those who prefer solitude should consider the months either side. The climate is mild and April to September are the driest months.

DON'T MISS:
Remains of an aboriginal fish weir, one of four archaeological sites to be found on Jedediah Island.

YOU SHOULD KNOW:
The first in a mysterious and gruesome series of discoveries that saw at least eight severed human feet found along British Columbia's shoreline was made on Jedediah by a visitor in August 2007. The lonesome foot was wearing a sock and size 12 Adidas training shoe.

Nootka Island

Waterborne adventure beckons for those willing to take to their boats and explore the fabulous waters that envelop Nootka Island off the wild west coast of Vancouver Island in British Columbia. The island is surrounded by Nootka Sound, Nuchatlitz Inlet, Esperanza Inlet, Tahsis Inlet and – last but by no means least – the mighty Pacific Ocean. There are a number of published kayak trails that offer inspiring vistas of breathtaking coastal scenery for those who prefer to remain afloat, but – however rewarding – that would mean ignoring the solid delights of Nootka Island itself.

The island covers an area of 534 sq km (206 sq mi). The main settlement is Yuquot (Friendly Cove), where modern-day British Columbia was born when the Royal Navy's Captain James Cook, who arrived in 1778, made the initial European contact with BC's First Nations people. The interior is a wilderness that cries out to be explored by the experienced hiker who loves solitude and magnificent scenery. Well-established trails along the island's awesome west coast and through the interior – that may be combined for a round trip – are not for the inexperienced.

Previous hikers have generally marked these routes but there are no man-made improvements, some of the terrain can be tricky and the risk of involuntary diversions in the wooded interior is ever present. Neither trail is excessively demanding, although the remoteness, unpredictable weather and lack of potential assistance in case of unexpected difficulties (take emergency medical supplies) makes exploring Nootka a true challenge. The circuit can be done in three days of hard tramping but a week is the ideal duration.

Approaching Yuquot on Nootka Island

There are black bears on the island so it is wise to avoid foods with a distinct aroma and store provisions high in a tree overnight.

Northern Rockies

In the top right-hand corner of British Columbia the Rocky Mountains offer amazing opportunities for lovers of wild places. Around 80 km (50 mi) to the southwest of Fort Nelson on the Alaska Highway is the Northern Rocky Mountains Provincial Park. Further along the road is Stone Mountain Provincial Park, while to the south is Kwadacha Wilderness Park. They offer a unique contiguous wilderness that encompasses much of BC's northeastern mountain landscape.

The largest is Northern Rocky Mountains Park. This expanse of valleys and ridges has a huge variety of water features – glaciers, lakes, large rivers, rushing mountain streams, waterfalls and white water. The smaller Stone Mountain Park encompasses some of Canada's finest scenery. For the truly dedicated backwoods explorer, the vast Kwadacha Wilderness does just what it says on the packet. It's accessed via a 150-km (93-mi) trail from the Alaska Highway at Trutch, or an alternative route from Sikanni Chief Canyon, and offers pristine wilderness untouched by the acquisitive hand of man. This one is for experienced trail hikers and horse riders only, although it is possible to be flown in.

HOW TO GET THERE:
Initial access is from the Alaska Highway but planned trips to the interior can be by helicopter, light aircraft, boat, horse . . . or on a pair of good old hiking feet.
WHEN TO GO:
May to mid September
DON'T MISS:
Magnificent vistas across Stone Mountain Park from the Alaska Highway – take a spare memory card for the camera.
YOU SHOULD KNOW:
It is essential to go equipped for every eventuality, even in summer. The parks are remote and weather conditions can change abruptly.

The diverse habitat of the three parks supports over 70 species of bird, including eagles, hawks, grebe, duck, various warblers and even the occasional Lapland longspur. Many and varied animals include bears (black and grizzly), wolves, wolverines, weasels, mountain goat, marten, moose, elk and deer. In addition to incomparable wildlife-watching, these parks together offer every sort of natural outdoor recreational activity. Hiking is pre-eminent, with plenty of opportunities to explore or follow established trails for anything from half a day to a week or more. To that may be added hunting, fishing, horse riding, boating, primitive camping and guided adventure tourism. Best of all, everything takes places against the backdrop of breathtaking Rocky-Mountain scenery.

Northern Rocky Mountains Provincial Park – serene at sunset

The Tarn at Jumbo Pass in the magnificent Purcell Mountains

Purcell Wilderness

It's a mouthful – namely the Purcell Wilderness Conservancy Provincial Park and Protected Area – but don't be put off by that. This is a magnificent 2,027-sq-km (783-sq-mi) mountainous landscape where no wheeled traffic whatsoever is permitted, and nor are the sort of helicopter drops well-heeled tourists sometimes use to reach remote wilderness destinations without doing the hard approach work. The park encompasses six large catchments that drain into the Columbia River and the original ecosystem is undamaged – remaining the only intact ecosystem in southeastern British Columbia. The park is located to the northeast of Nelson and northwest of Kimberley, not far from the US border with Washington, Idaho and Montana.

This is a truly wild place that offers determined explorers a choice of experiences to savour. Recreational opportunities include hunting, fishing, canoeing, horse riding, historic sites, climbing, wildlife observation and of course hiking. None of these is for the inexperienced, as the park contains no shelters, improved trails, public communications or supply points. Self-sufficient wilderness travellers will not be daunted, but indeed encouraged, by the opportunity to truly escape civilization. Even those who don't intend to venture into the park's rugged interior will find a day visit worthwhile, if only for splendid mountain scenery. Take plenty of food and drink plus warm clothing, as the weather can change rapidly and there are often violent thunderstorms in the summer months.

Overnight camping is permitted (beware of grizzly bears!) and there are established trails, notably the long Earl Grey Pass Trail (East and West) and the Fry Creek Trail. These should only be attempted with the help of proper equipment and trail maps. Other wildlife to look out for includes around 90 species of bird and animals such as elk, deer, wolverine, marten, beaver, coyote and wolves.

HOW TO GET THERE:
Drive to trailheads from Highway 31 at Meadow Creek (west side) or Highway 93/95 starting at Toby Creek (along gravelled roads used by heavy logging traffic).

WHEN TO GO:
May to September. Would-be hikers should note that many of the river crossings are difficult (or impossible) before the end of July, although a few have simple self-operated cable cars.

DON'T MISS:
Dewar Creek hot springs – too hot to bathe in, but an impressive sight as steaming water rich in minerals like sulphur, calcium and magnesium is expelled through a number of surface vents. The round trip (on foot or horseback only) should be made from the trail registry at the end of Dewar Creek Road. Allow four hours to hike there and back.

YOU SHOULD KNOW:
For those who don't like going it alone, there are a number of local guide-outfitters who offer hunting, fishing, wildlife viewing and hiking trips into the park, for one or more days.

Strathcona Provincial Park

Fishermen on Buttle Lake in Strathcona Provincial Park

Vancouver Island's largest provincial park was founded back in 1911, and now includes the UNESCO Biosphere Reserve at Clayoquot Sound, which encompasses three important watersheds in the western part of the park. Strathcona Provincial Park in the island's centre provides an unspoilt but relatively accessible tract of beautiful wild country. It can easily be reached from the surrounding communities of Gold River and Campbell River and – while there are no commercial tourist locations within the park – it does offer visitor facilities at Forbidden Plateau, Buttle Lake and Ralph River. These provide a choice of ideal bases with established campsites (mostly 'first come, first served') from which to sally forth into the surrounding wilderness, using a network of established trails.

Trekkers will find that this rugged wilderness offers a wonderful display of assorted wild flowers in the summer months, with mixed forest covering much of the park's valley areas and foothills. The most common trees are Western red cedar, Douglas fir, amabilis fir and Western hemlock. The intermediate slopes are home to creeping juniper, mountain hemlock and sub-alpine fir. Strathcona's rugged mountains remain snow-capped all year and higher elevations experience heavy snowfalls from November to March, with snow sometimes remaining on the ground, even at lower levels, until July.

The park is birdwatcher heaven, with unique Vancouver Island white-tailed ptarmigan to be found along with grouse, band-tailed pigeon, Steller's jay and many other species including chestnut-backed chickadee and red-breasted nuthatch. Many mammals common elsewhere in British Columbia are not found here, while some species are different from their mainland cousins. These include the Roosevelt elk, Vancouver Island marmot, Vancouver Island wolf and black-tailed deer. The most popular recreational activities are hiking, canoeing, climbing, cycling, fishing and snow sports. Horse riding is permitted only in the Kunlin area.

HOW TO GET THERE:
Car ferry from Vancouver or Horseshoe Bay to Nanaimo and drive north or, the shortest route, ferry from Powell River to the Comox Valley area and drive west. Alternatively fly-drive into Comox Valley or Campbell River, the principal access locations for the park.

WHEN TO GO:
This is an all-year destination but the park's campgrounds are only open from around the beginning of May to the end of September.

DON'T MISS:
Delta Falls in the southern section of the park – with an impressive drop of 440 m (1,440 ft) over three cascades, this is one of Canada's highest waterfalls.

YOU SHOULD KNOW:
Those interested in becoming proficient in backcountry exploration can take outdoor education courses in necessary wilderness skills at the Strathcona Park Lodge, cleverly combined with customized adventure holidays. This commercial facility is located close to the park along scenic Highway 28, the Gold River Highway.

Wood Buffalo National Park

Straddling the border between Northwest Territories and Alberta, south of Great Slave Lake, is Wood Buffalo National Park. The name contains a clue to the park's *raison d'etre* that would hardly tax Sherlock Holmes or Hercule Poirot – it was established in the 1920s to protect wood bison, a subspecies of the American bison (widely called 'buffalo') that once roamed North America's grasslands in huge numbers. Duly protected, the park's population of 5,000 is now the largest herd of free-ranging bison to be found anywhere.

The park is Canada's biggest, encompassing a vast tract of wilderness that ranges from Caribou Mountains to the Peace-Athabasca Delta, the world's most extensive inland delta. The park's headquarters is in the town of Fort Smith on Slave River, with an outstation at Fort Chipewyan, a hamlet dating from 1788 that is one of the oldest European settlements in Alberta. The park protects a perfect example of Canada's Northern Boreal Plains and enjoys UNESCO World Heritage Site status for its biological diversity.

In addition to the eponymous wood buffalo, the park contains much wildlife. Notable among many bird species is the critically endangered whooping crane. Animals include bears, moose, wolf, lynx, beaver and snowshoe hare. There is also a large population of garter snakes that have communal dens within the park. In addition to wildlife-watching, there are plenty of other attractions for intrepid adventurers. Not for the inexperienced, backcountry trips on foot or by canoe (along proven routes or breaking new ground) come as close to wilderness paradise as it's possible to get. The possibilities for hiking, canoeing, boating, camping and fishing – with or without guides – are virtually limitless. It's even worth the effort of going to Wood Buffalo National Park simply to enjoy the stunning landscapes.

Aspens turning a stunning shade of red in Wood Buffalo National Park.

Head-Smashed-In Buffalo Jump

If there's any lonely place in the world worth visiting for the name alone, it's surely this one. And Alberta's Head-Smashed-In Buffalo Jump tells it just as it is, or rather was. For this special natural feature provides an atmospheric reminder of the simple way of life followed by the indigenous people of Canada long before Europeans arrived – simple, perhaps, but certainly effective.

The location of this historic site is a point where prairie starts to give way to the foothills of the Rocky Mountains, close to the US border and not far from the town of Fort Macleod. The importance of this place in Native American history is underlined by its status as a UNESCO World Heritage Site and a fascinating museum of Blackfoot culture, consisting of an interpretive centre built naturalistically into a sandstone cliff. This presents archaeological evidence gathered from the area and explores the mythology, ecology, lifestyle and technology of the Blackfoot peoples. The centre also offers tepee camping and a number of special events take place throughout the year, including workshops on relevant aspects of native life such as moccasin-making and a Christmas festival that showcases the very best of First Nations' art and craft work.

But standing on the edge, the jump itself remains just as it has looked since time immemorial. This 10-m (33-ft) mini-cliff above a steep slope has been used to kill bison for at least five millennia. The buffalo were driven from a favoured grazing ground in the nearby Porcupine Hills, being channelled into narrowing lanes by many hundreds of artificial stone cairns before going off the 'jump' at full gallop. The resulting plunge broke legs and disabled these heavy beasts, allowing the hunters to finish them off at leisure and process the spoils at a nearby camp.

HOW TO GET THERE:
Drive for 18 km (11 mi) to the northwest of Fort Macleod on Highway 785.
WHEN TO GO:
Any time
DON'T MISS:
Fort Macleod's Fort Macleod – the town subsequently grew up around the North West Mounted Police barracks established in 1884 and now offers both the interesting NWMP Museum and a restored Main Street with original buildings dating back to 1874.
YOU SHOULD KNOW:
Don't be fooled into thinking that the correct name should be 'Broken-Leg Buffalo Jump'. According to legend, during one hunt a young Blackfoot decided to watch from below the jump, but was hit by falling buffalo and found dead beneath a pile of animals . . . with his head smashed in.

The poignant Head-Smashed-In Buffalo Jump

The strikingly ice-blue Moraine Lake

Valley of the Ten Peaks

Alberta's Banff National Park in the Rocky Mountains is Canada's oldest and covers an extensive 6,640 sq km (2,564 sq mi). It consists of mountainous terrain with many ice fields and glaciers. Dense pine forests that crowd the many lakes counterpoint the park's wonderful alpine landscapes. There has been tension between conservationists and developers since the park was established back in 1885, but one undoubted highlight of the park's protected wilderness is the magical Valley of the Ten Peaks, which contains ice-blue Moraine Lake.

Moraine Lake is an easy drive up from Banff along the Trans-Canada Highway (Highway 1), although a more scenic route is the parallel Bow Valley Parkway. There's parking at the lake's northeastern end, from whence the short but rewarding interpretive Rockpile Trail may be taken. It will take less than an hour to get to the top of the eponymous heap of rocks and back, with gentle ascent of rock-slab steps required. The effort will be rewarded by sensational vistas from viewpoints that overlook the lake and some of the famous Ten Peaks. The latter range from Deltaform Mountain at 3,424 m (11,234 ft) down to Mount Perren's still-impressive 3,051 m (10,010 ft). Together with nearby peaks like Mount Temple, Eiffel Peak and Mount Babel, they combine to create some of the most spectacular scenery to be found anywhere in the Rockies.

For those who want to overdose, a number of trails start at Moraine Lake, from two-hour round trips (Consolation Lakes) to five-hour there-and-back tramps (Eiffel Lake or Sentinel Pass) with unbelievable views all the way. Ultra-experienced wilderness hikers can follow the Perren Route – a hard day's climb up to the Neil Colgan Hut in a breathtaking location on the Fay Glacier.

HOW TO GET THERE:
From the small settlement of Lake Louise beside the Trans-Canada Highway, follow Moraine Lake Road to the south.
WHEN TO GO:
May to September. Awesome scenery means the Valley of Ten Peaks attracts a large number of visitors in high season (July and August).
DON'T MISS:
Photographing the stunning reflection of snow-capped peaks in the blue waters of Moraine Lake.
YOU SHOULD KNOW:
The Valley of the Ten Peaks featured on Canadian $20 bills issued in 1969 and 1979, and the exact spot from which the scene was captured is on the Rockpile Trail – known, inevitably, as 'Twenty-Dollar View'.

Writing-on-Stone Provincial Park

One of the most interesting places in Alberta contains both the works of nature and the impressive creations of Native Americans. The clue is in the name, for Writing-on-Stone Provincial Park contains the most concentrated collection of rock art to be found on the North American Great Plains. There are over 50 sites and literally thousands of pictographs (paintings) and petroglyphs (carvings), still held sacred by the Blackfoot people and other native tribes. The Canadian government has filed an application for UNESCO World Heritage Site status under the Blackfoot name *Áísínai'Pi*, meaning 'it is pictured'.

The park is a 17.8-sq-km (6.9-sq-mi) area of protected prairie, set against the glowering backdrop of Montana's volcanic Sweetgrass Hills to the south. It occupies part of the Milk River, where ancient grassland is broken by spectacular rocky outcrops. There are numerous coulees – low-lying areas with water in the bottom. This ideal habitat supports an impressive array of wildlife, which is high on the list of the park's sights. Animals include mule deer, pronghorn antelopes, bobcats, skunks, marmots, raccoons and northern pocket gophers. Among many bird species are prairie falcons, kestrels, cliff swallows and owls, along with pheasants and grey partridges. Reptiles include various frogs, spadefoot toads, tiger salamanders and assorted snakes.

But the park's unique attraction is the native rock art, dating back into the mists of time. Much was created by nomads passing through a sacred landscape consisting of the rocky hoodoos (stone spires) that adorn the park, and tells of the everyday lives and dramas of those who created them. From the mid 17th century the tales started to include the horses, guns and metal goods introduced by European incomers, whose influx would change and ultimately destroy the indigenous way of life in less than 150 years.

HOW TO GET THERE:
Drive in – the park is some 100 km (62 mi) southeast of Lethbridge and 45 km (28 mi) east of the Milk River settlement.

WHEN TO GO:
The park is open for camping at the official site (full facilities) all year round. High season is May to September.

DON'T MISS:
The fascinating North-West Mounted Police outpost, reconstructed exactly as was after a catastrophic fire destroyed the original shortly after World War I. It's part of the protected cultural site.

YOU SHOULD KNOW:
The most sensitive areas of the park have been named as a Provincial Historic Resource to protect the rock art from vandalism, graffiti and theft. Access to these areas is by official guided tour only. The Hoodoo Trail does provide access to freely available rock art but be warned – it gets very hot in summer.

Spectacular rocky outcrops are dotted throughout the park.

Agawa Canyon

There's an easy way and a hard way for those seeking to experience the natural delights of Northern Ontario's Agawa Canyon Wilderness Park. The park lies in a shallow canyon created by the erosive action of the Agawa River, between the Boreal Forest and Great Lakes-St Lawrence Forest regions. This ensures that the flora of both is represented along the well-wooded canyon, with an abundance of flowering plants in spring and summer.

The area was opened up when rail tracks were laid through the canyon in 1911, and exploited in the early 1950s when the railway company cleared a picnic area. And travelling by the Algoma Central Railway's Agawa Canyon tour train is still the easy way to visit the wilderness park, departing from the depot in downtown Sault Ste Marie. The city's grimy industrial area soon gives way to variegated woodland, rivers crossed by impressive trestle bridges and occasional panoramic vistas. It's over three hours each way, with just two hours to explore the canyon in between, choosing between five short nature trails that criss-cross the park area connecting a number of waterfalls. The experience is still very rewarding for anyone who does not have the time – or inclination – to hike in. That adds up to plenty of people and tour trains are usually packed.

But after the train has gone, those who make the effort to walk into this rugged wilderness park will more or less have the place to themselves. Even going the hard way is best essayed with a little help from the railway company. Seasoned hikers could plan their own expedition, but many prefer to opt for assistance from Algoma Central, which operates various lodges along the line. These offer the ideal starting point for a hiking trip to Agawa Canyon.

An aerial view of the railway line that runs through Agawa Canyon Wilderness Park

Algonquin Provincial Park

Smoke Lake in Algonquin Provincial Park

It may seem a curious suggestion, but the best place to start an exploration of Canada's oldest and most famous provincial park is in downtown Toronto. It is here that you will find the Art Gallery of Ontario, home to many of the works of Tom Thompson, Canada's greatest artist. Thompson spent every spring and summer hunting, fishing and canoeing in the park, and producing small studies of the landscape. He then returned to his studio in winter to develop these into larger oils on canvas which, almost unbelievably, were created using just four colours. Thompson's interpretations of Canada's wildernesses marked an epiphany in European settlers' attitudes to the country they had come to live in. The beauty of his work, as well as waking up a backward-looking art establishment, helped European Canadians to shake off their 'garrison mentality' and view the country around them no longer as 'Nature the Monster' but as a place of great beauty to be discovered and enjoyed.

It is possible to visit the museum in the morning, have a brunch of pancakes and maple syrup and be paddling a canoe on one of the park's many thousand pristine lakes in the afternoon. The park is vast and covers an area about one third the size of Wales. It has over 1,600 km (995 mi) of navigable waterways and innumerable hiking trails, which can be explored on skis, snowshoes or snowmobile in winter and on foot or on the water in summer. Its vast interior is characterized by maple-covered hills, fast-running streams, craggy ridges and spruce bogs. This environment supports a vast array of wildlife. Moose, black bear, beaver and wolves live alongside over 250 reported bird species and over 40 species of (non-poisonous) amphibians and reptiles. It is a place that the phrase 'Go explore' could have been written for.

HOW TO GET THERE:
Highway 60 runs through the south of the park; its northern section can be accessed from the trans-Canada Highway.
WHEN TO GO:
All year round
DON'T MISS:
Of all the sensory experiences available in the park, perhaps the most evocative of the Canadian wilderness is the howl of the wolf. Organized 'wolf howlings' take place in late summer when park staff encourage a wolf chorus by imitating their howls. Once the wolves get going on their own, they create a haunting melody that will live long in the memory.
YOU SHOULD KNOW:
Being within easy reach of Toronto and Ottawa, the park is very popular. Its sheer size means that it seldom seems crowded on the trails and waterways, but there is pressure on the campgrounds and chalets and advanced booking is recommended during the summer (July and August).

Sunset over George Lake in Killarney Provincial Park

Killarney Provincial Park

If there is one thing Ontario has in abundance it is well managed provincial parks ripe for exploration on foot, snowshoe or by canoe. Killarney Provincial Park, located by the shores of Georgian Bay, itself an arm of Lake Huron, is perhaps the most spectacular in terms of scenery. Although it is small for a Canadian park at just under 500 sq km (193 sq mi), it offers a spectacular variety of landscapes. Tectonic compression has changed the area's sandstone into brilliant white quartzite, producing the year-round appearance of snow-capped hills. This contrasts beautifully with the deep-blue lakes and the rich green of pine ridges. Ideally, active exploration should be punctuated with rests at the best vantage points to view the effects that sudden changes of light have on this striking palette. It was this landscape that drew the great artist A Y Jackson to the area and he later successfully lobbied for the creation of the Provincial Park, enjoyed by so many today.

Another Group of Seven artist, Franklin Carmichael, gave the world the iconic image of the park with his painting *La Cloche, Silhouette*, after which the park's most challenging trail is named. The La Cloche Silhouette Trail takes around a week to complete and leads the hiker into a sumptuous wilderness of glacial lakes, hardwood forest, rugged mountain peaks and stunning views over Georgian Bay. There are numerous shorter trails for those with less time or ambition. Each season clothes the park in a new kind of beauty and it provides the perfect habitat for bears, beavers, bobcats, moose and otters and over 100 species of birds.

HOW TO GET THERE:
Join Highway 637, 40 km (25 mi) south of Sudbury.
WHEN TO GO:
All year round
DON'T MISS:
The view of Silver Peak from the shores of David Lake
YOU SHOULD KNOW:
A compass and good navigational skills are a must, particularly for those thinking of going off-trail. The topography of the park can play tricks with the senses as the trails wind their way up and down this rugged terrain.

Point Pelee National Park

Point Pelee is a 20-sq-km (8-sq-mi) spit of land that juts out into Lake Erie, tapering gracefully to the point that marks the southernmost tip of mainland Canada. It sits on the same latitude as Northern California and has a climate that allows for the greatest biodiversity in Canada. Created by hunters in 1918 as an outdoor playground, soon the motorized transport that was liberating North Americans in their pursuit of pleasure started to strangle the park. Over the years the area became crammed with summer homes and campgrounds, and traffic jams often rivalled those of rush-hour in downtown Los Angeles.

Radical action was needed to restore the area to its former glory and, in 1972, a white knight duly arrived. Legislation was passed and all land was placed under the ownership of Parks Canada, traffic was greatly restricted and a transit service was introduced to ferry visitors deep into the park. Today, the area is home to a stunning array of wildlife. It marks the take-off point for a vast number of birds heading south and the assembly point for one of the greatest migrations on Earth. Each autumn, hundreds of thousands of monarch butterflies gather on the narrow peninsula, waiting for a kind wind to assist their passage over the Great Lake and eventually on down to Mexico.

Point Pelee contains an astonishing variety of terrain for an area of its size. Long sandy beaches invite a slow amble, while boardwalks take the visitor out deep into marshland. Canoeists can wend their way through reed beds and there are numerous trails suitable for navigation all year round. Large swathes of savannah grassland are framed by lush deciduous forest in a park that has something for everyone, whether they have two wings, four wings or none.

Point Pelee boardwalk enables visitors to wander deep into the marshes.

HOW TO GET THERE:
Follow the Parks Canada beaver signs from Highway 3 as you leave Leamington.
WHEN TO GO:
All year round – the shuttle service to the tip operates only from April to mid October.
DON'T MISS:
Standing at the very tip, virtually surrounded by the waters of Lake Erie, is probably the closest that a mere mortal can get to the feeling of walking on water.
YOU SHOULD KNOW:
While Point Pelee marks the most southerly point of mainland Canada, Pelee Island is its southernmost inhabited territory. Further out, the uninhabited Middle Island marks the most southerly point that flies the Maple Leaf flag.

Pukaskwa National Park

HOW TO GET THERE:
The only road access is via Highway 627, south of Marathon, Ontario.

WHEN TO GO:
The National Park is open all year round, but most of the facilities at the Hattie Cove campground are open only from May to October.

DON'T MISS:
Kayaking out from Hattie Cove as it joins the vast openness of Lake Superior (good weather only).

YOU SHOULD KNOW:
The lake shoreline is dotted with numerous sunken trenches known as the Pukaskwa Pits. They are anything up to 10,000 years old and were created by ancestors of the local Ojibwa people. Their function has caused much debate and theories about their use range from hunting hides to places of spiritual retreat.

Pukaskwa National Park is a place defined by its proximity to Lake Superior – the largest freshwater lake in the world. It is a body of water so vast that it can generate great storms capable of sinking large ships and hidden currents can have a dramatic effect even up stream, on the rivers that run into it. Its year-round average temperature is only a couple of degrees above freezing, perfect for alpine flora to blossom on its shores.

The park itself covers 1,878 sq km (725 sq mi) and is virtually all wilderness, with vehicular access available only to the administration office and the Hattie Cove campground. The landscape is boreal forest, typical of the Canadian Shield, where spruce and balsam mix with that most Canadian of trees – the Jack pine. Tip Top Mountain rises to a height of 630 m (2,067 ft) above sea level and marks the park's highest point, and a 60-km (37-mi) trail follows the shoreline of Lake Superior. A hop-on hop-off boat-hire service operates during the summer, allowing the hiker to experience this unique marine environment more intimately. The waters of Horseshoe Bay are shallow and calm enough to allow swimming in high summer and the shoreline is the perfect place to paddle a canoe.

Pukaskwa National Park includes land that is the domain of black bear, moose, beavers, wolves and the endangered woodland caribou. There is only one official campground (at Hattie Cove), but camping elsewhere in the park is allowed. It is important to be aware of the wildlife and secure all supplies above ground and adopt a policy of zero-trace camping by taking everything you brought in away with you.

Halfway Lake in Pukaskwa National Park

Cape Spear National Historic Site

Marking as it does the easternmost point of continental North America, Cape Spear attracts a lot of attention. People roll up to its historic lighthouse, take a quick photo as evidence that they were there and then roll away again. However, the centre of the Historic Site is well worth an hour or two of anyone's time. It contains the oldest surviving lighthouse in Newfoundland – dating back to 1836 – complete with renovated lighthouse-keeper's quarters. It was also the site of much activity in World War II, when a series of tunnels and fortifications was constructed. Two gun emplacements remain as a reminder of more troubled times.

The historic lighthouse on rugged Cape Spear

Venturing away from the man-made structures on show, the Cape has much to commend it to those looking for a rugged, if sometimes very bracing hike. The area has bird life in abundance, including shearwaters which can usually only be seen some distance out to sea. In late spring huge icebergs drift slowly down the coast like ghostly facsimiles of the rugged cape landscape. The headland is dotted with secluded coves which, in summer, provide the best land-based whale-watching in North America. Orca, minke and finback whales all come to feed on herring and capelin in the waters off the cape. Harbour seals, otters and dolphins may also be observed from these natural vantage points.

Great waves crash against the shore and high winds pummel the headland almost all year round. The cape has a good system of hiking trails and it is essential to keep to them, no matter how benign the weather may seem. It is a place of great beauty for those who like nature at its most raw. Standing on the edge of a mighty continent, it is easy to feel humbled by the forces of nature that have shaped this craggy promontory.

HOW TO GET THERE:
Take Highway 11 (Cape Spear Drive) from St John's, Newfoundland.
WHEN TO GO:
The grounds are open all year round. The lighthouse is open from mid May to mid October.
DON'T MISS:
Watching the waves roll in from Blackhead. This is particularly impressive in late spring when the water is laden with ice.
YOU SHOULD KNOW:
Cape Spear is so called not for its shape, although it does look like a giant blunt arrowhead. Rather it is a corruption of the Portuguese *Cabo da Esperança* – literally, Cape of Hope.

Cape St Mary's Ecological Reserve

Located at the very tip of Newfoundland's Avalon Peninsula, Cape St Mary's Ecological Reserve is about as wild a place as you could wish to find in North America. The wind roars so ferociously off the Atlantic Ocean that 100-year-old trees struggle to reach waist height. Waves crash against the rapidly eroding cliffs that mark the reserve's land boundary, while mist and fog shroud the peninsula most days.

Ecotourists come to admire the gannets that perch precariously on the rock face.

HOW TO GET THERE:
A two- or three-hour drive from St John's, Newfoundland, via Highway 90
WHEN TO GO:
Best between May and July.
DON'T MISS:
The performances put on by the gannets. They mate for life and have only one chick that spends the first weeks of its life perched perilously on the rock face, battered by wind and rain, held on by a harness-like nest of woven seaweed. Parent birds greet each other in both French and English styles (appropriately for Canada) – with a raised beak salute followed by alternating cheek beak taps.
YOU SHOULD KNOW:
The reserve has an interpretive centre which is the perfect place to start a visit to the area. Staff there will advise on current conditions and the best places to see the wildlife.

But when the wind abates and the fog clears one of the most beautiful seascapes on Earth is revealed. A lush green carpet of grass and moss covers the headlands and the land falls sharply away into the azure waters of the North Atlantic.

The reserve was established in 1983 and covers both the headland and the immediate waters around it. The main objective of the reserve was to create a low-pollution environment where birdlife could thrive. The result is a birdwatcher's paradise. Out to sea, the appropriately named Bird Rock is a limestone outcrop which has become separated from the mainland by years of erosion. Its detachment means that it is free from predators and pearly white gannets flourish to the point that every square inch of the island is occupied by them. Kittiwakes, gannets and murres all plunge into the fish-rich waters in their thousands, making the sea fizz with activity.

Great care should be taken while walking around the reserve, especially when conditions are misty or wet underfoot. As befits a wilderness, there are no signs warning you of the dangers. But, if you come well equipped and take extra care, the reserve offers many fantastic vantage points from which to witness the everyday trials and tribulations of vast colonies of majestic seabirds.

Gulf of St Lawrence

In geographical science the term 'gulf' is used to describe a partly landlocked sea and although the Gulf of St Lawrence (Golfe du Saint-Laurent) seems to fit the bill, it is a misnomer. In reality the 'Gulf' is the estuary of a 'super-river' formed at the end of the last ice age. The colossal erosive powers of the river carved out a huge basin and, once the melt had finished, the sea levels rose and saltwater pushed the freshwater of the river back to leave what is now the world's largest estuary.

The Gulf of St Lawrence is massive, covering an area of around 234,000 sq km (90,350 sq mi). It is bounded by Nova Scotia to the south, Newfoundland to the east, Labrador to the north, New Brunswick to the west and is of immense strategic value as it links the Great Lakes to the sea via the St Lawrence River and Seaway. It contains many of the Maritimes' most beautiful and formidable islands, including Prince Edward and Bonaventure Islands as well as the Magdalen Archipelago. Cruise ships that ply their trade in the Gulf in summer can take weeks to complete their tours, yet only scratch the surface of discovery.

The Gulf has long been of vital importance and many First Nations bands chose to live on its edge to exploit its fish-rich waters. Ever since its discovery by Europeans in 1534 it has been a vital shipping route into Canada and the point at which the Gulf flows into the river is named the Jacques Cartier Strait, after its European discoverer. The lands around the Gulf are home to moose, caribou, bears and beavers, while its waters contain over 200 species of fish, which provide food for vast colonies of seals and huge pods of whales.

HOW TO GET THERE:
By air to St John's, Newfoundland, or by boat from Quebec City
WHEN TO GO:
The Gulf is usually ice free from May to November.
DON'T MISS:
Port Aux Basques – a beautiful old French fishing station right at the very tip of Newfoundland as it juts out into the Gulf.
YOU SHOULD KNOW:
Although ice adds to the stark winter beauty of the area, ice floes are a hazard to shipping during the spring melt. The Canadian Coastguard runs a fleet of 18 icebreakers to keep their eastern trade routes open.

Limestone cliffs overlook the Gulf of St Lawrence.

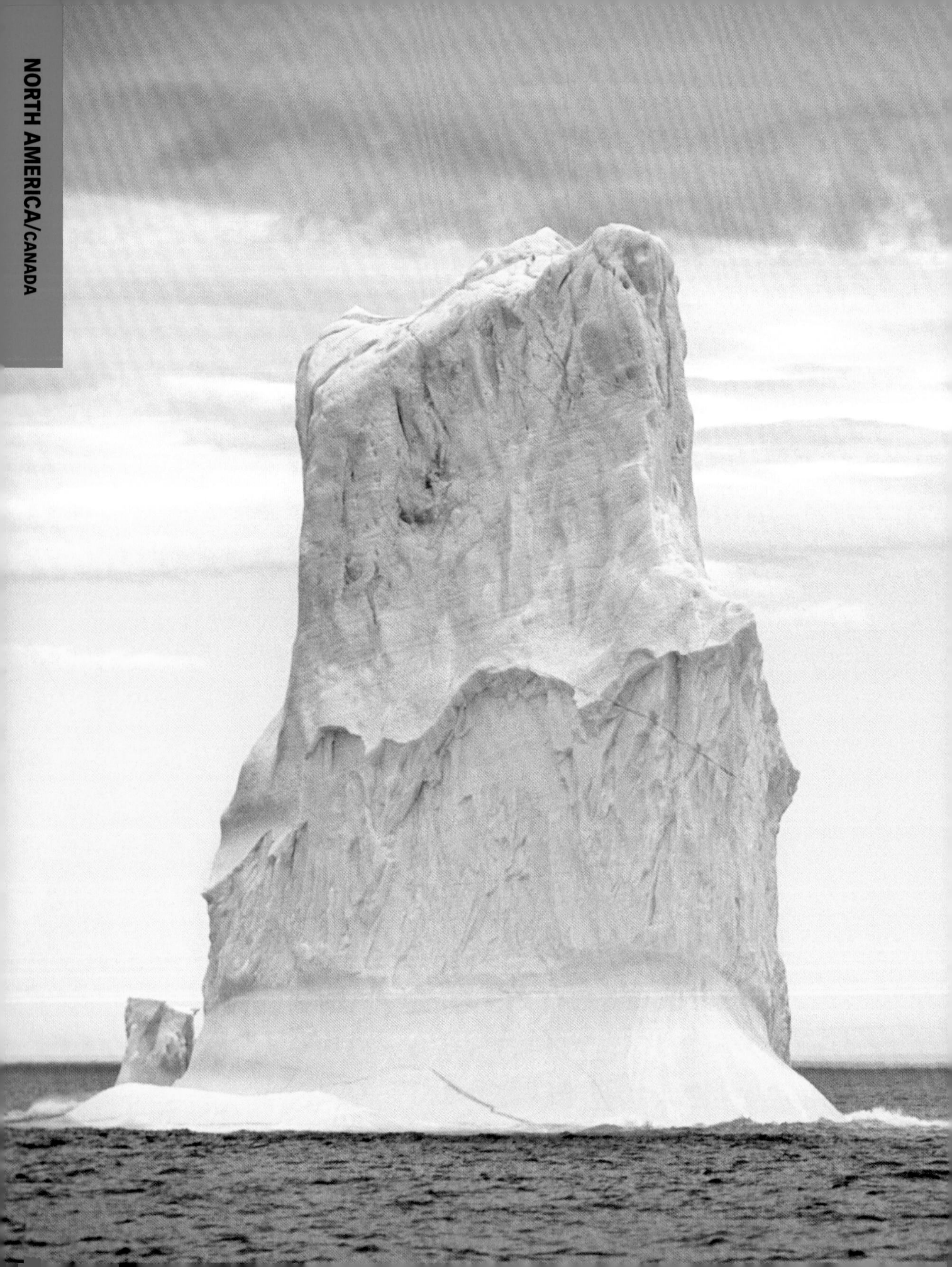

Witless Bay Ecological Reserve

If you have any fear of birds and maybe have to hide behind the sofa when watching Hitchcock's *The Birds*, it is probably best to give the superbly named Witless Bay Ecological Reserve a wide berth. The reserve consists of four craggy islands – Green, Great, Gull and Pee Pee – each of which is a protected area and home to hundreds of thousands of birds. The only access to the waters of the bay is via escorted tours by locals, many of whom take time out from their regular work to show visitors this amazing landscape.

If you visit the area before the end of June, you are treated to the sight of icebergs moving across the bay like giant ice cubes, slowly melting as they drift south to warmer waters. July sees the icebergs depart, only to be replaced by even more spectacular giants of the sea. Large pods of humpback, minke and finback whales come to the area to feed on capelin, a tiny fish found in abundance at this time of year. The finback whale can measure up to 30 m (98 ft) long and a fluke (tail) thrashing display is an awesome sight.

Finally it is time to get up close and personal with the birds. As you approach the islands you gradually realize that what seemed like the colour of the rocks is actually the plumage of birds. The islands are completely covered by them, like bees swarming around a hive. Murres, puffins and kittiwakes all jostle for position on these prime pieces of avian real estate. Murres are particularly argumentative little creatures but, as they nest at such high density that they often rub wings with their neighbours, that is hardly surprising.

HOW TO GET THERE:
It's a 30-km (19-mi) drive south from St John's, Newfoundland, along Route 10.
WHEN TO GO:
Tours run from June to September.
DON'T MISS:
A small detour takes you to The Spout – a giant wave-propelled geyser which squirts water at a ferocious speed through a small aperture in the rocks. Many of the guides include this in a tour of the islands.
YOU SHOULD KNOW:
Landing on the islands is prohibited except for those engaged in research. Keeping the islands safe for the birds has been highly successful since the islands were protected in 1962 and the total bird population has increased several hundredfold.

A whale-watching boat sails through icebergs in Witless Bay Ecological Reserve.

Magdalen Islands

Cap Herrise Lighthouse, Magdalen Islands

The Magdalen Islands (Îles de la Madeleine) form an archipelago located in the middle of the Gulf of St Lawrence, some 210 km (130 mi) from the Gaspé Peninsula. The islands, which are the visible peaks of a sub-marine ridge, run for over 60 km (37 mi) and comprise a dozen main islands along with innumerable rocky outcrops. Half of the islands are connected by long, slender sand dunes. The comparatively warm waters of the Gulf protect the island group from the harsh winters experienced on the Quebec mainland. The islanders are known as *les Madelinots* and are descendents of Acadians who escaped deportation to the south in 1755. Traditionally, agriculture and fisheries were the islands' mainstay, but farming has declined and only a small trawler fleet remains.

The islands' interiors are characterized by gently contoured verdant hills, while their shorelines are marked by fragile sandstone cliffs which have been eroded into spectacular arches, tunnels and caves by the combination of powerful winds and waves. The eroded stone from the cliffs impacts greatly on the islands' littoral zones and about one third of the islands' landmass is made up of dunes and sand bars. It is easy to find solitude along its many dune-lined strands, where only the roar of the sea and the squawks of seabirds can be heard. During the spring melt, seals can be observed hitching a ride on ice floes, while in summer the surrounding waters are ideal for windsurfing. When the wind drops, as it does every so often, the islands assume an appearance so benign that they might be from a lower latitude. But when it roars it provides a reminder that the elements govern the climate and topography of this remarkable archipelago.

Mingan Archipelago

A hiker walks through rock stacks on Niapiskau Island.

The Mingan Archipelago is a chain of around 30 islands and over 1,000 islets which runs for 150 km (93 mi) across Havre-Saint-Pierre on the north shore of the Gulf of Saint Lawrence. Comprised of limestone bedrock with granite outcrops, this ribbon of islands has, over millions of years, been sculpted by the awesome power of sea and wind into a remarkable landscape of natural monuments. Each of these huge rock stacks has weathered uniquely, some resembling giant monsters newly emerged from the sea, while others are reminiscent of the *inuksuit* (stone figures) left as markers by First Nations peoples.

Although the archipelago has the appearance of a fairly barren landscape, it is in fact part of a rich and diverse marine environment. The nutrient-laden waters of the Saint-Jean and Aguanish Rivers mix with the colder oxygen-rich waters of the Gulf to create ideal conditions for both flora and fauna. Grey, harbour and harp seals can be spotted sunning themselves on the rocks to raise their body temperature, in between fishing forays in the area's icy-cold waters. The abundance of fish and enormous shoals of plankton also attract dolphins and whales as well as Atlantic puffins, sea and eider ducks. On land, snowshoe hare, ermine and beaver flourish and the chief predators are red foxes and wolves.

The total landmass of the island chain may only be around 39 sq km (15 sq mi) but it boasts a dazzling array of landscapes. Peat bogs, coniferous forests, barrens and salt marshes as well as mile upon mile of shoreline all add up to a uniquely diverse ecosystem and the area is home to many rare and endangered wild flowers. There is also ample room for camping and hiking and, once the winter ice has melted, the surrounding waters are ripe for sea kayaking and diving.

HOW TO GET THERE:
It is a full day's drive along Highway 138 from Quebec – a bus also serves this route.
WHEN TO GO:
From May to September is best.
DON'T MISS:
Watching the sun rise or set behind the magnificent monoliths that line the islands.
YOU SHOULD KNOW:
Beavers, which are native to the area, favour lilies in their diet. The plant needs still water to grow, so the industrious beavers build dams so that the lilies flourish. The instinct to dam is so strong in the beaver, it has been demonstrated that even when played a tape recording of running water, the beaver will start building a barrier.

Restigouche Estuary

HOW TO GET THERE:
750 km (465 mi) by road from Montreal
WHEN TO GO:
All year round; the area gets a good covering of snow in the winter and the autumn colours are spectacular.
DON'T MISS:
Fort Listuguj, situated in the Restigouche First Nations Reservation. It's a great place to learn the legends of the area and find out about the bushcraft needed to survive in the Canadian wilderness.
YOU SHOULD KNOW:
The Restigouche Estuary was the scene of a decisive naval battle during the Seven Years War (1756–1763) and the defeat of the French forces by the British saw the latter gain control of the New World until the American Revolution in 1776.

The Restigouche (or Ristigouche) River marks the boundary between New Brunswick and Quebec and spills out into a large estuary at the western end of the Bay of Chaleur. At its most expansive the estuary is almost 8 km (5 mi) wide and only narrows some 25 km (16 mi) upstream at Campbellton. The estuary, although wide, is fairly shallow, allowing its waters to warm up quickly once the winter ice has melted. This encourages wildlife to flourish and the estuary is an important habitat for Atlantic salmon. Mussels and clams attract vast colonies of seabirds, including tens of thousands of black scoter which frequent the area in early spring.

The river's name is a corruption of the local First Nation word *Listuguj* – meaning five fingers. It is fed by fast-running streams that rise in the North Appalachians and which often teem with shoals of wild salmon. The shores of this bountiful river have for centuries been the home of the Mi'kmaq people who now live on reserved land at Pointe-à-la-Croix on the Quebec bank of the estuary. Although the surrounding land offers an opportunity for moderately challenging hiking, exploration of the area is best done on the water. A myriad of tributaries flow into the estuary and could not have been better designed for canoeing and rafting, but it is for fishing that the Restigouche is most renowned. The chance to catch and display a salmon as big as the fisherman has drawn people from around the world and the estuary was a favourite spot of former President Jimmy Carter. For all its bounty, the estuary is a delicate ecosystem and there have been numerous incidents when fish stocks have been all but exhausted by commercial fisheries. There is also still tension surrounding the First Nation people's ancestral fishing rights.

Grand Manan Island

It may be only an hour-and-a-half ferry ride from Blacks Harbour, but Grand Manan Island has a remoteness that belies its proximity to the mainland. Home to a year-round human population of fewer than 3,000, it is also a significant stopping-off point for North American bird migration and attracts birdwatchers from around the globe. The island's name is probably a shortening of *Mananook* – meaning island place in the local First Nation's language. For centuries the Malecite-Passamaquoddy Indians would risk life and limb to canoe across the often-turbulent waters to hunt, fish and collect seaweed. Norse explorers found the island over 1,000 years ago, but it was only settled by Europeans in the late 18th century.

Nearly all of the settlements are dotted around the southeast coast, in comfortable little coves that provide some degree of shelter from the often ferocious wind and sea. Away from the coast Manan has a rugged interior which becomes ever more spectacular the further north and west one travels. A network of trails takes the hiker over a barren landscape of 200-million-year-old igneous rock before the land falls away into the sea via towering 120 m (394 ft) cliffs. Never crowded, the 34-km (21-mi) long island has a good system of roads which are often no more than winding country lanes and best explored by bicycle. Away from the land, the nutrient-rich waters of the Bay of Fundy attract whales and a host of seabirds, while the shallower waters closer to the shore are the perfect place to learn sea kayaking. Each season on Manan brings its own beauty. The island is covered by a carpet of wild flowers in spring, and summer and winters are tempered by the comparative warmth of the sea.

HOW TO GET THERE:
By ferry from Blacks Harbour
WHEN TO GO:
All year round. The weather is best from May to September.
DON'T MISS:
The Seven Days Work cliff formation at Whale Cove
YOU SHOULD KNOW:
Although the island was ceded to Britain by the Treaty of Utrecht in 1713, the USA disputed its ownership until 1817 when they swapped the island for three that are now part of Maine.

Sunrise on the remote Grand Manan Island

Tobeatic Wilderness

The Tobeatic Wilderness Area, affectionately known as 'the Toby', straddles five counties of Nova Scotia and is the largest protected wild region in the Maritimes. Its name comes from the local Mi'kmaq language and means 'site of the alders'. It is an area sculpted by major glaciers of previous ice ages and its barren and semi-barren landscape is dotted with moraine and eskers. Its remoteness provides an undisturbed habitat for the rare Nova Scotia moose as well as a healthy population of black bear. The abundant wetlands of the area are also the ideal home for a vast array of bird life. Founded as a game reserve in 1927, the area has now grown to cover 1,040 sq km (400 sq mi). In 1968 it was afforded Wildlife Management Area status, which has helped to limit the impact of logging in the park.

Nine major river systems have their headwaters in 'the Toby' and their journeys to the Fundy and Atlantic coasts are interrupted by seemingly countless lakes. A network of streams, rivers and lakes makes for interesting and diverse canoeing expeditions and solitude is almost guaranteed as the canoeist heads even a little way into this remarkable wilderness.

In autumn the colours of the mixed woodland are spectacular, but this soon gives way to a long cold winter. It is then that the wilderness assumes an eerie calm. Covered in a blanket of snow and with the lakes frozen over, the mammals of the area take their long hibernation. On such nights, when the moon is full, the 'Toby' exudes an almost electric radiance and the silence is broken only by the hoot of the barred owl. April sees the ice melt and, as the black bears awake from their slumbers, the Tobeatic Wilderness springs back into life again.

A couple canoe down the Tusket River in the Tobeatic Wilderness.

Sable Island

Sable Island lies like a sleeping leviathan in the North Atlantic Ocean, detached from the coast of Nova Scotia by 160 km (100 mi) of often-turbulent water. It sits on the boundary between the warm Gulf Stream and the frigid Labrador Current, which often leads to the island being shrouded in thick fog. It is surrounded by barely submerged shifting sandbanks which, over the years, have first scuppered and then swallowed more than 300 ships. The treacherousness of its waters has earned it the tag 'Graveyard of the Atlantic'. Over the years it has been home to many stranded sailors, although today the only human inhabitants are scientists working for Canada's Environment Agency.

The island is long and narrow and is so battered by the elements that it is constantly changing shape. Since its discovery by Portuguese navigators, it has probably halved in size. Currently, it is around 40 km (25 mi) long and a mere 1.6 km (1 mi) wide at its broadest point. What it lacks in natural protection, the government of Canada has made up for in regulatory safeguards. Visitor numbers are strictly rationed and a code of practice must be adhered to. Indigenous wildlife includes harbour and grey seals that breed along the island's shoreline. However, there is one animal above all for which Sable Island is renown: a group of more than 250 displaced horses roam wild on the island, providing a curious sight in this harsh, treeless environment. While there are several interesting and conflicting stories about how these equine exiles happened to get to the island, it is probable that they were imported in the 18th century and then abandoned. Sable Island is a place like no other, starkly beautiful and wonderfully isolated, with a surreal charm all of its own.

Wild horses canter across the beach on Sable Island.

HOW TO GET THERE:
By small aeroplane (from Halifax, Nova Scotia) or by boat
WHEN TO GO:
From July to October
DON'T MISS:
For all its wild beauty the highlight of any trip to Sable has to be the horses. While there are numerous wild herds of horses in the world, few exist without some sort of interference by humans. The horses of Sable Island may not be indigenous, but they have adapted well to their environment and have no detrimental impact on the area's ecosystem.
YOU SHOULD KNOW:
In the early 20th century a plan was hatched to protect the island from erosion by planting tens of thousands of trees. Such was the ferocity of the wind, coupled with the paucity of the soil, that they all died – leaving just low-growth vegetation.

Alexander Archipelago

The Alexander Islands are named after Tsar Alexander II, the former owner, but proudly fly the Stars and Stripes nowadays – the USA purchased Russia's Alaska territories for less than two cents an acre, the bargain of the 19th century. The 485-km (300-mi) long archipelago is off Alaska's southern coastline and is a chain of over one thousand islands (although *not* the home of the famous salad dressing, that honour belonging to the Thousand Islands in the St Lawrence River). Once part of the mainland, these islands – the tops of submerged mountains – are close to shore. The northern section of the Inside Passage from Washington's Puget Sound to the Alaska Panhandle winds through the archipelago, which protects seagoing vessels from sometimes-violent Pacific weather.

These islands offer massive doses of everything wilderness addicts crave – they have steep coastlines with dramatic fjords, while rugged interiors have dense evergreen and temperate rain forests. Much terrain is officially protected and the Alexanders are thinly populated, offering resourceful travellers with the necessary survival skills every opportunity to find and explore virgin terrain without seeing another human being (apart from any like-minded companions) from one day's end to the next. There are indigenous occupants – the Tlingit and Kaigani Haidas and Tsimshians who arrived from British Columbia in the 1800s – plus those concerned with the main commercial activities of logging, fishing and tourism.

In the latter context, guides are available for those who love wild places but prefer not to go it alone. The main islands are Admiralty, Baranof, Chichagof, Dall, Kupreanof, Prince of Wales, Revillagigedo and Wrangell. These all have scattered communities that provide an ideal starting point for backcountry expeditions. But a visit can prove very rewarding for those who simply want to see and appreciate this unspoilt archipelago.

A humpback whale at sunset in Frederick Sound

Brooks Range

This impressive chain of mountains crosses Alaska from west to east, ending in Canada's Yukon. The Brooks Range is virtually uninhabited, having only a few tiny settlements such as Coldfoot and Deadhorse. Sole road access is from the Dalton Highway that runs through the Atigun Pass *en route* from Fairbanks to Prudhoe Bay's oilfields. The mountains include portions of the vast Arctic National Wildlife Refuge and encompass the Gates of the Arctic National Park. Together with the adjacent Noatak National Preserve, the latter is the USA's largest wilderness.

The Brooks Range marks the summer position of the Arctic front, ensuring that summers are relatively mild and providing a window of opportunity for visitors. It's possible to drive along the Dalton Highway and enjoy its rugged grandeur but, for those who want to see more, the answer is a trip organized by locals familiar with the spectacular but inhospitable terrain. Individual expeditions are possible, but even those experienced in self-sufficient wilderness travel should think twice before going it alone. The best way in is by floatplane and most adventurers wisely choose an expedition that includes hiking, kayaking or rafting with the help of experienced local guides.

The Brooks Range is the finest unspoilt mountain terrain in North America – a pristine wonderland of craggy granite, rivers and lakes teeming with wildlife. But it's that way for a reason. For the delights of the Brooks Range will never suffer the fate of so many natural wonders in the modern world – seeing a huge influx of the sort of visitors drawn to wild places whose presence ultimately devalues the very thing that attracted them in the first place. A visit to this magical place is simply too challenging for any but the most determined adventurers, able to dig deep into their wallets for the ultimate wilderness experience.

An aerial view of Atigun Pass in the stunning Brooks Range

HOW TO GET THERE:
Fly to a specific destination from Fairbanks or take the Dalton Highway and explore from there. Floatplane trips can be booked from Bettles.

WHEN TO GO:
Summer (June to August) is best.

DON'T MISS:
Wildlife watchers will be enchanted by the huge variety of fauna; be sure to witness the amazing caribou migrations through the mountains in spring and autumn.

YOU SHOULD KNOW:
Despite wilderness status and being almost entirely free from human disturbance, the Brooks Range is still home – at its western tip – to the world's largest zinc mine. The huge Red Dog opencast mine is responsible for around ten per cent of world zinc production and sits on land owned by the NANA Regional Corporation, created in 1972 to settle aboriginal land claims. The mine has operated since 1989 and hopes to continue extracting zinc, lead and silver until around 2030.

McNeil River Game Sanctuary

The main attraction in the remote McNeil River State Game Sanctuary is the world's largest gathering of Alaska brown bears, which takes place annually where a series of cascades on the McNeil River provides an obstacle for migrating chum salmon. This

Brown bear with yearlings on the McNeil River

makes them relatively easy prey for normally solitary bears, which duly congregate in large numbers to feast on Nature's bounty and fatten up for the harsh winter. A hundred or more turn up at the height of the salmon run in July to fight, play, feed and mate. A similar but smaller spectacle may been seen a little earlier at nearby Mikfik Creek, where up to 25 bears can be seen hunting red salmon in the ice-cold water.

The sanctuary extends to an unspoilt 462 sq km (178 sq mi) in southwestern Alaska. The nearest town is Dillingham, but the area has no roads and is untouched by modern development. The McNeil River originates high in the Aleutian Mountains and protected terrain surrounds the falls where the bears gather, close to the river's discharge point in lower Cook Inlet, 400 km (250 mi) from Anchorage as the light aircraft flies. A visit to this unique sanctuary to see the bears isn't a 'gimme'. In order to offer what the name suggests, access during the bear-watching season is strictly limited and permits – that should be applied for online to the Alaska Department of Fish and Game before March 1 each year – are issued by ballot.

Those who win a coveted four-day ticket to view form into small groups (consisting of no more than ten people plus a guide) that hike to prime bruin-watching spots to spend six or seven hours watching and photographing the congregation of bears, overnighting at an established campground and eating in a primitive cabin after a memorable wilderness experience.

HOW TO GET THERE:
The sanctuary is accessible by boat but most visitors fly in from Homer using one of several available air charters.
WHEN TO GO:
June 7 to August 26 is the period when permits are issued for bear-watching.
DON'T MISS:
The other wildlife to be seen in the refuge. Bears may be the main attraction, but those who don't make bear watch can still see (among others) moose, caribou, harbour seal, arctic ground squirrel, wolves and red fox – even the occasional lone bear – alongside numerous bird species including bald eagles and harlequin ducks.
YOU SHOULD KNOW:
No bears (or humans) have been injured since the restricted-access programme was introduced, but those lucky enough to take a bear-watching trip are reassured by the presence of an armed member of the sanctuary's staff.

North Cascades National Park

The Cascade Range begins in British Columbia and extends through Washington and Oregon into Northern California. The Washington section is known as the North Cascades, and there the national park of the same name may be found. In fact, the North Cascades National Park is a complex extending to around 2,800 sq km (1,080 sq mi) that consists of four linked areas – north and south park units plus Ross Lake and Lake Chelan National Recreation Areas. As 93 per cent of the park has been designated as wilderness, for those willing and able to survive in the wild there are plenty of opportunities to enjoy awesome mountain hiking in complete solitude.

The two recreation areas are destinations of choice for anyone keen to experience the ambiance of these rugged mountains without mounting a major backcountry expedition. Ross Lake National Recreation Area, close to the Canadian border, is the most accessible. This corridor along the Skagit River bisects the park's north and south units and encompasses three reservoirs used to generate power for Seattle, including eponymous Ross Lake.

Recreational activities include hunting, fishing, kayaking, canoeing, hiking and climbing. There are trailheads connecting to an extensive network of established hiking routes, including those that continue into adjoining wilderness. The North Cascades Highway passes through the recreation area from east to west, providing access and allowing travellers to enjoy superb mountain scenery that has earned the nickname 'American Alps'. There are a number of campsites along the road. The Lake Chelan National Recreation Area is more remote, but equally impressive. It covers just 250 sq km (95 sq mi) at the north end of the lake. The Pacific Coast Trail passes through and in summer there is an off-road bus service that connects the trail and the town of Chelan at the south end.

HOW TO GET THERE:
Ross Lake is accessible from North Cascades Highway or the gravel Silver Skagit Road to the Hozomeen campground. There's no road access to Lake Chelan, but it's possible to hike in, use the floatplane or take a ferry up the lake from Chelan.
WHEN TO GO:
April to October
DON'T MISS:
The North Cascades Visitor Centre and Skagit Visitor Centre, both to be found in Newhalem, Washington.

YOU SHOULD KNOW:
The magnificent vista seen from Desert Peak Lookout is reached by a 10 km (6 mi) trail from Ross Lake. The lookout is staffed in wildfire season and was manned in 1956 by Beat Generation writer Jack Kerouac, who used the experience as inspiration for his novel *Desolation Angels*.

Mount Shuksan, Washington

Trapper Creek Wilderness

HOW TO GET THERE:
There are no roads within the Trapper Creek drainage, but a number of primary and secondary unpaved forest roads skirt this wilderness area, which is just to the northwest of the town of Wind River.
WHEN TO GO:
May to September for the best weather
DON'T MISS:
The nearby Government Mineral Springs Recreation Area, where it's possible to imbibe – you guessed it – mineral water from the legendary Iron Mike Well.
YOU SHOULD KNOW:
The drive to Trapper Creek – just north of the Columbia River Gorge that divides Washington and Oregon – involves travelling the Columbia River Highway, built as a scenic route between 1913 and 1922. This has some spectacular sights, including Cascade Locks, the Bridge of the Gods and over 75 waterfalls.

The Gifford Pinchot National Forest in southern Washington stretches for 115 km (70 mi) along the western slopes of the Cascade Range, covering an impressive 5,300 sq km (2,050 sq mi). This vast area of wild country contains Mount St Helens National Volcanic Monument plus official wilderness areas such as Goat Rocks, Tatoosh, Mount Adams and Indian Heaven. One of the most interesting is the smallest – Trapper Creek drainage. This extends to a mere 240 sq km (93 sq mi) but is no less appealing for that. Trapper Creek Wilderness is a pristine area within the Wind River watershed and contains one of the largest blocks of original low-growth Douglas-fir forest in the state. To that may be added a rugged landscape full of rushing streams, waterfalls as tall as 30 m (100 ft) and huckleberry fields at higher elevations.

Anyone with limited time to explore the national forest would do well to focus on Trapper Creek, which offers accessible day hiking along established trails, although some are primitive and not for the inexperienced. For those capable of getting there (it requires physical effort and stamina), the outlook from the top of aptly named Observation Peak with its abandoned fire-watch post is awesome, encompassing Goat Rocks and Mounts Jefferson, Rainier, Adams and Hood. Catch it if you can! Soda Peaks Lake in the southwest corner of the drainage is another highlight that rewards a shortish hike.

Wildlife is varied and there is a good selection of birds – including barred and spotted owls, woodpeckers and goshawks – while commonly seen animals include Roosevelt elk, black-tailed deer and black bear. Rarer but still spotted occasionally are bobcat, cougar, pine marten and grizzly bear. For those with eyes to see beyond the striking scenery, it's a dimension that adds a special something to this beautiful wilderness.

Willamette National Forest

After the Cascade Range duly cascades down into Oregon its western slopes are occupied by the 180-km (112-mi) length of Willamette National Forest, a protected area that offers a hugely varied landscape of mountains, canyons, rushing streams and extensively wooded slopes. There are almost limitless possibilities for open-air recreation and touring – a point underlined by the fact that there are 10,300 km (6,400 mi) of roads within Willamette Forest, including designated scenic routes such as Aufderheide Memorial Drive, Clackamas-Breitenbush Road, Diamond Drive, Quartzville Creek Road and the McKenzie Pass-Santiam Pass loop.

But for those who do not have the luxury of limitless time to explore this vast wild place a narrower focus is required. The forest contains a number of wilderness areas sure to appeal to adventurous explorers, but with no fewer than 1,550 sq km (600 sq mi) of uninhabited terrain to choose from further refinement is called for. One sure-fire winner is the Diamond Peak wilderness, surrounding the shield volcano of the same name. This lonely place straddles the crest and is located within two national forests – Willamette to the west and Deschutes to the east. The Pacific Crest National Scenic Trail passes through and some 200 km (125 mi) of established routes may be found within the wilderness, including the 16-km (10-mi) Diamond Peak Trail. A jewel-like ring of small lakes surrounds the peak's snow-capped summit.

The area features impressive stands of mixed trees such as mountain hemlock, western white pine and lodgepole. Abundant alpine flowers provide bright colour in season along the trails, on lakeshores and in meadows. Other than hiking, popular activities are camping, horseback riding, fishing and mountain climbing. Good base camps for the ascent of Diamond Peak may be found at Divide Lake, Marie Lake and Rockpile Lake.

Proxy Falls in Willamette National Forest

HOW TO GET THERE:
Access the forest from the Salem, Albany and Eugene areas of the Willamette Valley. The main highways are US Route 20 and Oregon State Routes 22, 58 and 126. The nearest town to Diamond Peak is Oakridge.

WHEN TO GO:
Avoid winter conditions (November to March), unless the main attraction is cross-country skiing or snowshoe trekking.

DON'T MISS:
Abundant wildlife. Large animals to be seen around Diamond Peak are black-tailed and mule deer, elk and black bear. Small animals include foxes, pine martens, snowshoe rabbits and marmots. There are numerous feathered residents such as Clark's nutcracker, Oregon jays, ravens and water ouzels

YOU SHOULD KNOW:
Day or overnight trekkers entering the Diamond Peak wilderness area between Memorial Day (the last Monday in May) and October 31 must obtain a permit. These are free and can be self-issued at approved trailheads.

Kalmiopsis Wilderness

A ranger hiking by Western White Pine in Siskiyou National Forest

Tucked away at the heart of southwestern Oregon's Rogue River-Siskiyou National Forest is a hidden gem. The Kalmiopsis wilderness area is not small at around 730 sq km (282 sq mi), although that must be measured against the national forest's 7,300 sq km (2,820 sq mi). Even though it only occupies one tenth of the forest, Kalmiopsis is undoubtedly the star of the show. This unique wild place has extraordinary geology, with an amazing variety of rock formations supporting a huge diversity of plant life of great botanical interest that has evolved to survive in harsh soil conditions caused by high concentrations of heavy metals such as magnesium, iron, chromium and nickel leaching from serpentinite and peridotite rocks.

The landscape of this rugged wilderness ranges from a lowly 150 m (500 ft) to a maximum elevation of 1,554 m (5,098 ft) at Pearsoll Peak. It is characterized by sharp ridges and plunging tree-clad canyons carrying rushing streams and white-water sections of the Illinois, Chetco and North Fork Rivers that attract rafters prepared to carry their craft in. There are also nearly 250 km (155 mi) of hiking trails in the area. These can be challenging, as many are steep and rocky, and were not made easier by the major Biscuit Fire of 2002 that devastated much of the forest following a lightning strike. The flora is regenerating but damage to the tree cover is still apparent, making trails even more hazardous in places. Many routes incorporate sections of old mining roads and can become confusing, so a trail map is essential. Popular day hikes are those to Babyfoot and Vulcan Lakes. But those seeking solitude can take any other trail into the wilderness and be virtually guaranteed there will be no sight or sound of other people.

HOW TO GET THERE:
There are more than a dozen trailheads, most accessible by regular car. Easiest access is from Highway 199 near Cave Junction in the Illinois Valley or Highway 101 at Gold Beach or Brookings.

WHEN TO GO:
June to September inclusive are the 'dry' months. Snow often blocks roads to the trailheads into spring and the Illinois River cannot be forded at Collier Bar until August.

DON'T MISS:
Kalmiopsis leachiana, the plant after which this wilderness area is named. Discovered in 1930 by Lilla Leach, this evergreen has fabulous purple flowers, is a relic of the pre-ice age and the oldest known member of the *Ericaceae* (heather) family.

YOU SHOULD KNOW:
Don't be tempted to leave marked trails to travel cross-country – the terrain is steep and treacherous with dense vegetation.

Channel Islands National Park

Despite proximity to the urban sprawl of Los Angeles, the Channel Islands – close to California's southern coast – are largely unspoilt. Five of them form the Channel Islands National Park, a world apart from the bustling mainland. The islands offer a stunning display of wild flowers after the winter rains and have large seabird colonies, while surrounding waters support abundant marine life including whales, seals and sea lions.

Santa Cruz is the big one at around 245 sq km (95 sq mi) and preserves a fascinating microcosm of the Californian coastal environment as once it was. There are mountains, canyons, cliffs, tide pools, pristine beaches and sea caves – including one of the world's largest, the famous Painted Cave. There are numerous reminders of former occupants – both Chumash Indians and 19th-century incomers. Nearby Santa Rosa has cliffs, beaches and central peaks and – like its neighbours – supports a considerable diversity of flora and fauna, much of it unique to the islands.

The three islets of East, Middle and West Anacapa have towering cliffs, sea caves and the Arch Rock that serves as the park's symbol. In the summer on East Anacapa rangers dive in Landing Cove with video cameras, allowing visitors to glimpse the magical undersea world of the kelp forest . . . without getting wet. The smallest island is Santa Barbara, a 260-ha (640-ac) triangular rock with steep cliffs that is returning to its former self as the National Park Service reverses the effects of human interference like the introduction of rabbits and cats, which did huge damage to bird populations. Wild and windswept San Miguel is the outermost island, home to tens of thousands of pinnipeds (sea lions and seals by any other name) around Point Bennett, which may be viewed in season as part of a day-long hike guided by a ranger.

Anacapa islands at sunset

HOW TO GET THERE:
Other than by private craft, official concessionaire boats or light aircraft are the only way of reaching the islands – advance booking is recommended. A variety of trips to and around the various islands is offered and overnight camping is allowed (with a permit).
WHEN TO GO:
Any time
DON'T MISS:
The whales – grey whales are present from December to April and a large gathering of blue whales takes place in spring and summer. For those intent on spotting the world's largest animal, this is the place to go.
YOU SHOULD KNOW:
The park's headquarters and the informative Robert J Lagomarsino Visitor Centre are located on the mainland in Ventura, just across the water from the five islands that make up the Channel Islands National Park. There is an open-air visitor centre in Santa Barbara.

Death Valley National Park

HOW TO GET THERE:
California Highway 190 crosses
Death Valley National Park from west
to east, where US Route 95 runs
close to the park.

WHEN TO GO:
May to September should be
avoided. December and January are
the coolest months, with average
daytime temperatures of around
18°C (65°F). Spring is the most
popular season with visitors.

DON'T MISS:
Seeing Zabriskie Point – not the 1970
Michelangelo Antonioni movie, but
the original, that extraordinary
erosional landscape to be found in
the Amargosa Range within Death
Valley National Park.

YOU SHOULD KNOW:
A temperature of nearly 56.7°C
(134°F) was recorded at aptly named
Furnace Creek in 1913. That's
fractionally below the all-time world
high of 57.7°C (136°F) logged in Libya
a decade later.

If ever a descriptive name was appropriate, it must surely be Death Valley. This is the lowest, driest and hottest location just about anywhere, and must have seemed a fearsome place to pioneers crossing the uncharted southwestern USA during the California gold rush of 1849. Despite adverse conditions, the valley has been home to the Timbisha tribe (formerly called Panamint Shoshone) for a millennium.

Situated within the Mojave Desert, Death Valley boasts the lowest elevation in North America at 85.5 m (280 ft) below sea level. Ironically, less than 125 km (78 mi) east is the highest point in the contiguous USA – Mount Whitney's soaring 4,421-m (14,505-ft) peak. The 7,800-sq-km (3,012-sq-mi) hotspot of Death Valley is in the Great Basin, enclosed by the Sylvania and Owlshead Mountains, Panamint and Amargosa Ranges. It mostly lies in California, with small areas invading Nevada. The valley forms the greater part of the national park that bears its name, which also includes surrounding mountains, Saline Valley and most of Panamint Valley. Park headquarters is at Furnace Creek along with a visitor centre, museum, gas station, campgrounds, the world's lowest golf course and a desert resort. The visitor centre offers fascinating talks on a variety of valley-related subjects between mid October and mid April. To the north, Scotty's Castle makes a great stopover. This Spanish-style mansion was completed in the 1930s and guided tours of the interior and a network of underground tunnels are available.

Death Valley is not the place for inexperienced people to try backcountry exploring, although hiking, camping, mountain-biking and birdwatching are popular activities. A network of dirt roads allows exploration off the beaten track in a 4x4 vehicle, although precautions like notifying someone of plans are sensible, as the chance of finding help in remote locations is small to negligible.

*Leaving footprints in sand dunes
in Death Valley National Park.*

Inyo Mountains Wilderness

This stark place encompasses a large portion of the Inyo Mountains, a short range to the east of California's Sierra Nevada that stretches for 130 km (81 mi) from the Westgard Pass at the southern end of the White Mountains. The Inyos separate arid Owens Valley from the equally parched Saline Valley in the Mojave Desert. The Inyo Mountains Wilderness covers 810 sq km (313 sq mi) and to the north is the Inyo National Forest, home of the world's oldest tree (Methuselah, a Great Basin bristlecone pine at a secret location that's been around for nearly 4,850 years).

There is usually a good reason why wild places have remained uncolonized, and in this case it's the sheer ruggedness of the terrain. That doesn't stop the park showing evidence of long-abandoned mining activity like old cabins, decaying aerial tramways and an old stamp mill. Four hiking routes are historic mining trails. These are the Burgess Mine Trail, pivotal Lonesome Miner Trail, French Spring Trail and one of the most accessible hikes, the Snowflake Mine Trail starting from the Snowflake Talc Mine and climbing the Beveridge Ridge before dropping down to the old mill site. The Beveridge Canyon Trail leads to the main mining area in an isolated location in the Mojave Desert. These are not smartly waymarked trails, so can be hard to follow and are sometimes seriously overgrown or even lost altogether to rock slides.

This is, therefore, a destination only for experienced survivalists – although cautious day hikes are feasible. Most trailheads can only be reached using a 4x4 off-roader and the wilderness is hazardous territory with dense vegetation, while steep slopes covered in loose rocks wait to trap the unwary at every turn. Be warned that no assistance is available and few people use the trails.

HOW TO GET THERE:
The easiest access is from Lone Pine, Inyo County (on US Route 395).
WHEN TO GO:
April to October
DON'T MISS:
For those with the determination to get there, the ruined Five-Stamp Mill above Beveridge Canyon, surrounded by the remains of miners' cabins, serves as an atmospheric reminder that even more determined individuals once wrested valuable minerals from this inhospitable landscape. From the mill a well-defined trail leads up to historic Frenchy's Cabin, which is reasonably intact.
YOU SHOULD KNOW:
Although vehicles are not permitted in the USA's wilderness areas, the official boundaries in Inyo are 9 m (30 ft) back from unpaved roads and 90 m (100 ft) back from paved roads. Camping is allowed with a 14-day limit on one site, after which the camp must be shifted by at least 40 km (25 mi).

Inyo Mountains

Owens Peak Wilderness

HOW TO GET THERE:
The southern approach is from State Highway 178; from the east go via Indian Wells Canyon off US Route 395; from the north also use Route 395, then Ninemile Canyon Road.

WHEN TO GO:
Any time (in winter it's a good location for alpine skiing).

DON'T MISS:
The wildlife, which includes black bear, mule deer, mountain lion, prairie falcon and golden eagle.

YOU SHOULD KNOW:
The University of California has run a programme to improve the condition of this special wilderness, which has involved students undertaking activities like reopening then maintaining damaged dirt roads and scarifying selected areas to encourage water absorption and seed germination.

The highest point in the southern Sierra Nevada is Owens Peak at 2,574 m (8,445 ft), which gives its name to the 300-sq-km (115-sq-mi) wilderness occupying the broken eastern face of the mountains beneath this saw-tooth landmark. The steep terrain has an assortment of canyons, many of them expansive, some containing springs surrounded by lush growth. This Californian wilderness is located where three ecosystems meet – those of the Mojave Desert, Great Basin and Sierra Nevada – resulting in an interesting assortment of vegetation that ranges from creosote bush scrub, cacti, classic yuccas, low-level oak and cottonwood trees to juniper-pinyon woods with pine and sagebrush at higher elevations.

Some hardened backpackers will just be passing through – the Pacific Crest Trail crosses the wilderness – but this is a great place for a day hike, although camping is permitted for those who like to explore more thoroughly. Other recreational activities include horse riding, mountain-biking, scenic viewing from the network of dirt roads and climbing. Some of the most challenging climbs in the southern Sierras are to be found here, with names like Lamoont Spires, Sawtooth Peak and Spanish Needles telling the tale. Those willing and able to reach the higher elevations are rewarded with sensational mountain vistas, notably from anywhere along the 35-km (22-mi) stretch of Pacific Crest Trail. But be warned that it gets very hot in summer and there's no guarantee that water will be found, especially higher up.

A 4x4 vehicle is desirable and in most cases essential – many approaches and wilderness dirt roads are impassable to anything with low ground clearance. Although no vehicles are allowed in the wilderness itself, parking is permitted beside established roads for those tempted to get out and stretch their legs. Unfortunately, despite the rule, this wilderness attracts drivers who attempt extreme off-road feats.

Yosemite National Park

HOW TO GET THERE:
The key access road to Yosemite is California State Route 120, which runs through the park.

WHEN TO GO:
Any time (although tyre chains are often required on back roads in winter and some roads are closed).

Central California's Yosemite National Park attracts three-and-a-half million visitors each year to the western slopes of the Sierra Nevada range, but it's still a wild place. The park covers 3,100 sq km (1,200 sq mi) and the vast majority of those eager tourists are interested only in Yosemite Valley, a tiny 18-sq-km (7-sq-mi) fraction of the whole. This is the main entry point to the park and contains a concentration of visitor facilities – but also natural wonders that make this a scenic sensation to savour. It contains the Merced River, fed and carried down the valley by a succession of eye-catching waterfalls, while high granite walls rise to stunning rock features that

include the El Capitan monolith, Cathedral Rocks, Cathedral Spires, Sentinel Rock and the Three Brothers.

Yosemite Valley

Appreciating the enormity of these famous sights is mandatory, but for those who seek wide-open empty spaces there's plenty more to enjoy. Beyond the valley lies the 95 per cent of the park's area that has been designated as wilderness. This craggy landscape contains two major rivers, numerous streams and thousands of lakes and ponds. There are mountains, glaciers, meadows and forests within a vast expanse of unspoiled alpine scenery. The total area forms one of the largest undisturbed habitat blocks in the Sierra Nevada mountains, supporting a diversity of plants and animals within five distinct vegetation zones ranging from chaparral/oak woodland at lower levels up to alpine higher as the park's elevation rises from 600 m (1,970 ft) to 4,000 m (13,123 ft).

The park has 560 km (350 mi) of roads and an impressive 1,300-km (800-mi) network of hiking trails and provides limitless opportunities to strike out into the wilderness to find places where it seems no human foot can ever have fallen before.

DON'T MISS:
The most famous landmark in the entire Sierra Nevada, Half Dome, is situated where the Yosemite Valley forks. This extraordinary granite pile seems from the valley floor to be just a neatly domed mountain from which one half has mysteriously gone missing – but in fact this is an illusion, as the formation is entirely natural. Note that a permit is required to ascend the Half Dome on certain days (mostly weekends and holidays) using the cable walkway.

YOU SHOULD KNOW:
There's no guarantee that the awesome Yosemite Falls will actually be falling – the waterfall is fed mainly by snowmelt and often runs dry in August, remaining so until the winter snowfalls arrive.

Yellowstone National Park

America's first national park – established in 1872 – is still one of the most impressive. Yellowstone National Park is mainly in Wyoming, with small sections extending into Idaho and Montana. The park covers around 9,000 sq km (3,475 sq mi) and this huge landscape encompasses mountain ranges, canyons, lakes, waterfalls and rivers.

At its heart is the high-altitude Yellowstone Lake, situated over the caldera of America's largest active supervolcano. This is responsible for the lava flows and rocks scattered by ancient eruption that can be seen all over the park, including one of the world's largest petrified forests. Volcanic activity is also responsible for the huge number of geothermal features (half the recorded number in the world) found in Yellowstone. The world-famous Old Faithful geyser is but the highlight of the park's 10,000 dramatic hot springs, geysers and boiling-mud spectacles, many of which can be reached by the paved roads that give access to many of Yellowstone's key sights.

There are eight visitor centres within the park, some of which close in winter, each featuring a selection of interesting ecological and cultural subjects – Yellowstone is rich in flora and fauna and has a large number of archaeological sites. Among other services, they offer advice on where to observe animals such as grizzly bears, wolves, free-ranging bison and elk. A number of official suppliers offer visitor-support activities including transportation, boating, fishing, guided hiking and wildlife viewing, while a wide variety of ranger-guided activities can be booked. But for many the park's the star, and the opportunity to simply drive around, see some of the amazing hydrothermal features, spot wildlife and soak up the stunning scenery is all the stimulus needed to enjoy this extraordinary place, preserved for posterity in the 19th century by forward-thinking conservationists.

HOW TO GET THERE:
Fly into a local field like Cody, Jackson, Bozeman, Billings, Idaho Falls or West Yellowstone, many of which have linked bus services to the park. A network of roads surrounds the park (some roads traversing it) with good starting points being Butte (north or west entrance), Bozeman, Livingston and Billings (north entrance), Cody (east entrance), Jackson (south entrance) and Idaho Falls (south or west entrance).

WHEN TO GO:
Any time (but winter visits are best conducted as part of a guided tour using snow coaches or snowmobiles, as roads are only open to over-snow vehicles and most entrances are closed in November and March/April to prepare for and clear up after winter).

DON'T MISS:
The breathtaking Grand Canyon of the Yellowstone park, carved deep into the rock by the Yellowstone River, downstream of Yellowstone Falls.

YOU SHOULD KNOW:
An entrance fee is payable (valid for a week of unlimited re-entry), even by hikers on foot. It is not necessary to book Yellowstone in advance as there is no limit on visitor numbers.

ABOVE: *Colourful terraces atop Mammoth Hot Springs*

RIGHT: *An elk cow and calf standing beside the steaming geyser, Old Faithful*

52

Bryce Canyon National Park

Compared to many a vast American national park, Bryce Canyon has modest vital statistics, measuring just 145 sq km (56 sq mi), and its remote location ensures that this dramatic landscape is never overburdened with visitors. Many of those who do venture into the wilds of Utah confine themselves to the scenic drive that offers glorious views over a canyon that isn't really a canyon, but a stunning series of natural amphitheatres populated with huge arches and the extraordinary rock spires known as hoodoos. Indeed, many summer visitors don't even drive themselves, but prefer to park up and take the Bryce Canyon shuttle that tours the most popular viewpoints, thus allowing for uninterrupted sightseeing with no distracting need to watch the road.

Massed ranks of slender hoodoos that can rise to a height of 60 m (200 ft) create a spectacular multi-coloured jumble of red, orange and white rock seen from the canyon rim, which fluctuates between an elevation of 2,400 m (7,875 ft) and 2,700 m (8,860 ft). The 29-km (18-mi) scenic drive ends at the park's high spot, Rainbow Point, but those who prefer to get up close and personal with this unique place have other options.

There are eight waymarked walking trails that can be completed in less than a day, each taking from one to six hours for a round trip from trailheads. Two overnight trails (backcountry permits required) extend the total length of the park's various hiking routes to 80 km (50 mi). Anyone who prefers to let a horse do the hard work can book riding trips between April and October. There are two official campgrounds within the park for those who wish to explore at leisure or indulge in one of the park's most popular activities, landscape photography. Awesome sunrises and sunsets are favourite subjects.

HOW TO GET THERE:
The best access route is from US Route 89, then on to Bryce Canyon via Utah Routes 12 and 63.

WHEN TO GO:
Any time (many trails are passable on snowshoes in winter, when the park also has a number of marked cross-country ski routes).

DON'T MISS:
Seeing stars. Bryce Canyon is one of the darkest sports in the continental USA, offering stargazers the opportunity to see a blazing night sky filled with over 7,500 celestial bodies. There is an astronomy festival in the park every summer.

YOU SHOULD KNOW:
The reason so many of the USA's wilderness areas remain empty and unspoilt is that early pioneers found these barren places were incapable of sustaining them without a massive and ultimately unproductive effort. This is illustrated by the determined Mormon settler after whom the canyon is named – the Scot, Ebenezer Bryce – who made a log-cabin home for his family hereabouts during the 1870s but lasted for less than a decade before moving on to Arizona.

Navajo Loop Trail

Zion National Park

Attracting over three million visitors annually, Utah's most popular national park is renowned for breathtaking canyons. People are drawn to this 600-sq-km (230-sq-mi) park near Springfield by extraordinary features such as the enormous Kolob Arch, typical of amazing rock formations that abound. Zion Canyon itself is 24 km (15 mi) long and up to 800 m (2,625 ft) deep, winding between precipitous walls as the north fork of the Virgin River rushes along the canyon floor.

Zion National Park (so named when the original name of Mukuntuweap failed to roll off anyone's tongue) offers incredible views to those who prefer to remain firmly perched on top of four wheels and let the engine do the walking, but this is really a place to hike, climb, camp, bike or explore on horseback. It isn't a vast empty wilderness where no fellow-travellers will seen from one day to the next, but the nature of the landscape is such that there's plenty of opportunity to get away from the crowd and find deserted side canyons or rock scrambles to explore.

There are numerous trails within canyons and along the rims, rated from easy through moderate to strenuous and technical, so there's something for everyone. But the ultimate Zion experience is the Narrows hike, which follows the Virgin River and involves lots of time in the water – sometimes waist-deep pools. The hike is 26 km (16 mi) long and may be done from top to bottom, with or without camping overnight that allows time to check out tempting features like Kolob Creek and Orderville Gulch. It's possible to tackle the Narrows bottom-up, although only as far as Big Springs. A permit is needed for all but casual hikers at the lower end, to ensure that this wonderful experience is not devalued by processional use.

Zion National Park

Black Canyon

This precipitous gorge at the western edge of the Rocky Mountains is no place for those seeking the solitude of empty wilderness, although that is indeed the status of land surrounding Colorado's Black Canyon. Most people are drawn by one of the most awesome – and unsettling – natural wonders in the USA, and simply seeing it is satisfaction enough. The Black Canyon of the Gunnison National Park may be a bit of a mouthful – and the country's third-smallest national park – but few other experiences match the scary-yet-breathtaking opportunity to perch on the edge and peer down at the jagged rockscape far below.

The Painted Wall, Black Canyon

Carved deep into hard rock by the Gunnison River on its way to meet the Colorado River at Grand Junction, this spectacular canyon earned its name because it is so narrow – a mere 460 m (1,500 ft) across in places – and deep – over 610 m (2,000 ft) – that it remains in almost permanent gloom. The sun illuminates the canyon but briefly, and even then falls upon dark walls of volcanic schist. The main focus of visitor interest and most of the park's facilities are to be found on the Black Canyon's South Rim. The main entrance road is 13 km (8 mi) long, and passes the main viewpoints. There are 12 named overlooks, some requiring a short walk from the vehicle, plus opportunities for independent exploration.

The North Rim, accessed by a gravel road, is a better option for those who prefer relative solitude. It has overlooks that equal the spectacle to be seen from the South Rim, a primitive campground and three demanding trails down to the canyon floor – just the job for those who prefer 'I've been there and done it' to a rather less impressive 'I've seen it'.

HOW TO GET THERE:
Drive from Montrose, Delta or Gunnison, the nearest towns offering accommodation. There is a campground within the park. Access to the popular South Rim is from County Road 347, a short spur off US Route 50 – a main crossing of the Rockies. Find the North Rim road 18 km (11 mi) south of Crawford.

WHEN TO GO:
Any time (but the North Rim road is closed by snow in winter).

DON'T MISS:
Colorado's highest sheer cliff, seen from the South Rim. The Painted Wall is 685 m (2,250 ft) tall and shot through with light-coloured granite veins.

YOU SHOULD KNOW:
The 80-km (50-mi) Black Canyon has not remained untouched by the hand of man – two thirds of the upstream (eastern) section of the gorge have been flooded as part of a hydro-electric scheme and has become the Curecanti National Recreational Area, offering the usual outdoor activities associated with large artificial lakes.

Monument Valley

'Roll cameras, cue Indians' must have been words frequently uttered in Monument Valley by the great film director John Ford, who shot his first western in this iconic wilderness on the Utah-Arizona border. The movie saw the breakthrough of all-American tough-guy star John Wayne and *Stagecoach* became a classic. Ford returned to use the valley as a location time after time – there could scarcely be a more dramatic backdrop – and many more Hollywood film crews have followed him.

The Colorado Plateau has the greatest concentration of national parks and monuments in the USA, including the Grand Canyon, Canyonlands and the Petrified Forest. Monument Valley isn't among them – it lies within the Navajo Nation Reservation – but has unique scenic qualities that make this atmospheric place as special in its own way as any one of them. The arid floor consists of reddish siltstone and sand deposited by the ancient rivers that eroded the valley, dotted in places with low scrub vegetation. But the main attraction is the magnificent array of red sandstone spires and buttes, sculpted by wind and water over countless millennia into striking masterpieces that rise from the flatlands.

There's a fee for driving through the park on the 27-km (17-mi) dirt road (passenger-car friendly), open roughly from dawn to dusk and starting at the modest visitor centre and shop at Lookout Point, with its great valley views. Guided tours on wheels or foot are available on a choice of routes, including destinations such as Hunts Mesa or Mystery Valley not open to visitors without a Navajo guide. Excursions on horseback are offered at various locations around the park, ranging from an hour or two to a day and more in duration. Camping is available and – for the exotically minded – hot-air balloon rides.

HOW TO GET THERE:
Access is from US Route 63, part of the Trail of the Ancients National Scenic Byway.

WHEN TO GO:
Any time (be aware that the valley is full of visitors in the summer vacation period).

DON'T MISS:
A thunderstorm rolling across the valley – a truly awesome sight that explains why the Navajo place this natural phenomenon right at the top of their respect list. As these are rare, an excellent second prize is seeing the buttes by night, clearly silhouetted by the moon's harsh glow and burning starlight.

YOU SHOULD KNOW:
It's best not to plan a visit beginning or ending with an overnight stay in any sort of close proximity to Monument Valley – even the cheapest of motels (quality and moneywise) within an easily accessible radius are ruinously expensive.

A Navajo girl poses for the camera.

Chiricahua National Monument

It's billed as 'A Wonderland of Rocks' and the description is more than justified. This may not be America's largest untamed landscape – checking in at just 48 sq km (19 sq mi) – but there's still more than enough rugged terrain to allow an all-day vanishing act by those of solitary bent. Chiricahua National Monument in southern Arizona, some 190 km (120 mi) from Tucson, occupies a remote location. The Chiricahua Mountains are so-called 'sky islands', rising imperiously from a sea of surrounding grassland. The extraordinary rock formations are the main attraction, and these were grotesquely carved by water and ice over millions of years from rhyolite originally formed after the Turkey Creek Volcano erupted, a mere 27 million years ago – a sobering reminder of the human race's fleeting presence in a natural world of infinite age. This thought perhaps explains the awe experienced by those who see this enduring rockscape.

Exploring this special place may be done from the 13-km (8-mi) scenic drive on a paved road, or by using 27 km (17 mi) of hiking trails suitable for anything from short walks to day-long expeditions. There is a comprehensive trail guide available at the visitor centre. One day is the least amount of time anyone should want to spend at Chiricahua, and a select few use the 25-pitch campground to extend their stay (no pre-booking). Quite apart from stunning scenery, there's a fascinating opportunity to visit the Faraway Ranch Historic District, home of the Erickson family of Swedish immigrants who arrived in the late 1880s and subsequently developed a thriving homestead and guest ranch. The grounds may be explored and regular house tours take place. In the wild it's possible to spot black bear, mountain lion, white-tailed deer and assorted smaller creatures, plus a variety of bird life.

HOW TO GET THERE:
By car only. From Willcox (close to US Interstate 10) take Arizona State Highway 186 until reaching Arizona State Highway 181, turn left and find the national monument's entrance station. It's a 58-km (36-mi) journey.

WHEN TO GO:
Open all year (including visitor centre) although the scenic drive can be closed by adverse weather conditions in winter

DON'T MISS:
The one-room log cabin built by the first European settlers, Ja Hu Stafford and his wife Pauline, after they arrived here in 1880.

YOU SHOULD KNOW:
Fill the car's tank in Willcox – there are no gas stations on the lonely road between the town and Chiricahua National Monument.

Hikers on Echo Canyon Trail

Grand Canyon

HOW TO GET THERE:
The North Rim is served by Arizona State Route 67. State Route 64 runs along the South Rim to Grand Canyon Village.
WHEN TO GO:
Not winter, when the canyon may see heavy snowfalls that can prevent access to either rim. The North Rim sees greater precipitation and the single access road can be closed for months. Its facilities are closed from mid October until mid May.
DON'T MISS:
The amazing U-shaped Skywalk on Hualapai Indian lands at Grand Canyon West, jutting out above a vertical drop of 240 m (790 ft). This glass-floored engineering wonder has become a huge tourist attraction and is positioned over a side canyon, although it offers stunning views to the main canyon and Colorado River.
YOU SHOULD KNOW:
The first Europeans to see the Grand Canyon were a party of Spanish conquistadors in 1540, travelling up from the south under the leadership of Francisco de Coronado. After repeated unsuccessful attempts to descend to the river, they returned from whence they came and no awed European eyes fell on the canyon for another two centuries. The first non-native people – probably the first ever – to run the Colorado River through the entire length of the canyon were members of the waterborne expedition led by John Wesley Powell in 1869. With that track record he went on to head the US Geological Survey from 1881 to 1894.

Thanks to 17 million years of relentless effort by the Colorado River, Arizona has one of the world's great natural wonders. The Grand Canyon lives up to its billing at around 440 km (275 mi) long, ranging between 29 km (18 mi) and 6.5 km (4 mi) wide while plunging to a depth of up to over 1,800 m (5,900 ft). The canyon is a massive rift in the Colorado Plateau, creating a powerful rocky spectacle that may be viewed from either rim.

Most of this awesome gorge lies within Grand Canyon National Park, with headquarters in Grand Canyon Village on the South Rim. This historic settlement dates from the arrival of the Santa Fe railway in 1901 and has many building dating from that era. It is dedicated to servicing the needs of tourists and has numerous museums and information centres that add a dimension to the Grand Canyon experience.

For most, simply seeing this vertiginous canyon is enough, although it's worth noting that Desert View Watchtower at the eastern end of the South Rim, built on a promontory in 1932, is one of the few places from where the canyon floor and Colorado River can actually be observed. Most of the stunning views are of the opposite rim. The less-popular North Rim is considered to have the finest outlooks, yet ironically most visitors stick to the South Rim in order to enjoy the facilities at Grand Canyon Village. It's necessary to make the choice – the drive from one rim to the other is 345 km (215 mi) and takes five hours. For those who want more than scenery, the canyon offers unique hiking opportunities, but only for those prepared to hang tough and carry a lot of water in their backpacks.

Big sky above the canyons, buttes and plateaux of Grand Canyon National Park

Sonoran Desert

North America's largest and hottest place, covering 310,000 sq km (120,000 sq mi), is the Sonoran Desert. It extends all the way from California into Mexico, via Arizona – the latter's name confirming that arid desert terrain covers much of the state. For an apparently unforgiving wilderness, the desert contains a remarkable variety of flora and fauna. Over 2,000 plant types live and thrive in the harsh conditions, while the desert supports over 500 species of animals, birds and reptiles, plus countless insects.

The fact that such vast emptiness exists within the world's most advanced nation is surprising, and provides endless opportunities for those who love to escape from civilization and return to the wild for a few hours or days. Even so, this is America, so the desert must try to pay its way. It is exploited by – among others – animal grazers, so the Sonoran Desert National Monument has been established in Arizona to preserve an unspoilt tract. Find it to the south of Buckeye and Goodyear, east of Gila Bend. It's tiny in the context of the whole desert, but big in itself at 2,000 sq km (770 sq mi).

Perhaps the attraction of a journey of discovery through this extraordinary wilderness is best understood by quoting President Bill Clinton, after the national monument was established: 'The Sonoran Desert National Monument is a magnificent example of untrammelled Sonoran desert landscape. The area encompasses a functioning desert ecosystem with an extraordinary array of biological, scientific, and historic resources. The monument's biological resources include a spectacular diversity of plant and animal species. The monument also contains many significant archaeological and historic sites, including rock-art sites, lithic quarries, and scattered artefacts.' The same things can still be found in much of the Sonoran Desert by those prepared to look.

Springtime in the Sonoran Desert reveals saguaros, teddy bear cholla, and blooming yellow brittlebushes.

HOW TO GET THERE:
Access is a matter of choice. The two principal cities within the desert area are Phoenix and Tucson, which make good bases for exploration of a vast desert road network.

WHEN TO GO:
Any time – although it can be very hot in July and August.

DON'T MISS:
The tree-sized saguaro cactus with its distinctive upstretched arms. These grow nowhere else and have served as unpaid extras in countless Westerns.

YOU SHOULD KNOW:
California's Colorado Desert is part of the wider Sonoran Desert and home to the Anza-Borrego Desert State Park, which has 12 wilderness areas, numerous dirt roads and an extensive network of hiking trails.

Bisti Badlands

It's an evocative description, redolent of Wild West bandits and lawlessness, but actually the USA's badlands are just what the name suggests, consisting of arid ground – often with canyons, gullies and tortured rock formations – that early pioneers dismissed as 'bad lands' to settle on or travel through *en route* to more promising territory. The Bisti Badlands in the remote northwestern corner of New Mexico is just such a place – a scenic expanse of weirdly eroded rocks and colourful mounds to delight the modern backcountry explorer, which must have seemed a nightmare place to early 19th-century travellers as it interrupted steady progress across the prairie.

This little-visited 16-sq-km (6-sq-mi) patch of high desert is designated as the Bisti Wilderness Area, but the badlands actually extend much further than official boundaries. In truth, the latter are not much evident on the ground, although occasional fencing and barriers closing off dangerous washes may be seen, but beyond that there is little evidence of human interference – the Bisti Badlands remains an isolated

Tortured rock formations in Bisti Badlands

wild place rich in natural drama, much as Nature intended.

To make the most of this unique place a 4x4 vehicle is desirable. Assorted tracks criss-cross sandy hills at the southern boundary of the rocky areas, which are risky options for low-slung cars. The wilderness itself offers a vivid mix of colours – red, orange, brown and grey – and mostly consists of small hills, shallow ravines, dry washes and unusual rock formations, some of which look more like accomplished sculptures than natural artworks. Once away from the approach road, a surreal landscape envelops the bold interloper, going where there are no formal hiking trails and progress is generally made by following ravines with care – the terrain is often unstable and loose petrified wood litters the surface, often mixed with fossils.

DON'T MISS:
The Bisti Trading Post – a cluster of abandoned and decaying buildings, including an overgrown children's playground and simple church that is open to visitors. This windswept place is an evocative reminder of the enduring hostility of the adjacent badlands to human endeavour.

YOU SHOULD KNOW:
Those with the yen for total isolation should find the 16-km (10-mi) track that leads to the extensive De-na-zin Wilderness. It matches Bisti for colourful rock formations, but some are cloaked with scrub vegetation.

Sierra Blanca Wilderness

The Lincoln National Forest in New Mexico was established in 1902 and extends to an impressive 4,500 sq km (1,735 sq mi). The high-elevation forest is made up of major portions of four mountain ranges – The Capitans, Guadalupes, Sacramentos and its Sierra Blanca sub range. The latter is named for the extended blanket of snow up to 2 m (6.5 ft) deep that can cover the summits from November until as late as June. It is here that the White Mountain Wilderness Area may be found.

The wilderness soars to a breathtaking (literally) height of around 3,500 m (11,500 ft) and the mountains run in a north-south direction, bordering the Mescalero Apache Reservation at the southern end. The wilderness is about 20 km (12 mi) long and up to the same distance wide, straddling the crest and containing many ridges that branch off. The west side is steep and rugged with numerous rocky outcrops, while the east side is gentler with broad, forested canyons sometimes carrying small streams. The area is heavily wooded, but grassy oak savannahs and meadows are to be found, particularly towards the crest. This is a dramatic landscape of abrupt height changes, varied vegetation, rock promontories, bold escarpments and old avalanche slides.

Any backcountry explorer is sure to spot numerous representatives of the abundant wildlife with (among others) black bears, elk, mule deer, bobcats, coyotes, badgers, foxes, porcupines, skunks and squirrels in residence, along with a thriving bird population headed by wild turkeys. The chance to get among these creatures comes courtesy of a network of lonely wilderness trails, mostly following canyon bottoms and ridges. They range in difficulty from easy to strenuous and the ultimate challenge is the 32-km (20-mi) Crest Trail, offering views to die for in return for the effort required.

HOW TO GET THERE:
From the mountain resort town of Ruidoso, New Mexico, reached from US Route 70

WHEN TO GO:
Take your pick along with your pack – spring is windy, summer is hot, autumn is wet and winter sees prolonged snow.

DON'T MISS:
A visit to the Mescalero Apache's Cultural Museum on Route 70 south of Ruidoso, for fascinating insight into the history and culture of this ancient race.

YOU SHOULD KNOW:
Birders will be richly rewarded by a hike in the wilderness, and among many others will hope to spot one or more of the five species for which these mountains provide critical habitat – golden-crowned kinglets, Clarke's nutcrackers, red-breasted nuthatches, northern three-toed woodpeckers and Townsend's solitaires.

Lostwood National Wildlife Refuge

North Dakota contains one of the most important wildfowl breeding sites in the USA, and this area bordering both Montana and Canada is protected by the Lostwood National Wildlife Refuge. It lies in the so-called prairie pothole region – meaning it has a large number of lakes, ponds and boggy patches that provide a perfect habitat for geese, ducks and other aquatic birds. This has earned a designation as a Globally Important Bird Area, and the annual Burke County Birding Festival is held every June.

The 110-sq-km (42-sq-mi) block of old prairie was first settled in the early 1900s, but proved inhospitable to incoming farmers and has been reclaimed and restored since the mid 1930s with wildlife conservation a priority. In 1975, the Lostwood Wilderness Area was established within the refuge. This 23-sq-km (9-sq-mi) enclave provides further protection to the bird life, encompassing vital breeding sites and preventing disruptive activity. However, hiking and photography – plus cross-country trekking on skis or snowshoes in winter – are permitted. In the wider refuge, there are numerous trails providing the opportunity to explore.

Although the principal importance of the refuge lies in its 4,000 wetlands, Lostwood is within the Missouri Coteau region, which consists of prairie and hills. Nearly three quarters of the refuge is virgin prairie, making for a varied habitat that supports all sorts of creatures in addition to the large seasonal and resident bird population. There are around 250 bird species in the refuge, while animals to look out for include white-tailed deer, badger, coyote, fox, rabbit and weasel.

Badlands

South Dakota's Badlands National Park is the USA's largest mixed-grass prairie, preserved more or less in its original state. It serves as a poignant reminder of vast tracts of similar grassland – where buffalo roamed – that once covered much of America's Middle West, stretching from Saskatchewan down to Texas. The national park covers 990 sq km (380 sq mi), within which 260 sq km (100 sq mi) has been designated as the Badlands Wilderness. The rolling prairie shares this vast wild place with dramatic expanses of rock, eroded into fantastic shapes and patterns.

For centuries these badlands were the hunting ground of the Lakota Sioux tribe, and the last armed clashes between these proud indigenous people and the US Army took place hereabouts at the end of the 19th century. This story – plus a fascinating review of the park's long history from prehistoric times, as evidenced by the wealth of fossils to be found here – is brought to life at the Ben Reifel Visitor Centre, named after the Sioux Nation's first congressman, which has numerous interesting exhibits, some interactive, and a theatre showing the fascinating park movie.

A typical half-day tour consists of a session at the visitor centre during a run around the paved Badlands Loop Road, perhaps with a side trip along the gravelled Sage Creek Road, and pauses at four scenic overlooks. It's easily extended to a full day by using one of five waymarked hiking routes that require from half an hour to three hours for a round trip. There are ranger-guided activity programmes in summer, but those who prefer to stay away from the tourist trail can obtain a topographical map and break out the compass and backpack before heading into the wilderness to do their own thing.

HOW TO GET THERE:
The national park is best approached from Interstate 90 – exit 131 at Interior for the Northeast Entrance, exit 110 at Wall for the Pinnacle Entrance. Car rental available at Rapid City Regional Airport for those who fly in.

WHEN TO GO:
Spring to autumn is best (winters can be harsh), although the park is open all year.

DON'T MISS:
The nearby Minuteman Missile National Historic Site, just off Interstate 90 at exit 131. A reminder of the Cold War, this site preserves a Minuteman II ballistic missile system consisting of a launch control centre and missile-launch silo. Guided tours can be booked at the National Park Service office.

YOU SHOULD KNOW:
North America's most endangered land mammal – the black-footed ferret – has been successfully reintroduced to the Badlands Wilderness.

A fiery sunrise lights up the sky above countless peaks that make up the Badlands.

Big Bend National Park

This is a truly untouched wild place, much of it appearing today just as it did to the first European pioneers centuries ago. Big Bend National Park in West Texas is three parks in one – big river, desert and mountains. It lies in Brewster County, one of the USA's least-populated areas, and this fabulous park covers 3,250 sq km (1,255 sq mi), protecting much of the Chihuahuan Desert's unique ecology and topography. It also includes nearly 190 km (120 mi) of twisting Rio Grande, the border with Mexico, including a huge V-shaped sweep of river that gives the park its name. And the Chisos Mountains are here, the only range in the USA to be entirely contained within a single national park.

To be appreciated, even for a brief period that barely scratches the surface, this huge wilderness calls for a serious expedition rather than a simple visit. Once there, it is possible to enjoy a wide variety of activities. Simplest of all (and least strenuous) is viewing awesome desert landscape from one of many scenic drives on paved roads. For more adventurous types, the park has numerous unimproved dirt roads suitable only for reliable four-wheel-drive transport, allowing exploration of the remotest places, perhaps combined with backcountry camping (permit required). In either case, it's essential to leave the vehicle from time to time to merge with the landscape. Even from paved roads a few steps lead to timeless desert solitude, while those who want prolonged exposure can use the network of hiking trails.

Beyond that, rafting or kayaking the Rio Grande offers a hugely rewarding experience, through spectacular canyons with near-vertical walls like Santa Elena, Mariscal and Boquillas. It's possible to go solo (permit required) or with the help of many professional guides who organize trips.

Sunset on the Chisos Mountains in Big Bend National Park

Boundary Waters Canoe Area

The Superior National Forest in Minnesota's Arrowhead Region lies between the US-Canadian border and the North Shore of Lake Superior. In this 16,000-sq-km (6,180-sq-mi) tract of woods and water commercial activities like logging take place alongside the type of recreational activities offered by sparsely populated wild places. These include (in season where appropriate) berry picking, mountain-biking, camping, going afloat, hiking, fishing, hunting, cross-country skiing, snowshoeing, snowmobiling, driving scenic byways, off-roading, wildlife viewing and birding.

One of the most interesting and exciting possibilities is exploration within the Boundary Waters Canoe Area Wilderness (BWCAW), which extends along the national forest's northern limit. Renowned for pristine lakes – and the sporting fish that thrive therein – this is the USA's most-visited wilderness. But at 4,400 sq km (1,700 sq mi) there's little chance of this magical place to the east of Lake Superior becoming overcrowded. Actually, much of the BWCAW isn't the least bit canoe-friendly (although going afloat is a great way to explore), because it consists of both boreal forest and deciduous forest, including large tracts of old-growth timber that has never been logged.

For all that, the wilderness contains over 1,000 lakes and motorboats are prohibited on three quarters of them. Plenty of campgrounds that can be reached by vehicle surround the wilderness but, inside, 2,000 backcountry sites can only be reached by boat. With 1,600 km (1,000 mi) of established canoe routes, paddlers are spoiled for choice – although most require frequent portage between lakes. Popular entry points include Trout, Moose, Seagull and Sawbill Lakes, hinting at the abundant fish, animal and bird life to be seen in BWCAW. For those who get seasick on a boating pond, the wilderness has short hiking routes such as Eagle Mountain and Magnetic Rock, plus long-distance trails including the Kekekabic and Border Route trails.

Canoeing on Crooked Lake

HOW TO GET THERE:
There are many entry points to the wilderness for motorboats, paddlers and hikers – some for day use only, others for overnight trips. The nearest towns are Aurora, Ely, Isabella, Tofte and Grand Marais.

WHEN TO GO:
Any time, although winter is not the season to go afloat.

DON'T MISS:
Finding incised petroglyphs and painted pictographs on rocky ledges and cliff faces. There are hundreds within BWCAW, created by the Ojibwe people who once travelled these waters using birch-bark canoes and still live locally.

YOU SHOULD KNOW:
Overnight camping permits are required for all backcountry expeditions within BWCAW. In addition, advance-reservation permits are required for groups making motorized day or overnight journeys – plus overnight paddle-powered or hiking trips. These are on quota to ensure there's no overcrowding (issued on a first come, first served basis from May to September). At other times no reservation is required, but permits must still be filled out at entry points. The National Forest Service issues a comprehensive trip-planning guide (available online).

Mt Baldy sand dune and Lake Michigan at Indiana Dunes National Lakeshore

HOW TO GET THERE:
There are numerous access routes – Interstate 94, Interstate 80/90, US Route 20, State Highway 12 and various smaller roads. The Chicago & South Shore Train has stops in the park.

WHEN TO GO:
Any time. May to September are the kindest months weatherwise.

DON'T MISS:
The Heron Rookery near Pines Township in Porter County, Indiana, within the national lakeshore. Access to the eastern car park is from US Route 20. It consists of 28 ha (69 acres) set aside to protect the nesting grounds of the great blue heron, which has a wingspan of 2 m (6.5 ft). There is a trail along the Little Calumet River through hardwoods, and the birds may be seen nesting high in the trees on the opposite bank in season (late spring and early summer, when the wild flowers are also at their best).

Indiana Dunes National Lakeshore

This protected area on the southern shore of Lake Michigan is long and narrow –almost 40 km (25 mi) long, with a total area of just 61 sq km (24 sq mi). Gary is at the western end of Indiana Dunes National Lakeshore with Michigan City to the east. It is not contiguous, having two roughly equal sections and some privately owned property within the boundaries. However, it is a magnificent stretch of impressive lakeside landscape, dominated by sand dunes that can reach 60 m (200 ft) in height. But dunes, beaches and crashing waves are not the full story.

Although the long run of beaches along the lake is the principal recreational resource, the national lakeshore has much more than that to offer. It is a treasure house of natural delights, including areas of swamp, bog, marsh, prairie, riverbank, forest and oak savannah. The biological diversity is staggering, with around 1,100 ferns and flowering plant species to be found. The bird life is vibrant, with over 350 species recorded, including many migrants that rest before moving on. Birdwatching is therefore a popular activity, as is hiking along diverse trails that provide anything from a leisurely stroll to a day-long expedition.

This wonderful expanse of sculpted soft sand may be close to civilization and well used for recreational purposes, but it's still easy to get away from it all. The dunes are extensive, offering every opportunity to find a quiet spot. And by choosing one of the less-popular locations and going during the week it is perfectly possible to imagine that this magnificent lakeshore is the wildest of places scarcely touched by human hand. That's true in summer, so following an inland or dunes trail in the off-season (on skis or snowshoes if necessary!) virtually guarantees solitude.

YOU SHOULD KNOW:
Swimming in Lake Michigan is tempting, but there are only a few lifeguards on the most popular beaches (in season) and the lake is notorious for sudden rip currents. If caught, swimmers are advised not to fight the current – which will be too powerful for even strong swimmers – but to go with the flow until able to edge sideways out of the rip.

Lusk Creek Wilderness

Shawnee National Forest at the southern tip of Illinois is an oasis of natural wonders amid a (relative!) desert of intensively farmed land. Those seeking backcountry experiences are well served, and can concentrate on the wilderness areas within the national forest – Bald Knob, Bay Creek, Burden Falls, Clear Springs, Garden of the Gods, Panther Den and Lusk Creek. All seven are impressive wild places, but if one has to be singled out it is the Lusk Creek Wilderness – if only for the magnificent view that rejoices in the somewhat incongruous name of 'Indian Kitchen'.

This wilderness extends to a mere 28 sq km (11 sq mi), but for once that old saying doesn't stack up – size definitely *isn't* everything, as Lusk Creek is both the second-largest wilderness in the state and a miniature masterpiece to be savoured by lovers of unspoilt wild places. This perfectly formed mini-wilderness consists of rugged terrain and winding canyons – a type of landscape not common in Illinois – where broad ridge tops overlook terraces, narrow ravines and sheer rock walls. Lusk Creek Wilderness is dotted with sinkholes and caves, there is some old-growth timber and wild flowers are abundant in spring.

The wilderness may be accessed from one of two trailheads, at New Liberty Church and Indian Kitchen, and encompasses Lusk Creek itself. This is one of the purest streams in Illinois, attracting fishermen, canoeists and those who simply want to stroll the banks. Horse riding, hiking and camping are other recreational activities that may be practised, but most casual visitors find that simply walking around in tranquil yet dramatic surroundings is satisfaction enough – especially when the highlight is being surprised and delighted by one of the most spectacular overlooks in the state at a precipitous hairpin turn in Lusk Creek Canyon.

HOW TO GET THERE:
Lusk Creek has two trailheads. For New Liberty Church Trailhead leave Illinois State Highway 145 on Forest Road 404 then go south on Forest Road 488. For Indian Kitchen Trailhead (and that view) leave State Highway 145 on the Eddyville-Golconda Blacktop and follow the signs. The nearest town is Eddyville.
WHEN TO GO:
Any time (May to September for the best weather)
DON'T MISS:
The evocative reminders of ultimately fruitless human endeavour in Lusk Creek Wilderness, such as old homesteads, fruit trees, overgrown cemeteries and abandoned dirt roads.
YOU SHOULD KNOW:
The 255-km (160-mi) River-to-River Trail passes through Lusk Creek Wilderness shortly after commencing at Battery Rock, overlooking the Ohio River, before continuing westwards to its final destination on the banks of the Mississippi River at Grand Tower, Illinois.

Tupelo trees in the Cupola Pond Natural Area of Mark Twain National Forest

Mark Twain National Forest

HOW TO GET THERE:
Main roads through forest areas are Interstate 44 (east-west), US Route 63 (north-south) and US Route 60 (east-west).
WHEN TO GO:
Any time, but the show of brilliantly coloured turning Ozarks foliage from mid September into October is world-famous.
DON'T MISS:
Driving the 37-km (23-mi) Glade Top National Scenic Byway, a two-lane gravel road near Ava, Missouri, that winds through ridge tops above rolling countryside offering superb far-reaching views to the Springfield Plateau and Boston Mountains down in Arkansas.
YOU SHOULD KNOW:
Greer Spring in Oregon County, Missouri, is the largest spring on forest land in the USA. It discharges 840,360,000 l (185,000,000 gal) per day, which is 9,750 l (2,150 gal) per second. This dramatic scenic outflow can be reached and admired after a short hike from Missouri Highway 19.

Missouri native Mark Twain is commemorated by the national forest that bears his name, which consists of around a tenth of his home state's woodland. The Mark Twain National Forest (MTNF) covers some 6,100 sq km (2,350 sq mi) in south and central Missouri, spreading into 29 counties. The native timber had all been logged out when President Franklin D Roosevelt's Depression-era Civilian Conservation Corps – a New Deal work-creation programme – started replanting deforested areas and laid the foundations for what became MTNF, established in 1939 and mostly falling within the Ozark Highlands.

The forest is not in one block, but consists of nine separate tracts with six ranger districts and headquarters at Rolla, Missouri. It offers a variety of recreational opportunities for those who like to hunt, fish, hike, ride on horseback, camp or observe abundant wildlife, which includes over 300 species of birds, 75 types of mammal and 125 different amphibians or reptiles. Mountain-biking and driving are permitted on most forest roads, although not in wilderness areas, and there are also a number of roads where all-terrain vehicles may be used.

There are several prime locations for lovers of wild places. These include the rugged Bell Mountain Wilderness Area with

22 km (14 mi) of wilderness trails, and parts of the St Francois mountain section noted for streams, rivers, lakes, rocky bluffs, woodland trails and fine landscape views. The forest has recreation areas such as Sutton Bluff and Marble Creek with campgrounds and scenic trails. The latter is the trailhead for a section of the long-distance Ozark Trail that leads to Crane Lake. Other popular forest destinations are the Council Bluff Lake Recreation Area, surrounding the forest's largest stretch of open water, and the Silver Mines Recreation Area with its abandoned mine workings.

Kisatchie Hills Wilderness

Within Louisiana's Kisatchie National Forest may be found 35 sq km (14 sq mi) of the steepest and most interesting terrain in a state not noted for rugged grandeur. Kisatchie is the only national forest in Louisiana. It is located in seven parishes – Vernon, Rapides, Grant, Natchitoches, Webster, Claiborne and Winn – in the northern and central part of the state. The forest protects a wonderful natural world of bayous beneath old-growth pine and bald cypress stands. This magical place may be explored from a comprehensive 4,800-km (3,000-mi) network of forest roads where vehicles (including all-terrain vehicles) are mostly permitted.

One of the no-go motorized zones is the aforementioned Kisatchie Hills Wilderness Area, known locally as 'The Little Grand Canyon'. Relatively small but perfectly unspoilt, the only way of seeing this wilderness is to travel on foot or horseback. There are three established trailheads that provide easy access, although it's possible to enter from any direction. This scenic area features sandstone bluffs and outcrops, flat-topped mesas and varied woodland. There is a designated trail system but no restriction stopping hardy hikers from stepping into the unknown, and camping is permitted.

The four intersecting wilderness trails are for true adventurers. The Backbone Trail speaks for itself, and passes through 11 km (7 mi) of demanding terrain. The others are shorter – High Ridge Trail at 2.5 km (1.5 mi) and the Turpentine Hill Trail, of similar length. The shorter Explorer Trail provides a wonderful taste of wilderness hiking for those unwilling or unable to tackle the more demanding trails, but even there the wilderness is no place for casual strollers. Those who want to spend time in the district will find nine campgrounds in the area, all primitive and some not designed for vehicle use.

HOW TO GET THERE:
The wilderness trailheads are on Forest Road 59, the Longleaf Scenic Byway, and Forest Road 339. These may be reached from Interstate 49 using exit 119 and driving for 8 km (5 mi) down Louisiana Highway 119 to find FR 59, where the wilderness is on the right. A right turn onto FR 339 also borders the wilderness back to the point where it meets the forest proper.

WHEN TO GO:
Summer (late May to September)

DON'T MISS:
The opportunity to drive the Longleaf Scenic Byway from end to end – it's a 27 km (17 mi) paved road connecting Louisiana Highways 119 (east end) and 117 (west end). Better still, find time to add a visit to the Longleaf Vista Day-Use Complex and tramp the interpretive trail – a short loop through the woods with informative signs describing native flora. There are great glimpses of the adjacent wilderness and short spur trails lead to a mesa offering panoramic all-round views over the forest.

YOU SHOULD KNOW:
The four wilderness trails are all primitive and very remote and – although it is not compulsory – it is recommended that hikers or horse riders should come prepared to take risks and also leave a check-in form at their chosen trail entrance to inform the Forest Service of their presence and intentions – just to be on the safe side.

Black Creek Wilderness

HOW TO GET THERE:
The wilderness is located in Perry County east of Mississippi State Highway 29, north of Wiggins. The trailhead is at Big Creek Landing.
WHEN TO GO:
Any time (although high summer is seriously steamy and the insects can be voracious, so the other three seasons are generally favoured).
DON'T MISS:
De Soto National Forest's one other designated wilderness area, also of an aquatic nature – Leaf River Wilderness, between Benndale and McClain off State Highway 57. Although very similar to Black Creek, this is a smaller tract of flood plain, with rising ground at the western edge. It may be appreciated from the short Leaf Trail hiking route.
YOU SHOULD KNOW:
Firewood should never be taken into a forest area, even if campfires are permitted. This will help to prevent the spread of three alien wood-boring insects – emerald ash borer, Asian longhorned beetle and Sirex woodwasp – that can be brought in on firewood and, once established, will kill local trees.

On the Lower Coastal Plain of southern Mississippi, Black Creek is the state's largest wilderness at 20 sq km (8 sq mi). This peaceful enclave is located in the broad valley of Black Creek, a tributary of the Pascagoula River so named because the water is stained to a dark caramel colour by tannic acid from decaying vegetation. The creek is Mississippi's only designated Wild and Scenic River and bisects the wilderness. In truth, the emphasis should be on scenic rather than wild, for this is a gentle landscape of oxbow lakes and impressive clumps of old-growth timber that include bald cypress, loblolly pine, sweet gum, red maple, sweet bay and oak. This is not a place of rugged landscapes but rather low, rolling hills and unassuming ridges covered in the pinewoods of De Soto National Forest.

The Black Creek National Recreation Trail runs for 65 km (40 mi) along the Black Creek drainage. To be travelled only on foot, it passes through the length of the wilderness. Nothing motorized – a prohibition that includes bicycles – may enter the wilderness and horses are not permitted on the recreation trail. Hiking, camping, canoeing, kayaking and fishing (bass and panfish a speciality) are the principal activities on, in and around Black Creek. The river has plenty of wide sandbars ideal for pulling up a canoe, pitching camp or having a leisurely picnic in incomparable surroundings.

Black Creek cannot remotely be described as the USA's wildest wilderness, but it remains in pristine condition and on many days visitors will find it hard to believe that canoes have ever navigated the river or another human foot has fallen on this delightful flood plain. True solitude is a precious gift, and Black Creek can give generously.

Green Mountain National Forest

HOW TO GET THERE:
The two blocks of national forest are best explored from Rutland, Vermont, which lies between them. Going north use US Route 7 and Vermont Highway 116 (west) or US Route 4 and Vermont Highway 100 (east). Going south use US Route 7 (west) or Vermont Highways 103 and 100 (east). The state roads are super-scenic.
WHEN TO GO:
Any time (although winter conditions can be extreme and the autumn foliage has to be seen to be believed).

There is something for everyone here, for Green Mountain National Forest (GMNF) covers more than 1,600 sq km 620 (sq mi) of protected land in central and southwestern Vermont, forming an impressive north-south spine of public land down the middle of the state. The forest is characterized by great scenic beauty and a wonderful rural atmosphere, with rugged mountain scenery and extensive forests punctuated by charming traditional villages. The extensive forestation is of various age classes, but there are also small treeless upland habitats, wetlands, streams, ponds and lakes.

Three major trails pass through this largely untamed area – the Robert Frost National Recreation Trail, Appalachian National Scenic

Trail and Long National Recreation Trail. Beyond that, there are endless opportunities for wild-place action on the extensive 1,450-km (900-mi) network of local trails. These are used for hiking, primitive camping, cycling, horseback riding, snowshoeing, cross-country skiing and snowmobiling. The forest has three alpine and seven Nordic ski areas for winter sports enthusiasts who come out to play during the long winters that turn the forest into a white wonderland. Hunting (in season) and fishing are also popular pastimes. So, too, is wildlife-watching and photography, with numerous bird species and mammals including black bear, moose, beaver and white-tailed deer to be spotted. Boating opportunities exist, too, along with a number of developed campsites with good facilities.

Around 400 sq km (155 sq mi) are taken up by the eight officially designated wilderness areas within GMNF, a quarter of the total area. These are not for the inexperienced or faint-hearted. Management is minimal, with fallen trees left to rot and helpful aids like rough bridges and marked trails virtually non-existent. But those fit individuals motivated by the spirit of challenge, exploration and self-discovery will find wilderness heaven – total solitude plus awe-inspiring surroundings.

A view from Kelly Stand Road, Green Mountain National Forest

DON'T MISS:
A rewarding side trip to East Creek Natural Area near Orwell, Vermont. The creek flows into Lake Champlain and sustains wonderful wetlands that harbour rare flora and wildlife like the American bittern – but one among many bird species to be seen. Other notable inhabitants are painted and snapping turtles, muskrat, white-tailed deer, mink, bobcats and coyotes. Lower East Creek may be explored by rowboat for a special open-air experience.

YOU SHOULD KNOW:
The eight wilderness areas in GMNF (in ascending order of size) are Bristol Cliffs, George Aiken, Big Branch, Peru Peak, Joseph Battell, Lye Brook, Glastenbury and Breadloaf. Maps of each are available online at the US Department of Agriculture's Forest Service website.

White Mountain National Forest

HOW TO GET THERE:
The main access roads are Interstate 95 (Maine) or Interstates 93 and US Route 302 (New Hampshire). Principal towns are Portland, Laconia and Manchester, while Forest HQ is at Campton, New Hampshire.
WHEN TO GO:
Any time (there are lots of ski areas in or near the park for winter sporters).
DON'T MISS:
One or more of the visitors' centres that provide interesting insight into the forest's ecology, geology, flora, fauna and long history of human activity. Find them at Lincoln (in Grafton County), Campton (off Interstate 93), Lincoln Woods (on scenic Kancamagus Highway) and Bethel (Evans Notch Information Centre).
YOU SHOULD KNOW:
The Old Man of the Mountain, a rock formation on Cannon Mountain in Franconia Notch State Park near Lincoln looked just like the profile of a man's craggy face when viewed from a particular angle. The old boy was so distinctive that he became New Hampshire's much-loved state symbol, but he collapsed in 2003 and is no more.

It is big, beautiful, wild and spreads into two states – New Hampshire and Maine. It's the 3,175-sq-km (1,225-sq-mi) White Mountain National Forest (WMNF), unsurprisingly contained within the White Mountains. This range offers the most rugged upland terrain in New England and forms part of the mighty Appalachians. It may be big enough to allow wilderness seekers ample scope, but WMNF attracts six million visitors each year. Indeed, the only national site in the USA to draw more is the Great Smoky Mountains National Park, further south on the Tennessee-North Carolina border.

As for wilderness, there are five areas within WMNF, accounting for over 460 sq km (178 sq mi) of forest lands. The Presidential Range/Dry River Wilderness is notable for cloud-shrouded mountains named after prominent US citizens who made their mark on American history, including several presidents, and attracts serious peak-baggers. The Sandwich Range Wilderness consists of rugged terrain that rewards super-fit hikers with outstanding views over mountains, lakes and forest. The Great Gulf Wilderness is a small but spectacular *cirque*, a natural amphitheatre formed by glacial erosion. The largest is Maine's Caribou-Speckled Mountain Wilderness, a place of craggy rockscapes characterized by open ledges, deep notches and wooded ridges. The 'speckled' description comes from vivid splashes of autumn colour created by stands of hardwood trees. Pemigewasset Wilderness encompasses a river watershed surrounded by steep mountain ridges. It is the newest – and most widely used – of the forest's wilderness areas.

There are actually three disconnected areas within WMNF as a whole, together offering 1,900 km (1,180 mi) of hiking trails, numerous official campgrounds and all the usual outdoor recreational opportunities, from autumn foliage photography to zoological observation. As per federal regulations, wilderness areas cannot be commercially exploited and must be used only by non-motorized explorers.

A swift flowing river runs through White Mountain National Forest.

Catskill Forest Preserve

A view across the beautiful Catskill Mountains

The Catskill Forest Preserve consists of all state-owned land within Catskill Park, encompassing New York State's Catskill Mountains. The preserve amounts to an impressive 1,150 sq km (445 sq mi) that is, as the name suggests, mainly wooded. But it also includes wetlands and meadows, lakes, rivers, waterfalls and cliffs. It is a natural playground affording all sorts of recreational opportunities, not least of which is the ability to get away from civilization and enjoy the solitude of the woods, where the only companions are birds and forest animals, the latter including bear, coyote, bobcat and mink.

The 98 major peaks within Catskill Park form a stirring skyline, and forest preserve land is classified as one of three types – wilderness, wild forest and intensive use. The latter mainly consists of official campgrounds, most of which – while having vehicular access – offer only basic facilities. One exception is the huge North-South Lake campground with many pitches and swimming areas in both lakes.

Wild forest is mostly second- or third-growth woodland that has been disturbed by human activity before being allowed to regenerate. Certain vehicles are permitted on the old logging roads and those leading up to many fire towers that offer superb vantage points with panoramic views over the arboreal sea. These areas are popular with those who prefer driving, with or without accompanying woodland walks.

Wilderness areas must be 'untrammelled by man' and the forest park has four (review pending). These are Slide Mountain and Big-Indian Beaverkill in Ulster County, plus Indian Head and West Kill in Greene County. No mechanical intrusion is permitted – even chainsaws needed to clear fallen trees require a special permit – while trails are narrow woodland paths rather than old roads. It's here that backcountry hikers and birdwatchers can experience true solitude in the great outdoors.

HOW TO GET THERE:
Catskill Park has many routes that offer scenic touring and give good access to forest preserve areas. The park's vast network of minor roads is best reached from Interstate 87 (New York to Albany).

WHEN TO GO:
Any time (snow can be deep in winter, but there are still plenty of recreational opportunities like cross-country skiing and there are various winter sports facilities in Catskill Park, such as Belleayre Mountain Ski Centre).

DON'T MISS:
The view from the top of Slide Mountain, the highest peak in the Catskills – the main trail to the summit was built in 1892, the first hiking route constructed in the forest preserve at public expense.

YOU SHOULD KNOW:
Catskill Park is within a so-called 'Blue Line' encircling 2,800 sq km (1,100 sq mi) in Delaware, Greene, Sullivan and Ulster Counties. Deriving from the blue ink originally used to physically outline Catskill and Adirondack Parks on a map, this became a device ensuring that any land acquired by the state within Blue Lines must legally 'be forever kept as wild forest lands' and incorporated into existing forest preserves.

Ferns and hardwoods in Allegheny National Forest

Hickory Creek Wilderness

HOW TO GET THERE:
The Hickory Creek trailhead is close to Hearts Content Recreation Area, 24 km (15 mi) southwest of Warren, Pennsylvania, which is on US Route 6. Follow Scenic Route 3005 (Pleasant Drive) to the junction with Township Road 2002, which leads to Hearts Content with its campground.

WHEN TO GO:
Any time – October to enjoy the sensational colours of the autumn trees – although the wilderness trail itself is impassable to all but the most determined survivalists after snowfall.

DON'T MISS:
The interpretive Old Growth Trail, a stroll around a loop path from the picnic site at Hearts Content Recreation Area, through a lovely old-growth timber stand that was deliberately preserved by a logging company when all around came down in the mid 1800s. This is the centrepiece of the small but attractive Hearts Content Scenic Area, a National Natural Landmark.

YOU SHOULD KNOW:
The Hickory Creek Wilderness is one of only two such areas in the whole of Pennsylvania, the other being the Allegheny Islands Wilderness, consisting of seven islands along a 90-km (56-mi) stretch of the Allegheny River between Buckaloons Recreation Area and the town of Tionesta.

Pennsylvania's mighty Allegheny National Forest has much to offer, but nothing more self-contained and beguiling than the 15-sq-km (6-sq-mi) Hickory Creek Wilderness. This unspoiled gem is located in the forest's Bradford Ranger District in northwestern Pennsylvania and is characterized by beech and black cherry woodland, interspersed with open spaces dotted with stands of oak, maple, birch and hemlock, while at ground level there's a rich variety of mosses, ferns, shrubs and abundant wild flowers. The wilderness encompasses East and Middle Hickory Creeks, where native brook trout can be caught and black bears and deer lurk in the undergrowth along with shy wild turkeys. The trees are populated by the likes of barred owls and woodpeckers.

One of the most rewarding experiences within the national forest – and the only way to fully appreciate the wilderness atmosphere – is following the Hickory Creek Wilderness Trail. This 18 km (11 mi) loop offers a great experience for lovers of wild places, who will understand the lonely challenges faced by the first European pioneers as they explored the forest and empathize with their long-ago experiences.

The round trip is a strenuous day hike or rewarding overnight expedition. This is not one for the unfit or inexperienced walker, with map and compass essential aids. Occasional yellow blazes mark the trail, but these are being allowed to fade naturally and obstructions like fallen trees are mostly left untouched. If this sounds daunting rather than delightful, simply sampling the beginning of the trail gives a flavour of the place. Alternatively, plenty of easier yet worthwhile hiking opportunities are to be found on the 320-km (200-mi) network of well-developed and waymarked trails within the surrounding Allegheny National Forest's 2,075 sq km (800 sq mi) of largely wooded terrain.

Great Swamp National Wildlife Refuge

New Jersey's Morris and Somerset Counties are the places to find Great Swamp National Wildlife Refuge – an unspoiled corner of this well-developed state within 50 km (30 mi) of Manhattan that's so special it's one of the nation's 500+ wildlife refuges, has been declared a National Natural Landmark and is officially designated as wilderness. So what's so important about this relatively small area – 31 sq km (12 sq mi) – that very nearly became the site of a major international airport in the early 1960s?

The answer is 'birds'. The Great Swamp is within a watershed that provides the source of the Passaic River. Although habitat within the refuge is varied, its predominant character – as the name suggests – is wetland. This environment provides a home and refuge for a huge population of resident and migratory birds. Around 250 species have been recorded and the refuge serves as a vital stopping place on North America's eastern migration corridor. But the 'wildlife' tag applies to numerous four-footed denizens such as deer, coyote, fox, muskrat, raccoon, beaver, red and grey squirrel, plus the occasional bear. There are also turtles, snakes, amphibians, fish and innumerable insects, together enjoying a wonderful natural habitat rich in wild flowers and native vegetation.

There are roads through the Great Swamp at the western end, including Pleasant Plains Road where Refuge Headquarters and the Helen C Fenske Visitor Centre may be found, along with a nature shop. There's a wildlife observation centre on north-south Long Hill Road, which separates off the road-free eastern half of the refuge with its various rewarding hiking trails emanating from convenient trailheads with parking. There are related facilities surrounding the Great Swamp, such as an outdoor education centre in Chatham Township and the Somerset County Environmental Centre.

A boardwalk stretches across the unspoilt swamplands.

HOW TO GET THERE:
From US Interstate 78 (exit 40) take Hillcrest Road, Mountain Avenue and Meyersville Road. From US Interstate 287 take exit 30A and follow refuge signs.
WHEN TO GO:
Refuge grounds are open from sunrise to sunset all year round.
DON'T MISS:
The Raptor Trust – based in Millington, New Jersey, and surrounded by the Great Swamp. This is the place to see a huge collection of captive raptors and a large number of assorted wild birds recovering from injury.
YOU SHOULD KNOW:
Back in 1968, this was the very first of (currently) nearly 700 locations in the USA to receive official federal wilderness designation under the Wilderness Act of 1964.

Backbone Mountain

Maryland's Potomac-Garrett State Forest is a 47-sq-km (18-sq-mi) tract of rugged upland forest situated between the towns of Oakland and Westernport. This magical sweep of wild woodland, tumbling streams and deep valleys is a great place to start exploring Backbone Mountain, which straddles the border between Maryland and West Virginia. It is a prominent ridge of the Allegheny Mountains, part of the Appalachians and great Eastern Continental Divide, around 65 km (40 mi) long and runs on a northeast-southwest line from Maryland's Savage River Reservoir to Black Fork on the Cheat River in West Virginia.

Within the State Forest on its Maryland flank may be found Crabtree Woods, a fascinating remnant of the once-vast expanse of old-growth forest that has largely been logged out. It contains mixed hardwoods such as red oak, sugar maple, basswood and cucumber trees, offering a wonderful display of contrasting colours when the foliage starts to turn in late September or October. The forest as a whole offers fishing, trails to suit casual strollers and hardened hikers alike, plus a choice of mountain-bike routes.

Backbone Mountain is a watershed. While the north branch of the Potomac heads off into Maryland, West Virginia gets the white-water Youghiogheny, a tributary of the Monongahela River. The mountain's forested sides are criss-crossed with trails that allow backcountry hikers to enjoy the solitary splendours of nature and abundant wildlife. One feature worth visiting is the Olson Observation Tower at the southern end of the mountain. West Virginia's first fire tower was built there in 1922, although the present structure dates from the 1960s. The tower is not open to the public but, as befits a vital lookout, tree-top views from the last of the 133 steps leading up to it are truly spectacular.

Cranberry Wilderness

The last North American Ice Age sent its glacial fingers as far south as West Virginia. When they retreated, at their southernmost point they left behind a geological anomaly – a 3-sq-km (1.2-sq-mi) peat bog ecosystem. Maintained by chance microclimate, it's like a piece of Canadian taiga isolated in the dense, temperate woods and rushing mountain rivers of West Virginia's enormous Monongahela National Forest. The bog is called Cranberry Glades Botanical Area. Its spongy soil is so fragile and so full of site-specific flora, including orchids and carnivorous species like the pitcher-plant, that it can be crossed only on protective boardwalk trails.

Cranberry Glades is the jewel in the crown of the 145-sq-km (56-sq-mi) Cranberry Wilderness named after it – and of the additional 105-sq-km (40-sq-mi) 'Cranberry Backcountry' to its west, where wilderness restrictions are fewer). Cranberry Glades has survived untouched; Cranberry Wilderness is in reversion to its primeval state. In the 1970s it almost became West Virginia's biggest strip coal mine and, like most of the eastern United States, it was once clearcut by timber companies. Now, parts of Cranberry Wilderness have already had 100 years to recover. Along the Middle Fork of the Williams River, icy water tumbles across boulders in long cascades or runs through beautiful, tall ferns and broadleaf woods filled with exuberant outbursts of rhododendron. Side trails drop off the high ridges past waterfalls and into mysterious hollows. Others keep the high ground among red spruce and Appalachian hardwoods, with magnificent views across the broad mountains and deep valleys typical of the Allegheny Plateau. As a designated sanctuary for black bears, Cranberry Wilderness has become a haven for all forms of wildlife. It's a privilege to share it briefly with what the 1964 US Wilderness Act describes as 'a community of life . . . where man himself is a visitor who does not remain'.

A trio of pointed green leaves among a trio of crimson petals identifies this delicate spring wild flower as the Purple Trillium Blossom in the Cranberry Wilderness.

DON'T MISS:
'Hell For Certain' – a particularly lovely, isolated branch stream feeding into Middle Fork Williams River; white-water running in the rushing waters of springtime or lazy river tubing in placid late summer water; the secret hollows along the Big Beechy Trail.

YOU SHOULD KNOW:
Some rivers have 'catch-and-return' fishing rules on certain sections. Check licenses and permissions before you go. The Wilderness area is a black bear sanctuary. The backcountry is not. Wear brightly coloured clothing during the hunting season when hiking or camping near the fringes.

George Washington National Forest

The Appalachians, a glorious range of thickly wooded parallel ridges, deep valleys and shining rivers, sweep southwest, forming the Virginia–West Virginia border. The forests were home to Native Americans, then settlers, who cleared and farmed the fertile land. Logging and mining in the 19th century ravaged and scarred the landscape and almost wiped out the indigenous wildlife. Thanks to the vision and determination of those who recognized the threat to the nation's natural resources, the government intervened to purchase deforested mountains. In 1918, the area which later became the George Washington National Forest was one of the first acquisitions; now it is jointly administered with the Jefferson National Forest further south as a vast area of public land.

The forest is within easy reach for millions of city dwellers, who are drawn by its peace and grandeur and outdoor activities which include hunting, fishing, horse riding, camping and canoeing. Some spots can be quite crowded, but much of the more remote and undeveloped forest has been designated wilderness, and even at busy times walkers can find solitude on the hundreds of miles of hiking trails, which include part of the long-distance Appalachian Trail.

The varied terrain of the forest supports a huge variety of trees and plants and many animals and birds, including white-tailed deer and black bear, wild turkeys and bald eagles. It is splendid walking country and a climb to one of the higher ridges is rewarded with a stunning panorama of rolling, tree-clad ridges, in autumn dazzling with scarlet-and-gold foliage, receding into a softly misty distance. The US Forest Service aims to 'care for the land and serve the people', and here it does both superlatively.

Red River Gorge

More than 70 million years of weathering have formed the scenery surrounding the central section of Kentucky's Red River Gorge. Wind and water have sculpted sandstone cliffs, hollowing out rock shelters (caves) which slowly erode into arches and bridges and these are the best-known features of the gorge. Unspoilt woods and valleys between the rocky ridges are home to a wealth of plants and wildlife. When the railways opened up this remote countryside in the 19th century, city dwellers flocked here. Entrepreneurs opened hotels and the crowds enjoyed not just the wonders of nature, but restaurants, boating lakes and dance halls. Later, to protect this unique landscape, it was made part of the Daniel Boone National Forest. Red River Gorge is now a designated National Natural Landmark; orchestras no longer play, but there are miles of enjoyable short and long hiking trails.

The river offers excellent canoeing; the tough upper reaches suit experienced canoeists, while the quieter central section is normally safe and easy, with fine views of the rocks around the gorge. 'The Red' is also a world-renowned rock-climbing and abseiling location, with established routes in overhanging sandstone ranging from easy to very difficult.

While several of the spectacular rock arches, such as the famous Sky Bridge, are easily accessible and much visited, many more – there are around 100 – are found on quieter, more demanding trails and can be visited in peaceful solitude. Clifty Wilderness is a spacious, rugged, undeveloped part of the gorge, where a few longer trails wind through towering cliffs and narrow ravines. Traces of its earliest inhabitants, the Native Americans, and of pioneers and settlers can be seen in the area. These are treasured and protected by the Forest Service, which is diligent in its care for all aspects of this extraordinary landscape.

DON'T MISS:
The Gladie Cultural-Environmental Learning Center is excellent for background to the geology, wildlife and cultural heritage of the gorge, as well as for information on trails, climbing, camping, etc.
YOU SHOULD KNOW:
The cliff edges are often unstable; do not allow children to wander on their own. Canoeists should always check the river level – high water is too fast and low water too shallow for safety. New climbing routes must be approved by the Forest Service.

Unspoilt woods and valleys lie between the rocky ridges of Red River Gorge.

Fall Creek Falls State Park

The Cumberland Plateau is famous for its oak and hickory forests stretching from Kentucky down to Alabama. On its western edge in middle Tennessee, between Pikeville and Spencer, the plateau is creased by Cane Creek Gorge, the centrepiece of a geological formation that cuts into the stands of hardwood timber with streams, gorges, cascades and waterfalls. The region is powered by the waters that feed Cane Creek, but it takes its name from the highest of the waterfalls that make it so thrilling to visit: the 84-m (256-ft) Fall Creek Falls. Protected within a 81-sq-km (31-sq-mi) State Park, Falls Creek Falls is a compendium of some of temperate-zone America's most dramatic natural formations – with the added bonus of being highly accessible.

Cane Creek is fuelled by several streams even before it enters Cane Creek Gorge and drops hundreds of feet in less than a mile. Cane Creek Cascades drop 14 m (46 ft) before falling 26 m (85 ft) at Cane Creek Falls (into the same plunge pool as the 38-m (125-ft) Rockhouse Creek waterfall). Piney Falls tumble 29 m (95 ft) into a minor gorge above its confluence with Cane Creek; and even 76-m (250-ft) Coon Creek Falls seems inconspicuous right next to Fall Creek Falls itself. There are limestone sinks, cave systems, trails and swing bridges (slatted walkways, tethered at each end) high above the gorges. But there are also car parks close to the best overlooks, and facilities that owe nothing to nature.

Fall Creek Falls State Park is a scenic adventure of first magnitude. Away from the obvious choke points, it is still wild and ruggedly beautiful. Woven into its most popular sights are remote trails through mountain laurel, rhododendron and tulip poplar. Invariably, they re-emerge where moving water exercises its universal magic on human imagination – but nobody minds sharing that.

The scenic wonderland of Fall Creek Falls State Park

Congaree National Park

There used to be about 4,850 sq km (1,875 sq mi) of bottomland forest in South Carolina, part of a 210,450-sq-km (81,255-sq-mi) chain of forested swamp that looped from Chesapeake Bay to east Texas. Now just 52 sq km (20 sq mi) survive – 45 sq km (17 sq mi) of them in the protected 90-sq-km (35-sq-mi) wilderness of Congaree National Park. The astonishing old-growth bottomland hardwoods have no equal in the USA. Over 75 species, force-fed by constantly refreshed silts washed down in regular flooding, grow to record dimensions. Loblolly pines, incongruous in any floodplain, reach 52 m (171 ft) alongside giant swamp chestnuts, hickories, sycamores and bald cypresses over 8 m (26 ft) in circumference. Their collective canopy arches high, high above, chased by poison ivy and grapevines. In this silent, warm, watery cathedral, darting bright colours reveal some of the 173 species of birds that fill the forest. Among them are all eight species of southeastern woodpeckers, including the spectacular red-cockaded woodpecker.

In fact the area was only saved because it is a floodplain and not a true swamp. Neither farmers nor logging companies could capitalize on the regular flooding. The trees thrived in the rich wetlands but stayed too green to float down river. Although there are hiking trails, including a 4-km (2.5-mi) boardwalk over water, the best way to see it is by canoe. Cedar Creek meanders lazily through 32 km (20 mi) of oxbows, loops and bends before it joins the Congaree River. Heron, river otters, wild boar, box turtles and innumerable other wildlife in the dappled swamps and pools turn pleasant drifting into an adventure of slightly Jurassic wonder. For hikers, the Oakridge Trail guarantees getting close to the heart of the old-growth trees, especially magnificent old-growth oaks and beeches. There are giants here whose height is only exceeded by California's sequoias – but so many more of them.

HOW TO GET THERE:
Leave your car at the Harry Hampton Visitor Center at the entrance to Congaree National Park, 30 km (19 mi) southeast of Columbia off SC Route 48. Bring your canoe with you.
WHEN TO GO:
Any time. It's useful to ring before you go to check the state of flooding.
DON'T MISS:
The Low Boardwalk (trail) through bald cypress and water tupelo forest; the mystery of cypress 'knees' – the tangles of roots that grow up to 3 m (10 ft) in the air; wildlife along the King Snake Trail, one of the park's most remote.

Cypress Swamp,
Congaree National Park

YOU SHOULD KNOW:
On a floodplain, even giant trees have relatively shallow roots. When Hurricane Hugo smashed many of Congaree's tallest trees in 1989, it was considered a catastrophe – but the damage created dramatic holes in the leaf canopy which have greatly stimulated new growth on the forest floor.

Cumberland Island National Seashore

HOW TO GET THERE:
By ferry from St Mary's, Georgia, or by private boat from Fernandina Beach, Amelia Island, Florida.
WHEN TO GO:
Any time. Winter is particularly good for beachcombing.
DON'T MISS:
The wild turkey courtship dance of March/April; loggerhead turtles nesting from mid May; the 1898 Georgian-revival Plum Orchard Mansion; the marine wilderness flora and fauna around Lake Whitney on the Roller Coaster Trail.
YOU SHOULD KNOW:
In September 1996, the late John F Kennedy Jr and Carolyn Bessette chose to be married in the single-room wooden shack First African Baptist Church, in 'The Settlement' established in the 1890s for African-American workers.

A wind-bent oak on Cumberland Island

The largest and southernmost of the Atlantic barrier islands protecting the coast of Georgia, Cumberland Island also includes the biggest island wilderness in the entire USA. It's a vision of an entirely pristine America without noise or light pollution, where native species like wild turkeys, otters, white-tailed deer and armadillos are commonplace among the wild horses, alligators and occasional bobcats that share the fertile island paradise. The island is 28 km (17 mi) long and 5 km (3 mi) wide, big enough to support three distinct ecosystems. Towards the ocean, a perfect sand beach (one of America's top ten) runs up to a kilometre deep the length of the island, backed by dunes which give way to dense palmetto stands, pines and – magically – sun-dappled pastures and woods of ancient oaks festooned with Spanish moss. On the west coast woods and meadows yield to 69 sq km (27 sq mi) of marshes, creeks and tidal mudflats, teeming with 300 species of waders, sea birds and dazzling migrants.

Cumberland Island's haunting beauty is emphasized by the few traces of human occupation that still endure at its north and south ends. Once owned by the Carnegie family, part of the island remains private and closed to visitors; but palatial mansions remain, as ruins or restored luxury hotels, along with the more poignant chattel houses of 'the Settlement' where a small community of fishermen and farmers long ago sweated a living. Hotel guests get a special kind of access to the island's secrets, including wildlife-watching at dawn and dusk when other visitors have mostly gone. Rangers try to keep visitor numbers down to about 300 at any time – and although some arrive by private boat as well as on the daily ferry, Cumberland Island is never crowded. It is one of the Carnegie family's most prescient and valuable gifts to America.

Florida Bay

Florida Bay is a vast triangle of ultra-shallow sea at the tip of the Florida Peninsular, protected from the Atlantic by the arc of the Florida Keys. To its north the bay's coast is porous. It's where the 80-km (50-mi) wide, slow-moving mass of the Florida Everglades freshwater 'river' merges with the sea in a symbiotic exchange of salt and fresh water critical to the huge variety of subtropical wetland flora and fauna for which the Everglades are so famous. It's not surprising that most of the bay's 2,218 sq km (855 sq mi) are included in the Everglades National Park, because its average depth is under 1 m (3 ft). Here, land and sea are defined by the same topographic and ecological integrity, and mutually dependent. Beneath Florida Bay's shimmering surface lies a marine wilderness as rich in novelty, colour and rarity as any of the Everglades' mainland natural marvels.

An aerial view of Florida Bay

The shallow sea only just covers gigantic meadows of seagrass. As a nursery for hundreds of marine species, and food for larger creatures like the manatee and green sea turtle, the grasses ultimately sustain the whole of Florida Bay's ecosystem. Bigger fish lurk round the mangrove islands and in the coastal estuaries and brackish waterways where mangroves form long tunnels and the channels of water run slightly deeper.

Guided boat tours apart, the only way to explore Florida Bay is by canoe or small, powered boat. With Polaroid (non-reflective) glasses you can see deep into the water – as vital for navigating shallow channels as for enjoying the full range of marine wildlife. Canoes are easy (and quiet) to manoeuvre among both mangroves and mudflats, and offer the best opportunities of seeing anything from a saltwater crocodile to some of America's rarest and most beautiful wading birds.

HOW TO GET THERE:
By boat from Key Largo or by car from Miami to Flamingo village, where you can rent a boat or canoe, or sign up for a boat tour.
WHEN TO GO:
November to April
DON'T MISS:
The birdlife around the Eco Pond, close to Flamingo; pottering among the tidal waterways such as Alligator Creek and Terrapin Bay.
YOU SHOULD KNOW:
There are marked channels for travelling across Florida Bay: missing them risks a steep fine and almost inevitably running aground. Getting towed off is expensive and extremely damaging to the fragile seagrass prairie – so take the time to study the free navigation charts available at the Flamingo Visitor Center.

Calakmul Biosphere Reserve

HOW TO GET THERE:
By car or bus from Merida or Cancun, to one of the small communities like Xpujil along the east–west or north–south access roads between core and buffer areas. Then on foot, with a guide.

WHEN TO GO:
Any time

DON'T MISS:
The view from the top of the Mayan pyramids; howler and spider monkeys – possibly teasing a crocodile.

YOU SHOULD KNOW:
Calakmul is part of the Mesoamerican 'biological corridor' of tropical forests that includes the Yucatan Peninsula, the Isthmus of Tehuantepec and El Peten. Restoring it is vital for far-ranging species like jaguar and migratory birds. Currently Calakmul is working to create a direct wildlife corridor with the Sian Ka'an Biosphere Reserve.

In the language of the ancient Central American Maya culture *Calakmul* means city of twin pyramids. Calakmul was among the Maya civilization's most important sites, second only to Tikal in Guatemala. Its massive pyramids have long been reclaimed by tropical forest and jungle, but the Calakmul Biosphere Reserve, of which the ten square miles of Mayan ruins are only a small part, is intended to protect archaeological history as much as the precarious regional ecosystem. The reserve covers 7,300 sq km (2,820 sq mi) – rather more than the US State of Delaware – bounded by Quintana Roo to the east and Guatemala to the south. It is the biggest tropical forest reserve in Mexico.

The forest would be familiar to a returning Mayan. Five of Mexico's six 'big cats' (jaguar, puma, ocelot, margay and jaguarondi) share the regrown wilderness with 80 other mammals, 358 bird species, reptiles, fish, butterflies, bats and amphibians. Tropical fauna make splashes of colour in the halls of green trees where monkeys swing and parrots chatter. At dusk every day, between two and five million bats wheel into the sky from Calakmul's bat cave to forage for insects. The taxonomy of such rich biodiversity even includes the family of man. The reserve needs to sustain humans, too, and it's in the forefront of the UNESCO 'Man and the Biosphere' (MAB) programme.

It's a balancing act. Calakmul is already expanding both its core wilderness areas and the buffer zones which contain the Mayan ruins and where the *ejidos* (Mexican communities living on communal land) can benefit directly from the forest. The scheme will be successful when the *ejidos* take over the management of the forest, and as guides for ecotourism. The advantage to visitors is beyond price – access to local expertise in one of the world's most stunning tropical ecologies.

Cumbres de Majalca National Park

It is epic terrain. South of the US–Mexican border on the Rio Bravo, the wide-open hill country familiar from Texas becomes even wilder and more rugged. Chihuahua is Mexico's biggest state (half the size of Spain, or the whole of Britain), where the purple mountains of the Sierra Occidental descend to the southeastern plateau of the Chihuahua Desert. The state capital, also called Chihuahua, is one of just two sizeable local cities (the other is Juarez on the US border). The rest is a geological badlands of mountain bluffs and box canyons, where outstanding natural beauty has been baked and then frozen into the land itself. The harsh climate and difficult access have helped preserve its natural secrets. Cumbres de Majalca National Park is one of its best.

It is completely unexpected. The volcanic mountains of the Sierra de Majalca sub-range rise only to 2,600 m (8,530 ft), but from them spring a number of *arroyos* (fast-flowing streams) that cut dozens of valleys into the 1,000-m (3,280-ft) high plateau. Most of it is mantled by thick oak and pine forest; but after rain, every clearing is carpeted with green and dotted with the wild flowers of the high prairie. Everywhere, enormous boulders or chimneys (*cumbres*) of volcanic rock stand isolated – whittled, split and smoothed by water and wind. Like Easter Island statues, the extraordinary volcanic sculptures seem to have individual characters, but share the natural majesty of simply being immense. The dominant forest is typical of its altitude and the extreme hot and cold temperatures. It is a perfect habitat for the black bears who live here, among coyote, eagles, falcons, woodpeckers, and deer.

Visitors come for the hiking, mountain-biking and rock climbing, and become smitten by the Cumbres' sheer beauty. Fortunately, the dramatic geological oddities share their grandeur with more wildlife than people.

HOW TO GET THERE:
By car from Chihuahua City – 30 km (19 mi) north on Highway 45, then left on a gravel track for the same distance.

WHEN TO GO:
Any time – but in mid winter the high ground is likely to be under snow.

DON'T MISS:
The boulders of Salsipuedas (especially if you enjoy rock climbing); the geometry eroded into the Penon de El Cuadrado rock formation; the imaginative formations known as Sleeping Beauty, Soldier's Peak and Eagle's Nest.

YOU SHOULD KNOW:
The Mexican phrase to express being dumbstruck with amazement is *Ay Chihuahua!* (Don't ask: just practise). The boundary between the Cumbres de Majalca National Park and the backcountry is not clear. Be prepared to meet police or soldiers looking for the *bandidos* regularly alleged to patrol the area.

Nevado de Colima

HOW TO GET THERE:
By car from Colima or bus from Ciudad Guzman to the edge of the park; or by 4x4 to La Joya. Within the park, apart from that track, only hiking and horse riding are allowed.
WHEN TO GO:
November to March, the dry season
DON'T MISS:
Carizalillo Lake, where weekenders come to camp, kayak and picnic high on El Nevado; swimming in the stone pool fed by the spring at the bottom of a canyon below the campsite clearing at 3,521 m (11,550 ft); the green water of Laguna Maria, on the trail to El Volcan, a perfect alpine mirror reflecting the smoking crater.
YOU SHOULD KNOW:
In the Nahuatl language, *Colima* means God of fire who rules, and refers to Volcan de Fuego's belching eruptions. Yet although both volcanoes have Colima as part of their names, they are both in fact in the State of Jalisco.

From any angle – north to Guadalajara or southwest to Colima on Mexico's Pacific coast – the twin cone peaks of Nevado de Colima (El Nevado) and Volcan de Fuego de Colima (El Volcan) stand out from a distance. El Volcan is active, with a history of major eruptions and semi-permanent fizzing and growling. At any time it can, and does, spill showers of red-hot rocks over its flanks, and as recently as 2005 shot columns of ash 5 km (3 mi) high into the sky. It's a dangerous but fascinating force of nature, still growing in the old caldera formed by the much older and completely dormant El Nevado, a just-comfortable 9 km (5.5 mi) out of range. Between and surrounding the two lie thick forest and scrub, the 204 sq km (79 sq mi) Nevado de Colima National Park. Snowcapped El Nevado looks down from 4,335 m (14,220 ft) on its fiery, 3,900 m (12,795 ft) neighbour. Hiking the first is the best way to see the second.

El Nevado rises out of hot, dusty (and now deforested) plains, through increasingly cooler subtropical and temperate zones of lush coniferous forest near the top. The trees are full of movement, of white-tailed deer, coyote and endemic birds like the highland guan, Aztec thrush and thick-billed parrot as well as woodpeckers, doves and hawks. Reaching El Nevado's summit is a strenuous two-day hike from the edge of the park; but in a 4x4 you can get to La Joya, a solitary cabin at the end of the track from where a short but demanding hike brings you to some of El Nevado's loveliest terrain, and a grandstand view of El Volcan. Stay the night at La Joya and you stand the best chance of seeing the astonishing wildlife dramas that occur during the early hours of daylight.

Ria Celestun Biosphere Reserve

This is the place where the word 'ecotourism' was invented in 1983. The Ria Celestun Biosphere Reserve protects some of the best-preserved wetlands in the northwestern Yucatan Peninsular, on Mexico's Gulf coast. Its centrepiece is the estuary (*ria*) close to the fishing port and resort of Celestun. The river emerges onto a shelf of shallow sea lined with sand dunes, swamps and mangroves that form domes and tunnels around the coastal lagoons, flooded pastures and lowland jungle on 'shore'. It is bursting with glorious life. Enormous flocks of intensely pink flamingoes (up to 18,000 at a time) strut and flap offshore like a pink Mexican wave. There are storks, egrets, parrots, cardinals, pelicans and hummingbirds among the 320 species here. Crab and shrimp crowd the brackish water where mangroves thrive, and there are turtles, crocodiles, manatee and spider monkeys above and below. Jaguars, tapirs and anteaters are among 75 mammals in the jungle areas. They add up to a dazzling demonstration of species and habitat interdependence, completed by a boat ride at night time. The nocturnal wildlife action in the maze of mangrove waterways gives wings to the imagination.

Ria Celestun Biosphere Reserve is not especially big – 591 sq km (228 sq mi) – but it has added significance in being the source of most of the fresh groundwater in northwestern Yucatan (where all fresh water comes from underground sinkholes). Every development on its increasingly crowded fringes interrupts the free exchange of fresh and saline water, and impacts immediately on the fragile balance of the ecosystem. A new bridge slightly diverted a freshwater channel, causing a reed marsh to stagnate and a large flamingo feeding area to close down. Threats like these to such a beautiful exhibition of natural dynamics can be removed only by inspiring the local economy to put ecotourism first. Which means, go soon and help keep Ria Celestun pristine.

HOW TO GET THERE:
Head for Celestun port and rent a boat or bicycle, or take tour boats to different parts of the reserve.
WHEN TO GO:
Any time. Flamingoes are most numerous in winter.
DON'T MISS:
The 'petrified forest' of hundreds of sun-bleached, long-dead trees – a surreal landscape; swimming 'underground' in a freshwater sinkhole (*ojo de agua*); the reed marsh habitats and fishing grounds.
YOU SHOULD KNOW:
Typically, a flamingo hoovers up 2,000 l (440 gal) of water per day, filter-fishing. Celestun has adopted the American Flamingo – the biggest and most deeply coloured of the world's six species – as its 'signature bird'.

Flamingoes feed in their thousands at the Ria Celestun Biosphere Reserve.

Sierra Gorda Biosphere Reserve

HOW TO GET THERE:
By car or bus to Jalpan de Serra, at the centre of the reserve in north Queretaro. Transport is fairly easy in the area because Sierra Gorda's small towns are a tourist destination in their own right.
WHEN TO GO:
Any time
DON'T MISS:
The rare opportunity to sample radically different ecosystems in a short time, and without having to carry lots of supplies. Wilderness areas are seldom as accessible or fringed by such a choice of facilities.
YOU SHOULD KNOW:
Sierra Gorda's fame as a tourist hot spot rests chiefly on a group of five villages known as 'the Missions of Sierra Gorda' – five Franciscan convents built in the 18th century and among the best examples of Mexican Baroque architecture and art of the colonial era. They were built for the Pame and Chichimeca indigenous peoples whose fierce resistance to the colonial Spanish lasted until the mid-19th century. Somewhat contrarily, they accepted evangelizing friars and conversion to Christianity centuries earlier. The villages have World Heritage status.

The state of Queretaro in Mexico's central highlands is the meeting point of north and south bio-regions, and it makes Sierra Gorda Biosphere Reserve the most ecologically diverse in the country. The range is vast within a compact area. Mean altitudes go from 300–3,500 m (985–11,500 ft), and local microclimates produce a huge variation in rainfall. The reserve includes deciduous and evergreen tropical forests, cloud forest and dense oak and pine; spiny shrubs and giant barrel cacti in its arid semi-desert areas; and barely penetrable jungle bursting out of its canyons and deep valleys, watered by huge sinkholes and underground river systems. Historically difficult to access, and with a small population bound by poverty, the Biosphere Reserve was established by integrating Sierra Gorda's farms and villages into co-dependency with habitat conservation. There are roads and villages, and some industry – but local people have encouraged the wilderness areas to creep in and around them. Across almost a third of the whole state of Queretaro, their efforts have increased tourism but reduced its environmental impact. It is welcome evidence of an unusual empathy between man and nature.

Sierra Gorda is on the monarch butterfly's flight path. Its mountains and canyons echo with 300 kinds of migrant and native birds, and it's a matter of mood which kind of leafy glade, cooling waterfall or earthy-smelling oak forest to hike in. One of the area's most exciting hikes (or mule rides) is to the Sotano de Barro (Mud Basement) through jungle and across hill country. It's a huge sinkhole 600 m (1,970 ft) across and 450 m (1,475 ft) deep. Every night, it fills with a raucous colony of military macaws roosting; and the sight of them flooding out *en masse* at dawn is as colourful as Queretaro's famous woven shawls.

Sumidero Canyon

A view of the spectacular Sumidero Canyon

Sumidero Canyon, east of Tuxtla Gutierrez in Mexico's extreme southeast, began as a seismic event on the edges of the North American, Cocos and Caribbean plates. It evolved over millions of years from a gash on the edge of the Chiapas High Plains to a majestic chasm carved a kilometre deep out of limestone and basalt by the Grijalva River. The Sumidero Canyon National Park encloses the canyon along 30 km (19 mi) of the river. The topography of its roughly 219 sq km (84 sq mi) varies between 360–1,729 m (1,180–5,670 ft), and a road connects a series of vantage points called *miradores* from which to look down on the canyon's finest features. Hiking the area is tough and uncomfortable. It's better to head straight for the Ecological Reserve established on the river bank. It nestles in a crook of the river before the canyon proper. The lower ground encourages huge ferns and dense jungle foliage around small pools and marshy ground, the habitat of crocodiles and spider monkeys.

Like the Ecological Reserve, the canyon is only accessible by boat. These *lanchas* leave from the town of Chiapa de Corzo (you may have to wait on the jetty for enough people to fill a boat) for the 35 km (22 mi) ride to the lagoon of the Chicoasen Dam. The twisting Grijalva River runs placid and deep, the home of egrets, herons, kingfishers, vultures and cormorants perched on rocky outcrops. Huge crocodiles bask on tiny beaches. The walls of the canyon rise and rise, almost sheer, to 1,000 m (3,280 ft). They are lined with caves, and a magnificent formation called 'the Christmas Tree'. It's a yuletide lookalike made of calcium deposits on trailing mosses, which becomes a waterfall in the rainy season. It fits perfectly into the strange, lost world of Sumidero Canyon.

HOW TO GET THERE:
By boat, from Chiapa de Corzo or Cahuare
WHEN TO GO:
Any time, in daylight (boats won't operate after dark).
DON'T MISS:
Cueva de Colores (Cave of Colours); the sunset view from the *mirador* called *La Coyota*; *Cascada Velo de Novia* (Bride's Veil Waterfall); the giant *Crocodylus acutus*, the American crocodiles for which Sumidero is a perfect, and rare, habitat.
YOU SHOULD KNOW:
Sumidero Canyon is both exciting and spooky. Its *ambiente* is coloured by its history, of enduring significance to the indigenous Chiapanecas people who still live in the area. Centuries ago, when the Spanish conquistadors over-ran them, the Chiapanecas of Sumidero committed mass suicide in the canyon rather than face slavery.

The Maya Mountains

Bladen Nature Reserve

There are no roads in the Bladen Nature Reserve. Visitors are forbidden. Bladen's 403 sq km (156 sq mi) are set aside as true wilderness where the lavish biological diversity of Belize can 'perpetuate itself' without human intervention. The only way to go there is on a pre-arranged educational research tour or as a volunteer researcher for the scientific teams permitted to do medical or environmental research. Even with a permit, the reserve is difficult to get to. It is entirely surrounded by other protected areas which provide a natural buffer zone against encroachment on its own, pristine rainforest. Bladen is in the Toledo district of southwest Belize. The Maya Mountains and Deep River Forest Reserves lie to the south, the Columbia Forest to the southwest, Chiquibul National Park to the north and the Trio Reserve to the east. Any and all of them are magnificent – but the Bladen Nature Reserve surpasses the best of the rest.

It's breathtakingly lovely – but rugged. The reserve descends the southeast slope of the Maya Mountains and across the Bladen Branch of the Monkey River. The limestone karst under its southern half is full of conical hills and outcrops honeycombed with sinkholes, cave systems and underground streams. The conditions produce towering palms and 70 species of trees; and make giants of the lianas, herbs, ferns, flowers and fruits that crowd round jungle pools and waterfall cascades. In this sanctuary even rare species are commonplace and visible. Peccary, tapir and jaguar are among 300 mammal species; the crested guan and great curassow among the 200 birds; and the reptiles and amphibians are the richest in Belize.

Nobody has lived in the area since the Mayans and, although attempts are made at illegal activities like logging, Bladen has never been much disturbed. It is a verifiable tropical Eden, the adventure of a lifetime, and well worth the effort.

HOW TO GET THERE:
By vehicle from Danriga to Mile 59 Southern Highway, then on foot 10 km (6 mi) to the BFREE (Belize Foundation for Research and Environmental Education) field station on the edge of the reserve. Given notice, they might send a 4x4 to collect you.
WHEN TO GO:
November to May
DON'T MISS:
Hiking in the forest with a local Mayan who teaches ethno-botany and is expert in traditional forest lore; and be sure to swim in one of the rock pools below one of the many falls in the completely pure waters of the Bladen Branch River.
YOU SHOULD KNOW:
Visiting the Bladen Nature Reserve is not for everyone. You look creation full in the face – and discover that its exalted beauty lacks even rudimentary comfort for casual visitors. The dedicated can apply for voluntary internships with BFREE; and the Ya'axche Conservation Trust (aka simply 'Ya'axche') rangers sometimes accept volunteers on extended patrol to help observe illegal (usually commercial) forest incursions (Ya'axche recently caught the Belize Hydroelectric Company trying to build a wholly illegal dam in Bladen – without being noticed!).

Cockscomb Basin Wildlife Sanctuary

Isolated in the far south of Belize between the Maya Mountains and the coast, the Cockscomb Basin Wildlife Sanctuary is the world's only jaguar reserve. It is also one of the few reserves that accept casual visitors on the same basis as serious naturalists. This rudimentary respect stimulates visitors' curiosity and sense of adventure: it's a very effective method of sharpening vision and hearing before hiking into the great unknown.

Learning to 'read' the forest is paramount at Cockscomb. The reserve's 728 sq km (280 sq mi) of jungle are watered by dozens of streams and underground watercourses that emerge in sparkling waterfalls and clear, deep pools ringed by boulders. As in every kind of terrain, but here especially, pug marks and broken vegetation speak for the teeming wildlife – adrenalin-pumping proof of fabled big cats too canny to be easily spotted. There are several trails (graded by difficulty and physical ability) where you can feel completely absorbed into the patterns of nature the sanctuary is at pains to illustrate. The all-day hike to Outlier Mountain covers most important habitats from jungle swamp and tropical rainforest to the rugged tangle of the mountain itself; but shorter trails are intended to be as much about fun as learning something. For the really committed, the four-day hike to 1,120 m (3,675 ft) Victoria Peak is a lifetime opportunity. You need a permit from the Belize Audubon Society and a licensed guide. The area has not yet been fully explored since it was returned to a wilderness decades ago, and you can expect to discover unknown orchids and encounter rare animals.

Cockscomb Basin's willingness to treat serious conservation as potential recreation should be a blueprint for other wildlife sanctuaries of similar stature. Not many of them encourage inner-tubing down their rivers for the thrill of 'looking a crocodile in the eye at its own level'.

HOW TO GET THERE:
By car or bus from Danriga to the Maya Center on the Southern Highway (the bus will stop by request). At the Maya Center Women's Group Gift Shop you pay the entrance fee to the reserve; then it's a 10-km (6-mi) hike or local taxi drive on a dirt road to the Cockscomb Basin Visitors' Center.

WHEN TO GO:
December to May (the dry season, and the only months Victoria Peak may be visited) – although wildlife generally is much more active from June to July (the start of the rainy season). December is best for migrant birds.

DON'T MISS:
Ben's Bluff Trail, a hike through the transition zone of rainforest to mountain pine forest, ending with a swim beneath a 6-m (20-ft) waterfall; inner-tubing on the Stann Creek River; or the antics of Montezuma's oropendola and the white-collared manakin, two of the world's most hyperactive birds.

YOU SHOULD KNOW:
The Visitor Center is built on the remnants of what used to be a logging camp, so the reserve is able to offer basic facilities like a small convenience store, bunkhouses and a few guest cottages as well as a campsite. Take advantage of them: they are as much comfort as you'll ever find in the wild.

A stunning jaguar on the prowl in the Cockscomb Basin Wildlife Sanctuary.

Sarstoon/Temash National Park

HOW TO GET THERE:
By very small plane to the airstrip close to Barranco; by boat from Punta Gorda; or by local 'bus' from Punta Gorda to Barranco if you are on foot.

WHEN TO GO:
Any time

DON'T MISS:
Belize's only example of comfrey palm forest, on the banks of the Sarstoon River; the red mangrove forest – the best in Central America; lingering in Barranco for a glimpse of Garifuna (descendants of the original Carib peoples) culture and folklore.

YOU SHOULD KNOW:
In the heat and humidity it's easy to drift into somnolence. Stay awake and aware on land and water in Sarstoon/Temash – the crocodiles are not the only creatures who mean business.

The Sarstoon River forms Belize's southern border with Guatemala. The Temash River opens onto the Gulf of Honduras 16 km (10 mi) up the coast in Amatique Bay. Sandwiched between the two deltas are 170 sq km (66 sq mi) of mangrove forests, sandbar and silt-filled creeks, swamps and marshes merging into some of Belize's most pristine jungle forests. It is an ancient place of innumerable shades of green shadow, splashed with flashes of primary brilliance. It is home to species not found elsewhere in Belize, like the scarlet macaw, white-faced capuchin monkey, countless butterflies and Morelet's crocodile. Seldom disturbed by human intrusion, the deeper forests are full of fresh tracks of bigger, rarer mammals like the tapir, jaguar and ocelot – legends of invisibility, but frequently glimpsed.

The crowning glory of the Temash River are the towering red mangroves reaching up on both banks to 31 m (100 ft) or more, and stretching for miles into and along the coast. Orchids and bromeliads decorate the solid 3-m (10-ft) wall of their roots. Between the rivers, the delta of shallow, brackish waters nourishes underwater grass plains where manatee feed and shoals of fish flit away their nursery years. Sea birds wheel in search of the rich pickings of shrimp; and snook and tarpon patrol far upriver.

You need a guide to come here, and a boat to enjoy it. Boats can be rented in Punta Gorda, the biggest community in the Toledo District. More interesting (and easier if you use the little airstrip near the park), is to look for a guide at the thatched Garifuna village of Barraco, known as the 'gateway to the park'. With expert local guidance, you'll be helping to fulfil the park's commitment to sustainable activities – and be certain of getting close to its most extraordinary natural secrets.

Indio-Maiz Biological Reserve

Nelson did it for glory. Cornelius Vanderbilt did it for gold. Mark Twain called it 'an earthly paradise'. Now, the reason for ascending the San Juan River on Nicaragua's border with Costa Rica is because it is one of only two ways to enter what UCLA (University of Southern California at Los Angeles) biologists called 'the gem of Central American nature reserves'.

The Indio-Maiz Biological Reserve is the biggest area of contiguous rainforest outside the Amazon. Much of it is still not fully explored, but from the Caribbean side it is permitted to use the Indio River (via the San Juan) to get deep inside the 2,590-sq-km (1,000-sq-mi) reserve, most of which is prohibited except to scientists. The only other access point is from the west, via the Bartola River near the historic settlement of El Castillo. This route also connects to the San Juan River, but is used by many more people for frequent, shorter, token visits just inside the reserve.

Visitors must have a guide, and the guide must be a Rama Indian. In a supreme irony of modern 'conservation', the Rama people are no longer allowed to live along the Indio River as they have done for centuries, but visitors can use their former homes to camp within the reserve for a few nights. That aside, their expert knowledge brings the richness of the jungle forest to vivid life. There are deer, sloths, giant anteaters, boars, pacas, pumas, howler and spider monkeys, manatees, freshwater sharks (the world's only species), turtles, crocodiles, caimans, iguanas, yellow-and-black poison dart frogs, reptiles of every hue, toucans, hummingbirds, parrots, and whole rainbows of butterflies, orchids and other tropical flowers – very probably, all of them before lunch. The Indio-Maiz Biological Reserve is where you go to stock the ark; and Mark Twain was right.

HOW TO GET THERE:
By road or plane to San Carlos at the foot of Lake Nicaragua on the west side; or by boat or plane (airstrip) to San Juan del Norte on the Caribbean. If necessary, the trip can be organized in advance from Managua.
WHEN TO GO:
Any time
DON'T MISS:
Staying at least one night within the reserve. It's the only way to get a real impression of the species' diversity and behaviour – even though night-time jungle noises can be spine-chilling. The reward for sleeplessness is the magic of dawn and the reawakening world – and the prospect of seeing twice as many animals and birds as on a short, daytime visit.
YOU SHOULD KNOW:
Incredibly, this is not a region for mosquitoes (perhaps because of all the frogs). Be afraid of the caimans and some of the snakes, but not of being bitten by something you can't see.

93

La Flor Wildlife Refuge

HOW TO GET THERE:
By 'bus' (four-wheel drive) with a guide from San Juan del Sur, 18km (11 mi) away.

WHEN TO GO:
The season runs from July to January, peaking in October and November – but there are turtle landings throughout the year.

DON'T MISS:
The chance to camp on or near La Flor beach (if possible around the time of a full moon). It takes at least 24 hours to see how the ocean, beach and forest interact on behalf of the turtles, their eggs, and their predators, with some degree of success for them all.

YOU SHOULD KNOW:
The hatchlings emerge simultaneously, millions at a time, after about 50 days and there are usually seven or eight major *arribadas* each season. La Flor is open day and night, subject to an entrance fee and camping fees. No facilities are available.

One of Nicaragua's most beautiful beaches lies on the Pacific coast just north of the border with Costa Rica. It looks like a scene from an Elvis movie: the deep crescent of pure white sand is backed by swaying palms, rising cliffs and tropical dry forest, and buffered at each end by thick clumps of mangroves. The rather theatrical perfection is appropriate. This is La Flor, the annual site of a spectacular natural drama. Between July and January, hundreds of thousands of sea turtles haul themselves out of the ocean to nest and lay their eggs here.

How turtles recognize the beach where they were born is as much a mystery as how they synchronize their mass invasions, known as *arribadas* (arrivals). La Flor is one of only two beaches on Nicaragua's Pacific Coast they use; and although all kinds of turtle can be seen there, it is olive Ridley's turtles (known as *paslama* in Nicaragua) which appear night after night, sometimes in groups of 30,000–50,000. They've got to be quick. They have to struggle through the fine, soft sand, competing for the best spaces; laboriously clear a hollow in which to lay around 100 eggs; cover it so that the eggs can develop at the correct temperature; and escape back to sea before they are spotted by hovering predators. Predators are everywhere. La Flor exists primarily to protect the turtles, but its forests are big enough to house monkeys, iguanas and big bird colonies which treat the newly laid eggs – and subsequent hatchlings – as a convenient larder. Their only safety is in their colossal numbers.

Witnessing an *arribada* can be emotional. La Flor is close to Central America's well-trodden surfer and backpacker trails, but inside its boundaries visitors are hushed by its sudden, primal silence; then spellbound by the dawning significance of its almost nightly, natural spectacle.

Penas Blancas Massif

The Penas Blancas (White Rocks) Massif in north central Nicaragua takes its name from the calcium streaking the rockface. The massif, part of the vast Bosawas Biosphere Reserve, is the highest part of the Isabella Mountains range spanning the Jinotega and Matagalpa districts, the watershed between the Bocay and Coco Rivers on one side, and the Tuma on the other. On a bigger scale, its position between the Pacific and the Caribbean magnifies the significance of its height: it is the key to weather patterns and the life-giving water balance of a much, much larger area. In the recent past, the massif's generous fertility encouraged the development of coffee and other farms on its lower slopes. The realization that stripping the mountains of its rainforest damaged its vital but fragile ecosystem caused a dramatic rethink. Now the lower slopes have been returned to nature, and the Penas Blancas Massif can be appreciated for its unique contribution to the region's biodiversity.

It is unique because the Massif is self-enclosed, and above 1,000 m (3,280 ft) where it has never been developed, its steep valleys and multiple peaks are a mist-filled realm of untouched cloud forest. Evergreen flora grow to giant size with trees reaching 50 m (164 ft). Black oak, granadillo and walnut trees shelter giant ferns, heleconias, orchids and bromeliads. Birds love it. Among the colourful parakeets, warblers, hummingbirds and tanagers the resplendent quetzal is the loveliest, and restricted to its mountain habitat. Waterfalls crash jawdropping distances from the massif's sheer rock walls, and the network of streams and creeks makes hiking wearily wet. There is no prolonged summer interval of hot days. The sun may shine, but the massif's microclimate maintains a year-round temperature 20–24°C (68–75°F) and a steady drip. Damp hikers will appreciate that this is why the scenery and wildlife are so spectacular.

HOW TO GET THERE:
By bus or car from Matagalpa to km 195 on the road to El Cua, then on foot or by 4x4 to Penas Blancas community.

WHEN TO GO:
Any time. (The prevailing, uniform weather pattern means take warm clothing.)

DON'T MISS:
La Pavona, one of the most beautiful waterfalls; *La Media Luna* – a difficult, unmarked hike through utterly compelling cloud forest landscapes; *El Horno* – an adventure hike with an expert guide, high into primary forest to a campsite from where, early in the morning, you can see quetzals flying out to breakfast.

YOU SHOULD KNOW:
The Penas Blancas Massif was revered by the Mayans as a sacred sanctuary. Water was the element foremost in their rituals. Each year, during Easter Week, the small population of Mayans still living in the massif cover themselves in white clay and bathe in the streams and rivers. A few people come from several other Central American countries, especially Guatemala, to share the ritual. So can you.

Braulio Carrillo National Park

HOW TO GET THERE:
By car or bus (stops on request) along the Guapiles highway – park up in a hidden spot and hike. It's best to leave the car at a Ranger Station; hikers have been held up, robbed and carjacked on the deserted highway.

WHEN TO GO:
Any time. There is less rain in March and April.

DON'T MISS:
The Rainforest Aerial Tram through the canopy layers, or the zipline through the canopy itself.

YOU SHOULD KNOW:
The 'green miracle' of Braulio Carillo National Park is that, so far, it has protected central Costa Rica's most important water catchment from the real threats of deforestation and settlement common elsewhere, despite the relatively new road running through it. It's a victory for Costa Rican common sense, only slightly marred by bandits' willingness to point guns at unvigilant visitors.

It takes 30 minutes to go from Costa Rica's capital, San Jose, to Braulio Carrillo National Park, and it's like time-travelling. Although Costa Rica was slow to recognize its own environmental wealth, it responded with enthusiasm to the challenge of preserving it. More of the country is protected as wilderness or an ecological buffer zone than – proportionately – anywhere else in the world. Braulio Carrillo National Park is one of Costa Rica's biggest and best, and it's right on the capital's doorstep.

It covers the western side of the volcanic Cordillera Central, from the edge of the coffee farms and cattle ranches on the highland plateau straight up the mountains to the chilly mists of cloud forest between extinct volcanoes; and then down the Caribbean slope to La Selva's great swathes of humid lowland jungle. Crossing it is a tough four- or five-day adventure with a guide (and permission). It's dangerous, too; from top to bottom 84 per cent of it is primary forest and jungle, and the wildlife includes some of the world's most lethal snakes, touch-poisonous amphibians and other colourful, murderously attractive threats. Fortunately, three Ranger stations on the park's edge provide easier access to short, marked trails. The Barva Station is the start of a climb to the

lake in the crater of the dormant Barva Volcano. The cloud forest here harbours local heroes like the strawberry poison arrow frog, the terrifying *fer-de-lance* snake, and the continent's biggest venomous snake, the bushmaster. Zurqui Station has two major trails taking in the rivers and waterfalls of different forest ecosystems full of howler and spider monkeys, deer, tapir, and the luminous, shimmering glory of quetzals, scarlet-rumpled tanagers, toucans and golden hummingbirds. The old-growth trees, butterflies and burgeoning wildlife have flourished here for thousands of years – untouched and virtually unseen until Braulio Carrillo was declared a national park. There's no easier place to sample such extraordinary diversity.

Tourists take an aerial tram through rainforest canopy near Braulio Carrillo National Park.

Cordillera de Talamanca

Still largely unexplored, the Cordillera de Talamanca is the southern spine of Costa Rica, the continental divide between North and South America and the watershed between the Pacific and the Caribbean. The range soars upwards to Costa Rica's highest peak, Cerro Chirripo – 3,820 m (12,530 ft) – towering over a forbidding wilderness of plunging valleys, glacial lakes and some of the rarest terrain in the whole world: the high-altitude, neotropical ecosystem called *paramo*. It looks like science fiction: peat bogs and swampy grasslands peppered with enormous spiked plants and strange shrubs in profusion. The *paramo* is one of an astonishing number of habitats in the Cordillera, created by differences in altitude, weather patterns, soil and topography. Since every one of them is a mix of flora and fauna from north and south, Talamanca's wildlife is among the world's most abundant and diverse. The isolation of the lush forests of Talamanca's valleys harbours 600 kinds of bird, 500 species of trees and bushes, 150 kinds of orchids and around 265 amphibians and reptiles. Ocelots, tapirs, anteaters, pumas and jaguars are not rare here. People are.

The lower half of the Costa Rican section of the Talamanca range is even better. It's part of a Biosphere Reserve shared with Panama. Known to both as the Amistad National Park, it's the biggest wilderness in either country, and a concentration of colourful and numerous species as rich as anywhere on earth. The terrain is more difficult (even the Conquistadors gave up), but the rewards are phenomenal. Camping and hiking are allowed, but there are no facilities. It's worth the effort to stay a while; of the Cordillera's nine major ecosystems, three are found only on the Pacific side and four on the Caribbean. Between them, the Talamanca range is believed to be home to no less than four per cent of all the species on earth.

Banana plantations in the Cordillera de Talamanca range

HOW TO GET THERE:
On foot, from the Inter-American Highway. The easiest access is via Las Tablas, near the Las Cruces biological field station at San Vito de Coto Brus.

WHEN TO GO:
Any time. Seasons don't really exist in the Cordillera de Talamanca – but the west slope is a little drier from December to March.

DON'T MISS:
The surreal rarity of the *paramo* landscape: it's a once-in-a-lifetime chance and worth the necessary altitude acclimatization. Getting there and back provides another chance to spot the red-and-green magnificence of the quetzal among the great virgin forests of moss-covered oak and bromeliad-trailing cypress.

YOU SHOULD KNOW:
Among the geomorphic surprises of the Talamanca Range around Chirripo, one of the strangest is the discovery of several perfectly preserved glacial features.

Rio Bongo Estuary

HOW TO GET THERE:
On foot, from Manzanillo in Puntarenas, or from Playa Coyote in Guanacaste; or by boat from the port of Puntarenas around the tip of the peninsular

WHEN TO GO:
November to April, for sunshine and the cooling Papagayo offshore breeze; or the beginning of the rainy season in May, for the revival of the lush green flora and the best multi-coloured sunsets. October is a washout.

DON'T MISS:
Following the Rio Bongo a little way upstream, past deep pools and small lagoons where countless birds nest in the thickets and somnolent crocodiles swarm on sandbanks.

YOU SHOULD KNOW:
The tourist industry has recently become aware of the Rio Bongo's ecological rarity and is proposing wildlife-spotting boat trips. Officially there are no regulations to restrict this because Rio Bongo is not a Reserve. Please remember that visitors enjoy it (and are welcome) by courtesy of its owner, and should respect his ambition to keep it unspoilt by over-intrusion.

The Pacific coast of Costa Rica's Nicoya Peninsular is an endlessly scenic series of curving white beaches punctuated by rocky headlands and mangrove-filled river estuaries. Nicoya's northern section is a mecca for surfing *cognoscenti*, intrepid backpackers and world-weary travellers who recognize that life seldom gets much better than this. The southern section is paradise itself – and the Rio Bongo estuary is its pristine heart. Reaching it involves a 7-km (4-mi) hike north from the village of Manzanillo. It's easy to be entranced by the thick forest crowding the edge of an enormous sweep of fine sand. Be wary. The beach becomes a long spit running parallel to the river. Where it emerges into the sea it's only waist deep, but ford it at your peril. The Rio Bongo is famous for its large colony of crocodiles, once compared in size to African Nile crocs. They flourish for some way up the river, scouting the thick mangroves and sandbanks of its meanders and oxbows; and occasionally startled swimmers find them in the open ocean, miles from the estuary.

Crocs aren't the only giants to survive from the age of dinosaurs. The Rio Bongo beach is one of the most important nesting sites for leatherback sea turtles in the eastern Pacific – and the 1.8–2.4 m (6–8 ft) *colossi* are very picky about their habitat. Happily, the whole beach is protected by a private landowner who refuses to allow any kind of development that might disturb them. His sensible rules include prohibiting camping, but permitting 'night hiking' so visitors can witness the leatherbacks' ancient ritual. Take the opportunity. The sight is as rare as finding a true, tropical beach wilderness – and between the swaying palms, the rhythmic pounding of the ocean, and the river's serene tranquillity, Rio Bongo genuinely reflects nature in harmony.

Tortuguero National Park

The waterworld of Tortuguero National Park on northeast Costa Rica's Caribbean coast is an ecological adventure playground. It covers a huge region of lowland palm swamps, tropical wet rainforest and mangroves, criss-crossed with natural channels and connected lagoons as well as the freshwater creeks that feed the Tortuguero River itself. Boating on its lazy currents is the only way to get close to its many secrets and electrifying surprises – although the park includes some montane rainforest where volcanic hills climb to 100–300 m (328–985 ft). Hiking among its waterfalls and swimming in rock pools is a beautiful experience, but Tortuguero's magic is in its water margins, where freshwater and saltwater mix and all four elements merge.

With such a wide variety of habitats and the comparative rarity of visitors (in a whole day gliding through the network of canals and rivers, it's possible never to come across another boat), the region is alive with movement. More than half of all Costa Rica's bird and reptile species live here. Monkeys, sloths, anteaters, lizards, caimans and crocodiles exist in the kind of profusion that makes sightings inevitable, even from a boat. Every corner is a nest, breeding ground, or habitat for something in the canopy, mangroves or dense jungle forest islands. Four kinds of marine turtles lay eggs on Tortuguero's sandbanks, including the biggest visiting population of green sea turtles anywhere on the Caribbean coast. Visitors can join 'night walks' to see them crowd ashore (but only the mandatory guide may carry a flashlight, to prevent disorienting the turtles).

The downside of Tortuguero's fertility and abundance is the threat from commercial interests like logging, which can only upset the ecological balance. In practice, that means the more people who come to admire its natural beauty, the more likely Tortuguero can be properly protected.

HOW TO GET THERE:
By boat from Moin, north of Limon, or from Puerto Viejo de Sarapiqui
WHEN TO GO:
February to April is the nesting season for giant leatherbacks; July to October for green sea turtles.
DON'T MISS:
The 2-km (1.2-mi) jungle trail running from the Park Ranger HQ known as *Cuatro Esquinas* near Tortuguero village; and remember the wonderland underwater – with Polaroid lenses it's easy to see the seven kinds of river turtles, manatees, river otters and 50 fish species (including the menacing alligator gar) weaving through the seagrasses below the boat
YOU SHOULD KNOW:
The long boat ride to Tortuguero from Puerto Viejo is worth the physical discomfort because it transits the stunningly beautiful Barra del Colorado Wildlife Refuge. It also passes from the Sarapiqui River to the San Juan River, which is technically inside Nicaragua. Be prepared for border checks, in and out.

Trees overhang the waters in Tortuguero National Park.

Chiriqui Highlands

HOW TO GET THERE:
By plane to David, then car or bus to Boquete

WHEN TO GO:
Any time. Temperatures vary enormously according to altitude rather than season, and the park is a network of microclimates.

DON'T MISS:
Central America's finest white-water rafting on the Chiriqui River (the only way to access some of the most spectacular natural features). Listen out for the ethereal call of the black-faced solitaire in the forest canopy, and the ringing croak of the three-wattled bellbird in the shrubs.

YOU SHOULD KNOW:
Visitors to Chiriqui may encounter a large community of Ngobe-Bugle (aka Guaymi), Panama's largest indigenous tribe. They come to the highlands for the coffee-picking season, the centre of their social culture. Ngobe-Bugle women wear *naguas*, beautifully crafted dresses in vivid blues, greens and reds, and carry *chacaras*, woven bags decorated the same way. They are accomplished examples of folk art, directly inspired by the colour schemes of Chiriqui's forest birds.

The province of Chiriqui forms Panama's border with Costa Rica on the Pacific slope of the continental divide. Its coastal lowlands are a mix of dense jungles and lively surfing resorts, backed by miles of orderly farmland where the volcanic soil guarantees astonishing fertility. The region is famous for its coffee farms stretching high up into the Chiriqui Highlands, quilting the slopes of Panama's highest peak and only volcano, the dormant 3,478 m (11,410 ft) Baru Volcano. As the farms thin out, montane rainforest takes over, dotted with small villages perched on rocky crags in a landscape of waterfalls and tall trees. It's suspiciously European, and no surprise to discover that most of the villages were built by engineers who came to work on the Panama Canal. Higher still lies a wilderness of primary cloud forest, a cool, misty world filled with the clamour of birds of the brightest colours and fanciest names. Between the mountain villages of Boquete and Cerro Punto, the Quetzal Trail follows a high ridge around the Baru Volcano. Besides the legendary sacred bird of the Aztecs and Mayas, the oak, cedar and laurel trees and the ferns and mosses harbour the spectacled foliage-gleaner, the prong-billed barbet, the buffy tufted-cheek and a jeweller's display of hummingbirds. They share a landscape of rare beauty.

On Baru's Caribbean side the Chiriqui Highlands descend through changing flora and fauna until they merge with the slopes of the Panamanian extension of the Cordillera de Talamanca. This region falls within the Amistad Biosphere Reserve, Central America's biggest reserve, and a pure wilderness. Amistad is shared with Costa Rica, and its Panamanian section forms a biological corridor connected through the Chiriqui Highlands to the lowland jungles and islands of Bocas del Toro. That puts Chiriqui at the heart of one of the planet's boldest ecological endeavours.

Daybreak over Baru Volcano in Chiriqui province

Isla Bastimentos

Of the 68 Bocas del Toro islands spread across 100 km (62 mi) of the Gulf of Chiriqui on Panama's Caribbean coast, only Isla Bastimentos anchors a National Marine Park. Amazingly, it flourishes in the middle of a growing tourist industry centred on the town of Bocas, visible (and sometimes audible) from Bastimentos itself. The 52 sq km (20 sq mi) island is one of Panama's biggest, and although it is a trackless jungle accessible only by boat, it is populated at either end. Only the central section belongs within the park, providing a land bridge between three enormous and mutually dependent marine tracts which are the highlight of any visit to Bocas del Toro. The real wonder is that the indigenous villages and tourist developments on the island see eco-conservation as serving their own interests: Bastimentos is an advanced model of how to combine leisure with ecotourism.

There's plenty to explore. The 16.6 sq km (6.4 sq mi) of interior land corridor is primary rainforest with a full complement of monkeys, sloths, turtles, frogs, lizards, caimans, armadillos, colourful birds, ferns, hardwood trees, bromeliads and orchids. To the south the forest floods to become Panama's largest red and white mangrove swamp, opening onto the shallows of Almirante Lagoon – a sub-marine meadow of waving seagrass dotted with mangrove islands, sandbars and coral reefs.

HOW TO GET THERE:
By boat from Bocas town on the tip of Colon Island
WHEN TO GO:
Any time, but the turtles come to nest between April and October.
DON'T MISS:
Playa Larga (Long Beach), worth braving rough sea and rocks to land on, and Red Frog Beach, named after the numerous bright-red poison dart frogs that swarm there and nowhere else. Red Frog beach is on the edge of the park, and threatened by development.
YOU SHOULD KNOW:
Isla Bastimentos, like Bocas del Toro in general, was settled by West Indians centuries ago. The village of Bastimentos used to be called Old Bank and people still speak *Gali-Gali*, a local Creole dialect combining Afro-Antillean English, Spanish and Ngobe-Bugle. At the other end of the island is the purely Ngobe-Bugle village of Quebrada Sal.

To the north, the jungle canopy overhangs a coastline of rocky outcrops, sheer cliff faces and freshwater creeks interspersed with long stretches of white beach where four kinds of marine turtle come to nest and lay their eggs. The east end of the marine park takes in the beautiful, uninhabited Zapotilla Cays, part of the barrier reef around Bastimentos, with an underwater landscape of pinnacles, crags, rock chutes and tunnels that make spectacular diving and snorkelling. Afterwards, the cays make a great venue for playing Robinson Crusoe.

Red Frog Beach

A view looking west along the Rio Dulce from the bridge at the village of the same name.

Rio Dulce

The eastern corner of Guatemala between Belize and Honduras is a self-contained watery wonderland called Rio Dulce. The Dulce River itself is short – 42 km (26 mi) – but it is the central feature of a much bigger region of small rivers and jungle islands, of protected swamps, mangroves, and primary tropical rainforest. The river is the outlet for Lake Izabal, Guatemala's biggest, which is fed in turn by the rivers running off the Sierra de las Minas into the Polochic Valley. The glorious logic of this topography and the climate is the ripeness and fertility of all the different kinds of wilderness the region supports. The feeling remains strong despite a thriving tourist industry based on several small towns and villages on its banks, and the major road bridge that crosses it. The human presence actually makes access to Rio Dulce's secrets easier: without it, the jungle would be forbidding and, frankly, scary. But even with its civilization, the giant-size vegetation feels all-consuming.

The Garifuna town of Livingston, on Amatique Bay at the mouth of the Rio Dulce is the only large community at one with its environment – so it's the place to find a guide as well as to have fun.

HOW TO GET THERE:
By bus to the town of Mariscos on the south shore of Lake Izabal; or by boat to Livingston
WHEN TO GO:
Any time. The rainy season expands the wetland jungle delta where the Polochic River enters the lake, and the wildlife explodes all along the Rio Dulce.
DON'T MISS:
Turning off the outboard and paddling your own *cayuco* among the untouched and seldom-visited pristine jungles and crystal-clear freshwater rivers like Rio Obscuro and Rio Zarquito on the southwest bank of Lake Izabal. Return via the Biotopo de Chacon Machacas – the manatee sanctuary in the seagrass lagoons of the Golfete, a 5-km (3-mi) wide section of the Rio Dulce edged by a lattice of mangrove channels.

Since Livingston is accessible only by boat, Rio Dulce's fabulous natural riches are on the doorstep. There are hundreds of connecting channels overhung by trees trailing flowers and filled by chattering monkeys, long-beaked waterbirds and screaming parrots. There are 'hot' waterfalls created by underwater geysers, huge 'meadows' of packed lily pads in bloom, a 10 km (6 mi) white limestone gorge with 120-m (400-ft) high walls festooned with trailing greenery and orchids, and acres of reed beds. A motorized dugout (*cayuco*) opens up the most remote, toucan-friendly creeks and provides a water taxi to some of the amazing jungle trails.

YOU SHOULD KNOW:
When pirates roved the Spanish Main, Lake Izabal was a popular pirate haven. The little town of El Estor got its name from English pirates who used to sail up the Rio Dulce to replenish supplies at 'The Store' – *El Estor*. The Castillo, the fort of San Felipe de Lara upstream of the present-day road bridge, was built by the Spanish to repel the Englishmen's regular visits.

Sierra de las Minas

Undisturbed since the Olmecs and Maya mined jade and obsidian – and gave the mountains their name – the Sierra de las Minas has been protected by the deterrence of its geography. Its shallow soil and steep slopes discouraged farming, and its topography caused local microclimates of opposite and irregular extremes. Scientists love its integrity: six ecosystems and three eco-regions operating in symbiotic harmony, but with different results from anywhere else with a similar range. This is because the Sierra is 3.2 km (2 mi) high, 48 km (30 mi) wide and runs east-west for about 160 km (100 mi) through Guatemala's northeast highlands. Its shape causes 'weather-shadows'. Visitors expect to find the florid glory of tropical exuberance at the lower levels of valleys and ravines, but not dry pine-oak forests below the biggest cloud forest in Central America, and still less the arid rarity of the Motagua valley thorn scrub forest right next to the region's most verdant wetlands around Lake Izabal.

The astonishing variety and quantity of the wildlife can only be appreciated by taking in the Sierra's entire altitudinal range. Between San Agustin Acasaguastlan and Chelasco on the Biosphere Reserve's northern edge there is a 32 km (20 mi) wilderness trail which more than justifies the strenuous effort required. From the bird-filled cloud forests of mossy hardwoods and bamboo stands the trail winds down through evergreen forest so perfect that the Sierra is referred to as 'one of the world's most important tropical gene banks for conifer endoplasm' (it means seed banks are a good thing). It's certainly beautiful, and the descent proves repeatedly that there's more wildlife and more varied fauna even than in the legendary Peten area to the north. It's an extra hike to visit the Motagua Valley – but Motagua has the added attraction of being *chaparral* country, perfect for a cowboy vacation.

HOW TO GET THERE:
By bus to Chilasco, Salama or San Agustin Acasaguastlan, in any of which permission and a guide may be sought from Defensores de la Naturaleza (the Guatemalan agency in charge).
WHEN TO GO:
Any time. The lowest rainfall is between January and March.
DON'T MISS:
Tasting the utter purity of the water – the dense forests of the Biosphere's northern section filter it repeatedly. The montane forest species include very rare survivals of yew and maple stands, where resplendent quetzals are quite usual. The Sierra de las Minas has a big population and it is also an important flyway for North American migrants and overwintering birds.
YOU SHOULD KNOW:
Despite considerable efforts since the 1950s to locate them, the Olmecs' sources of jade were considered lost forever – until in 1998 Hurricane Mitch flooded the Motagua River to a height 9.5 m (31 ft) above its flood level, and revealed alluvial deposits which were traced back into the mountains to a jadeite vein 2 m (6.5 ft) wide by 45 m (148 ft), alongside boulders of jade 'as big as a bus'.

Western Highlands

Guatemala and Central America's highest peak is 4,220 m (13,845 ft) Tajamulco, one of the chain of 37 volcanoes whose steep cones dominate the Sierra Madre highlands of western Guatemala. Parallel to and north of the Sierra Madre is the Sierra de los Cuchumatanes, Central America's highest entirely non-volcanic mountains. Between the two ranges lies an upland plateau of ripe fertility, a temperate network of plunging valleys, waterfalls and craggy granite ridges. In springtime, sheer mountainsides of deep green explode with the colour of wild flowers; but at any time the region is the most spectacularly beautiful in all Guatemala. Its beauty is at odds with its history of violence – yet it remains culturally as well as geographically enclosed. Running down from the spine of the Cuchumatanes is the network of valleys and fast mountain rivers known as the Ixcan, centred on the Ixil Triangle. Conflict as much as location has always isolated the Ixil people, and their language is spoken nowhere else. Their wariness towards strangers originated before the Conquistadors – so it isn't personal – but it adds to visitors' feelings of slight alienation, despite the authentic welcome offered in every Ixil village.

Getting the most from visiting the Western Highlands means revising the usual definitions of nature in the wild. The Sierra Madre's three active volcanoes spit regular fire and fumes, yet their flanks are still terraced for crops wherever possible. In the rain-drenched highlands, forests at every elevation grow giants of their species, with dense under-brush to match. Only the summits are treeless *altiplano*, a mist-wreathed, chilly grassland broken by worn boulders. Yet both landscapes are productive in the hands of the indigenous farmers and shepherds. The Western Highlands and its people have evolved together and belong to each other. It is their symbiosis that makes the region so bewitching.

Early morning fishing on Lake Atitlan

Pico Bonito

The resort beaches lining the Caribbean at La Ceiba are dominated by the looming bulk of Pico Bonito. The highest – 2,436 m (8,000 ft) – peak in the Nombre de Dios range, Pico Bonito rears up from sea level immediately behind the resort. Its jagged silhouette stretches away into the blue yonder, an invitation to an adventure that starts just a few minutes' drive away. The lure is the diversity of wildlife habitats in close proximity; the coastal jungle rises through strata of tropical wet, broadleaf and lowland dry forest, diversifying into cloud forest at around 1,200 m (4,000 ft) – a rare combination guaranteeing the best chance of seeing the widest variety of endemic species. These strata are subdivided by another influence – the mountain's unusually steep valley formations. Tumbling rivers and rushing streams create dozens of cascades and waterfalls on every level. Each harbours its own population of birds, butterflies and bigger animals, from monkeys to river otters. Their abundance is dependent on the harsh topography, which makes Pico Bonito very hard to access, but correspondingly rewarding.

The Biosphere Reserve to which Pico Bonito gives its name remains one of the least explored in Honduras. Some of the most difficult terrain will stay that way, because access is forbidden to everyone other than professional climbing teams with permission to make ascents. It doesn't matter. Most of the best of the reserve is accessible near its perimeter and at intermediate height. There are eight-cable zipline tours beneath the forest canopy and white-water rafting on the Rio Bonito and the Rio Cangrejal (in the park's buffer zone). Cross the swaying suspension bridge to the visitor centre (one of only two entrances to the park) and a trail system unfolds taking visitors to beautiful waterfalls hung with orchids and guarded by scarlet macaws. The balance between visitor entertainment and nature conservation is sympathetic to both. Bravo.

Pico Bonito and its surrounding lush coastal jungle

Rio Platano Biosphere Reserve

The 'Banana' River used to be the source of 'red gold' – the mahogany that furnished Europe. It is the major river of the Mosquito Coast and is still home to the remnants of three of Honduras' indigenous peoples: the Miskito, Pech and Garifuna. The biosphere reserve was created as much to provide a sanctuary for these cultures as to protect the fabulously complete coastal ecosystems in which, historically, they thrived. It is a humid, haunting wilderness of steaming mangroves, islets of jungle, coastal lagoons and creeks draped in moss-shrouded rainforest. It is the sudden splash and whirling water of the caiman in the shadows, and the squawking crash of flocks of parrots bursting from the canopy. Most of all, it is the silent wariness of the traveller in a dugout, watching, watching.

Canoeing along the Rio Platano river.

It is also extraordinarily beautiful and full of surprises. The best are to be found with the guidance of one of the villagers. Each guide is part of the region's living continuity, familiar with its wildlife and weather and alert to the drama hidden in the landscape. Near the Rio Platano's headwaters at Warsaka, and at Lancetillal nearby, there are 1,500-year-old petroglyphs incorporated into major ruins whose occupants used the rainforest as larder and pharmacy just as its current residents do. Descending the river by *cayuco* (motorized dugout) to Las Marias – a Miskito and Pech village on the edge of the vast mangrove forest – provides a glimpse of the subtle complexities controlling every kind of life in these isolated wetlands and shows how Miskito culture is integrated into the fragile eco-chain. There are quicker ways to sample Rio Platano's natural marvels, but the region's rarity is its human connection. Take the time and have the adventure. This is a long, long way from the city.

HOW TO GET THERE:
By plane to Palacios, then by boat (five hours) from Raista on the coast upriver to Las Marias. Using a tour company might be less complicated.

WHEN TO GO:
Any time

DON'T MISS:
Spending as much time as possible in a *pipante* (dugout) or on a raft on the Rio Platano. It's the best vantage point to see every kind of wildlife. The river also passes some of the best archaeological sites, such as the 1,000-year-old village of Los Metates, as well as natural features like El Subterraneo – a white-water gorge lined with flat slabs of rock and full of monkeys, macaws and toucans.

YOU SHOULD KNOW:
The Mosquito Coast gets its name from the Meskito people, not because it's a mosquito-infested swamp. Although, in fact, it is.

Sierra Maestra

The biggest mountain range in Cuba, the Sierra Maestra rises steeply from the southeast coast. Pico Turquino, at over 1,970 m (6,465 ft) the country's highest mountain, is named for its colour – its slopes are clad in misty, greenish-blue vegetation. Now a national park, the sierra has special historical and emotional significance for the Cubans as a place of refuge. From the Taino Indians' flight from the Spanish in the 16th century to the 20th century when the Castro brothers escaped into the lush greenery and mists to organize the struggle against Batista, these inaccessible wooded valleys and precipitous gorges have sheltered revolutionaries and rebels.

The ascent of Pico Turquino is a long, challenging hike best undertaken as a two- or three-day guided trek. Walkers usually start the climb by heading east from Alto del Naranjo, northwest of the peak, and either return there or continue south, descending to the coast at Las Cuevas. This stretch of the southern coastline, with plunging mountains and quiet beaches, is spectacular. The peak can be scaled from here, although this ascent is very steep. Refuges are spaced out along the whole route and guides will organize overnight stops. The walk combines green valleys, open uplands affording panoramas of unfolding mountain ranges and the brilliant-blue Caribbean, and cool forests rich in flora and fauna (pygmy owls and hummingbirds are often spotted).

The Comandancia de La Plata, Castro's revolutionary base, is a shorter hike and can be completed in a day. After the steep road from Santo Domingo to Alto del Naranjo, this trail runs west along sheer ridges to where, in a deep gully, hidden under a canopy of trees, Fidel and Raul built their settlement. Here, visitors can inspect a scatter of huts, including dormitories and stores, Castro's operational headquarters and Che Guevara's hospital. A little museum displays photographs and memorabilia, such as Fidel's fountain pen and the radio equipment used by Che for his Radio Rebelde broadcasts to the nation.

The lush scenery in the Sierra Maestra Mountains

HOW TO GET THERE:
Flight or long-distance bus to Bayamo, road to Santo Domingo and jeep taxi to Alto del Naranjo.

WHEN TO GO:
December to June

DON'T MISS:
Santo Domingo, in its deep, verdant valley, is a delightful village and a good base for visits to the Sierra Maestra, gentler rambles in the foothills and swimming in the river. What is now accommodation for walkers was once another camp for the revolutionaries. The life of the dignified rural community has changed little since then.

YOU SHOULD KNOW:
All walks must be guided. The trails are sometimes closed for reasons ranging from bad weather to official visits. Photography is not permitted in La Plata. El Cobre, a copper-mining town west of Santiago de Cuba, is home to the Virgin of Charity, the patron saint of Cuba, whose shrine was visited by Pope John Paul II. Among the many offerings is one from the mother of the Castro brothers and, although it is now locked away, John Steinbeck's 1954 Nobel Prize medal.

Culebra National Wildlife Refuge

The Flamenco Peninsula

Culebra was declared a National Wildlife Refuge in 1909 but was, effectively, a firing range for the US Navy until 1975. Now administered by the US Fish and Wildlife Service, the refuge includes the deeply indented coastline, palm-fringed beaches, parts of the rocky, forested interior and all the satellite islets; all this, and its exceptional wildlife, attracts visitors to this small island with its easy-going brand of ecotourism.

Limited development means wonderfully clean seawater and Culebra's fringe and barrier reefs are some of the most vibrant in the Caribbean. They provide excellent feeding for seabirds and large fish and some very fine snorkelling – anything from angelfish to barracuda may be encountered in the brilliant, glassy waters.

Large coastal mangrove swamps are roosting sites for the endangered brown pelican and nurseries for fish and crustaceans, while the isolated beaches (most are accessible only by tracks) and untouched forest (the Mount Resaca area can be explored by trail) are perfect habitats for a multitude of nesting birds. Terns are particularly numerous on Culebra – a large colony of sooty terns colonizes the Flamenco Peninsula, while roseate, sandwich, bridled and royal terns are widespread. Other birds frequently seen include boobies, tropicbirds and ospreys.

The northern beaches and tiny Isla Culebrita are also nesting sites for endangered sea turtles. Loggerhead, hawksbill, green and leatherback turtles all bury their eggs in the soft sand; the sites are closed during the summer hatching season.

Culebra is only about 11 km (7 mi) long and there is little traffic on the few roads; mountain bikes are a good transport option. By day, the empty beaches of Cayo Luis Pena and Isla Culebrita can be reached by water taxi, although a kayak is a pleasing and ecologically sound way to visit these little desert islands.

HOW TO GET THERE:
Flights from San Juan and Fajardo airports; regular ferry service from Fajardo
WHEN TO GO:
November to July
DON'T MISS:
Summer visitors who volunteer early enough are recruited to assist wildlife refuge rangers count and protect sea turtle nests and hatchlings. Seeing the tiny turtles struggle out of the sand and scuttle to the water's edge is a thrilling and moving experience.
YOU SHOULD KNOW:
Keep to the trails as some parts of the island are littered with a legacy of the target practice years – unexploded bombs. The deep, sheltered bay of Ensenada Honda was used by pirates, including Captain Henry Morgan, as refuge from enemies and hurricanes.

El Yunque

Sometimes the rich Taino, European and African heritage of Puerto Rico seems overshadowed by modern American life, but the island probably owes the survival of its rainforests and rich biodiversity to US colonial rule. Logging and rapid urban expansion resulted in serious deforestation and soil erosion, but in the 1920s extensive areas of conservation forest were set aside and now thousands of tropical plant, bird and animal species flourish in a variety of natural habitats.

Much of eastern Puerto Rico is covered by the forests, hills, streams and waterfalls of El Yunque (previously known as the Caribbean National Forest), the only tropical rainforest under US administration. Now a UNESCO Biosphere Reserve, it is carefully managed and has hiking trails and visitor and research centres. A range of forest types grows here, including most of Puerto Rico's ancient virgin forest – many of the reddish-barked Palo Colorado trees, with their trailing vines, are around 1,000 years old. Sierra palms, ferns and mosses thrive in wetter conditions and, on peaks and ridges, heavy rain and constant winds bend and stunt the cloud, or dwarf, forest. This sumptuously diverse landscape supports a wealth of wildlife. Although the endangered Puerto Rican parrot (which nests in the Palo Colorado trees) is rarely seen, more than 50 bird species, many unique, inhabit the reserve. Resident reptiles include the Puerto Rican boa.

Some of the shorter, paved trails to popular destinations (waterfalls, viewing towers and peaks) can get busy, but longer wilderness trails in the undeveloped south of the forest are often deserted. Serious walkers may leave the crowds behind and relish the cool, pristine beauty of this mountainous subtropical rainforest.

HOW TO GET THERE:
There is no public transport to El Yunque, but Highway 191 (off Highway 3 from San Juan) runs right into the forest.

WHEN TO GO:
April to June are quiet months in the forest; in the hot summers, islanders flock there to cool down; winter (high season) can be hectic.

DON'T MISS:
A night in the rainforest. Camping is permitted off-trail, but it is very basic. Several hotels around the forest perimeter provide an enticing combination of comfort with the unforgettable music of the creatures of dusk and darkness.

YOU SHOULD KNOW:
Do not attempt the longer trails without a good map and compass as it is easy to get lost in a rainforest. It rains, so take suitable clothing. The piercing two-note call of the *coqui* frog, the Puerto Rican mascot, is the sound of the forest. This tree frog deposits its eggs in crevices in trees and then guards them. The tadpoles develop inside the eggs and emerge as tiny froglets.

Palms in the rainforest at El Yunque

Armando Bermudez National Park

HOW TO GET THERE:
Take a pre-arranged tour, or make your way to the park's office in La Cienega, near Jarabacoa. The adventurous can travel to San Juan de la Maguana by car or public transport and arrange the trip from there.
WHEN TO GO:
December to February and July to August.
DON'T MISS:
The Dominican Republic's carnival takes place in February – and you might see whales in Samana then, too.
YOU SHOULD KNOW:
This region is cool, with an average temperature of 12–21°C (54–70°F). But in December and January it can drop to 0°C (32°F) during the early hours.

The Dominican Republic is the eastern two thirds of the island of Hispaniola, with Haiti to its west. It has the second largest economy in the Caribbean, a large portion of which is tourism. Most visitors content themselves with the beautiful beaches and sparkling nightlife, but that means missing the spectacular mountainous interior.

The Armando Bermudez National Park, the first to be established here, is now one of several. Covering the north of the island's highest mountain range – the Cordillera Central – and bordering another national park, this region boasts the four highest mountains in the Caribbean, with Pico Duarte rising to 3,087 m (10,130 ft).

The scenery is glorious; the forested slopes, including most of the surviving virgin rainforest, encompass the largest areas of the country's originally forested landscape. Rivers allow a lush subtropical mixture of West Indian cedar, orchids, palms, bamboo and tree ferns to thrive; at higher elevations, the trees are mainly Caribbean pines. This is twitcher paradise where Hispaniolan parrots, palmchats – the national bird – Hispaniolan trogons, loggerhead flycatchers and several endangered species such as the La Selle thrush can all be seen. Mammals – wild boar and the endangered Hispaniolan solenodons, a creature like a large shrew – are far less visible.

The park draws those who love the great outdoors. Campsites and trails bring climbers and hikers, but for others the goal is the summit of Pico Duarte. To attempt this, you must take a guide and a mule with you and camp *en route*. The trek is not for the faint-hearted although, after travelling through aromatic pine forests with the occasional meadow affording fabulous views, the tough push to the ancient, barren summit is worthwhile. Once there you feel that you are standing on top of the Caribbean, if not the world.

Light streams through a cloud forest high in the mountains of Cordillera Central in Armando Bermudez National Park.

Eastern National Park

One of the largest marine parks in the Caribbean, the Eastern National Park is situated on the thickly wooded southeastern peninsula of the Dominican Republic, near Bayahibe. To the south is Calderas Bay, opposite which is Saona Island, and to the west the small, uninhabited Catalina Island. Formed in 1975, and a UNESCO World Heritage Site, the park is 808 sq km (312 sq mi), of which 388 sq km (150 sq mi) are marine.

A pristine beach on Saona Island

Formed from limestone, the peninsula has shoreline cliffs, white sandy beaches, rocky spurs and mangroves and is riddled with tunnels and caves where pre-Columbian pictographs may be seen. The park is famously hot, with no freshwater streams or lakes; rainwater flows through the porous limestone and collects in sinkholes. The easiest cave to visit is Cueva del Puente, but it's a tough hike nevertheless. Whether approaching from land or sea, take water with you. Around 112 species of birds are to be found here, including the ashy-faced owl and the Hispaniolan lizard cuckoo, both of which are endemic.

However, the shoreline, sea and islands are the greatest attraction in the park. The coastal ecosystem provides habitats for hundreds of species of plants, birds, fish and marine mammals, such as the rhinoceros iguana, bottlenose dolphins, manatees, and several different species of sea turtle. Catalina Island has a wealth of glorious white sandy beaches with crystal-clear waters, so the snorkelling and diving is renowned. Camping permits can be arranged.

Saona Island has two small communities and excellent anchorage. There are no hotels, so visit for the day or anchor offshore and stay longer. It, too, is beautiful with many coconut palm-fringed beaches and fabulous swimming and diving. Many hours can be spent snorkelling over coral reefs and seagrass beds, viewing hundreds of fish, corals, sponges and crustaceans. You may see dolphins and, perhaps, whales in winter.

HOW TO GET THERE:
Take your own boat or hire a boat and a guide from Bayahibe harbour and settle the price before you set off. There are entrances near Bayahibe and Boca de Yuma if you go by car. Don't forget to buy entrance tickets from the ranger stations, and hire a guide.
WHEN TO GO:
December to February and July to August.
DON'T MISS:
The natural swimming pool on Saona Island. Not more than 1 m (3.3 ft) in depth, you can see all kinds of starfish and other marine creatures in this lovely spot.
YOU SHOULD KNOW:
Saona Island's original name was Adamanay, but in 1494 Christopher Columbus changed it to Savonesa, which has become Saona over the course of time.

Jaragua National Park

HOW TO GET THERE:
By 4x4 or boat. The park office is near Oviedo, but there are no facilities or guided tours available.
WHEN TO GO:
December to February or July to August.
DON'T MISS:
Bahia de las Aguilas – 8 km (5 mi) of glorious white sand, fringed by spectacular coral reefs. The tourism industry has its eye on these beaches, but there is also a strong lobby for careful, sustainable ecotourism, which would provide jobs for the local population and would in turn ensure the safety and health of this unique national park.
YOU SHOULD KNOW:
Originally Hispaniola was two islands, each of which had its own plants and animals. Some 20,000 to 30,000 years ago the islands were united and the Bahoruco Mountains were formed. These extend into Haiti and are the reason that so many endemic species are found here. *Jaragua* comes from the Taino Indian language and this region was once part of their land.

The white sand beaches of Bahia de las Aguilas are fringed by spectacular coral reefs.

The largest protected area in the Caribbean, Jaragua National Park lies in the southwest of the Dominican Republic's Barahona Peninsula. Jaragua is unusual in that the third of it on land includes the southern slopes of Bahoruco Mountains, while the remainder consists of protected waters that include Beata and Alto Velo Islands, and a recently formed and still-growing reef platform called Los Frailes.

The park is a fascinating place to explore. The dry, thorny forest hosts a preponderance of cacti alongside endemic shrubs such as the medicinal canelilla, and guanito palms. The land is dotted with caves and many are decorated with petroglyphs and pictographs dating back to 2590 BC; they provide shelter for 11 species of bat. More than 50 endemic species live here: 36 in Hispaniola, 26 in Jaragua itself, four on Beata Island and three on Alto Velo Island. Among these are two iguanas and, at 16 mm (0.6 in) the world's tiniest reptile, the Jaragua Sphaero – a dwarf gecko.

The park is also home to 130 species of birds – some 60 per cent of the country's total – over half of which are seabirds. The country's largest population of pink flamingoes lives at Oviedo lagoon and vast colonies of white-crowned pigeons and the largest known colony of the plain pigeon, a West Indian endangered species, can be found here, too. On the islands and cays the sooty tern has formed its largest Caribbean colony.

Closer to the coast are mangroves. The beaches, many of which are empty and truly idyllic, are nesting sites for leatherback, hawksbill, loggerhead and green turtles which inhabit the extensive coral reefs and seagrass beds – as do queen conch, spiny lobsters and the endangered West Indian manatee. Dolphins are often seen playing in the waters near Alto Velo Island.

Lake Enriquillo

The largest lake in the entire Caribbean, Lake Enriquillo is unique. Situated some 44 m (144 ft) below sea level in the southwestern area of the island, it is just 20 km (12 mi) south of the border with Haiti. Part of the ancient sea channel that once divided Hispaniola, its fascinating ecosystem is due to its hypersalinity. Not only twice as salty as the sea, it is also sulphurous. The depth varies considerably as the water evaporates quickly, and storms are required to replenish its volume because the region receives little rainfall.

Lake Enriquillo was declared a National Park in 1995, although in 1974 Cabritos Island – one of three islands in the lake – became a National Park in its own right. The lake is named after Enriquillo, the Taino Indian chief who resisted the Spanish colonizers while hiding in this area; his statue can be seen at a museum in Santo Domingo.

These difficult conditions provide a habitat for a large number of birds and reptiles, including the American crocodile. The largest population in the world may be found here; each day they swim to the mouths of freshwater streams and spend their nights and lay their eggs on Cabritos Island – a flat, arid six-mile-long island where cacti grow in profusion. Two species of iguana – Ricord's and rhinoceros – abound. Some are so tame that they approach visitors in the hope of being fed.

This is also flamingo country and thousands of these lovely birds can be seen. Among the many other species are burrowing owls, West Indian nighthawks, Hispaniolan parrots and several types of heron – altogether some 97 species of land and aquatic birds make their home here. A harshly beautiful area, Lake Enriquillo is well worth a visit.

HOW TO GET THERE:
By car from Barahona to La Descubierta – the National Park Station is 2 km (1.2 mi) east of town. Here you can hire a boat and a guide to take you to Cabritos Island. You could also join a tour in Santo Domingo.
WHEN TO GO:
December to February and July to August.
DON'T MISS:
A strange illusion that can be experienced at Polo Magnetico. As you drive there from Cabral the car will feel heavy although the road is flat. At Polo Magnetico, where the road seems to rise, put the car into neutral and feel it pick up speed as it appears to go uphill.
YOU SHOULD KNOW:
On a hill close to the lake is the Las Caritas Indian Cave where you'll find Taino engravings of faces. It is thought that Enriquillo himself hid from the Spanish in this small cave. It has fabulous views of the lake and is extremely hot, so take plenty of water.

Beyond the cacti – Lago Enriquillo

Cockpit Country – home to more than three quarters of Jamaica's birds

Cockpit Country

One of the joys of flying from Montego Bay are the views of an extraordinary and beautiful region of Jamaica. From this bird's-eye viewpoint, it looks like a vast inverted egg box: all verdant mounds and hollows, unscarred by roads or settlements. This is Jamaica's unique Cockpit Country. In 1665 the British army took Jamaica from its Spanish colonists, many of whom released their slaves and fled to Cuba. In western Jamaica, the slaves, or Maroons, hid in this wilderness. After many years of guerrilla warfare, they forced the British to cede land, autonomy and freedom to them in the treaty of 1738, and their descendents live there still.

Formed 12 million years ago, subsequent erosion of the limestone plateau produced a large area of regularly spaced, rounded conical hills and flat-bottomed pits, or sinks, probably caused by collapsing cave systems. During storms, soil is brought down from the hills into the valleys, some of which are cultivated and only accessible by trails from surrounding villages. Much of the region remains impenetrable virgin forest.

The region is extremely important for wildlife. More than three quarters of Jamaica's birds are found here, including both the black- and yellow-billed parrot. The island's largest predator, the Jamaican boa, makes its home here, too, as do the endemic blue swallowtail and Jamaican giant swallowtail butterflies and many kinds of bat that roost in the 300 or so caves. At least 101 unique species of plant can be found, some growing on a single hill. These include ferns, bromeliads and six varieties of orchid. You'll need to take a local guide when hiking here – it's easy to get lost and dangerous to go off trail, as you can fall through thin layers of limestone into a deep sinkhole below.

HOW TO GET THERE:
The Cockpits are easiest to explore from Accompong, just north of Maggotty. Guided hikes can be taken into the interior, or you can visit with a tour company.
WHEN TO GO:
December to March if you are going to camp. For short hikes, early morning is the best time as it is still cool.
DON'T MISS:
Wait-a-Bit, the visitor centre at the entrance to Cockpit Country, and the Peace Cave where Cudjoe, the Maroon's Ashanti leader, and the British signed the peace treaty.
YOU SHOULD KNOW:
In the 17th century the British chose the name Cockpit Country because the area reminded them of the cock-fighting pits that were prevalent across Jamaica at that time. Cock fighting is now illegal, although it still takes place occasionally.

Central Rainforest Reserve

St Lucia is one of the Caribbean's Windward Islands and best known for its tourism. It is an extremely beautiful island with superb natural harbours and stunning beaches. Most visitors either visit on cruise ships or remain in their all-inclusive holiday resorts. In recent years, however, the Forestry Department has actively promoted the beauty of the mountainous interior. Clad in tropical rainforest, it contains many rivers that tumble down to the sea.

The Central Rainforest Reserve encompasses 77 sq km (30 sq mi) of the central mountain range. Mount Gimie, the highest peak in the region, rises to 958 m (3145 ft) and is a steep, tough hike of about seven hours. Many shorter hikes are available, however, such as the Enbas Saut Falls trail, which starts 9.6 km (6 mi) east of Soufrière on the island's southwestern coast.

An hour-long trip at the base of Mount Gimie takes you, via many wooden steps, to two waterfalls and natural pools at the head of the Troumassee River. Most hikes require a forestry guide, but this trail can be followed without one. There are splendid mahogany and mahoe trees to be seen and some huge ferns. The trail includes both true rainforest and cloud forest and it's good for spotting birds. The St Lucia black finch, the blue-hooded euphonia, the mountain whistler and even the St Lucian parrot, endemic to the island, may be sighted here.

Hike from coast to coast in a morning, following an old trail used by slaves and their masters during the 17th and 18th centuries. Arrange a birdwatching trip with the Forestry Department and you may see other rare, endemic birds such as the St Lucia peewee and the St Lucia oriole. Along the way you'll spot many beautiful tropical flowers, fruits, orchids and bromeliads.

HOW TO GET THERE:
From Soufrière or Vieux Fort
WHEN TO GO:
The dry season is from December to June, but don't forget there can be frequent sharp showers in the rainforest.
DON'T MISS:
The fabulous World Heritage Site twin peaks of Gros and Petit Piton – ancient forested volcanic cones that rise from the sea on the southwestern coast of the island.
YOU SHOULD KNOW:
It is an offence not to have a permit when entering the rainforest. These are available at every trailhead. At about one-and-a-half times the size of the Isle of Wight, St Lucia was named after Saint Lucy of Syracuse by the island's first colonizers, the French.

Tropical rainforest in the interior of St Lucia

Caravelle Peninsula

HOW TO GET THERE:
By road from the town of La Trinité to Château Dubuc.
WHEN TO GO:
Avoid the rainy season between July and November.
DON'T MISS:
The small but fascinating museum at Château Dubuc, where you will not only see the old slave dungeon, but also learn about the Caravelle Peninsula's colourful history. Be sure to visit the lighthouse, from the top of which you can see the entire length of Martinique's Atlantic coast.
YOU SHOULD KNOW:
In 1902 Martinique's highest peak, Mount Pelée, erupted, devastating the town of St Pierre and killing 28,000 people. The grey-and-black sand beaches in the north were formed by volcanic ash. Don't forget that the currency on Martinique is the Euro.

Martinique, an island lying between Dominica and St Lucia, is an overseas *département* of France and its general standard of living is higher than that of most Caribbean islands. The south, with its fine, white sand beaches, is its most popular region, while the north, dominated by mountains and extinct volcanoes, is carpeted with lush rainforest.

The Caravelle Peninsula is a nature reserve that juts out into the Atlantic on the northeastern side of the island and is an excellent place in which to hike. The peninsula is quite different from the rest of Martinique, being arid with varied landscapes and offering stunning views of the rocky coastline. It is also beautiful.

Start your trip at the 17th-century Château Dubuc, a ruined plantation with wonderful vistas across Treasury Bay. From here hike one of the two paths that lead through the reserve, or go off-piste. The longer trail is 12 km (7.5 mi) and takes some three-and-a-half hours to traverse. It gives the hiker an opportunity to see the different ecosystems of the Caravelle, as well as many types of flora and fauna – some 80 species of sea and land birds, including rare and endangered species, frequent the area.

The trail, shaded by trees such as red gum, passes through

A view of the Caravelle Peninsula looking towards the mainland.

mangrove swamps. Wooden boards provide safe passage across the wettest areas, where thousands of small crabs can be seen clinging and scuttling about the aerial roots. Subsequently it becomes a beautiful coastal path, cutting across the tip of the peninsula and affording splendid views of Treasury Bay and out to the open sea, which crashes and foams against the rocky cliffs below. Here the trail has no shade – a hat, sunscreen and plenty of water are essential.

Morne Trois Pitons National Park

Rugged little Dominica lacks beaches and has avoided mass tourism, but its waters are perfect for diving and whale-watching, its mountainous, forested interior rewarding for birdwatchers and walkers. Much of this 'nature island' is protected and the Morne Trois Pitons National Park is also a UNESCO World Heritage Site because of its rare combination of volcanoes, fumaroles and hot springs with pristine rainforest and a remarkable biodiversity.

Much of the park is accessible via a network of walking trails. Some very popular short walks, such as the Trafalgar Falls and Emerald Pool Trails, pass through luxuriant rainforest where ancient, towering trees with massive, buttressed trunks are festooned in creepers and bright with flowers, to reach cool lakes, plunge pools and waterfalls. Longer trails lead to high, secluded lakes and volcanic peaks – the easiest to climb is the Morne Anglais, in the south of the park. From high ridges where trees are dwarfed by wind and rain, there are views over remote waterfalls and valleys to the circling sea.

The most demanding and exciting hike is to the Boiling Lake and the Valley of Desolation. A three-hour guided climb through rainforest brings the walker to a ridge above the lake, whose water is heated by geothermal activity. It is unwise to linger long here, for the ever-present dense clouds of steam and vapour over the lake are sulphurous. The invisible water can be heard churning as it simmers at just below boiling point. The floor of the Valley of Desolation steams, hisses and belches with numerous scalding geysers, bubbling mud pots, hot springs and steam vents in a blighted expanse of sulphur-stained rocks. On the return path, a dip in Titou Gorge can be very welcome.

Trafalgar Falls

HOW TO GET THERE:
Buses run from Roseau to most of the trailhead villages.
WHEN TO GO:
February to June
DON'T MISS:
The aerial tramway near Titou Gorge gives a unique view up to the rainforest canopy and down through clouds of birds and butterflies to the forest floor, where agoutis (rather like long-legged guinea pigs) may be spotted rummaging.
YOU SHOULD KNOW:
Guides are essential for longer walks – after rain, the going can be treacherous and mists descend very quickly; when the cruise ships are in, Trafalgar Falls is packed with day-trippers; Dominica is the only island where Caribs (the pre-Columbian residents) still live – their culture and skills survive and they are still expert canoe carvers and navigators.

Tayrona National Park

HOW TO GET THERE:
Domestic flights are available to
Santa Marta, from where there are
regular buses to the park entrance.
WHEN TO GO:
Any time of year, although you might
prefer to avoid the two rainy seasons
(May to June and September to
November).
DON'T MISS:
If you can tear yourself away from
the beach, it's worth making the
two-hour trek through the rainforest
to the ruins of a pre-Columbian
native village at Pueblito.
YOU SHOULD KNOW:
A key part of Tayrona's appeal is its
lack of development so you should
come well prepared with your own
supplies of essentials such as sun
screen and mosquito repellent.

Colombia has made huge strides in recent times to clean up its image
as a dangerous, crime-infested country where powerful drug barons
operated largely unchecked by the forces of law. Now it has become
once again a relatively safe and desirable tourism destination.
Nowhere is the transformation more dramatically apparent than in the
Tayrona National Park in the remote far north of the country. What
was until relatively recently a no-go zone for visitors where Marxist
guerrillas battled with right-wing paramilitary groups for control of the
cocaine business, has now reverted to a secluded paradise containing
some of the Caribbean's most stunning unspoilt beaches and most
pristine tropical forest.

Tayrona was designated a national park in 1964. Its 150 sq km
(58 sq mi) are remarkable for their biological diversity. The park is
flanked on its southern edge by the foothills of the world's highest
coastal range, the Sierra Nevada de Santa Marta, which includes the
country's tallest peak, at 5,775 m (18,950 ft). Tayrona is one of the few

places on the planet where you can stand on a
tropical beach and see snow-capped
mountains. It is home to more than 200
species of bird, including the extraordinary
royal flycatcher, and mammals such as howler
monkeys, collared peccaries and the elusive
jaguar (a nocturnal hunter which you are most
unlikely to see).

Tayrona is situated 35 km (22 mi) east of
the old coastal city of Santa Marta. There are
no roads inside the park so you have to walk
or hire a horse for the 45-minute trek through
the jungle to the coast at Arrecifes, where
a sequence of glorious beaches unfolds to
the west.

*Arenilla Beach in Tayrona
National Park*

Canaima National Park

The name of this vast park, encompassing some 30,000 sq km (11,600 sq mi) of remote jungle in the southeast corner of Venezuela, may not be a familiar one but Canaima includes within its borders one of the planet's great natural wonders, the mighty Salto Ángel or Angel Falls. Only discovered by the outside world in 1937 after American bush pilot Jimmie Angel crash-landed his light plane on top of Auyantepui table mountain, Angel is the world's highest waterfall; at 980 m (3,215 ft) it is 16 times the height of Niagara Falls. The phenomenon is caused by the Churún River plunging dramatically off the edge of the Auyantepui plateau into the dense rainforest below. So high is the drop that before the water hits the pool at the base, much of it has turned to mist.

In spite of it being the country's number one tourist destination Angel Falls is not an easy place to reach, although you are unlikely to regret the effort involved. You can arrange to view the waterfall by flying over it in a small plane but it is far better to take your time with an overland trip. This typically takes three days and involves

HOW TO GET THERE:
Light plane from Ciudad Bolívar to Canaima, then motorized canoe up two rivers, and a final 1.5-hour trek through the jungle.

WHEN TO GO:
The rainy season (June to October) when Angel Falls is at its fullest and most spectacular (although visibility may be affected by cloud and mist cover at the top).

DON'T MISS:
The darkly brooding cliffs of Cañón del Diablo (Devil's Canyon) at the base of Angel Falls.

YOU SHOULD KNOW:
If you visit Angel Falls in the dry season not only will you see a diminished cascade but you may also have to help carry your boat overland at certain points because of low river levels.

flights, river travel and hiking. The sense of anticipation as you trek the final leg through the rainforest is palpable; you hear the dull roar of the huge cascade long before it comes into view. And spending a night in a simple camp at the base of the east-facing falls means that you see them in the magical light of sunrise.

Canaima offers much more than Angel Falls, though. The beautiful lagoon beside Canaima village, for example, is surrounded by half a dozen smaller waterfalls, including one that you can actually walk behind.

Mist enshrouds Angel Falls – the world's highest waterfall.

Roraima

Until the last 100 years the large plateau forming the summit of Roraima in the southeast corner of Venezuela was largely cut off from the impact of humans. Known as a *tepui* (a local Indian word meaning 'house of the gods'), Roraima is one of over a hundred such plateaus scattered throughout the remote Gran Sabana region. The distinctive 'table-top' profiles of these sandstone mountains, with their flat summits and near-vertical sides rising up out of the surrounding rainforest, are the result of geological processes two billion years ago, making them among the most ancient formations on the planet. Roraima's impenetrable flanks have produced a unique ecosystem on the plateau: endemic species of plants, insects and small creatures found nowhere else on earth. The reports which the first Victorian explorers to reach the summit brought back fired the imagination of Sir Arthur Conan Doyle and inspired his famous adventure story *The Lost World*.

Roraima may not offer the dinosaurs conjured up by Conan Doyle, but the many endemic species of flora and fauna found nowhere else but here make the six-day trek up onto the 2,800-m (9,200-ft) plateau a thoroughly rewarding one for anyone possessing reasonable levels of fitness and stamina. The climb requires no technical skills but it is a long and demanding one. The pay-off is a genuinely other-worldly experience of a kind that is increasingly rare on this crowded planet. The mysterious atmosphere on the barren surface of the summit with its strange rock formations, glinting quartz crystals and bizarre plant life is only enhanced by the frequent mists that cover it. The microclimate on top means that visitors must travel prepared for wet and chilly conditions as well as the heat and humidity of the encircling savannah and rainforest.

Sunset at Mount Roraima

Iwokrama Rainforest

As most of Guyana's population lives on the coastal belt you lose the crowds in no time at all when you head inland. Travelling some 160 km (100 mi) south of Georgetown, the capital, brings you to a very special place. Iwokrama is an area of unsullied tropical rainforest which owes its remarkable survival to a pioneering initiative of the Guyanese government in 1996 to establish an internationally funded project for the conservation and sustainable development of the rainforest. A key feature of the Iwokrama approach is the active involvement of local communities. The Makushi Indian people, whose traditional homeland this is, have been given support and training to develop new and non-destructive ways of earning their living, such as low-impact harvesting of timber and opportunities to work in ecotourism.

The Iwokrama reserve covers an area of 3,710 sq km (1,430 sq mi) and boasts a range of habitats in addition to rainforest, including lakes, river systems, savannah and, at its heart, a 1,000-m (3,280-ft) mountain range from which the area takes its name. Inviting as all this may sound to the intrepid traveller, the strict rules governing the management of the reserve mean that you are not allowed to explore the reserve on your own. Your base is the international field station beside the Essequibo River where you live alongside scientists conducting ongoing conservation and research into Iwokrama's extraordinary profusion of flora and fauna. Nearly 500 species of bird, 130 different mammals and over 400 types of fish (including South America's biggest) are found here and the field station offers lots of nature walks with expert local guides to help you spot the wildlife. With so many creatures hunting at night, nocturnal safaris are also not to be missed.

*A red and green macaw (*Ara chloroptera*) flies through the Iwokrama Rainforest.*

HOW TO GET THERE:
4x4 transport from Georgetown or a flight to Annai and 4x4 transfer to the field station
WHEN TO GO:
September to March
DON'T MISS:
In the southwest of the reserve there is a 150-m (500-ft) suspended walkway which takes you through the forest canopy, giving a unique view of the treetops and the forest floor 30 m (100 ft) below.
YOU SHOULD KNOW:
Although there can be absolutely no guarantees, Iwokrama gives you a better chance than most places of sighting South America's great cat, the shy and elusive jaguar.

127

Cotopaxi and Chimborazo volcanoes preside majestically over Ecuador's central highlands.

Chimborazo

The snow-capped peak of Chimborazo presides majestically over the central highlands of Ecuador. At 6,310 m (20,700 ft) this extinct volcano is the country's highest mountain and sits at the southern end of what the 19th-century German explorer Alexander von Humboldt dubbed the 'Avenue of the Volcanoes'. The Andes at this point is formed of two parallel mountain chains, with Chimborazo part of the western range. Unlike its famous counterpart Cotopaxi in the eastern range, Chimborazo is no longer an active volcano and its landscape today is one of extinct craters, huge glaciers and ice fields. Cotopaxi may be the world's highest active volcano but Chimborazo has its own claim to fame: lying only a couple of degrees south of the equator, the planet's bulge makes it the world's tallest peak when measured from the earth's core.

Although it is technically not a difficult climb, basic mountaineering experience of snow and ice conditions is required for the ascent of Chimborazo; this normally takes three days with an organized expedition. Because there is a real risk of avalanches during the warm daylight hours, the final eight-hour summit climb is undertaken at night. If you are not in this league, however, it is still possible to appreciate the magnificent landscape with day-treks; for example, by climbing close to the snowline between the two refuges, an ascent of 200 m (655 ft). The highlands surrounding the mountain are protected as a forest reserve and hiking here will familiarize you with the unusual native vegetation and also give you the chance to see llamas and alpacas roaming freely.

HOW TO GET THERE:
There is a good road from the town of Riobamba, 30 km (19 mi) to the southeast. A bus will take you to the entrance of the reserve, or a taxi all the way to one of the trailheads.
WHEN TO GO:
June and July or December to early January
DON'T MISS:
The *quinoa* plant, sacred to the Incas, grows wild in the reserve.
YOU SHOULD KNOW:
Bear in mind that serious trekking at Chimborazo is at high altitude – over 3,500 m (11,500 ft) – so you should take care to acclimatize well beforehand.

128

Galápagos Islands

So many stories and myths surround the Galápagos Islands that it is sometimes hard to believe that they exist at all but rather inhabit a parallel universe beloved of natural history film makers. Exist they most certainly do, however, in a remote location in the Pacific 1,000 km (620 mi) west of the Ecuador mainland. It was, of course, Charles Darwin who first brought the Galápagos to the world's attention when he visited the archipelago in 1835 and used his observations of the islands' wildlife to formulate his revolutionary theory of evolution. What made such an impression on Darwin was the extraordinarily rich ecosystem which had developed in an isolated location untroubled by man and other major predators.

This ecosystem may be rich but it is also incredibly fragile and struggling nowadays to deal with the pressures of the modern world, not least those resulting from mass tourism. The Galápagos Islands are high on the destination list of most serious nature lovers but be warned that visiting them does not come cheap; indeed the authorities now deliberately hike the prices in an effort to restrict the human flow. Although you can plot your own itinerary once there, you will definitely see more of the remarkable wildlife on an organized boat tour; a typical tour offers onboard accommodation as you cruise among the islands, and numerous onshore excursions. There are opportunities aplenty for observing the astonishing number of species that are unique to the Galápagos, including the world's most northerly penguins, frigate birds, blue-footed boobies, Darwin's celebrated finches, the ubiquitous sea lions, marine iguanas (the world's only seagoing lizards) and, most famously of all, the majestic giant tortoises. Nowhere else on earth can you get up as close and personal to wild creatures which seem so unfazed by your presence.

HOW TO GET THERE:
There are flights from the Ecuador mainland to Baltra and San Cristóbal. Public ferries connect the major islands if you are not on an organized boat tour.
WHEN TO GO:
Any time of year. You have a choice between warm and wet – and busier (January to June), and cool and dry (July to December).
DON'T MISS:
If your visit coincides with the mating season, you should see one of nature's more bizarre spectacles: the courting ritual of the male frigate bird which inflates a flap of scarlet skin on his chest to the size of a balloon.
YOU SHOULD KNOW:
UNESCO now has the Galápagos Islands on its Danger List. The pressures on its unique environment have now become so extreme that any responsible traveller should consider seriously the morality of a visit.

A view of Pinnacle Rock on Bartolome Island

Machalilla National Park

On Ecuador's central Pacific coast Machalilla National Park was created in 1979 to preserve its most beautiful stretch of coastline and one of the few remaining expanses of tropical dry forest on the continent. The park covers an area of 600 sq km (230 sq mi), one third of which comprises ocean. Tranquil and isolated beaches are backed by coastal scrub and densely forested hills, while inland the terrain rises and the dry forest gives way to the lush vegetation of a cloud forest. A pass to visit Machalilla can be obtained from the park headquarters in the small coastal town of Puerto López and is valid for five days. There are few maps or waymarkers, however, so you will be dependent on the expertise of local guides. Mighty ceibo trees tower above you on the various hiking trails through the virgin forest as your guide points out exotic orchids and numerous endemic plant species, such as the ivory palm.

You will certainly hear if not see howler monkeys and, if you are lucky, spot anteaters and two rare species of deer, as well as over 350 types of bird. Agua Blanca is a small village in the park with noted archaeological remains from pre-Columbian times. A nearby sulphur pool offers an enticing and refreshing dip, in spite of its pungent odour. For a change of habitat, you can take a boat trip from Puerto López to Isla de la Plata, one of several offshore islands incorporated in the national park. The island provides important breeding grounds for frigate birds and boobies. Pelicans and albatrosses may also be seen and in the winter months the surrounding seas are host to one of nature's great spectacles as humpback whales arrive for the mating season.

Yasuní National Park

The extensive area of Ecuador east of the Andes range is known, appropriately enough, as the Oriente. And in the far east of this region, brushing up against the border with Peru, lies Yasuní National Park. Covering nearly 10,000 sq km (3,860 sq mi), Yasuní is the largest mainland national park in the country and one of Ecuador's last true wildernesses. Most of the park consists of upland tropical forest, but there is a liberal sprinkling of lakes, rivers and other distinctive wetland environments, too, such as seasonally flooded forest and *igapó*, lowlands that are more or less permanently under water.

What makes Yasuní so special for biologists and nature lovers alike, is the fact that for reasons that are still not clear this area was spared the ravages of the last ice age; as a consequence it has retained a degree of biodiversity found in few other places on earth. Yasuní is home to more than 500 species of bird and nearly two thirds of the mammals found in Ecuador, including three of the continent's 'Big Five' – the tapir, jaguar and giant otter. A recent botanical study discovered 473 different tree species in a single hectare (2.5 acres) – thought to be a world record. The fecundity of this remarkable place has been recognized by UNESCO, which in 1989 declared it an international biosphere reserve.

It comes as no surprise that such a well-preserved natural environment should be a long way from civilization. It is not an easy place to get to and you certainly should not visit the park without a guide (it is a jungle out there, after all). Most people savour the delights of Yasuní on organized tours which are plentiful and relatively cheap; arrange one in advance when you are in Quito.

A dusky titi monkey at Napo Wildlife Center, Yasuní

HOW TO GET THERE:
The oil town of Coca, eight to 10 hours by bus from the capital, Quito, is the main jumping-off point for Yasuní. To reach the park from here involves a 90-minute drive followed by a two-hour river trip.

WHEN TO GO:
Any time of year (but note that May to July are the wettest months).

DON'T MISS:
The formidable harpy eagle, one of the world's largest birds of prey.

YOU SHOULD KNOW:
Lucrative oil deposits in Yasuní mean an uneasy co-existence prevails at present between the ecology lobby and the oil industry.

Altiplano

HOW TO GET THERE:
There are spectacular views of the Andes on the nine-hour train journey from Cuzco to the lakeside town of Puno (but note that the train is subject to cancellation at short notice if passenger numbers are low, so you might be better advised to take the bus – seven hours – instead).
WHEN TO GO:
May to October, although at this altitude you should be prepared for cold nights, with temperatures below freezing at times, as well as sunny days.

Altiplano means 'high plain' in Spanish and the term is now used to denote a vast plateau in the central Andes that spreads into Bolivia, Argentina and northern Chile as well as southern Peru. The wide, empty grasslands of the Altiplano occur at altitudes of 3,500 m (11,480 ft) or more so it is essential to acclimatize yourself properly before visiting the region – a good reason, in addition to the environmental one, for travelling overland to get there rather than flying in. After Tibet, the Andean Altiplano is the most extensive area of high plateau on the planet; it really does feel like being on the roof of the world here. The rarefied air at this altitude is exceptionally clear, affording wonderful views of seemingly limitless horizons beneath stunning cobalt skies.

The most significant feature of the Altiplano is Lake Titicaca, at 3,811 m (12,500 ft) the world's highest navigable lake. Straddling the border with Bolivia the lake is also one of the largest, with a length of 170 km (106 mi) and an average width of 60 km (37 mi). A boat trip on the lake to explore some of the 70 or so islands is an unmissable experience, giving the visitor a chance to witness the fishing communities of the local Quechua Indians as they struggle to retain their distinctive culture against the onslaught of modern commerce and tourism. These communities are also to be found on Titicaca's remarkable floating islands. Resembling enormous rafts, these islands are built from the buoyant *totora* reeds which grow in abundance around the lake and which are also used in the construction of the traditional fishing boats.

DON'T MISS:
The *chullpas* at Sillustani and Cutimbo. These extraordinary cylindrical burial towers dominate the landscape in the flat plains to the west of Titicaca and are reminders of an ancient pre-Inca culture that once flourished in the region.
YOU SHOULD KNOW:
The Incas believed that Lake Titicaca was the birthplace of the sun and that the first Inca, Manco Capac, rose out of its waters.

A church and snow-topped mountain on the Altiplano

Chachapoyas

If you harbour Indiana Jones-style fantasies of coming across mysterious archaeological remains as you hack your way through dense jungle, then a trip to the Chachapoyas region in Peru's Northern Highlands is a must. There may be established trails now which spare you the hacking but this is still a remote and undeveloped area which does not reveal its surprises easily. The virgin cloud forests surrounding the little market town of Chachapoyas are littered with archaeological sites testifying to an enigmatic ancient culture which at one time rivalled the Incas. Chachapoyas, indeed, was the Incas' name for this culture and may be derived from Quechua words meaning 'people of the clouds'.

The Chachapoyas were a fierce warrior people who liked to show off their trophies of conquest and also practised human sacrifice. Buses and shared taxis run along unsealed roads in some valleys but the only way to reach most of the ruins is on foot or horseback. Many of the remains have been reclaimed by the jungle and are hard to spot so, even if you decide to strike out on your own, you would be well advised to hire a local guide for any serious exploration. The most spectacular ancient site (and a relatively accessible one) is the mighty stone citadel of Kuélap, perched breathtakingly on a mountain-top surrounded by thick forest. Location and vistas rival Machu Picchu, without the crowds.

Only disclosed to the outside world a few years ago, the Gocta Falls deep in the jungle north of Chachapoyas are one of the world's tallest waterfalls, at 771 m (2,530 ft). It's a tough five-hour trek but worth it if you want to see the falls before the inevitable happens and they are opened up to organized tourism.

Laguna de los Condores in the Chachapoyas region

HOW TO GET THERE:
An 11-hour bus ride from Chiclayo to Chachapoyas. Once there, shared taxis (*colectivos*) are a cheap and efficient way of getting around.
WHEN TO GO:
May to September
DON'T MISS:
You'll think you've found Shangri La when you first set eyes on the Belén valley west of Chachapoyas, with its river lazily meandering through a fabulously green valley floor and ringed about by mist-covered hills.
YOU SHOULD KNOW:
The Gocta Falls remained unknown for so long because the local people feared the curse of a beautiful resident mermaid if they disclosed its whereabouts.

133

Lomas de Lachay National Reserve

HOW TO GET THERE:
The entrance to the reserve is 4 km (2.5 mi) east of the Pan-American Highway. There are no buses so, if you are not on a tour, you will require your own vehicle or else have to walk from the highway.
WHEN TO GO:
August to October, when the wild flowers are in full bloom and the hills are at their greenest.
DON'T MISS:
Keep your eyes peeled for the vizcacha, a rodent which looks more like a rabbit than the chinchilla to which it is closely related.
YOU SHOULD KNOW:
As the best time to visit is during the wet season, you should be prepared for fog and high levels of humidity. A waterproof jacket is essential.

A little over 100 km (62 mi) north of Lima, the bleakness of the Sechura desert which fringes the coast all the way to the border with Ecuador is unexpectedly punctured by the Lomas de Lachay, a spur running down from the Andes. The exposure of these foothills (*lomas* means 'mounds' in Spanish) to the ocean currents created by Pacific trade winds has created a microclimate in sharp contrast to the aridity of the surrounding coastal plain. The rolling mists that blow in off the sea in the winter months produce condensation in the hills which triggers an explosion of growth and life. No fewer than 74 plant species have been recorded in this relatively confined area, one third of which are now on the critically endangered list. Among the 55 types of bird found here are several species of the delicate hummingbird. Mammals to look out for include the *zorro* (red fox), Andean skunk, and grey deer which have been successfully re-introduced in recent years.

The Peruvian government was quick to recognize the significance of this unusual ecosystem and an area of 51 sq km (20 sq mi) is now protected as a *Reserva Nacional*. There may be few other facilities in the reserve but it does offer good waymarked trails and a number of camping areas. Among the profusion of flora and fauna there are also strange rock formations, the result of forces eroding the local granite; some have been given fanciful names, such as *Cerro la Virgen*, said to resemble a praying Virgin Mary. Although these hills are now uninhabited, rock paintings provide evidence that they were once the home of ancient tribes.

Manu River

Peru takes its responsibility to protect its wilderness areas rather more seriously than its neighbour Brazil, and nowhere is this better demonstrated than in the Manu area deep in the southern Amazon basin. Here the entire watershed of the Manu River is contained within the Manu National Park, the country's largest. Rising on the eastern slopes of the Andes, the river makes its sluggish way south to Boca Manu where it joins the Madre de Dios, which in turn flows eventually (yes, you've guessed) into the mighty Amazon. As with most of the Amazon jungle the river provides the only means of getting around. It takes some six hours to travel upstream by boat from the park entrance to the lake of Cocha Salvador, where one of the park's two lodges is situated.

Manu National Park is half the size of Switzerland but a mere one fifth is open to visitors (the rest is accessible only to indigenous tribes and authorized scientists), so even spending a week here means you are only ever going to scratch its surface. But what a surface! Manu is right up there as one of the most biodiverse spots on the planet; not for nothing did UNESCO declare it a Biosphere Reserve in 1977 (and a World Heritage Site a decade later). The park's boundaries encompass altitudes ranging from 365 m (1,200 ft) to 4,000 m (13,120 ft), and the resulting variety of environments, from lowland jungle to mountain cloud forests, is home to a staggering array of vegetation and wildlife. The numbers are almost unbelievable – there are 13 types of monkey and 1,200 butterfly species alone – but it does mean that, with the help of an experienced guide, you should be richly rewarded with sightings.

The Manu River

HOW TO GET THERE:
Make this the adventure it deserves to be and travel overland from Cuzco. It's a 24-hour boneshaking drive to Atalaya or Shintuya where you board a boat for the day's river journey to the Manu park entrance.

WHEN TO GO:
May to October, when it is hot and humid but the tropical downpours are fewer.

DON'T MISS:
The giant catahua tree in the rainforest, used by the native tribes to make their dugout canoes.

YOU SHOULD KNOW:
It is illegal to enter the park without a guide. Visitor numbers are carefully controlled by the authorities so it is essential to book your tour well in advance (in Cuzco or Lima).

Beni Biosphere Reserve

HOW TO GET THERE:
It is a 24-hour journey by bus from the capital, La Paz, but as this includes a section through the mountains which has been designated the world's most dangerous road, this may be one occasion when it makes sense to overcome any environmental qualms and take a flight instead to San Borja or Trinidad.
WHEN TO GO:
May to October (but note that even though the climate is tropical the area is subject to the occasional *surazo* – a cold wind blowing up from the Argentine pampas – so some warm clothing is advisable).
DON'T MISS:
If you are visiting at the end of July the three-day village fiesta at nearby San Ignacio de Moxos is one of the most colourful and exciting in the country.
YOU SHOULD KNOW:
In recent years the Chimane homelands and the fringes of the Beni Reserve have come under increasing threat from commercial logging interests.

The enormous Amazon Basin in the northeast of Bolivia still contains great swathes of pristine tropical forest. One of the best is the Biosphere Reserve of Beni which lies in the Llanos de Moxos region west of Trinidad. The reserve protects 1,350 sq km (520 sq mi) of mixed savannah and rainforest and, as its label suggests, is rich in flora and fauna. Around 500 bird species have been recorded here and 100 different types of mammal, including big favourites like the anteater, peccary, jaguar, river otter and spider monkey (although as usual you can count yourself fortunate if you see any of the stars as most are shy and elusive, often hunting or foraging at night). A large adjacent area of forest has been set aside for the exclusive use of the local Chimane people.

The only visitor facilities in the reserve are at El Porvenir on its southern edge, close to the main road between La Paz and Trinidad. This is savannah and the forest proper is some way away but various tours are offered from the visitor centre, a former ranch which offers basic accommodation. You can either take day-long guided hikes out into the jungle or tours on horseback around the more open areas. Viewing towers give you a different perspective on the wildlife. A popular excursion (although that is a relative term in this remote spot) is the river trip by canoe to the Laguna Normandia, a lake filled with rare black caimans. These impressive amphibians may look entirely at home in this lovely setting but in fact they are the descendants of creatures rescued from a failed leather business in the city.

Laguna Colorada

HOW TO GET THERE:
This is a sparsely populated area with few facilities so you should not consider visiting it other than on an organized tour. Three- or four-day tours by 4x4 can be arranged in the nearby towns of Uyuni and Tupiza.
WHEN TO GO:
July to October (but remember that the high altitude means that it can be bitterly cold, with temperatures at night falling well below freezing).
DON'T MISS:
If you can brave the cold, the night skies of the Altiplano are some of the best you will ever see.
YOU SHOULD KNOW:
Flamingoes have a remarkably sophisticated filtering system in their large bills for extracting nutrients from the lake's saline waters.

High up on the *puna* grasslands of Bolivia's southern Altiplano sits a very unusual lake. The name, Laguna Colorada or 'Coloured Lake', provides a clue. Forget the palette of blues, greys and browns you would normally associate with a lake; this one has a striking reddish hue, caused by the algae that flourish in these mineral-rich waters. If you walk around the shores of the lake you can see evidence of the minerals themselves in deposits of white sodium and magnesium. Although the lake covers an area of 60 sq km (23 sq mi), its average depth is a mere 0.8 m (2.6 ft), making it a haven for waders and other waterfowl. Many different species of duck and geese flourish in these brackish waters but the undoubted stars of the Laguna Colorada show, and what most people come here to see, are the flamingoes. All three of the continent's native species are to be seen here, including the world's largest population of the smaller James

flamingo. The stupendous array of colours in this harsh, other-worldly landscape – the lake's waters, the greens of the *puna* scrub, the delicate pinks of the flamingoes, the snow-capped peaks on the horizon, and all beneath a brilliant blue sky – takes your breath away; literally so, since the altitude is well over 4,000 m (13,120 ft).

The Laguna Colorada is in the north of the large Eduardo Avaroa Wildlife Reserve which extends over 100 km (62 mi) down to the borders with Chile and Argentina. Herds of wild llama and vicuña roam the wide open plains and the reserve contains a number of unusual features, including other coloured lakes, a volcano (which can be climbed) and geothermal areas with hot springs, bubbling mud pools and steaming fumaroles.

A small herd of llamas walks along the shoreline of Laguna Colorado.

Salar de Uyuni

HOW TO GET THERE:
The town of Uyuni is the main base for expeditions into the Salar. Uyuni is seven hours by train or eight hours by bus from Ororo. It is advisable to buy your tickets a day or two in advance.
WHEN TO GO:
July to October for the best climate, although an autumn visit (March and April) gives you a greater chance of seeing the reflective surfaces.
DON'T MISS:
Consider making your immersion in the saline world a total one by staying at one of several 'salt hotels' which are entirely constructed from the stuff.
YOU SHOULD KNOW:
Few of the hotels and hostels in the area offer central heating so a well-insulated sleeping bag is an essential travel requirement.

You may want to rethink the phrase 'flat as a pancake' once you have gazed on the vast expanse of the Salar de Uyuni in southwestern Bolivia. This extraordinary landscape is like no other; it is a desert, yes, but instead of the more familiar golden hues of sand your eyes are assaulted by a dazzling whiteness. Uyuni is a salt pan, the world's largest, covering more than 12,000 sq km (4,630 sq mi). The Altiplano (high plain) here has no outlet to the sea so mineral-rich waters off the surrounding mountains once collected at the lowest point; high salinity levels left salt deposits which formed a giant saltwater lake. A permanent cover of water has long since evaporated thanks to the fierce Andean sun but beneath the thick surface crust of salt the ground remains largely saturated.

There is an awful lot of salt around and, not surprisingly, there is an industry devoted to its extraction and processing. It is a tough way to earn a living and many locals have realized that a more lucrative avenue is to sell curios and artefacts made from the white stuff to the growing tourist market. Most people visiting the Salar take an organized 4x4 tour which generally involves one night on the salt flats in fairly basic accommodation. Longer tours also take in the Eduardo Avaroa Wildlife Reserve to the south. The desert is entirely flat and featureless apart from a few 'islands', such as Isla Incahuasi with its strange, cactus-covered mounds.

If you are fortunate enough to see the salt flat just after rainfall, you can enjoy the reflections of the sky and clouds in the surface water – an astonishing optical effect where the horizon seems to disappear altogether.

A fantastic view across the salt lake – Salar de Uyuni

Chaco Forest

Paraguay lags behind most other South American countries in the development of tourism, largely because of the long-lasting and repressive Stroessner regime which only came to an end in 1989. What this small, land-locked nation lacks in the way of facilities for the traveller, however, is more than compensated by the integrity and lack of degradation of much of its natural landscapes. Occupying 60 per cent of the country west of the Paraguay River, the Chaco is one of the continent's great remaining wildernesses and its second-largest ecosystem after the Amazon.

*The stunning flower of a midnight queen (*Harrisia bonplandii*)*

With both tropical and subtropical climates, the Chaco encompasses a range of environments; wide plains and seasonally flooded savannahs characterize the lowlands which provide major feeding grounds for waterbirds. The real adventure, however, begins in the High Chaco to the north where the huge dry forest of El Gran Chaco extends over the borders into Bolivia, Brazil and Argentina, covering an area of more than 1,000,000 sq km (386,100 sq mi). It is a harsh, unforgiving landscape of prickly scrub and stunted trees where searing temperatures and fiercely hot winds hold sway. But, unpromising as it sounds, it is also one of the best places to seek out the continent's larger mammals. Both great cats – the puma and the jaguar – live in the Gran Chaco, as well as peccaries, tapirs, anteaters, giant armadillos and the guanaco, a member of the camelid family that includes the llama and alpaca. The best chance of spotting animals is on a night walk. Patience and a torch are the most useful aids, especially at a waterhole or salt lick. Look out, too, for the unique night monkey – the only nocturnal monkey in the Americas.

HOW TO GET THERE:
There is only one highway through the Chaco. A bus from Asunción, the Paraguayan capital, takes 16 hours to get into the heart of the Gran Chaco.
WHEN TO GO:
May to September
DON'T MISS:
You are also likely to spot the rhea, the giant flightless bird that is South America's equivalent of the ostrich and emu.
YOU SHOULD KNOW:
If you make your own arrangements to tour the Chaco you will have to hire a 4x4 and travel with plenty of fuel, food and water as there are no supplies available locally.

139

*An aerial view of the
Anavilhanas Archipelago*

Anavilhanas Archipelago

The Rio Negro or Black River in western Brazil is one of the major
tributaries of the Amazon. Rising in the mountains on the
Venezuelan border it joins with the Rio Solimões at Manaus to form
the Amazon proper. A day's boat journey upstream from Manaus
brings you to the small jungle town of Novo Aírão, gateway to the
world's largest group of freshwater islands – the Anavilhanas
Archipelago. Over time geological barriers downstream caused the
river to flow in narrower channels and the resulting water pressure
backed up to create a huge lake-like area up to 20 km (12.5 mi)
wide, which is studded by more than 400 densely forested islands –
the consequences of sedimentary deposits. Much of the forest here
is seasonally flooded, known in Portuguese as *igapó*; during the wet
season, indeed, many of the islands in the archipelago are
completely submerged.

Riverboat tours introduce you to the delights of the Anavilhanas
Archipelago, which has its own ecosystem and an abundance of
plant and animal life. Those flamboyant and noisy jungle-dwellers,
macaws and parrots, are a common sight, as are toucans and howler
monkeys. Among the river creatures you are likely to see are
delightful Amazonian dolphins. The dry season exposes some
superb beaches on a number of the islands, their fine white sands
making a vivid contrast with the unmistakable black waters of the
river. It may not be the seaside but you can still enjoy chilling out on
these beaches, especially as the Negro's acidic waters mean there
are far fewer mosquitoes around than normally in the jungle.

HOW TO GET THERE:
Anavilhanas is an eight-hour boat
ride from Manaus. (It's a little quicker
by bus but it's much more
atmospheric to be on the river.)
WHEN TO GO:
Any time of year. This region gets a
lot of rain; if you really want to avoid
the wet stuff, June to October tends
to be the driest period.
DON'T MISS:
If you get the chance, try your hand
at a spot of piranha fishing (don't
worry, despite the fish's fearsome
reputation you are unlikely to lose a
finger let alone your hand!).
YOU SHOULD KNOW:
Your odds on spotting wildlife will
increase greatly if you can decamp
from the main boat and explore the
side channels in the peace and quiet
of a canoe.

Aparados da Serra National Park

In the far south of Brazil the dominant landscape feature is an extensive highland plateau, its rock formations the result of layer upon layer of sediment deposited from the nearby Atlantic Ocean. Volcanic and other subterranean activity some 150 million years ago covered the tableland with a thick crust of basalt rock. The forces of wind and water subsequently carved out great cracks in the basalt at the plateau's edges, creating a series of magnificent canyons for the modern visitor to wonder at. The most impressive of these is Itaimbezinho, which forms the centrepiece of the Aparados da Serra National Park. The canyon is nearly 6 km (3.75 mi) long, 720 m (2,360 ft) deep and between 600 m (1,970 ft) and 2 km (1.25 mi) wide. It is a sublime spectacle at any time, but its grandeur is enhanced still further by the regular fogs that roll in off the Atlantic.

The canyon's most striking feature is its sheer rock escarpments; unlike those of the Grand Canyon, though, these surfaces are mostly covered with vegetation. The park lies in a temperate zone, with well-defined seasons, but the special topography of the Itaimbezinho canyon means that it hosts two distinct habitats: the canyon floor is subtropical, while the slopes and higher levels which see relatively little rainfall, display a thick cover of cloud forest. The surrounding tableland is dotted with stands of araucaria pine with their distinctive umbrella shape.

Guided trails, including one that runs around the canyon rim and a more challenging one that descends to its floor, take you into the heart of the park. Aparados da Serra is home to an abundance of bird and animal life. The maned wolf, puma, ocelot and tapir can be found here.

HOW TO GET THERE:
The park lies 66 km (41 mi) northeast of São Francisco de Paula. It is a difficult place to get to unless you take a guided tour or have your own transport (4x4 advisable).

WHEN TO GO:
Winter (May to August) is the best time to visit; it may be cold but the visibility is clearest and there is less chance of sea fogs spoiling the views. Spring (October and November) can also be chilly but offers a dazzling display of wild flowers.

DON'T MISS:
The canyon contains two spectacular waterfalls.

YOU SHOULD KNOW:
Visitor numbers to the park are limited to 1,000 per day so if you are not on an organized tour you are advised to book your visit in advance.

Winter in the Aparados Da Serra National Park

Boipeba Island

HOW TO GET THERE:
Although you can travel over from
Tinharé, the best way to reach
Boipeba is direct by boat from the
coastal town of Valença (four hours
by normal boat or one hour in a
speedboat).
WHEN TO GO:
Any time of year (although you may
want to avoid the rainy season,
April to July).

*Boipeba Island is separated
from Tinharé by the Rio
de Inferno.*

Like most good things the Ilha de Boipeba does not come to you on
a plate. It takes some effort to access its various delights but you
are unlikely to come away disappointed. Boipeba is one of the three
main islands of the Tinharé Archipelago which lies just off the
Bahia coast, 100 km (62 mi) south of Salvador. Its larger neighbour,
the Ilha de Tinharé, is a famous holiday destination popular with
the Brazilian cool set as well as foreign sun-seekers. Boipeba to the
south is separated from Tinharé by the vividly named Rio de
Inferno (Hell River). The change of atmosphere crossing this
narrow and, in spite of its name, relatively placid channel is quite
remarkable; the crowds and the buzz that surround the beaches of
Morro de São Paulo on Tinharé vanish completely when you step

onto its unassuming neighbour. Yet Boipeba has beaches every bit as sensational but considerably less developed than Tinharé's.

This is a place where you can really slow down and forget the pace of modern life for a while. There are no roads and no cars, just the odd tractor and jeep, so the only ways to get around are on foot or by boat. Besides the palm-fringed beaches the landscape is one of sand dunes, salt marshes, extensive mangrove swamps and, in the interior, dense Atlantic rainforest. The waters around the island are crystal clear most of the year and are superb for snorkelling and diving, especially the coral reefs off the Ponta de Castelhauos at the southern tip of the island. If you are feeling more energetic, surfing, canoeing and horse riding are also available.

DON'T MISS:
The amazing array of sea life to be seen in the natural pools that form off the beaches at low tide.
YOU SHOULD KNOW:
The island's name is derived from a native Indian word for flat snake, referring to the sea turtles that frequent the local waters.

Caatinga Wilderness

This vast and sparsely populated region covering 750,000 sq km (290,000 sq mi) of the interior of northeastern Brazil gets its name from the thorny scrub which is its dominant vegetation. Only the hardiest of plants survive in the harsh, semi-desert conditions of these uplands. One of the toughest of all, the cactus, is a common feature of the landscape. Other kinds of tree have adapted to the intense heat and drought-like conditions by remaining leafless for long periods. An integral part of the *sertão*, the Brazilian bush or outback, the Caatinga is a bleak and lonely place where scattered communities eke out a living from subsistence farming. It is little visited by travellers but possesses all the same a raw and unvarnished beauty which feels a world away from the hectic life of the coast.

The towns of Campina Grande and Caruaru are the main gateways for exploring the region if you are heading inland from the coast. The São Francisco River is also an important artery and a vital green lung through what is the largest area of dry forest on the whole continent. With a mere one per cent of it enjoying any form of protection, however, the Caatinga is very much at the mercy of commercial pressures and human activity. The large ranches with their herds of grazing cattle and *vaqueiros* cowboys may look picturesque enough but the introduction of new and intensive agricultural practices is accelerating a process of desertification throughout the region. This is particularly bad news for the bird life, which is surprisingly rich given the unpromising habitat.

HOW TO GET THERE:
Distances are huge and public transport erratic so you will need to hire a 4x4 for any serious exploration of the Caatinga.
WHEN TO GO:
It is hot and mainly dry all year round, with a rainy season from March to June.
DON'T MISS:
If you are here in the wet season you will see much of the landscape transformed by wild flowers and lush new growth.
YOU SHOULD KNOW:
In times of severest drought even cactus plants – thorns and all - are used as cattle feed.

143

The Chapada dos Guimarães still feels remote and mysterious.

Chapada dos Guimarães

The Mato Grosso in western Brazil is a region of flat uplands which extend to the horizon in every direction. At its centre is the Chapada dos Guimarães, a sandstone plateau that rises over 350 m (1,150 ft) from the surrounding plains. As you draw nearer on the road that climbs steadily out of the city of Cuiabá, the precipitous curtain of rock confronting you looks ever more daunting and impenetrable. Do not be intimidated, though, because the national park that covers much of the plateau – 300 sq km (116 sq mi) of it – holds an array of spectacular natural sights you won't want to miss. Although the Chapada is an increasingly popular attraction, it still retains a distinct aura of remoteness and mystery. It can claim, however, to be at the heart of things in one very specific sense, lying as it does at the geodesic centre of the South American continent (it is equidistant between the Pacific and Atlantic oceans).

There are a number of hiking trails around the national park, some of which can only be undertaken with a guide. Natural features include waterfalls, canyons, caves and bizarre rock formations. The Véu de Noiva (Bridal Veil) waterfall drops 86 m (282 ft) down a sheer cliff, while the Cidade de Pedra (City of Stone) is a mesmerizing collection of sandstone shapes around the canyon edges. A flash of blue seen here belongs most probably to macaws which build their nests on the cliff faces. At several sites ancient rock paintings have been preserved. From the highest point of the plateau, São Jeronimo (850 m, 2,790 ft), there are panoramic views of the *cerrado* (high plain) and the Pantanal wetlands to the south.

HOW TO GET THERE:
The gateway to the park is the small town of the same name, which is 65 km (40 mi) from Cuiabá. Although you can get there by bus, having your own vehicle is recommended as the distances between the various sights in the park are considerable.
WHEN TO GO:
Any time of year
DON'T MISS:
The vertical walls of dark-red rock assume a special grandeur at sunset.
YOU SHOULD KNOW:
In recent years the Chapada has become popular with New Age followers, attracted by its spiritual qualities and other-worldly atmosphere.

Itatiaia National Park

Established in 1937, Itatiaia was Brazil's first national park and is still a place where you can escape the crowds and get back to nature with relative ease. It is located in the far west of Rio de Janeiro state, 165 km (103 mi) from the city and close to the state borders with Minas Gerais and São Paulo. The unusual name comes from an indigenous word referring to 'rocks with sharp edges'. The park covers an area of 120 sq km (46 sq mi) on the slopes of the Mantiqueira mountain range; the variation in altitude it encompasses makes for a startling diversity of landscapes, from dense Atlantic forest in the foothills (a type of forest that is now critically endangered in Brazil) through treeless, grassy slopes at higher levels and on up to the mountains themselves. Within the park's borders are two major peaks: Agulhas Negras at 2,787 m (9,145 ft) and Prateleira at 2,540 m (8,335 ft), both of which are popular climbs for those with mountaineering experience.

Because the area escaped use for coffee cultivation or other agricultural purposes its ecology has remained remarkably intact and unchanged. On the various walking trails through the park you will see giant tree ferns, bromeliads, orchids and other characteristic features of subtropical forest. Itatiaia is graced with numerous waterfalls and natural springs which feed the Paraíba River (an important source for Rio's water supply). The water may be bracing, but on a hot day you will probably be very grateful for a refreshing dip in one of the natural pools.

Itatiaia is a paradise for birdwatchers; hummingbirds, owls and toucans are all much in evidence. The park's visitor centre provides a good introduction to the flora and fauna to be seen.

HOW TO GET THERE:
By 4x4 or local bus from the town of Itatiaia which lies on the main highway between Rio and São Paulo.
WHEN TO GO:
May to August, when it is generally dry but can be chilly at night.
DON'T MISS:
Lago Azul (blue lake) with its beautiful setting and clear waters that are ideal for bathing.
YOU SHOULD KNOW:
The park is still recovering from a disastrous bushfire in 1988 which swept through one fifth of its area.

Giant tree ferns can be seen from the walking trails.

145

Lençóis Maranhenses National Park

HOW TO GET THERE:
The park is three to four hours by road from the state capital São Luis. Most tours start from the town of Barreirinhas.

WHEN TO GO:
June to September, when the lagoons are filled. It is always hot and humid but there is occasional relief from cooling sea breezes.

DON'T MISS:
The beaches at Lençóis Maranhenses are exceptional by any standards and you will almost certainly have them to yourself.

YOU SHOULD KNOW:
Since access to the national park is carefully controlled you will have to hire an accredited guide if you are planning your own visit.

Brazil is a huge country but it's a fair bet you won't see anything else quite like the Parque Nacional dos Lençóis Maranhenses. Located on the coast of the northeastern state of Maranhão, the park's name translates from Portuguese as 'bedsheets', a suitably graphic description for this unique landscape. When you are only a few hundred kilometres from the Amazon delta you do not expect to find a desert, but that is what you get at Lençóis Maranhenses: an area of over 1,500 sq km (580 sq mi) composed in the main of giant white sand dunes. Their dramatic shapes have been formed over thousands of years from sand deposited by rivers at their mouths, which has then been swept back inland by winds and ocean currents. The dunes now stretch up to 50 km (31 mi) inland and extend 43 km (27 mi) along the coastline.

The play of sunlight and shadow on the dunes is a captivating sight, not least for anyone who fancies themselves behind a lens. But this is an equatorial climate, with little of the aridity of the Sahara or Arabian deserts. When it rains in the first half of the year it does so with a vengeance and the flat areas between the dunes fill with water, creating hundreds of freshwater lagoons. Some, like Lagoa Bonita and Lagoa da Gaivota, are enormous and provide wonderful swimming opportunities in their crystal-clear waters. Other activities to enjoy in the park include boat trips on the Preguiças river and around the mangrove swamps and riding the dunes in a jeep (authorized drivers only!).

Sunset over the desert

Rio Negro Forest Reserve

There aren't many places on the planet that can still lay claim to being uncharted territory but the upper reaches of the Rio Negro in the far northwest of the Amazon basin come as close as any. The Rio Negro, or Black River, is a major tributary of the Amazon, its characteristic dark waters (more the colour of tea than jet black) joining with those of the Rio Solimões at the Meeting of the Waters below Manaus to form the main Amazon River. The Negro has its source in the Colombian uplands 2,230 km (1,390 mi) away. Close to the source, and hard up against the border with Colombia, lies the Rio Negro Forest Reserve, a protected area covering 38,000 sq km (14,670 sq mi) of virgin tropical forest. Bounded on one side by the Rio Negro and on the other by its tributary the Uaupés, the reserve contains significant swathes of *igapó*, seasonally flooded forest, as well as primary rainforest and *caatinga* scrubland.

There are virtually no facilities in this remote area and the only way to explore the reserve is by hiring a local guide to take you on day treks or camping trips. The town of São Gabriel, a few hours downstream, is the place to arrange this. In terms of wildlife the Rio Negro Forest Reserve is the Amazon at its extravagant best; over half of all the species recorded in the Amazon basin can be found here, although as usual you will need a good deal of patience and luck to spot the rarer and more elusive creatures. Multi-coloured toucans and parrots, pink dolphins frolicking in the river and capuchin monkeys swinging through the canopy should provide ample compensation for any other disappointments.

*Amazon River dolphins (*Inia geoffrensis*) frolic in the Ariaú River, a tributary of the Rio Negro.*

HOW TO GET THERE:
A fast boat upstream from Manaus takes five days.
WHEN TO GO:
During the dry season, June to November
DON'T MISS:
If you're lucky your guide will help you spot the golden-backed uacari, one of South America's most charming but least-known monkeys.
YOU SHOULD KNOW:
Unfortunately, the very remoteness of the area has attracted less savoury elements and drug running across the national frontier is a significant problem. You should take official advice before planning a visit to the reserve.

Serra do Cipó National Park

A pair of black tufted-ear marmosets

The Espinhaço Mountains bisect the state of Minas Gerais from north to south, dividing the central Brazilian Highlands from the coastal plain to the east. At the southern end of the range lies the Parque Nacional Serra do Cipó, established to protect a typical *cerrado* landscape of high-altitude grasslands and open savannah of a kind that is increasingly threatened with degradation from human settlement and commercial exploitation. Covering an area of 338 sq km (130 sq mi), the park is criss-crossed by a series of watercourses forming part of the São Francisco basin. Formidable canyons and gorges have been created where the valleys have cut through the mountains; the Cānion dos Confins and the gorge of the Rio do Peixe are two of the best. The park is also blessed with an abundance of beautiful waterfalls, most of which can be reached easily enough on a network of walking trails.

Serra do Cipó is renowned for its biodiversity and boasts a high proportion of endemic species. The conditions in this harsh scrubland hardly seem propitious for growth but a remarkable variety of unusual plants manage to prosper in the sparse and sandy soil, helped by the proximity of fresh water. Among more than 50 species of mammal found here are anteaters, deer, armadillos, monkeys, ocelots and otters. This is also classic habitat for the capybara; you should have no difficulty spotting the world's largest rodent. Besides trekking, Serra do Cipó offers opportunities for horse riding and for kayaking on the Cipó River. As you explore the area keep an eye out for traces in the foothills of the old stone road built by slaves for the prospectors who came looking for gold and precious stones in centuries past.

HOW TO GET THERE:
The national park is 100 km (62 mi) northeast of Belo Horizonte, the state capital.
WHEN TO GO:
Serra do Cipó has a tropical lowland climate. The best time to visit is between April and October.
DON'T MISS:
The clear waters in the pool beneath the Great Waterfall make a marvellous bathing spot.
YOU SHOULD KNOW:
North of Serra do Cipó are the towns of Diamantina and Serro, two examples of the *cidades históricas* (historic cities), founded as mining camps in the early 18th century.

Atacama Desert

If the name Atacama has a familiar ring about it this is probably because in a school geography lesson you will have learned about it as the driest place on earth. In parts of the Atacama, rainfall has never been recorded. The world's highest desert occupies the entire far north of Chile, extending 1,000 km (620 mi) south from the Peruvian border. It is a huge region but its most spectacular sights are to be found in a relatively compact area at the desert's heart, clustered around the town of San Pedro de Atacama. Here you can experience the best of the Atacama in microcosm: a dazzling *altiplano* (high plains) landscape of salt flats, sand dunes, lagoons and hot springs, set against a backdrop of snow-capped volcanoes.

Immediately south of San Pedro the rough white crust of Chile's largest salt flat stretches away as far as the eye can see. The monotone visual palette is dramatically punctured by large flocks of flamingo and other waders attracted to the shallow lakes scattered around the saltpan. On its northern edge the aptly named Valle de la Luna is a world of strange rock formations, the result of millions of years of erosion. The valley is at its most striking at either end of the day when the sun's rays bathe the encircling peaks in hues of pink, gold and purple.

In the other direction El Tatio is the world's highest geothermal field, at 4,320 m (14,170 ft). Early morning is the best time to see the geysers at full strength; the sight of steaming fumaroles against the brilliant azure of the *altiplano* sky is one of many memorable images the Atacama has to offer.

HOW TO GET THERE:
The nearest transport hub is the copper-mining city of Calama, 106 km (66 mi) to the west. Regular buses run between Calama and San Pedro.
WHEN TO GO:
Any time of year (but remember you are at considerable altitude so nights can get very chilly).
DON'T MISS:
A relaxing soak in one of the thermal pools at El Tatio.
YOU SHOULD KNOW:
The atmospheric conditions in the Atacama Desert make it a famous location for star-gazing and there are a number of observatories in the area.

Hikers on the salt flats along the Tuyajito Lagoon in the Atacama Desert

Bernardo O'Higgins National Park

HOW TO GET THERE:
Most visits to the park start from Puerto Natales, 50 km (31 mi) to the south. The nearest airport is at Punta Arenas.
WHEN TO GO:
December to March
DON'T MISS:
If the weather and season are right, the chance to kayak among floating icebergs on a meltwater lake.
YOU SHOULD KNOW:
Most of the tours involve kayaking and have a minimum age restriction (usually 12).

Bernardo O'Higgins was the unlikely sounding name of Chile's first head of state after the country had shaken off the Spanish colonial yoke and gained its independence in 1818. A fully paid-up member of the Chilean liberation struggle, O'Higgins was the illegitimate son of an Irishman who is now remembered as one of the nation's founding fathers. His name crops up frequently, but certainly nowhere more substantially than in Chile's largest national park. Straddling the 50° latitude in the deep south of Patagonia, the Bernardo O'Higgins National Park covers a staggering 35,000 sq km (13,510 sq mi). The park has been much less touched by human hands than its more famous neighbour, the Torres del Paine, largely because it is only accessible by boat.

The granite pillars of Torres del Paine may be justly famous among the trekking community but Bernardo O'Higgins is the place to come if you want to hike away from the crowds. Including much of the Southern Patagonian Ice Field within its boundaries, this is a truly elemental world of glaciers, waterfalls, lakes, craggy peaks and untouched fjords. Huge swathes of native forest are interrupted by pampas and the occasional isolated *estancia*. This is the realm of the condor but also of the guanaco, a smaller relative of the llama. It takes several hours to reach the park by boat up the Última Esperanza sound. The name translates as 'Last Hope' but you should certainly not despair as the views on the way are astonishing, as is your eventual arrival at the base of the Serrano glacier, beautiful Mount Balmaceda rising up behind. The only way to do the park full justice, though, is to take one of the longer escorted tours which involves kayaking and camping.

The west side of Cerro Torre – 3,102 m (10,180 ft) – and neighbouring peaks, from the Southern Patagonian Icefield

Pumalín Park

Parque Pumalín (Pumalín Park) is the creation of one man, the American clothing magnate and entrepreneur Doug Tompkins. Tompkins is one of a new breed of environmental philanthropists dedicated to supporting innovative projects in conservation and sustainable living. He purchased his first parcel of land in the area 20 years ago and has added to it steadily since, so that today the park covers an area of nearly 3,000 sq km (1,160 sq mi) in northern Patagonia, running south from outside Hornopirén to just north of Chaitén. This has always been one of Chile's wildest and most rugged regions and Doug Tompkins wants to keep it that way, while at the same time giving visitors an experience of the natural world that is both enriching and humbling.

Pumalín preserves a pristine landscape of temperate forest and pasture criss-crossed by sparkling upland rivers. A jagged coastline with deep inlets carved out by the ocean adds to the drama. By local standards the visitor facilities in the park are exemplary and could serve as a model for the country's national parks. As well as a network of well-marked hiking trails there are sensitively sited lodges and campsites, all designed to have minimum impact on the environment. Tompkins has been careful to involve the local communities; small farms continue to operate privately within the park where the emphasis is on low-impact practices and sustainable agriculture.

There are two points of access to the park. Most people visit from the south where there is a visitors' centre and other facilities at the small cove of Caleta Gonzalo, 60 km (37 mi) north of Chaitén. It is the northern end, however, accessed by boat from Hornopirén, that is wilder and more spectacular and offers the added attraction of hot springs.

HOW TO GET THERE:
There is a daily ferry sailing in the summer months between Hornopirén and Caleta Gonzalo.

WHEN TO GO:
December to March (in spite of the latitude the sun's rays are still strong so you should always wear sun screen).

DON'T MISS:
The giant alerce tree, a member of the cypress family. This hardy evergreen can grow to over 60 m (200 ft), making it the largest tree species on the continent.

YOU SHOULD KNOW:
After the eruption of Chaitén volcano in May 2008 many of the facilities in the south of the park were closed. You should check the current status before embarking on a visit.

A river within Pumalín Park

Torres del Paine, Patagonia

Torres del Paine

Mention the words Torres del Paine to a serious walker and the chances are you will be met with an expression of awed reverie. This national park in the far south of Chile has long been a legendary destination among the trekking community and the eponymous 'Towers' – a cluster of 2,600-m (8,530-ft) granite pillars that make up the Paine Massif at the heart of the park – have become the defining image of Patagonia in many people's minds. There are enough different aspects of elemental nature here to satisfy the most seasoned of travellers: rugged mountain terrain, thundering rivers in deep-sided valleys, wide-open steppes and dense green forests. And being so far south you find a magical extra ingredient in the mix:

HOW TO GET THERE:
By bus from Puerto Natales, 150 km (93 mi) to the south on a reasonable gravel road
WHEN TO GO:
October to April (although hardened and experienced trekkers might choose to go in the quieter winter months).

152

huge glaciers and lakes with floating chunks of shimmering blue ice the size of a house. The most accessible is the Grey glacier and its associated lake (which is anything but that colour), although it is still a long day's hike to the base of the glacier.

The breathtaking scenery in this national park fully deserves its reputation but it does mean that it is a popular place and can get very busy with hikers in the summer months. Most walkers come to tackle the 'W', one of the world's classic treks, so called because of the route's shape on the map. The 'W' takes four to five days to complete and there are good campsites and mountain shelters throughout the park. The route includes a number of fantastic viewpoints (*miradores*) and the Valle Francés, a steep-sided valley with spectacular mountain views on both sides. If you have the time and the stamina, the Circuit Trail (seven to ten days) takes you round the back of the peaks and gets you away from the crowds.

DON'T MISS:
Being at the Las Torres viewpoint at dawn to watch the peaks suffused by the first rays of the sun.
YOU SHOULD KNOW:
In peak season (January and February) it is essential to make advance reservations for your sleeping arrangements while in the park.

Valdivian Coastal Range

The Valdivian Coastal Range forms part of the Cordillera de la Costa, the western range of the Andes mountains which hugs much of Chile's Pacific coast. Also known as the Cordillera de Mahuidanchi, the range lies towards the southern end of the whole chain. Its ecological significance lies in the fact that it is a rare surviving example of temperate rainforest, a habitat which has been particularly vulnerable throughout the world to intensive logging and other commercial interests. Broadleaf evergreens are the dominant tree type; they flourish in the moist and humid climate created by the prevailing westerly winds blowing off the ocean. The elegant canelo tree is a particularly common sight in the Valdivian forest with its shiny whitish-green leaves. Its durability and adaptation to harsh conditions has given it the nickname of 'winter's bark'.

Although a less-visited part of the country, the Valdivian hills and forests have much to offer the lover of nature. A good place to sample the area's delights is in the Parque Oncol, a 754-hectare (1,860-acre) reserve centred around Cerro Oncol, at 714 m (2,340 ft) the region's highest point. Numerous walking trails and viewing platforms give excellent views of the ocean as well as the area's many volcanoes further inland. The park makes for a good day trip from the city of Valdivia. If you are feeling adventurous there is an extensive canopy tour which provides an excitingly different perspective on the wildlife. Among the animals you might see in the reserve are wild boar and *pudú*, the world's smallest deer.

HOW TO GET THERE:
A 4x4 is recommended for the 32-km (20-mi) trip from Valdivia.
WHEN TO GO:
Any time of year
DON'T MISS:
Chile's national flower, the copihue, grows in these forests. The distinctive shape of its red flowers gives it its common name of Chilean bellflower.
YOU SHOULD KNOW:
The canelo tree was considered sacred by the Mapuche Indians who used to inhabit these hills and forests.

Aconcagua

The Andes mountain chain runs the entire length of the continent but it is Argentina that can claim the loftiest peak of all within its borders. At 6,960 m (22,835 ft) Mount Aconcagua is the highest summit in both the western and southern hemispheres. It is also one of the most accessible of the world's great peaks, attracting hundreds of climbers every year to its three routes to the top. Provided you are fit and have some experience of climbing at altitude there is no reason why you shouldn't undertake an organized ascent with professional guides, although you won't be able to take the family and you will need to allow a good two weeks.

If you hadn't planned on such hardcore activity you can still enjoy many of the splendours of the Alta Montaña on a tour of the Andes highlands west of Mendoza. Beyond the city the road soon starts to climb, leaving behind fertile slopes covered in vineyards (this is Argentina's premier wine-growing area). The hills become increasingly barren and denuded of vegetation as the ascent continues. Pastures and grassland give way to mountain streams,

sudden deep valleys and rocks of strikingly varied hues. Just beyond the winter ski resort of Los Penitentes and at an altitude of 2,700 m (8,860 ft) you encounter one of the region's great sights, the Puente del Inca. This natural stone bridge over the Rio de las Cuevas owes its extraordinary coppery-gold colour to minerals in the water.

A short distance further brings you to the entrance to the Aconcagua Provincial Park. If you have not signed up for the full climbing experience you can still enjoy hugely rewarding day and overnight treks to base camps and mountain shelters beneath the snow line.

Mount Aconcagua in the Andes Mountain Range

Los Glaciares

HOW TO GET THERE:
The Perito Moreno glacier is 80 km (50 mi) west of El Calafate, where there is an airport. The main base for the northern section of the park is El Chaltén, reached by a two-and-a-half-hour drive on a paved road from El Calafate.

WHEN TO GO:
November to April

DON'T MISS:
The opportunity to try your hand (and feet) at a spot of ice trekking on the glacier – equipment and full instruction provided, but not available to children under 12.

YOU SHOULD KNOW:
Scientists studying these glaciers to gauge the effects of climate change have reported clear evidence that many are receding at an alarming rate.

The Los Glaciares National Park is formed from the eastern slopes of the Andes in southern Patagonia. Extending for 170 km (106 mi) along the national frontier with Chile, the 6,000-sq-km (2,320-sq-mi) park encompasses a range of habitats as its terrain spreads down from the mountains: to the east lies Patagonian steppe, giving way, as the ground rises, to huge montane beech forests. What most people come to this national park for (and the reason why it is a UNESCO World Heritage Site) is hinted at in its name: *glaciares* is Spanish for glaciers and there are 47 of them in the park, occupying close on half its total surface area. This extraordinary fact becomes more credible when you consider the mind-boggling dimensions of the larger glaciers like Upsala and Viedma; the latter is the biggest in the country at nearly 1,000 sq km (385 sq mi). Together they make up the Southern Patagonian Ice Field, the largest ice mass on the planet after Antarctica and Greenland.

The most celebrated and visited of the park's glaciers is the Glaciar Perito Moreno in its southern section. Although there are fabulous views of the glacier from the well-sited walkways on the Península de Magellanes, the best way to appreciate the splendours of this frozen world is to take a boat tour on Lago Argentino. As well as visiting several smaller glaciers, the boat weaves its way between giant icebergs floating on the lake as it draws close (but not too close!) to Perito Moreno's 60-m (197-ft) high ice wall. If you are very lucky you may experience the phenomenon known as 'calving' in which huge chunks of ice succumb to water pressure and break away from the face of the wall.

Perito Moreno Glacier and Lago Argentino

Lapataia Bay

Were you so inclined you could follow the Route 3 highway out of Buenos Aires all the way south to the very toe of the country where the road finally runs out at Lapataia Bay, a mind-boggling distance of 3,242 km (2,015 mi). A few kilometres west of Ushuaia, the world's southernmost city, Lapataia is a wide south-facing bay overlooking Beagle Channel, which separates the mainland from the islands of Cape Horn. The narrow channel is named in tribute to Darwin's ship which famously cruised these waters. Lapataia Bay lies within the extensive Tierra del Fuego National Park, 630 sq km (243 sq mi) of mountains, forests, lakes, glaciated valleys and unspoilt coastline. Inviting as all this may sound, only a very small proportion of the park (less than five per cent) is open to visitors; this is the section around Lapataia and neighbouring Ensenada Bay. It is more than enough, though, to showcase the very special atmosphere here and to leave you with an indefinable yet potent end-of-the-world feeling.

Extending north across Lago Fagnano, the park encompasses vast swathes of southern beech forest. Walking among the trees as the wind gently rustles the fragrant leaves is a wonderfully refreshing experience. There are half-a-dozen short trails which acquaint you with the park's range of natural features and make for excellent day treks. One trail runs for 8 km (5 mi) along the shoreline while another heads inland along Lago Roca to the national border with Chile. If you are looking for a tougher challenge, the steep climb up Cerro Guanaco – 973 m (3,190 ft) – will reward you with panoramic views from the summit.

HOW TO GET THERE:
Lapataia Bay is an easy 12-km (7.5-mi) bus or car ride from Ushuaia. A more atmospheric, if slower, way to reach the park is to take the old narrow-gauge railway which once transported convicts to hard labour in the forests.
WHEN TO GO:
November to April
DON'T MISS:
If you are here in March or April the trees put on a stunning display of autumn colours.
YOU SHOULD KNOW:
It is hard to believe that you would find a species of parrot this far south, but you may be lucky and catch a glimpse of the austral parakeet in the trees.

Lapataia Bay lies within Tierra del Fuego National Park.

A Magellanic penguin with her chicks

Cabo dos Bahias

HOW TO GET THERE:
The reserve is about 30 km (19 mi) south of Camarones by the RP1, a slow, gravel road.
WHEN TO GO:
October to March for penguins, although the reserve is a fascinating place all year round.
DON'T MISS:
Meeting the penguins. Although the nesting area is fenced off, they potter about and are naturally curious. Visitors who sit and wait will be rewarded, although penguins do nip if anyone gets too close. Land-based residents will also approach, and are not at all camera-shy.
YOU SHOULD KNOW:
Gaiman, a small town north of Camarones, which was settled by the Welsh in the 19th century, is famous for afternoon tea. Tearooms and family homes serve strong tea with delicious pies, jams and fruitcake.

Patagonia's coastal highway runs almost all the way to Tierra del Fuego. The landscape is often hypnotically vast and empty, although in places the road is within sight and sound of the ocean. Here, an extraordinary abundance of wildlife – whales and dolphins, seals and sea lions, penguins and seabirds – nest, breed and feed. The Valdes Peninsula in the north is a prime whale-watching location, while the popular Punto Tombo Reserve is home to South America's largest nesting colony of penguins. Cabo dos Bahias, south of Camarones, is an isolated wilderness of scrub and rugged shore, where land and sea creatures thrive in a peaceful, protected reserve.

Large numbers of Patagonian foxes and the usually timid guanacos (wild llamas) and ostrich-like, flightless rheas, wander fearlessly inland. Seals and big, aggressive sea lions colonize the rocky foreshore and killer whales (orcas), which are actually large dolphins, patrol the waters for sustenance. Numerous resident seabirds include cormorants, skuas and petrels. In spring and summer, beach and hinterland become an enormous nursery where some 25,000 pairs of Magellanic penguins raise their young.

These strikingly marked birds – elegant black-and-white stripes divide dark backs from white fronts – have discordant calls and are also known as jackass penguins. Males come ashore and dig burrows where females lay eggs in October; parents share feeding duties until the chicks learn to swim in February. In March, the young start their migration north, followed by the adults. Watching thousands of penguins seemingly 'planted' in holes and surrounded by grazing guanacos is fascinating – and rather surreal.

Calchaquí Valleys

The Andean northwest of Argentina is a dry, semi-desert world of striking rockscapes and sparse vegetation that is far removed from the lush pampas to the south. Even so, such an unpromising landscape can yield surprising pockets of fertility, such as the Valles Calchaquíes region. The dramatic contrasts between green valleys, surrounding sun-parched uplands and an ever-present backdrop of snow-capped mountains help to explain the particular appeal of this remote area, lying south and west of the provincial capital Salta. The main artery through the region is the Calchaquí River and most of the valleys link to it. Tumbling mountain torrents have carved a number of remarkable canyons out of the sandstone plateau.

In this thinly populated landscape the few scattered settlements are oases of shade and tranquillity, offering traditional adobe houses, cobblestones, pretty squares and artisan workshops. Cachi is a typical example and boasts an unbeatable setting beneath the towering profile of Mount Nevado del Cachi – 6,380 m (20,930 ft). An area of 650 sq km (250 sq mi) at the heart of the Valles was designated a national park as recently as 1996; the Los Cardones park takes its name from the ubiquitous *cardón* or candelabra cactus, one of the few plants to flourish in these parts. With no other trees growing here, the wood of this giant cactus, which can grow to over 5 m (16 ft), is widely used by local communities as a construction material and for furniture. Its unmistakable profile will certainly be one of your abiding images of a visit to the Valles.

HOW TO GET THERE:
The road from Salta to Cachi, which climbs up and over the Cuesta del Obispo, is one of Argentina's most spectacular drives.
WHEN TO GO:
Any time of year, although it can get brutally hot in summer (December to February).
DON'T MISS:
If you are visiting in the autumn (March to May) you will see lines of red peppers drying in the sun on many of the hillsides.
YOU SHOULD KNOW:
The vineyards which proliferate as you approach Cafayate on the southern edge of the Valles Calchaquíes are among the highest in the world.

The striking rockscape of Calchaquí Valley

Ibera Wetlands

The Esteros del Iberá or Ibera Wetlands are one of Argentina's most important wildlife havens. Situated in the subtropical northeast of the country in the Entre Ríos or Mesopotamia region – so called because it is bounded by the two great rivers of the Paraná and the Uruguay – the Esteros del Iberá were once part of the main course of the Río Paraná. Sluggish currents have combined with silting and sedimentation over time to form the present patchwork of lakes, water channels, swamps, densely wooded marshes and savannah. Floating islands, known as *embalsados*, are a special feature of the waterways, a consequence of aquatic plants and other vegetation accumulating on the water's surface.

This is no ordinary wetland; covering a total area of 13,700 sq km (5,290 sq mi), the Esteros del Iberá is the second-largest wetland in the world after the Pantanal in Brazil. In recent years it has been afforded a measure of protection as a nature reserve but environmentalists, worried about continuing threats to its delicate ecosystem, carry on campaigning for tougher controls and greater regulation. There are no paved roads in the reserve so most visitors don't take their vehicle in. Even though you are largely leaving behind the sounds of human activity it is surprising to discover just how noisy the natural world can be, especially when you are talking about howler monkeys and more than 350 bird species. Waders feature prominently of course, among them the splendid Jabiru stork and the ruddy tiger heron. There can be few more magical experiences than being poled through the marshes in a noiseless flat-bottomed boat as the air around you is filled with the rich and raucous polyphony of the natural world.

The Ibera Wetlands – the largest protected area in Argentina

HOW TO GET THERE:
It's a four-hour bus journey from Mercedes on a dirt road to the centre of the reserve at Laguna Iberá.

WHEN TO GO:
Any time of year but you might want to avoid the fierce heat of high summer (June and July).

DON'T MISS:
The capybara, the world's largest rodent. Luckily, unlike many of the other South American mammals, the capybara is far from reclusive and can often be seen grazing in large family groups at the water's edge.

YOU SHOULD KNOW:
In the language of the pre-Columbian people who once inhabited the area Iberá means 'glittering water'. When the sun is setting or beneath a full moon it is easy to see why.

Misiones Forest

The magnificent Iguazú Falls

The province of Misiones lies in the far northeast of Argentina, in a strip of land that extends like a crooked finger between Paraguay and Brazil. The climate and topography are subtropical and Misiones has some of the largest and least spoilt areas of surviving Atlantic rainforest, a habitat that has been particularly vulnerable to logging and other agricultural activities. In Misiones, where controls on development and commercial exploitation are limited and there are comparatively few areas under government protection, these threats remain acute. As a result it is not as easy as you'd think to find accessible examples of pristine forest for that jungle experience you'd always promised yourself.

Your best bet is to head up to the Brazilian border and avail yourself of the services and infrastructure that have been established around the Iguazú Falls. The magnificent falls are one of the planet's top natural wonders and what of course everyone comes here to see. But set as they are within a sizeable national park which has left the surrounding jungle largely undisturbed, it is surprisingly simple to escape the visitor crowds and head off on a nature trail as it plunges into the depths of the forest. The dense canopy and the luxuriant undergrowth support a staggering array of plants and wildlife. In no time at all the sounds of human activity are behind you and, provided you are patient and tread softly, you should be rewarded with plenty of sightings. While all the stars of the South American animal kingdom can be found here, you can count yourself fortunate indeed if you spot any; what you will see aplenty are multi-coloured butterflies and gorgeous tropical birds like toucans and parrots.

HOW TO GET THERE:
The nearest town is Puerto Iguazú, 20 km (12.5 mi) to the northwest, from where regular buses run to the park entrance.
WHEN TO GO:
Any time of year
DON'T MISS:
An early morning walk in the forest is the best time to see the birdlife.
YOU SHOULD KNOW:
If you really want to immerse yourself in the rhythms and moods of the jungle, a stay at a jungle lodge is strongly recommended.

Valley of the Moon

HOW TO GET THERE:
The park is 80 km (50 mi) north of
San Agustin de Valle Fertil, where
some organized tours start.
WHEN TO GO:
April to September. Afternoon tours
offer the added bonus of a
wonderful sunset.
DON'T MISS:
The museum has displays on
evolution and palaeontology and the
history and work of the park. A must
for anyone with an interest in
dinosaurs, there are fossils,
reconstructions and dioramas of the
palaeoenvironments.
YOU SHOULD KNOW:
The rangers usually speak only
Spanish; information in the museum
is also in Spanish, but making sense
of the written word is rather easier.
The roads in the park are gravel and
may become impassable after (rare)
rain. The countryside west of the
park, in the foothills of the Andes, is
delightfully fertile and supports a
thriving wine industry. The San Juan
Wine Route tour is a very refreshing
change from the desert.

Ischigualasto Provincial Park lies high in the semi-arid Sierra de Valle
Fertil amid the lower ranges of the Andes in northwestern Argentina.
This name derives from the Diaguita for 'land without life'. The park
is an extensive area – around 600 sq km, (230 sq mi) – of barren,
eerie emptiness scattered with twisted rock formations. Millions of
years ago its dramatic red-sandstone canyons contained rivers whose
swirling waters eroded the rocks, which were further sculpted by
millennia of weather into strangely shaped red and ash-grey
monoliths. This lifeless landscape is known as the Valley of the Moon.

Much more than a geological curiosity, the valley is a
palaeontological treasure trove. The park is a UNESCO World
Heritage Site, for its fossil-bearing rocks form a unique, undisturbed
sequence of deposits, with perfectly preserved fossils representing

*A typical sight in the Valley of
the Moon in San Juan
province, land of the first
dinosaurs*

the entire Triassic period. Among the important dinosaur fossils are the remains of the carnivorous *Herrerasaurus* and of the small predator *Eoraptor lunensis*, the 'dawn raptor', one of the earliest dinosaurs ever discovered. Fossils of other vertebrates and of ferns, horsetails and giant tree trunks have given palaeontologists a chance to study the evolution of dinosaurs and mammals and to build up a picture of their environment. The lunar landscape was, around 200 million years ago, a flood plain with meandering rivers and dense vegetation.

Rangers lead regular convoys around the park. Tours, which last about three hours and include a visit to the museum, stop at several important and photogenic spots for information and exploration. Special events include magical full moon tours.

AFRICA

Farafra Oasis and the White Desert

HOW TO GET THERE:
Regular buses run between Cairo and Farafra via Bahariya and will drop passengers off in the White Desert. Many tours of the area start in Bahariya, fewer in Farafra.

WHEN TO GO:
November to March. Nights in the desert can be extremely cold in winter and the White Desert gets very crowded during Egyptian holidays.

DON'T MISS:
Seeing the White Desert under different light conditions. At sunrise and sunset, the weird chalk shapes take on a strange life, glowing pink and orange, while by moonlight an eerie, silvery, ghostly chill envelops them.

YOU SHOULD KNOW:
Although the old name Land of the Cow probably referred to Farafra's association with the cow-headed goddess Hathor, cattle in the oasis still look strikingly like those depicted on tomb and temple walls in Luxor.

White inselbergs and yellow sand dunes are characteristic features of the El Qabur area of Egypt's White Desert.

A huge fertile depression in the Libyan Desert, the Farafra Oasis is the most isolated and least populated of Egypt's oases. No archaeological evidence of occupation in pharaonic times has been found, although it is known that during the reign of Rameses II it was called Ta-iht, the Land of the Cow. It is bordered to the west by the impenetrable Great Sand Sea where, it is said, the army of the Persian king Cambyses disappeared *en route* to Siwa. Repeated searches have revealed no trace of the lost men.

All that remains of an important Roman settlement is a tumbled fort, although a ruined Roman cemetery lies outside the town and evidence of Roman and Byzantine travellers is scattered around springs and pools all over the oasis, particularly at Ain Hadra, an important watering place on the ancient caravan route. Now sleepy Farafra is home to Bedouin who live in traditional mud-brick houses, often painted blue to ward off the evil eye. At nearby Bir Sitta, a sulphurous spring offers a soak after a day in the desert.

The extraordinary White Desert begins about 32 km (20 mi) north of the town; the vast, flat, milky wasteland is broken by hundreds of jagged, blindingly white chalk rocks, shaped by millennia of desert winds into pinnacles, twisted spires, misshapen mushrooms and a bewildering menagerie of mutant creatures. West of the road stand the *inselbergs* – steep, symmetrical rock cones with flattened tops, strangely similar to those seen on Mars. These give some welcome shade for walkers and campers. This surreal landscape is much visited by tour groups, but away from the most popular clusters of photogenic chalk formations, its mystery is compelling.

Valley of the Whales

Southwest of the Faium Oasis, the Wadi al-Rayan is a protected area of lakes and waterfalls popular with birds and animals and with weekend Cairenes escaping the city's heat. A long unpaved track leads from the wadi out into the desert to a level, pale expanse broken by occasional rocky outcrops. This is the Valley of the Whales which, in 2005, became Egypt's first Natural World Heritage Site. More than 40 million years ago, when oceans covered much of the Sahara, this arid spot was very like the Florida Everglades – a swampy coastal region whose waters teemed with fish and marine life and whose banks swarmed with reptiles, animals and birds.

A remarkable variety of well-preserved fossils, including mangrove roots, sharks and turtles, give palaeontologists a vivid picture of life before the waters ebbed, but it is the fossilized skeletons of whales that give the valley its name and importance. This extinct subspecies of whale, the *archaeoceti*, was carnivorous, streamlined, 18 m (59 ft) long, and land-based. Many of these fossils have not only flippers but also hind legs, feet and toes, and represent a major stage in evolution: the emergence of the whale as an ocean-dwelling mammal.

This incomparable open-air museum is now carefully managed by UNESCO. Marked walking tracks lead around the exhibits, where fossilized whale skeletons (many have been unearthed since the first was found in the 1902–1903 season) lie stretched out on the sand, ringed by stones and low ropes. The site's remoteness and scale are impressive and slightly disorientating. A visitor gazing over the endless surrounding waves of sand which lap around the steep islands of rock, may experience a brief vision of whales slithering between tangled mangrove roots into the ebbing ocean.

HOW TO GET THERE:
Organized tour with 4x4s
WHEN TO GO:
November to April
DON'T MISS:
The visitor centre and information booths around the site. They may seem incongruous, but they are sympathetically built and the maps and information are invaluable.
YOU SHOULD KNOW:
The site is so sensitive and important that access is restricted, although pre-arranged tour groups are allowed to camp in the valley. None of the fossils should be touched and there are very heavy penalties for removing anything from the valley.

Fossilized bones of ancient whales in Egypt's Valley of the Whales

Green Mountains

HOW TO GET THERE:
Several good roads lead from the main coastal road up into the hills.

WHEN TO GO:
April to November

DON'T MISS:
Outside Slonta, a little hill town, stands a tiny temple dedicated to a pre-Greek deity. The naively carved human faces and animals are unlike anything else in Libya. Nothing is known of the cult.

YOU SHOULD KNOW:
The Green Mountain Sustainable Development Area was initiated in 2007. This ecotourism initiative aims to protect classical sites and the rugged landscape – which has been described as 'one of the last ten paradises of the Mediterranean' – from haphazard tourist development.

Most of Libya's vast, barren landscape does not receive sufficient rainfall for settled agriculture. Desert lakes are salt and the network of wadis, apart from brief periods after rain, is dry. The Green Mountains (Jebel al-Akhdar) of northern Cyrenaica, where streams and waterfalls flow almost year round, are the exception. The mountains, with their cover of pine, wild olives, cypress and juniper trees, are gloriously verdant. In the south, the desert stretches to the Chad border; to the north, the range drops precipitously to a coastal plain which curves from Benghazi to Derna. Cyrenaica was a province of ancient Greece and several important cities lay on the coast. Then, the lovely Green Mountains were a precious granary; now, this area is little known.

It is possible to explore the Green Mountains from Al-Bayda and Shahat and visit some of Libya's finest classical sites. These include Ptolemaia, Apollonia and magnificent Cyrene, the most complete of the Greek cities. Inland sites like the Temple of Aesculapius at Al-Bayda are less visited. In Qasr Libya a museum displays the remarkable mosaics found in two small Byzantine churches. Laid in AD 539, most depict paradisiacal scenes of flowers and wildlife, although one shows the Pharos Lighthouse at Alexandria. Wadi al-Kuf was the scene of fierce battles in 1927 when, until they were bombed, Libyan resistance fighters halted the advance of the Italian forces. The caves where the guerrillas sheltered can be seen in the steep, rocky walls of the valley.

The fertile rounded hills of the Green Mountains still produce cereals, potatoes and fruit. This is one of the few areas in Libya with a pleasant summer climate, and cliffs, canyons, springs, woodland and deep, shady valleys make for marvellous, relatively cool walking in beautiful, unspoilt countryside.

Jebel Nafusa

HOW TO GET THERE:
Regular shared taxis run between Tripoli and Nalut or Gharyan. Less frequent services link the towns and villages.

WHEN TO GO:
March to May, October and November

Towns and villages – many deserted and derelict – cling to the rocky hillsides of the Jebel Nafusa. This narrow east-west range rises steeply from the arid coastal lowlands and its southern slopes merge with an immense, empty gravel plain. The landscape appears harsh and inhospitable, yet sheep and goats graze the uplands and, in places, the plateau is golden with grain, shaded by fig and apricot orchards, and scattered with silvery olive groves; regular winter rains support agriculture here.

In the seventh century the Berbers retreated to these mountains. Here they built underground houses, *dammous*, to protect them from the advancing Arabs and the weather. The most impressive of these are dwellings built into the sides of wide, deep pits, reached by tunnels. From a distance, they are invisible. Huge, fortress-like granaries, *qasrs*, some of which are still in use, protected their treasure – the crops. Although now living in modern homes, most of Libya's Berbers still farm the Jebel Nafusa.

Three towns make good bases for exploration. Nalut, near the Algerian border, has an old town built on a rocky bluff and Gharyan, at the eastern end of the range, has some well-preserved underground homes. In the middle, Yefren, built among woods high above the coastal plain, is a lovely old town. A large Jewish community once lived here and a fascinating, ancient synagogue survives.

Steep slopes, deep ravines and high, sunny pastures with breathtaking views north and south make for exhilarating walking. Several villages merit a detour, notably photogenic Tarmesia, whose deserted stone houses blend almost organically into the crags where they perch.

DON'T MISS:
The spectacular granary at Qasr al-Haj, an ancient village north of Yefren. This enormous 12th-century 'fortress' stored olive oil in the underground area and grain in the upper three storeys. Some of the rooms, sealed with palm wood doors, are still used; grain stored in these cool, dry spaces stays fresh for years.

YOU SHOULD KNOW:
Gharyan is famous for its pottery. Roadside stalls sell wares ranging from intricately decorated bowls and *tagines* to timeless terracotta jars and ewers. The Libyan authorities sometimes restrict access to the more remote parts of the country at short notice.

Abandoned Berber village in the Jebel Nafusa

Ubari Dunes and Lakes

HOW TO GET THERE:
Flight from Tripoli or Benghazi to Sebha, then 4x4 or regular shared taxi to Tekerkiba, Germa and Ubari.

WHEN TO GO:
October to April. Winter night temperatures in the desert can drop below zero.

DON'T MISS:
Near Germa are the important remains of Garama, the city of the Garamantians from the first century AD. They ruled southern Libya for hundreds of years and controlled the Saharan trade routes, but their great secret was understanding how to tap the ancient aquifers for water, enabling them to farm the desert. They died out when the water dried up.

YOU SHOULD KNOW:
To avoid offending the locals, cover up when bathing in the Ubari lakes. Libya's ambitious Great Manmade River project uses the Garamantians' skills on a vast scale, bringing water from deep under the Sahara for hundreds of miles to irrigate the populous north.

Much of the desert which covers Libya is a flat, gravel wasteland. To experience the thrill and romance of the Sahara dunes, visitors must head for one of the sand seas. The most accessible is the Ubari Sand Sea, which is easily reached from three towns – Tekerkiba, Germa and Ubari. Although much visited, it is not hard to escape the noisy convoys of 4x4s for this is a boundless expanse of reddish sand waves – crescent and ridge dunes which, with their compacted bases, are relatively stable. Early and late, they glow with rosy sunlight and their shadowy valleys make perfect campsites. As the temperature drops and the campfire crackles, the brilliance of the stars in an inky sky and the total silence are awe inspiring. Although 4x4s are a quick and easy option, they do break up the surface of the dunes and a trip into the sand sea by camel is infinitely more satisfactory. As well as being ecologically sound, it allows a glimpse of the true majesty and magic of the desert.

A first sight of the Ubari lakes from the heights of the dunes is unforgettable, for they lie in the tawny sands like gleaming slivers of lapis lazuli set in the deep green of palms and reeds. There are several north of Tekerkiba, and three – Umm al-Maa, Mavo and Gebraoun – are sizeable. A fourth large lake, famous for its changing colour, has almost dried up, as have several of the smaller ones. They are remnants of a wetter past and are now very salt, so that bathing in them – Gebraoun is the easiest to get into – is a float rather than a swim. Lying back in the buoyant, warm water surrounded by towering sand cliffs is a wonderful experience.

A group of date palms among the sand dunes

Bouhedma National Park

Probably Tunisia's most important national park, Bouhedma was created in 1980 and is now a UNESCO Biosphere Reserve. The 165-sq-km (64-sq-mi) park is dominated by a type of gumtree and scrub, the last traces of the savannah that once spread along the northern edges of the Sahara desert.

Lying beneath the Bouhedma Escarpment, but including the rocky slopes, the park is unique in North Africa and looks and feels more like parts of Kenya or Tanzania. This is the place to visit if mammals are of particular interest to you. Dorcas gazelles, scimitar-horned oryx, golden jackals, Cape hares and Ruppell's foxes can be seen, as well as gundis – rodents that live on the rocky foothills of the escarpment. Bouhedma has needed some protection as grazing livestock, land clearance and poaching had begun to degrade the landscape. As part of this effort several animals, such as addax and dama gazelles, have been successfully re-introduced. There are also about 300 plant species and many birds. These include ostriches and several species of raptor, such as golden eagles, Lanner falcons and Pharaoh eagle owls.

The highest peak, which reaches 840 m (2,756 ft), is home to juniper, olive and *Pistacia* – a genus of trees in the cashew family.

Both permanent and seasonal watercourses can be found here, the most important of which is the source of Ain Cherchera. Be alert as you walk, however: there are scorpions all across Tunisia, including some that are potentially deadly.

A small eco-museum and forest station is situated at the entrance to the park, the former offering excellent guidance on its flora and fauna. For those with walking difficulties, there are a few enclosures nearby to ensure that every visitor can see some of the wildlife.

HOW TO GET THERE:
By road from Gabès
WHEN TO GO:
During the winter months – the summer is far too hot.
DON'T MISS:
The remnants of ancient civilizations that occupied this area. There are Neolithic places of worship, Berber tombs, a prehistoric site and old mines to be seen.
YOU SHOULD KNOW:
This is one of the few remaining places in the world where the sand or dune cat has been sighted, although no specimens have been collected. Sand cats have very furry feet and can live in extremes of heat and cold, as long as there are enough small rodents for them to eat.

Ichkeul National Park

HOW TO GET THERE:
Arrange a taxi from Menzel
Bourguiba or Bizerte, or choose a
tour when in Tunis.
WHEN TO GO:
Winter or spring
DON'T MISS:
The small eco-museum just inside
the entrance to the park. Your guide
will be able to explain all the exhibits
if you don't speak French or Arabic.
YOU SHOULD KNOW:
Between 1996 and 2006, Lake
Ichkeul was on the World Heritage
Sites endangered list. However, the
Tunisian government stepped in and
measures were taken to rehabilitate
the lake. It had become too salty,
causing a reduction in the numbers
of birds relying upon it. In 2006, the
park was removed from the
endangered list.

Comprising a large lake and wetland area by the side of Ichkeul Mountain, Ichkeul National Park is the only natural area in North Africa to be recognized as a World Heritage Site. Easily reached from the capital, Tunis, this is a wonderful place to visit.

Connected to a large lagoon which is itself connected to the ocean, the 85-sq-km (33-sq-mi) shallow and brackish Lake Ichkeul is an essential refuge for more than 200 species of trans-Saharan migratory birds that gather here each spring and autumn. During the winter season between 200,000 and 300,000 birds can be seen on the lake and its surrounding marshlands. Herons, white storks, spoonbills, flamingoes, ducks, geese, waders and endangered white-headed ducks rest up while, overhead, buzzards, kites, ospreys, falcons and harriers hunt for the perfect meal.

The lake itself is full of life, including otters, frogs, toads, snakes, turtles, crabs and fish such as eels, sole, sea bass and anchovies. Plenty of pondweed provides both food and shelter for many species.

On Mount Ichkeul, jackal, genet, wild cat, porcupine, wild boar and mongoose thrive – there is even a large boa population. During winter, when the area receives the most rainfall, the mountainside is carpeted with flowers and, just at the entrance, a small herd of water buffalo can be seen, often with white egrets on their backs, eating the insects bothering their hosts.

During summer the lake becomes more saline as the rains depart and salt-loving plants begin to colonize the edges. The locals have been known to use lake water for drinking and irrigation and, despite being illegal, cattle, sheep and goats graze in the park, too. Hunting, fishing and quarrying also continues, albeit clandestinely.

Khroumirie Mountains

The Khroumirie Mountains are situated in the eastern reaches of the Atlas Mountains, which stretch from Morocco through to northern Tunisia. The average height of these peaks is 800 m (2,625 ft) and their 550 km (340 mi) of footpaths and trails provide a wonderful hiking experience. At 1,014 m (3,327 ft), the highest peak is Jebel Biri.

This region enjoys a Mediterranean climate and the town of Ain Draham, deep in the Khroumirie Mountains and developed by the French as a hunting resort, has a European look with its steeply sloped red roofs. It is an excellent base for a visit, surrounded as it is by many paths and tracks leading through this lovely forested region. Trees include mimosa, eucalyptus, pine, juniper and – the dominant species – cork oak. These last are large evergreens with gnarled and twisted branches that live for about 150 years, growing a thick layer of rough bark that can be harvested without damage to the tree about 12 times during their lifespan. The cork layer regenerates, making the trees a renewable resource.

This woodland habitat shelters mammals such as deer, wild boar, jackals, wild cats, porcupines, foxes and mongoose, as well as birds such as partridges, green woodpeckers and cuckoos. Tortoises may be seen trudging about on sunny slopes and rocky verges. Hiking through this shady cork forest, with its springs and waterfalls, valleys and glorious panoramic views is an absolute joy. The region receives more rainfall than most in North Africa, and some snow falls during winter. Much of the wildlife suffered from over hunting by the local population, so steps were taken to protect it. This has been successful in the main but you will probably see more boars' heads mounted on walls than while exploring the forest.

HOW TO GET THERE:
By car or public transport from Tabarka or Bizerte on the coast, south to Ain Draham.
WHEN TO GO:
It is possible to go at any time of year, but be aware of possible winter snow. Even at the height of summer the Khroumirie Mountains remain reasonably cool.
DON'T MISS:
Ain Draham's Women's Weaving Cooperative. Here you can see carpets being woven by hand and buy them from the showroom.
YOU SHOULD KNOW:
Tunisia's cork forests are owned by the state and looked after by Forest Administration. The country's main water reservoirs are located here. Locals have the right to graze livestock and gather firewood, some of which is made into charcoal to provide another source of income.

Erg Chebbi

HOW TO GET THERE:
Organized tours can be arranged
from most major Moroccan cities,
but Merzouga can also be reached
by public transport, rental car or 4x4
with a driver.
WHEN TO GO:
April, May, June, September and
October are the best months to
experience the dunes. In July and
August many Moroccans visit for
sand bathing, a traditional treatment
for arthritis and rheumatism.
DON'T MISS:
Merzouga and its surrounding area.
You may visit Berber villages and an
oasis where date palms provide
shade and the air is moist and cool.
The neat patchwork of fields of
vegetables, wheat and alfalfa and the
sound of trickling water is a relief
after the relentless heat of the desert
around you.
YOU SHOULD KNOW:
Local folklore has it that Erg Chebbi
was formed as a punishment from
God. A woman and child were
refused shelter by the villagers of
Merzouga, which was situated where
the dunes are today. As a result, an
enormous sandstorm blew up and
buried the whole village.

The Erg Chebbi dunes near the village of Merzouga are the most
impressive of the two ergs in southeast Morocco. The landscape is
flat, desolate, stony desert, but suddenly, and seemingly out of
nowhere, these vast Saharan sand dunes rise up to 150 m (490 ft)
high, blown there by the wind. They cover an area 22 km (14 mi)
long and 5 km (3 mi) wide and are an astonishing sight.

This is the closest to being in the full-on Sahara without first
participating in some extremely intrepid travelling, and it is a
remarkable experience. It is possible to take a camel ride to the top
of the dunes, or hire a quad bike, but the very best way to
experience them is on foot. Go to watch the sunset – it will be like
no other: an awe-inspiring visual feast of red, pink, orange, yellow
and purple – and if luck is on your side, you might even see a
green flash.

A walk into the dunes in the dark is also exciting, lit only by the
moon and a myriad of sparkling stars in the sky above. Infinitely
more stars are visible when there is no ambient light, and the
realization of the immensity of the universe is humbling. It is cold
at night and, because it is so hot during the day, the body feels the
drop in temperature very strongly, so dress accordingly. Sunrise is
another good time to be on the dunes.

During the day try dune boarding or have fun just sliding or
rolling down the dunes. In the summer months the daytime
temperature is often over 45°C (113°F), so remember to take
plenty of water, a hat, sunglasses and sunscreen. Visitors may stay
in traditional camel-and-goat-hair tents.

*The impressive Erg
Chebbi dunes*

Jbel Tazzeka National Park

Located in the Middle Atlas Mountains some 97 km (60 mi) east of Fez is the old garrison town of Taza, which is the perfect base from which to explore Jbel Tazzeka. This 1,980-m (6,496-ft) peak rises in the centre of the surrounding national park, which is famed for its scenic beauty. There are many routes to take, short or long, but on reaching the summit of Jbel Tazzeka the reward is majestic views of the surrounding forested mountains and snowy peaks in the distance.

The park is a great area for hiking through forests of cedar, cork oak and even olive trees; splashing through clear springs; marvelling at waterfalls and lakes; and exploring canyons and caves. The undergrowth is largely tall ferns and bracken, interspersed with pink cistus – a good habitat for large frogs, brilliantly colourful lizards and birds such as rollers, shrikes, short-toed treecreepers and hoopoes. During spring and summer gorgeous butterflies abound. Don't be surprised to meet goat herders or farmers ploughing small plots with oxen or donkeys. Crops are surrounded by yellow-and-white daisies and blood-red poppies, which add to the pleasure of walking here.

Dayat Chiker is an interesting, large, dry lake with strange rock formations and fault lines. For much of the year crops are grown here and animals are grazed. But the best-known feature in the park is an enormous cave system. Discovered some 80 years ago by Norbert Casteret, a French citizen, the Friouato caves form the largest cave system in North Africa and have yet to be fully explored. They are entered via a 100-m (330-ft) deep shaft, with 580 steep steps down. Then chamber follows chamber, each with spectacular stalactites, stalagmites and even stalactite curtains.

HOW TO GET THERE:
By road from Taza
WHEN TO GO:
May to November
DON'T MISS:
Even if cities aren't your thing, visit Fez. The ancient walled city, Fez el Bali, is a UNESCO World Heritage Site. Utterly fascinating, it is unlike anywhere else in the world.
YOU SHOULD KNOW:
If time is short, there is a beautiful 112 km (70 mi) scenic drive through Jbel Tazzeka National Park. It is a good way of seeing a great deal in just one day.

Sheer rock walls line the dramatic Todra Gorge.

The Dades and Todra Gorges

Morocco bursts with dramatic natural beauty and the Dades and Todra Gorges rank high on the list of memorable sights. The pair lie fairly close to each other in the Atlas Mountains, 110 km (70 mi) northeast of Ouarzazate.

At full flow during winter, a river runs through the Dades valley, irrigating wheat, figs, dates, argan and almond trees. In early spring the almond blossom is enchanting, softening the spectacularly vivid red and rocky landscape. Historically, the Berbers fortified this fertile area with hundreds of *kasbahs*: great, castellated buildings made of red mud, straw and lime, their turrets and walls decorated with carvings. Some are inhabited but many stand empty, gradually being reclaimed by the earth.

The entrance to the Dades is by paved track, although it is far more interesting to hike than to attempt to drive. There are fantastic rock formations and a walk through the gorge, with its sheer rock walls, is unforgettable. Both gorges are a big draw for rock climbers, with many different routes to attempt.

The Todra Gorge is the more dramatic of the two. It is 600 m (656 yd) long and cuts through the mountains, the 300-m (985-ft) walls guarding a passage at some points a mere 10 m (33 ft) in width. As sunshine only reaches the bottom of the gorge in the mornings, the stream here is very cold and at night the temperature can drop to freezing. A few families live and farm nearby and can often be seen with sheep, goats or camels, making their way along the dirt track to settlements at the other end.

In the past this area rarely saw tourists and although those days are gone, the sheer drama of the gorges and their surrounding mountains and valleys make them definitely worth visiting.

HOW TO GET THERE:
Public transport, shared or privately hired taxi, rental car or organized tours can be arranged from Ouarzazate.

WHEN TO GO:
Spring or autumn. The best time for photography in the gorges is between 08.00 and 13.00.

DON'T MISS:
El Kelaa M'Gouna, an oasis in the Dades valley that is the centre of Moroccan rose cultivation. It is a great hiking area and every May a traditional Rose Festival is held.

YOU SHOULD KNOW:
Berbers lived in North Africa long before the Arabs arrived. Many Moroccans have Berber origins but, as they are often perceived to be 'backward' due largely to their homelands in the most traditional and rural parts of the country, many deny their roots. The Berber language is entirely different from Arabic, and sadly is not recognized as an official language in Morocco, but French is.

Pico de Fogo

Some 483 km (300 mi) from the coast of Senegal, West Africa, lies the Republic of Cape Verde. An archipelago of ten islands and eight islets, its capital, Praia, is on the largest island, Santiago. Fogo is Cape Verde's fourth largest island and the only one with an active volcano: Pico de Fogo.

Two eruptions shook the island during the last century. In 1951 lava poured down the southern flanks of the volcano and created two new cones. The 1995 eruption was incredibly dramatic. After days of small earthquakes, flaming lava shot 400 m (1,310 ft) into the sky, raining down into the crater and forcing the inhabitants to run for their lives. An ash cloud 5 km (3 mi) high covered Fogo and it was seven weeks before the lava stopped flowing altogether. One village was effectively destroyed.

At 2,892 m (9,488 ft) and dominating every view, Pico de Fogo looms high, and a hike or two around and into the caldera is hard work and exhilarating, providing extraordinary views not only of the volcano itself but also of Santiago. The volcano's eastern slopes are covered with dark lava from eruptions that have occurred over hundreds of thousands of years.

Volcanoes are famously fertile and Pico de Fogo is no exception. The crater is known as Cha das Caldeiras and within it the vast floor is relatively flat, although strewn with lumps of lava. Two small villages exist here, cultivating vegetables and fruit, including grapes that are turned into locally renowned wine. The valleys of the northeastern slopes are also used for agriculture – coffee and vines grow here, amidst eucalyptus trees.

There are many hikes to enjoy: to the summit of Pico, round the crater rim or floor, to the 1995 peak, or the steep descent to the town of Mosteiros, caught between the mountain and the sea.

HOW TO GET THERE:
There are daily flights from Praia, and twice-weekly ferries. Those arriving by yacht can anchor at the harbour north of São Felipe, Fogo's capital. An *aluguer* (shared taxi), rental car or a conventional taxi is the best way of getting around once there.
WHEN TO GO:
November to July
DON'T MISS:
The Cooperativa in the crater, where you can enjoy music and dancing in the evenings; the Bandeira de São Felipe, Fogo's liveliest festival that takes place at the end of April; São Felipe's historic centre.
YOU SHOULD KNOW:
The people who live in and around Pico de Fogo are straight haired, sometimes blonde and blue eyed, with light skin. They are believed to be descended from the French Duc de Montrond, who fled here to escape a duel in the 19th century, bringing with him the vines that are now so productive.

Pico de Fogo dominates the surrounding lanscape.

Pelicans inhabit the many sandbanks and small islands.

The Langue de Barbarie National Park

HOW TO GET THERE:
By public or rented transport from Dakar, then *pirogue* from the park headquarters. It is possible to stay in very basic *campements* on the Langue de Barbarie itself, rather than in Saint-Louis.
WHEN TO GO:
November to May is best.
DON'T MISS:
The bird-count tours. On the 24th of each month a walking tour takes place and, on the 28th of the month, boats tour the full length of the park. On both occasions visitors may help the professionals spot water birds.
YOU SHOULD KNOW:
The name *Langue de Barbarie* was taken from the prickly or Barbary pears that once grew here in profusion. Although the park is just 25 km (15 mi) long, the entire length of the sand stretches from Nouadibou in Mauritania, to Saint-Louis – a matter of some 600 km (375 mi).

The West African city of Saint-Louis is situated on a narrow island some 25 km (15 mi) from the mouth of the Senegal River. A UNESCO World Heritage Site since 2000, this charmingly dilapidated city is in three parts. The historic centre is on the island itself, while Sor, with its tidal marshlands, is on the eastern mainland, separated from the island by the river. To the west the river is separated from the Atlantic by a narrow sand spit, the Langue de Barbarie.

At 30 km (19 mi) long, the sand spit itself has little vegetation – mostly casuarina trees that have been encouraged to grow to help prevent erosion – and can best be explored by *pirogue*. These small, flat-bottomed boats are used by local fishermen and can be easily handled in shallow water – paddled, punted or used with a small sail or outboard motor. The trip alone is interesting as the *pirogue* gently moves through the many sandbanks and small islands. This is an area of great importance to migratory birds, as well as being a haven for marine turtles, many of which nest here.

From early spring until autumn, multitudes of birds breed here, while others overwinter. White and grey pelicans waddle about and pink flamingoes pick their way carefully around the water's edge. Terns and swallows swoop and dive while lapwings and weavers and glamorous sunbirds busy themselves nest building. Herons and ducks are ubiquitous, as are cormorants, which fly steadily over the water, occasionally diving in and capturing an unwary fish. Pata monkeys, lizards and crabs abound, although it is rare to see a turtle – they just come ashore during the summer months to lay their eggs, departing immediately afterwards. The turtles are closely monitored as they are an endangered species, and unfortunately poaching still occurs.

Kiang West National Park

Kiang West National Park is probably the most important and least visited wildlife park in The Gambia. Located on the south bank of the Gambia River, it is only 145 km (90 mi) from the capital, Banjul. The journey, however, is hard as the road is in poor repair. Established in 1987, the river forms the park's northern boundary.

Kiang West is uninhabited, flat and low. Three *bolongs*, or creeks, run through the interior, which mainly consists of savannah and deciduous woodland, with mangroves and tidal flats. There are many trees: red acacia, kapok, and several species native to the Sahelian biogeographic area that divides the Sahara desert from the southern savannahs.

Most of The Gambia's mammals are found here, including antelopes, warthogs, spotted hyenas, leopards, servals and caracals. This is habitat for marsh mongoose, pythons, cobras and Nile crocodiles. West African manatees and humpback dolphins can sometimes be spotted in the Jarin creek.

The Gambia is famous for its birds and this area is home to half the country's species – more than 300 have been recorded. During the dry season many raptors are found such as eagles – including the bateleur, Kiang West's logo – hawks, harriers, falcons and the ubiquitous vultures. Other birds include hornbills, with their recognizably awkward flight, weavers, parrots, kingfishers, sandgrouse and chats. It is not essential to take a guide, but they are knowledgeable and quick to point out birds that you might otherwise miss.

Make for Tubabkollon Point. Here you are close to the river and antelopes and warthogs can be spotted from the nearby escarpment. A waterhole within walking distance can be observed from a viewing shelter. Here you'll see many animals, including monkeys, coming to drink as the dry season tightens its grip.

HOW TO GET THERE:
4x4 on the southern Trans-Gambia highway to Dumbuto, the main base of Kiang West. You can also take tours that go partly by road and the remainder of the way by river boat.
WHEN TO GO:
During the dry season, from November to April
DON'T MISS:
The Nganingkoi Bolon tidal creek where you will see many wading birds, and possibly marsh mongoose hunting for crabs.
YOU SHOULD KNOW:
Kiang West National Park warrants more than a quick look, and it is easy to stay nearby. You can organize this independently or through a tour company.

179

Pendjari Biosphere Reserve

Situated in the northwest of Benin, Pendjari National Park, some 12,000 sq km (4,635 sq mi) in size, is part of the largest complex of Protected Areas in West Africa, crossing the borders of Benin, Niger and Burkino Faso. During the 1950s Benin, then part of French West Africa, listed Pendjari as a Protected Area and it became a hunting ground for French colonials.

Today, Pendjari still retains three areas for hunters and their professional guides, under the ownership, control and supervision of the local people. A percentage of the fees received for hunting permits is used to improve the lives of those living near the park boundaries; the remainder helps preserve and improve the Biosphere Reserve, which it became in 1986. Much emphasis is placed on the growth of ecotourism and research, and this is a fantastic area through which to hike, go mountain-biking, take canoe trips, join organized safaris or drive independently.

Renowned for its populations of large mammals, the savannah and grassland is home to cheetahs, lions, leopards, hyena, African wild dogs and jackals. Other large mammals include elephants, buffalo and hippos. Pendjari contains several types of antelope and monkeys, but most of all, there are birds.

With a backdrop of the Atakora range and its rocky cliffs, Pendjari park is lush in part, thanks to the eponymous broad river winding through it, bordered by thick, canopied forest. Within its boundaries over 300 species of bird can be found. Birds of prey include kestrels, kites, harriers and eagles such as the booted eagle and the African fish eagle. Smaller species include chats, babblers, waxbills, whydah, white-throated francolin and many more. Purple glossy starlings flash past, their iridescent plumage almost shockingly vivid, disappearing into the shelter of baobabs, palms and other African tree and shrub species.

Gola Forest

Bordered by the Atlantic Ocean, Guinea and Liberia, Sierra Leone is severely underdeveloped. Its inhabitants still suffer from the after effects of a disastrous civil war, only resolved in 2000. Deforestation has increased since the end of the war, but in 2005 the RSPB and Bird Life International, alongside the Forestry Department and the Conservation Society, joined forces to work on a conservation and sustainable development project in the Gola Forest. It is hoped that by 2012, the forest will achieve national park status.

Gola Forest is the largest area of lowland rainforest in Sierra Leone. It is divided into four distinct areas. Gola North is rugged, fairly high and drained by the Mogbai River, while Gola East and West, separated by the Mano River, are low-lying and swampy. Tiwai Island, situated in the Moa River to the west of Gola West, is a game sanctuary.

The closed canopy forest, which contains 200 species of tree, supports most of West Africa's wildlife. Around 50 species of mammal live in Gola, including ten primates. Several species are vulnerable or endangered, including chimpanzees, elephants and pygmy hippopotami. Other species have only recently been found, such as the leopard, zebra duiker and bongo. There are about 330 different birds. Nine are threatened, six are vulnerable and one, the rufous fishing owl, is endangered. The 770 species of flowering plants in the forest help the very high diversity of butterflies to flourish; over 600 species have been found there, three of which are new discoveries.

It is possible to visit the Gola Forest in a 4x4, with a guide, just for the day. But for a much more interesting visit, full camping kit, complete with porters and a cook can be arranged. If rainforests are of interest, Gola should be visited. This is why the park is known as the country's 'green diamond'.

HOW TO GET THERE:
Gola is located in the southeast of Sierra Leone and is accessible by road. The nearest big town, Kenema, is a six-hour drive southwest of Freetown, the capital.

WHEN TO GO:
The dry season is between December and May. The average temperature is 26°C (78.8°F) but it can fall to 16°C (60.8°F) at night.

DON'T MISS:
The pygmy hippopotamus, the white-necked picathartes which nests in colonies on cliffs in the forest, and the very rare Gola malimbe.

YOU SHOULD KNOW:
Despite all efforts, Gola is threatened by logging, hunting and mining, including for diamonds. Famously, blood diamonds were used to finance the civil war. Sierra Leone is rich in diamonds, and corruption is rife. Drug cartels have started to use the country as a place from which to ship drugs to Europe, which may turn it into a narco-state similar to neighbouring Guinea Bissau.

Comoe National Park

HOW TO GET THERE:
Comoe National Park is 410 km
(255 mi) by road from Abidjan. A
4x4 is essential.
WHEN TO GO:
The park is open to visitors from
December to May.
DON'T MISS:
Big-game fishing is available on the
Comoe River if hiking doesn't appeal.
YOU SHOULD KNOW:
The country is edging towards civil
war, which has exacerbated the
constant problems with poaching,
particularly of elephants, overgrazing
of cattle and the burning of land for
agricultural purposes in Comoe
National Park.

Located in northeastern Côte d'Ivoire, south of the country's border with Burkino Faso, is Comoe National Park. West Africa's largest game park was inscribed on the UNESCO World Heritage Site list in 1983, but added to the endangered sites list in 2003. The political turmoil that has overtaken the country during recent years has made 65 per cent of the park 'beyond the control of the staff'.

The Comoe River, which flows south from the northeastern section of the park, is the reason Comoe contains such remarkable plant diversity, including shrub savannahs and dense rainforest normally found much further south. It is best visited when its floodplains seasonally become tall grasslands, tempting many species to leave the forest in search of food.

The park contains a great many birds and mammals. Among these are 17 types of carnivore, including African wild dogs and leopards. Chimpanzees, baboons, colobus monkeys and the endangered Diana monkey can be found here, as can duikers,

bongos, hartebeests, kobs and bushbucks. African elephants, buffaloes, warthogs and hippos are also present, but in fairly small numbers.

Comoe is also known for its birds. Some 494 species include five species of vulture, 50 species of other raptors and ten species of heron, including the goliath heron. It is possible to sit by the river's edge with binoculars and observe many of these creatures at close range.

This is a park for adventurous explorers looking for a truly authentic experience. During the dry season, when the park is open to visitors, 500 km (310 mi) of tracks are available. Some of these are rugged and hard to follow, and it is wise to employ a guide. Two tourist zones have been established, but there is an area that is strictly off limits.

*An aerial view of a village
in Comoe National Park*

Tai National Park

Declared a Forest and Wildlife Refuge in 1926, Tai National Park became a UNESCO World Heritage Site in 1982, 46 years later. Situated between the Cavally and Sassandra rivers in the southwest of Côte d'Ivoire, this is the largest area of primary tropical rainforest in the whole of West Africa.

Vast trees soar to heights of 46 m (150 ft), their massive trunks using supporting roots for extra strength. The dense canopy excludes sunlight, making for good hiking as it keeps the undergrowth down. Tai has two recognizable types of forest: the north and southeast supports trees such as palms and ebony on poor, thin soil, while in the southwest the trees are all tropical, rain-loving species, 150 of which are endemic.

There are 47 species of large mammal living in this forest, five of which are endangered. It is not particularly easy to see large mammals – many are elusive – but there are African elephants, leopards, golden cats, various species of duiker, pygmy hippos, Cape buffaloes and colobus monkeys. The chimpanzees of Tai National Park have become famous thanks to years of study carried out by Swiss researchers. The apes live in groups of 70–80, and during the dry season visitors can hear them cracking nuts open with stones. The elephants, which are on the endangered list, aid the region's ecosystem, as secondary forest springs from dung deposited in clearings.

Areas around the rivers are the best places from which to spot both large mammals and birds. There are no fewer than 230 bird species here, eight of which are endangered. Among these is the white-breasted guinea fowl. Tai is protected by a buffer zone some 5 km (3 mi) wide, part of which is farmed, but there are on-going problems with poaching, illegal tree felling and gold mining.

HOW TO GET THERE:
Visit the Tai National Park Headquarters in San Pedro for a permit, and take their advice as to which method of visiting the park would suit you best.
WHEN TO GO:
The dry season is between December and February.
DON'T MISS:
Hiking up Mount Nienokoue, in the south of the park. The effort is more than worth the view of a never-ending sea of green rainforest, and you are likely to see animals and birds *en route*.
YOU SHOULD KNOW:
A new strain of Ebola virus has been isolated in Tai National Park. Chimpanzee meat, which has been linked with spreading the virus, is frequently eaten locally. Côte d'Ivoire has been relatively peaceful since 2007, but it is a potentially explosive country. Visit only if you are already familiar with it or if you have family or friends there.

Walking through the towering trees in Tai National Park.

Crystal Mountains National Park

Gabon lies on the equator and contains three well-defined areas: mountains, savannah and the coastal plain. Unusually in sub-Saharan Africa, the economy – boosted by oil revenues – is relatively well distributed and the government has made conservation a high priority. Some 10 per cent of the country is protected in 13 national parks, boosting revenue from tourism as well as protecting Gabon's natural treasures.

The Crystal Mountains National Park is a section of a wide, rocky escarpment situated in the northwest of the country between Equatorial Guinea and the Ogooué River. Mount Iboundji, in the north of the mountain range, reaches just 1,575 m (5,167 ft) and is the highest peak in Gabon.

Stunningly beautiful, the park is the epitome of a tropical African jungle – teeming with life and famed as a biodiversity hotspot. An American research team has been working here since 2004. The flora is exceptional. Trees include hardwoods such as ebony, mahogany and purpleheart, as well as *okoumé* and *ozigo*, all of which produce valuable timber, and there is an extraordinary array of flowers, including endemic orchids and begonias. At higher elevations, clouds envelop the forest, producing a mystical landscape of tangled undergrowth, trees shrouded in lianas, and climbing vines.

This equatorial rainforest provides habitat for a wide variety of wildlife. Elephants, leopards, antelopes, jackals and zebras roam the savannah; crocodiles and hippos haunt the river; lowland gorillas and many other primates swing through branches in chattering groups. Pythons and vipers hunt for small prey at ground level, while toucans and parrots screech in the canopy above.

Take a wildlife safari to the Crystal Mountains and visit the Kinguele Falls in the heart of the region, on the M'Bei River. It is a marvellous opportunity to experience the African rainforest, normally only seen on television screens.

Loango National Park

In 2002 Gabon's president Omar Bongo Ondimba created 13 national parks. The existing Petit Loango and Iguéla Reserves were joined to form Loango National Park. Its habitat includes forest, savannah and lagoons as well as swamps and untamed coastline, and it quickly became a popular spot for ex-pats living in Libreville. Situated between the Nkomi and Ndogo lagoons, south of the capital, and based on the concept 'tourism pays for conservation', it became the focus of small-scale, low-impact, high-end tourism.

The coastline boasts the largest number and variety of whale and dolphin species, including humpback and killer whales, with the exception of South Africa. The ocean also contains many large fish, and Loango is renowned for its record-sized Atlantic tarpon. Fishing in these waters is an exciting experience.

Four types of sea turtle breed on this coastline, including the Olive Ridley and the leatherback, both of which are endangered. From November to February, visitors may join the data-collection team, going out at night in search of nests or hatchlings. Three species of crocodile may also be seen on such a night-time trek.

A Western lowland gorilla in Loango National Park

Fabulous wildlife abounds in Loango throughout the year and, although the animals are shy, there is a good chance of a sighting from a 4x4, on foot, from a hide or from a boat. Trips around Iguéla lagoon are very rewarding and birdwatching expeditions can be arranged. Expect to see Pel's and vermiculated fishing owls, Forbes's plover, and African river martins among others.

The savannah and forest is home to many mammals, large and small, and although Loango is not like the big game parks in East Africa, on a safari there is a good chance of observing several species such as zebras, herds of buffalo, lowland gorillas and chimpanzees in unusual settings.

WHEN TO GO:
The best time for little rain and clear skies is December. In the dry season, from June to September, the sky is overcast. Some months are better than others for seeing particular animals, so check before booking if you have a particular interest.
DON'T MISS:
Elephants and forest buffaloes walking on the beach at sunset or the whale-watching season from July to September.
YOU SHOULD KNOW:
Africa's last Eden, as Loango is often known, is where *National Geographic* photographer Michael Nichols took his photographs of surfing hippos.

185

Tourists on the tree-top walkway in Kakum Conservation Area

Kakum Conservation Area

Just an hour by road from Cape Coast, the Kakum Conservation Area covers 350 sq km (135 sq mi) of dense tropical rainforest. The area supports a rich diversity of wildlife, including the white-bearded colobus monkey, bush pigs, porcupines and the timid forest elephant. Many species of birds and butterflies also flourish in this lavish land of plenty and the noise of competing wildlife provides a wonderful, if none too peaceful, soundtrack to Kakum.

The conservation area has a number of hiking trails that take ramblers deep into the forest to a land of fast-flowing tropical rivers and spectacular rapids. Park guides are available to explain the area's economic and cultural significance to local people, as well as to lead the way through the dense undergrowth.

It is the 65-m (213-ft) tall giant hardwood trees, however, that are the main attraction in Kakum. Ghana is by no means unique in suffering rapid deforestation and the need for food, timber and even firewood means that what takes hundreds of years to grow can often be destroyed in the blink of an eye. To their credit, the administrators in Kakum have come up with an ingenious way of giving their trees greater economic value by leaving them *in situ* than they would have if they were chopped down. Visitors can now climb high into the canopy by way of a 500-m (547-yd) long tree-top walkway to experience the environment of the high-tree dwellers. A good head for heights is required as the walkway is little more than a narrow width of wood held in a rope cradle. If vertigo can be avoided, it is a magnificent way to view a world that is seen only by canopy dwellers and wildlife cameramen.

HOW TO GET THERE:
By bus from Pedu Junction in Cape Coast

WHEN TO GO:
All year round, but it's driest from May to August.

DON'T MISS:
The area is best seen just after a sharp shower. The mist caused by evaporating rainfall shrouds the dense vegetation in a cloak of tiny water particles.

YOU SHOULD KNOW:
Kakum is not the best place to get close to wildlife. Forest dwellers are generally shy and chances are they will hear people before people see them. The best way to view animals in the park is by way of a night-time stakeout, when there is the possibility of sighting the elusive forest elephant.

Banc d'Arguin National Park

Mauritania is a vast country in West Africa on the western fringes of the Sahara Desert. Its boundaries, save for the Senegal River to the south, are little more than lines in the sand. Its main resource, other than some low-level mining, comes from its Atlantic coastline in the form of fishing. But even here the right to fish very often belongs to others. This makes the National Park of Banc d'Arguin all the more vital for the protection of the ecology of the area.

The park covers the largely desert coastal region of the country between the capital Nouakchott and Nouadhibou. Most of its interior is made up of sand blown by strong Saharan winds but, away from the arid core, Banc d'Arguin contains an astonishing variety of habitats. The area of most significance to the biodiversity of the region is a large expanse of mudflats, particularly those adjacent to the island of Tidra – the largest of 15 significant islands off the coast. Millions of birds head south to escape the European winter and breed in the park, making the mudflats of Banc d'Arguin the largest bird conservation area on Earth. The fish-rich waters are also a magnet for dolphins and sea turtles.

Perhaps the most surprising and remarkable part of the park is its large mangrove swamp. As well as containing the most diverse flora in the park, it offers up clues about the area's very different geological past and about our ever-changing planet. The fact that Banc d'Arguin contains such an assortment of fertile grounds is largely due to its once having been the huge estuary of a river system that flowed from the now-parched Sahara Desert.

HOW TO GET THERE:
By road from Nouakchott – a 4x4 vehicle is essential.
WHEN TO GO:
All year round – wildlife-watching is best from November to March.
DON'T MISS:
Birdwatching – especially from the island of Niroumi – where the colonies of bar-tailed godwit, ringed plover and dunlin represent over half of the total Atlantic population.
YOU SHOULD KNOW:
Travel to and within Mauritania is difficult. Advice on safety and security should be taken from the Foreign Office (UK) or State Department (US) before travelling.

Greater flamingoes are one of many species that breed in the park.

Bandiagara Escarpment

When journeying through the flat, unexciting and scorched landscape of Mali, the traveller could be forgiven for recalling the words of Samuel Johnson, who said that there are places 'worth seeing, but not worth going to see'. Such thoughts are quickly dismissed as the road begins a steady incline and one of Africa's greatest natural wonders rises mirage-like out of the desolate landscape. The gigantic Bandiagara Escarpment – a 150-km (94-mi) long towering sandstone cliff of rich ochre colour – runs from Ouo in the west to the Honbori mountains in the southeast and, as well as being a geological phenomenon, is a place of no little human intrigue.

The cliff face itself varies in height from 100 m (328 ft) to 500 m (1,640 ft) and is broken by deep ravines and scree-lined passages. The higher levels of the escarpment have a rich and diverse flora which has all but disappeared at lower levels. Archaeological research has revealed that high up in the cliffs a system of caves and tunnels was created over 2,000 years ago. The caves then lay empty for over a thousand years until the Tellem pygmies arrived and built houses in the crevices. The remains of these elevated structures can still be seen. Today, the cliffs act as protection for a string of over 300 villages belonging to the local Dogon people.

It is hard to leave the area without the feeling that you've visited a place out of time. The flat-topped and cone-roofed clusters of Dogon buildings blend in to seem part of nature and the people themselves have an animist system of beliefs and rituals that is far removed from anything else on Earth.

The spectacular cliffs of the Bandiagara Escarpment

Air and Tenere Natural Reserves

Located in northern Niger towards the border with Algeria, the Air and Tenere Natural Reserves together form the largest protected area in Africa. At 77,000 sq km (29,730 sq mi) they cover an area of arid and semi-arid land on the edge of the Sahara Desert that is roughly the size of Scotland. The combined reserve was created in 1988 and includes the western portion of the Tenere Desert and the eastern peaks of the Air Mountains. Its mission was to provide an environment where wildlife could flourish and it was hoped that sustainable populations of desert fauna could be established in the area. However, years of civil strife have seen wildlife numbers plummet. The addax antelope, ostrich, and dama gazelle have all but disappeared from the region, while the once numerous Barbary sheep and Dorcas gazelle are now seldom seen.

Although denuded of much in the way of wildlife, the reserve is still a place of unusual beauty. The Tenere Desert contains one of the world's largest sand seas and some of the highest barchan dunes in the Sahara. It is a bleak landscape punctuated only by the odd sand-blasted tree whose spiky leaves have evolved to withstand sandstorms and intense heat.

The Air Mountains are positively verdant by comparison. Comprising several massifs above a craggy plateau, they support a wide variety of grasses, shrubs and small trees. The mountains are also a good landmark for migrating birds and their relative greenness provides welcome respite in a land where water is at a premium.

The area was established as a UNESCO World Heritage Site in 1991 and was almost immediately put on its endangered list. Things are now moving in the right direction and one sixth of the reserve is working well as a sanctuary for the addax antelope.

Sand dunes in the Tenere Desert meet the Air Mountains.

HOW TO GET THERE:
Travel by road from Niger's capital, Niamey, or (more difficult) from Algeria.
WHEN TO GO:
During the 'cold' season (October to February) when the heat is less oppressive.
DON'T MISS:
The distant view of the Air Mountains that appear to bubble up out of the desert.
YOU SHOULD KNOW:
The north of Niger has pretty much been a zone of conflict for the past 30 years. Advice on safety and security should be taken from the Foreign Office (UK) or State Department (US) before travelling.

Mount Cameroon is the region's highest peak.

Mount Cameroon

Dubbed 'the roof of West Africa', Mount Cameroon at 4,095 m (13,435 ft) above sea level is not only the region's highest peak but is also the only active volcano of mainland tropical Africa west of the Rift Valley. It is part of a basalt ridge that rises from the Gulf of Guinea and is a truly awesome sight when viewed from the sea. It is also as wet as it gets. The region surrounding the mountain receives some of the heaviest rainfall on Earth at an incredible average of 10 m (33 ft) per year. This, coupled with the tropical heat of the lower slopes of the mountain, creates a hothouse environment for a diverse and spectacular range of plant life. Some of the insect-attracting plants that thrive there have heads as big as bicycle wheels.

Despite its elevation, the mountain is more of a hike than a climb, but the vertical journey takes the traveller through four distinct habitats. At sea level the area is characterized by dense mangrove forest, which soon gives way to lush evergreen lowland forest. The tall luxuriant growth of the lowlands is then replaced by thinner mountain forest until the land turns to savannah above 2,000 m (6,560 ft). Once at the top the hiker can explore recent volcanic action in the form of craters, lava streams and crater lakes.

The area around the mountain is administered by the youthful and vibrant Mount Cameroon Inter Communal Ecotourism Board which seeks to preserve the area by marrying the mountain's well-deserved popularity with the needs of local people. Portage is compulsory (no bad thing, given the heat and humidity) and there is a series of huts on the mountain for overnight stays.

HOW TO GET THERE:
By road from Cape Coast or bus from Limbe
WHEN TO GO:
All year round, but the rain is most intense in the months between June and October. The hottest months are between March and May.
DON'T MISS:
The view over the Atlantic from the summit. Because the mountain is often shrouded in cloud, it is worth allowing extra time on any climb to have a greater chance of clear weather.
YOU SHOULD KNOW:
The climber should arrive prepared for all weathers. The mountain is stiflingly hot at the lower gradients while, at the top, a dusting of snow is not uncommon in the cooler season (September to February).

Zakouma National Park

The *raison d'etre* of a game reserve is to bring people close to the wild animals they would normally have little access to. This is a happy marriage, as the visitors bring much-needed revenue, which in turn goes towards preserving the animals' habitat. Safety and security in exchange for the disturbance created by a few motor vehicles is no bad deal. For the staff and wildlife at Zakouma National Park this would be a great luxury. Its close proximity to the war in Darfur has had a catastrophic impact on the area and poaching has become endemic. Some wildlife has been killed for food, but one animal has suffered more than most. In a land where *per capita* income is less than $200 a year, the elephant has been targeted by organized criminal gangs for its tusks, which can fetch $100,000 a pair when sold in China or Thailand. In 1970 the elephant population in Chad stood at over 300,000, today it is below 10,000 and falling.

Travel through the park is possible only by journeying with the park rangers who, by necessity, must be as heavily armed as are the poachers. But Zakouma soon reveals itself to be a beautiful place. It is a land of wide open plains broken only by a few clumps of trees, where lions take shelter before heading into the cover of the long parched grass to stalk their prey. This is a magical place, where heat haze distorts distance and clouds of dust rise out of the sun-baked earth, disturbed by the hooves of jinking gazelles. But it is the mighty African elephant that most symbolizes the park. As sensitive as it is strong, its plight is shaming, although it is hoped that, with the help of the Wildlife Conservation Society, it may once again flourish in the region.

HOW TO GET THERE:
By plane to N'Djamena, then overland by car
WHEN TO GO:
The wet season, from June to September, is less oppressively hot.
DON'T MISS:
The sight of a moving elephant which, uniquely among mammals, spreads the burden of its weight evenly between front and rear legs, making it the four-wheel drive of the animal kingdom.
YOU SHOULD KNOW:
Currently it is not advisable to travel outside of N'Djamena. Check with the Foreign Office (UK) or State Department (US) before travelling.

Trou au Natron is a caldera in the Tibesti Mountains where the Toubou people gather rock salt.

Tibesti Mountains

The inhospitable plains of the Sahara Desert extend across North Africa from its Atlantic coastline in the west to the Nile Delta in the east. At 9 million sq km (3.5 million sq mi) and growing steadily still, it is the largest arid region on Earth. It is characterized by vast shifting sands that blind and disorientate the traveller. Only the camel has adapted to this extreme environment through its ability to store fat and the development of an extra eyelid that acts as a windshield.

Rising out of this seemingly endless and monotonous landscape are two mountain groups – the Ahaggar in the west and the larger and more imposing Tibesti Mountains in the east. The Tibesti Mountains appear like a mirage from the desert. Composed of black basalt from a now-dormant volcanic chain, they have over the years been sandblasted into a stunning lunar-like landscape. Travel through the range is beset with problems. Sand gets into everything and the area is subject to the largest diurnal temperature range on Earth. Morning temperatures can be below freezing, while by midday they can have soared to half boiling point (in Fahrenheit the range is an astonishing 100 degrees).

Emi Koussi, at 3,415 m (11,204 ft) is the highest and most challenging peak of the area. Surrounded by a corona of dramatic volcanic spires, it provides a test for even the most experienced mountaineer. But, without doubt, the most stunning spectacle the area has to offer is a 5-km (3-mi) wide 750-m (2,460-ft) deep salt-filled crater, Trou au Natron. The contrast between the black mountains and the blinding white of the crater as the sun beats off both provides one of the world's most extraordinary sights.

HOW TO GET THERE:
Travel overland from N'Djamena, Chad, or (more difficult) from southern Libya.
WHEN TO GO:
The heat is less searing from December to February.
DON'T MISS:
The view of Emi Koussi from Tarso Taro
YOU SHOULD KNOW:
Travel to and within Chad is difficult. Roads are few and far between and the only public transport is aboard cargo lorries. Advice on safety and security should be taken from the Foreign Office (UK) or State Department (US) before travelling.

Bale Mountains

There are always wild places to be discovered in this world – often fascinating destinations where sheer remoteness has until recently precluded a visit. One such area is the Bale Mountains in southeastern Ethiopia. This lush landscape of forested mountains and pristine streams offers superb scenic satisfaction, but also introduces visitors to local culture in a manner that provides a blueprint for sustainable ecotourism. As with much of Africa, however, it's a clear case of 'the sooner the better'. There is increasing clearance within forested areas and the level ground at the foot of the mountains is no longer used for pastoral livestock herding. Instead, the land is being cultivated with increasing intensity.

But the locals are friendly and guides may be found to lead visitors into the forest, either on foot or mounted on horseback. Bold trekkers will be rewarded with a wealth of tree and plant life, with distinctly different flora as the elevation increases, right up to heather-covered moors at the highest levels. The hillsides are aflame with torch lilies between June and November, while the bright-yellow flowers of *Hypericum lanceolatum* are everywhere. Honey production is a significant activity and there are far worse tipples than the punchy mead that much of it mysteriously becomes.

The Adaba-Dodola forests harbour a wealth of birdlife, from Abyssinian catbirds to yellow-fronted parrots. These will be more visible than the forest animals – although the likes of Menelik's bushbuck, assorted monkeys, baboons, spotted hyenas, porcupines, warthogs, mongoose, jackals and Ethiopian wolves (among others) are there to be spotted by those with sharp eyes and a light tread. The chances of getting lucky – and enjoying a good all-round experience – are much increased for visitors who book one of the organized mountain expeditions that use primitive but established camps.

HOW TO GET THERE:
The gateways to the Bale Mountains are Dodola and Adaba, in the Regional State of Oromia.
WHEN TO GO:
Any time. The dry season (November to May) is best, although the mountain climate is generally cool. The rains come in July and August, when damp discomfort is counterbalanced by the intensity and freshness of the vegetation.
DON'T MISS:
A daytrip from Dodola town to the Lensho River and spectacular Shebelle Waterfalls
YOU SHOULD KNOW:
There is a real threat of terrorist activity in Ethiopia, and not even Addis Ababa is deemed entirely safe for visitors. Extreme vigilance is essential, especially at transport hubs and places regularly frequented by expatriates and foreign travellers.

The lush landscape of the remote Bale Mountains

Omo Valley

The important Omo River falls entirely within southern Ethiopia, rising in the Shewan Highlands and rushing down to Lake Turkana in the Great Rift Valley. Ethiopia's most remote wilderness surrounds the Omo Valley. The valley's natural beauty may be stunning and justify a visit in its own right, but the opportunity to visit colourful local villages adds a fascinating extra dimension. This UNESCO World Heritage Site is a cultural melting pot where the earliest-known fossil remains of *Homo sapiens* were discovered.

The river flows through two national parks – Omo and Mago – but these have few if any facilities and are defined more by lines on maps than much evidence on the ground. With just one significant road providing access – from Konso via Woito to Bako or Omorate – this really is a splendid opportunity for adventurous types to organize the expedition of a lifetime. But however ambitious the journey, there simply won't be time to see and do everything. Photography, birdwatching, wildlife-viewing, fishing, nature hiking and exploring in a 4x4 are just some of the tempting possibilities, but the real joy of this place is people-watching.

There are at least 20 different African tribes within the area – all interesting, all with their own customs, all living a traditional way of life that may be seen today but will inevitably be swept away by 'progress' within a few more generations. Peoples of the lower Omo Valley include the Dizi, Dorze, Hamar, Me'en, Mursi, Nyangatom and Suri. The villages contain mud-and-thatch houses – often of beehive form – and this is the place to see the extraordinary sight of women with mouths stretched to accommodate huge round clay plates. The effort of getting to the Omo Valley may be considerable, but the reward will be a storehouse of memories to treasure.

Hamar men tending their cattle.

Goda Mountains

Located to the northwest of the Gulf of Tadjoura in North Africa's smallest country, the Goda Mountains rise to a height of 1,750 m (5,741 ft) and are Djibouti's largest 'green' enclave – a vegetated oasis amid the country's stony desert landscapes and an area where mist often rises above the lush green slopes and it actually rains sometimes. Small mountain villages like Bankoualé, Dittilou and Randa seem a world apart from the scorching plains at the foot of the mountains and offer the blessed relief of a cooler climate.

It is possible to enjoy a day's hike in the mountains or find accommodation there at a few locally run campsites or in simple huts reserved for tourists in unspoilt areas, either of which can provide a base to explore before it's too late. Much of the forest has been cleared over the past 200 years and only one tenth of its original area remains. Drought, fires, deforestation and overgrazing by ubiquitous livestock are, sadly, continuing the process.

The Day Forest National Park, accessed from the National 9 road, aims to protect much of what is left and contains most of Djibouti's biodiversity. One of three national parks in Djibouti, it is small but has a unique ambiance. It harbours rare plants and birds, some – like the Djibouti francolin – endemic. Birdwatching attracts visitors, while animals such as warthog, monkeys and antelope may also be seen. The forest is located where the plateau of the Goda Mountains is bordered by the Goh and Hamboka cliffs. The Day Massif contains juniper trees and an impressively dense pine forest. However, the attempt to preserve the junipers seems to be a losing battle, as there are now almost too few to ensure survival, let alone mass regeneration.

HOW TO GET THERE:
A hired 4x4 vehicle is the transport of choice, with or without the services of a local guide.
WHEN TO GO:
Favoured months to visit Djibouti are October to April.
DON'T MISS:
A visit to Tadjoura, on the gulf of the Tadjoura Sea and overlooked by the Goda Mountains. Once a slave-trading centre, Djibouti's oldest town is now a busy port notable for white-washed houses and splendid nearby beaches.
YOU SHOULD KNOW:
The Djibouti-Eritrea border is disputed and best avoided under all circumstances. There is a general threat of terrorist activity and petty crime such as mugging and bag snatching is not uncommon in Djibouti, which is nonetheless a stable and relatively prosperous country. French is widely spoken in this *petit* former colony, once French Somaliland.

The green slopes of the Goda Mountains

195

Lake Assal

HOW TO GET THERE:
Hire 4x4 transport or – more economically but perhaps less satisfyingly – join an organized tour from Djibouti City.
WHEN TO GO:
Avoid high summer, when the heat can be unbearable.

Anyone who's ever wanted to walk on water must head for Lake Assal, a crater lake 120 km (75 mi) to the west of Djibouti City. There, the impossible almost becomes possible, for this amazing body of water is fed by salt springs that make it more saline than a more publicity-conscious pretender: the Dead Sea. Lake Assal is an impressive 157 m (515 ft) below sea level – making it the lowest point in Africa. The effort required to get there isn't wasted, for remoteness and fierce climate combine to ensure that this eerie landscape remains largely untouched by the heavy hand of tourism.

DON'T MISS:
Aficionados of science-fiction landscapes should make the effort to visit Djibouti's other extraordinary lake – Abbé, set in surreal surroundings where endless limestone pillars dot the plain, many belching steam. It's sufficiently out of this world to have served as the set for the sci-fi movie *Planet of the Apes* and is guaranteed to refresh even the most jaded tourist palate.
YOU SHOULD KNOW:
It is possible to go in to the water at Lake Assal to frolic (drowning an impossibility, sitting up almost feasible) – but it's advisable to wear shoes as the bottom is littered with sharp salt crystals.

Lake Assal – the lowest point in Africa

The lake is in the Danakil Desert and extends to an area of 54 sq km (21 sq mi). It is surrounded by brooding volcanoes (happily dormant) whose dark presence contrasts dramatically with the lake's brilliant aquamarine colour. A visit to Lake Assal is not for those who like gentle scenery and a temperate climate. It is in an inhospitable area seared by desert winds that is one of the hottest places in Africa, with temperatures capable of reaching nearly 60°C (140°F) and light so bright that a good pair of polarizing sunglasses is an essential travelling companion. But for lovers of wild places and dramatic landscapes its austere charms will be deeply satisfying.

The banks are covered in large salt crystals and saltpans surround the lake. The local Afar people still produce salt to trade into Ethiopia, as they have for centuries, and may be seen coming and going with their camels. The visitor is likely to be offered an unusual souvenir – a large bag of Lake Assal refined salt, costing only a few francs.

Meru National Park

Zebra in the Meru National Park

International fame came to Meru National Park when Joy Adamson's book *Born Free* chronicled the reintroduction of the lioness Elsa to the Kenyan wilderness back in the late 1950s. This was an important step forward for the conservation movement yet, despite such a positive association, many tourists overlook Meru. This may be a legacy of mismanagement in the 1970s and 1980s, when poaching was endemic and visitors wisely stayed away. Today, that situation has been remedied after an intensive rehabilitation programme conducted by the Kenya Wildlife Service, supported by the International Fund for Animal Welfare. So Meru is once again a haven for wildlife and a stimulating destination but, happily for those who appreciate wilderness exploration, it remains one of Kenya's lesser-known – and visited – parks. That said, there are lodges and self-catering accommodation in Meru along with campsites public and private. Overnight camping is a great experience for those not thrown by the myriad noises of an African night.

The 870-sq-km (335-sq-mi) park consists of riverine palm forests, with wooded grasslands in the west and thorny bush land to the north. The area experiences high rainfall that encourages the growth of tall grass and nourishes extensive swampland, which means that animals are sometimes difficult to spot. But with or without the help of an experienced guide it is possible to see many species, including lion, leopard, cheetah, giraffe (not so hard to detect!), zebra, elephant and hippopotamus, black rhino and rare antelopes. In addition, the bird population is thriving and more than 300 species have been recorded within park boundaries. The park is within sight of Mount Kenya and natural highlights are the Tana River and Adamson's Falls. Game viewing, birdwatching, photography and simply soaking up the scenery of this special place are the principal activities.

HOW TO GET THERE:
Meru National Park is around 350 km (220 mi) from Nairobi and most visitors fly in to the Mulika Lodge Airport within the park. Road access is by the main entrance, Murera Gate – 35 km (22 mi) from Maua.

WHEN TO GO:
Any time (the hottest months are generally February and March, the coolest July and August).

DON'T MISS:
The Meru home of George and Joy Adamson of *Born Free* fame. Elsa herself is buried in the park and some of Joy Adamson's ashes were scattered over the grave of her beloved lioness after the pioneering conservationist was murdered in 1980.

YOU SHOULD KNOW:
There is a real terrorist threat in Kenya, which has experienced indiscriminate attacks – notably on places frequented by expatriates and foreign travellers. It is unwise to enter slum and township areas, where crime rates are high. The border area with Somalia is also dangerous and several kidnaps of aid workers and nuns have been recently reported.

Clark's anemonefish swimming through magnificent anemone.

Watamu Marine National Reserve

HOW TO GET THERE:
Watamu is 120 km (75 mi) north of Mombasa and 28 km (17 mi) south of Malindi. The reserve is some 11 km (7 mi) off the main Mombasa-Malindi road – turn towards the Indian Ocean at Gede. It's possible to fly in to Malindi Airport and hire a vehicle or get onward transport from there.

WHEN TO GO:
Any time. The coastal lowlands are not as temperate as most of Kenya and have high temperatures and humidity, although these extremes are tempered by sea breezes.

DON'T MISS:
Gede ruins – the remains of a 12th-century Swahili village, mysteriously abandoned around 1400 and now an atmospheric place overgrown with baobab and tamarind trees. This National Museum merits exploration and should be followed by a visit to the Kipepeo Butterfly Project – by Gede's entrance – where locals breed forest butterflies for export to live display centres around the world. Another nearby attraction close to the main road is the Malindi Crocodile Farm and Snake Park. Feeding time is 16.00 on Wednesdays and Fridays (volunteers welcome!).

YOU SHOULD KNOW:
Neither Malindi nor Watamu is plastic-friendly – both reserves have an entry fee that must be paid in cash, either Kenyan shillings or US dollars are the acceptable currencies.

The jewel in the crown of Kenya's 50-plus national parks, reserves and sanctuaries must surely be the tiny but glittering Watamu Marine National Reserve, itself part of the much larger Malindi Marine National Reserve. Watamu may seem geographically insignificant but that's not the full story. As the name suggests, the glory of this special place lies in its extraordinary marine environment.

This consists of the Mida Creek mangrove forest with its teeming bird-like intertidal rocks, sandy beaches, mud flats, coral cliffs, fringing reefs and a glorious coral garden. The latter lies less than 300 m (328 yd) from shore in the azure Indian Ocean, crying out to be explored by glass-bottomed boat. Snorkelling or diving are even better options for those who want to become part of this unique underwater world, however briefly (snorkels, masks and fins are available for hire). Water temperature ranges from 20°C to 30°C (68°F to 86°F) so immersion is pleasant indeed. Expert guides are on hand to add detailed information to the experience, if required, and there are other splendid snorkelling possibilities outside the main coral garden.

Quite apart from corals – there are around 150 species here, hard and soft, including sponges, brain and fan corals – over 500 types of fish inhabit the waters. The larger denizens include whale shark, barracuda, manta rays and giant octopus, while there are countless brightly coloured reef fish. Another major attraction is the green turtle population, actively encouraged in this haven by a serious conservation programme that involves the active co-operation of local fishermen. Also to be seen is the occasional dugong – the fabled sea cow said to be the inspiration behind mermaid legends. Watamu may not be the wildest place in Kenya, but it's certainly one of the most interesting and colourful.

Mahale Mountains

In the west of Tanzania, bordering Lake Tanganyika, is a magical wild place. The Mahale Mountains National Park represents the heart of Africa unspoilt, a place with no roads just 100 km (62 mi) from where Stanley found the object of his prolonged search and (allegedly) uttered the immortal words 'Dr Livingstone, I presume'. The park covers 1,600 sq km (620 sq mi) of lakeshore and spectacular upland terrain, with beaches and azure water easily mistaken for those of an Indian Ocean paradise island. The added dimension is mysterious, jungle-clad mountains that tower above the lake, rising to the dramatic heights of 2,460-m (8,070-ft) Nkungwe – the park's loftiest peak.

A chimpanzee in the Mahale Mountains National Park

For those sufficiently determined to reach this remote place, the star attraction may well be chimpanzees, for the park is home to around 800 of the agile tree-dwellers – one of the largest cohesive populations left in Africa. There's every chance of a sighting – about 60 of them belong to the M Group, which has become used to humans as a result of a research programme dating back to the 1960s.

But the park has more to offer than charismatic primates. Some visitors may get no further than the waterside – swimming, snorkelling or fishing in the pristine waters of the world's least-polluted freshwater lake. Others will be seduced by camping safaris to the interior, where forested slopes are home to an amazing array of colourful birds and easily observed red colobus, red-tailed, and blue monkeys. Most will want to do a bit of both, to wring every last drop of rewarding experience from the trip of a lifetime. In season there are three permanent tented camps – with almost every mod con – plus a large general campsite and two small rest houses.

HOW TO GET THERE:
Take a charter flight to the park from Arusha, Dar es Salaam or Kigoma. Alternatively, go by boat – charter a private or park motorboat from Kigoma (four hours). The weekly steamer from Kigoma takes seven hours, after which a local fishing boat or park boat (by prior arrangement) completes the journey.
WHEN TO GO:
The dry season (May to October) is best for forest hiking, although November's light rains are not really problematical.
DON'T MISS:
The very special opportunity to see a complete troupe of chimpanzees in the wild (allow two days for the expedition). It's also possible to see chimps acclimatized to human presence in nearby Gombe Stream National Park, a small but beautiful enclave on the lakeshore.
YOU SHOULD KNOW:
Be aware of an underlying terrorist threat in Tanzania. However, a more pressing cause of concern should be long-distance buses, which tend to be ill maintained and liable to become involved in accidents, often with fatal consequences. Armed robberies have occurred in the Arusha region and areas bordering Burundi can be hazardous. Once there, however, the Mahale Mountains are quite safe.

Ruaha National Park

The name of the game is game, and this is the place to see game galore. Ruaha in Central Tanzania is the country's second-largest national park at almost 10,350 sq km (4,000 sq mi), and this vast wilderness consists of semi-arid bush country that is home to a teeming population of animals and birds. The arteries of this rugged landscape are the Great Ruaha River and its tributaries along the park's eastern boundary – raging torrents in the rainy season, dwindling thereafter to a series of still-vital pools amidst a desert of rock and sand.

Africa's most iconic animals are here in numbers. The park has 10,000 elephants, the greatest number in any East African park. There are giraffe, zebras galore, many large lion prides, leopard, cheetah, hippo and crocodile, along with numerous great kudu – characterized by the males' magnificent corkscrew horns, the latter serving as the park's emblem. Among other species to be seen (it's not too hard in dry season, when animals congregate around the remaining waterholes) are lesser kudu, striped and spotted hyena, packs of rare African wild dogs, Grant's gazelle, sable and roan antelope, impala and waterbuck. The bird population is equally impressive, with some 450 different species to 'twitch', including the trilling crested barbet and handsome natives such as the ashy starling and yellow-collared lovebird.

There is a network of tracks designed to facilitate dry-season wildlife-watching along the Great Ruaha River and its seasonal tributaries. These may be driven or hiked, while many visitors with a love of wild places simply can't resist the opportunity to take day walks or a hiking safari through untouched bush land, allowing them to share the wonderment of the first Europeans to explore the African interior's solitary splendour.

A bull elephant in Ruaha National Park

Serengeti

Migrating wildebeest

Tanzania's largest, oldest and most popular national park is a world-famous UNESCO World Heritage Site – with good reason. For Serengeti is home to one of the most awesome events in the animal world, when six million hooves pound the plains during an annual migration that sends a million wildebeest, 300,000 Thomson's gazelle and 200,000 zebra in search of fresh grazing to support a population explosion of 8,000 calves every day, before the 1,000-km (620-mi) return journey sorts out the weak from the strong.

The 40-km (25-mi) columns of animals are a moving spectacle as they brave crocodile-infested river crossings to fulfil their annual destiny, but Serengeti has much more to offer. This land of parched savannah, wooded hills, termite mounds and orange dust has different faces, becoming transformed in the rainy season to a green expanse spangled with flowers. The variety of wildlife is extraordinary and this is one of the best places in Africa to watch game doing its own thing in the wild. Apart from the great migration, a highlight of any visit is the sight of one of the great predators pursuing a kill. The park has lion, leopard, cheetah, buffalo, giraffe, elephant, rhino, eland, topi, impala, jackal, hyena and many more, right down to the insect-eating aardwolf. There are also at least 500 bird species.

Serengeti has ample in-park accommodation, from luxury lodges through quality standing tented camps to regular campsites for pitch-it-yourself travellers. Even so, the park is so vast that even a full complement of visitors can quickly vanish into the blue yonder, allowing everyone so minded to enjoy undisturbed solitude in this wonderful wilderness. One exotic activity is a hot-air-balloon safari, while other organized possibilities include guided game-viewing drives, walking safaris, bush picnics or *al fresco* lunch/dinner parties served in Africa's great outdoors.

HOW TO GET THERE:
Scheduled or charter flights from Arusha, Lake Manyara and Mwanza. Long-distance road access from the same three starting points, or nearby Ngorongoro Crater.
WHEN TO GO:
Depending on the desired spectacle, December to July to follow the wildebeest migration or June to October to best observe predators going about their deadly business.
DON'T MISS:
Fascinating rock paintings executed by the indigenous Maasai people – ask in the village of Kolo for a guide to the cave site where they may be viewed.
YOU SHOULD KNOW:
Allow at least three days to be sure of seeing wildebeest moving during the great migration – both route and timing can be unpredictable – then add another couple of days if the visit is to include a look at Serengeti's main predators in action.

The Kitulo Plateau

The glittering jewel in the crown of Tanzania's Southern Highlands is the Kitulo Plateau. Locals call Kitulo *Bustani ya Mungu* – the Garden of God – and anyone lucky enough to reach this enchanting place will instantly understand why it has earned that name. For this is where one of the world's most impressive floral displays may be seen during the rainy season. Around 350 types of vascular plant erupt into a botanical spectacle of extraordinary diversity from November onwards, dazzling visitors with sheer variety and scale. Prominent alongside 45 different ground orchids are plants such as aloes, asters, geraniums, giant lobelias, lilies and brilliant red-hot pokers, together creating a riot of competing colour.

The plateau levels out at 2,600 m (8,530 ft) and is protected by Kitulo National Park, which extends to an area of around 415 sq km (160 sq mi). This is an important watershed for the Great Ruaha River, with well-watered volcanic soils supporting the country's most important montane grassland. In addition to this rolling grassland, the area has rounded hills, rivers, waterfalls, crater lakes and forest. Visitors should aim to find the Numbi Valley, a picturesque spot where small streams emerge from grassy hillsides as if by magic.

There are good hiking trails on the plateau, offering easy walking over open grassland and giving access to flowers and a vibrant bird population. The latter is so beguiling that it attracts birdwatchers who see Kitulo's flowers and brilliant butterflies as a great backdrop to the main attraction – rare avian treasures such as Denham's bustard, blue swallow, mountain marsh widow and *Cisticola njombe*. It is also possible to go beyond the plateau to enjoy strenuous hill climbing through sometimes-dense vegetation amidst the rugged surrounding peaks of the Livingstone, Poroto and Kipengere Mountains.

Kibale Forest

It's a primary primate destination – a beautiful 775-sq-km (300-sq-mi) tract of preserved Ugandan tropical rainforest that supports no fewer than 13 primate species, from chimpanzees to several types of Central African monkey, such as L'Hoest's, Ugandan red colobus and Ugandan mangabey. But for most the main attraction of Kibale National Park will be those appealing chimps. They're sufficiently used to people to go about their lives undeterred by human intrusion – playing, squabbling and grooming in trees bearing the juiciest fruit, demonstrating sublime unconcern for camera-toting visitors with cricked necks.

A network of shaded trails offers almost unlimited hiking possibilities within the forest, also giving opportunities to visitors with a specialist interest. Birdwatchers are drawn by over 300 species, including African grey parrots, noisy hornbills, African pitas, green-breasted pitas and the endemic Prirogrine's ground thrush. Lepidopterists are attracted by shimmering displays of butterflies while botanists (including university researchers) come for the varied flora. In addition to seeing numerous agile primates, animal watchers may be delighted by occasional encounters with buffalo, leopard, bush pig, otter or assorted antelopes. The park's forest elephants (smaller and hairier than plains counterparts) commute to and fro from Kibale to the adjacent Queen Elizabeth National Park, the two protected areas together providing one of the country's most important ecotourism areas. In fact, the latter is Uganda's most-visited game reserve.

Although it looks entirely authentic to the untrained eye, Kibale owes its survival to colonial-era status as a forest reserve that could be (and was) sustainably logged. The national park was created in 1993, alien replanting was removed and the forest has been regenerating ever since. This provides encouraging evidence of the way in which important examples of Africa's rapidly vanishing natural habitats are being preserved thanks to the economic desirability of carefully managed tourism.

Chimpanzees can often be seen grooming each other.

HOW TO GET THERE:
Access is from Fort Portal in the west of Uganda – Kibale Forest is 35 km (22 mi) away via a dirt road and there is (somewhat erratic) public transport. Fort Portal itself is 320 km (200 mi) from Kampala along a (mostly) paved road.
WHEN TO GO:
Any time – the climate is hot but bearable all year. The rainy season is from March to May.
DON'T MISS:
The sights and more particularly sounds of the forest on a guided night walk – an unforgettable experience
YOU SHOULD KNOW:
It is essential to obtain comprehensive travel and medical insurance before visiting Uganda. Road travel by night outside major towns is not recommended. Kibale itself is safe, with in-park lodges (upmarket and budget) plus a luxury tented camp providing secure accommodation.

A view across the plains of Kidepo Valley

Kidepo Valley

HOW TO GET THERE:
By air, either using a private charter from Entebbe International Airport or Eagle Air's thrice-weekly scheduled service. The Karamoja region is potentially dangerous and overland travel is not recommended, as violent poachers or cattle rustlers may be encountered. Those who do risk the 700-km (435-mi) road trip from Kampala (a sturdy 4x4 is essential) are officially recommended to hire armed guards for the final leg. This rigmarole may be justified as a 4x4 vehicle is the best way of seeing as much of the park as possible.

WHEN TO GO:
Any time (although March and April are prime months for birdwatchers, when all the specials and many transient migrants are present).

DON'T MISS:
A visit to the local Karamajong community, which welcomes visitors interested in their timeless way of life. Cultural entertainers will put on a splendid show of traditional dancing for a small fee.

YOU SHOULD KNOW:
The Uganda Wildlife Authority's Apoka Rest Camp offers comfortable in-park *bandas* and chalets. Visitors should bring their own food, which can then be cooked for them. For those with bottomless pockets, the exclusive Apoka Lodge in the centre of the park offers every mod con. For visitors on a tight budget, there are two primitive campsites for those with their own equipment.

The Kidepo Valley National Park in the Karamoja region is tucked away in Uganda's northeastern corner, where it meets Sudan. It's the country's most remote national park, boasting rugged landscapes unsurpassed in any other. Kidepo is the ultimate destination for true lovers of unspoilt wild places, for this pristine 1,500-sq-km (580-sq-mi) wilderness of semi-arid valleys is little visited by tourists. Indeed, the word best used to describe those who do make the pilgrimage is 'adventurers'.

Many determined travellers who make the effort needed to visit Kidepo Valley are birdwatchers – often as part of organized ornithological expeditions – attracted by the huge variety of feathered species (around 475) to be found in the varied habitat of semi-desert scrub, open thorn scrub, grassy savannas, assorted woodland and granite outcrops. Among 'specials' not found in any other Ugandan park are some of East Africa's rarest birds, including the Karamoja apalis and black-breasted barbet. But the range is eye watering, from ostrich down to a huge variety of colourful songbirds, with an awesome selection of birds of prey. The animal population suffered during Uganda's catastrophic Idi Amin years, but has recovered. Over 80 mammal species live in Kidepo, including nearly 30 found in no other park. Along with rarities like the bat-eared fox and caracal, visitors can expect to spot the likes of giraffe, elephant, buffalo, lion, leopard, cheetah, reedbuck, waterbuck, kongoni, orobis, kudu, klipspringer, dik dik, zebra, warthog, jackal and mongoose, plus a healthy reptile population.

Guided walks (perhaps augmented by spotlit night drives) offer the ideal opportunity to see the maximum number of animals and birds in the time available. But for those happy to regard the wildlife as part of a rewarding wilderness trek rather than an end in itself, merely being in this magical wilderness is enough.

Lake Mburo

For a relatively compact national park by African standards, with an area of just 260 sq km (100 sq mi), Lake Mburo offers a very special experience. The name is something of a misnomer, for there are actually five lakes within the park – home to hippos, crocodiles and numerous water birds. The lakes are fringed with swamps that give sanctuary to papyrus specialists like the Sitatunga antelope and the rare Papyrus gonolek, a striking red, black and yellow bird.

This gives a clue to Lake Mburo National Park's key attractions – animal watching and birdwatching. This part of Uganda is covered in acacia woodland, with rich biodiversity supporting its own distinctive fauna. Those intent on seeing a wide variety of game will not be disappointed. There are nearly 70 species of animal to be found within the park, including Uganda's most visible population of giant eland plus impala, topi, the rare roan antelope, zebra and buffalo, with predators like leopard, jackal and hyena waiting to pounce on all but the fittest. Birders have 360 recorded species to pursue, including half a dozen forest rarities and 60 different water birds. The park has strategically placed hides overlooking salt licks where animals may constantly be observed coming and going, while boat trips on Lake Mburo provide an unmissable perspective on the park's flora on fauna, including those wily crocs, hippos and birds such as pelican, fish eagle and the rare shoebill stork.

There is a selection of accommodation (from luxury to budget) in Mbarara, while there is a permanent tented camp at Rwonyo park headquarters. There are three strategically located public campsites within the park and meals may be ordered from the Lake Mburo dining shelter. However, visitors are advised to bring enough food and drink to last for the duration of their stay.

HOW TO GET THERE:
By road. The park is about a four-hour drive from Kampala, in the Mbarara District. Turn off the Mbarara to Kampala highway at clearly signed junctions for one of the park's two gates: Sanga or Nshara.
WHEN TO GO:
Any time
DON'T MISS:
The opportunity to explore swampy Rubanga forest on a ranger-guided trip. It is small but has a closed canopy in places, formed by a rich variety of trees. Look out for fine specimens of Africa's famous flame trees.
YOU SHOULD KNOW:
While wandering in the park on foot can be an exciting opportunity to experience nature as nature intended, it is actually mandatory to be accompanied on any such expedition by an armed park official.

Lake Mburo National Park

Sempaya hot springs are rich in salt and sulphur.

Semuliki Valley

A remote section of the Semuliki Forest in western Uganda is an extension to the Congo's vast Ituri Forest. This 220-sq-km (85-sq-mi) ecosystem on the Uganda-DRC (Democratic Republic of Congo) border is enclosed by the Semuliki River to the west and north and by the Fort Portal to Bundibugyo road on the other two sides. The land is flat, in marked contrast to the rugged grandeur of the nearby Rwenzori Mountains, and was gazetted in 1993 – thus becoming the only national park in the country to consist primarily of tropical lowland forest.

It provides a wonderful chance to escape Uganda's regular tourist circuit and experience the only real jungle in East Africa. There is accommodation in Fort Portal from which to sally forth, but the very best way of enjoying Semuliki Valley is to camp within the park and spend time exploring on foot. There's much to be seen. A hike along the winding Semuliki River will seem like paradise for birdwatchers, while everyone can enjoy the bright butterflies and perhaps glimpse animals such as pygmy hippo, crocodile, forest elephant, buffalo, leopard and assorted primates (including chimps). For anglers, the river offers great sport fishing. There are campsites within the park (tents supplied or bring your own). An associated canteen offers food and drink with meals prepared to order, but most visitors bring their own provisions. For those with loftier aspirations, the park has a few 'executive *bandas*'.

One unmissable highlight is Semuliki's hot springs, located in a section of mineral-rich swamp land that attracts a fascinating variety of wildlife and is served by a network of trails. The highlights are a jet of super-heated water and pool of boiling water that bubbles up from the depths. The park's party trick is to take some food and boil it on site – eggs a speciality.

HOW TO GET THERE:
Starting from Fort Portal (reached by two good routes from Kampala), it's 4x4 country. About 50 km (30 mi) along the rough road to Bundibugyo is the park's Sempaya Gate, with park headquarters at Ntandi a bit further along. For true daredevils, regular public transport there and back (until around 16.00) is available from Fort Portal's taxi park. There are also local outfits in Fort Portal that will organize a custom visit.

WHEN TO GO:
Any time (but localized flooding occurs during the rainy months – March, April, May, September, October and November).

DON'T MISS:
A side trip to Mungilo Waterfall, just outside the park boundary. Another 'must' is the view over the park from the Bundibugyo road as it meanders through the Rwenzori escarpments, with a spectacular panorama visible from Mungu Ni Mukunwa.

YOU SHOULD KNOW:
Visitors travelling to Fort Portal from Kampala often choose the longer route via Masaka, Mbarara and Kasese, as this provides the opportunity to visit Lake Mburo National Park, Kyambura Wildlife Reserve, Rwenzori Mountains National Park and Queen Elizabeth National Park along the way.

Akagera National Park

The most remote source of the Nile is northeast Rwanda's Akagera River, meandering through a landscape of lakes and swamps on the Tanzanian border. The river is surrounded by typical African savannah that consists of open grassland and acacia woodland – terrain in marked contrast to the country's generally hilly character. In 1936 a 2,500-sq-km (965-sq-mi) area to the west of the river was reserved to form Akagera National Park, one of Africa's finest in terms of flora, fauna and outstanding natural beauty.

All the classic African animals were well represented, including hippo, crocodile, lion, leopard, elephant, giraffe, zebra and many types of antelope, along with a stunning bird population numbering around 500 species. But the preservation of this fabulous place was inevitably set back by the tragic events of the 1990s, when over a million Rwandans died as a result of ethnically motivated genocide. Dedicated conservationists did their best to maintain the park's integrity, but it was an uphill struggle. Refugees returning after the civil war flooded the savannah and this severe human pressure drove much of the wildlife back into the park's more remote areas. The influx resulted in two thirds of the park's original area being degazetted.

However, enough unspoilt terrain remains to ensure a memorable visit, and there is every hope that the lure of hard tourist currency will ensure the park's continuing rehabilitation. This remains big game country with every chance of spotting the big ones – giraffe, elephant, buffalo and zebra herds, plus occasional lions and leopards on the prowl. A dozen species of antelope still inhabits the park, including impala and the statuesque Cape eland. The birdlife is amazing, with some of Africa's greatest concentrations of water birds to be seen along the river, lakeshores and in marshy areas.

HOW TO GET THERE:
Akagera is best explored from the town of Kagitumba on the park's northern boundary, reached from Goma by road via Ruhengen and Kabale – a roundabout journey of some 200 km (125 mi).

WHEN TO GO:
Avoid the rainy months (December, March and April) when many routes become impassable.

DON'T MISS:
The opportunity to camp alongside one of Akagera's lakes, experiencing the true majesty of the African bush as pods of hippos splutter and grunt all day long, large crocodiles sunbathe, and assorted wildlife appears to drink at dawn and dusk – all accompanied by an extraordinary display of colourful birdlife.

YOU SHOULD KNOW:
The country is now generally safe but rural areas bordering the Democratic Republic of Congo or Burundi are best avoided. There have been occasional grenade-throwing incidents in Kigali but these seem to be related to local disputes rather than indicate any sort of general terrorist threat.

Desert-dwelling elephant

Nyungwe Forest

Southwestern Rwanda's Nyungwe National Park is located on the Burundi border south of Lake Kivu. A long-established forest reserve, it gained national park status in 2004 and covers an area of 970 sq km (375 sq mi). It contains the largest tract of montane forest left in East or Central Africa. Nyungwe Forest with its high canopy is a wonderland of 250 types of tree including ebonies and mahoganies, towering tree ferns, tangled vegetation and orchids galore. Notable among the flora is the spectacular giant lobelia. Nyungwe is home to 275 bird species, countless butterflies, 80 different mammals including 13 primate species, plus assorted amphibians and reptiles. The biodiversity within this area is exceptional by African standards but remains threatened by Rwanda's burgeoning population.

There is an extensive network of well-maintained hiking trails in the national park, designed to show off the huge variety of flora and ensure that all the best scenic valleys, waterfalls and viewing points are accessible. Excellent day walks range in duration from one to seven hours, with guides available to lead the way. For those sufficiently seduced to spend two or more days in Nyungwe National Park, Uwinka Tourism Reception Centre has a good rustic rest house and campsite conveniently located at the edge of the forest, providing an ideal base for extended exploration.

The latter option is definitely worthwhile. Birders will have to look hard to spot feathered gems, with 24 specials endemic to this part of the Rift Valley high on the list. These include giant hornbills, great blue turacos and red-breasted sparrowhawks, so the effort is worthwhile. Looking for primates is hugely satisfying, with chimpanzees ever-popular quarry but plenty of other possibilities to pursue, such as huge troupes of Ruwenzori colobus monkeys, grey-cheeked mangabeys and L'Hoest's monkeys.

Early morning mists in the Nyungwe Forest National Park

Volcanoes National Park

In the far northwest of Rwanda, towering to an impressive 4,500 m (14,760 ft), the Virunga Mountains are home to the oh-so-rare mountain gorilla. The flanks of this rugged range are protected by Volcanoes National Park (officially Parc National des Volcans) – Africa's first national park, gazetted in 1925 to protect those priceless primates. The foothills of the Virungas are cultivated, but as soon as ascending trails enter the park visitors are transported to a different world – a rich cocktail of montane ecosystems consisting of bamboo and evergreen forest, heath and open grassland, lake and swamp.

This elevated rainforest is alive with the sound of birds and a bright array of feathered inhabitants rewards those with the patience to wait and watch. Evidence of the forest's elusive population of buffalo and elephant will be plainly visible, a fleeing bush duiker may be glimpsed and rare golden monkeys chatter in the trees above. Arrow-head mountaintops will be visible through gaps in the canopy, beckoning those with the energy and stamina to tackle some of Africa's highest volcanic peaks, including Bisoke (one day) or Karisimbi (two days).

But the park's main attraction is the gorillas, saved from extinction after eminent American primatologist Dian Fossey brought their plight to international attention. She founded the Karisoke Research Centre in the 1960s and devoted the rest of her life to studying these amazing animals. She was murdered at her home in 1985 – probably by poachers – and is buried in the park among a gorilla population that owes its continued existence to her efforts. Seeing these magnificent but gentle creatures up close in their natural habitat is one of the world's most moving wildlife experiences and a fitting memorial to Dian Fossey, whose story was told in the film *Gorillas in the Mist*.

HOW TO GET THERE:
A good starting point is the bustling town of Ruhengeri, in its scenic setting at the foot of the mountains.

WHEN TO GO:
Any time (it was famously said of the Virungas by Dian Fossey that 'they're so high up that you shiver more than you sweat').

DON'T MISS:
The bridge at Musanze, just outside Ruhengeri. It's an extraordinary natural marvel formed from a solidified lava flow dating from the ancient volcanic eruptions that shaped this dramatic area. A worthwhile side trip is to the remote but beautiful Lakes Burera, Ruhondo and Karago – easily visited and appreciated on a daytrip.

YOU SHOULD KNOW:
Permits to visit the mountain gorillas are not cheap, and guided parties are limited to a maximum of eight visitors (and four parties per day), leaving the ORTPN (Rwanda Tourist Board) offices in Musanze after an early morning briefing. Although these magnificent animals may be approached at close quarters – but no nearer than 7 m (23 ft) – gorillas are susceptible to human diseases and anyone with a contagious illness, such as a cold or flu, should not attempt the trip.

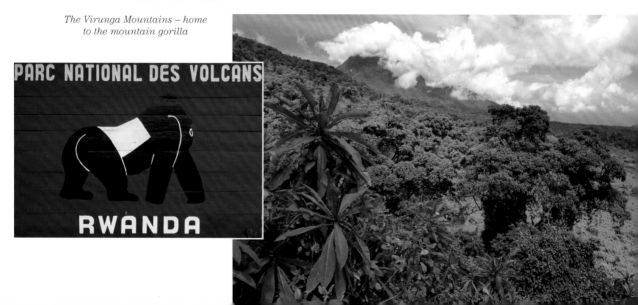

The Virunga Mountains – home to the mountain gorilla

Nankhumba Peninsula

HOW TO GET THERE:
Visitors to tourist lodges either fly in to the Nankhumba Peninsula on a charter or arrive by private launch. It is possible to drive from Lilongwe to the national park in about three hours, with road improvements promising to speed the journey in future (local roads are generally unmade and potholed and can become impassable in rainy season).

WHEN TO GO:
May to October is the prime season for visitors.

DON'T MISS:
Chembe village on Cape Maclear – a fishing community at the end of a dirt road from Monkey Bay with a few basic facilities, offering an ideal opportunity to see how the locals live.

YOU SHOULD KNOW:
As Africa goes, Malawi is one of the safer destinations. But driving – especially at night – can be hazardous, and the many mini-buses that ply for trade are decidedly accident-prone. Malawi is known as 'The friendly heart of Africa' and Malawians welcome visitors warmly.

Malawi is landlocked, but it certainly isn't short of water – the country is dominated by and shares a name with Africa's third-largest lake, which is surrounded by exceptional landscapes characterized by high mountains, plateaux, rocky outcrops . . . and sensational vistas across the continent's most beautiful lake from the rim of the Great Rift Valley. Combined with a vibrant local economy involving bustling towns, traditional villages, lively markets, endless roadside produce stalls and numerous cottage industries, this creates one of Africa's more tempting destinations – a country that is both relaxed and stimulating.

One of the most attractive sections of Lake Malawi's long shoreline is Nankhumba Peninsula at the picturesque southern end of the lake. The peninsula is a serious tourist destination, capitalizing on the lake's undoubted charms. Lake Malawi National Park encompasses the peninsula's northern tip and is a UNESCO World Heritage Site, the citation referring to its importance in the study of evolution as a result of the incredibly varied endemic fish population. The park is also home to important Neolithic sites. At scenic Cape Maclear within the park, upmarket lodges offer the combination of luxury accommodation and the usual watersports (no jet skis allowed, happily). The main settlement is Monkey Bay.

Those fish are the main attraction, providing an extraordinary display of kaleidoscopic colour and seeming entirely devoid of fear, feeding from the hand and swirling boldly around snorkellers. But the lake is (much!) bigger than the park's relative unobtrusive tourist facilities and the Nankhumba Peninsula as a whole remains an achingly beautiful place, with backcountry that contains wildlife like antelope and baboon and a pristine shoreline. The birdlife is abundant – with squabbling fish eagles ruling the roost – and the adventurous traveller can easily find complete solitude in this truly magical place.

Nyika National Park

Malawi's largest national park covers an area of 3,200 sq km (1,235 sq mi) and this unique wild place does just what the name suggests. The translation of *Nyika* is 'source of the water' and the national park is indeed one of the country's most important catchments. It extends across a great plateau in northern Malawi and is a vast granite dome hosting an environment like no other in Africa, consisting of rolling grassy hills interspersed with wooded valleys, surrounded by steep escarpments.

The grasslands are richly endowed with wild flowers, including over 200 types of orchid, and the montane vegetation attracts large numbers of antelopes – which in turn serve as a generous larder for one of Central Africa's most concentrated leopard populations. The occasional lion or elephant may be seen, along with zebra and smaller animals like bush pig or warthog. Over 400 species of bird have been recorded in Nyika National Park. Notable among the latter are the endemic red-winged francolin, wattled crane and rare Denham's bustard.

The park attracts specialist visitors like birdwatchers and landscape photographers, but also makes a superb destination for those who simply want to get away from civilization and enjoy this atmospheric wilderness, which is often shrouded in cloud during the rainy season. There are all sorts of attractions to be found, such as a Neolithic shelter, waterfalls, trout pools and the pretty Lake Kaulime. The area may be explored from park headquarters at Chelina Camp, in the centre of the Nyika Plateau, where the log-cabin lodge provides good accommodation that makes a perfect base. Safaris may be undertaken on foot, mountain-bike or horseback, and 4x4 excursions are the easiest way to see as much as possible of this striking country if time is limited.

HOW TO GET THERE:
Access is by one dirt road branching off the highway to Katumbi border post, some 60 km (37 mi) north of the town of Rumphi. It continues across the plateau (where it delineates the border with Zambia) before reaching Chisenga border post.

WHEN TO GO:
In the rainy season (November to April) to see Nyika's fabulous display of wild flowers.

DON'T MISS:
A side trip to Vwaza Marsh Game Reserve – just 50 km (31 mi) south of Nyiki. This remote reserve is not much visited, but its mopane and miombo woodland provides an exceptional opportunity to view a great variety of animals and rich birdlife.

YOU SHOULD KNOW:
A small 80-sq-km (31-sq-mi) section of the Nyika Plateau (also called Nyika National Park) falls inside Zambia, but there is no road access so all visitors from that side of the border have to travel via Malawi to see Zambia's own small but perfectly formed wild gem.

Getting away from it all in Nyika National Park.

Zomba Plateau

HOW TO GET THERE:
The old 'up' road was a nightmare, but there's now a new paved road to the top of the plateau, well signed from bustling Zomba town, Malawi's former capital (but note that the 'down' road from the plateau is stony and unsurfaced).

WHEN TO GO:
Any time. But be aware that the rainy season is from November to April (although rainfall varies and is heavier on the plateau than around Lake Malawi). The driest months are September and October.

DON'T MISS:
Emperor's View – with one of the very finest viewpoints on a Zomba Plateau over-endowed with wonderful distant views, this crowning glory was presumably named for Queen-Emperor Victoria by 19th-century British pioneers, who undoubtedly had to work much harder to experience this awesome outlook than today's motorist (although, to be fair, many choose to make the scenic hike to Emperor's View instead of driving).

YOU SHOULD KNOW:
Unfortunately, cars left unattended while the occupants explore the plateau are sometimes broken into, so tempting items should be concealed within the locked vehicle.

Mist hangs over the Zomba Plateau.

In the south of Malawi is a great massif that rises to 1,800 m (5,900 ft). It supports vast tracts of cypress, cedar and pine woodland, interspersed with a riot of mixed vegetation. Although there are plenty of animals and birds galore, Zomba is not the place to attract dedicated wildlife-watchers – the animals are shy and, although leopards, bushbuck or baboons may occasionally be glimpsed, the cover is so dense that such events are a rarity. However, one type of impressive sighting is guaranteed – brilliantly coloured giant butterflies are everywhere – and more visible birds include the ubiquitous white-necked raven and green louries with their vivid red underwings.

But the main attraction here is stunning scenery. Colonizing Brits in pith helmets once described the sweeping panoramas to be seen from Zomba Plateau as 'The finest views in the British Empire' and it's breathtakingly apparent why they came to that bold conclusion. Far-reaching vistas overlook Lake Chilwa to the north, Shire River to the west and Mount Mulanje to the southeast.

Most of the plateau is managed by Malawi's Department of Forestry, which is doing a fairly sensitive job that respects the original ecosystem. This means that a good network of dirt roads exists, which is ideal for 4x4 sightseeing excursions around this wonderland of tumbling streams, waterfalls and lakes. Other popular recreational activities are trout fishing in season, hiking and horseback riding. For those tempted to spend more than a day enjoying this unique landscape, there is a luxury hotel on the edge of the plateau, along with a large campsite with facilities like hot-water showers and proper sanitation. Another, more primitive campsite is located on the west side of the plateau, an ideal base for those who like getting away from more obvious tourist bases.

Chimanimani Mountains

This rugged range – part of a chain stretching from Cape Town to the high mountains of East Africa – straddles the frontier between Mozambique and Zimbabwe, mostly falling within the Chimanimani Transfrontier Conservation Area. A national park on the Zimbabwean side is an established destination for organized expeditions, but Mozambique's Reserva Nacional de Chimanimani in Manica Province was only established in 2003 and is as yet undeveloped. It has the country's highest peak – Monte Binga at 2,436 m (7,992 ft) – and offers a number of primitive campsites, staffed by friendly AK-47-toting rangers in smart green uniforms who are happy to offer help and advice. Tourism may be a major contributor to the area's future but for now it is still a truly wild place – with lushly forested slopes that provide the opportunity to explore on foot and highlands that remain a wilderness – that progress (apart from those ubiquitous AK47s) seems to have passed by.

The biodiversity of the Chimanimani Mountains is legendary, but to enjoy their solitude it is first necessary to leave the cultivated areas around villages behind, and avoid many illegal panners working the streams in the hope of finding glinting gold. Local guides are easily found, and essential for everything but the most cursory day hike. For anything longer, it is sensible to hire porters who will act both as guides and carry camping equipment. With their help, it is possible to reach the plateau with its sensational rock formations and far-reaching views, where curious animals such as klipspringers are likely to take a close look at the intruders to their lofty domain. Elephants are quite common lower down, where the forest birdlife is abundant and the butterflies are vivid. Other sights include rock paintings and there are opportunities for canoeing.

HOW TO GET THERE:
With considerable patience and much bumping on unmade roads. From the coast, take the EN1 and – after crossing the Buzi River – turn off the paved road and head for Dombe and thereafter find an entrance to the reserve on the Sussundega road.

WHEN TO GO:
Tropical cyclone season (November to March) is best avoided, as heavy rain is inevitable and widespread flooding not unusual.

DON'T MISS:
The spectacular waterfall of the Muvumodzi River within the reserve (also known as the Martin Falls), plunging dramatically into a deep, rocky bowl.

YOU SHOULD KNOW:
Mozambique's Ministry of Tourism is working with the World Bank to develop a programme of ecotourism that will make the Chimanimanias more accessible, rather than calling for the sort of fairly determined individual expedition currently required to explore this unspoilt wild place.

The Chimanimani Mountains offer some of the most spectacular mountain landscapes in Africa.

Maputo Special Reserve

HOW TO GET THERE:
From Matupo to Catembe by ferry across Maputo Bay, or by paved road to Boane (4x4 transport necessary for the final gravelled stretch from Boane or the South African border post and Ponta de Ouro).

WHEN TO GO:
Any time – temperature and humidity are relatively stable throughout the year. The wet season is November to March but rainfall is heavier in other areas of the country.

DON'T MISS:
The traditional sight of groups of local fishermen netting fish from the shore.

YOU SHOULD KNOW:
Mozambique is generally a safe destination, but health facilities are minimal and local providers do not always accept insurance payments, requiring affected travellers to pay now and claim later. Car-jacking is a threat in Maputo, so drivers should be vigilant in the city and car doors are best kept locked. The reserve itself is considered to be relatively risk free although, as always, caution is advised.

Around 80 km (50 mi) south of Mozambique's capital of Maputo is a world apart from the bustling city with its teeming streets, cultural diversity and fascinating museums. Although sharing its name, the Maputo Special Reserve (formerly Elephant Reserve, a name still widely used) on Santa Maria Peninsula in the country's southern part is an area of outstanding natural beauty forming part of the Lubombo Transfrontier Conservation Area – a grouping of national parks from South Africa, Swaziland and Mozambique itself.

Happily for lovers of wild places, in the aftermath of prolonged civil war Mozambique is some way behind its neighbours in catering for the well-heeled local and international visitors who will eventually transform the national economy. But there's a downside to go with the fact that the reserve therefore remains wild and unspoilt by over-exploitation for tourism (three ecotourist sites planned but as yet unbuilt). That downside is that a 1975 stocking of the reserve from South Africa's Umfolozi Game Reserve introduced a huge population of elephant and rhino that was undone by civil war. Just 200 elephants and no rhinos survived the conflict. However, numbers are now recovering well with a splendid selection of wildlife to be seen – such as expanding elephant herds, hippos, crocodiles, leopards, lions, antelope, zebra, armadillos and red squirrels – within the reserve's sparsely populated 800-sq-km (310-sq-mi) territory. Birds flourish in assorted habitats and there are many rare species, with avian riches attracting birders from all over the world.

Visitors are treated to an extraordinary stretch of pristine coastline on the Indian Ocean with limpid waters offering stimulating diving possibilities. There are also dunes, fabulous beaches and important mango ecosystems. Interior tracts of forest and grassland offer great hiking potential and some splendid wildlife-viewing opportunities.

Quirimbas Archipelago

The Quirimbas Archipelago is a chain of mesmerizing islands.

Northern Mozambique's Quirimbas Archipelago is a mesmerizing chain of 31 islands in the Indian Ocean that contains some of the world's richest coral reefs, supporting a fabulous array of marine life that equals snorkelling and scuba-diving heaven. For non-swimmers, simply seeing the Quirimbas could be the experience of a lifetime. Still, the archipelago's seductive attractions are a relatively well-kept secret and these enchanting tropical islands have never been seriously exploited for tourism and remain a conservation jewel all but untouched by intrusive development – reflected in recently acquired UNESCO World Heritage status and the fact that 11 of the southernmost islands have been integrated into the Quirimbas National Park, established in 2002.

The islands stretch from the coastal town of Pemba up to Cape Delgado and the Tanzanian border, a distance of around 320 km (200 mi). Some are linked to the mainland by coral reefs, sand bars and mangroves. The fortunate few who stray from the beaten track to pay one or more of them a visit are richly rewarded. It won't always be so, for Mozambique's proactive Ministry of Tourism is busy planning a serious campaign to make the most effective economic use of the country's abundant natural wonders, with the buzzword being 'ecotourism'.

It doesn't come much more eco that the Quirimbas. These fine islands – some tiny, some uninhabited, some with lodges built of local materials that hardly seem to intrude on the beauty that surrounds them – are formed of rugged coral punctuated by golden beaches where it is truly possible to feel isolated from the cares of the modern world. Key islands include Ibo, Quisiva and Matemo, which harbour former Portuguese outposts that supplanted pre-colonial settlements – a striking example being Stone Town on Ibo, a monument to Swahili culture over the centuries.

HOW TO GET THERE:
By air direct to Pemba from Johannesburg (a five-hour flight thrice weekly) or Dar es Salaam in Tanzania (a 45-minute flight five times a week). Internal flights from Maputo get to Pemba in the end, via a circuitous route. Thereafter it's a matter of making local arrangements for onward travel to the islands (by boat or light aircraft).

WHEN TO GO:
It's an any-time adventure.

DON'T MISS:
Those who like the Quirimbas Archipelago will also adore the Bazaruto Archipelago, to the south – a national park that has no roads, shops or tourist attractions . . . just breathtaking beaches, pristine waters and stunning coral reefs. Expect to see the fabled dugong, or sea cow, for Africa's largest concentrated population lives here.

YOU SHOULD KNOW:
The small island of Medjumbe has a ruined lighthouse plus a hotel that offers chalet accommodation and a pace of life all its own. Medjumbe time (an hour ahead of the mainland) operates and visitors are ceremonially issued with watches set accordingly.

Kasanka National Park

This is not a national park in the conventional sense, for Kasanka in Zambia's Central Province is operated by a non-profit-making charitable trust that aims to secure the park's biodiversity and make it self-sustaining with the help of carefully managed tourism. The park has assorted habitats – lakes, rivers, swamps, dambos (shallow drainage channels), riverine forest, grassland – and is handsomely endowed with the miombo woodlands characteristic of the area. It is considered to be one of the most picturesque parks in the country.

Despite being relatively small at 450 sq km (175 sq mi), Kasanka is a well-preserved wilderness that serves as a haven for many endangered species – including Sitatunga antelope and blue monkeys from the animal kingdom, plus Ross's lourie and wattled crane from the wonderful world of birds, which here numbers over 400 recorded species. The latter figure underlines the fact that Kasanka has a rich diversity of flora and fauna. There are no vast herds of animals but it's possible to spot a variety of interesting creatures. In addition to the rarities, visitors can look for hartebeest, antelope, bush pig, warthog, duiker, baboon, leopard, waterbuck, reedbuck, hippo, crocodile, otter, elephant, jackal, civet, mongoose and more.

There are three affordable campsites with basic facilities in the park, requiring visitors to bring their own camping equipment. It is wise to check in advance rather than simply turning up, as conditions may preclude camping, or all three sites may be fully booked. It is also possible to stay at one of Kasanka's two lodges, an option which many combine with a trip to nearby Shebill Island Camp in the vast Bangweulu Wetlands. Wasa Lodge and Luwomba Lodges offer the choice of budget self-catering chalets or a more expensive full-board package that includes some seasonal activities.

Punting in a dug-out canoe on Lake Wasa in Kasanka National Park.

HOW TO GET THERE:
By private air charter to a strip in the park. Driving takes around five to six hours from Lusaka or the Copperbelt, using the paved Great North Road to Kapiri town from either direction and turning there towards Mpika and Tanzania.

WHEN TO GO:
If a visit can be made at any time, go for November and December when Kasanka sees a spectacular congregation of several million fruit bats. The least favoured months are January to May.

DON'T MISS:
The opportunity to visit the Livingstone Memorial, marking the spot where the great explorer died in 1873. It is about 30 km (20 mi) north of Kasanka.

YOU SHOULD KNOW:
Petty crime is a problem in Zambia, with bag-snatching, mugging and thefts from parked cars not uncommon. Walking alone after dark is not recommended and there are occasional attacks on tourists in remote areas. However, Kasanka's protected environment is entirely safe.

Lower Zambezi National Park

Still relatively undeveloped, Zambia's newest national park is an unspoilt wilderness that extends to an impressive 4,000 sq km (1,545 sq mi). It lies some 450 km (280 mi) downriver from Victoria Falls, where the mighty Zambezi River crosses the fertile floodplains of the Lower Zambezi Valley. Across the river is Zimbabwe's Mana Pools Reserve, and the two parks combine to create a huge wildlife sanctuary. There is a steep escarpment along the northern boundary of the park, confining most animals to the plain. The river's edge is characterized by lush vegetation, the floodplain is fringed with winterthorn trees and mopane forest, while broadleaf woodland cloaks the surrounding hills.

A canoe safari gets close to a bull elephant.

There may not be as many different animal species in Lower Zambezi National Park as can be found in some other parks, but they are present in vast quantities and this place offers keen wildlife-watchers a unique experience. This involves taking to the water and observing the likes of abundant hippos, large elephant herds, crocodile, impala, buffalo, zebra, kudu, puku antelope and baboons, all seeming relatively unfussed by waterborne intruders, thus allowing canoeists to get very close. The birdlife is exceptional with a huge variety of species to be spotted, including fish eagles, trumpeter hornbill, Meyer's parrot, Lilian's lovebird, crested guinea fowl, black eagle and vast flocks of quelea.

Day safaris are offered by park lodges – guided or unguided – that allow adventurous visitors to drift downstream at a leisurely pace all day, before being spared the need to paddle back by the arrival of the lodge's motorboat as dusk approaches with the welcome offer of a return tow. Several operators run canoeing trips extending to several days, with nights spent at comfortable bushcamps on the banks. Some established lodges and camps offer vehicular game drives or guided walking safaris.

HOW TO GET THERE:
It's possible to drive to the park (using a 4x4) from Chirundu or Luangwa Town. But it's too new to have established vehicle access and most visitors prefer to be picked up from Lusaka or Chirundu after booking in advance with lodge or canoe-safari operators.

WHEN TO GO:
Any time, although April to September are the best months, with June to September being the park's high season.

DON'T MISS:
If there's one place where the cost of booking a bushcamp or safari lodge is justified by the return, this is it – the park has some of the very best in Africa.

YOU SHOULD KNOW:
Fishing (for tiger fish, bream and vundu catfish) is a popular recreational activity in the park and – strangely – the canny locals have discovered that pungent cheap soap is a top bait.

Sesriem Canyon and Sossusvlei

The dunes of the Namib Desert are 30 million years old. Whipped by fierce winds into sharp, undulating ridges like colossal red-and-black waves in a granulated ocean, they cover 32,500 sq km (12,550 sq mi), stretching 300 km (186 mi) north up Namibia's coast from Luderitz, and as much as 140 km (87 mi) inland. Nowhere in that vast region are their changing colours and moods more spectacular than in the alien magnificence of Sossusvlei. These are the tallest dunes in the world, over 300 m (1,000 ft). Just to gaze on them is humbling. Between the hours of dawn and dusk they might be coloured blood red, lilac, palest gold, deep yellow or intense orange like rust; and shadowed by a patchwork of soft blue and green, deepening to ultramarine and black.

Incredibly, the bone-dry Sossusvlei dunes mark the estuary of the Tsauchab River, swamped in mid flow by the encroaching desert. The river evaporates into white clay pans like Dead Vlei and Nara Vlei on the edge of Sossusvlei. Sometimes enough water reaches the pans to provide a mirror reflecting some of Africa's most spectacular views, and to bring the desert alive with flowers and birds. But visitors may not stay here: camping is a 63-km (39-mi) drive 'upriver' at Sesriem. A trail from the campsites leads to the 40-m (131-ft) deep and 1 km (0.6 mi) long Sesriem Canyon, carved over a million years by the Tsauchab River. Even from a few metres' distance, the canyon is invisible among the camelthorn trees and scrub. In many places its walls almost meet overhead, and the pools of water it retains are a magnet for all manner of scrambling desert creatures and birds. To get the best of it, start early in the morning and follow the arcing sun from the gorge up onto the dunes.

Sesriem Canyon

The untouched Skeleton Coast

Skeleton Coast

The Bushmen called it 'The Land God Made in Anger'. To the Portuguese it was 'The Gates of Hell'. The Skeleton Coast used to mean the whole of Namibia's Atlantic coastline. Now it refers to the 20,000 sq km (7,720 sq mi) National Park that protects the northern one third of Namibia's coast, from the Ugab River to the Angolan border. It is an untouched world shrouded in chilling mists and prolonged fog. The cold Benguela Current sweeps north, pushing Antarctic air into the arid African heat. Although it never freezes, the Skeleton Coast is spitefully inhospitable – but it is a sanctuary to fur seals and marine and wading birds for which the nutrient-rich sea is a perpetually full larder. Inland, huge crescent, hummock and transverse dune systems lie between canyons of rust-coloured rock; and in this rainless transition zone desert scrub is watered by the mist. It's the transition that brings so much wildlife to the area. Rare desert elephants live here, with oryx, springbok, giraffe, ostrich, hyena, black rhino and even lion. Most find refuge in the depths of the canyons and dry river beds where the temperature is higher – pursuers and pursued using the foggy world for hunting cover.

Between the Hoanib and Kunene Rivers the Skeleton Coast may only be visited as part of a 'fly-in safari' that must be organized by a government-licensed concessionary. This northern section is where the coast's hostile reputation is confirmed. The shore is littered with long-ago shipwrecks, surreal sculptures of mechanical bones wedged in the sands. Somehow they are simultaneously pathetic and magnificent: failures in a contest with the raw power of unforgiving nature. Yet for some of Africa's most threatened creatures, the harsh struggle to stay alive here is their shield. The dynamism of that wilderness struggle is what brings visitors, and it's worth seeing.

HOW TO GET THERE:
By car to either Ugabmund or Springbokwasser, the only two entrances to the park's southern area; or by pre-arranged 'fly-in safari' to the north.

WHEN TO GO:
Any time. From May to September a strong wind blows the fog further inland, bringing moisture and reviving plant and animal life.

DON'T MISS:
Giving yourself time. The Kunene River harbours turtles and a big colony of crocodiles. Elephant and lion occasionally scavenge on the beaches, but you are more likely to see them and a huge variety of other creatures further inland. The park has over 250 species of birds and, close inshore, there are dolphins, humpback and killer whales besides the seals. Every habitat on the Skeleton Coast is teeming, if only you have time to explore it.

YOU SHOULD KNOW:
The Skeleton Coast is literally a geological jewel. Some of its beaches, especially near Mowe Bay, consist of gemstones polished by wave action. They can include red and maroon garnets, amethysts, quartzes, agate and carnelians. Legend has it that shipwrecked sailors often found alluvial diamonds at their feet – then died of thirst on those interminable beaches, with the wealth of a Croesus in their pockets.

219

Spitzkoppe has the silhouette of a sleeping dinosaur.

Spitzkoppe

HOW TO GET THERE:
By car, on the long gravel turn-off from the road to Henties Bay.
WHEN TO GO:
Any time
DON'T MISS:
The details – birds in the air, and the flora and fauna of the rock formations and the cracks in the massif. Equally important to Spitzkoppe's compelling sense of identity are the various sites of Bushmen rock paintings. The most complex – and complete – are at 'Bushman's Paradise', where you use a chain handhold to clamber up a smooth slope to see them, on the underside of a long rocky overhang.
YOU SHOULD KNOW:
Spitzkoppe is famous among photographers for its fabulous colours and shapes. In Namibia, the massif is considered so beautiful and unusual that images of it inspire a kind of reverence.

On the flat, arid scrub desert of Namibia's coastal plain between Usakos and Swakopmund, Spitzkoppe rears on the horizon as the jagged silhouette of a sleeping dinosaur. Sometimes called the 'Matterhorn of Namibia', the granite massif is the eroded remnant of a volcano that collapsed 100 million years ago. Its twin peaks reach 1,800 m and 1,584 m (5,905 ft and 5,197 ft), but their effect is made much more dramatic by rising, sheer, over 700 m (2,300 ft) above the plain. Wind and rain have sculpted the rocks into weird and wonderful formations, carving out gullies and caves which harbour unusual flora like the yellow butter tree and the poison tree, which oozes a white sap used by Bushmen to poison their hunting arrows. Several sheltered rock faces carry ancient paintings by this indigenous San people.

Spitzkoppe is a magnet for experienced climbers, who over the years have established a system of permanent lines for hikers to pull themselves over rocky obstacles along the various trails. This act of mercy opens up the mountain for less athletic visitors. There are so many trails to so many beautiful, hidden corners, and they cater to every level of fitness. They lead to spectacular views across the plains to the Pondok Mountains (the name comes from the Afrikaans for 'looks like an African hut'), or to vistas along the spine of the Klein Spitzkoppe 10 km (6 mi) to the west. Climbing is much harder than it may look. Even for experts the rock can be too hot to touch, and the round, weathered surfaces defy any sane grip – but outside the summer there are climbing tours to the summit which require spending three nights on the mountain. The less committed will be content with the lower campsites sited in isolated privacy among boulders, with fantastic views and skyscapes.

Sibebe Rock

Swaziland is landlocked by Mozambique to the east and South Africa everywhere else. It's a topographical jigsaw, with highlands predominant in the west, and hot, dry lowlands to the east, both crammed into an area no bigger than Wales in the UK or New Jersey in the USA. In a single day visitors can easily drive from the cool mountains, forests and waterfalls of the highveld, through hilly central grasslands, to the open savannah of acacia and broadleaf and the baking bushveld of stunted thickets, knobthorn and dry riverine forests. Many drive straight through to South Africa, cheating themselves of some of Africa's loveliest landscapes, and missing world-class geological oddities for which Swaziland is famous.

Outside Mbabane, Swaziland's capital at the northern end of the Ezulwini Valley, a gravel road follows the Mbuluzi River as it winds down the incomparable Pine Valley. The villages and rondavel homesteads seem to grow naturally out of this pastoral beauty: it's made for hiking or horse riding. Then quite suddenly, as river and road loop round a protruding bluff of smooth rock, the trees and shrubs fall away to reveal the bald rock crown of a truly massive granite dome pushing into the blue sky. This is Sibebe, second only to Australia's Uluru as the world's largest single rock. Close-to, it's impossible to guess its real size. The colossal granite monolith is only visible from far away, sheer on all sides, and unbroken anywhere except by gullies formed by erosion. It's even more spectacular from its own summit. It feels like being on top of the world, with views (on a clear day) as far east as the great 'big five' game reserves of Hlane and Mkhaya, and to the south, the twin peaks called Sheba's Breasts, the legendary site of King Solomon's Mines. Informally, Swazis call Sibebe Rock 'the tumescence of Swaziland' – and they might not be joking.

HOW TO GET THERE:
By car or bus. There are official 'entrances', but access is permitted across most private land on the perimeter.
WHEN TO GO:
June to November, when the western highlands are drier but cooler.
DON'T MISS:
The short hiking trails on Sibebe Rock (if the summit proves too ambitious), and guided hikes in the vicinity – like the Mlilwane Hippo Trail or the Lion Cavern, celebrated as the oldest known human mine workings, dating back to 43000 BC.
YOU SHOULD KNOW:
Swaziland is sometimes called Africa's last truly traditional kingdom. 'Kingship', personified in the Swazi royal family, is also a mystical notion that informs everyone's daily life and provides the glue securing traditional culture to modern customs. The whole country stops for two major annual rituals – the Incwala, or sacred ceremony of Kingship, and the Umhlanga Reed Dance, in which unmarried girls collect reeds (umhlanga) to make a symbolic windbreak demonstrating their protective loyalty to the Queen Mother, known universally as Indlovukazi, or 'She-Elephant'.

Kgalagadi Transfrontier Park

HOW TO GET THERE:
By light plane, with prior permission, to the South African entrance at Twee Rivieren (Two Rivers); or by 4x4 to one of the park's five entrances.

WHEN TO GO:
Park travel is easiest in winter, between May and September, but at any time travellers can expect extremes of heat and cold. Between November and April rain is irregular, but can cause flash floods in the pans and riverbeds: best for birds.

DON'T MISS:
The Gemsbok Wilderness Trail, Mabuasehube Wilderness Trail, or the Nossob 4x4 Eco Trail, each of which is expertly planned to take in the highlights of different areas and habitats.

YOU SHOULD KNOW:
One of Kgalagadi's useful maxims for visitors is the reminder that 'stopping for little things often produces interesting things that were not apparent'. The actual rules are stricter: visitors must plan their day to reach their destination before sundown. Driving or any kind of travelling at night is forbidden. In the Botswana section of the park, visitors can't even go it alone in a single vehicle: there must be at least two in any travel group.

Formerly known as Kalahari Gemsbok National Park, Kgalagadi is a joint enterprise by Botswana and South Africa on their Namibian border. With only five park entrances from the three countries, visitors may have to jump through a few bureaucratic hoops to fulfil border as well as park controls. Frankly, it's worth every effort to gain access to one of Africa's and the world's great open wilderness areas. In size alone Kgalagadi represents the rare phenomenon of an entire ecosystem with minimal human interference. The park covers 36,000 sq km (13,900 sq mi) of semi-desert savannah, red dune systems, acacia scrub and woodland, and endless sparse tracts of Kalahari couch grass covered in camelthorn bushes. They are landscapes that belong naturally to huge herds of antelope, and visitors will find migrating oryx, blue wildebeest, grey duiker, red hartebeest, steenbok, impala, gemsbok and the occasional rare eland.

Where they go, the predators follow. No campfire is complete without an evening serenade of the grunts, screams, snarls and coughing roars belonging to some of Africa's most famous carnivores, but a much better time to see them is around midday when leopard, cheetah, spotted hyena and the giant, black-maned Kalahari lion can often be found resting in the shade of camelthorn or acacia trees. Mammals of all sizes concentrate in or near the dry courses of the Auob and Nossob Rivers, including meerkat, pangolin (aka the scaly anteater), honey badger and bat-eared fox. The Nossob is also a byword for spotting an unusual variety of raptors, like the bateleur, snake eagle, lappet-faced vulture, pygmy falcon, kestrel, kite and pale chanting goshawk. With 200 other migratory and resident species, the birds participate in Kgalagadi's magnificent annual cycle of regeneration. The visitor's privilege is to be able to follow its wildlife cast of millions, playing out the game of life in all its glorious, gory detail. Amazing.

A lion in Kgalagadi Transfrontier Park

Tsodilo Hills

Rock paintings of the San Bushmen in the Tsodilo Hills

From a distance the desert horizon is a flat line broken by a series of quartzite cliffs rising sheer from the savannah to 410 m (1,345 ft). This is the highest peak in Botswana, and one of four in a line of descending height called the Tsodilo Hills. Standing alone in the western corner of the Kalahari Desert, in Ngamiland near the edge of the Okavango swamps, the hills have a history to match their geological oddity. Alternately baked and scoured by freezing winds, they are the repository of the world's biggest collection of indigenous rock paintings, the summary of 100,000 years of known religious worship and sacred ritual. Throughout that time the Tsodilo Hills have been physical representations of the San Bushmen's spiritual culture. According to height, they are 'the male', 'the female' and 'the child' (with the nameless fourth knoll ascribed to 'the male's first, discarded wife') in the San creation myth, and the resting place of ancestral spirits. Even now, a San guide taking visitors to what is known collectively as the 'Rock that Whispers' will first ask 'permission' from the hill deities to do so.

The 4,500 rock paintings (and thousands of other artefacts) are spread between 400 sites across 10 sq km (3.8 sq mi) of the hills. Most of them, including the best, are on the northern side of 'the female' and, significantly, they are different in style and content from any other known rock art. The feeling of being in a place of mystery and magic can be overwhelming: visitors may come for the archaeology or the cultural aesthetics, but they leave with a profound sense of human indomitability. By investing their enduring faith in these barren, inhospitable and isolated hills, the San Bushmen have created an ark of beauty out of burning hot rock.

HOW TO GET THERE:
By small plane to the Tsodilo airstrip; or by 4x4 on a track just south of Sepupa in the Panhandle region

WHEN TO GO:
Any time

DON'T MISS:
The symbology which challenges presumptions about how long human cultures have been capable of abstract thought. The Tsodilo Hills paintings aren't the only demonstrations of ancient ideas: in one of the rock grottos on 'the female' (from which the gods ruled the world) the stones have been crudely fashioned into a 2-m (7-ft) high, and 6-m (20-ft) long python's head. The python is and has always been central to San culture as the creator of mankind, and the arid stream beds around the hills are held to be the python's tracks, searching for water.

YOU SHOULD KNOW:
Some visitors think it is fanciful to ascribe spiritual significance to four outcrops of rock. Some feel their atmosphere so keenly they cannot bear to stay in the area. Many not only feel the strong emotions that the hills engender, but also report feeling an 'unlooked-for empathy' with the San belief that hunting or causing death of any kind in the vicinity will bring misfortune.

Sehlabathebe National Park

HOW TO GET THERE:
From Lesotho travel on foot or horseback along the Top of the Berg Trail from Sani Top – 40 km (25 mi); or journey by 4x4 or bus from Qacha's Nek to Sehlabathebe village – 100 km (62 mi). From South Africa it's a six-hour trek (on a highly dramatic trail) from Bushman's Nek to the park's Nkonkoana Gate. There are no other ways.
WHEN TO GO:
Any time. Summer rain means frequent thick mists; but it is cold in winter and light snow is common.
DON'T MISS:
Driving the legendary Sani Pass before you start trekking. It's one of Africa's most spectacular mountain roads, a long sequence of banked, hairpin bends. Another route follows the Patiseng River valley up past several Basotho villages to Ha Ramaepho, and the breathtaking views from 3,000 m (9,840 ft) Makoaneng Pass. Both backcountry and park are full of ancient Basotho cultural sites.
YOU SHOULD KNOW:
With a pre-arranged permit, camping is allowed throughout the park. It's the best way to see it, but staying in the villages outside can also be fun.

The Sani Pass, which goes from South Africa to Lesotho, through the Drakensburg Mountains.

If the 'Kingdom of the Sky' has a garden, it is Sehlabathebe National Park. Like the fabled Shangri-La it is an impossibly remote, sub-alpine paradise protected by its average altitude of 2,450 m (8,038 ft) and its position on Lesotho's eastern border with South Africa, on the lip of the Drakensberg Escarpment. A tectonic quirk raised the Sehlabathebe area higher than its surroundings, pushing a very rare outcrop of Clarens formation (cream-coloured) sandstone clear of the Drakensberg basalt which forms southern Africa's highest mountains immediately to the north. Whittled by the Tsoelikane and other tributaries of the nascent Orange River to the west, the sandstone contributes sensational landscapes like near-vertical cliff faces, river gorges, weird rock formations riddled with caves, waterfalls, magnificent promontories looking over plateaus studded with small lakes – and the sandy sediments which fill its valleys and provide the mineral sustenance for some of the planet's loveliest open grasslands. There are marshes and meadows at every altitude, completing the conditions for an unusual range of biodiversity. Game is restricted to rhebuck, eland, baboons, oribi antelope, mongoose, otters, wild cats and jackals, but the birdlife is magnificent, especially in the highest tarns. With all this, and vast skies and distant views, Sehlabathebe makes gods of hikers and riders. There are no fences.

Sehlabathebe is a designated wilderness that shares a boundary with South Africa's uKhahlamba Drakensberg Park, and a position at the southern end of the 300-km (186-mi) Maloti-Drakensberg Transfrontier Project which rings north and east Lesotho. Although visitors bask in the park's remote perfection, the beautiful surrounding backcountry adds to the quality of the experience by reintroducing the human element. The wilderness survives only if the Basotho people can benefit from it. It's possible to drive to the park – but it's far, far more rewarding to trek in through the surrounding Basotho villages.

Tsehlanyane National Park

Small by international standards, Tsehlanyane is the jewel in a much larger environmental scheme, and of growing importance to its ultimate success. The park covers 56 sq km (21.5 sq mi) of the highest and most rugged terrain in the Lesotho Highlands. Set deep in the Front Range of the Maloti Mountains, Tsehlanyane's plunging valleys have an altitude range of 1,940–3,112 m (6,365–10,210 ft) and are predominantly sub-alpine. Their beauty is not exclusive – the whole Maloti range is breathtaking – but it is of rare quality. Tsehlanyane includes one of Lesotho's very few remaining old-growth indigenous forests, and preserving it is proving crucial to the Maloti Mountains' role as a source of pure, fresh water, and to a high level of endemism.

The much larger scheme is the development of the Maloti-Drakensberg Transfrontier Project. Tsehlanyane and its environs represent a massive extension of a biological corridor that now runs for hundreds of miles around northern Lesotho along the Drakensberg range that forms its border with South Africa. It is a fragile ecosystem, challenged by human encroachment of every kind – but it's proving to be a model of sustainable development, benefiting the Basotho people as much as the wildlife. Already visitors to Tsehlanyane can see previously non-existent herds of migrating eland, troops of baboons, grey rhebuck and 20 other frequently sighted medium-sized mammals. Even leopard have returned. Yet Tsehlanyane is not a wholly pristine wilderness. There are still villages dotted about. The Maloti Mountains are full of archaeological sites charting Basotho culture over several millennia. Tsehlanyane's forests include che-che woodland and stands of berg bamboo among local flora and fauna that have direct cultural significance for the Basotho. For visitors, trekking on foot or horseback through such natural beauty, it's a joy to participate in a culture so enthusiastic about living in harmony with nature.

HOW TO GET THERE:
By car along the Hlotse River valley to the park entrance just past Khabo village. Then by hiking or surefooted Lesotho pony.

WHEN TO GO:
Any time – but winter is always cold and snow is not unusual.

DON'T MISS:
Riding. It's the ideal travel mode for the steep hillside trails. Tsehlanyane is full of streams, cascades and rock pools for a super-bracing dip, and a really stunning 39-km (24-mi) trail connects the park with Bokong Nature Reserve, perched on a cliff overlooking the Lepagoa Valley and home of the Lepagoa Falls.

YOU SHOULD KNOW:
Visitors will find a very friendly welcome in Basotho villages. In typically rural areas like this, Basotho people wear trademark blankets in very bright colours – but only tourists wear the traditional, conical, Basotho headgear. Travellers who enter or leave Tsehlanyane by way of Butha-Buthe should pause to see the fossilized dinosaur footprints on the banks of the nearby Subeng River.

Maloti Mountains in the Lesotho Highlands

225

Timbavati Game Reserve

HOW TO GET THERE:
By 4x4 to the Timbavati control gate, or by private charter light plane to an authorized bush strip.
WHEN TO GO:
April to September, when it is drier and cooler.
DON'T MISS:
The 'white lions' of Timbavati. Lion prides in the region carry the recessive gene which can result in an ultra pale-furred lion. Nobody can guarantee seeing one (and there are intervals when none exist), but doing so is the experience of a lifetime. Sometimes whole prides can be 'white'.
YOU SHOULD KNOW:
You can go it alone and drive yourself, staying in excellent government rest camps – but you have to stick to a few, mostly paved, roads and you are not allowed to leave your car. With a guide in a concessionary area, you see much more. However you travel, there is a strict etiquette to going on safari. Most of it is common sense, like not damaging vegetation and trusting your guide or driver to decide how close to get to a pride of lunching lions, but every camp has its own rules and customs.

South Africa's Kruger National Park is an enormous wilderness showcasing Africa's most spectacular wildlife. Timbavati borders the Kruger's central section, one of a number of private concessions along the Kruger's length which benefit from having no fences to hinder game moving freely between them. Timbavati's 680 sq km (262 sq mi) of low bushveld is the meeting place of the mopane woodlands and the Timbavati floodplain. The combination of savannah grasslands and dense shelter makes the region one of southern Africa's best for viewing all kinds of game. Besides the 'big five' of lion, leopard, buffalo, elephant and rhino, visitors are almost certain to see impala, kudu, giraffe, baboons, zebra, monkeys, cheetah, hippos and crocodiles. Early morning and late afternoon safaris are adventures into the real world of dangerous predators – and even from a vehicle it's not unusual to have to back off quickly if an elephant or buffalo feels threatened.

Of course, getting as close as possible to some of Earth's greatest living creatures is the whole point. Timbavati is organized so that it's never crowded, although it can feel like it during the dry season when three or four land rovers are tracking game to the same waterhole. It takes expert knowledge to get the best from going on safari, which means staying at one of Timbavati's private lodges. Some are bushcamps, others are five-star luxury eco-resorts camouflaged in the vegetation next to waterholes for easy viewing. Each has a speciality, like night tours, or tracking lion on foot, or river trips by dug-out canoe among crocodiles and Africa's most dangerous mammal, the hippo. Some are better placed to see the 500 bird species that regularly visit the Kruger and its environs. The joy of Timbavati is that so much variety is on its doorstep.

A young lion cub climbing on its mother.

Madikwe

Between the little town of Groot-Marico in South Africa's North West province and the Botswana border lies one of the country's biggest game reserves. Madikwe includes 750 sq km (290 sq mi) of acacia-studded grasslands and bushveld plains that disappear in a blue haze on the horizon, broken only by outcrops of burnished rock and the occasional solitary hill (called an *inselberg*). It is a transition zone between the desperately arid Kalahari thornveld and the dense forests watered by a permanent river and seasonal wetlands in the foothills of the majestic Dwarsberg Mountains. Madikwe is how travellers imagine the African wilderness, with columns of elephant and buffalo shimmering under a heat haze, and the inky blackness of the night canopy. With its varied terrain it supports a phenomenal number and variety of game. The 'big five' are all there, with the biggest elephant herd outside the Kruger, and of buffalo anywhere; white and black rhinos; cheetah, giraffe, hyena, zebra, kudu, springbok and dozens of other species; and a mixture of desert, plains and wetland species among its 300 birds.

Madikwe's success as a reserve has been bolstered by Operation Phoenix, the world's biggest translocation programme. With the enthusiastic support of its residents, in little more than 20 years Madikwe has seen re-introduced species like wild dog and black rhino flourish and spread as former farm and ranching land was returned to a wilderness that would attract the big herds. Local enthusiasm has been crucial, and one of its cornerstones has been the local desire not just to create South Africa's 'best' reserve, but to make it especially attractive to children. Throughout Madikwe, the camps and lodges make a concerted effort to be family-friendly. The facilities for children (and their parents) are unmatched in any other reserve – and best of all, Madikwe is entirely malaria-free.

White rhinoceros in Madikwe Game Reserve

HOW TO GET THERE:
By 4x4 from Johannesburg – 360 km (224 mi); or Gaborone in Botswana – 28 km (17 mi) to the Abjagterskop reserve gate. This is usually arranged through a lodge concessionary since day visits are not permitted.

WHEN TO GO:
July to September, when sparse vegetation makes viewing easier and animals congregate at the remaining waterholes.

DON'T MISS:
Bringing the children. The guides at Madikwe love explaining things to kids, and most of the camps have special activities for them, including 'game drives' for under eights! But that doesn't mean they will infantilize the safari for adults – it's a measure of the care that has gone into making Madikwe such a winner. And (say it often) the reserve is *malaria-free*.

YOU SHOULD KNOW:
The region of Madikwe is immortalized in the works of Herman Charles Bosman (1905–1951), the South African writer and poet. His most famous story is called *The Mafeking Road*, after the track which runs straight through the reserve. Bosman also wrote – of the contemplative mysticism Madikwe inspires – "It does strange things to you, the Marico moon, and in your heart are wild and fragrant fancies, and your thoughts go very far away." Visitors often feel the same.

Fish River Canyon is one of Africa's most amazing natural wonders.

|Ai-|Ais/Richtersveld Transfrontier Park

HOW TO GET THERE:
By four-wheel drive. Visitors from South Africa must go via the Sendelingsdrift border post, and use the recently reactivated pontoon ferry over the Orange River – or face a 485 km (300 mi) detour!

WHEN TO GO:
April to October. Depending on good rains, springtime (July to October) brings out the full floral splendour of |Ai-|Ais/Richtersveld.

DON'T MISS:
Booking ahead. Numbers are restricted on the Fish River Canyon Trails – Vensterval (four days), Lelieshoek (three days) and Kodaspiek (two days) – to preserve the delicate ecosystem. Ask a local Nama guide to point out the Apollo 11 caves, which contain Namibia's oldest rock paintings, and the 2,000-year-old Khoi rock engravings at sites all over the park. A guide can also explain the importance of *malmokkies*, the cold fog from the Atlantic Ocean that brings moisture to sustain the birds, reptiles and smaller mammals.

YOU SHOULD KNOW:
In the Nama language, |Ai-|Ais means 'burning water', and refers to the thermal springs gushing up into the desert at the place where the Fish River Canyon hike ends.

Nobody does camouflage better than Nature. The unification of Namibia's |Ai-|Ais reserve and South Africa's Richtersveld appears to be the twinning of two equally inhospitable mountainous deserts that face each other across a loop of the mighty Orange River. A closer inspection reveals that the two halves of the Transfrontier Park complete each other to form a single botanical hotspot called the Succulent Karoo biome. The apparently barren landscape of interminable rocky hills scarred by rugged *kloofs* (gullies), dry river beds and valleys filled with immense boulders is a fragile ecosystem adapted to over 1,700 plant species, most of them rare, and over a 100 of which are endemic. As the eye adjusts to the spectacular topography, it begins to take in the enormous variety of life forms it supports. Many are bizarre, like the *halfmens boom* (half-person tree), a 3 m (10 ft) cactus with a crown of leaves like dreadlocks. Wild animals are also numerous, although elusive in Richtersveld's vastness. Even so, hikers will come across klipspringer, springbok and steenbok, baboon, mountain zebra and leopard. The unfamiliar flora attracts 150 specialist bird species, and in the Orange River and some of the larger pools elsewhere, the region has its own endemic fish, like the yellowfish, Orange River mudfish and the sharptooth catfish.

On the Namibian side are two of southern Africa's most amazing natural wonders. One is the hot springs at |Ai-|Ais itself. The other is the second-largest natural canyon in the world. Hiking 90 km (56 mi) of the 166 km (103 mi) Fish River Canyon is one of the great African adventures. There's no marked trail. Hikers take five days to pick their way down the bluffs of the canyon and follow the intermittently flowing Fish River through a chasm with sheer walls 550 m (1,800 ft) high to a world of magnificent, alien beauty.

Royal Natal National Park

Royal Natal National Park was created long before anyone realized the importance of bio-corridors in conserving flora and wildlife. Now it forms part of the mighty uKhahlamba Drakensberg Park, itself subsumed into the Maloti-Drakensberg Transfrontier Project that rings the border between Lesotho and KwaZulu-Natal. As interest shifts towards the grander plan, it's easy to overlook the jewel in the Drakensberg crown: the original nature reserve, Royal Natal.

It is dominated by the Drakensberg Amphitheatre, a wall of rock 5 km (3 mi) long standing 500 m (1,640 ft) straight up from the surrounding plain. Two 3,000-m (9,840-ft) peaks, the Sentinel and Eastern Buttress, guard each end and several large domes rise from the summit plateau. A French missionary christened the highest of these *Mont-aux-Sources* because seven rivers begin here, including the Orange River. It is a spectacular landscape at any level and from every angle. Experienced hikers get the best of it on the two-day, 45-km (28-mi) *Mont-aux-Sources* Trail; although it's possible to drive to the top as well. A network of shorter trails adapted to every level of competence covers the Amphitheatre. One of the most scenic leads visitors boulder-hopping along the Tugela Gorge, through thick forest with stands of yellowwood trees, over flower-studded grassland and up a chain ladder through a rock tunnel to a cliff with an eye-popping view of Tugela Falls. Tugela is one of the world's highest waterfalls, dropping 948 m (3,110 ft) in five distinct leaps. After heavy rain, the flooding Tugela River can tumble in as many as 18 separate cascades from the lip of the Amphitheatre; and in winter they freeze into enormous sculptured ice pillars. Less crowded now, Royal Natal National Park has never been more beautiful – and it has first-class visitor facilities to match.

HOW TO GET THERE:
By car
WHEN TO GO:
Any time
DON'T MISS:
Swimming in the rock bowls at the top of Gudu Falls, then using chain ladders to climb the cliff chimney called 'The Crack' for the reward of seeing the vast panorama of the rugged Drakensberg; return by clambering down the near-vertical 'Mudslide'.
YOU SHOULD KNOW:
Anyone can apply to run the *Mont-aux-Sources* Challenge, an annual 50-km (30-mi) cross-country race usually held in September. Competitors race from the entrance to Royal Natal National Park to the top of the Sentinel peak, and back again. The field is restricted to 250 runners and is popular with 'extreme athletes' – so book early, because there is a waiting list.

The Drakensberg Amphitheatre, Royal Natal National Park

iMfolozi Wilderness

HOW TO GET THERE:
By car, either to a lodge, or as a daytrip in the Hluhluwe section. iMfolozi Wilderness may only be entered on foot, on horseback, or in a canoe on the White and Black iMfolozi Rivers.

WHEN TO GO:
Any time is excellent for birdwatching. Game-viewing is best between May and August.

DON'T MISS:
The guided walking trails – Emoyeni Mpila, Enkulu and Masinda Ncane – led by local community members who use each one to try and impart different aspects of the meaning of 'wilderness' while taking visitors up close and personal to startlingly 'wild' animals. Hearing and smelling carnivorous predators moving through the hot grasses before your eyes is dangerously thrilling.

YOU SHOULD KNOW:
Winter temperatures can change rapidly, so wear layers of clothing. Children under 14 may not be permitted on certain trails or night safaris. Take precautions against malaria.

Both iMfolozi and its neighbour Hluhluwe had been game reserves for a century when they were officially amalgamated as the 960-sq-km (370-sq-mi) Hluhluwe-iMfolozi Game Reserve in 1989. Game conservation had not always been completely unselfish: iMfolozi (formerly Umfolozi) was once the private hunting precinct of King Shaka Zulu, and both sections have been threatened by hunting warriors as well as poachers. Hluhluwe in the north is more mountainous, broken by canyons, fast rivers and tropical forests filled with the colours of exotic birds. Its hills and dense shrubbery are the ideal habitat for black rhino, which thrive here. To the south, iMfolozi flattens into a wilderness of acacia-dotted savannah and undulating, thicket-cloaked hills squeezed between two branches of the iMfolozi River.

It is predator and big game country. iMfolozi Wilderness is (relatively) crammed with Africa's biggest and best, and in numbers that make seeing them all but guaranteed. The reserve is famous as a sanctuary for both black and white rhino, and visitors staying at the various park camps and lodges can expect game drives and guided trail safaris to the hides overlooking wilderness pans and waterholes to which all wildlife must come. Elephant, lion, cheetah, leopard, hyena, buffalo, warthog, wildebeest, baboon and jackal pass in a pageant of African splendour. At any time on the savannah they may be joined by zebra, giraffe, waterbuck, nyala, kudu, bushbuck and great herds of impala. The grasslands themselves harbour wild dog, meerkat and dozens of smaller species, and everywhere colourful tropical birds fill the air or patrol the mudflats round the waterholes and river banks. At iMfolozi it really is possible to believe in the notion of an ark of creation. In conjunction with Hluhluwe, the reserve offers the greatest concentration of easily visible big game in Africa.

Burchell's zebra

Kosi Bay

Fish traps in Kosi Bay

In the northeastern corner of Maputaland, on the border with Mozambique, Kosi Bay sustains an African microculture that has survived there for over 700 years. Kosi Bay is inhabited exclusively by Maputaland's three oldest existing communities of kwaDapha, eMalangeni and Nkovukeni peoples, members of the Tembe tribal group indigenous to the area. They live in symbiotic harmony with the 12-km (7.5-mi) long system of Kosi Bay's four lakes, which they maintain as the fundamental element of their very existence.

It is a fragile ecosystem. The chain of lakes is connected by a series of channels that lead to the most pristine estuary in South Africa – a sandbar-choked lagoon with just one narrow exit into the Indian Ocean. High tides constantly refresh the system, and the differing salinity of each lake supports a colossal variety of plant life on its banks, including rare forests of raffia palm, five mangrove species, figs, orchids and papyrus. The lakes themselves are strung with a web of fish *kraals*, sited to make the most of every twist in the watercourse and every flood and eddy in the water itself. The fish are so plentiful that Kosi Bay is known as 'the aquarium', and its crystal-clear waters are great for snorkelling and scuba-diving. However, even fishing can be a risky business. Zambesi sharks come up the channels, and hippos and crocodiles live among its marshes, reed beds and overhanging swamp forests. Lots of them. The forests are also home to bushbuck, duiker and several kinds of monkey, and the variety of the terrain brings some of the world's rarest and most beautiful birds in a rainbow of colour to its wetland splendour.

Kosi Bay has the endlessly fascinating charm of undisturbed nature at its most subtle. It is stunning, and deserves to be the destination of choice of every visitor to Africa.

HOW TO GET THERE:
By 4x4, slowly and carefully
WHEN TO GO:
Any time – but in December and January loggerhead and leatherback turtles come to the beaches to lay their eggs; and humpback whales pass close inshore on their way to calve off Mozambique.
DON'T MISS:
Birds to set your imagination ablaze, like the bluemantled flycatcher, pinkthroated longclaw, crab plover, African finfoot, Pel's fishing owl and hundreds more.
YOU SHOULD KNOW:
Visitor numbers are restricted, and permits are necessary both to visit and to fish (take-and-return). But with Tembe Elephant Reserve on its doorstep (home to the 'big five' and a lot more), making the effort to see Kosi Bay is doubly worth it. Technically, Kosi Bay is part of the iSimangaliso Wetlands World Heritage Site centred on St Lucia Bay much further south – but that's as much as they have in common. Note that Kosi Bay is a high-risk malaria area.

Tsitsikamma National Park

HOW TO GET THERE:
By car along Route 62, a tiny road passing the edge of the Formosa Nature Reserve, reminiscent of the USA's Route 66 in Arizona and New Mexico. It is lined with a string of small towns preserved since the 1940s and 1950s. Stop and hike into the wilderness.

WHEN TO GO:
Any time

DON'T MISS:
The Tsitsikamma range rises suddenly east of the Keurbooms River north of Plettenberg Bay, and the area is particularly rich in colourful birds like the giant kingfisher, Knysna lourie, Knysna woodpecker, and sunbirds galore. Head for the mountains' highest peak, 1,675-m (5,495-ft) Formosa, for glorious views over Nature's Valley and the fertile coastal forest.

YOU SHOULD KNOW:
Tsitsikamma means 'place of many waters', and was named by the Khoi San indigenous people of the region. The National Park and the Tsitsikamma Mountains are full of ancient Khoi cultural sites, including caves, shell middens and rock art.

A beautiful bay on the Cape Garden Route

Most South Africans think of Tsitsikamma as an eco-playground and adventure centre for extreme sports, with Tsitsikamma National Park as its heart. The park includes a marine section extending 5 km (3 mi) into the Indian Ocean, and an 80-km (50-mi) stretch of coast that forms part of the Cape Garden Route, internationally celebrated for its rugged beauty and colourful flora and fauna. Tsitsikamma Forest sits on a 200-m (656-ft) high, thickly forested plateau rising sheer from the waves, bounded by the Bloukrans River to the west and the Eerste River to the east. Its owes its conservation to the development of trails and facilities for mountain-biking, group hiking, bungee-jumping (Bloukrans Bridge over the Storms River gorge is the highest bungee jump in the world), quad bikes, scuba diving, canopy ziplining and trail-driving – yet wildlife flourishes and Tsitsikamma's beauty remains legendary. Visitors love its setting between the ocean and the Tsitsikamma Mountains, assuming both belong to the National Park. They look, but they seldom see.

The Tsitsikamma Mountains are a true wilderness with no formal trails or activities. Their solitude is enhanced by their location within the Formosa Nature Reserve, which itself lies between the remotest part of Tsitsikamma National Park and the Bavvianskloof Wilderness Area inland towards the Great Karoo. The only crowds are of birds which fill the rich afromontane forests, ravines, river banks and towering ferns and shrubs of the wet *fynbos*. Near the pools below mountain cascades there may be bushpig or blue duiker, leopard or elephant; or more likely, butterflies and amphibians and smaller mammals.

The name 'Tsitsikamma' is used to refer to so many other geographical delights that few people realize how incredibly isolated the Tsitsikamma Mountains really are – or how very extraordinary it is that such a pristine region of Africa could still exist untouched, so close to one of the country's major tourist attractions.

Eastern Cape – The Wild Coast

The remote Wild Coast

Not so long ago South Africa's apartheid culture banished 'unwanted blacks' west and north of the Kei River, creating the semi-autonomous Transkei, an unloved territory deprived of economic opportunity and subsidy. For decades Transkei was ignored as a deeply rural backwater, while the rest of South Africa's beautiful Cape coast was heavily developed in the name of local and international tourism. Known as 'The Garden Route', it's still beautiful – but Transkei's pristine coastal dunes, beaches and bays are both beautiful and empty. Rolling hills and grasslands reach back from the rock cliffs and dune systems. Aloe groves fill deep ravines. Dense forests are folded into the land, lining its rivers and dramatic, tidal estuaries. For roughly 250 km (155 mi) from the Great Kei to the Mtanvuna River, the Wild Coast is a gift of nature, unpolluted by light or noise, and accessible only to those willing to hike or ride a horse to get there.

The only communities are the long-established thatched rondavels of fishermen, and the occasional backpacker lodge or small hotel, managed and owned by local people. When democracy turned South Africa on its head, the Xhosa communities of the Wild Coast quickly realized the value of preserving their natural asset intact. Nowhere else in the world is there such an idyllic coastline with a benign, all-year climate, and still virtually undeveloped. The Wild Coast does include several small nature reserves like the tiny Silaka Reserve which protects an enclave of towering forest and lush grasslands; but most are like the Hluleka Reserve south of Port St Johns, useful signposts to areas of unspoilt natural beauty and tranquillity. It's an addictive combination and visitors will discover that the more they entrust themselves to local knowledge about the Wild Coast, the more they will be enriched by its isolated charm.

HOW TO GET THERE:
On foot or horseback. Access by 4x4 is strictly limited – and unlike most other places in South Africa, it isn't at all easy just to 'fly in' for the day or weekend.
WHEN TO GO:
Any time
DON'T MISS:
The coastal hike from Coffee Shack past Baby Hole and Hlungwane Waterfall to the spectacular 'Hole in the Wall' – a pierced rock formation in which crashing waves set up a rhythmic slapping. Closer to Mthatha, the regional capital, Luchaba Nature Reserve is a series of wetlands, grasslands and forest glades that explodes with birds and wildlife. For isolated beaches try Mbotyi in Pondoland.
YOU SHOULD KNOW:
Nelson Mandela was born in the Wild Coast region of the Eastern Cape. It is the Xhosa heartland, and Xhosa is the majority first language. The more visitors know of Xhosa traditions and customs, the more they will understand Mandela – and vice-versa.

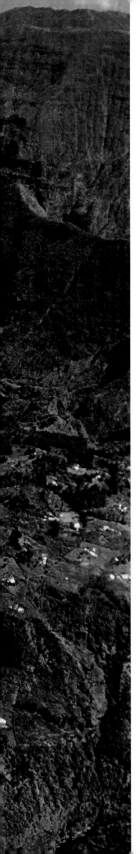

Cirque Mafate, Réunion

Conan Doyle would recognize it as his *Lost World*, accessible only by helicopter or long, hard trek. Summit peaks of bald rock lance the tropical sky, almost strangled by a cloak of thick forest and green jungle that plunges down to absurd, handkerchief-sized clearings between the mountains. Separated by huge crags, ravines and waterfalls, the isolated clearings are connected only by difficult trails that wind through tumbled boulders overrun by rainforest vines and giant ferns. The Cirque Mafate is the Indian Ocean volcanic island of Réunion's 'island within an island', one of a 'three-leaf clover' of adjacent calderas (*cirques*) in the north of Reunion (the only active volcano is in the south), each differing radically from the others and from the rest of Reunion. Cirque Cilaos is the most developed. Cirque Salazie is the most exuberantly florescent, and famous for the perfect straw to make straw hats. Mafate is the most remote, protected by inaccessibility. It has always been so: it was untouched until it became the refuge for a few maroons centuries ago. Eventually some stayed, founding the eight *ilets* ('islets', or villages) on the only flat ground they could clear between the almost sheer mountain walls. Each has a different character, although the biggest (La Nouvelle) has only 150 residents. To hike between them, succinctly placed in staggering landscapes of rock and sky and falling water, is to enter enchantment. There is a tamarind forest where the trees grow to 20 m (66 ft), bent by wind and covered in trailing bearded capuchin. Grass-covered ledges skirt precipices, and swaying bridges cross fearsome gorges. Every turn holds a surprise and, with a Mafate guide, every trail becomes a jaw-dropping adventure into raw wilderness.

The incredible Cirque Mafate

HOW TO GET THERE:
By helicopter or on foot
WHEN TO GO:
Any time
DON'T MISS:
The Creole culture that persists in Cirque Mafate. It includes a relaxed version of French café culture, and several *ilets* are centred on the *bonhomie* of curiosity and conversation in the communal cafe. Join in to find a congenial guide, willing to take you to places like Ilet Aurere at the foot of Piton Cabris, connected to Ilet a Malheur via a hair-raising bridge over the Bemale gorge.
YOU SHOULD KNOW:
The hiking is world-class, with or without a guide. Being French (Réunion is a *Departement d'Outre Mer*, or Overseas Territory) Mafate trails are marked using the *Grande Randonnee* system.

Ranomafana National Park

HOW TO GET THERE:
By the scenic road from
Antananarivo, 400 km (250 mi) to the
park entrance; then on foot with a
compulsory (and necessary) guide.
WHEN TO GO:
Any time
DON'T MISS:
The unique plants and wildlife at the
very top of Mount Maharira in the
south of the park, found only in this
one spot. In general, Ranomafana
bombards the visitor's sense of
wonder with the frequency of rare
wildlife sightings. Night walks
between September and May are
especially good; with a torch it's easy
to pick out the frogs, chameleons,
sportive and mouse lemurs, dazzling
moths, seven species of tenrec, two
of mongoose, and hundreds of other
nocturnal species.
YOU SHOULD KNOW:
Visitors are not allowed to enter
Ranomafana's core wilderness at
night – so 'night walks' take place
along the perimeter trails through the
rainforest. In the context of the
buzzing tropical darkness, night
walks like this are much more
adventurous than they might sound.

When Madagascar split from the African continent it became a living laboratory of evolution and diversity. Isolation prevented almost all forms of species exchange, so that 90 per cent of its flora and fauna is now endemic and exclusive. Yet four fifths of all Madagascar's landmass has been stripped and ransacked for short-term commercial gain. Rainforest once covered the coastal flatlands that now produce just a few corporate export crops like coffee, and more is disappearing as Malagasy farmers are forced to farm on higher ground. Ranomafana National Park protects the best of what's left. About 60 km (40 mi) east of Fianarantsoa, Ranomafama is proof of the richness of the rainforest that once extended along the whole of Madagascar's east coast.

The National Park owes its existence to the golden lemur. Its discovery in 1986 prompted research which revealed 30 species of lemur monkeys, and 60 more in the extended lemur family. Some are really bizarre. The indri has panda markings and somersaults from tree to tree, wailing like a humpback whale. The aye-aye is the stuff of nightmares, with bat's ears, teeth that never stop growing, and a Scrooge-like long skinny finger that enables it to perform the role of a woodpecker where no woodpeckers otherwise exist. Ranomafana's montane rainforest covers 416 sq km (160 sq mi) of teeming wilderness at altitudes between 400–1,200 m (1,310–3,940 ft). Watered by dozens of streams feeding the Namorona River (which crashes out of the eastern escarpment in spectacular falls close to the park entrance), it nourishes more orchid species than in the whole of Africa and flora and fauna like nowhere else on Earth. It is full of colour and beauty, and endlessly exciting encounters with strange life forms: there is no more productive wilderness on the planet.

A female red-bellied lemur

Tsingy de Bemaraha

Just getting in is the hard part, like crossing Manhattan by having to climb up and over each skyscraper in the way. The *tsingys* of western Madagascar are plateaux of karst limestone undercut by groundwater into cavern systems and tunnel fissures, and simultaneously eroded from the top. Collapsed caverns form slot canyons up to 120 m (395 ft) deep with sheer rock walls cracked into a series of razor-sharp pinnacles. Crammed together so tightly they are impassable, *tsingys* (Malagasy for 'where you can not walk barefoot') are labyrinths of jagged rock edges and fluted spikes.

Entering the Tsingy de Bemaraha may be like crossing sky-high fences topped with broken glass, but it's not all bad. The dissected limestone extends over much of the 1,519-sq-km (586-sq-mi) Bemaraha World Heritage Site of untouched forests, lakes, rivers, grasslands and even mangrove swamps. Over half is a 'Strict Nature Reserve', accessible only for research – but the whole region is a biofortress protected by its impenetrable geography. It's full of unknown, unnamed flora and fauna, besides a legion of known species endemic not just to the reserve, but often to specific altitudes on specific pinnacles. The forest crams into the spaces at the foot of each *tsingy*, often creating its own microclimate, and three or four distinct habitats chart its height and exposure to the extreme heat and humidity. These are magic mini-worlds, variants of Bemaraha's greater ecology – but travellers willing to risk its real dangers (just to stumble is to be lacerated) will find lemurs, amphibians, butterflies and birds among wildlife and landscapes that simply don't exist anywhere else. Lemurs at Tsingy de Bemaraha are dominated by the troops of acrobatic sifaka adapted to balancing on razors – and there's a lemur species with long legs and a silly walk named after the British comedian, John Cleese.

An aerial view of tsingys

HOW TO GET THERE:
By 4x4 from Morondava – 150 km (93 mi) or one day, with luck; by chartered plane from Antananarivo to Antsalova, near the reserve; or by *pirogue* (dugout canoe) with a tour expedition on the Manambolo River.

WHEN TO GO:
April to November (closed during the rainy season December to March)

DON'T MISS:
The short trail on Great Tsingy, one of the two limestone formations accessible to visitors, goes deep into the 'forest of dagger blades', crossing the pinnacles on hair-raising rope bridges; but a river expedition up the spectacular Manambolo Gorge combines the greatest variety of wildlife-spotting opportunities (like the world's only 'cave crocodiles') with an introduction to indigenous Vazimba culture as well as an easier path into the *tsingy*. Within the park the two- or three-day Anjohimanintsy Trail takes in the highlights of *tsingy* endemism.

YOU SHOULD KNOW:
The *tsingys* cannot be underestimated. One hiker who fell described the damage 'like being flensed', and even the stoutest climbing boots get lacerated. On the other hand, Tsingy de Bemaraha is the most fascinating of all Madagascar's marvellously alien wildernesses.

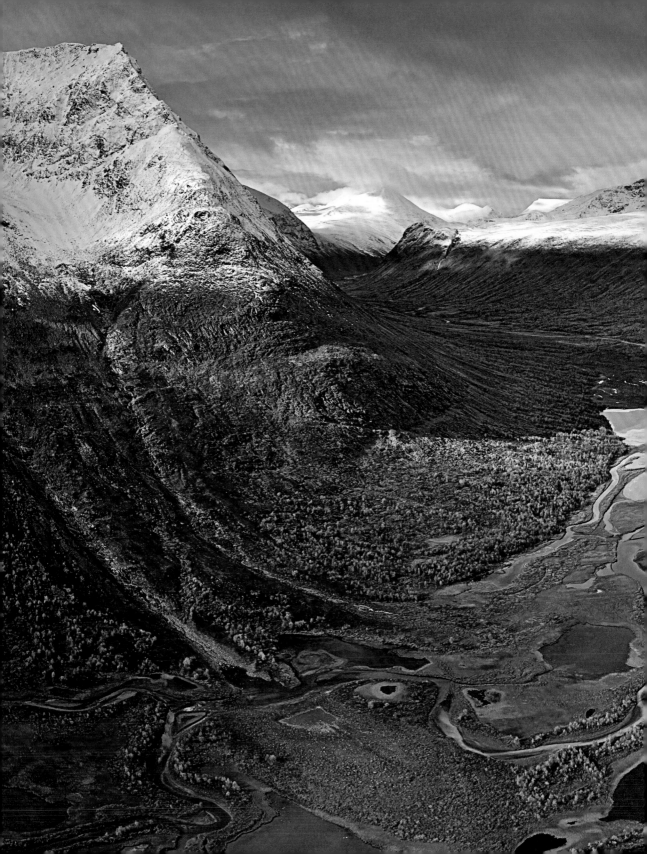

EUROPE

Hornstrandir

Like a barnacle-encrusted Neptune's triton, the three peninsulars of Iceland's West Fjords region look on the map to be stuck haphazardly to the rest of the country, connected only by a narrow isthmus. The region is as isolated as it looks – and Hornstrandir, at the tip of the most northerly 'prong', is the most remote and solitary of all. It has a coastline out of all proportion to its actual size, made up of deeply incised fjords of widely differing character. The variety – of chilling precipices of black rock, grassy slopes tumbling down to sandy coves, wave-smashed pinnacles and beaches formed from crushed shells – lends itself to constantly evolving marine landscapes that change according to both the weather and the shape-shifting illusions of its spectacular topography. Inland, Hornstrandir's majestic cliff formations are backed by vivid-green grasslands. Everywhere, vistas across lakes and streams to faraway promontories and snow-touched peaks are also reminders of the austerity that living creatures here must endure. It takes a full summer for the ice of the previous winter to melt – so every blade of grass and every field mouse survives on the edge, and visitors need to be hypersensitive to scuffing mosses that may have taken years to root properly. Ungrazed for decades, rare botanicals flourish among Hornstrandir's 260 flowering plants and ferns. Once polar bears roamed here; now it's the domain of arctic foxes and

huge colonies of eider ducks, the sea eagle and the screams of seabirds raging against the wind.

Hornstrandir is about purity. It is free from all man-made pollution. The colours of the sky and land are more vivid and more subtle. It's beauty is a heart-wrenching happiness of living creation going on all around – being. Go there. It's hard work, but you will rejoice.

Hornstrandir's majestic cliff formations are backed by vivid-green grasslands and wildflowers.

Thingvellir

A view across the stunning rift valley of Thingvellir

Thingvellir means 'plains of parliament', and it is where Iceland instituted the world's first legislative assembly, the Althing, in the year 980. As a geographic metaphor for democracy, it could hardly be bettered. Thingvellir is a broad, flat plain big enough for any size of public gathering, fringed by a high ridge to the west from which any speaker can be seen and heard. Far beyond the green plain, touched with glistening lakes and rivers, blue mountains blur into the mists. It is a majestic vista with the kind of open natural beauty that inspires visitors to optimism and a sense of reverence – and that's an opinion voiced and written down by visitors to Thingvellir for a thousand years.

Geologically, Thingvellir is just astounding. It is a major rift valley set out like a textbook illustration of plate tectonics. It is where the North American and Eurasian plates drift apart – visibly. A small Natural History Exhibition with an overview of the whole valley explains the significance of the shield volcanoes, glaciers, lava fields and the 114-m (374-ft) deep Lake Thingvallavatn spread below; and visitors can walk down one of the largest faults, Almannagja, to the Oxararfoss waterfalls. Most of the lake's water flows out through Flosagja and its tributary fissures to the east. The greatest adventure at Thingvellir is to go 'fissure diving' in Silfra, one of the world's top-ten dive sites. It is literally the crack in the Earth's crust between the plates, and divers swim 'from Europe to America' between the two faces of rock, wafted effortlessly along on the gentle current. Silfra is 40 m (130 ft) deep in open water, and 60 m (197 ft) in its side caves. Below the surface, the clear water turns a surreal, bright blue. Non-divers may prefer to discuss Viking politics while basking in Thingvellir's hot springs.

HOW TO GET THERE:
By car or bus
WHEN TO GO:
Any time (note that the weather has no influence on fissure-diving).
DON'T MISS:
Exploring the geology of the fissures along Thingvellir's western rim, and along the water margins and meanders of the Oxara River just below it.
YOU SHOULD KNOW:
Thingvellir is more than a nature conservation area. Officially it is a 'protected national shrine'. Its unique status derives from the Logberg, or 'Law Rock', from which the 'Law Speaker' proclaimed the laws of the Icelandic Commonwealth. He was supposed to memorize the laws, and was given three years to recite them all; but he had to recite the procedural rules at each summer gathering. The original Logberg was the 'Spongin', the long spit of lava between the branches of the Flosagja fissure.

241

Surtsey

Iceland grows about one inch wider each year as Europe and North America continue to pull apart. Tension between the two tectonic plates creates a weak fault line in the earth's crust which cracks under pressure of the welling core magma. Over tens of millions of years the process threw up the submerged mountain chain called the mid-Atlantic Ridge, and pushed Iceland above sea level. Surtsey, newest of the 45 rocky outcrops of the Vestmannaeyjar (Westmann Islands) off Iceland's south coast, is a rare surface demonstration of our planet's dynamic fundamental geology. In June 1963, fishermen saw the sea boil as fiery lava broke the surface, vented from a volcano that rose 130 m (426 ft) from the sea floor in a day, and continued to challenge ice with fire for nearly four more years. By then Surtsey had grown to 2.8 sq km (1.1 sq mi) of still-smoking lava, but although it was already being nibbled by wave and wind, it was untouched by human intervention. In fact, since its birth, only scientists have been permitted to set foot on it, to take advantage of the unrivalled opportunity to chart both its raw geology, and its gradual colonization by coastal flora and fauna. It is an utterly pristine work of nature, in all its forms of development.

Visitors may be forbidden on Surtsey but the other Westmann Islands were formed by the identical process, and Heimeay suffered its own volcanic eruption in 1973. Side by side, visitors can compare the newly created terrain of crusty lava with the beautiful, austere, sub-arctic landscapes into which it might mature. It's already happening on Surtsey. By boat (and the smaller the better), it's quite easy to study the colonizing vegetation and tentative animal life – and to enjoy it at least by analogy on Heimeay, so close by.

HOW TO GET THERE:
By air from Reykjavik, or air-taxi from several points along the coast to Heimeay; or by ferry from Thorlakshofn. Small boats for island-hopping can be hired on Heimeay.

WHEN TO GO:
June to September

DON'T MISS:
Kittiwakes, puffins, razorbills and guillemots wheeling round the caves, cliffs and sea-stacks of volcanic rock between the Westmann skerries and islands. On Heimeay, hike up Eldfell past steaming fissures and vents to the brilliantly coloured mineral deposits at the top.

YOU SHOULD KNOW:
Surtsey was named for Sutur, the Norse giant of fire. Its original eruption blasted columns of ash 9,150 m (30,000 ft) into the sky to the accompaniment of non-stop lightning storms. Travellers are asked to applaud this demonstration of Icelandic mythology and not reveal that volcanic ash clouds create electrical charges by friction, just like clouds of vapour.

A volcanic crater on Surtsey Island

242

Thorsmork National Park

Thorsmork is Iceland's sacred, hidden valley. For at least a thousand years it has been dedicated to Thor, the Norse god of thunder and lightning. Thorsmork means 'Thor's Woods', and in a country that plundered all but one per cent of its trees for firewood, Thorsmork's forested beauty confirms its continuing status. It is approached across 30 km (19 mi) of lichen-covered gravel cut by the myriad shallow channels of the Markarfljot River, braided with its tributary glacial streams. They converge where the mountains rise up on either side into the glaciers of Tindfjallajokull and Eyjafjallajokull. As the river turns north through the hills, it reveals an outlet finger of the Gigjokull spur glacier pushing down a side-gully into a steel-blue lagoon, and magnificent box canyons like Stakkholtsgja gorge, where the towering rock walls narrow to the feathery waterfall at its far end. Another turn in the river and suddenly Thorsmork opens out, an oasis of green vegetation in the rain shadow of the huge glacial and volcanic complexes of Eyjafjallajokull and Myrdalsjokull – both ice caps over major volcanoes. Its microclimate is warmer and less windy than its surroundings. Birds fill the air, attracted by the lichens, mosses, alpine flowers, grassland and birch trees that soften the dynamic geology of volcanic glaciers, moraine and lakes.

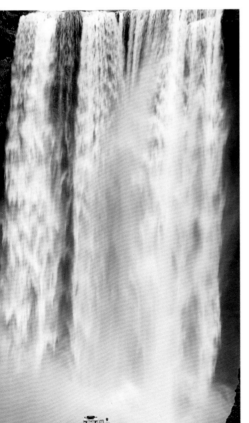

Thorsmork is an outstanding destination for hiking and, especially, horse riding. Icelandic horses deal with fording rivers better than any vehicle, besides doing minimal damage to the ultra-fragile ecosystem. The most popular trek is from the lush valley up across the rocky fastness of Fimmvorduhals Pass between the glaciers, to the glorious 60 m (197 ft) waterfall of Skogarfoss near the coast. The descent passes 20 major cascades before the main falls' sheer drop over the escarpment – where a double rainbow forms in the spray every time the sun shines.

HOW TO GET THERE:
By 4x4, with a driver experienced in fording rivers, from Reykjavik –160 km (100 mi) away. Horses are available locally.
WHEN TO GO:
June to September/October
DON'T MISS:
The *Laugavegurinn* or 'Hot Spring Trail' to Thorsmork from the north, including the colourful rhyolite area near Torfajokull and its 11 obsidian lava fields, to Lake Alftavatn (the 'Lake of the Whooper Swans') and the ultimate wilderness beauty of Thorsmork, seen from the multiple-river plain near Fremri-Botnar.
YOU SHOULD KNOW:
In March 2010, after 200 dormant years and without any warning at all, two brand-new volcanic fissures several hundred metres long opened on the Fimmvorduhals Pass. The eruption sent molten lava spilling into the Hrunagil and Hvannargil gorges, transforming the Krossa River into a torrent of meltwater, and threatening Thorsmork. Authorities evacuated the entire area. Scientists fear it could trigger a future catastrophic eruption of Katla, the colossus buried under the Myrdalsjokull icecap overlooking the pass – but instability is the chief characteristic of Iceland's vulcanology. Visitors should be aware of the risks and be prepared for the worst.

Skogarfoss waterfall

Lysefjord

HOW TO GET THERE:
By bus or car to various highlights along Lysefjord's rim; by boat from Stavanger, or summer ferry from Lauvik, to Lysebotn

WHEN TO GO:
Any time – but there are many more boats, buses and functioning facilities between June and September.

DON'T MISS:
Sailing as close as possible to 400-m (1,312-ft) high Hengjanefossen, plunging down the cliff face. The waterfall looks good from the north rim, too, but the major shoreline attraction is Preikestolen (Pulpit Rock), a 600-sq-m (6,460-sq-ft) flat mountain ledge towering 604 m (1,981 ft) above Lysefjord. Drivers will appreciate Lysevegen, a spectacular road with 27 hairpin bends rising 900 m (2,950 ft) out of Lysebotn. It is closed in winter.

YOU SHOULD KNOW:
Victor Hugo visited Lysefjord in 1866. Its atmospheric menace inspired sections of *Les Travailleurs de la Mer* (*The Toilers of the Sea*), in which a blighted Guernsey seaman seeks his dream among the malevolent rocks of a fictitious Channel reef. Hugo declared that Lysefjord was 'the most terrifying of all ocean reefs' – and some of his fictional descriptions exactly fit the reality of the rock formations you can see there. For once, Hugo didn't have to depend on poetic licence.

The two southernmost of Norway's major fjords meet near the 'oil city' of Stavanger. Lysefjord heads eastwards off Hogsfjord, through a cleft in the rock like the Pillars of Hercules in the Bosphorus. It looks even more like a creation of the gods as it suddenly opens up a dramatic vista along most of its 40 km (25 mi) length, revealing walls of rock facing each other over just 2 km (1.5 mi) of water, and rising to peaks over 1,000 m (3,280 ft) high. The effect of the sheer slabs of light-coloured granite (*Lyse* means 'light') is magnified by the water's other-worldly shade of deep green where it plunges to its maximum depth of 422 m (1,384 ft). Lysefjord was carved by brutal glacial action into the kind of austere landscape that inspired Norse sagas. Its sides are so steep and inhospitable that nobody can live there, and nobody tries. That means one of Norway's most characteristic natural wonders remains a pristine wilderness, easy to access, and highly popular as a destination for both afternoon hikes and serious trekking.

A walker admires the stunning view from Pulpit Rock 604 m (1,981 ft) above Lysefjord.

There are two ways to see Lysefjord – from the top or by boat. Boating is glamorous and comfortable. From Lysebotn, the ancient (and only) community at the fjord's innermost end, Lysefjord stretches straight ahead in an overwhelming geometric perspective of sky, rock and water. Almost the same view from the Kjerag Boulder – a giant sphere of rock wedged in a crevice over a sheer, 1,000-m (3,280-ft) drop into the water – feels like looking across the roof of the world, and visitors feel this sense of majesty wherever they look across the fjord to faraway mountain ranges. Fortunately, it's easy to combine a boat trip with a hike to Lysefjord's rim in the same day.

Utladalen Canyon

Sognefjord, north of Bergen, is Norway's longest. It snakes 205 km (127 mi) inland towards the country's spine, the great mountain wilderness of Jotunheimen National Park. The connecting link is the gigantic glacial canyon of Utladalen, an extension of Sognefjord that remained above sea level when the glaciers melted. Now Utladalen is the southwestern gateway to the biggest concentration of high mountains in Norway. Geologically, it belongs to them, because the whole Jotunheimen is composed of gabbro rock, an ancient and exceptionally hard form of granite that resisted primary glacial erosion. The unusual result is a series of sharp peaks and abrupt rock buttresses, separated by many short, hanging valleys. It took a much bigger secondary glacier to scour out the huge, steep-sided canyon of Utladalen – and the silts it left behind are the reason that Utladalen is so very much more pastoral than the wild, jagged peaks around it (the location, incidentally, of Peer Gynt's frenzied flight on a reindeer's back, in Act One of the opera).

Utladalen is the gentler face of Jotunheimen's dramatic landscapes. Its pine forests are old, and a sheltering cloak to remote hill farms. The rugged terrain is softened by grassy spurs and slopes of scree or shale, and dozens of streams and waterfalls. The occasional farms lend an air of domesticity in tune with, but quite different from the harsh extremities of the alpine Hurrungane mountain region which soars up alongside. The contrast is what attracts both ramblers and the many hikers for whom Utladalen is part of a highway. It has only one obvious attraction – Norway's highest free-falling waterfall, 275 m (902 ft) Vettisfossen – but the valley holds more unregulated major waterfalls than anywhere else anyway. Outstandingly beautiful, geologically fascinating and spiritually fulfilling, Utladalen is a manifestation of the compelling chain that binds human enterprise to nature at its most robust.

HOW TO GET THERE:
By car from Ovre Ardal to the Hjellefossen waterfall car park; then on foot
WHEN TO GO:
Any time. In winter the waterfalls can become gigantic spears and columns of ice.
DON'T MISS:
Exploring the web of trails that criss-crosses the Utla River in search of ever more spectacular mountain panoramas. Short trails like the path from Vetti to the falls make a great day out. Others can be 160 km (100 mi) long and cross from the high tops and glaciers of Jotunheimen, through Utladalen, to the wonders of Sognefjord.
YOU SHOULD KNOW:
Jotunheimen is the 'Home of the Giants' of Norwegian folk lore. In fact it has over 50 peaks higher than 2,000 m (6,560 ft), and is the highest section of *Kjolen* (the Keel), the spine of Scandinavia running the whole way north between Norway and Sweden, that looks like the keel of an upturned boat.

Kullaberg Nature Reserve

HOW TO GET THERE:
By car, bus or train to Molle
WHEN TO GO:
Any time
DON'T MISS:
On the north side, pick your way from the cliff-top forest down to the sea through a ramshackle extravaganza of driftwood towers and tunnels that has grown into a whole maze over 27 years. Called Nimis, the structure is owned by the artist Christo (of Reichstag-wrapping fame), but was created by Lars Vilks, who in 1996 declared the land around it to be an 'independent republic' called Ladonia. Visitors are invited to pay $12 and join the Ladonian nobility. Nimis is still growing, but remains an illegal structure.
YOU SHOULD KNOW:
Carl Linnaeus, primogenitor of modern scientific classification and giant of avifauna in particular (as in the Linnaean Society), adored Kullaberg when he came in 1749. You can see why so many birds visit the place – the birch, pine, beech and oak forests with their understorey of juniper, wild honeysuckle and blackthorn, added to the intertidal marine habitats, appeal to an almost unique combination of species.

Part nature reserve and part civic amenity, Kullaberg occupies the very tip of the Kullen peninsula that points a finger of rock northwest into the southern end of the Kattegat. The promontory marks the entrance to the Oresund strait between Sweden and Denmark, a few miles north of its narrowest point, where Helsingborg faces Danish Helsingor (home of Hamlet) across the water. Kullaberg is Sweden's most westerly point – but its fame rests on being the only 'mountain' of any kind at all in Skane, the country's remorselessly flat and featureless southern region.

Kullaberg packs an extraordinary variety of terrain into its 35 sq km (13.5 sq mi). Its highest point is 187-m (613-ft) Hakull, but between this 'peak' and the 40-m (131-ft) cliffs of ancient archean rock that rear above the sea on Kullaberg's north and south sides, there are beech forests, meadows filled with wild flowers, steep gullies and promontories that drop off the central ridge where climbers come to practise. The cliffs themselves are mined by the sea into secret swimming holes, tide pools and prehistoric caves that were inhabited 10,000 years ago. Many of the best are accessible only from the water, but visitors can rent kayaks locally to reach them and some of the 800 climbing routes with intriguing names like Napoleon's Hat or The Kulla Man's Door. The lighthouse at Kullaberg's tip stands only 70 m (230 ft) above the sea, but is visible for 50 km (31 mi); in one form or another it has signalled the murderous dangers of the peninsula for nearly 1,000 years. On misty evenings there is a lovely walk from the lighthouse bluff through woods of gnarled juniper and hawthorn to a place of low stone walls, curled like elfin ramparts in a troll forest. Kullaberg is full of imaginative surprises.

Sarek National Park

HOW TO GET THERE:
By car or bus from Jokkmokk to Ritsem, then by Lapp boat across Lake Akkajaure; or on foot via the Kungsleden or Padjelanta marked trails through adjoining national parks.
WHEN TO GO:
Any time. The Northern Lights are usually at their best between November and February.

Rapa Valley in autumn in Sarek National Park

The World Heritage Site of Laponia is known more prosaically as Sweden's northernmost province of Norrbotten, and it is the ancestral home of the nomadic Sami reindeer herders. It is a harsh, remote world, far above the Arctic Circle, of glacial lakes and valley wetlands, alpine massifs, ravines, rivers and spectacular mountain peaks rising above glittering icefields and glaciers. Most of it is a trackless wilderness, protected by a series of national parks that border Norway to the west, and stretch almost to Finland in the east. Each park has a signature terrain, but their common heart is Sarek, where Sweden's greatest concentration of high peaks sits in icy majesty. Of some 250 distinct mountains, 87 are over 1,800 m

(5,900 ft) and eight soar over 2,000 m (6,560 ft), packed into a rough circle spanning 50 km (31 mi). Although the park contains nearly 100 glaciers, it suffers a lot of rain which can turn streams into torrents without warning. In fact, crossing rivers is a major hazard in Sarek, where two bridges over key trail junctions are the only facilities available to help hikers. The bridge over the Smaila River at the park's centre is all-important, and visitors use it as both destination and meeting point. From the outside it takes two to three days to reach – from Rinim through the Pastavagge; from Kisuris through the Ruotesvagge; or, most magically of all, from Aktse along Rapadalen.

Rapadalen is Sarek's main artery. Fed by the waters of 30 glaciers, the Rapapaato River flows like threads, braided and spread across the broad valley floor, settling in ponds and small lakes. The water is coloured a bright, ice green against the emerald shrubs on its soggy banks, and fingers of mist shroud nearby mountain tops and hover in side canyons. It's one of Europe's most beautiful places, and worth every effort to see.

DON'T MISS:
Laddepakte, Skarjatjakka and Skierfe are easily accessible mountain peaks, with some of the best panoramas over Sarek. Look out for the bizarrely exuberant herbaceous flora of Rapadalen, and dense stands of mountain birch and osier that encourage the presence of bear, arctic fox, lynx, wolverine and the large elk of the region.

YOU SHOULD KNOW:
Sarek National Park is not for the inexperienced. Professional polar explorers come here to train, and so do climbers practising for major assaults. Some of the hiking is fairly easy (especially in summer, although the downside is zillions of swarms of mosquitoes), but beginners can be caught out by conditions changing from benign to treacherous in seconds.

A sailing boat moored amongst the islets in the Stockholm Archipelago.

Stockholm Archipelago

Swedes call it the 'garden of skerries' (rocky islets) or *Skargarden*. The archipelago of more than 24,000 islands radiates from Sweden's capital city, Stockholm, in an arc 70 km (44 mi) deep and 150 km (93 mi) from north to south. The largest and most heavily forested islands are closest to the city (and include some fully fledged suburbs). Size and vegetation diminish with distance, so that the smallest outcrops of bare, black rock are closest to the lashing storms of open water. In a continuous geological process, the whole land mass has been rising infinitesimally, exposing new skerries and enlarging the existing islands; and uniquely among the world's major archipelagoes, the islands are extremely close together – many only 100 m (328 ft) apart. Since they are typically formed from the mixture of volcanic ash, sand and clay called greywracke, a bedrock created billions of years ago, Skargarden is simultaneously very old and very young.

It is also very beautiful. The larger, inhabited islands like Fjaderholmarna, 17th-century Vaxholm, or 12th-century Uto, famous as much for its mining heritage as for its nature reserve, combine carefree resorts with idyllic, pastoral interiors of swimming ponds, streams, meadows and forests. Thousands of others show nature at its most deliciously varied and delicate, with sandy beaches, picturesque rock formations, and lush grassy clearings in their thick woods, full of wild flowers and berries. Even where visitors see a summer house discreetly sheltered by the trees, they have *Allemansratten* – every person's legal right to land anywhere (except immediately next to someone's house) and set up camp for as long as they like, anchor their boat, pick berries and mushrooms, and enjoy the fields and woods. The countless seaways are busy in summer with canoes, sailing boats, skiffs and even punts: the Stockholm Archipelago can absorb thousands in their personal quests for solitude within its amphibian magnificence.

HOW TO GET THERE:
By ferry along specified routes or by rented craft to wherever you like.
WHEN TO GO:
Any time, but note that winter ferry services are greatly curtailed.
DON'T MISS:
Vaxholm, which used to defend the all-important sea route to Stockholm, and Grinda, the 'green island' full of tranquil lanes through its pastoral beauty and small enough to enable visitors to connect with nature without abandoning social comfort. Both islands are a reminder of Skargarden's importance in Swedish culture and history.
YOU SHOULD KNOW:
The smallest islands are uninhabited and will probably stay that way because of recent legislation prohibiting new building within 300 m (1,000 ft) of the shoreline. Some Swedes call it the 'Robinson Crusoe charter', because it is an encouragement to find your very own piece of pristine solitude.

Lake Saimaa

The Saimaa lake district of southeast Finland is a shimmering, watery maze of thousands of lakes, 14,000 islands and skerries, green forests, reed beds and narrow strings of grassland dividing one water course from another. Water covers 1,700 sq km (656 sq mi) of the 4,400 sq km (1,692 sq mi) lake district, an area roughly the size of Belgium. Created by uniform glacial upheaval, most of the lakes run roughly parallel to each other, and water flows slowly from north to south through the vast system of connecting channels above and below ground. The twisted, elongated shapes of the lakes and the islands together offer 15,000 km (9,320 mi) of pristine shoreline. In such a huge outdoors, visitors can sail or hike, or both, for days without seeing another person. Even the little summer houses visible on many small islands, or among the forests crowding the shore, are too discreet to disturb the tranquil beauty that characterizes the majority of the region. Visitors can stay in some of them, although facilities are suitably Spartan. Part of Lake Saimaa's ethos is demonstrating rugged individualism, and that includes cooking on an open fire on fish caught locally, as well as hurling yourself into freezing water for fun.

Lake Saimaa itself lies at the heart of the system, and through it run some of the region's 3,000 km (1,865 mi) of canoe or sailing routes, including one running all the way from Helsinki, via the Saimaa Canal and lake, to the resort town of Savonlinna and far beyond. Savonlinna is famous for its opera festival, held at the magnificent medieval castle of Olavinlinna, and from late June to August it's full of vacationers and weekenders. Visitors in search of Saimaa's treasure house of natural wonders will have no difficulty in finding more peaceful domains to call their own.

HOW TO GET THERE:
By train to Savonlinna, where boats of every kind can be rented; or by car or bus. Most lakes have a designated slipway to launch boats from car trailers.
WHEN TO GO:
Mid June to September – although Saimaa is beautiful in winter, too.
DON'T MISS:
Saimaa seals, among the world's rarest creatures and exclusive to Lake Saimaa. They are found only in fresh water, and only 270 remain in the wild. For sheer adventure, sail to Haukivesi, a gigantic lake within the Saimaa system. You can follow the Linnonpoiku Nature Trail in Linnansaari National Park – which is self-contained, with its own, internal lake system, on a 40-km (25-mi) island in the middle of Haukivesi.
YOU SHOULD KNOW:
The Saimaa lake district has always been a favourite haunt of visiting Russian elites. Tsar Alexander III came regularly, and visitors can join a luxury cruise that follows the 'Tsar's route' through the Kotka archipelago in the Gulf of Finland to the medieval town of Lappeenranta and Savonlinna. Soviet elites continued the fashion – but now the region's many Russian visitors include the less exalted.

A low sun over the shimmering Lake Saimaa

Lemmenjoki National Park

HOW TO GET THERE:
By car to Repojoki or to the
Lemmenjoki Nature Information Hut
at Njurkulahti, from where there is a
motor boat service to the park's
wilderness area.
WHEN TO GO:
June to August
DON'T MISS:
The introductory 4 km (2.5 mi)
Lemmenjoki Nature Trail; taking a boat
down the Lemmenjoki River valley; or
the 26.5-km (16-mi) circular trail from
Ravadasjarvi Lake to Morgamoja Brook
– the centre of the 1940s to 1950s
Lemmenjoki Gold Rush – and on to
Ravadaskongas waterfall. Visitors may
still encounter the occasional gold
prospector – be advised that they are
characteristically solitary.
YOU SHOULD KNOW:
Lemmenjoki is divided into three
areas. All the marked hiking and
canoeing/boating trails are in the
'basic zone', but visitors can go
anywhere within it, although
campsites are designated. In the
'wilderness zone' there are no marked
trails and hikers are trusted to use
their discretion when choosing camp
or fire sites. In the 'restricted' area,
walking is *only* allowed on marked
trails, to prevent erosion and protect
fragile root systems.

Lemmenjoki National Park

Nothing else in Europe matches the size of Lemmenjoki National Park as an uninhabited, roadless wilderness. It covers 2,850 sq km (1,100 sq mi) of forests, rivers, low fells and huge mires in the arctic north of Finnish Lapland. At the 'top of Europe', Lemmenjoki shares one boundary with a Norwegian national park (which greatly extends their mutual viability as wilderness); and both Swedish and Russian Lapland are close.

The fragile ecosystem that Lemmenjoki protects has a cultural as well as ecological importance. The park combines natural features which enable the nomadic Lapp people to survive from one year to the next. Along the Repojoki River, the Sallivaara Reindeer Round-up site of round-up fences and cabins is a reminder of the herders' harsh way of life – but Lapps know that Lemmenjoki can also be a garden of opportunity. The slopes of the 70-km (43-mi) long Lemmenjoki River valley and the banks of both Kietsimajoki and Vaskojoki are thick with typically Lappish, short and wide, old-growth pine trees called *aihki*, which are favoured by succulent moose. Above the river valleys pine gives way to birch and the habitat of the rock ptarmigan on the bald hilltops and fells. Where the valleys are broad, *aapa* bogs and deep mires crammed with rarities of arctic flora buzz with a sub-stratum of birds and insect life; and although the spruce forests reach their northern limit in Lemmenjoki's south, the park is permanent home to brown bears, wolverines and golden eagles as well as the foxes, moose and reindeer which thrive here.

Lemmenjoki has unequivocal grandeur, as though its big sky, vast forests and great rivers shake their combined fist at the brutal harshness of the elements; but it also demonstrates how richly varied and fulfilling life – in all its forms – can be on the margins.

Oulanka National Park

Oulanka National Park sits in the cross-hair of the Arctic Circle and Finland's border with Russia, roughly equidistant from Kuusamo and Salla. It's a Finnish 'National Landscape' which celebrates a uniquely Finnish version of the northern boreal forest zone that encircles the world. The hilly uplands range only from 380 m (1,246 ft) to 150 m (492 ft) in the lowest river valleys, but they are carved by two major rivers and their tributaries into a series of canyons and gorges famous for their white-water rapids, waterfalls, and long, shallow cascades. In the valley bottoms, rich silts deposited by river meanders and oxbows encourage lush meadows full of sub-arctic wild flowers, boreal moths, and butterflies like the copper violet. Big temperature variations between the fells and meadows support even greater species versatility; and the region's calcium-rich bedrock gives a further twist to the selection of rare flora, especially close to Oulanka's chalk springs and ponds. The herb-scented forests higher up shelter mosses where visitors will find plants like the dark-red helleborine, dwarf milkwort, and the calypso orchid (Oulanka Park's symbol). Hiking here is heaven on the senses.

Oulanka's dramas are played out on and by the rivers. The Oulanka River enters the park as rip-roaring rapids plunging down the Oulanka Canyon, and descends a series of stunning ravines to meet the Kitkajoki just before the Russian frontier. Hiking down the Oulanka takes visitors through a selection of the park's finest scenery, across hanging bridges where streams come hurtling in from the side, past Rupakivi Rock and the deafening roar of the Klutakongas waterfalls and rapids, to eventual tranquillity in the water margins of its eastern edge. Not surprisingly, Oulanka's charms make it one of Finland's favourite destinations, for hiking, water-rafting, rapid-running and even swimming, as well as botanizing for idle pleasure. It's a glorious bit of nature.

A blaze of colour in the forests of Oulanka National Park

HOW TO GET THERE:
By car, to entrances at north and south, or in the middle of the park at the visitor centre close to Oulanka Canyon.

WHEN TO GO:
Any time – the new winter Rytisuo Snowshoeing Trail takes in small, open mires, spacious pine forests, and peaceful riverscapes.

DON'T MISS:
The breathtaking scenery along the lower course of the Kitkajoki River, from Juuma to the Russian border. Less challenging, and more suitable for families who like canoeing or boating, are the calm waters of the lower Oulanka, from Kiutakongas to Jakalamutka.

YOU SHOULD KNOW:
Berry and mushroom picking is (unusually) allowed within the National Park, and there is a profusion of lingonberry, blueberry and crowberry as well as wild strawberry and arctic bramble. Unfortunately, the park's *aapa* bogs and fens produce few cloudberries; and you have to get to any mushrooms before early rising reindeer beat you to it.

251

Mols Bjerge National Park

In a country as flat as Denmark, rolling hills and coastal cliffs have special significance. Mols Bjerge National Park takes its name from the 137-m (450-ft) hill-top of Mols itself – the best-known natural feature of a much bigger, 180-sq-km (69-sq-mi) reserve that includes heath, pastureland, forests, bogs, meadows and a whole range of coastal and marine features. It sits on the twin headlands of southern Djursland, east of Arhus, and extends north as far as Ronde in the west, across to Hyllested on the Kattegat coast. It even includes the open water of Begtrup Bay and much of Ebeltoft Bay, two stretches along the Kattegat, and the offshore island of Hjelm.

Mols Bjerge is a representative catalogue of Denmark's finest landscapes, all of it discreetly signed with trails that make those highlights accessible to hikers and ramblers of every level of experience, and as special as possible for children and the wheelchair-bound. The trail from the Forest and Nature Agency Visitor Centre at Ovre Strandkaer, next to Mols, is typical. It runs through pine and broadleaf woods and across gentle open hills full of grazing longhorn cattle to a spot with far-flung views over

Wild lupin in Mols Bjerge National Park

252

Ebeltoft Bay. Ebeltoft is an historic, 13th-century market town of huge charm and has an ancient harbour flanked by sandy coves. To its south the fascinating salt marsh of Ahl Plantage is crammed with wild flowers, herbs and grasses adapted to its brackish moisture, right next to what was once the mighty Bjornkaer and Egedal forest of oak which fuelled the 17th-century salt-extraction process, and is now recovering its grandeur. A lovely 6-km (4-mi) nature path north to Gravlev passes rich meadows and mixed broadleaf woods. This is nature at its most reticent and domestic – but as dramatic in its detail as anything in the world.

Rold Skov

One of Denmarks's largest forests, Rold Skov covers about 80 sq km (31 sq mi) in the Himmerland region between Aalborg and Randers on the Jutland peninsular. The forest is an agglomerate of state- and many privately-owned small forests, brought together by common interest not in preservation for its own sake, but in the development of an ecologically integrated plan for a reserve which necessarily spreads in and around villages, farmsteads and small towns. For visitors it helps that Rold Skov is a patchwork of discrete sections. In one, prominence is given to restoring great plantations of North American spruce and fir species, adding to existing forests of dense, old fir which flourish in the moraine soil of sand and gravel. With the considerable rain it gets, Rold Skov is one of the best conifer habitats in Denmark. Elsewhere, in the Rebild Hills and Bjergeskov sections, there are wonderful – and big – growths of natural, old beech forest, where the gnarled and twisted trees have survived long-ago pruning and damage from game. Two sections, Troldeskoven and Urskoven, are set aside to revert eventually to virgin forest. With no human intervention trees will fall, creating their own glades and new flora to fill them; and it is closest to these sections that visitors will see most game and most birds.

Almost equally important as the forest ecology itself are the cultural artefacts and associations scattered throughout Rold Skov, linking the restoration of its forests to those who lived in symbiosis with it. The Northern Well is 600–700 years old, and the Bjergeskoven section alone holds Bronze Age burial mounds, the Stenstuen dolmen, and several ancient, parallel sunken roads. Evidence of various methods of charcoal-burning is everywhere. Hiking through its forest glades, springs and lakes, visitors find that Rold Skov in its entirety forms a really uplifting ecological narrative.

HOW TO GET THERE:
By bus or car to Rold or Gravlev; or by train to Skorping
WHEN TO GO:
Any time. Each season has distinct flora and fauna.
DON'T MISS:
The 'erosion holes' caused by acidified rainwater penetrating cracks and dissolving the lime in the soil, which collapses into serious cavities invisible beneath the forest carpet. In June, you can see Denmark's largest orchid, the Lady's Slipper, in the Bjergeskoven forest – although it's behind railings for its own safety.
YOU SHOULD KNOW:
Hikers may like to spice up their journey through Rold Skov with a sudden and unprovoked 'attack' by leering, dirt-smeared, masked bandits of uncivilized mien. This is a service that can be pre-arranged. For a fee, you get three (sort of) medieval 'robbers' (five or six for big occasions) who will ambush you and your party in the forest, at your convenience. With luck, this 'unpleasant half-hour' encounter will end jocularly with a *roverbjaesk*, a drink from a hip-flask. Rold Skov is the only official Danish nature reserve to offer this service.

Skagen, Grenen and the Raabjerg Mile

HOW TO GET THERE:
By car, bus, or train to Skagen, but by bike or on foot on the sands of Grenen

WHEN TO GO:
Any time. Skagen is always a birdwatcher's paradise, but May is spectacular for raptors and many other migrants.

DON'T MISS:
The 14th-century *Tilsandede Kirke* (Buried Church) abandoned in 1795 when relentless sand drifts overwhelmed its walls. The pathos of its marooned tower is a reminder that for all the radiant light, and the distinctive ambience of typical 'Skagen yellow' houses with their white picket fences and red roofs, Skagen belongs to Nature. The picturesque cross-hatched waves at Grenen are also a warning of ferocious currents that make swimming lethal.

YOU SHOULD KNOW:
In the 19th century, Grenen's land and seascapes captured the imaginations of the 'Skagen painters', who popularized the area, bringing with them Denmark's greatest writers, musicians, composers and aesthetes. Peter Severin Kroyer's internationally famous painting *Sommeraften ved Skagens Strand* (Summer Evening on the Beach at Skagen) looks like a romanticized interpretation, but it captures the physical reality as well as the soul of the place.

If the Jutland peninsula were a silhouette portrait, Skagen would be the cowlick on top of its Pompadour hairstyle. Skagen (pronounced 'skayn') is Denmark's northernmost point, the tip of the spit separating Denmark from Norway across the Skagerrak, and from Sweden across the Kattegat. It is the meeting point of the Baltic and the North Sea, a place of colliding white water and achingly beautiful, blue and gold luminescence, where the elements shimmer in perpetual motion.

History clings like seaweed to the region. Empires have been won and lost on Skagen's whimsical meteorological vagaries: 'the Skaw' (the *Ska* of Skagerrak) is notorious for breaking mariners' hearts. In fact the eccentric resort town of Skagen anchors local geography with its system of stabilized dunes, and the opposing forces of the Skagerrak and Kattegat have gradually moved their principal battleground to Grenen, the curling tongue of sand on Skagen's northern edge which consequently grows by 8 m (26 ft) each year and shifts its shape from day to day. Visitors can ride a blue-and-red tractor-train called the *Sandormen* (Sandworm) from the dunes to the water's edge, and stand with a foot in each sea. Less than a dot in this universe of sky and water, a visitor can almost touch the eternal in Grenen's majestic interplay of light and reflection.

Southwest of Grenen, the 'Raabjerg Mile' demonstrates the colossal natural forces determining the region's character. The Raabjerg Mile is one of Europe's biggest migrating coastal dunes, up to 40 m (131 ft) high and composed of roughly 3.5 million cubic metres of sand, generating a miniature desert of almost a square kilometre (0.3 sq mi). In 300 years it has moved 5 km (3 mi), burying villages and forests which will one day reappear as it continues northeast at an average speed of 18 m (60 ft) a year. It is held in such awe that it is not even desecrated by litter.

Windswept sand dunes at the Raabjerg Mile, Skagen

Llechwedd Slate Caverns

Not all the world's wild places remain so because they are unsullied by human hand. Nowhere is this truer than in the confines of the British Isles, where much of the landscape has been shaped by the expansion of agriculture, industry and commerce since time immemorial. But paradoxically, once some enterprises have served their purpose and been abandoned the result can be natural drama of the highest order.

The slate industry is active around Blaenau Ffestiniog in North Wales, where quarries still produce this valuable commodity and spoil tips continue to grow. But Llechwedd Slate Caverns is one example of a not-so-natural wonder once created by industrial activity. This is the place to learn about the Welsh slate industry and the life and times of the hardy miners who made it possible, when huge demand for this quality roofing material arose in the 19th century.

Today, the abandoned caverns offer a unique journey back in time. At the surface is a re-created Victorian Village with pubs, shops, a lock-up, bank and smithy, plus a collection of narrow-gauge wagons once used to haul slate. Below ground it's possible to enjoy two special experiences – riding the Miners' Underground Tramway through a network of tunnels and vast chambers enlivened by tableaux, then exploring the Deep Mine on foot, where dramatic *son et lumière* presentations re-create Victorian mining conditions.

After enjoying the brilliant re-creation of yesteryear above and below ground, the abiding memory of Llechwedd Slate Caverns will surely be the truly awesome grandeur of those magnificent underground cathedrals of commerce, hewn from the living rock with the help of no more than basic tools, gunpowder and muscle power. Long after those tough miners are no more than a memory, their work remains as a dramatic spectacle that Mother Nature herself might envy.

Clwydian Range

One of only eight protected landscapes in Wales, the wild and wonderful Clwydian Range is a 35-km (22-mi) chain of heather-clad hills stretching from Prestatyn Hillside in the north to the Nany y Garth pass in the south, from the Vale of Clwyd in the west towards the Dee Estuary in the east. Denbigh and Ruthin are in the vale and Mold is on the Dee side.

This is one of the most precious tracts of countryside in North Wales, rising from fertile farmland through coppice woodland and small, hedged fields on the lower slopes to open heather moorland punctuated

Heather-covered slopes of the
Clwydian Range leading up to
the summit of Moel Famau

with limestone outcrops and wooded escarpments on the tops. Deep valleys slash the flanks, notably those carrying the Rivers Alyn and Wheeler. Where the limestone breaks through, there are grasslands rich with orchids and other wild flowers.

The Clwydian Range is best viewed from the Vale of Clwyd, but most folk will want to do more than look. These hills offer the opportunity for every sort of recreational activity, from thrill-seeking challenges like paragliding, abseiling or rock climbing through horse riding, cycling and walking to fishing. Although long popular as a 'green lung' for visitors from Merseyside and Cheshire, these delightful hills have enough roaming room to ensure that anybody who wants to get away from it all need never feel crowded, especially if avoiding summer weekends.

A popular stopping-off point is Gweryd Lakes, towards the south of the range. In enviable surroundings, it offers coarse and trout fishing and is an excellent base for sallying forth into the hills. Afterwards, hikers will find that unspoilt local villages provide a welcome chance to visit traditional pubs such as the Cross Foxes in Nannach, Blue Lion in Cwm, Raven in Llanarmon or Druids in Llanferres.

WHEN TO GO:
Any time (although the weather can, to say the least, be unwelcoming to those unprepared for the rigours of winter).

DON'T MISS:
One or both of the range's two delightful country parks. Loggerheads has a beautiful wooded valley, dramatic cliffs and limestone outcrops. Moel Famau consists of heather moorland, plus the remains of a tower constructed to celebrate George III's Golden Jubilee – and sensational views.

YOU SHOULD KNOW:
The Offa's Dyke National Trail runs for almost the entire length of the Clwydian Range's ridge. Much of the Clwydian Range is open-access land, but there are private areas where walkers are asked to remain on signed public rights of way.

Nicholaston Burrows

HOW TO GET THERE:
The Burrows may be found to the south of Nicholaston on the A4118 Swansea-Port Eynort Road, between Oxwich Bay to the west and Tor Bay to the east.

WHEN TO GO:
From late spring to early autumn if lazy beach time is a priority. Avoid July and August if solitude is a desirable part of the package.

DON'T MISS:
At least one of the Gower's six castles as an interesting side visit. The ruined Norman Oystermouth Castle overlooking Swansea Bay is good. So too is Weobley Castle above Llanrhidan Marsh and the Loughor Estuary. The other four (Oxwich, Pennard, Penrice and Landimore – the latter completely overgrown and hard to find) are little more than interesting, but decayed, ruins.

YOU SHOULD KNOW:
Take everything needed for a self-sufficient outing when visiting Nicholaston Burrows for the day. It's a 50-minute round-trip tramp to the car park and back, while the nearest facilities are at the Oxwich Bay Hotel, around 40 minutes away along the beach.

Oxwich Bay

The Gower Peninsula in southwest Wales has plenty of splendid marine scenery along its southern coastline, fronting the Bristol Channel, and back in 1956 the Gower was the first place in the UK to be designated as an Area of Outstanding Natural Beauty. Considering its proximity to bustling Swansea, Nicholaston Burrows can seem incredibly remote, especially out of season. Even in high summer it does not get crowded, because getting there requires a hike through extensive Nicholaston Woods (home to protected ash trees and rare plants such as purple bromwell, butcher's broom and bloody cranesbill), where it's quite possible to spend a rewarding hour before even reaching the Burrows (dunes and beach).

Those in search of sea, sand, scenery and solitude should put Nicholaston Burrows high on their list of must-visit destinations. This unspoilt seaside gem is backed by extensive sand dunes held together by scrub vegetation, themselves well worth exploring on the way to the beach. The western part of Oxwich Bay (where there's car parking) can get crowded in summer, but even then the eastern end next to Nicholaston Burrows never gets too busy, and those with a keen interest in nature may care to explore the Oxwich Burrows reserve, a wonderful expanse of salt- and freshwater marshes.

In the other direction lies Three Cliffs Bay with its impressive jutting rock formations. There's an excellent short walk looping out along the cliff tops looking down, and returning along the beach looking up. When the tide is out beachcombing often produces dividends, especially for lovers of seafood such as cockles and scallops. It's easy to spend a couple of active days exploring the Burrows and environs, but those who simply prefer messing about on a beautiful beach will find ample satisfaction doing just that.

Brecon Beacons

Good enough for the tough-as-nails SAS to use as a training ground, these stern hills to the south of Brecon are neither over-populated nor the easiest of terrain – particularly in winter, when the local mountain rescue team is frequently called into action. That said, at other times of year the Brecon Beacons offer rewarding outdoor opportunities, although they are notorious for sudden weather changes. The range consists of peaks forming a horseshoe around the head of Taf Fechan River, including Pen y Fan, Corn Du, Cribyn and Fan y Big. They're connected by an extended ridge with long parallel spurs.

These are the core of the Brecon Beacons National Park, but there are other sections, giving an overall area of 1,350 sq km (520 sq mi). The Black Mountain is to the west and then comes the sandstone massif of Fforest Fawr. To the east of the beacons lie the Black Mountains on the English border. The park contains some of the most spectacular upland formations in southern Britain and the landscape is mainly high moorland, with forestry plantations and pastureland in the many valleys.

Sightseeing from the comfort of a car is satisfying, with so much rugged scenery to appreciate, but the national park is made for those who enjoy outdoor activities. These include a gamut of leisure possibilities, including hang-gliding, parascending, caving, rock climbing, water sports, canoeing, fishing, horse riding, cycling, mountain-biking, walking and camping. The park's rich past and natural heritage offer another dimension, with numerous archaeological and historical sites to be found. Around 170,000 visitors come each year, which is far too few to deny the secretive SAS their lonely, undisturbed route marches in the park's remote wilderness areas.

HOW TO GET THERE:
Working clockwise from the west, the main towns surrounding the Brecon Beacons National Park are Llandeilo, Llandovery, Brecon, Hay-on-Wye, Abergavenny, Pontypool, Blaenavon, Brynmawr, Merthyr Tydfil, Glyn Neath and Ystradgynlais. Several good roads cross the park from north to south and the A40 runs from east to west.

WHEN TO GO:
Spring, summer or autumn.

DON'T MISS:
Waterfalls. There are dozens in the national park, mainly towards the southern edge, the tallest of which is Sgwd Henrhyd with a drop of 27 m (90 ft), on National Trust land near Coelbren.

YOU SHOULD KNOW:
In 2005 the first hiking route to cover the entire length of the Brecon Beacons National Park was inaugurated. The Beacons Way runs from the village of Bethlehem in Carmarthenshire to the foot of Ysgyryd Fawr near Abergavenny, the most easterly of the Black Mountains. The long-distance Taff Trail from Brecon to Cardiff also passes through the national park.

A view across the Brecon Beacons

Porthcurno Beach

Porthcurno

The Cornish coastline is world famous, and Porthcurno is an ideal place to appreciate its visual grandeur. This little village is almost at the tip of England – an honour reserved for nearby Land's End – but with its triangular beach and flanking cliffs Porthcurno delivers all the rugged splendour anyone could want. The steeply shelving beach has coarse sand and faces to the southeast. It is tucked neatly into the western end of Porthcurno Bay, a sweep of awesome cliffs punctuated by tantalizing coves culminating in rectangular Logan's Rock to the east.

The coastline around Porthcurno is designated as an Area of Outstanding Natural Beauty. The granite cliffs are up to 70 m (230 ft) tall and can be appreciated by exploring the many footpaths, one of which is the long-distance South West Coast Path. Green Bay is a small sandy cove immediately adjacent to Porthcurno Beach that can be reached at low tide. Further towards Logan Rock is Pedn Vounder, another small beach accessed by a steep path from the cliff top. Near the top is a white granite pyramid that serves as a navigational aid. It replaced the building that housed the terminal of an undersea telegraph cable to France, laid in 1880. In the other direction is Porth Chapel Beach, which is named for a ruined medieval chapel.

Lifeguards are on duty at Porthcurno between Whitsun and mid September (there can be dangerous rip-tides off the beach) and a dog ban is in force on the beach from Easter to the end of September. Cornwall cheerfully overdoses on holidaymakers in high season and Porthcurno is a justifiably popular destination, but at other times of year it is possible to find total solitude amid some of the Cornwall's most dramatic coastal scenery.

Prawle Point

Devon's southern extremity is Prawle Point, a jutting coastal headland. It is to the east of Plymouth in the area known as the South Hams, across the Kingsbridge Estuary from the popular waterside town of Salcombe in the direction of Start Point. The land is mostly owned by the National Trust and the point itself is a ten-minute (uphill) walk from the NT car park. The building on the cliff above the point is a watch station manned by National Coastwatch Institution volunteers (visitors welcome to pop in for a chat and see the display housed there). The volunteers are not alone in observing passing traffic out to sea, as this superb vantage point is a magnet for ship spotters (really!).

Actually, this is not a place to go with the intention of doing particular stuff, because the real joy is being there, surrounded by magnificent coastal scenery in a remote and unspoilt place. That said, ornithologists might beg to differ. The Devon Bird Watching & Preservation Society has a small reserve that features a modest superstar – the sparrow-sized cirl bunting, found only in South Devon. Birdlife is abundant, with major migrations in spring and autumn and a large cast of regulars, including assorted sea birds, ravens and raptors like buzzard, red kite and hobby.

Apart from being a birdwatcher's paradise, Prawle Point will appeal to those who simply want to appreciate the rugged grandeur of this beautiful coastline. The South West Coast Path passes through and it's possible to scramble down to little coves with shingle beaches and explore rocky shelves that run unevenly out to sea from the base of the cliffs. Just to the west is Macely Cove, with its enticing strip of sand enclosed by towering granite walls.

HOW TO GET THERE:
From the village of East Prawle (reached via a number of alternative minor roads from Frogmore or Chillington on the A379 from Kingsbridge to Dartmouth), using a single-track road to the National Trust car park.

WHEN TO GO:
Any time – even in high summer the place doesn't get overcrowded.

DON'T MISS:
Summer nature watch – apart from the birdlife, look out for rare butterflies such as the clouded yellow or green hairstreak on land, while basking sharks and grey seals can be spotted in the water.

YOU SHOULD KNOW:
Just after leaving East Prawle, the tall post in a field was erected to play the role of a ship's mast, allowing coastguard crews to practise the use of rocket apparatus – once a crucial aid in shore-to-ship rescues. It was often deployed locally, for many a ship has run aground on Prawle Point over the years. The strange-looking bunker on the left just before the climb to the point is a leftover from one of two radar stations built in World War II.

Remote Prawle Point

Exmoor

The Exmoor National Park is very special and sure to appeal to anyone who loves wild and lonely places. But there's much more than moor to be seen in this 700-sq-km (270-sq-mi) area of outstanding natural beauty that includes the Vale of Porlock and Brendon Hills. It spans the borders of Devon and Somerset, with nearly three quarters located in the latter county. Exmoor has over 200 scheduled ancient monuments and countless historic sights ranging from prehistoric hill forts and mine workings to pretty medieval villages with wonderful old churches. Red deer roam free, as do Exmoor ponies, while sheep graze everywhere and the thriving bird population is represented by species as different as the peregrine falcon and Dartford warbler.

But the landscape's the star and that, too, is hugely varied. The rugged northern boundary is a Heritage Coast 55 km (34 mi) long, a stretch of dramatic coastal scenery that includes Britain's highest cliff – the grimly named Great Hangman near Combe Martin, soaring to an impressive 318 m (1,040 ft) with a sheer face of 250 m (820 ft). The shoreline is often wooded and exploring the coast reveals a wonderland of cliffs, caves and huge waterfalls. There are few settlements on the water – only Lynton-Lynmouth (connected by a cliff railway) and Porlock Weir – so mostly this awesome coast is accessible only to the most determined adventurers.

The park predominately consists of heather-covered moorland, lightly peppered with hamlets and small villages. This hilly former royal hunting ground also has extensive areas of broadleaf and conifer woodlands. There are numerous rivers, notably the River Exe and its tributaries flowing south and several that flow out into the Bristol Channel in the north, and it would be easy to spend a month or more exploring Exmoor's beguiling features.

HOW TO GET THERE:
The Exmoor National Park is crossed by two main roads – the A39 from Barnstaple to Minehead and the A396 (from Dunster, off the A39 south of Minehead, to Tiverton). The moor itself has a network of minor roads.

WHEN TO GO:
Any time, although extreme care should be exercised if venturing onto the moor proper in winter, when weather conditions can change for the worse with dramatic suddenness and swirling mist can pose a particular threat to walkers. Set against the risk factors, the moor's stern winter face has an austere beauty and when Exmoor is covered in snow it has an ethereal appeal.

DON'T MISS:
A stroll across the famous Tarr Steps, an ancient clapper bridge across the River Barle between Withypool and Dulverton.

YOU SHOULD KNOW:
Does the Beast of Exmoor really exist? This huge cat is said to stalk the woods and pastures of Exmoor – killing the occasional sheep, leaving the odd large paw print in soft mud and exciting the media every time there's a new sighting. True or false, Exmoor is definitely big and lonely enough to provide sanctuary for shy, night-hunting predators.

An Exmoor pony grazes on heather-carpeted moorland.

Orford Ness

Nearly but not quite as far to the east as it's possible to get in the British Isles lies Orford Ness – a remote natural marvel off the Suffolk coast. The largest shingle spit in Europe is joined to the mainland at Aldeburgh and stretches south past Orford to North Weir Point, opposite the hamlet of Shingle Street. The Ness is separated from the mainland by the River Alde and is an internationally important example of rare and fragile European vegetated shingle habitat. Together with nearby Havergate Island, the spit has been designated as Orford Ness National Nature Reserve.

The Ness is 15 km (9 mi) long – an atmospheric strip of marsh and mudflat, lagoons and tidal river, shingle and sand, grassland and scrub, flowers and shells. This should be a lonely outpost untouched by the hand of man, but instead it has a lighthouse dating from 1792 and an extraordinary collection of abandoned buildings. Damaging one of the world's largest vegetated shingle habitats was of little concern to the British War Office in the first half of the 20th century – had such a thing then been deemed valuable or even defined – and the legacy of the Ness's history as a closed site for weapons testing and other research purposes may be read from a bizarre assortment of structures dating from two hot world wars and one Cold War. Early radar experiments took place in the 1930s and the distinctive 'pagodas' were used for testing nuclear triggers after World War II. The National Trust purchased the site in 1993 and has chosen to preserve the military detritus.

The combination of lonely wild place, wide-open spaces and big skies with a 'mystique of secrecy' generated by the former military establishment makes for weird contrasts and a fascinating visit. The National Trust's self-guiding booklet reveals all.

HOW TO GET THERE:
Access is strictly limited to protect the natural habitat, and may be (officially) obtained only by using the National Trust ferry from Orford town quay on a 'first come, first served' basis.

WHEN TO GO:
Between April and the end of October, with Saturday sailings only except in July, August and September when open days are Tuesday to Saturday. Crossings to the Ness are between 10.00 and 14.00, with the last boat returning at 17.00.

DON'T MISS:
The great Martello Tower built at the top of the Ness, the most northerly of those sturdy round gun platforms built to deter a Napoleonic invasion that never came.

YOU SHOULD KNOW:
This is not a wheelchair-friendly place. Access to the ferry launch is via steep and slippery steps, some tracks on the Ness are rough and/or unsurfaced and once there the entire circuit involves traversing shingle areas. Most buildings that may be entered have narrow doorways, thresholds and steps.

The atmospheric Orford Ness

North Norfolk Coast

HOW TO GET THERE:
Use the A149 that runs from Hunstanton (north of King's Lynn, passing Sandringham) along the coast to Sheringham and Cromer, due north of Norwich.
WHEN TO GO:
Any time – winter to find a tourist-free zone and see the large number of migrating wildfowl on the marshes, notably protected Brent geese that can gather in their thousands.
DON'T MISS:
The famous seals off Blakeney Point. Boat trips run from Morston or Blakeney Quay daily in season (April to October), less frequently in the off season. Up to 500 common and grey seals will be seen basking on the sandbanks and some will inquisitively surround the boat. Many trips land on Blakeney Point to allow visitors to study the abundant birdlife, stroll to the Old Lifeboat House, splash about in the water or lie in the sun.
YOU SHOULD KNOW:
Lord Nelson spent many boyhood days exploring this coast from his home at Burnham Thorpe, where his father was rector. One of 11 children, young Horatio didn't have that much time to run wild on the salt marshes – he joined the Royal Navy in 1771 aged just 13.

A summer evening at Holkham Bay on the North Norfolk Coast

The trendy North Norfolk Coast has become known as 'Chelsea on Sea' after the large number of well-heeled Londoners who have holiday homes in charming small towns and villages that line the water or lie just inland. These include (from west to east) Brancaster, Burnham Deepdale, Burnham Market, Burnham Overy, Holkham, Wells-next-the-Sea, Stiffkey, Morston, Blakeney and Cley Next the Sea. Appealing as these delightful places may be to second-homers, there is another aspect of this fascinating coast that will appeal mightily to everyone who loves wild and lonely places, huge skies, the haunting call of passing curlew and total solitude.

For this Area of Outstanding Natural Beauty (AONB) is a land of extensive marshes and mudflats, creeks and tidal pools, beaches and sand dunes. This is where low tide can see the sea retreating beyond sight from the shoreline, only to rush back when the tide turns, filling the gutters with extraordinary rapidity and threatening to cut off the unwary from dry land with no more warning than the ominous rumble of waves driven by a following wind. Local knowledge is helpful and tide tables are an essential aid for any would-be foreshore explorer.

Wonderful walks may be enjoyed in the Holkham National Nature Reserve. It stretches from Burnham Norton to Blakeney and has every feature that makes this unique coastline so special – foreshore, reclaimed marshland, salt marsh, pinewoods, scrub and dunes. A good spot to start is Holkham Bay, right in the middle of the reserve (a small charge for parking in the convenient access point of Lady Ann's Drive is payable during the summer months). There are some impressive dunes at Holkham, but the very best system of the coast is Winterton Dunes at the eastern end of the Area of Outstanding Natural Beauty.

Pendle Hill

The old mill towns of Burnley, Nelson, Clithero and Colne in northeastern Lancashire are grouped around isolated Pendle Hill, rising to a moorland crest 557 m (1,827 ft) above sea level. It is part neither of the Pennines to the east nor of the nearby Forest of Bowland, although included within the latter's designation as an Area of Outstanding National Beauty (AONB). The moist climate that underpinned the area's cotton-producing industry is enshrined in the local saying 'when you can see Pendle Hill it's about to rain, when you can't, it's already started'. Despite that, on a rare clear day it's possible to see the sea from the summit.

This crouching mound has inspired people since prehistoric times – there's a Bronze Age burial site on the summit but Halloween is the time for a completely different historical hike – large numbers gather to climb the supposedly haunted hill each year in memory of the infamous Pendle witch trials of 1612 that accused a dozen locals (including two men) of murdering ten people by witchcraft. One 'witch' died in prison, one was acquitted and ten were found guilty . . . and hanged by the neck until dead. Those who can't (or won't!) make Halloween can follow a signed Witches' Trail on foot at any time to visit key sites.

Pendle Hill is one of those places too wild to be tamed, and has therefore remained much as nature intended. Away from regular paths to the summit it offers compete peace and solitude, while those who like to be organized can follow cycling or walking tours designed to showcase the natural beauty of this great hill and its pastoral surroundings. These include the Pendle Three Peaks Trail, the 70-km (43-mi) circular Pendle Way and Grand Cycle Tour of Pendle.

Pendle Hill seen from the Ribble Valley.

HOW TO GET THERE:
The most popular – and steepest – ascent of Pendle Hill begins in the village of Barley to the east. Other villages around the hill are Newchurch-in-Pendle, Twiston, Downham, Mearley, Pendleton and Sabden. Pendle Hill is north of the M65 at Burnley, with the A59 running to the west and A682 to the east.
WHEN TO GO:
Any time (but winter conditions call for hill-walking experience).
DON'T MISS:
The British in India Museum in nearby Colne's Hendon Mill, dedicated to telling the story of the British Raj with the help of coins, ivory carvings, commemorative boxes and plates, weapons, photographs, uniforms and model soldiers (open weekdays, find it off Craddock Road in the town centre).
YOU SHOULD KNOW:
It was here in 1652 that George Fox, famous founder of the Religious Society of Friends (Quakers), experienced a vision that became enshrined in Quaker consciousness. Those tempted to ascend the hill today should perhaps note his words before starting out on their journey: 'We came near a very great hill called Pendle Hill and I was moved of the Lord to go to the top of it, which I did with difficulty, it was so very steep and high'.

A view of Ennerdale Water from the northern shore

Ennerdale Water

The remote hidden gem in Cumbria's crown is Ennerdale Water. This glacial lake is the most westerly stretch of water in the Lake District National Park and one of the smallest, with a surface area of just 3 sq km (1 sq mi). Although surrounded by famous peaks such as Brandreth, Great Gable, Green Gable, High Crag, Pillar and Steeple, this pristine little lake and its shoreline remain undeveloped and completely unspoilt, helped by the absence of any public road entering its snug Ennerdale Valley location.

Ennerdale Water is fed by the River Liza and various fell streams, before discharging into the River Ehen and thence into the Irish Sea. The water level has been artificially raised to support the lake's role as a reservoir (owned by United Utilities) serving the Whitehaven area. The Forestry Commission manages the environs, ensuring that there is no intrusive tourist-orientated development. Despite proximity to the towns of Egremont and Cleator Moor, the lake is not well known and is little visited in comparison to more popular Lake District destinations, making it all the more special for those who appreciate the solitude of wild places.

Beyond Ennerdale Water's western end the broad vista of the West Cumbrian Plain stretches away to the sea, in marked contrast to the eastern end where awesome crags and fells rise sharply. Along the northern shore of the lake is a favoured path to the summit of the great Pillar – a satisfying climb that will be rewarded with sensational views from on high. Other peaks can be reached from the lake, but the routes are more challenging. The lake itself can be circumnavigated, but those walkers who take it on should be ultra-careful when using the testing path beneath Anglers Crag along the southern shore.

HOW TO GET THERE:
The easiest access point for walkers or cyclists is Ennerdale Bridge, a delightful small village reached by minor roads from the B5295/A5086 Egremont to Cockermouth road.

WHEN TO GO:
Any time (weather conditions permitting in winter)

DON'T MISS:
The magnificent view of Ennerdale Water from the top of Anglers Crag. There may be equally spectacular views in the Lake District National Park, but none can better it.

YOU SHOULD KNOW:
The annual Ennerdale Show takes place in the last week of August each year – a typically lively Cumbrian event at Ennerdale Bridge that brings country people together to be entertained by agricultural displays, local arts and crafts, assorted competitions, music and general revelry.

North York Moors

True Brits (and many others around the globe) who watch the long-running TV series *Heartbeat* will be familiar with regular locations like Aidensfield (actually the village of Goathland) and the stunning scenery of the surrounding North York Moors. The 1,425-sq-km (550-sq-mi) national park is sparsely populated and boasts one of the UK's largest unbroken expanses of heather moorland. This stunning landscape is a place where it's possible to walk for long distances without seeing a soul, listening to the calls of upland birds and enjoying the wide sweep of open moors.

Seductive as wild and lonely places may be, there's much more to the North York Moors National Park than that. Quite apart from the wonderful heather moors, there are ancient woodlands, rivers and a wonderful stretch of Heritage Coast that includes the fascinating old port of Whitby, plus beaches and dramatic cliffs. In addition, there are picturesque sandstone villages, castles, medieval abbeys and churches to be found by those fascinated by built history.

To see how much this special place has to offer, drive – or take the Moorland Explorer bus – to The Moors National Park Centre at Danby and enjoy the interactive exhibition, tearoom, arts and crafts gallery, indoor and outdoor play areas and grounds. The centre also has details of eight specific routes for wheelchairs and pushchairs, encompassing the park's various attractions – high moorland, Heritage Coast, riversides, lakes and an important archaeological site. Superb views are on offer from the network of roads on the moorland plateau without climbing or hiking a single step. It's a place that everyone can enjoy at their own pace, in their own way.

HOW TO GET THERE:
The Moorbus Network offers a comprehensive public transport network from April to October in an attempt to reduce the pressure of private cars. Park and Ride (free with a Moorbus ticket) is available at Sutton Bank National Park Centre, The Moors National Park Centre at Danby, Hutton le Hole, Thornton le Dale and Newton under Roseberry. Drive in from any of the surrounding towns – Saltburn, Guisborough, Stokesley, Northallerton, Thirsk, Pickering or Scarborough.
WHEN TO GO:
Any time
DON'T MISS:
A nostalgic trip on the huffing, puffing NYMR (North Yorkshire Moors Railway). This authentic slice of yesteryear offers steam locos, wood-panelled carriages, old-fashioned conductor service and around 30 km (19 mi) of preserved track through exceptional moorland scenery. Hop on and off at will to explore between late March and the end of October. Grosmont is the terminus for the scenic Esk Valley line that also crosses the park.
YOU SHOULD KNOW:
In the 12th century the abbot of Rievaulx Abbey made a timeless comment that happily is as true today as it was then: 'Everywhere peace, everywhere serenity and a marvellous freedom from the tumult of the world.'

Escape the hustle and bustle of modern life on the North York Moors.

267

North Pennines

The special character of the North Pennines – stretching down from Carlisle to Darlington – is recognized by salutations galore. This low-rise range has been designated as an Area of Outstanding Natural Beauty and at 2,000 sq km (772 sq mi) is the second-largest AONB in England, outranked only by the Cotswolds. As a result of unique geological heritage – unusual flora (including rare alpine plants not found elsewhere in the British Isles) and threatened fauna such as red squirrel – the North Pennines have also achieved UNESCO European and Global Geopark status.

Quite apart from official recognition, everyone who appreciates wide open spaces and the ability to escape into the great outdoors will be instantly captivated by huge expanses of open heather moor, blanket bog, hay meadows bright with wild flowers in season, enticing dales, rushing rivers, waterfalls and wonderful woodland.

Traditional stone-built villages house welcoming traditional communities and the North Pennines has a fascinating industrial past, with evidence of extensive lead mining and quarrying in past centuries still to be found, providing an added dimension to this striking landscape that spans three counties – Cumbria, Durham and Northumberland.

The North Pennines are a magnet to birdwatchers. Thousands of wading birds nest in the area, raptors are easily spotted and so are black grouse, with 80 per cent of England's population here. Horse riding, cycling (on and off road) and hiking are the best ways of appreciating the outstanding qualities of the North Pennines.

For those who prefer organized tramping rather than wandering at will, a major section of the long-distance Pennine Way falls within the Area of Outstanding Natural Beauty. Or try Isaac's Tea Trail – a 58-km (36-mi) loop walk that takes in the villages of Ninebanks, Allendale, Nenthead and Alston. This trail is named after Isaac Holden, a lead miner-turned-tea-seller-cum-Methodist-preacher who roamed these parts in the 19th century.

High Cup Nick is a spectacular U-shaped glacial valley.

Galloway Forest Park

A view over to Meikle Millyea

Welcome to the Scottish Borders – one of Britain's most pleasing tracts of unspoilt countryside. Once there, the 775 sq km (300 sq mi) of Galloway Forest Park provides a wonderful opportunity to experience the natural beauty of the Borders at first hand. As the name suggests, this is a woodland park. It is operated by the Forestry Commission, an organization that majors on commercial conifer plantations, and this is indeed the predominant characteristic of Galloway Forest Park. But this is a mixed landscape of forest and moor, lochs and rivers, seashore and mountains – a combination that attracts over a quarter of a million fresh-air enthusiasts who visit every year.

Their motivation is understandable. The park is in Dumfries and Galloway and encompasses much of the Galloway Hills, part of Scotland's Southern Uplands. This is a wild and uninhabited area, allowing enormous scope for independent exploration in the sure and certain knowledge that – despite all those visitors – total solitude is never far away. There is more than enough lonely backcountry to get lost in (hopefully not literally) and there are 27 waymarked trails, covering every type of landscape within the park and catering for every level of ability. Wild camping is a popular summer option, and other recreational opportunities include fishing in stunning surroundings for trout and salmon (in season), canoeing, mountain-biking, horse riding and wildlife-watching (top sightings are red deer, pine marten, otter and red squirrel, golden eagles, black grouse and nightjar).

There are three first-class visitor centres to help point newcomers in their desired direction: Kirroughtree (reached from Newton Stewart or New Galloway), Glentrool (reached from Newton Stewart) and Clatteringshaws (reached from New Galloway). The latter is on the Galloway Red Kite Trail and has a superb interactive wildlife exhibition.

HOW TO GET THERE:
Enter the park from any of the surrounding villages – Newton Stewart, New Galloway, Gatehouse of Fleet, Dalmellington or Castle Douglas. The main road to Newton Stewart is the A75. There are three single-track access roads into the Galloway Hills – one from the A712 near the dam at Clatteringshaws reservoir to Craigencallie; one forestry toll road to Loch Doon, Loch Doon Castle and Stinchar Bridge near Dalmellington; and one from Glentrool village to Bruce's Stone.

WHEN TO GO:
Any time (even if a winter visit goes no further than Kirroughtree Visitor Centre to introduce the kids to Santa and pick up a sustainably grown Scottish Christmas tree).

DON'T MISS:
A visit to Bruce's Stone, high on the northern shore of Loch Trool, which can be reached by car (see above). This memorial commemorates Robert the Bruce's first victory over the English, when he was a fugitive hiding in the Galloway Hills.

YOU SHOULD KNOW:
In 2009 Galloway Forest Park was the first place in the United Kingdom to be awarded Dark-Sky Park status by the International Dark-Sky Association, on the grounds of having a UK night sky unusually free of light pollution.

Isle of Jura

HOW TO GET THERE:
There's a small and chunky car ferry that operates all year round from Port Askaig on the east coast of the adjacent island of Islay to Feolin slipway on Jura. There's a direct summer service between Tayvallich on the mainland and Craighouse.
WHEN TO GO:
Spring to autumn to avoid fierce winter gales.
DON'T MISS:
A taste of Isle of Jura Single Malt. The distillery has been operating since 1810 at Craighouse, and produces a smooth, light whisky up to 21 years old – plus one named Superstition for the island's mystical heritage and the many traditional superstitions respected by islanders. The distillery may be visited by appointment.
YOU SHOULD KNOW:
The writer George Orwell – known to the locals by his given name of Eric Blair – lived on Jura towards the premature end to his life (he died of tuberculosis, aged 46, in 1950). The *Animal Farm* author moved to the island in 1946 to escape the pressures of London literary life, taking over remote and abandoned Barnhill farmhouse at the north end of the island where he wrote his famous dystopian novel *1984*, which put the world 'Orwellian' into the English language.

The Paps of Jura

Once the exclusive fiefdom of the powerful Campbell clan, the Isle of Jura in the Inner Hebrides is now split into different estates. There are lots more red deer than people on Jura and deer stalking is a principal contributor to the island's economy. The other is tourism. With an area of around 370 sq km (143 sq mi) and some 200 inhabitants, this starkly beautiful island remains a classic unspoilt Scottish wilderness that draws visitors who love wild and lonely places.

Most people live in the pretty village of Craighouse on the east coast, which has a post-office shop, hotel, tearoom, village hall and church. A narrow road (pretentiously titled the A846) follows the eastern and southern coasts. Jura House in the south has the sheltered Walled Garden, open to the public, featuring many exotic species from the Antipodes. Respecting the awesome power of Atlantic gales, the rugged and unsheltered west coast is uninhabited, but has a number of raised beaches (rocky marine shelves above sea level). The island's western side is dominated by three conical peaks known as the Paps of Jura. These are included in the challenging annual Isle of Jura Fell Race sponsored by the local distillery. Between the northern tip of Jura and neighbouring Scarba is the Gulf of Corryvreckan, complete with notorious whirlpool.

Jura has many historical sites, including Iron Age forts and prehistoric standing stones, but the landscape is the main attraction. The island has assorted habitats – lough, woodland, bog, heather, grassland, mountains, cliffs, bays and beaches – and is a walkers' paradise. Along the way it's impossible not to see red deer, and perfectly possible to spot a wealth of wildlife such as seals, otters, golden eagles, sea eagles, hen harriers, buzzards, assorted songbirds and many species of sea bird.

Knoydart Peninsula

A house nestled in the tranquil haven of the Knoydart Peninsula.

Travellers tempted to visit Scotland's last great protected wilderness will even enjoy the bit that is sometimes frustrating when it comes to such adventures – getting there. Because, for all but seafarers or those rich enough to hire a helicopter, a visit to the remote Knoydart Peninsula will start with a drive up *Rathad nan Eilan* – the Road to the Isles. This starts at Fort William and goes through breathtaking coastal scenery as it passes through Glenfinnan and Arisaig *en route* to the port of Mallaig. A good alternative is making the same journey by train, using the spectacular West Highland Line.

The peninsula is sandwiched between Lochs Nevis and Hourn. This National Scenic Area, known locally as the 'rough bounds', attracts sailors, hill walkers and mountaineers – the latter including those intent on Munro-bagging, with two of these must-climb mountains on offer. The pretty whitewashed village of Inverie crouches below conifer woodland on the north side of Loch Nevis, beneath the intimidating bulk of Sgurr Coire Choinnichean. The peninsula's one metalled road goes nowhere, making Inverie the largest mainland settlement in Britain not connected to the national road network. Inverie is the ideal base from which to explore Knoydart's dramatic landscape. There are guided ranger walks on Wednesdays that allow day visitors to experience this extraordinary place without staying over, timed to end before the last return ferry to Mallaig.

There are a number of excellent B&B establishments in and around the village of Inverie, and also some self-catering cottages, farmhouses, converted barns and bothies. It's advisable to book early if summer accommodation is required – or take a tent – for some visitors return year after year to recharge their batteries in this tranquil haven far from the hustle and bustle of modern life.

HOW TO GET THERE:
By boat from Mallaig, or on foot – a modest 30-km (19-mi) hike through rough country. There is also the Arnisdale Ferry Service, from the village of the same name on Loch Hourn – custom trips to the north side of Knoydart Peninsula by small boat a speciality.

WHEN TO GO:
Any time, although the peninsula can be bleak in winter.

DON'T MISS:
A swift half at the remotest pub in Britain, the Old Forge at Inverie. It has six moorings, offers good food, is open all day for 364 days a year . . . and has that all-important clothes-drying rack by a roaring fire.

YOU SHOULD KNOW:
The peninsula is now owned and managed by the Knoydart Foundation, a partnership set up to maintain and manage 70 sq km (27 sq mi) of the wildest county in Britain. This put the peninsula's future back in the hands of the local community, 150 years after most of the inhabitants were evicted and sent to Canada as part of the infamous Highland Clearances.

Rannoch Moor

HOW TO GET THERE:
The A82 crosses Rannoch Moor on its way north from Bridge of Orchy to Gen Coe and Fort William, as does the West Highland Line.

WHEN TO GO:
Spring to autumn, unless extreme winter sports are the objective.

DON'T MISS:
Breathtaking Loch Ossian, tucked away in the northeastern corner of Rannoch Moor, far from public roads (but just a short hike from remote Corrour rail station on the West Highland Line).

Rannoch Moor can seem like the last place on Earth when the weather closes in, as cloud swirls down from the hills and relentless rain starts falling. This large triangular expanse of boggy Highland moorland stands on its inverted apex to the west of Loch Rannoch and extends to around 130 sq km (50 sq mi). The moor is a level plateau surrounded by mountains and consists of innumerable lochs and lochans, streams and peat bogs, heather and scrub.

The moor is crossed by one road and a railway, but still remains one of Scotland's loneliest enclaves, described thus by Robert Louis Stevenson in his novel *Kidnapped*: 'A wearier-looking desert a man never saw'. He must have seen it on a bad day, for when the sun comes out this dour other-worldly place takes on a sparkle all its own. Weary hikers plodding across the moor on the West Highland Way are re-energized. Others are tempted to park their cars and roam through this extraordinary landscape, while some let the train take the initial strain before doing the same. Achallader is at the moor's southern apex, Rannoch Station is at the northeastern corner, while the northwest is delineated by the mouth of Glen Coe.

The isolated situation of the moor and the fact there is no west-east road crossing is underlined by the realization that anyone who decides to walk the 16-km (10-mi) track between the Youth Hostel near Rannoch Station and the Kings House Hotel on the main A82 road for a refreshing drink is in for a 32-km (20-mi) hike. There's no chance of getting a lift or taking a taxi back to rest weary feet, for the shortest route back to Rannoch Station by road is over 160 km (100 mi) long.

YOU SHOULD KNOW:
Those who prefer to look rather than do can get a feel for Rannoch Moor by riding the aforementioned West Highland Line, whose Victorian builders had to support the tracks on a base of imported earth and ashes laced with timber and brushwood to reinforce the boggy ground. It's not a bad option – the 'Iron Road to the Isles' is one of the most scenic railway routes in Britain and is considered to be one of the world's best rail journeys.

The jagged Cuillin Hills on the Isle of Skye are seen here from Loch Coruisk.

Loch Coruisk

'Speed, bonnie boat, like a bird on the wing . . . Over the sea to Skye' is part of a famous Jacobite lament for the lost cause of Bonnie Prince Charlie in the 18th century, commemorating the Young Pretender's flight from Uist to the Isle of Skye with the help of Flora MacDonald, following his defeat at the Battle of Culloden in 1746. In fact, the origins of *The Skye Boat Song* are not traditional – for it is a Victorian invention written after one Annie MacLeod heard and remembered the melody of her oarsmen's Gaelic rowing song in a boat on Loch Coruisk.

Whatever the origins, it's a haunting song, and people are still going over the sea to enjoy the stunning natural beauty of Skye. One of the highlights of any trip to the island must be a visit to that self-same Loch Coruisk, a freshwater lake that takes its name from the Gaelic *Coire Uisg* (Cauldron of Waters). This must surely be one of the most wild and dramatic visions in all the Scottish Highlands. The northern end of the loch is surrounded by the jagged fangs of the Black Cullin range and it is hidden by those inhospitable basalt mountains. A small rill from the southern end discharges into Loch Scavaig, a sea loch.

This fact is a life-saver for those who lack the time, energy or fitness to reach this compelling but isolated natural wonder on foot, for boat trips from various starting points on and off the island deposit people at the iron steps on Lock Scavaig that give access to the short but rocky walk to Scotland's most magnificent freshwater loch. The boat trip alone is worth the entry fee, with Loch Coruisk itself a stunning visual bonus.

HOW TO GET THERE:
First get yourself to Skye. Thereafter take a boat from Elgol on the shores of Loch Scavaig at the end of Srathaird Peninsula (easy way) or hike the same trip along the shoreline (hard way, a long walk along a path with difficult sections including the notorious Bad Step above a vertical drop to the sea). An alternative 11-km (7-mi) rough tramp is from Sligachan down Glen Sligachan.

WHEN TO GO:
April to October for the boat trip from Elgol

DON'T MISS:
A scenic boat trip to Loch Coruisk followed by a couple of hours exploring the environs of this inspiring lake after fellow-passengers have departed, before returning to Elgol on foot along one of the most impressive coastal paths in Scotland.

YOU SHOULD KNOW:
Loch Coruisk has inspired many a painter – including the well-travelled J W M Turner – and attracted a number of literary giants such as James Boswell and Samuel Johnson.

Sandwood Bay

Where's Great Britain's finest beach? You've guessed it – the answer that would be disputed by none who have been there is Sandwood Bay, facing the restless Atlantic Ocean close to the northwestern tip of Scotland. The beach is a 2-km (1-mi) stretch of wide pinkish sand backed by impressive sand dunes and a small loch, which curves between craggy cliffs. An imposing sea stack guards the southern end. For sheer majesty, this place takes some beating, but perhaps its true appeal is that there's every chance of having private use of this beautiful wild place.

Even in high summer it is likely that only a few determined souls will share this special strand, for a real effort is required to get there. Once, it was possible to keep driving after the road started to peter out into a rough track, abandoning the car when further progress was impossible and walking from there. Nowadays, there's a mandatory car park at the dead end of the nearest road, after which a gate and well-defined 6-km (4-mi) path leads across undulating moorland to the beach, passing Sandwood Loch on the way. As the descent to the beach begins, roofless Sandwood Cottage is on the right – providing a good spot to camp for those who think one day in this special place isn't enough.

They're not wrong. Simply sitting on the beach soaking up the stark beauty of this lonely beach is a great beginning, but after that comes the urge to explore – the sand, the dunes, Sandwood Loch, adjoining cliffs. Some imbued with pioneering spirit even set out to follow the shore up to Cape Wrath, a name that says everything about this Atlantic coastline.

HOW TO GET THERE:
A minor road leads north from Rhiconich, just past Achlyness on the A838. It winds alongside Loch Inchard to Kinlochbervie and on to Oldshoremore, after which the road expires at Blairmore. Park at the end and walk northwards towards the beach.

WHEN TO GO:
Any time – the beach is delightful in summer, but truly magisterial in winter when angry Atlantic waves lash the beach and flying spray clouds the cold air, beneath a dark and steely sky.

DON'T MISS:
The honesty box in the car park – Sandwood Bay is owned by the John Muir Trust and contributions help to preserve this priceless beach.

YOU SHOULD KNOW:
Not seeing doesn't add up to not believing – powerful local superstition suggests the ghost of a bearded sailor whose Spanish Armada galleon was wrecked on the rocky coast used to knock on the windows of Sandwood Cottage and he still haunts the bay – perhaps intent on pursuing the mermaids said to disport themselves on shore when nobody is around. Approach quietly, just in case.

The sun sets over Sandwood Bay.

Glens of Antrim

Known by locals as 'The Glens', this Area of Outstanding Natural Beauty in Northern Ireland is officially designated as the Glens of Antrim. There are nine of these stunning valleys, together offering a concentrated cocktail of awe-inspiring scenery within an area of some 50 sq km (19 sq mi), which includes glacial valleys and tundra plateau, boglands and grazing, rivers and waterfalls, vertical cliffs and sandy beaches.

The Glens radiate from the Antrim Plateau down to the northwest coast and serve as a major tourist attraction. But there's more than enough dramatic scenery to go around so there's no need to feel crowded, especially if avoiding high summer and making an effort to stray from the well-beaten visitors' track. Famed in Irish poetry, song and myth, these lush green valleys seem like secret wonderlands alive with the sound of running water and birdsong.

Each glen has its own character, each merits leisurely exploration. Glenarm – the glen of the army – has a village of the same name. Glencloy is the glen of the hedges. Fertile Glenariff is the so-called Queen of the Glens. Glenballyemon is geographically the middle glen of nine. Rugged Glenaan is the site of legendary Ossian's grave. Glencorp is the glen of the slaughtered, named for a long-forgotten event in Ireland's violent past. Glendun, spanned by a viaduct carrying the main Cushendall-Ballycastle road, is the glen of the brown river. Glenshesk is the sedgey glen and Glentaisie is named for the princess of nearby Rathin Island. It would take a lifetime to explore them all, so it's a case of 'take your pick'. Whichever is chosen there are a few roads, but this is a mission best undertaken on foot armed with no more than a map, stout shoes, a flask of tea and camera with spare memory card.

Glanariff – 'Queen of the Glens'

Mourne Mountains

The very words have a romantic ring, and the Mourne Mountains in County Down do not disappoint, for this Area of Outstanding Natural Beauty is generally regarded as the most picturesque mountain region in Ireland. Thanks to the words of the popular song penned by Percy French in 1896 ('Where the Mountains of Mourne sweep down to the sea'), they are also Ireland's most famous mountains.

This compact range due south of Belfast overlooks Carlingford Lough close to the Irish Republic. The mountains are contained within a rough triangle just 24 km (15 mi) long by 13 km (8 mi) wide with apex-points formed by Newcastle, Warrenpoint and Kilkeel. Among around 60 high tops in the Mournes are a dozen granite peaks rising to a height of 600 m (2,000 ft) or more, including Northern Ireland's highest – Slieve Donard. Others in this wild landscape have quaint names such as Slieve Muck, Brandy Pad, Butter Mountain, Buzzard's Roost, Cock and Hen Mountains, Devil's Coach Road, Eagle Mountain and Pigeon Rock.

With rugged mountains, grazing pastures, heather moorland, forests, drumlins, lakes, rivers, coastal plains and wonderful sandy beaches, the area is a magnet for get-up-and-go outdoor enthusiasts. Walking is a major activity, with everyone from afternoon strollers to serious hill walkers finding more than enough to satisfy them. Climbers, too, can find pitches to test every level of competence. Seven signed cycle trails offer varying degrees of difficulty and length, while dedicated mountain-bikers with thighs like tree trunks have their own marked course. Fishing and horse riding are also popular options. For those who prefer not to wander yonder on spec, there are wonderful reserves to enjoy (Castlewellan, Tollymore and Kilbroney Forest Parks, Donard Forest, Silent Valley, Cranfield Beach and Murlough Bay).

Sand dunes at Murlough Nature Reserve with views to Dundrum Bay and the Mourne Mountains

HOW TO GET THERE:
The Mournes can be accessed using a network of minor roads from Castlewellan and Newcastle in the north and Rostrevor in the south, or various turnings off the main A2 coast road from Newcastle to Rostrevor via Kilkeel.

WHEN TO GO:
Any time

DON'T MISS:
The chance to partake of some *al fresco* dining out in a beautiful spot that has been voted as one of Britain's Top 20 Picnic Sites – Tollymore Forest Park near Newcastle, which offers excellent views of the sea and surrounding Mourne Mountains and is itself handsomely endowed with woodland, green sward and delightful rivers.

YOU SHOULD KNOW:
The Great Wall of County Down (actually it's a simple but rather long dry-stone wall more prosaically called the Mourne Wall) runs for 35 km (22 mi) and links 15 mountain summits. It dates from the early years of the 20th century and was built over two decades to define the boundary of an area purchased by Belfast's water authorities to ensure security of supply for Ireland's growing industrial powerhouse. Silent Valley reservoir is a scenic reminder of their efforts.

Lough Allen

This beautiful lake atop the River Shannon is shared between Counties Leitrim and Roscommon, with the former having the lion's share and the latter a mere morsel. This is the uppermost of three loughs on Ireland's great river and lies beneath the Iron Mountains near the Shannon's source on Cuilcagh Mountain. Lough Allen is 13 km (8 mi) long and 5 km (3 mi) wide. The water level is controlled by sluice gates and can therefore fluctuate by as much as 2.5 m (8 ft), revealing many ancient crannog dwelling sites when low.

Lough Allen has suffered from insensitive examples of modern tourist development, but by and large remains an unspoilt gem set in stunning Leitrim countryside. This is a traditional tract of rural Ireland that is sparsely populated, with the lough separating the hilly northwest from a relatively flat southeast. It is a land of extraordinary pastoral beauty, with soaring mountains and plunging valleys, rolling pastures and woodland, lakes and rivers – plus a short stretch of Atlantic coastline.

The lake itself is a wonderful stretch of water, fed by numerous small streams that descend the slopes of adjacent mountains, which are steep but not precipitous.

This is wild country – a place of bogs, heather and rocks with some relatively recent woodland planting. The lake is a noted angling hotspot, and eco-friendly watersports such as windsurfing and kayaking are popular. The limit of the Shannon navigation is at the north shore of the lake, with access from the extensive Shannon waterway system via scenic Lough Allen Canal at the southern end, originally built to carry coal from the nearby Aringa mines in the early 1800s. There are many signed walking routes around the lake and various stables offer the means to explore the shore and surrounding countryside on horseback.

The Burren

If there's a more bizarre landscape in all Ireland, it remains a secret – for surely nothing can wrest that quirky crown from The Burren. This karst limestone region – one of Europe's largest – extends to around 300 sq km (115 sq mi) bounded by the Atlantic to the west and Galway Bay to the north. The name comes from the Irish *Boireann*, meaning 'Great Rock', and it's certainly that. These rolling hills are made up of limestone pavements criss-crossed with a distinctive pattern (*karren*) of cracks (*grikes*) and isolated rocks (*clints*).

The Burren seems like a barren wilderness at a first distant glance, but closer inspection reveals rich vegetation growing in the narrow cracks. This habitat is so unusual that Mediterranean, arctic and alpine plants live side by side, with one alpine – the blue spring gentian – serving as The Burren's tourist-board symbol. This wild and empty place will not appeal to people who like their natural wonders to be big and bold, yet more discerning explorers will be captivated by green lanes where it's possible to walk for long distances amidst this unique landscape without seeing a soul. Along the way will be innumerable signs of The Burren's rich heritage – dozens of megalithic tombs, standing stones, Celtic crosses and traces of villages abandoned during the Great Famine.

And those who only do 'big and bold' need not despair, for The Burren's muscular coastline is magnificent – coming to a dramatic high point at the Cliffs of Moher towards the southwestern boundary. These are as big and bold as they come, towering up to 214 m (702 ft) above the Atlantic. There are spectacular coastal views from the top, but these have to be shared. The cliffs attract over one million visitors a year.

HOW TO GET THERE:
The Burren is roughly delineated by a circle formed by the villages of Ballyvaughan, Kinvara, Tubber, Corofin, Kilfenora and Lisdoonvarna in northwest County Clare.
WHEN TO GO:
Any time (spring for the fabulous wild flowers)
DON'T MISS:
The annual Doolin Festival, held over the weekend following the last Friday in February. Dedicated to the world-famous local musician Micho Russell and notable for the West Clare style of lively concertina playing, this is also a wonderful showcase for traditional Irish musicians from all over the country. This small fishing village beneath the Cliffs of Moher describes itself as 'a doorway to The Burren', and visitors who don't make the festival can still enjoy nightly Irish music at any one of three pubs.
YOU SHOULD KNOW:
During Oliver Cromwell's brutal mid-17th-century campaign in Ireland his lieutenant general of horse, one Edmund Ludlow, uttered a phrase that has never been forgotten and is enshrined in local history. During the course of operations to suppress resistance in The Burren, he sourly commented 'It is a country where there is not enough water to drown a man, wood enough to hang him nor earth enough to bury him.'

Limestone criss-crossed with a distinctive pattern of cracks and isolated rocks – a typical Burren landscape

The rural coastal countryside of the Beara Peninsula

Beara Peninsula

The Wild West of Ireland isn't what it used to be, with tourist pressures and prosperity brought by Celtic Tiger years inevitably changing this once-remote area. But even though the lower slopes of coastal mountains are now dotted with the white rectangles of new bungalows, one beside each abandoned stone cottage, these are no more than small blemishes on the face of a hauntingly beautiful landscape. One place that – despite some development in its settlements – retains its traditional character is the Beara Peninsula in the far southwest of the country.

Marooned between the Kenmare River to the north (in true Irish fashion, a bay) and Bantry Bay to the south, the Beara Peninsula was once the stronghold of the O'Sullivan clan and it's easy to understand why it was one of the last strongholds to resist the conquering English in Elizabeth I's reign. Today, the established tourist trail is the Ring of Beara, a 195-km (120-mi) circumnavigation of the untamed peninsula that allows motorists to enjoy some of Ireland's most magical coastline and imagine that – but for their modern chariot and others like it – they have gone back in time.

The ring begins in Kenmare and ends at Glengarriff, passing through Adrigole, Castletown Bere and Allihies along the way. Top attractions include ruined Dunboy Castle, Puxley Mansion, a copper-mining museum and Derreen Gardens. There are also various tourist traps, but for those who like to get away from it all there are countless opportunities to explore the rugged shoreline and/or vanish into one of two mountain ranges that run down the centre, the Caha and Slieve Kish, bisected only by two roads along their entire length. For determined off-road hikers, the breathtaking Beara Way also runs right round the peninsula.

HOW TO GET THERE:
Kenmare and Glengarriff are on the N70 coast road.
WHEN TO GO:
Any time
DON'T MISS:
The wonderful coastal vista to be seen from the top of Healy Pass, which connects north and south coasts of the peninsula south of Lauragh, with a commanding outlook over Beara that stretches away to the neighbouring Iveragh Peninsula.
YOU SHOULD KNOW:
Anyone with a day to spare should take the Dursey Island cable car – the only one in Europe specifically used to span a stretch of water, in this case treacherous Dursey Sound with its powerful tidal race. Go in the off season and this wild and lonely isle can be shared with fewer than a dozen inhabitants and their livestock . . . some of which may occasionally be encountered in the cable car as it goes to or comes back from market.

Marquenterre Dunes

The estuary of the River Somme on the Picardy coast is the largest in northern France at 72 sq km (28 sq mi), but it's shrinking steadily as a result of sedimentation. That means the estuary is a rich vegetated habitat and the prolonged process of silting has created one of Europe's most extensive sand-dune complexes between the Somme and Canche estuaries. Le Marquenterre is an impressive expanse of dunes fronting La Manche (the English Channel) that have been stabilized by pinewood plantations. The place is home to an assortment of interesting wildlife, including a colony of seals, but – apart from satisfying those who can't resist the lure of exploring wild and lonely places – the real attraction is birds, birds, birds.

In addition to a varied resident population, Le Marquenterre provides refuge for an enormous number of migrating birds stopping off to rest and refuel during the long two-way journey from Scandinavia to Africa. This strange land of dunes, pine forests and tamarisk, with salty meres and ponds rich with water plants, provides an ideal habitat and it's possible to wander undisturbed for hours and spot many of the birds that occupy this haunting landscape. But those who need or welcome expert guidance should take their binoculars to the Marquenterre Ornithological Park, one of only two bird reserves in France.

It offers three waymarked walks – a short one taking around 90 minutes and two longer ones needing perhaps three hours. The beauty of these is that they were designed to pass numerous points ideal for observing birds. There are many strategically placed hides along the way, some of which may be manned by knowledgeable guides and have telescopes trained on nesting sites in the breeding season. The park also offers informative ranger-guided walks.

HOW TO GET THERE:
The Marquenterre Ornithological Park is situated off the D940 near Rue, an attractive former fishing village marooned inland as the Somme silted up. The extensive dune system is bounded to the east by the D940, which runs north from Le Crotoy on the Somme Estuary via Rue to Conchil-le-Temple, and is roughly parallel to the main A16 road.

WHEN TO GO:
Any time (winter visiting to the park between November and March is possible only at weekends, as part of an official guided tour). The northern bird migration takes place in April and May, the return journey from August to October.

DON'T MISS:
Ornithologists (and others) will be fascinated by the Maison de l'Oiseau (House of Birds). Find it between Cayeux-sur-Mer and St-Valéry-sur-Somme on the other side of the estuary.

YOU SHOULD KNOW:
As one of France's only two bird sanctuaries, Marquenterre is not quite the safe haven the word 'sanctuary' might suggest – as soon as the French waterfowl season opens, the surrounds of the relatively small reserve echo with the sound of gunfire as sporting shooters take full toll of their feathered quarry.

Le Marquenterre – one of Europe's most extensive sand dune complexes

Iles d'Ouessant

In the wild Atlantic Ocean, close to Cape Finistère, lies the one place in Brittany that has a different name in English. Ushant is a corruption of Ouessant, one of only two inhabited islands (the other is Molène, to the southeast) in the rocky Iles d'Ouessant – rocky granite outposts separated from the mainland by treacherous seas. A visit to Ushant involves taking the car ferry – capacity just two cars, so don't bother taking yours as the island's main road extends to just 6 km (4 mi) long and the whole island is only 8 km (5 mi) long and half as wide.

Ushant has one significant settlement. Lampaul has all the necessary facilities, including four hotels, and there is also a campsite for do-it-yourself visitors. Although it is a popular destination, Ushant never gets overrun and this windswept place remains a wild and unspoilt destination even in high summer. The island is surrounded by towering cliffs that plunge into the sea, with nary a guard rail in sight, and intrepid observers can find innumerable spectacular vantage points from which to study this dramatic coastline in all its moods. The interior is a virtually treeless plateau covered in heather and springy turf, with occasional stunted trees and low scrub crouching in hollows. There is gorse and a kaleidoscope of wild flowers in season.

There are few established paths so walkers go where they please, while bicycles may be hired from the ferry terminal by those who prefer pedal-power. Ornithologists love the Iles d'Ouessant, for this craggy archipelago is a welcome stopping-off point for numerous migratory birds such as the wheatear and ring ouzel, with around 350 species recorded. Beyond that, the obvious wildlife seems confined to the large rabbit population and lizards sunning themselves on dry-stone walls.

Haut Allier

The Auvergne has been described as 'France's best-kept secret' and, if it is, a place that even most French open-air enthusiasts have yet to discover, the unspoilt Haut Allier is even less well known. Located in the western half of the Haute-Loire department in southern Auvergne (although the principal river is actually the Allier, a Loire tributary), this is the driest and sunniest part of the Auvergne, which constantly provides a reminder that the South of France is not far away.

The Haut Allier – unexploited for mass tourism – is emblematic of authentic rural France at its best. The landscape is stunning and includes large tracts of wild country. The River Allier rises in the Cevennes Mountains and features extraordinary riverscapes with awesome rock formations. The river runs through and is surrounded by stunning gorges – usually having no road access – that are often densely wooded. This is France's last great wild river and the area is renowned among those in the know as white-water rafting and canoeing heaven. Primitive camping, backpacking, rambling, day-hiking and mountain-biking are also popular, using an extensive network of paths through this natural playground. Anglers come for the trout and salmon (there is an extensive fry-stocking programme designed to maintain the salmon run).

The Haut-Allier (high valley of the upper Allier) is a place where it's possible to get up close and personal with Mother Nature – either at a leisurely pace or as part of an action-packed adventure, which could be anything from rock climbing through bungee-jumping to dog-sledding in winter. To that may be added the heritage dimension – discovering castles, abbeys, old churches, mills and delightful medieval villages full of vernacular buildings in the mellow local stone, many with traditional weekly markets.

HOW TO GET THERE:
The Haut Allier lies to the south of Brioude, a delightful settlement on the banks of the River Allier. Brioude is to the south of Clermont-Ferrand on the N102 road, which strikes off to the east from the A75.

WHEN TO GO:
Any time (winter brings enough snow to satisfy any self-respecting cross-country skier).

DON'T MISS:
The magnificent Basilica of St Julien in Brioude, constructed between the 11th and 14th centuries – the largest church in the Auvergne, this splendid building has some wonderfully colourful frescoes.

YOU SHOULD KNOW:
There is an annual series of summer concerts put on in some of Haut Allier's beautiful medieval churches, running from late June until August and reinforcing the area's status as a *Pays d'art et d'histoire* (Rural place of outstanding artistic and historical merit).

Millevaches Regional Nature Park

HOW TO GET THERE:
The park is criss-crossed by a network of lanes and minor roads. Good starting points for a journey of exploration are the N141-D941 Saint-Léonard-de-Noblat to Aubusson road in the north or the A89 Tulle-Ussel road in the south.

WHEN TO GO:
Any time (but note that summer mornings can be very misty and winter days can be very chilly).

DON'T MISS:
Millevaches Regional Nature Park at a glance. This unique experience is available at purpose-built Mont Bessou viewing tower at the southeastern edge of the plateau at its high point. Set in an area of woodland just north of Meymac, the tower affords stunning vistas across the park and to the distant Cantal mountains in the south.

YOU SHOULD KNOW:
Don't make the assumption that the park is called after the brown Limousin cattle that may be seen everywhere. It is perhaps named for distinctive rock formations that look like cows (*vaches*) – or possibly as a combination of the Celtic *melo* (high) and Latin *vacua* (empty). Take your pick – it has thousands of Limousin cattle, lots of rock formations that look like cows (with a little imagination) and it's definitely both high and mostly empty of human habitation.

Unwilling to do anything by halves, when the authorities created Millevaches Regional Nature Park in 2004 they ensured it fell within all three of Limousin's departments – Corrèze, Creuse and Haute-Vienne. Equivalent to the UK's Areas of Outstanding Natural Beauty, regional nature parks aim to preserve the best of the nation's fine countryside – an asset that France happily still possesses in abundance. Millevaches makes the point in spades.

This marvellous tract of wild landscape is located in the foothills of the awesome Massif Central. It covers an area of 3,150 sq km (1,216 sq mi), thinly populated by around 40,000 people who mainly live in the villages and small towns around the edge of the park that are characterized by wonderful vernacular stone buildings. An extensive granite plateau offers heather moorland and peat bogs, open grasslands and wildflower meadows, deciduous, coniferous and mixed forests, bubbling springs, rushing rivers and lakes. In fact, it is more of a gentle dome than a plateau, ranging in height from 600 m (1,968 ft) to 1,000 m (3,280 ft). The River Varre rises here, flowing north to feed the Loire, and the Vézère originates nearby but flows south into the Dordogne River.

The higher areas are heavily forested with little agricultural activity. Otherwise, a pleasing patchwork of woods and meadows is punctuated by the occasional field of sunflowers or maize. As is to be expected, Limousin cattle are everywhere. This is an area that provides real satisfaction to those who like exploring unspoilt places where they can be alone amid the vastness of nature. But for those who like a little conventional tourist fun, large reservoirs are nearby. These have beaches, campsites and picnic areas, while sailing and boating should appeal to the nautically minded.

La Coubre Forest

The Avert Peninsula at the mouth of the Gironde Estuary borders the coast and its tip offers the opportunity to go down to the woods – and shore – without feeling in the least bit crowded. With around 500 sq km (193 sq mi) to explore, La Coubre Forest is a real get-away-from-it-all destination. As with so many things in the modern world, La Coubre Forest is not quite so original as it now appears, having been planted in the 19th century to stabilize a large area of sand dunes. Also, this is a commercial woodland and there are tracts of clear felling awaiting replanting – although compared to the vast presence of the whole, these hardly intrude.

It's possible to drive through the forest and see some worthwhile sights – including Bonne Anse Bay, La Coubre lighthouse, La Bouverie forest lodge and Pointe Espagnol, where a path from the car park leads to a particularly fine beach with far-reaching views that was named for a Spanish vessel wrecked in 1823. For those who like being beside the seaside in a natural environment entirely unspoiled by tourist trappings, La Coubre's sandy Côte Sauvage is a terrific find.

That should be part of any itinerary, but in truth La Coubre deserves to be explored at leisure, on foot or two wheels. The considerable expanse of this light-and-airy pine forest is criss-crossed with established trails. Serious hikers will be tempted by the long-distance path from Royan to Ronce-les-Bains and the island of Oléron, although walkers can roam the forest unchecked. For cyclists who prefer established routes to pedalling at will, there is a cycle track from Saint-Palais-sur-Mer to Ronce-les-Bains, a 60-km (37-mi) round trip that takes in both coast and woodland. There are also marked mountain-bike routes in the forest.

HOW TO GET THERE:
The D25 road between Ronce-les-Bains and La Palmyre passes through the middle of the forest, a drive of some 20 km (12 mi).

WHEN TO GO:
At any time, although July and August do see plenty of visitors, so those who prefer going alone might prefer the off season.

DON'T MISS:
The splendid outlook from the base of the Tour de Gardour, a metal communications tower just off the D25. Follow the arrow sign from the road and park, then take the short footpath and enjoy a breathtaking panorama that takes in the forest, Atlantic Ocean and Gironde Estuary.

YOU SHOULD KNOW:
Be aware that certain paths and areas within the forest may be restricted on Thursdays, the day reserved for hunting. Guided walks are offered every day in season (barring Sundays and public holidays), starting at 10.00 from La Bouverie on the Côte Sauvage (take signposted road 44 from the D25).

Chaîne des Puys

A *puy* is a volcanic mountain with a rounded outline. And one of the best places for seeing lots of these shapely domes is the Massif Central's Chaîne des Puys. This run of eight lava domes, 48 cinder cones and 15 maars (volcanic explosion craters) stretches for just 40 km (25 mi) and reaches the high point at the Puy de Dôme towards the middle. This is the highest point in the Auvergne, attracting half a million visitors annually.

There's a regular bus to the summit from Clemont-Ferrand station in summer and there's parking at the lofty visitor centre, but for many the objective is not so much the destination – impressive though that may be – but getting there unaided. This involves ascending an old Roman road, Le sentier des muletiers, or taking the northern path via the Nid de la Poule crater. Cyclists can emulate some famous stage finishes on the Tour de France by using the road during limited periods when it is closed to motor traffic. To be fair, some people aren't that interested in the going up – for numerous paragliders coming down is the high.

If that sounds a bit touristy, the rest of the Chaîne des Puys maintains its unyielding rocky character without any compromise with the modern world. Rocky tops rise above tree-clad flanks, maars have become lonely lakes and occasional isolated farmsteads may be found in the valleys below. Those drawn to wild places can have free rein and it's possible to tramp through this unspoilt mountain landscape for hours without seeing anyone. The Auvergne is an area of great natural beauty where the timeless traditions of rural France are kept alive beneath the watchful gaze of extinct volcanoes, and nowhere is this truer than around the Chaîne des Puys.

An extinct volcano in the Chaîne des Puys

HOW TO GET THERE:
The Chaîne des Puys is just to the east of Clermont-Ferrand and runs on a north-south axis. Puy de Dôme is just off the A75 road.

WHEN TO GO:
Winter to avoid the tourist hordes – and to admire the view of the Chaîne des Puys from the top of Puy de Dôme when there's snow on the ground, which can only be described as breathtaking.

DON'T MISS:
It is thought that the summit of the Puy de Dôme has served as a gathering place for special ceremonies since prehistoric times, and the Romans were certainly no exception – be sure to inspect the ruined Gallo-Roman temple built there and dedicated to Mercury.

YOU SHOULD KNOW:
When the 6-km (4-mi) road up the Puy de Dôme is too busy in summer motorists are required to park at the foot of the mountain and take a shuttle bus to the summit.

Massif du Sancy

This ancient stratovolcano in the Auvergne's Puy-de-Dôme department has been inactive for over ten millennia, so it's reasonable to suppose that no eruption is imminent. The Massif du Sancy was created around 250,000 years ago when molten rock exploded through the Earth's crust to spawn a basalt giant. Today, the massif rises majestically from the middle of a plateau and at a soaraway 1,186 m (3,890 ft) takes the crown as the highest mountain in the centre of France – outgunned nationally only by those big guys in the Alps and Pyrenees. Over time it has eroded to a chaotic jumble of steep valleys and spiky needles.

The Massif du Sancy is an imposing sight from afar, a steep-sided monolith crouching along the skyline wearing a white cap of snow long after the surrounding countryside has thawed. Both northern and southern slopes are popular skiing locations, with a number of cable cars and lifts to make the going up easy (although biting winds call for warm clothing, even in summer). Determined mountaineers who prefer doing it the hard way will not be disappointed – some of the routes up the massif's rugged flanks are extremely testing. Despite winter-sports infrastructure, this remains an empty expanse of jumbled rock surrounded by rolling backcountry with fir woods, pastures, rushing streams and waterfalls that echo the mountain's lonely grandeur. The nature of the place may be judged from the evocative names of features such as Hell's Valley and the Devil's Teeth.

The town of Mont-Dore in the valley to the north has a dozen thermal springs known to and enjoyed by the Romans. The restorative waters contain iron, bicarbonate of soda and arsenic, the latter happily in non-lethal concentrations. The park alongside the River Dordogne contains relics of the Roman baths.

HOW TO GET THERE:
The nearest big town with an airport is Clermont-Ferrand, from whence a right turn from the southbound A75 onto the D229 at Coudes will morph into the D996 to Mont-Dore. The D203 loops around to the south of the Massif du Sancy.

WHEN TO GO:
The climate is severe and the main visitor season for non-winter-sporters is from mid June to mid September, when the autumn foliage is already turning.

DON'T MISS:
The truly awesome panoramic view from the Massif du Sancy summit – just reward for those fit enough to beat the meandering yet demanding Puy de Sancy summit trail . . . although lazybones can instead skip up 850 steps to the top from the cable-car station above Le Mont-Dore.

YOU SHOULD KNOW:
The valley to the north of the Massif du Sancy contains two streams called the Dore and Dogne that with relentless etymological logic merge to form the River Dordogne.

The imposing Massif du Sancy

Livradois-Forez Regional Nature Park

HOW TO GET THERE:
The park is to the east of Clermont-Ferrand and may be reached from the A75 road. The A72 to Thiers crosses the park from west to east and loops down the east side. The park itself has a network of country roads.
WHEN TO GO:
Any time
DON'T MISS:
An authentic taste of rural France in the welcoming town of Ambert in the centre of the park – the taste in question being that of Fourme d'Ambert, a delicious blue-veined cheese that is the local gastronomic speciality.
YOU SHOULD KNOW:
For those debating how to spend their time in the park, an excellent first stop is the visitor centre (Maison du Parc) in Saint-Gervais-sous-Meymont. Those who prefer to view some of the park's scenic charms through eddying steam will leap aboard the heritage steam train complete with observation car that runs (in season) between Courpière in the Puy-de-Dôme department and La Chaise-Dieu in Haute Loire.

They're not big as mountains go, but the Forez Mountains on the borders of Auvergne's Puy-de-Dôme and Haute-Loire departments have pine forests that seem a timeless haven of arboreal tranquillity. Across the Dore river valley is the Livradois, a wooded area of undulating plateau with granite outcrops. Together with gentle hills and slopes around Billom in the west, rolling forested valleys in the southwest and the fringes of the Auvergne's volcanic mountains in the southeast, these contrasting landscapes make up the Livradois-Forez Regional Nature Park, which – in addition to dramatic scenery – is as good a place as any in the land to experience the timeless rhythms of traditional French rural life.

The park has Chateldon and the famous French cutlery capital of Thiers in the north, Ambert and Usson in the middle and Brioude, Lavaudieu and La Chaise-Dieu towards the southern end. But this vast area that stretches from the plains of Limagne to the peaks of the Forez Mountains is essentially a rural backwater dotted with small villages and isolated hamlets. The contrasting terrain gives visitors with limited time available some regional food for thought – there's so much to see that it's hard to decide where to start and what to cram in.

Perhaps the answer is to follow the Route des Métiers – a fascinating circuit that includes castles, ancient monuments, museums and the workshops of craftsmen who still practise country skills passed down over time immemorial in the 21st century. This is not only a great opportunity to appreciate the heritage of this delightful area, but also provides an opportunity to make impulsive diversions into the extensive woodlands, explore river banks, swim in lakes or tramp across unspoilt high moors as the mood dictates. Whatever the choices, this magical nature park rarely disappoints.

Chartreuse Mountains

HOW TO GET THERE:
The mountains fall within a triangle formed by Grenoble, Chambéry and (at a distance) Lyon. The A41 road from Grenoble to Chambéry runs along the eastern flank of the Chartreuses, the A43 Chambéry to Lyon road crosses to the north and the A48 Grenoble to Lyon road provides access to the southwest. There is a network of minor roads within the mountains.

Eastern France's Chartreuse Mountains stretch down from the Lac du Bourget towards Grenoble. They are 45 km (28 mi) long and 25 km (15 mi) wide, forming the most southerly extension of the Jura Mountains and containing many impressive peaks. This limestone range is riddled with underground passages and caves, including the famous *Dent de Crolles* system that extends to an impressive 60 km (37 mi) in length. Above ground, the mountainous terrain makes a great backdrop for a few centres that cater for skiers, although the undeveloped Chartreuse Mountains serve mainly as a magnet for climbers and summer hikers.

They follow in illustrious footsteps. These wild and beautiful uplands were a regular calling point on 18th-century grand tours and subsequently attracted such artistic luminaries as painter J W M Turner and poet William Wordsworth. The mountains remain wild and beautiful, as confirmed by Regional Nature Park status awarded for scenic excellence and interesting cultural heritage. The eastern flanks fall abruptly into the Isère Valley, while the western slopes fall away more gently towards the Rhône Valley. The high ground consists of peaks and valleys. The tallest peak is Chamechaude at 2,082 m (6,831 ft), with other notable summits including Grand Som and Mont Granier.

The internal valleys have small rural communities supported by pastoral farming and sustainable forestry. These little settlements have distinctive vernacular architecture. Square houses sit beneath steeply pitched tile roofs, while shingle-roofed barns with massive cornerstones are constructed with irregular reddish stone. From the inhabited valleys wooded slopes rise to dramatic cliffs, above which the fit and determined hiker will find a magical world of high plateaus and secret valleys covered in grassland and stunted vegetation, beneath those impressive peaks. As wild places go, the Chartreuse Mountains are pretty special.

WHEN TO GO:
Summer is best for the backcountry walking, winter for slippery sports centred on Chamechaude.
DON'T MISS:
Le Fort du St Eynard, a well-restored 19th-century fortress just south of Le Sappey-en-Chartreuse, perched on a cliff top overlooking Grenoble. The fort is interesting, the views are magnificent and may be enjoyed during some excellent short walks.
YOU SHOULD KNOW:
Yes, the famous liqueur is made hereabouts, in the town of Voiron. It consists of distilled alcohol blended with an (inevitably secret) infusion of 130 herbal extracts that improves with age in the bottle. Originally created by monks at the Grand Chartreuse Monastery in the 18th century, revenue generated still helps to support the Carthusian order to this day.

The superb view from Charmant Som

Plateau du Vercors

The Vercors is a series of plateaux and mountains in the Isère and Drôme departments, surrounded by vertical limestone cliffs and divided by deep canyons. This remote and lonely place was the scene of fierce fighting between German troops and French Resistance *maquisards* during World War II, as the Maquis de Vercors group gallantly rose to tie up enemy forces that would otherwise have been available to counter the D-Day landings in June 1944. The doomed uprising is commemorated by a memorial and cemetery at the village of Vassieux-en-Vercors in the heart of the massif, where it all began.

Today's visitor can easily understand why this place was ideal for resisting the German conquerors (and collaborating French Militia) during the war. Today, the Vercors massif is a picturesque Regional Nature Park. But those daunting cliffs and broken terrain remain the same, explaining why it took 10,000 German soldiers delivered by glider and parachute to defeat 4,000 guerrilla fighters operating in territory perfect for ambush and evasion.

The Vercors has distinct sectors. These are the heavily forested Coulmes area in the northwest, the northern plateau nicknamed 'The Four Mountains' for obvious reasons, small western plateaus with their high summer pastures and deep gorges, plus the high plateaus that are the wildest and most remote part of the park. Such contrasting areas give the Plateau du Vercors enormous visual variety, but all of it is impressive. The massif is popular with get-away-from-it-all hikers and there are many signed and well-maintained trails. Many caverns can be explored without special equipment (or undue risk), while paragliding and white-water canoeing are other possibilities. Happily for the action-averse, sightseeing from the relative safety of a car offers breathtaking vistas from some of the most vertiginous roads in France (try the likes of the D76, D518 and D22 through precipitous gorges).

A lone hiker on the northern ridge of Mount Jocou walks towards the Col de Seysse with views of the Plateau du Vercors beyond.

The Gorges de la Dourbie and the mill (Moulin de Corps) by the river's edge

Dourbie Valley

The stunning grandeur of the three Tarn gorges takes the breath away, and of these natural masterpieces the Dourbie Valley is the most picturesque. Its wild slopes are wooded or covered with sparse vegetation at higher levels where the bare rock breaks through, and the stunning array of wild flowers has to be seen to be believed. The smallish but perfectly formed River Dourbie winds down this green valley from its source near Le Vigan in the Cévennes Mountains to join the Tarn at Millau.

The upper valley narrows into two spectacular granite and schist gorges that are 300 m (985 ft) deep. In the Cévennes foothills the river flows through the lush 'Garden of Aveyron', a peaceful green oasis where the charming villages of Nant and Saint Jean de Bruel are located. The Dourbie then begins its home run to the Tarn, snaking between the Causse Noir and Causse du Larzac down an austere yet grandiose valley.

Favoured leisure activities in the Dourbie Valley are rock climbing, white-water canoeing or rafting, birdwatching, horse riding, cycling, strolling beside this lovely river, enjoying some of the best trout fishing in France or hiking up to the limestone plateaus above to find solitude beneath a big sky populated with lazily circling vultures. For some, the scenery ensures that simple sightseeing is enough. In addition to its scenic qualities, the Dourbie Valley has quaint stone-built villages like La Roque-St-Marguerite with its 11th-century church and mill, located near the river below Montpellier-le-Vieux, an impressive labyrinth of rock that simply must be explored. It appears almost man made but was carved by water. The village also has impressive Montcalm Castle. Other medieval villages like Saint Véran and Cantobre cling to the cliffside with stunning views down the valley.

HOW TO GET THERE:
The Dourbie Valley is accessible from the A75 at Millau, with the D991 actually going up the valley to La Roque-St-Marguerite, Saint Véran, Saint-Sauveur and Nant.

WHEN TO GO:
Any time (the winter valley looks great beneath a covering of snow, with not so much as a solitary tourist to be seen).

DON'T MISS:
A jar (or two) of the local honey to take home. Made by bees that forage among the Dourbie Valley's pollen-laden expanses of wild flowers, it is said (admittedly by the locals) to be the tastiest in all France.

YOU SHOULD KNOW:
Millau's famous Tarn Valley viaduct is the world's highest bridge. Its tallest mast is higher than the Eiffel Tower and falls just short of New York's Empire State Building. This cable-stayed road bridge was designed by Sir Norman Foster.

Cévennes National Park

Created in 1970, the spectacular Cévennes National Park in the Languedoc-Roussillon region stretches across the departments of Lozère, Gard and Ardèche. Its importance is reflected in a UNESCO World Biosphere Reserve classification. One of the park's objectives is to promote tourism, but happily only the sustainable sort that does not damage this precious landscape of mountains, *causses* (limestone plateaus), deep valleys, forests and alpine meadows. The park has three eco-centres and attracts over 800,000 visitors every year, but this is still a place where it's possible to escape into the vastness of the Cévennes Mountains and enjoy peaceful solitude amid awe-inspiring natural beauty.

Elevations within the park vary from 380 m (1,250 ft) to 1,700 m (5,600 ft) and the climate varies from the continental north to the maritime south. Coupled with differing soil types this ensures an extraordinary variety of flora, with over 2,250 species. Notable among them are huge plantations of chestnut trees and the carnivorous sundew plant, while both alpine and subtropical species may also be found. Animal and bird life is equally diverse, with nearly 2,500 different creatures recorded. Animals such as deer, wild boar, mouflon (wild sheep with large curved horns), beaver and otter roam free, while more visible birds include vultures, woodpeckers and grouse.

There is a network of established trails that extends to 1,800 km (1,120 mi), many designed to be sufficiently user-friendly to encourage visits by families with children. But the park also has more *Grande Routes* (GR long-distance walking paths) than any other French national park, plus bridlepaths, cycleways and winter cross-country skiing routes. There are a large number of *gîtes d'escape* (simple refuges) and rural *gîtes* available in the park for those who want to spend time in this haven of natural tranquillity.

HOW TO GET THERE:
The A75 road skirts the park's western side and the N106 runs from Nîmes to Alès, a great starting point from which to start exploring the park.

WHEN TO GO:
Any time (take skis or snowshoes in winter).

DON'T MISS:
Nobody should visit Cévennes National Park without taking in Aven Armand, north of Meyruis off the D986 road. Discovered at the end of the 19th century on the Méjan Causse by one Louis Armand, this amazing limestone cavern is a fairyland of stalagmites, including the world's largest known example at 30 m (100 ft) tall. Bold visitors can descend a natural shaft on a rope, following the route used by Louis Armand, although most will prefer to use the lift.

YOU SHOULD KNOW:
Camping is not allowed in the central area, nor are camper vans or caravans. Visitors' cars, motorbikes or bicycles are not permitted to go off road anywhere in Cévennes National Park, which remains dedicated to preserving the peaceful, unspoilt character of this beautiful area.

Vultures perch on limestone rocks in the Cévennes National Park.

Cirques de Gavarnie and d'Estaubé

HOW TO GET THERE:
This is not one for casual sightseers – the natural glories of Cirque de Gavarnie can only be enjoyed after a two-hour uphill tramp from the small mountain village of Gavarnie, close to the Spanish border in the Hautes-Pyrenees. Cirque d'Estaubé calls for a demanding hike via the Gave d'Estaubé (from the D176 south of Luz-Saint-Sauveur).

WHEN TO GO:
Summertime, when the going is (relatively) easy and the weather is (usually) in clement mood.

The stunning Cirque de Gavarnie

The Pyrenees has rugged mountainscapes aplenty, but two adjoining features that should not be missed are the Cirque de Gavarnie and the Cirque d'Estaubé. In this context a *cirque* (circus) is a valley-head formed like an amphitheatre, open on the downhill side to form a flatter area corresponding to a stage with the valley falling away behind. The upper part of the bowl is a steeper section that might represent the sloping seating area.

The Cirque de Gavarnie is a famous example of the feature. It is around 800 m (2,625 ft) across at the low point and 3,000 m (9,840 ft) wide at the top. It has an impressive natural gap in the surrounding steep cliffs called Le Brèche de Roland. Legend has it that this jagged aperture was cut by Charlemagne's nephew, Count Roland, following his defeat by the Saracens in a nearby battle, as

he unsuccessfully attempted to destroy the legendary sword Durendal to prevent it falling into infidel hands. It's a good story, showing at the very least that memories in these parts are long. The Cirque de Gavarnie also boasts France's highest waterfall, the Grand Cascade de Gavarnie, a tiered falls down a rugged cliff face with a drop of 422 m (1,385 ft). This awesome natural bowl is far from human habitation and ranks as a scenic masterpiece.

The Cirque d'Estaubé is another 4 km (2.5 mi) to the east. It is neither as well known nor quite so spectacular, but this secret grassy enclave amidst encircling mountains is well worth the effort required to get there, although this is really one for serious mountain walkers who are equipped with all-weather clothing and for whom the destination is less important than the journey.

DON'T MISS:
A *cirque* hat trick – add the tranquil Cirque de Troumouse to the other pair and admire its amazing curved rock wall that's 10 km (6 mi) long and 1,000 m (3,280 ft) tall. It is not far from the Cirque d'Estaubé and the nearest road is the D922.

YOU SHOULD KNOW:
The two *cirques* fall within the Pyrenees National Park on the Franco-Spanish border, an unspoiled mountainous landscape without fences or walls where animals roam free and biodiversity is maintained. The park is home to 70 species of animal and has a wide variety of flora.

Orlu Nature Reserve

The Ariege Department to the south of Toulouse is little known outside France. The land rises to the high Pyrenees and is steeped in history, as the ruins of numerous romantic Cathar castles atop their rocky outcrops testify. One little gem tucked away in the dramatic mountain landscape of southeastern Ariege is Orlu Nature Reserve. This 40-sq-km (15-sq-mi) chunk of mountain terrain rises from 930 m (3,050 ft) to 2,765 m (9,070 ft) and is sufficiently demanding to ensure that – despite its relatively small size amidst the general grandeur of the surrounding Pyrenees – the determined explorer must still put in a real effort to appreciate everything this special wild place has to offer.

The expedition can start with a quick visit to the museum at the bottom of the reserve, to discover the rationale behind its status as a national hunting reserve – a rarity in a country where anything that moves is likely to end up in the pot. Rangers ensure that the wildlife is protected, scientists study it and intrepid members of the public watch it. Orlu requires the donning of stout shoes and walking. There is an easy hike in the Gaudu Valley and a more demanding three-hour climb to a sanctuary in the middle of the reserve where it's possible to stay overnight.

Orlu Nature Reserve is a place of lush alpine wildflower meadows and forest, tumbled rocks and rushing water. The Oriege cascades down the Orlu Gorge, a splendid mountain torrent that attracts white-water canoeists. There is also an aerial adventure course with zip lines and tree climbing, but this place is really about easily observable wildlife. The stars are chamois and marmots. Birds include vultures, capercaille and ptarmigan.

HOW TO GET THERE:
The reserve is near Ax-les-Thermes, on the E09-N20 road between Tarascon-sur-Ariège and Hospitalet près l'Andorre.

WHEN TO GO:
Any time (there are four skiing stations for winter-sports enthusiasts).

DON'T MISS:
A side trip to Andorra, as one of over ten million annual visitors to this beguiling mountain principality who take full advantage of its duty-free status and enjoy the scenery, usually in that order. Andorra has a joint monarchy, the duties bizarrely being shared by the President of the French Republic and the Bishop of Urgell in Catalonia – not many people know that.

YOU SHOULD KNOW:
In the Orlu Valley beneath the Baxouillade peak rumour has it that a Roman gold mine is waiting to be found, although a determined search in the 19th century failed to unearth it. Legend suggests a rich seam is there somewhere, because a long-ago Count of Carcassonne knew the secret and used the bounty to fund the building of his city walls.

Gorges de Spelunca

HOW TO GET THERE:
By road from Porto, or by foot from
Evisa or Ota.
WHEN TO GO:
Any time of year, but the best time is
between April and November.
DON'T MISS:
The Forêt d'Aitone National Park, just
to the west of Evisa.
YOU SHOULD KNOW:
Corsica is renowned for its food and
its forests are home to many wild
boar. Try the wild boar ham, smoked
sausages and stews.

Some 30 km (19 mi) south of Calvi – a popular destination on Corsica's northwest coast – and a short distance inland from the beautiful little resort of Porto, a UNESCO World Heritage Site, is the Gorges de Spelunca.

Set between the mountain villages of Ota and Evisa, this 2-km (1.2-mi) long canyon cuts between the two, its steep, red, granite walls plunging down to the eponymous river below. The gorge is one of Corsica's famous natural sites and it is possible to walk or hike there all year round. Although there are excellent views of much of the gorge from the road, it is more rewarding to make for the mountains, where there is shade and the air is fresh and clean.

Although the gorge is accessible from both villages, most people start from the cemetery just outside Evisa. The descent, at first quite gentle, becomes steeper lower down. The trail leads through shady woods, passing wind-scoured rock pinnacles and bare rock faces to the bottom of the valley and the elegant old Genoese stone bridge, Pont de Zaglia – one of two here. The track through the gorge was once an important communications link, enabling heavily laden mules to be sent from Porto into the mountain villages. Today, the path has been restored using original stones, but it can often feel more like jumping than walking.

Children will also enjoy the gorge, although it will be too strenuous for very little ones. Curiously shaped tiers of boulders, sometimes with one balanced, apparently precariously, on top of another, lead to mini waterfalls and several natural bathing pools. Keep an eye open for the Corsican salamander – this is a great place to see one.

West Frisian Islands

Germany and the Netherlands share the North Sea's Frisian Islands, with Holland having the best of the deal – it has 14 West Frisians (five inhabited) as opposed to Germany's 12 East Frisians (seven inhabited). In truth, most of the uninhabited Frisians are little more than shifting sandbars that barely stay above water at high tide and even the populated ones are sparsely settled. They are barrier islands, sheltering the shallow Waddenzee from the North Sea proper.

Starting in the west, the largest and best-populated island is Texel. A third of Texel is a nature reserve. The landscape of sand dunes has a network of cycle paths that encourage two-wheeled exploration. Next along is Vlieland, with one major settlement at Oost-Vlieland. Again, dunes are the predominant feature, leavened by meadows and woods. Historic Terschelling is notable for (surprisingly) cranberries. Inhabitants have long used bounty brought by the sea to build eccentric houses and barns, and a barrel of cranberries was washed ashore in 1840. The canny islanders planted them, they thrived and today bakeries and restaurants vie to offer the best cranberry delicacies. Ameland has just four small villages and consists mostly of dunes, but nonetheless has extraordinary biodiversity. Tiny Schiermonnikoog – heavily fortified by the Germans in World War II – hosts Holland's first nature reserve. Small and flat, it nonetheless attracts huge numbers of summer visitors, including many day-trippers.

Island-hopping ferries offer tickets that allow visitors to go at their own pace and check out inhabited islands in turn. This is ideal for hikers and – this is two-wheel-savvy Holland – the many touring cyclists. The West Frisians, particularly outside summer's high season, are wonderfully atmospheric wild places for those who love challenging the elements surrounded by big skies, lonely dunes and restless sea.

HOW TO GET THERE:
The islands can easily be reached from Amsterdam by car and ferry from Den Helder. The more easterly islands can be accessed from Harlingen or Holward on the mainland, but Vlieland and Schiermonnikoog do not allow visitors to bring their cars. The latter is served by regular ferries from Lauwersoog.

WHEN TO GO:
Any time. Winter can be very bleak, but promises dramatic solitude in return for defying the angry marine elements.

DON'T MISS:
The ten-day Oerol Festival on the island of Terschelling. It takes place in mid June and the whole island becomes a stage for the arts, with theatre, music and visual arts put on in the unlikeliest of places - barns, boathouses, meadows, dunes - as well as utilizing the two purpose-built main stages. Tickets are sold as 'passports' allowing people onto the island for all or part of the week and tens of thousands attend this unique event.

YOU SHOULD KNOW:
The uninhabited islands of Griend, Rottumerplaat and Rottumeroog are nature reserves that may only be visited if a permit is obtained in advance. However, one 'island' can be visited without going afloat - Wieringen became joined to the mainland after reclamation work in the 1930s.

A windmill at sunrise on the island of Texel

Amrum Island

HOW TO GET THERE:
The ferry from Dagebüll Hafen on the mainland takes 90 minutes for the crossing to Wittdün. A bus service connects the island villages.

WHEN TO GO:
April to October (especially August and September when the purple heather is in blossom).

DON'T MISS:
Look out for seals sunning themselves on the sandbanks close to the shore.

YOU SHOULD KNOW:
Much of the island is a fragile environment and enjoys protected status. You should take care to keep to marked paths and boardwalks, especially through the dunes.

Amrum is the smallest of the North Frisian group of islands which lie in the North Sea off the west coast of Germany. It is also the least commercialized and offers a very different experience from its lively and sophisticated neighbour Sylt. Amrum is a place to come to unwind and allow your biological clock to slow down to a gentler and simpler rhythm of life. At little more than 20 km (12 mi) long and never wider than a couple of kilometres (just over a mile), the island can be cycled in a few hours and even walked around inside a day. Considering its size Amrum contains a remarkable variety of habitats, including pine forests, heathland and marshes. Its crowning glory, though, and what draws people back to the island year after year, is the Kniepsand, a huge expanse of fine white sand extending for 12 km (7.5 mi) down the entire western side of the island. If you grow tired of the fantastic beaches, the large patchwork of dunes behind await exploration. These cover almost half the area of the island, with some rising to as much as 32 m (105 ft) above sea level.

A single road runs down the spine of the island, linking its five villages. There is a good walk from the lighthouse at Wittdün in the south (the tallest on Germany's coast) through dunes and forests to Norddorf. On the way it is well worth stopping to admire the traditional Frisian houses in the pretty village of Nebel, as well as its well-preserved windmill. A more unusual walk – and one you should only undertake with a local guide – allows you to cross the Wadden Sea at low tide to the island of Föhr.

An aerial view of Amrum Island

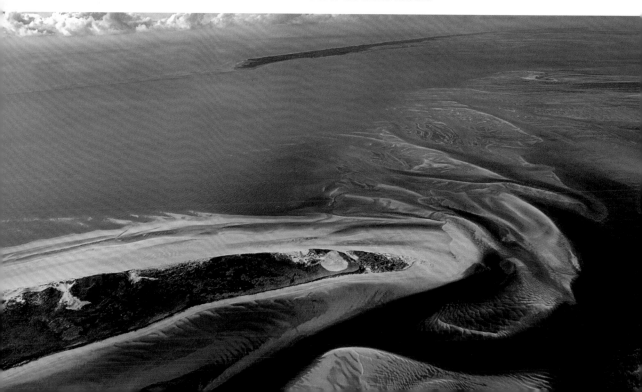

Jasmund National Park

Rügen is a popular holiday island just off Germany's Baltic coast, famous for its fine sandy beaches and rugged coastline. In the 19th century the already fashionable resorts here used to attract the elite of Prussian society during the warm summer months. Writers and artists were also drawn to the island's natural beauty, especially the great German Romantic painter Caspar David Friedrich, who was born in the nearby town of Greifswald. His canvases of Rügen's splendid white chalk cliffs have become not only the island's defining image but also a key icon of European landscape art.

Friedrich was a regular visitor to Rügen and his favourite spot on the island was an area at the end of the Jasmund Peninsula – the Stubbenkammer – from which there are outstanding views of the chalk cliffs stretching south.

This coastline, extending some 10 km (6 mi) to Sassnitz, is now protected as a national park. The cliffs here are the highest sea cliffs in Germany and demonstrate vividly the effects of coastal erosion. The highest of all is the Königsstuhl (king's seat) which plunges 118 m (387 ft) into the emerald-green sea. It is a popular viewpoint, although for a view of the cliff itself you need to head a few hundred metres further along the coast to the Victoriasicht viewpoint. A superb cliff-top walk takes in the entire coastline between the Königsstuhl and Sassnitz, including the craggy Wissower Klinken cliffs.

Although a small park, Jasmund also has fine examples of marsh, wetland and mixed broadleaf woodland; its other claim to fame is the Stubnitz forest of ancient oak and beech trees, some of which are over 700 years old.

The stunning chalk cliffs of Jasmund National Park

HOW TO GET THERE:
Sassnitz is well connected to the road and rail network. In summer you must leave your car at Hagen and take the shuttle bus or walk the remaining 3 km (2 mi) if you are visiting the Königsstuhl.
WHEN TO GO:
April to October
DON'T MISS:
A ride on the Rasender Roland narrow-gauge steam train which runs between Putbus and Göhren.
YOU SHOULD KNOW:
Jasmund gets very busy in the holiday season.

Harz National Park

HOW TO GET THERE:
The Harz Mountains are reached easily from the A7 motorway and from the nearest main railway station at Goslar. As well as the steam railway, an extensive local bus network covers the region.
WHEN TO GO:
April to October (but there is also excellent cross-country skiing in the winter months).

Rising above the North German Plain, the Harz Mountains cover an area 100 km (62 mi) by 30 km (19 mi) which straddles the border that once divided the country into East and West Germany. In 2006 the Nationalpark Harz was created out of the amalgamation of two former parks on either side of the old border. The new park protects 158 sq km (61 sq mi) of mountainous granite terrain, much of it covered in dense forests, but there are also areas of high moorland and hidden valleys where birdsong and the babbling of crystal-clear streams are the only sounds you will hear.

At the heart of the national park stands the Brocken, at 1,142 m (3,747 ft) the highest point in the Harz range. You can trek to the top or else take the delightful narrow-gauge steam railway; as it puffs and wheezes its way up the steep gradient you may wonder at times

Hiking on the Brocken

whether it is going to make it, but these plucky little engines have been making this journey successfully for well over 100 years. The Brocken itself is steeped in legend and the mists that often shroud the summit serve only to enhance the air of mystery. It is the legendary site of the great witches' gathering on the pagan festival of Walpurgisnacht; lively celebrations in the local towns and villages take place on the night in question (April 30), when lots of locals dress up as – you've guessed – witches and devils.

With some 8,000 km (5,000 mi) of walking trails the Harz National Park is a well-established area for hiking enthusiasts, offering everything from leisurely strolls around beauty spots to long-distance routes such as the Kaiserweg (Imperial Way) and the Hexensteig (Witches' Way) which runs east-west across the entire park.

DON'T MISS:
The Grüne Band (Green Line), a 75-km (47-mi) walking trail which follows the line of the old Iron Curtain border.
YOU SHOULD KNOW:
Goethe used the Brocken as the setting for the Walpurgisnacht scene in his great drama *Faust*. More prosaically, the Soviet Union used it as an observation post during the Cold War.

Spreewald

Journey little more than an hour from the centre of Berlin and you could be on a different planet. The Spreewald in the southeast of the state of Brandenburg is one of Germany's most surprising landscapes. This extensive network of rivers, streams and canals was formed when mineral deposits during the Ice Age created natural barriers that forced the River Spree to divert its course and split into a multitude of channels. The resulting marshes and wetlands, with their numerous small lakes and sandy islands, constitute an important ecosystem rare in central Europe; it was duly recognized as such when in 1990 UNESCO declared the region a biosphere reserve.

The Spreewald has over 400 km (250 mi) of idyllic green waterways, many of which are navigable. You can explore them yourself in a canoe or kayak, or else take a trip in a characteristic flat-bottomed boat and enjoy the local knowledge and anecdotes dispensed by your ferryman as he propels you gently along with his pole. These punts are an integral part of a traditional way of life here; in the summer months the post is still delivered by boat to the outlying villages! The wetlands are a haven for water birds and you should have no difficulty spotting many different species, especially at either end of the day.

Another factor which makes the Spreewald such a distinctive place is that it is the historic home of Germany's only indigenous minority, the Sorbs. At festivals and on special days you can still see them in their traditional costumes. The open-air museum at Lehde has fine examples of old Sorbian thatched houses and farm buildings.

HOW TO GET THERE:
The twin towns of Lübben and Lübbenau in the heart of the Spreewald are one hour by train from Berlin.
WHEN TO GO:
April to October
DON'T MISS:
With no hills and a well-developed network of trails running alongside the streams and canals this is a great cycling area for family outings.
YOU SHOULD KNOW:
The Spreewald is famous throughout the country for its flavoursome gherkins.

Lower Oder Valley

The Oder is a name which resonates in postwar European history. The river has formed a significant frontier for hundreds of years and currently marks the border between Germany and Poland. Flowing into the Baltic Sea by Szczecin in Poland, the Oder possesses one of the few delta regions in Europe that have remained largely undisturbed by human interference. A cross-border reserve has been created in its lower reaches to protect and preserve this exceptional environment. The greater part, 105 sq km (40 sq mi), is on the German side where it is known as the Lower Oder Valley National Park. The park covers a 60-km (37-mi) stretch of the River Oder with idyllic riverbank scenery, water meadows, marshes, mixed riparian forests and dry grassland on the surrounding hillsides.

The biodiversity of this relatively compact area is outstanding in Europe. The floodplain is a breeding ground for over 120 kinds of birds, including several endangered species such as the black stork and the sea eagle. Conservation methods have become more radical in recent years and large parts of the park are now completely off-limits to human activity. Even so, the Lower Oder Valley remains a Mecca for serious birdwatchers who are able to get close to the wildlife on foot, on bicycle or by canoe along the riverbank. The visitor centre in the village of Criewen has lots of useful information and is a good starting-point for tours of the park. A recommended day walk is the 14-km (9-mi) circuit of the polder at Schwedt; walking on the raised dyke gives you a good vantage-point for spotting birdlife. Serious cyclists can also do a round trip up and down the two riverbanks (passport needed for the Polish section).

Saxon Switzerland

Many parts of Europe have had the 'Swiss' epithet applied to them by virtue of their putative resemblance to that country's alpine scenery, although few live up to the grandeur of the real thing. One that does is the region known as Sächsische Schweiz, or Saxon Switzerland, which occupies the land between Dresden and the border with the Czech Republic. It may not boast the snow-covered peaks of its namesake, but Saxon Switzerland possesses drama of a different kind. Soaring sandstone cliffs, canyon-like gorges and flat-topped mountains combine to create a landscape like no other in Germany.

The area, which is also known as the Elbsandsteingebirge (Elbe Sandstone Mountains), owes its existence to the mighty River Elbe which has here carved a tortuous path through the Lusatian Mountains. It is well known for the extraordinary sandstone and basalt rock formations which crop up everywhere, the result of erosion by wind and water. Tall columns with weird shapes and names like Barbarine and the Pillars of Hercules are popular among rock-climbers, but you do not have to go to such lengths yourself to get a buzz from this landscape. It is a paradise for children who love venturing into the myriad gullies and clefts and scrambling up the gentler rock faces. Climb to the top of a sandstone plateau like the Pfaffenstein or the Lilienstein and you are rewarded with magnificent panoramic views of the Elbe valley and the surrounding countryside. The ruins of a medieval fortress are an additional attraction on top of the Bastei rocks which tower 305 m (1,000 ft) above the open fields and rolling hills. An alternative and less strenuous way of appreciating the scenery is on one of the lovely old paddle steamers which ply the Elbe between Dresden and Schmilka.

Bastei Bridge and the Lilienstein Plateau in Saxon Switzerland

Kellerwald-Edersee National Park

HOW TO GET THERE:
Kellerwald-Edersee is 30 minutes' drive southwest of Kassel. The nearest rail stations are Bad Wildungen and Frankenberg.
WHEN TO GO:
Any time of year
DON'T MISS:
Look out for the pretty Cheddar pink flower, also known as firewitch, which grows in the cracks of rock faces around the Edersee.
YOU SHOULD KNOW:
The Kellerwald is one of the last remaining habitats in central Europe of the wild cat and the eagle owl.

Once upon a time much of central Europe was covered in beech forests but the inevitable pressures of human settlement and exploitation have led to their steady decline, with the result that today they are found only in isolated pockets. The largest such pocket is in the north of the state of Hesse in the so-called 'green heart' of Germany. Such is its importance as a habitat that in 2004 the Kellerwald-Edersee National Park was established to preserve it for future generations. The broad swathe of ancient, gnarled beech trees which makes up the Kellerwald – many several hundred years old – owes its survival to having been a hunting ground for the local nobility in centuries past, which protected it from logging and other forms of exploitation. The majestic red deer is still a common sight in the park but thankfully is no longer hunted.

The beech may be the dominant tree here but it does allow other deciduous species to make an occasional appearance, such as large-leaved limes, ancient oaks and the ash and mountain elms found in the damp gullies which proliferate throughout the park. Numerous nature trails take you along crystal-clear streams, past rock and boulder fields (relics of the last Ice Age) and over meadows covered in wild flowers. The northern boundary of the park is marked by the Edersee, an artificial lake formed by a dam which offers all kinds of water-based activities. A 70-km (43-mi) walking trail takes you right around the lake, while the Kellerwaldsteig is twice as long and links up with the adjacent nature park to the south.

Kellerwald-Edersee National Park – the 'green heart' of Germany

Hainich National Park

A forest path in Hainich National Park

Covering an area of 160 sq km (62 sq mi), Hainich Forest is the largest unbroken expanse of mixed deciduous woodland in Germany. In 1997 the southern half of this western Thuringian forest became a national park and a visitor infrastructure was created to promote exploration of the beautiful beech and oak woods. Hainich was formerly part the GDR (East Germany); situated close to the once-sensitive border with West Germany, it was used formerly as a military training area and was off-limits to visitors. There are not many reasons to remember with affection that period of the country's history when Germany was a divided nation, but in this case it meant that Hainich, in common with other rural areas along the heavily fortified border, was for many years spared the pressures of mass tourism. Nowadays it is a delightfully green and peaceful place to visit, with plenty of walking opportunities. One of the more unusual is a high-level walkway near the park's visitor centre at Thiemsburg which takes you through the tree-tops to an observation tower in the heart of the forest, 44 m (144 ft) above the ground. Children will appreciate the different perspective on the forest, as they will the 'Wild Cat Children's Forest', an adventure playground fashioned out of fallen trees and natural materials.

Hainich National Park is in the northwestern corner of the Thüringerwald (the Thuringian Forest), an area of thickly wooded hills and picturesque valleys which was once a favoured haunt of artists of the German Romantic movement. The unhurried lifestyle and relative lack of commercialism which once attracted them still prevail, although the region has sadly suffered significant environmental damage from decades of unchecked industrial pollution during the GDR era.

HOW TO GET THERE:
The historic town of Eisenach, on the main east-west A4 motorway to the south, is the best base for visits to the park.
WHEN TO GO:
Any time of year. Spring and autumn are particularly good times to visit for, respectively, the wild flowers and the changing tree colours.
DON'T MISS:
Eisenach is the birthplace of Bach and the site of Germany's greatest medieval castle, the Wartburg.
YOU SHOULD KNOW:
One of the country's best long-distance trails, the Rennsteig, starts outside Eisenach and runs for 168 km (104 mi) through the Thuringian Forest to Blankenstein on the Saale River.

Wutach Gorge

The 'Grand Canyon of the Black Forest', as it is sometimes billed in the tourist brochures, may be overdoing it a tad, but the Wutach Gorge is an undeniably impressive sight, the more so for being so unexpected in this part of the continent. The River Wutach rises on the Feldberg, the highest point of the Black Forest, and flows east and south before joining the Rhine near Waldshut. This is the far southwest of Germany, close to the Swiss border and to the European Watershed – the line dividing the basins of the country's two great rivers, the Danube and the Rhine. At one time the Wutach was a tributary of the Danube but geologists have yet to solve the puzzle of what caused the river to change its course by 90 degrees in favour of the Rhine.

Outside the small town of Bonndorf the Wutach River has punched its way through the Black Forest rocks to create a spectacular ravine with jagged, near-vertical cliffs which soar skywards and keep the valley in shadow for large parts of the day. The damp, shady conditions have generated a microclimate where unusual plants grow. Well over 1,000 types of wild flower have

The River Wutach flows through the Black Forest.

HOW TO GET THERE:
There is a good local bus network which offers special passes for exploring the area. The Wutach Gorge is 80 km (50 mi) east of the Rhine motorway linking Basel and Frankfurt. The nearest railway station is Seebrugg, 10 km (6 mi) to the west.

been recorded in this astonishingly fertile environment, which in turn attracts rare birds such as the grey egret and a glorious variety of butterflies and insects. The best way to appreciate this remarkable landscape is to hike the length of the gorge.

The trail runs beside the river between the Schattenmühle and the Wutachmühle. It is 13 km (8 mi) long and takes between four-and-a-half and five hours. It is part of the much longer 118-km (74-mi) path, the Schluchtensteig (Gorge Way), which links the towns of Wehr and Stühlingen.

WHEN TO GO:
Any time of year (bring warm clothes as it can be cool in the gorge).
DON'T MISS:
If you want somewhere even wilder and more remote, the detour on the gorge trail to the Lotenbach Glen is definitely worth tackling.
YOU SHOULD KNOW:
You should take special care on the paths, which are steep in places and tend to be wet and slippery.

Swabian-Franconian Forest Nature Park

Germany can boast a huge variety of scenery within its borders. While the wooded hills of northeast Baden-Württemberg may not be among the star offerings, they do come as close as any other to presenting what for many is the archetypal German landscape – a mosaic of forests, valleys, fields, gentle uplands, water meadows and pastures where sheep and cattle graze.

Much of this area is now contained within the Naturpark Schwäbisch-Fränkischer Wald. Covering 900 sq km (347 sq mi), the Swabian-Franconian Nature Park gets its name from the fact that it straddles the historical frontier between the medieval duchies of Swabia and Franconia. The border itself ran along the ridge above the valley of the Murr River which more or less cuts the park in two on an east-west course to join the Neckar near Marbach.

The park provides a good example of a reasonably harmonious co-existence between man and nature which has lasted hundreds of years. It is lovely country for walking and cycling excursions and there are any number of marked trails leading you to hidden valleys, viewpoints and peaceful lakes in the woods where a refreshing dip can be very welcome on a hot summer's day. On your wanderings through the spruce and beech forests look out for signs of the *Limes* (pronounced 'lee-mays') – the frontier which for 250 years marked the northern limit of the Roman Empire in central Europe. Unlike Hadrian's Wall, the *Limes* was a timber-and-earthwork fortification and you can still find good traces of the ditch and earth rampart in many places; the foundations of some of the stone watch-towers are also still visible. A walking trail with information panels enables you to follow the course of the *Limes* right across the park.

HOW TO GET THERE:
The park headquarters and visitor centre is at Murrhardt, 45 km (28 mi) northeast of Stuttgart.
WHEN TO GO:
April to October
DON'T MISS:
The archaeological park near Welzheim, which includes a full-scale reconstruction of a twin-towered gateway to a Roman fort.
YOU SHOULD KNOW:
In a pioneering venture, the nature park currently offers GPS satellite navigation to its walkers and cyclists.

Bavarian Forest

HOW TO GET THERE:
There are railway stations at Cham, Zwiesel and Bayerisch Eisenstein, and a good network of local buses, especially in the holiday season when good-value day passes are available for unlimited travel around the forest area.

WHEN TO GO:
April to October (although if you like snow-walking or cross-country skiing and don't mind the cold, winter in the forest can also be very inviting).

DON'T MISS:
The large wildlife enclosure in the national park will appeal particularly to children. You can walk all the way around its 7-km (4.3-mi) perimeter for great views of animals such as bison and wolves, which used to be natives of these forests.

Along with the Bohemian Forest across the border in the Czech Republic, the Bavarian Forest (Bayerischer Wald) forms the largest continuous area of woodland in Europe. It covers most of the land between the north bank of the Danube and the Czech border, an area of some 6,000 sq km (2,317 sq mi) on a southeast axis extending from Regensburg to Passau. For a country as heavily populated and highly developed as Germany the Bavarian Forest is a surprisingly wild and unspoilt region and it is certainly a place to come if you want to fill your lungs with green and fresh air. These uplands, which in parts rise to nearly 1,500 m (4,920 ft), are covered almost entirely in dense forest – largely spruce, but beech, oak and pine also feature. Here you can see ancient trees that have grown to gigantic proportions, some as high as 50 m (164 ft) and with girths of 2 m (6.5 ft) and more. Their enormous scale certainly enhances the sense of this being a primeval wilderness.

Although mostly wooded, the Bavarian Forest also has lakes, mountain streams, pastures and areas of high moorland. The landscape is dotted with isolated little villages and farming

A pair of European lynx

communities. At its southern end is Germany's first national park, also called the Bavarian Forest, which in 2010 celebrated its 40th anniversary. Together with the ?umava National Park in the Czech Republic, it forms the largest area of protected forest in central Europe. With hundreds of kilometres of walking and cycling trails, the park is a nature-lover's paradise and one where you might be lucky enough to spot rare wildlife such as the lynx and the capercaillie (a type of grouse).

YOU SHOULD KNOW:
Thanks to the local rock's high quartz component the area has long been famous for its hand-blown glass making. You can visit workshops in Zwiesel and Frauenau to see the ancient craft still being practised.

Fichtelgebirge

The name of these mountains tells it as it always was and happily still is today – for Fichtelgebirge translates as 'Spruce Mountains' and that pretty much describes this extensive range in northeastern Bavaria. The Fichtelgebirge stretch from the Red Main River Valley to the Czech border and form part of the distinct upland region known as the Thuringian-Franconian Highlands. In truth, these are more like rolling wooded hills than mountains, serving as a reminder that Germany has enough territory to ensure that several large areas of peaceful forest can be allowed to remain relatively undeveloped.

There are numerous towns and pretty villages within the Fichtelgebirge, but this does not detract from the area's natural charms and its unspoilt rural character attracts tourists all year round. For many, simply driving around and seeing the sights is enough, for this is a place of extraordinary granite rock formations and huge tracts of attractive woodland interspersed with moorland, meadows, wetlands and rivers. But Germany wouldn't be Germany without large numbers of enthusiastic visitors bent on embracing bracing open-air activities. These include camping, hiking and mountain-biking in the warmer months, quickly switching to alpine skiing, snowboarding, cross-country skiing and sledding when the snow comes. More pampered incomers head for traditional spas like Fichtelberg, Bad Berneck or Bad Alexandersbad that have morphed into thoroughly modern health resorts offering thermal baths with all the luxury trimmings.

For those who like to get away from the hustle and bustle of modern life, the Fichtelgebirge is an ideal destination. Touring by car offers scenic satisfaction around little-used back roads, plus the opportunity to stop off and picnic or explore tempting corners without seeing another soul. For those on two feet or two wheels, the huge network of forest trails is hiking/biking heaven.

HOW TO GET THERE:
The Fichtelgebirge lie between Hof and Weiden, with Bayreuth close to the western fringe. There is good access from *Autobahnen* A 93 and A 9, while Marktredwitz within the Fichtelgebirge has good rail links and is an excellent base for those not equipped with wheels.
WHEN TO GO:
Any time
DON'T MISS:
The chairlift ride (from either Flecki to the south or Bischofsgruen in the north) to the summit of Ochsenkopf (Ox Head) Mountain, second highest in the Fichtelgebirge range. The views are sensational and it's possible to enjoy them from the Asenturm outlook tower, which conveniently has a restaurant.
YOU SHOULD KNOW:
The Fichtelgebirge are the continental divide between the North Sea and the Black Sea and this region is known as 'The Navel of Europe', because four rivers rise in the mountains, each heading off towards a different point of the compass.

La Pierreuse Nature Reserve

La Pierreuse is the largest nature reserve in Romandie, the historical name for the French-speaking part of Switzerland which makes up the west of the country. It packs a good deal into its 34 sq km (13 sq mi). These foothills to the east of Lake Geneva constitute a prime example of a sub-alpine landscape, with cliffs, meadows, moorland and forests. The reserve is situated south of the town of Château d'Oex on the left bank of the River Sarine. Its core is a broad valley basin which is surrounded by mountains – Le Rocher du Midi to the west, La Videmanette to the east and, to the south, by the sheer limestone wall of the Gummfluh range, which rises to 2,458 m (8,064 ft). There is certainly no escaping the aptness of the name – La Pierreuse translates as 'the stony one' – for the whole area is strewn with large rocks and boulders.

Ibex and chamois are at home here on the screes and rocky slopes, while black grouse live on the moors and birds of prey include falcons and golden eagles. The variety of scenery in a relatively confined area, together with the surprise factor of the scattered rocks, makes La Pierreuse an excellent place for day walks. One of the best begins at the mountain station of the Videmanette cable car and runs through the reserve, crossing over four hills before finishing in L'Etivaz. It is a tough but rewarding six-hour hike with a difference in elevation of 1,000 m (3,280 ft); an easier variation is to walk down from the same starting point to the valley floor at Château d'Oex.

Lötschental

Tucked into the southern fringes of the Bernese Oberland, the high alpine valley of Lötschental can lay claim more justly than most to its promotional tag as the 'hidden valley'. A mere 100 years ago it was still completely cut off from the outside world. It took the arrival of the railway and the engineering feat of a tunnel constructed through the Lötschberg in 1913 to begin the process of opening up the valley. The tunnel links Kandersteg to the north with Goppenstein at the western entrance to Lötschental. Ringed by steep-sided mountains, this is a classic glacial valley through which the River Lonza flows on its journey south to join the Rhône. Although the modern era has caught up with a vengeance and the valley is now a popular winter sports and summer hiking area with the high standard of facilities you expect of the Swiss, its isolation until relatively recently has meant that it has remained largely unspoilt and less developed than many other mountain resorts.

This is wonderful walking terrain during the summer months. From the top of the Wiler cable car the Lötschentaler Höhenweg (high path) takes you high along the northern side of the valley, offering sweeping views before descending to the valley head at Fafleralp. Another classic walk starts from the Lauchernalp ski area and crosses the Lötschen pass into the Gasterntal and Kandersteg.

A further consequence of the valley's isolation has been the survival of old folk customs, including the carnival ritual of Tschäggätta in which local villagers parade through their communities wearing animal skins and fearsome wooden masks. The religious festival of Corpus Christi is marked with a similarly colourful procession.

The River Lonza runs through the high alpine valley of Lötschental.

Murgtal

HOW TO GET THERE:
The main railway line and motorway
through the area runs along the
south shore of the Walensee.
WHEN TO GO:
July to October
DON'T MISS:
A cruise on the Walensee
YOU SHOULD KNOW:
This region is now marketed as
'Heidiland' as it was the fictional
setting for *Heidi*, Johanna Spyri's
classic of children's literature.

The Walensee in eastern Switzerland
is one of the country's prettiest lakes.
Lying close to the Liechtenstein
border, this long and slender stretch
of water is framed by dramatic
mountain scenery that invites further
exploration. The village of Murg on
the lake's southern shore marks the
entrance to the Murgtal, a valley
which plunges into the southern
massif. The mountains here may not
be as immediately striking as the
imposing Churfirsten range on the
north shore but they still possess a
wild and untamed air. Their unspoilt
grandeur has been maintained thanks
to a large part of the valley having
been designated a nature reserve.
The reason for the area's protected
status is the mighty stone pine trees
that grow in what are the largest such
forests in the northern Alps. There
are deciduous woods here too and,
close to the lake, the unexpected
sight of large stands of chestnut.

The best way to appreciate the
scenery is to trek through the
chestnut forests and on up the valley
from Murg. Alternatively, you can
make your way to the head of the
valley at Merlen from where a superb
14-km (8.75-mi) circular hike takes
you right round the Hochmättli peak.
Climbing up to 1,800 m (5,900 ft) the
route takes you over moorland
meadows, past bogs and waterfalls
and yields outstanding views in every
direction. It also passes a sequence of
three classic little mountain lakes –
sumptuous watery jewels in this
remote fastness.

*Beautiful Lake Walensee in
Switzerland's 'Heidiland' region*

Eisenwurzen Nature Park

Tucked away in the far north of Styria, close to the provincial borders with Salzburg and Upper Austria, the beautiful alpine landscape that makes up the Eisenwurzen Nature Park looks entirely natural and unspoilt. Appearances can be deceptive, though; scratch below the surface and you will find many indicators of man's effect on the valleys, slopes, pastures and pine forests. Parts of this landscape would have looked very different 500 years ago when the mining of iron ore from the surrounding hills was a flourishing industry. Centred on the town of Eisenerz 25 km (15 mi) to the south, the mines were a major element in the livelihoods of the various small communities scattered throughout the Eisenwurzen region. Whether ferrying logs on wooden rafts down fast-flowing mountain rivers to feed the furnaces, or working in the area's many mills, the locals did well out of the industry until mining ceased in the 19th century. Nowadays virtually all traces of it have disappeared and it is hard to believe that it was ever here. A few old mills still stand, including three flour mills close to the village of Gams.

Eisenwurzen is Austria's largest nature park, covering an area of 586 sq km (226 sq mi). As well as its industrial heritage the park has the lovely valley of the River Enns and boasts many important geological features in the karst landscape, including caves, gorges and a lake which has no inlets (it is fed by water entering through natural springs in the lake bed). There are dramatic walkways along the narrow Noth and Water-Hole gorges; in the latter the waters originate from inside a huge limestone cave before dropping 300 m (984 ft) in a series of five falls into the Salza valley.

Stubai Alps

The Alps attract visitors at all times of the year, whether for winter sports or summer walking, and it is not always easy to find that lonely communion with nature you are seeking. One area where you stand a better chance than most is the Stubai Alps, a glaciated mountain chain forming part of the central Alps. Considering their proximity and ease of access to Innsbruck to the northeast, the Stubai Alps are a surprisingly quiet and unexplored section of the mountains; it is not difficult to get away from the crowds, especially if you are willing to tackle multi-day hikes.

This wild and remote region is made up of a network of steep escarpments and criss-crossing ridges, with many summits topping 3,000 m (9,840 ft). The principal ridge in the range forms the border with Italy and includes the highest peak of the Stubai group, the Zuckerhüttl (literally, 'little sugar loaf') at 3,507 m (11,506 ft). The main access into these mountains is along the Stubaital, a long steep-sided valley which ends at the village of Mutterberg, from where a cable car whisks you up to high-level trekking or, if you are so minded, to skiing on the Stubai glacier. Halfway down the valley the village of Neustift is the starting point for the Stubaier Höhenweg, one of the best long-distance hikes in the whole of the Alps. You need a good week for this challenging route and to ensure enough time to relish the stunning scenery, but it should be manageable by any adult who is reasonably fit. The route crosses several passes at around the 2,700-m (8,860-ft) mark, and paths can be rough and steep, with occasional fixed ropes and ladders to be negotiated in places.

DON'T MISS:
If you are a skier, the chance to ski on the Stubai glacier in high summer.
YOU SHOULD KNOW:
Austria maintains a well-developed system of mountain huts which provide simple but comfortable accommodation for long-distance hikers.

A view from Mount Patscherkofel over the Wipptal and Stubai valleys

Bohemian Switzerland

HOW TO GET THERE:
Bohemian Switzerland is a 90-minute drive from Prague and a two-hour rail journey to the nearest main town, Decín. There are regular buses between Decín and Hrensko and from Hrensko to the heart of the region at Mezná.
WHEN TO GO:
April to October

It was two Swiss artists of the Romantic movement who first coined the phrase 'Bohemian Switzerland' (*Ceské Švýcarsko* in Czech) in the late 18th century to describe this area of northern Bohemia, although in fact, aside from the occasional meadows and Swiss-style chalets, it is not really alpine in character at all. Striking the landscape undoubtedly is, however, featuring broad expanses of dense woodland covering an elaborate network of bluffs and small canyons where outcrops of sandstone rock have punched their way above the dark-green carpet. Wind and rain have sculpted the soft rock into many strange shapes, creating a paradise for climbers and a gallery of sculptural delights for walkers.

A peaceful boat trip along the Kamenice Gorge

Part of Bohemian Switzerland is now a national park of the same name, but this only accounts for a small proportion of the region which is bounded to the west by the Labe (Elbe) valley and extends eastwards from the German border at Hrensko to Ceská Kamenice. There are many well-marked trails to help you explore the area, of which the most popular is a 17-km (10.5-mi) round route from Hrensko which is manageable in a long day. This trail takes in the region's two most spectacular sights: the Pravcická brána, a huge stone arch that is the largest natural bridge in Europe, and the gorge of the Kamenice River which carves its way through Bohemian Switzerland before joining the Labe at Hrensko. In the east of the region, near Ceská Kamenice, the Panská skála presents another geological curiosity: stacks of basalt columns which, although much smaller in scale, are reminiscent of Northern Ireland's Giant's Causeway.

DON'T MISS:
The boat trip along the Kamenice Gorge, a short but dramatic ride in which a ferryman poles you along as you float noiselessly between towering sheer-sided cliffs that rarely see the sun.
YOU SHOULD KNOW:
The same geological features spill over the border into Germany where the area is known as Sächsische Schweiz, or Saxon Switzerland.

Broumov Highlands

A special feature of the central European forests which cover the borderlands of the Czech Republic, Poland and Slovakia are the so-called 'rock towns' (*skalní mesta*). Several are to be found in the Broumov Highlands, an area covering over 400 sq km (154 sq mi) in the far east of the country hard up against the Polish border. Visiting these mysterious landscapes where plateaus, gorges, cliffs and caves are interspersed with strangely anthropomorphic rock formations, it is easy to believe that you are walking through deserted settlements. Two of the best such 'rock towns' are situated next to one another at Adršpach and Teplice in the north of the highlands. Well-signposted trails ensure you don't miss the most interesting rocks and the bizarre shapes which weathering has wrought in the soft sandstone. Grandmother's Armchair, Sugar Cone and the Hand are some of the names that have been applied to nature's work. And at a height of nearly 100 m (328 ft) the Courting Couple at Adršpach is the tallest sandstone pillar in the country.

Another striking section of the highlands are the Broumov walls, a long thin sandstone ridge which effectively cuts off the town of Broumov to the east from the rest of the country. Approaching from the west in this thickly wooded region you would hardly know the 'walls' were there before coming to the edge of a precipice and being presented all of a sudden with a stupendous panorama of the plain below as it stretches away into Poland. A good vantage point is the little chapel of Panna Maria Snežná, a Baroque jewel built by the great 18th-century architect Dientzenhofer who contributed so much to the cityscape of Prague.

HOW TO GET THERE:
The train journey from Trutnov to Broumov may be slow but it gives you plenty of time to savour the scenery.
WHEN TO GO:
April to October
DON'T MISS:
The evocatively named Sibir (Siberia) Gorge at the Teplice rock town, which has its own microclimate where cool and damp prevail and towering tree-ferns thrive.
YOU SHOULD KNOW:
The great German writer Goethe was one of the first people to put the area on the map when he visited in the 1770s.

Šumava National Park

HOW TO GET THERE:
Šumava is four hours by bus and five
hours by train from Prague. Local
buses link the main towns and
villages in the region but the more
scenic way to travel is on the two
charming single-track railway lines
that traverse the eastern and central
sectors of the park.
WHEN TO GO:
Any time of year
DON'T MISS:
The Boubín Virgin Forest, one of the
world's first nature reserves founded
as far back as 1858.
YOU SHOULD KNOW:
The Šumava runs along what was
once one of the most heavily fortified
sections of the Iron Curtain, a factor
which ironically has helped spare it
subsequent over-development.

The Šumava is one of very few remaining parts of the crowded continent of Europe that can be legitimately described as a wilderness area. Situated on the southwestern fringe of the Czech Republic, this sparsely populated region forms part of the much larger Bohemian Forest which spills over into neighbouring Germany. It is a land of rolling hills, dark pine forests, meadows, peat bogs and low, humpbacked mountains. With few gradients of serious consequence it is ideal terrain for cycling as well as offering magnificent hiking possibilities. A network of trails gives access to hidden valleys and tiny isolated villages which seem to have grown organically out of their natural surroundings. It may be a deservedly popular destination for lovers of the great outdoors, especially those from Germany and Austria, but the size of the Šumava means there's no problem in getting away from the crowds.

Established only after the collapse of communism in 1991, the Šumava National Park, together with its buffer zone which has the status of a Protected Landscape, covers an area of 1,630 sq km (630 sq mi). The country's most famous river, the mighty Vltava, has its source in the western hills and flows through the length of the park before turning north to Ceský Krumlov. Along the way a dam has created a large artificial lake at Lake Lipno, a popular recreation and watersports area in the summer months. The park becomes ever quieter and more remote and the woods ever thicker the further west you go. The area around Železná Ruda is particularly unspoilt, with two glacial lakes and the lovely Bilá Strž waterfall.

The confluence of the Cold and Hot Vltava rivers

Beskidy Mountains

It's easy to escape the crowds on the Beskidy Mountains.

Running for 320 km (200 mi) along the Polish border with the Czech Republic and Slovakia, the Beskidy Mountains form part of the Carpathians, one of Europe's principal mountain chains. With summits rarely topping 1,200 m (3,940 ft) they are not in the same league as the Tatras, their more spectacular neighbours to the west, but these gentle slopes and enticing valleys have an unpretentious and timeless appeal which the discerning visitor can hardly fail to appreciate. The two principal ranges in the central section of these mountains, the Beskid Niski and the Beskid Sàdecki, make for excellent hiking and are well supplied with short day walks and long-distance trails.

Beech and fir are the main trees in these densely forested hills where you will have little difficulty escaping the crowds and communing with nature. You are sharing the woods with bears, wolves, lynx, and wildcats but you need not fret unduly about a close encounter with a predator since these are generally discreet and reclusive hunters who prefer not to be seen. What you will have no difficulty spotting – and one of the special delights of the region – are the wooden churches, some hundreds of years old, which are scattered across the landscape. These extraordinary edifices with their onion domes and richly decorated interiors stand as silent witnesses to a distinctive and almost vanished folk culture which once flourished in these hills. Dedicated to the Orthodox faith, the churches were built by the Lemko people – descendants of nomadic Slavic groups which migrated from the south and east to the Beskidy Mountains in the 13th century; they still speak a dialect that is closer to Ukrainian than Polish.

HOW TO GET THERE:
There is a good network of roads along the valleys which penetrate the mountain ranges. Krosno and Gorlice are the best bases from which to explore the Beskid Niski, while Nowy Sàcz and the spa town of Krynica serve the Beskid Sàdecki.
WHEN TO GO:
April to October
DON'T MISS:
The Poprad River running south from Nowy Sàcz is a particularly beautiful valley in the Beskid Sàdecki hills.
YOU SHOULD KNOW:
In the mid-19th century the Beskid Niski area experienced a major economic boom when oil was discovered.

319

Kaszuby Lakes

HOW TO GET THERE:
The area's main town, Kartuzy, and the lakeside resort of Chmielno are the best bases for a visit. Public transport is fairly thin so you will need your own means of getting about to get the most out of a visit.
WHEN TO GO:
April to October
DON'T MISS:
The Kashubians are enthusiasts for snuff. Look out for the hand-carved snuffboxes they carry around.
YOU SHOULD KNOW:
The Kashubian is considered a genial and free-spirited character but with a reputation also for obstinacy. There is a phrase in Polish which translates as 'stubborn as a Kaszub'.

Sunset over the lakes

The historical region of Pomerania covers the northwest of present-day Poland and has been one of Europe's most bitterly contested territories, changing hands many times over the centuries between Polish, Germanic and Scandinavian overlords. One fascinating legacy of this troubled history is the area of Kashubia (Kazuby), home to one of Poland's most distinctive folk cultures. Kashubia extends for some 100 km (62 mi) southwest of Gdansk and is noted for its tranquil landscapes and serene beauty. This area is not one of nature's scene-stealers but one which wears its modest charms easily and appealingly to anyone seeking a less hurried pace of life and an insight into how the Polish peasantry lived 100 years ago. It is a world of low hills and quiet woodlands dotted with quaint villages containing many examples of the traditional wooden and half-timbered buildings characteristic of Kashubian domestic architecture.

The area's most distinctive features are the many lakes scattered across the countryside – according to legend the footprints of giants

who created the region. A local saying has it that 'wherever you throw a stone in Kashubia, it will land in water'; not surprisingly, the area is a haven for canoeists and kayakers. The Radunia Circle is a particular favourite – a 60-km (37-mi) aquatic loop which takes in ten lakes, all connected by the Radunia River. The loop is in the countryside between Kartuzy and Koscierzyna, a landscape of hills and lakes known popularly as Kashub Switzerland.

You will still hear older Kashubians speaking a dialect of Polish that is thought to derive from an ancient Pomeranian tongue. If you want to learn more about their culture, the outstanding *skansen* (open-air museum) at Wdzydze Kiszewskie in the south of the region is the place to go.

Stolowe Mountains

Part of the Sudetes Mountains which run for over 250 km (155 mi) along the Polish-Czech border, the Góry Stolowe or Stolowe Mountains have been attracting visitors to this corner of Lower Silesia for more than 200 years. The curious rock formations that are their particular fascination are certainly found nowhere else in Poland. When you look at the characteristic flat-topped profiles of these mountains it is not difficult to see why they are known as the Table Mountains (*stolowe* in Polish). These plateaus were formed as a result of deposits of soft sandstone building up in horizontal strata. Over time the forces of erosion have worn away the softer rock to leave the harder stuff exposed beneath. Inevitably the bizarre shapes thus created have been given names, such as Camel, Elephant, Hen and Pulpit, although it takes quite an effort of the imagination in some cases to appreciate the likeness.

The Góry Stolowe are now a national park. At 63 sq km (24 sq mi) it is relatively small by national park standards, which means you should be able to explore its principal sights in a couple of days. Numerous hiking trails and cycle paths lead through the spruce forests that constitute 90 per cent of the park area, including one that takes you on a large loop from the village of Karlów past various viewpoints and rock formations. After climbing nearly 700 stone steps to the Szczeliniec Wielki, at 919 m (3,015 ft) the highest outcrop in the range, you pass by other striking natural features, including a 20-m (66-ft) deep chasm in the rock appropriately named Little Hell. Elsewhere in the park there is a large group of scattered rocks known as the Petrified Mushrooms and the Bledne Skaly, a huge labyrinth composed of gigantic boulders.

HOW TO GET THERE:
The small town of Kudowa-Zdrój on the Czech border to the southwest is the best base for a visit to the Stolowe Mountains. The popular health resort lies on the main Warsaw to Prague highway.
WHEN TO GO:
April to October (but be advised that you may still find snow at the bottom of the Little Hell crevice as late as June).
DON'T MISS:
If you are in the area you should certainly not miss the Chapel of Skulls in Czermna on the outskirts of Kudowa-Zdrój, a *memento mori* if ever there was one.
YOU SHOULD KNOW:
The waters from the area's natural springs have long been known for their curative and restorative properties. There are a number of elegant spa towns close to the Stolowe Mountains.

Aukštaitija National Park

HOW TO GET THERE:
Start from the Aukštaitija National Park Visitor Information Centre in Palūšše where helpful staff can offer advice on things to see and do; good routes to follow on roads, water or on foot; and accommodation.

WHEN TO GO:
Avoid early November to late March when the sun never shines, there are deep snowfalls and the weather (particularly in January) can be bitterly cold. Summers are warm but wet.

DON'T MISS:
The wonderful vista over lakes and woods from the top of the park's most famous viewpoint, Ladakalnis Hill, or the ornate wooden 18th-century church of St Jezefa in Palūšše that appears on the Lithuanian 1 litas banknote.

YOU SHOULD KNOW:
Although Aukštaitija National Park occupies but one per cent of Lithuania, it contains 59 per cent of the country's plant species.

Lithuania's Lake District has lots of lakes, including 126 in Aukštaitija National Park. None match up sizewise to England's famous equivalents, as the largest is comparatively diminutive Lake Kretuonas with an area of just 8 sq km (3 sq mi). Nor are there dramatic fells, for Lithuania's lakes are scattered among wonderful country consisting of woods, meadows and gentle hills. The park is crossed by the River Žeimena, which is fed by numerous streams and occupies an area of around 400 sq km (154 sq mi) centred on the village of Palūšše, 100 km (62 mi) north of Vilnius beside Lake Lušiai.

Although there are 115 traditional villages within the park, home to over 2,000 people, human presence does not detract from the area's outstanding natural beauty. Three quarters of the terrain is wooded and much of the rest is water, ensuring great biodiversity undamaged by the intrusive scars of modern development. Indeed, some two per cent of Aukštaitija National Park is classified as 'strictly protected' and these sensitive zones may be entered only if accompanied by a member of the park's staff.

The area has a long history – the park has 11 hill forts – and this heritage adds a pleasing dimension to any visit. Stripeikiai is the park's oldest village and hosts the quaintly named Lithuanian Museum of Ancient Beekeeping. Another worthwhile destination is Ginuciai, with its original watermill. But the lakes are magnetic and, since the park was established in 1974, water tourism has become the major leisure activity. Kayaks are easy to hire and a wonderful way of exploring this special landscape, with waterside campsites to encourage extended expeditions. Everyone who takes to the water should be sure to visit Baluošas Lake to explore the seven islands therein, one of which has a mini-lake of its own.

Aukštaitija National Park – land of lakes and hills

Gauja National Park

Latvia's largest national park is one of four in the country and was established in 1973 in the region of Vidzeme. Running from northeast of Sigulda to southwest of Cesis, Gauja National Park occupies an area of 920 sq km (355 sq mi) along the Gauja River Valley – 60 km (37 mi) long and between 10 km (6 mi) and 30 km (17 mi) wide. Although it follows the river's course, the park also contains lakes – the largest being Lake Ungurs – and around half the terrain consists of dense forest, mainly spruce and pine.

Spectacular sandstone cliffs along the Gauja River soar to 90 m (300 ft) in some places and feature strongly in the park's wilder northern sections around Sigulda, where strict preservation rules apply. There are many amazing rock formations and numerous caves carved from sandstone by wind, weather and water over many millennia. The southwestern parts of the park are more leisure orientated and a natural playground popular with the inhabitants of Riga, who enjoy rafting and canoeing on the river, or hiking, biking and horse riding. The forests provide a home for over 900 plant species, 150 types of bird and nearly 50 different wild animals. There are a number of campsites in the park, including some for river users.

But quite apart from this carefully husbanded nature reserve, those who explore the park will find over 500 monuments testifying to the area's long and colourful history. There are overgrown castle mounds as well as real castles, archaeological sites, old churches, windmills and watermills, fortresses and ancient manors.

The town of Ligatne, which is within the park, has its own fascinating nature park, complete with trails.

HOW TO GET THERE:
The historic towns of Sigulda, Ligatne and Cesis are all in the park, while Valmiera is close by and they all provide an ideal jumping-off point for exploration. Sigulda is 50 km (31 mi) east of Riga.
WHEN TO GO:
Any time. Winters are short and sharp (generally from January to March). Summers are usually mild but wet.
DON'T MISS:
The beautifully reconstructed medieval Turaida Castle, right across the River Gauja from Sigulda. In addition to the original structure begun in 1214, the surrounding museum reserve includes an ancient wooden church and the Dainu Hill sculpture park.
YOU SHOULD KNOW:
Gauja National Park and its environs boast the title 'Livonian Switzerland', named for the area's ancient inhabitants and its spectacular scenery. It has been a popular tourist destination since the late 19th century.

Pine forest in Gauja National Park

323

Matsalu National Park

Every spring and autumn, most of the waterfowl which breed in the arctic tundra migrate along the southern coast of the Baltic Sea. Geese, swans, ducks and waders in their hundreds of thousands stop in western Estonia, on and around the Kasari River delta where it flows into Matsalu Bay and the Vainameri Sea. The entire area falls within 486 sq km (188 sq mi) Matsalu National Park, one of Europe's largest and most important migratory stopovers. It is distinguished both by the extraordinary coincidence of geophysical circumstances that make it so attractive to birds and by the ethereal beauty of its unusual coastal landscapes.

Matsalu belongs to neither land nor sea. Protected by the brackish shallows of the Vainameri Sea from the full onslaught of the open Baltic, Matsalu Bay has no real tides to scour the rich silts that infuse the coastal meadows, reed beds, swamps, bogs, floodplains and slick mudflats that meld into the shoreline. The bay is 18 km (11 mi) long and 6 km (4 mi) long, but barely 1.5 m (5 ft) deep, a sanctuary from everything except the wind and winter ice, which is thicker here, and lasts longer, because of its sheltered position. The 236 sq km (91 sq mi) of open sea within the reserve includes 40 islands which greatly extend the variety of nesting and rest sites available to the two million waterfowl which settle in Matsalu. It's hard to take in their magnificence. On the greyest day, to see 20,000 Bewick's swans materialize from a waterlogged horizon, and listen to the urgent thunder of 100,000 beating wings as greylag and barnacle geese slap down on the water, is to participate in some sort of homage to creation. At dawn in springtime, or in the reddening vastness of a fine-weather dusk, Matsalu is paradise.

Soomaa National Park

Between Viljandi and Parnu in Estonia's southwest, Soomaa National Park protects and celebrates a hydrological anomaly left over from the great Ice Ages. Deep beneath the bogs and forests of the region, the bedrock is inclined at an angle which causes its rivers and streams to drain into a single major river, the Halliste, which then flows into the Navesti River at 160 degrees against its stream. The almost head-on collision of water causes biblical floods every year. In fact, flooding is known locally as 'the fifth season'. Over millennia the same sequence has created five huge bogs separated by thick swamp forests and enormous flood plains; and over centuries, the people who live there have incorporated this bizarre wetland into their own, unique version of rural Estonian culture. For visitors,

Soomaa's international importance as a RAMSAR wetland and World Heritage Site means that every facility now exists to enable them to enjoy both the cultural and ecological highlights of the region.

The best way to get around is by dug-out log canoe, used in Soomaa since the Stone Age, although there are foot and bicycle trails which use traditional trestle bridges erected in times of flood. It's hard to believe the ways water can modify landscapes – especially in the swamp forests (known also as 'carrs') where beaver and otter create river meanders with their building works; the alluvial meadows and river banks coloured blue with wild iris, and harbouring 200 other species including orchids; or the fens and bogs where you might see bear, wolves or lynx. Each of these geographic features is without direct parallel elsewhere in the world. Soomaa is an evolutionary laboratory on a colossal scale, and even its flora and fauna are adaptive. Its peculiar natural history of flooding makes it the most exciting wetland in Europe.

A view over the swamp forests of Soomaa National Park in early spring

YOU SHOULD KNOW:
Soomaa is full of so many anomalous natural forces that some visitors can start to feel light-headed. The more effort visitors make to see and understand how local communities have adapted, the easier it is to give free rein to enthusiasm, without losing the sense of wonder that makes Soomaa so special.

Teberdinsky Nature Reserve

The Caucasus mountain range on Russia's southeastern border has exercised a potent hold on the European imagination ever since Alexander Pushkin, Russia's national bard, celebrated the region's elemental grandeur and exotic atmosphere in richly romantic verse after being exiled there in the 1820s. In spite of these magnificent mountains being involuntary witnesses to many of the fiercest territorial disputes which have flared up in the aftermath of the break-up of the former Soviet Union (Chechnya is the most notorious), their mystique and rugged beauty have been preserved remarkably intact. The Communist regime was taking no chances, though, and in 1936 designated the lands surrounding the upper reaches of the Teberda River as a nature reserve.

The Teberdinsky Nature Reserve encompasses an area of 851 sq km (328 sq mi) on the northern spurs of the western Caucasus. With a vertical elevation of nearly 3,000 m (9,840 ft) within its boundaries the reserve displays an astonishing range of environments, from temperate mixed woodlands through dense conifer forests to high alpine meadows above the tree-line. Teberdinsky protects one of the most unspoilt and biodiverse ecosystems in Europe, a fact recognized internationally in 1997 when it was awarded biosphere reserve status by UNESCO.

The reserve offers splendid hiking opportunities but you should take a local guide with you, especially in the southern reaches which abut a sensitive national frontier (Abkhazia, a small breakaway republic from neighbouring Georgia, is on the other side). The forests are home to brown bears, bison, lynx and wild boars while on the rocky higher slopes you should have no difficulty spotting chamois and *tur*, the wild goats which with their large curved horns are found only in the Caucasus.

HOW TO GET THERE:
The nearest railhead is at Cherkessk, from where it is a three-hour bus journey south to the village of Dombay, a winter sports resort and the best place from which to organize your visit to the reserve.
WHEN TO GO:
May to September
DON'T MISS:
The gorgeous displays of wild flowers in the high meadows during the summer months
YOU SHOULD KNOW:
The Caucasian bison is Europe's largest native mammal. By the 1920s it had been hunted to extinction in the region but has been re-introduced to the Teberdinsky reserve.

The Teberda River, near Dombay

Kaluzhskie Zaseki Nature Reserve

In times past the vast forests of the central Russian uplands formed a natural defensive barrier protecting the fledgling principalities of northern Russia from marauding tribes and horsemen invading off the great southern steppes. City-states such as Novgorod and Muscovy (modern-day Moscow) relied on the impenetrability of these forests, although local rulers strengthened them still further with fortifications of their own. The use of felled trees stacked one on top of another was one such defensive measure; referred to normally by the French term *abatis*, its Russian name, *zaseki*, has been given to one of Russia's newest nature reserves, created since the end of the Soviet Union.

The Kaluzhskie Zaseki Nature Reserve is situated in the Kaluga region southwest of Moscow. Large parts of this region were formerly covered by mixed deciduous woodlands but, once the military threats from the south had diminished, the forests fell prey to logging and other forms of human exploitation and dwindled fast. Although a country as big as Russia can still hold plenty of secrets, scientists were surprised when as recently as the early 1990s they came across an undisturbed tract of old-growth broadleaf forest. Considering the political turmoil of the times it was quite an achievement that they were able to safeguard this precious survival by establishing an area of 185 sq km (71 sq mi) as a nature reserve.

The reserve is criss-crossed by streams and wetlands but the vast majority of it is woodland and home to a remarkable proliferation of wildlife. Moose, deer, wild boar and wolves are the larger mammals that inhabit the forest; it is also home to over 160 different birds, including golden eagles, hawks and other birds of prey. No fewer than 189 species of mushroom have been recorded.

Kostomukshsky Forest

The province of Karelia in Russia's far northwest has always been a land alive with legend and shrouded in romance. Inside the huge dark forest an air of mystery mingles with an almost oppressive stillness and, as you contemplate the serried rows of pines receding into the far distance, it becomes easy to imagine the spirits of the woodland that populate the rich folklore of the region. Indeed, it was on the banks of Lake Kamennoye that the poems and songs of the *Kalevala* had their probable origin (the great national epic of Finland which has proved such a fertile source of inspiration for the country's artists, most notably the composer Jean Sibelius).

The 10,500-ha (25,946-ac) Lake Kamennoye is the largest of some 250 lakes found in the Kostomukshsky Nature Reserve in northern Karelia. The reserve was established in 1983 to protect 476 sq km (184 sq mi) of virgin coniferous forest along Russia's border with Finland. This is a classic landscape of the boreal or northern taiga: dense pine and spruce forests interspersed with waterways, swamps and peat bogs. It is home to large animals like the reindeer and brown bear, and to predators like the wolf and the lynx. Sadly, reindeer numbers in the reserve have halved over the past two decades, partly because of poaching but also because the barbed-wire border fence has impeded the creatures' natural east-west migrations. Among the birds to be found in Kostomukshsky are the capercaillie and black grouse, and birds of prey such as the golden eagle, osprey and great grey owl.

HOW TO GET THERE:
The nearest town, Kostomuksha, is located 200 km (124 mi) west of the main St Petersburg to Murmansk railway line.
WHEN TO GO:
June to August
DON'T MISS:
They may be an endangered species but you should be lucky enough to spot white-tailed sea eagles, either in their lofty bankside perches or circling and swooping over the rivers and lakes.
YOU SHOULD KNOW:
Thanks to a special joint agreement, Kostomukshsky is now part of a much larger green belt which incorporates other reserves across the border in Finland.

Yugyd Va National Park

HOW TO GET THERE:
The northern part of the park is reached from the towns of Pechora and Inta, both on the Moscow to Vorkuta railway line. The southern part is best reached via Vuktyl, 230 km (143 mi) east of Ukhta rail station. Vuktyl is also home to the park headquarters.
WHEN TO GO:
May to September (the spring snow melts offer the best rafting conditions).
DON'T MISS:
The neighbouring Pechoro-Ilych Nature Reserve which, together with Yugyd Va, comprises the UNESCO World Heritage Site known as the Virgin Komi Forests.
YOU SHOULD KNOW:
Yugyd Va is situated within the Komi Republic, one of 21 autonomous republics that make up the Russian Federation.

It is only fitting that a national park within the largest country on Earth should be on a similarly epic scale and Yugyd Va certainly does not disappoint. At almost 19,000 sq km (7,336 sq mi) it is practically the size of Wales and covers a 400-km (248-mi) length of the northern Urals. This mountain range forms the continental border with Asia, although Yugyd Va is firmly on the western, European side of the mountains. The park includes prime examples of taiga and Europe's largest remaining expanses of virgin spruce forest. As you move east into the foothills, the landscape changes to predominantly tundra. The Urals are not a high range – the highest peak, Mount Narodnaya, which is located within Yugyd Va, is less than 2,000 m (6,562 ft) – but the park lies just outside the Arctic Circle so it comes as no surprise to find glaciers and frozen lakes.

If the Siberian spruce dominates the landscape of the lower slopes, the monotony of dark green is relieved occasionally by broad stands of that most evocative of Russian trees – the birch. There are established populations of elk, reindeer, sable and brown bears in the park, and you are likely to hear wolves even if you don't see them. Yugyd Va covers much of the basin of the River Pechora, one of Europe's longest, which flows north into the Barents Sea. Adventure rafting on its feeder rivers as they tumble down from the mountains is an increasingly popular activity but Yugyd Va is still seriously off the beaten track; with relatively few visitor facilities in the park the only practicable way to experience its many delights is to sign up for a guided tour with camping under canvas or in primitive shelters.

Tsentralno Chernozyomny Nature Reserve

The city of Kursk lies 500 km (310 mi) south of Moscow on the northern fringes of Russia's fabled Chernozyom, or Black Earth belt. This region, much of it now in present-day Ukraine, was once known as the breadbasket of the Russian Empire, thanks to its deep, nutrient-rich soil. A well-drained humus layer, as much as 1 m (3 ft) deep, has provided one of the most fertile and productive agricultural landscapes anywhere on Earth. One 19th-century writer, indeed, called the Chernozyom 'the Tsar of soils, more valuable than oil, more precious than gold'. Unsurprisingly, it has been intensively farmed over the centuries, which makes the 130 sq km (50 sq mi, including buffer zone) of the Tsentralno Chernozyomny Nature Reserve outside Kursk all the more astonishing a survival.

The reserve is important because it protects a small but precious area of pristine steppe habitat that has never fallen under the plough. It marks the point where the wide open plains meet the belt of temperate forest to the north; roughly half its area consists of broadleaf woodlands. Fringed by the basins of two of Russia's mightiest rivers, the Don and the Dnieper, Tsentralno Chernozyomny also has its fair share of swamps and marshland. The forests are home to elk, roe deer and wild boar while smaller mammals include the Siberian polecat and the stone marten. Black kites are a common sight hovering overhead and the exotic hoopoe with its striking feathered crest and pinkish colouring can also be found here. The grasslands in the reserve put on a fine display of wild flowers in the spring.

HOW TO GET THERE:
Kursk is connected to Moscow by bus and rail services. The journey by train takes eight hours.
WHEN TO GO:
April to October
DON'T MISS:
The beautiful flute-like song of the golden oriole, a summer visitor to the reserve which you are unlikely to see, however, as the bird tends to stay in the tree-tops.
YOU SHOULD KNOW:
Because the reserve is divided into six separate tracts it is more vulnerable to pressures from surrounding settlements. Conservationists are trying to establish a system of linking corridors.

Mount Elbrus

HOW TO GET THERE:
The city of Nalchik in the foothills to
the north is the base for visits to the
Elbrus region. Connected by rail (38
hours) and by air to Moscow, Nalchik
is a three-hour bus journey from the
head of the Baksan valley.
WHEN TO GO:
June to September (but note that
there is also a skiing and winter
sports season from December to
May).
DON'T MISS:
The park's many beautiful waterfalls
and the natural mineral springs near
Baydaevo.
YOU SHOULD KNOW:
The walking routes that go up the
southern slopes of the valley
towards the border with Georgia
require you to have a border permit.
This is a free document but can
involve you in a lot of bureaucracy
so you might prefer to join a tour
which will take care of the
formalities for you.

If you accept that the Caucasus Mountains are part of Europe
(some people consider them to be in Asia), then Mount Elbrus is
the highest peak in Europe at 5,642 m (18,510 ft) – significantly
superior to Mont Blanc in France. Its distinctive twin peaks, under a
permanent cover of snow, are an impressive sight at any time of
year but, unless you are an experienced climber or a winter sports
fanatic, you will need to come in the summer months if you want to
see them. Elbrus is situated at the head of the Baksan River valley,
on a spur projecting north from the central Caucasus range. The
mountain forms the heart of the Prielbrusye National Park, a vast
wilderness area comprising 1,000 sq km (386 sq mi) of alpine
meadows and pine and birch forests in addition to the mountains
themselves. Jagged ridges and lofty peaks flank the valley on both
sides, offering spectacular panoramas in every direction.

Various trails lead off from the valley floor along smaller side
valleys, presenting options for easy day-treks or longer, more
strenuous hikes involving overnight stays in campsites or shelters.
You cannot see the summit of Mount Elbrus itself from the Baksan
valley, but a three-hour walk up the Terskol valley brings you to a
dramatic hanging glacier (one of several in the park) where great
shards of ice 'drip' over the cliff edge; from here there is a fine view
of the twin peaks. The more popular and less effortful way of seeing
the summit, though, is to take the cable car at the end of the valley
to the Mir Bar station at 3,500 m (11,483 ft).

Mount Elbrus, Europe's
tallest peak

Shulgan-Tash

There are many reasons for protecting our precious natural environment but few can be stranger than the one which has given birth to Shulgan-Tash Nature Reserve in the rolling hills of the southern Urals. The reserve was established in 1990 in order to protect the natural habitat of the humble Burzyan honeybee. Renowned for the quality of sweet golden honey they produce, these wild bees are able to survive very cold weather and Shulgan-Tash is the only place in the world where they are still found in the wild. The bees colonize hollows in trees and feed on nectar from linden trees and the fireweed plant (more popularly known in Britain as rosebay willowherb). The hives are now tended by rangers on the reserve, many of whom have inherited beekeeping skills passed down through generations of Bashkir families.

Bounded on its northern edge by the Nugush River and by the Belaya River to the south, Shulgan-Tash reserve is located in the autonomous republic of Bashkortostan, some 200 km (124 mi) south of the capital Ufa. The landscape is predominantly one of old-growth deciduous forests which cover the hills and low mountains and are occasionally punctuated by clearings of meadow and grassland. Mountain tributaries of the main rivers wind their way through the terrain, creating dramatic canyons through the limestone ridges. Besides the bees, Shulgan-Tash's other claim to fame is the Kapov Caves, a huge underground complex of grottos and passages carved out of the karst by the Shulgan river. The caves, which can be visited on guided tours, contain some of Europe's most ancient rock paintings, estimated to be at least 15,000 years old.

Some of Europe's most ancient rock paintings can be found in the Kapov Caves within the Shulgan-Tash Nature Reserve.

HOW TO GET THERE:
The nearest point of access on the railway network is the industrial centre of Magnitogorsk, 100 km (62 mi) to the east.
WHEN TO GO:
May to September
DON'T MISS:
The chance to sample the product of those busy bees. The amber nectar may not come cheap but is rightly prized by the local population.
YOU SHOULD KNOW:
Conservationists are currently campaigning against a proposed hydro-electric dam on the Belaya River which they fear would flood important habitats in Shulgan-Tash.

Dilijan National Park

HOW TO GET THERE:
By minibus van from Yerevan to the upper Avtokayaran, then another to Ijevan that will stop at Dilijan. That said, a taxi from Yerevan is not expensive, even for budget travellers. Car hire offers freedom to see more of the park and its environs.

WHEN TO GO:
The Armenian climate varies considerably according to specific location, but the preferred time to explore Dilijan National Park is during the cool and moist summer. Autumn visitors will be delighted by the turning foliage, however.

DON'T MISS:
The fabulous Haghartsin Monastery, in a beautiful wooded hillside setting near Dilijan. Constructed between the 10th and 14th centuries, it has many impressive buildings (some ruined) and the centrepiece is St Astvatsatsin Church with a wonderful dome that has no fewer than 16 facets.

YOU SHOULD KNOW:
The resort of Dilijan is actually a modest spa town, renowned for its energizing mineral waters – although definitely not quite so grand as Bath or Buxton.

It initially seems somewhat chaotic. Dilijan National Park in northeastern Armenia's Tavush Province – one of two national parks in the country – was created in 2002 to succeed a state nature reserve, itself the scene of forestry enterprises until the late 1950s. Although it spreads across slopes of the Pembak, Areguni, Miapor, Ijevan and Halab mountains, all the high pastures are actually excluded from the park. There are numerous cultural monuments and settlements located within the park – including eponymous Dilijan town – and a railway line passes right through the middle. Tension between well-meaning nature conservation and commercial activity is endemic.

Sounds . . . unpromising? Actually, the largely forested Dilijan National Park is rather good, with plenty of unspoilt, wild terrain awaiting the adventurous traveller looking for an unusual destination. Dilijan itself is a charming old town nestling in the picturesque hills, and provides an ideal base for sallies into the surrounding countryside. This may remind visitors of Switzerland, as it has forests and alpine meadows very reminiscent of the land of alpenhorns and tinkling cowbells. Happily, this remote corner of Europe is gnome-free and anything but a tourist hotspot – seeming all the better for that.

The park cries out to be explored and is rich in flora and fauna. There are over a thousand plant species and a wide variety of trees, including oak, beech, hornbeam, lime, maple, ash, pine, juniper and many wild fruit trees. Around 150 species of bird have been recorded, including real corkers like golden eagle, goshawk, black kite, honey buzzard, black grouse, Caspian snowcock and eagle owl. The animal population is scarcely less impressive, numbering the likes of brown bear, wolf, lynx, wild boar, wildcat and red deer among its 50 or so members.

Chornohora Mountain Ridge

The mighty Carpathian Mountains frown down on Ukraine, and remain one of Europe's great unspoilt wilderness areas. The Chornohora Mountain Ridge is the highest section, and gives access to the country's tallest peak – Hoverla mountain in western Ukraine at 2,061 m (6,762 ft). Chornohora's main range extends for some 40 km (25 mi) from the Chorna Tysa River in the west to the Chornyi River in the east. The ridge forms the watershed between the rivers Prut and Tysa and is divided by a deep pass. The western end is jagged and the monolithic eastern massif contains the highest peaks, including Hoverla, Pip Ivan, Shpytsi and Tomnatyk. The geology has been shaped by glacial action in the last Ice Age, as evidenced by many lateral and terminal moraines.

Postglacial depressions bottom out in lakes or peat bogs and narrow valleys slash the slopes of Chornohora. The lower elevations are heavily forested with beech and spruce trees, then there's a belt of alder and juniper brush before the alpine meadows and barren rock fields that make up the ridge. The local Hutsul people are mainly occupied with traditional animal herding on high pastures during a five-month season, although tourism is starting to play an increasingly important role in the regional economy.

That said, the mountains are still isolated, lonely and potentially hazardous. So this is really one for an organized hiking tour led by a guide who knows the rugged terrain intimately. A number of treks are offered, lasting from one day to a week. Go-it-alone types should not be tempted to tackle the Chornohora Mountain Ridge unless their self-sufficiency skills and backcountry experience are well honed, although modest day hikes are comfortably within the reach of anyone who is reasonably fit and active.

HOW TO GET THERE:
Tourism in the Ukrainian Carpathians centres on the towns of Bystrets, Rakhiv, Verkhovyna and Vorokhta. The best starting points for Chornohora are Bohdan in the Bila Tysa River Valley and Yasinia in the Chorna Tysa River Valley. The nearest rail station to the latter is at Ivano-Frankifsk.

WHEN TO GO:
For something very different, be around on August 24, Ukraine's Independence Day, when thousands of Ukrainians make a pilgrimage to the summit of Hoverla. If that's not on, any time in summer is good and any time in the long winter is bad.

DON'T MISS:
Anyone tackling the all-day ascent of Hoverla Mountain should be sure to take the short diversion south of the main trail to view the impressive waterfall on the Prut River, a tributary of the Danube. Alternatively, this is a worthwhile hike in its own right if the summit climb is too demanding.

YOU SHOULD KNOW:
Continuing tension between Ukraine and Russia was reflected in 2007 when vandals suspected of being Russian activists defaced official Ukrainian national symbols at the summit of Hoverla.

Synevyr Lake

Ukraine's largest mountain lake is in the picturesque heart of the Synevyr National Nature Park, the country's third such protected area. This impressive tract of mountainous landscape extends to 400 sq km (154 sq mi) in the southern part of the Gorgany Mountains, themselves the centre of the Ukrainian section of the mighty Carpathians. Wooded slopes and mixed habitats provide refuge for a variety of wildlife, including brown bear, wolf, lynx, deer, ermine, badger and marten. Among protected bird species, the rare horned owl stands out.

Synevyr Lake itself is at an elevation of nearly 1,000 m (3,280 ft). It has an outflow into the Tereblya River and was formed when a landslide dammed the steep valley it occupies. It rejoices in the title 'Blue Eye of the Carpathians', encouraged by the presence of a tiny island in the centre that represents the pupil. This small but deep lake has recently been classified as a wetland of international importance. Although the surrounding mountains are wild and lonely – an ideal challenge for the hardy hiker who loves self-sufficient wilderness exploration – the lake is a popular destination.

The drive to the lake is an experience in itself, as the road winds up the steep Synevyrskiy Pass, far above the white dwellings of Svnevry village which are scattered around the silver thread of the Tereblya River. To see the lake in its marvellous setting from afar before actually going there, continue to the summit of nearby Ozirna Mountain before returning to the lake (road open in summer only). A word to the wise – Synevyr Lake's crystal-clear waters may look tempting, and often attract hardy swimmers, but think carefully before joining them. The water temperature rarely rises above 5°C (41°F), which makes the average cold shower seem, well, warm.

Grand Canyon

Forget travelling all the way to the USA – Europe has its very own Grand Canyon, tucked away in southern Ukraine. The Grand Canyon of Crimea may be found on the peninsula of the same name, which juts into the Black Sea and is an autonomous republic within Ukraine. This geological marvel is situated on the northern slopes of Ai-Petri Mountain, behind Yalta, and in no way measures up to its cousin in Arizona when it comes to the awesome natural wonder stakes – although it is still a sublimely beautiful wild place.

The canyon walls tower up to an impressive height of 320 m

(1,050 ft) and – amazingly – it is a mere 3 m (10ft) wide at the narrowest point. The fast-flowing Kuru-Uzen races along the canyon's rocky floor, creating dynamic small waterfalls, pools and white-water rapids before joining the Auzun-Uzen River towards the canyon exit. Despite those dizzying rock faces, much of the canyon has shallower sides. They – along with the canyon surrounds and floor – are densely wooded.

There are two routes for hikers who want to travel along the Grand Canyon and enjoy its astonishing rock formations close up. One route follows the canyon floor beside the water, another passes along the right flank of the canyon. The former is impassable in winter and spring, when a raging torrent invariably overwhelms the path, but the latter may be used all year round. The favoured direction for hiking is from the upper to the lower end. This through-trek can be done in a day but is anything but a casual stroll. A good level of fitness is essential, for either route is demanding physically. In addition, there are side paths that lead nowhere and anyone tempted to follow one can end up hopelessly lost amidst tangled vegetation.

The walls of the Grand Canyon of Crimea tower up to a height of 320 m (1,050 ft).

DON'T MISS:
A short day-hike along the canyon floor from the car park, to find the popular Blue Pond and Bath of Youth pools – anyone tempted by the promise implicit in the latter should be aware that the water temperature never rises above 11°C (51.8°F) and is often colder.

YOU SHOULD KNOW:
Those exploring the canyon floor should have small-denomination used notes handy – rangers usually expect a non-voluntary 'contribution'.

Malá Fatra National Park

HOW TO GET THERE:
There is a regular bus service from Žilina, 25 km (15.5 mi) to the west of Malá Fatra.
WHEN TO GO:
Any time of year. May and September are particularly good months if you want to escape the crowds and the snows.
DON'T MISS:
Golden eagles nest in these mountains; you may be lucky to see these majestic birds circling high overhead on the thermals.
YOU SHOULD KNOW:
Terchová is famous in Slovakia as the birthplace of a Robin Hood-like folk hero called Juraj Jánošík.

The Malá Fatra is a mountain range in central Slovakia, 226 km (140 mi) of which is protected as a national park. The focus of the park is the beautiful valley formed by the Vrátna River as it carves its way deep into the mountains. The village of Terchová stands at the entrance to the valley but the real gateway comes a short distance south as you enter the dramatic rockscape of the Tiesňavy gorge, with sheer cliffs and towering limestone pinnacles on every side. Further up the valley, exciting vistas open up of mountain-tops rising above slopes which are covered in pine and beech forests. The valley is completely encircled by brooding peaks which leave you in no doubt that raw nature holds sway here. From Chatna Vrátna at the head of the valley, 7 km (4.3 mi) south of Terchová, you can take a cable car 750 m (2,460 ft) up the mountain to the Snilovské saddle from where it is a 40-minute hike to the summit of Velký Kriváň, at 1,709 m (5,607 ft) the highest peak in the park. If the weather holds you will be rewarded with panoramic views not only of the Vrátna valley but also over the Vel'ká Fatra range to the south.

There are some terrific hikes through the Malá Fatra; some include steep sections featuring ladders and chains which are not for the faint-hearted. The trek to the Rozsutec massif in the east of the park is a particularly satisfying one, giving you access to a cave below Mount Malý Rozsutec as well as a number of hidden valleys and the narrow Dolné Diery gorge.

Limestone cliffs in Malá Fatra National Park

Pieniny Mountains

Tri Koruny peak in the mighty Pieniny Mountains

The Pieniny Mountains form part of the border between Slovakia and Poland. A northern spur of the Carpathians, this small range lies in the shadow of the High Tatras to the west, and while it may lack the grandeur of its mighty neighbour, its unspoilt landscapes possess an undeniable appeal. This is in no small part due to a small national park which, together with a sister park on the north bank in Poland, exists primarily to protect the lovely valley of the Dunajec River which forms the actual frontier. Jagged limestone peaks rise above the thick forests which cover nearly half of the park's 21 sq km (8 sq mi). Much of the rest is given over to small fields and richly grassed meadows, testimony to a traditional way of farming largely untouched by the modern age.

The best way to appreciate the mountains is from the river. Although it is what everyone comes to the Pieniny for, you should definitely not miss the trip downriver on one of the large wooden rafts. Starting at the 14th-century Red Monastery, the 90-minute journey takes you down a jaw-dropping 8.5-km (5.3-mi) gorge past cliffs which rise sheer from the water and tower over you. This is no white-water trip so you have plenty of time to admire the dramatic scenery as you are poled along by rafters in their traditional embroidered waistcoats. The views change constantly as the river winds its way through the limestone hills. Your guide will point out the main features, such as the three rocks known as the Stone Monks and the Tri Koruny (Three Crowns); at 982 m (3,222 ft) these are the highest peaks in the range, but Poland claims them as they are on the north bank.

HOW TO GET THERE:
The Pieniny Mountains are 120 km (75 mi) from Košice, the main city in East Slovakia. Buses are infrequent so it is best if you have your own transport.
WHEN TO GO:
May to October
DON'T MISS:
Look out for otters in the water or on the riverbanks.
YOU SHOULD KNOW:
At the end of the raft ride at Lesnica you can return to your starting-point on a riverside trail, either on foot or by hiring a bicycle.

339

Vihorlat Highlands

HOW TO GET THERE:
There are railway stations at Humenné and Michalovce, from where local buses reach the heart of Vihorlat at Remetské Hámre, a village 7 km (4.3 mi) south of the lake.
WHEN TO GO:
April to October
DON'T MISS:
The traditional wooden churches of the area, a curious blend of western Catholicism and eastern Orthodoxy and the most visible reminder of the local Rusyn culture.
YOU SHOULD KNOW:
Late September/early October is a particularly rewarding time to visit the Vihorlat Highlands when the beech woods are a blaze of autumn colours.

In the easternmost part of Slovakia the Vihorlat Highlands are a range of tree-covered volcanic hills which provide some of the country's best walking. With the highest points barely scraping 1,000 m (3,300 ft) there are no flamboyant peaks here but the nature-lover will find more than enough compensation in the varied vistas and the peace and serenity of an area that has been designated a Protected Landscape. The woodlands of the Vihorlat are composed mainly of mixed deciduous trees, with beech being the predominant species. In 2007 parts of these woods, along with counterparts in Ukraine, were inscribed on UNESCO's World Heritage List as Primeval Beech Forests of the Carpathians.

A hidden gem in the Vihorlat Highlands is the Morské oko lake, perhaps the most beautiful and unspoilt in the whole of Slovakia. This glacial lake owes its unusual name (*morské oko* means 'sea eye') to its distinctive blue-green colour. If you sit quietly on the shore you may see the black storks which nest in these parts and honey buzzards and eagles as they circle high overhead. From the northern lake shore it is a two-hour hike to another natural marvel of the region, the Snina stone, a great slab of rock which rises precipitously above the tree line. The strenuous climb to the top is up steep iron ladders attached to the cliff face but the outstanding views from the table-top summit, 1,005 m (3,297 ft) high, make the effort eminently worthwhile. On a clear day you can see all the way over the eastern border into Ukraine.

Hortobágy National Park

Rather like the Prairie in North America, the Steppes in Russia or the Veldt in South Africa, the Puszta not only indicates a vast flat grassy area, but also carries with it a meaning that portrays a way of life. The great Hungarian Plain is not only the largest natural grassland in Europe but is also a place of special harmony between humans and nature. On the Puszta herdsmen on horseback tend their grey cattle and Racka sheep, while oxen haul trailers brim full with bales of hay. It is a traditional place little changed since before the birth of Christ.

Within this great plain lies Hortobágy National Park. Created in 1973, it was the first to acquire national park status in Hungary and its unique ecosystem was further recognized and protected when it was afforded World Heritage status in 1999. The park covers 800 sq km (309 sq mi) of meadows, low-lying scrub, bogs and lakes which provide a diverse range of habitats for a wide array of flora and fauna. Over 300 bird species have been identified in the park. One in particular provides one of the most spectacular avian displays in the world when, in the late autumn (October) evenings, cranes gather in numbers as great as 80,000 to rest on the park's lakes – in flight they almost block out the sky.

The neoclassical white Nine Span Bridge, completed in 1833, is the most famous man-made landmark in the Hortobágy and at 170 m (558 ft) is the longest stone bridge in Europe.

The Hungarian Puszta is an exceptional example of a cultural landscape shaped by the pastoral activities of mankind. In a world of ever more intensive agriculture and increasing carbon footprints, it is a special place worthy of preservation.

HOW TO GET THERE:
By train from Budapest to Debrecen (Hungary has an excellent railway system).
WHEN TO GO:
It's best from April to October.
DON'T MISS:
The Tisza Lake Water Trail – a 1.6-km (1-mi) boardwalk into the lake's wetlands, complete with watch towers and hides
YOU SHOULD KNOW:
The Hortobágy once filled Hungarian dissidents with terror. The former communist rulers built labour camps there in an effort to quell rebellion after World War II.

Cranes fly over the great Hungarian Plain at Hortobágy National Park.

Bicaz Canyon and Red Lake

HOW TO GET THERE:
Red Lake can be reached from Ghoergheni by taking the national road 12/C and then following the road through to the canyon.

WHEN TO GO:
It's beautiful all year round but clear of snow from April to October. The area is most beautiful in autumn (September and October) when the trees change colour.

DON'T MISS:
The view of Red Lake from the slopes of Killer Mountain

YOU SHOULD KNOW:
It is said that when the mountainside came down to form Red Lake, shepherds and their sheep were buried beneath the rubble. Legend has it that their cries can still be heard over the lake.

Located in the northeast of Romania, Bicaz Canyon (Cheile Bicazulu) is a deep gorge burrowed out by the fast-flowing Bicaz River. The canyon is not only a destination in itself but also acts as a corridor linking the regions of Transylvania and Moldavia via a precipitous snaking road – which is definitely not for the faint-hearted – for 8 km (5 mi). Within the limestone walls of this most imposing canyon are hidden two remarkable caverns: the Black Cave and Waterfall Cave. As well as offering ample opportunity for a spot of spelunking (cave exploration), the canyon is a favourite among rock climbers. Huge walls up to 300 m (984 ft) high rise to fantastic hanging ceilings, with deep scars in the rocks and huge clear spaces providing an adrenalin-filled climb for those skilled enough to take up the challenge.

Upstream from the canyon lies a spectacular lake, which in geological terms is barely out of the maternity ward. Sometime in the summer of 1837, after a huge storm system hit the area, an

enormous chunk of Killer Mountain became dislodged and blocked three creeks, producing a natural dam which flooded the valley. The result was Red Lake (Lacu Rosu) – made red by alluvial deposits and the reflection from the purple flanks of Suhardu Mic Mountain in the water. The lake has an eerie appearance as stumps of pine trees poke out from beneath its surface. In winter it freezes and the gorge is covered by a blanket of snow, while in summer the lake is the perfect place for a leisurely row.

Bicaz Canyon – a favoured spot for adrenaline-seeking rock climbers.

Piatra Craiului

Piatra Craiului (pronounced Cry-ooh-loo-e) is a 150 sq km (58 sq mi) national park in the Carpathian Mountains of Romania dominated by a mountainous ridge from which it takes its name. The north of the park, near the Barsa River, is made up of sloping intense-green pastureland which in spring and summer is dappled with wild blue orchids and yellow buttercups. But it is the spectacularly stark 25-km (15.5-mi) long black ridge, marbled with snow, that is the main attraction in the park. Hiking along the sharp-crested serrated ridge takes two to three days and, as well as offering spectacular panoramic views, takes the walker into the domain of *Ursus arctos* – the northern brown bear. Unlike the Alps or the Pyrenees, where bears have been hunted to virtual extinction, Piatra Craiului has a healthy population with estimates put at around 5,000.

Storm clouds gather over Mount Piatra Craiului.

Chamois (a goat-like antelope) forage along the precipitous mountain slopes, nimble and fleet of foot so as to elude the wolves and lynx that prowl the area. Falcons soar on the thermals thrown up by the sun-warmed scree, scouring the ground for the slightest movement that might indicate a meal. An area's environmental wellbeing can be measured by the number and diversity of its bird and butterfly populations, and Piatra Craiului triumphs on both counts as 120 species of birds have been identified in the park and more than twice as many species of butterflies. Of the thousand species of plants to be found, one-fifth are unique to the area.

The highest peak of the ridge – Vârful La Om at 2,238 m (7,342 ft) – may be only half the height of Mont Blanc, but the climb is so arduous that it has the feel of a much greater mountain.

HOW TO GET THERE:
By bus from Brasov to Zarnesti, which acts as a gateway to the park.
WHEN TO GO:
From May to September is best for hiking on the ridge.
DON'T MISS:
The views of the Barsa Valley from the Crapaturii Saddle (a relatively easy hike)
YOU SHOULD KNOW:
In geological terms the ridge is an *arête*, formed at the head of two opposing glaciers. Post-glaciation, the slopes have been further steepened by the action of frost and winter ice breaking rocks into scree.

Autumn in the Zsil Valley in the Retezat Mountains

Retezat Mountains

Sometimes called the Transylvanian Alps, Retezat is the highest section of the Southern Carpathian range in Romania and covers around 500 sq km (193 sq mi). The range has a distinct 'H' shape with two parallel rims (Retezat and Little Retezat) connected by a short ridge. The spectacular scenery of the area was carved out by glaciers of the Pleistocene epoch and the range, which has an average elevation of more than 1,500 m (4,920 ft), comprises spectacular granite and limestone massifs speckled with numerous turquoise tarns.

Although starkly beautiful when covered by snow in winter, the mountains gradually come to life after the spring melt. Alpine meadows blossom on the middle elevations in an area that boasts over 1,000 different plant species, with around 100 being unique to the region. The melting ice gives added force to the many waterfalls that cascade down the mountainsides, as bears and marmots slowly shake off their winter sleep. Lynx, otters, chamois and wolves all add to the remarkable diversity of life, while salamanders and vipers seek out sun-warmed rocks to raise their body temperatures.

The most spectacular scenery is to be found on the route between Mount Peleaga and Mount Judele, where a series of stunning lakes on the southern slope of Judele culminates in Lake Bucura, Romania's largest glacial lake. The area is ideal for hiking and in late summer the smaller mountain lakes warm up enough to provide pleasant conditions for swimming. However, frost-cracking means that the higher elevations are formed of unstable scree which can make progress difficult. Serious climbing can be had on the twin peaks of Bucura mountain in the northern ridge of the range, where the northeast ascent of Bucura II is via a sheer rock face.

HOW TO GET THERE:
By train from Deva or Petrosani to Ohaba de Sub Piatra, then by bus to Cabana Cârnic.

WHEN TO GO:
All year round – it's warmest from May to October but wettest in June.

DON'T MISS:
The view of the chain of mountain lakes from the higher elevations of Mount Peleaga.

YOU SHOULD KNOW:
Any exploration of the higher elevations of the range should be approached with caution. The area is notorious for its hostile weather, winds of over 80 kph (50 mph) are not uncommon, and when it rains, it pours.

344

Cape Kaliakra

Located on Bulgaria's Black Sea coast near the border with Romania, Cape Kaliakra is a formidable place – so formidable that even the colour of its rocks is said to come from the blood of those who have defended it (although iron oxide in the soil provides a more prosaic explanation). It is where East meets West and where history and legend meld into one story. Dragons have been slain, great treasure lost in its caves and maidens have leapt to their deaths to avoid religious conversion.

The word *kaliakra* is of Medieval Greek origin and can be translated as 'Beautiful Fortress' – a fitting description of the cape on both counts. Formed of limestone created beneath the prehistoric Sarmat Sea, it stretches 2 km (1.25 mi) into the sea and is protected by 70-m (230-ft) high sheer cliffs. The inaccessibility of the place made it ideal for the construction of a citadel – named Tirisis – which was successively used by Thracians, Romans and Byzantines. A small yet informative museum houses relics left behind by the ancient settlers.

In 1941 Kaliakra was declared a nature reserve which encompasses not only the land of the cape but also the waters around it. It has healthy populations of bird species all year round. Grebes and cormorants flourish in winter while eagle owls, alpine swifts and black-headed bunting breed here. Dolphins are a common sight out to sea, but the plight of the monk seal has brought into sharp focus the fragility of the cape's ecosystem. Once a common sight, they are now rarely seen.

Hiking along the top of the cape is popular, but great care should be taken as its rocks are subject to constant erosion. The Black Sea can be accessed via steep steps.

HOW TO GET THERE:
Take the coast road north from Varna (Bulgaria) or south from Constanta (Romania).
WHEN TO GO:
All year round, but it's very warm in July and August.
DON'T MISS:
The museum, which as well as being a treasure trove, has the bonus of being housed inside a cave.
YOU SHOULD KNOW:
Of all the legends associated with Kaliakra, perhaps the most poignant is that of the 40 maidens. It is said the young women wove their hair together and jumped *en masse* into the sea to avoid capture by the Turks, and hence conversion to Islam. An obelisk called 'The Gate of the 40 Virgins' stands on the spot in their honour.

Cape Kaliakra, where East meets West.

Central Balkan National Park

The Central Balkan National Park is one of the largest and most important protected areas in Eastern Europe. Established in 1991, the park covers 720 sq km (278 sq mi) and encompasses nine distinct nature reserves. The park's topography includes alpine meadows, sheer rock faces, deep gorges, waterfalls and rapids, as well as 20 peaks above 2,000 m (6,562 ft). Old-growth forest of beech, spruce, fir, hornbeam and sessile oak cover over half of the park.

The area is home to bears, wolves and otters as well as around 120 species of birds, including the eagle owl and golden eagle. Of equal importance are the hundreds of species of fungi, moss and algae, and over 100 medicinal plants, that grow there. The park is popular with those seeking outdoor thrills and has ample opportunity for rock climbing, mountain-biking, mountaineering and caving. Exploration of the park can be undertaken on horseback or by hiking.

The reserves contain many astounding geological features. The granite and sandstone bedrock has been sculpted by erosion into weirdly wonderful shapes, most notably the fragile vertical stone pillars of Kalchovi Kamani and the rock bridge, Skalniya Most. Another breathtaking formation is a chain of ravines in the valleys of the Stara Reka and Cherni Osam Rivers. Underwater springs feed fast-flowing rivers and at many points their passage is interrupted by impermeable bedrock, thus creating many impressive cascades and waterfalls.

The park is of global significance and its management board seeks not only to preserve its unique natural scenery, but also the heritage and livelihood of the 31 communities contained within its boundaries. An increased demand for ecotourism is making their task easier.

Snow-covered Central Balkan National Park

Rhodope Mountains

The Rhodope Mountains start south of the Bulgarian capital, Sofia, and run for around 240 km (150 mi) across the border into Greece. They have throughout the ages been the home of Thracians, Ancient Greeks, Romans and Slavs and each has left its mark not only on the architecture of the area but also on the myths and legends associated with this enigmatically beautiful landscape. The area was reputedly the home of Orpheus, who is said to have visited the underworld and returned; perhaps the region's many caves and gorges acted as portals in his journey.

The range is split geologically between east and west. The western section is classic karst terrain – limestone bedrock cut by deep gorges and pitted with caves. To the east, the younger igneous rocks have been eroded to leave rock mushrooms and sharp peaks. The western section has the more spectacular scenery, most notably at Trigrad Gorge – a deep canyon bounded by sheer marble rocks. It is here that the Trigradska River is diverted underground into the Dyavolskoto Garlo (Devil's Throat) Cave, one of the highest underground waterfalls in Europe.

About 8 km (5 mi) from Trigrad is one of the most impressive caves in Europe. The Yagodina cave is on five levels and is around 10 km (6 mi) long. Tours take the visitor into a subterranean wonderland of illuminated stalactites and stalagmites which was home to a troglodyte clan in prehistoric times. Other natural wonders are to be found near the Aidarsko Dere River, in the shadow of the Chernatitsa Ridge. The Chudnite Mostove (Wondrous Bridges) Arches are possibly the remnants of a collapsed cave system where, over time, the elements have sculpted two natural marble bridges.

A summer landscape in the Rhodope Mountains

HOW TO GET THERE:
A bus links the gateway villages of Kesten, Trigrad and Devin.
WHEN TO GO:
From May to October is best
DON'T MISS:
Orlovi Skali (Eagle's Rocks) – a relic of ancient Thracian culture
YOU SHOULD KNOW:
The Rhodope Mountains is a huge range covering 14,750 sq km (5,700 sq mi) which would take months to explore fully. The village of Trigrad is a useful base, being close to several places of interest and easy to get to.

Dadia Forest

Towards the end of the 20th century, the black vulture faced extinction in Europe. The Dadia Forest in northeastern Greece was still home to a few pairs and, with active support from the World Wildlife Fund, an inner zone was set up – a protected reserve where black vultures and griffon vultures (also very rare in Europe) are now well established. The forest reserve covers a succession of volcanic ridges and its diverse habitats are home to a huge variety of flora and fauna, but it is most famous for birds. Its position on major migration routes attracts countless visiting species, but its prime importance is as a refuge for birds of prey. Of Europe's 38 diurnal raptors, 36 are seen here, including imperial and golden eagles, falcons and hawks.

A visit to Dadia Forest begins at the Ecotourist Centre, with informative displays and videos on the birds and on the work of the reserve. This includes augmenting the vultures' food as the greatest threat to their health comes from eating carrion picked up outside the reserve, which may be poisoned. A van takes visitors up to the well-designed observation area where binoculars, telescopes and knowledgeable staff help birdwatchers identify species. There is a very good chance of seeing vultures feeding in the canyon below the hide. Marked trails through the sunlit clearings and the shady, hushed depths of the forest allow silent walkers the sight of rare birds among the trees, or silhouetted high above. Birds of prey can be seen at closer quarters as they take to the air, and a night in the Ecotourist Hostel gives a marvellous early-morning opportunity to watch them soar and take advantage of the first thermals.

Pindos Mountains

The magnificent Pindos Mountains stretch south of Metsovo and Ioannina from the Albanian border. Logging, road building and ski slopes have partly denuded the range but two national parks safeguard large areas of diverse, unspoilt landscapes and endangered wildlife. With deep river valleys, thick conifer and broadleaf forests and sweeping alpine pastures, both are superb trekking country.

The remote, northern Pindos National Park is home to some of Greece's rarest large animals. Lynx, jackals, wolves and brown bears are not often seen, but at dawn and dusk deserted hillsides echo with the howling of wolves. Zagori, south of the Aoos River, is more accessible but no less wildly beautiful. The Vikos-Aoos National Park covers part of a region which is remarkable not only for its dramatic, rugged landscape but also for the *Zagorohoria* – its numerous, traditional villages. Built on mountain ledges – level ground is used for cultivation – these were winter settlements for the shepherds, who traditionally spent summers on the mountains with their flocks. Greek-speaking Sarakatsani, and Vlachs who speak an ancient Romance language, still make up most of the settled population, although many abandoned the harsh seasonal life. The almost deserted villages are now being restored and some of the traditional stone houses and the surprisingly grand 18th- and 19th-century mansions are guesthouses.

The towering peaks of the Pindos, including Smolikas, the highest in the range at 2,640 m (8,660 ft), and Gamila, whose sheer face drops hundreds of metres to the river below, are long and challenging ascents even for experienced climbers. But the whole area is crossed by tracks – many used by shepherds for centuries – through ravines and forests, over uplands and ridges, to isolated villages and high lakes.

YOU SHOULD KNOW:
Even experienced climbers must have specialist guides and equipment and should never climb alone. There is no formal mountain rescue service in the Pindos and the weather changes rapidly – check conditions with the Ioannina Tourist Office. All walkers need sticks, not just for the terrain, but for fending off the all-too-common semi-wild dogs. The steeply arched, slender packhorse bridges which span rivers and link the stony mountain trails were, until the mid 20th century, the only routes between villages and were built, mainly in the 19th century, by groups of itinerant workers who practised their skilled craft around the Balkans.

Rousanou Monastery in the magnificent Pindos Mountains

Detail of a fossilized tree in the Petrified Forest

Petrified Forest, Lesvos

Lesvos is a large island and most of its hilly terrain is very fertile, with fields of grain, orchards and olive groves interspersed by dense forests of oak and pine. For the Romans, this was a holiday island and for the Ottoman Turks, a productive larder. But the landscape of the far west is, in surprising contrast, almost desert, with spectacularly bare hills and stony, barren plains. A massive prehistoric eruption buried and transformed – completely and forever – the forested countryside around the volcano. A thick layer of volcanic ash and the action of heavily mineralized water turned all living things to stone, making this strange part of Lesvos a treasury of fossils.

Sigri, the little west-coast harbour town, has an excellent museum with permanent exhibitions on the primeval landscape and

HOW TO GET THERE:
Regular charter and internal flights and ferries to Lesvos. Infrequent buses between the capital, Mytilini, and Sigri pass not too far from the forest.
WHEN TO GO:
Although the forest is open all year, it is very bleak in winter and shadeless and parched in summer.

the geology and evolution of the Aegean which will enhance a later visit to the Petrified Forest with vivid images of this ancient world. On display are the fossilized trunks, twigs and leaves of the trees and plants which grew here between 15 and 20 million years ago, and a few fossils of creatures that inhabited the forests. Although sequoia and palm have disappeared from Lesvos, a surprisingly large number of the fossilized trees – which include beech, oak, cypress, walnut and plane – still grow here and examples are planted around the museum alongside the standing stumps of petrified trees. To the east of Sigri, the Petrified Forest covers the sun-baked eastern face of the extinct volcano, Ordhymnos. About 3 km (2 mi) of walks are laid out for visitors around the strange, scattered logs and stumps. There is an evocative ancient and lonely atmosphere in this place of eerie, almost lunar, beauty.

DON'T MISS:
The Byzantine monastery of Ipsilou, close to the Petrified Forest, is dedicated to St John the Theologian. It is surrounded by a fittingly apocalyptic wasteland, scattered with a few fossilized tree trunks. In contrast, the courtyard is filled with flowers, the interior sumptuous and the small museum excellent.

YOU SHOULD KNOW:
Lesvos produces half the world's supply of ouzo. Some of the island's small distillers use secret recipes and produce outstanding spirits. Pre-ouzo rituals among the island's many imbibers include rapping the bottle three times to prevent the contents harming the drinker.

Island of Evia

Although in some places less than 50 m (165 ft) from the mainland, Evia, which is more than 150 km (93 mi) long, is Greece's second largest island. Very easily reached by road-bridge or one of several short ferry hops, it has long been a favourite with Greek holidaymakers, although relatively few foreign tourists visit. The ancient name, Euboea, means 'rich in cattle' and, although now better known for lamb and kid, Evia remains famously fertile. Particularly popular with Athenians are the picturesque fishing villages and beaches and the world-famous spa, Loutro Edipsou (visited by celebrities from Aristotle to Greta Garbo), on the accessible and sheltered west and north coasts.

Most of inland and eastern Evia is remote, with forested mountains, shady hillside villages and unspoilt beaches. In spring, the countryside becomes a flower garden and, in autumn, open slopes are bright with cyclamen and autumn crocuses. On hills and cliffs, resident and migratory birds of prey include falcons, eagles and buzzards, while coastal wetlands and the reed beds of Lake Dystos are home to large numbers of waders and waterfowl.

Evia has two wonderfully untouched mountain ranges. From the delightful village of Steni there are good treks around the forested foothills of Mount Dirfys and to some lovely, deserted beaches on the central east coast; but the peak itself is a very difficult climb. Mount Ohi is also demanding, although the walk up limestone slopes above the village of Myli is an easier approach. This route passes ancient quarries scattered with chunks of marble and unfinished columns. The southern port and resort, Karystos, is a good base for exploration.

HOW TO GET THERE:
Rail and bus from Athens to the capital, Halkida; ferries to points north and south. Buses from Halkida run to some of the larger villages.

WHEN TO GO:
May and June or September and October. At weekends, accommodation can be scarce.

DON'T MISS:
A cluster of massive stone arches, like Stonehenge's trilithons, stands north of the village of Syra and a single, even larger, one near the summit of Mount Ohi. They are known as *dhrakospita*, dragon houses, because whoever shifted the blocks had to be superhuman. They may be 6th-century BC temples.

YOU SHOULD KNOW:
Neither of the peaks should be attempted without the right equipment. The Halkida Alpine Club can provide maps, trail guides and advice. Every few hours, the current in the narrow Evripos Straits changes direction – it can be watched from the old drawbridge at Halkida. Aristotle was reputedly so enraged by his failure to explain the phenomenon that he threw himself into the water; scientists remain baffled.

Lousios Gorge

Central Arcadia, with its green hillsides, beautiful old villages, fertile valleys, olive groves, orchards and flowery meadows sweet with herbs and tinkling with sheep bells, seems touched by ancient, idyllic magic. The narrow, serpentine road between Dimitsana and Stemnitsa allows glimpses of the Lousios Gorge, one of Greece's loveliest and most interesting hikes.

The trail from Dimitsana – a fascinating little town with fine 18th-century mansions and glorious views into the valley – descends through garden plots to the deep, wooded valley whose flanks narrow into sheer rock faces which, in places, reach almost 300 m (985 ft). Marked hiking trails cross the river at several points and, hidden among the trees, a clutch of monasteries cling to the crags. On the west side of the narrows, Nea Filosofou monastery has some fascinating 17th-century frescoes and the remains of the 10th-century Palea Filosofou monastery seem to merge into the surrounding stone. The remarkable Prodromou monastery clasps the eastern face of the gorge; it is built into the rocks, tucked away like a martin's nest, and occupied by about a dozen young monks. A long track zigzags to the road above.

The path up to the charming village of Stemnitsa, once an important metalworking town and now home to a school for gold and silversmiths, branches off a little further downstream. It is also worth walking along the valley to the Kokkoras Bridge – a high, elegantly arched medieval structure, once a major road link for Arcadia. This spot, with dappled shade and the cold, clean, fast-flowing river, is popular with trout fishermen and with walkers. Although the actual gorge is only about 5 km (3 mi) long, time becomes mysteriously elastic in this entrancing Arcadian landscape.

Taygetos Mountains and the Mani

From the olive groves of Kalamata to the very south of mainland Greece, the middle 'finger' of the Peloponnese is dominated by the Taygetos Mountains, which divide the Mani east-west into 'Sunward' and 'Shadowed' coasts. North of Areopolis, Outer Mani's landscape is one of dramatic peaks, snow covered until May, steep slopes whose thick forests were, sadly, devastated by recent summer fires, and a narrow coastal plain, watered by mountain streams. South, the mountains taper to craggy bare hills in the remote, sparsely populated Inner Mani, which is generally visited only as part of a daytrip. Fishing villages are scattered along the rocky and rather inaccessible east coast, while in the west, stony tracks over the austerely beautiful ochre and tan landscapes lead to villages of towers, sprouting from the hillsides, and tiny, richly frescoed and isolated Byzantine churches.

Further north is Gytheio. This attractive, friendly port provides a comfortable base on the east coast; on the west coast there are two popular resorts – Stoupa with its fine sand beaches and Kardamyli, where the highest point in the Taygetos, 2404-m (7887-ft) Mount Profitis Ilias, soars above the coast. The peak can be attempted by experienced climbers from the Vyros or Rindoma Gorges, along steep, rocky escarpments and knife-edged ridges, or by hikers via the saddle between the sharp, pyramidal summit and a summer settlement reached by a dirt road.

Around Kardamyli, *kalderimi* (cobbled mule tracks) fan out into the foothills and offer a number of excellent hikes, including a short walk to a pair of burial chambers known as the tombs of the Dioskouri – the Gemini twins. One of the tracks from Exohorio, a hamlet high above the Vyros Gorge, descends into the ravine where two monasteries shelter beneath towering rock faces.

WHEN TO GO:
Late April (late May for climbers) to June and from September to early October

DON'T MISS:
The spectacular road from Sparta to Kalamata crosses the high mountains, climbing through plane-shaded river valleys and ridge after ridge of jagged peaks. In the starkly dramatic Langada Gorge is a rock where the ancient Spartans abandoned infants considered too weak to become soldiers, and the Langada Pass – highest point 1,524 m (5,000 ft) – is reached by a dizzying series of hairpin bends.

YOU SHOULD KNOW:
The Taygetos is one of the most beautiful ranges in Greece but is also very hazardous. All climbers, even experienced ones, should seek information and advice on routes.

The rocky shoreline of the Mani Peninsula

Imbros Gorge

HOW TO GET THERE:
Imbros is on the bus route from Hania to Hora Sfakion. A less frequent service runs from Plakias to Hora Sfakion through Komitades.

WHEN TO GO:
May and June or September and October. The gorge is open all year, but in early spring snowmelt and rain may swell the stream dangerously.

DON'T MISS:
The road above the gorge has wonderful views into the ravine and, as the long zigzag down to Hora Sfakion begins, there is a panorama over the shining sea. To the west, rocky ridges tumble darkly into the water, fading to shadows in the distance. It is stupendously theatrical at sunset.

YOU SHOULD KNOW:
There is no drinking water in the gorge. In Sfakia, many of the village elders and shepherds wear magnificent Cretan costume, or elements of it. Voluminous black trousers are belted by a long sash and tucked into high leather boots. Fringed black kerchiefs are knotted round the head and, often, a rifle or a Cretan knife with a curling ram's horn handle completes the outfit.

Although Crete's White Mountains – the Lefka Ori – are capped in snow for half the year, they are named for their sun-bleached limestone. The journey south from Hania passes isolated villages, high plains and pockets of fertility among the barren, tumultuous peaks. Hora Sfakion, squeezed between steep mountains and the sea, is the chief town of Sfakia, Crete's stoniest and most independent region. The little port is regularly packed with crowds making their way to and from the Samaria Gorge, but the White Mountains are carved by a dozen or so other deep canyons and 'local' gorge hikes include the very challenging Aradhena to the west and the delightful Imbros to the east.

The distance from Imbros to Komitades is about 10 km (6 mi); before the road was built, the ravine was the main route towards the coast and it is generally well cobbled and undemanding – an excellent walk for anyone not seeking an endurance test. For years, Imbros was something of a secret, but it is now on the coach-tour itinerary. The first bus up from Hora Sfakion, or a tranquil night staying in Imbros village, ensures a head start and a peaceful and lovely walk down a path following the stream through steep green valleys, under a rock bridge and into narrow, sheer canyons. In this gaunt landscape, only plants inaccessible to hungry goats thrive, and in spring these steep cliffs are a flower-decked, vertical rock garden and the air is sweet with oregano, thyme and dittany, a favourite Cretan hangover cure. Green and golden lizards scuttle, butterflies dance and songbirds and cicadas chirp in the thick vegetation which shades much of the gorge. High overhead, huge birds of prey hang motionless in the bright day.

Gavdos

HOW TO GET THERE:
Regular ferries from Hora Sfakion take about 2.5 hours.

WHEN TO GO:
May, June, late September or October. In early September, popular beaches display the aftermath of the summer crowds.

DON'T MISS:
The lighthouse near the west coast hamlet of Ambelos has been restored as a café and lighthouse museum. The top of the tower is a marvellous spot to watch the sunset flaming behind the distant, dark, jagged coast of Crete.

In recent years, the island of Gavdos has changed. There is a big new concrete dock, some newly asphalted roads, new wells and – although the rumble of beachside diesel generators still augments the evening chorus of cicadas – an electricity station. In summer Cretans and mainland Greeks occupy ramshackle beach houses at Sarakiniko and Korfos, or join campers and nudists for a bohemian interlude. But, off-season, the little island retains its magic.

The appeal is not the landscape, as scrub covers much of the low-lying interior, or the architecture – the few 'villages' and even the 'capital', Kastri, are no more than clusters of simple cottages, mostly deserted. Its archaeological remains are fragments of Neolithic and Minoan pottery and its history, apart from a Byzantine period when the population of 8,000 included a bishop, is unremarkable. By the 20th century, when it was used as a place of exile for political prisoners, many of Gavdos's inhabitants had chosen an easier life in Crete.

A visit, though, can be potently nostalgic. The island is about 10 km (6 mi) long and there are good tracks over the undemanding terrain. The longest hike is to rocky Tripiti, the southernmost point of Europe, where swimmers in the crystal-clear waters find themselves surrounded by small fish. The many beaches – sand or pebble, rocky or dune-backed and tamarisk-shaded – are often deserted. Tents can be pitched anywhere and driftwood fires, the slap of wavelets, and a star-jewelled inky sky, are alluring options. But it is the small permanent population (about 50 residents from six families) that makes a long stay feasible and enjoyable. With friendly tavernas, barbecued fish, boat trips, even beer *en route* to Tripiti, Gavdos is a desert island without tears and offers a delightful, illusory isolation.

YOU SHOULD KNOW:
In autumn, the 50 km (31 mi) of deep water between Gavdos and Crete is often rough and ferries may be delayed or cancelled. Although Gavdos has plenty of fish, lamb, kid and some locally grown vegetables, most supplies are shipped from Crete. The local thyme honey is delicious, but long-staying vegetarians may go hungry. Gavdos is one of several suggested locations for Calypso's enchanted island, where Odysseus stayed longer than he intended on his way home, but it is better documented as a pirate's lair.

Agios Ioannis beach

Lura National Park

HOW TO GET THERE:
The closest town is Peshkopi, 25 km (15 mi) to the east. The easiest route from Tirana is north through Miloti, then west via Rreshen.
WHEN TO GO:
April to October, although in winter the snowy forest and the frozen lakes are lovely.
DON'T MISS:
One of the southern lakes is named the Lake of Flowers because it is covered with water lilies. When they bloom, the water is invisible beneath the overlapping leaves and the galaxies of starry white flowers.
YOU SHOULD KNOW:
Although this park was established in 1966, it has been little developed. A new ecotourism initiative aims to establish 'adventure activities', guides and facilities, and to encourage the involvement of the local community. It is to be hoped that the untouched peace of the Lura Lakes can survive.

Until 1990 Albania was a closed communist country and it remains somewhat mysterious. Despite a sorry legacy of ecological vandalism, much of its rural interior is unspoilt and now industrial activity is monitored and national parks preserve landscape and wildlife. The Lura Mountains, northeast of Tirana, are part of Albania's mountainous spine. On the eastern slopes of the mountain massif known as Lura's Crown, Lura National Park protects a wide belt of forest and a glacial landscape of ridges, ravines and high lakes.

The beautiful, cool forest consists chiefly of beech, fir and pine, and is home to many animals and birds. Pine marten, roe deer and capercaillie may be spotted, while the remote and inaccessible parts of the forest are said to shelter rare and elusive animals, such as brown bears, lynxes and wolves. Amphibians, including newts, live in the chilly waters. The Lura Lakes are well known to Albanians, but little visited by tourists. Numbering about a dozen, they lie like jewels among the trees; some are inky dark, reflecting the conifers, others bright with the blue of the open sky. From the upland village of Fushe Lura several circular walks begin, looping round the upper or lower group of lakes, or climbing the heights of Lura's Crown before descending through the forest. A large swathe of alpine pasture in the south of the park, the 'Field of Mares' is a popular place to relax. In spring and summer it is absolutely radiant, a glorious tapestry of wild flowers.

Djavolja Varos

Devil's Town (Djavolja Varos) occupies the watershed of two steep ravines – Devil's Valley and Infernal Valley – on the slopes of Mount Radan in southern Serbia. About 200 elongated cones, many over 15 m (49 ft) high, topped by flat, dark stone caps stand crowded together like a multitude of tall, silent, sinister giants. Thousands of years of water erosion carved them from the soft red stone and their evolution continues – old towers change shape and crumble away, others grow slowly from the ground. When the wind blows, they seem to shriek, sigh, groan and wail. Close by, traces of habitation can be seen, as well as the ruins of a church, still visited despite the oak tree which has grown up through the altar. Those who once lived here invented stories about the place and named it – and the two highly mineralized springs – the Devil's Water and the Devil's Well.

Similar geological oddities exist worldwide, but these 'devils' are unusually tall and closely packed – it is almost impossible to squeeze between them – and Devil's Town was recently nominated for the new 'Seven Natural Wonders' list. Although it was not placed, visitor numbers have increased and current development projects will provide amenities and floodlighting for night tours. Independent travellers who want the place to themselves can walk there from Prolom Spa. The enjoyable 9 km (5.5 mi) hike, the Path of Health, crosses fertile farmland and climbs past isolated hamlets before descending through thick woods to the site. There is a strange, unsettling beauty to the twisted towers in a desert of reddish scree, surrounded by the watchful green forest.

HOW TO GET THERE:
Regular buses run from Nis and Kursumlija to Prolom Spa. The tourist office in Kursumlija can arrange visits.

WHEN TO GO:
May to September

DON'T MISS:
A detour from the Path of Health. After the last hamlet, the main path turns downhill, but an uphill track between two ancient oaks (one is roughly carved with *Dj. Varos*) leads to the edge of a precipitous gorge, high above the 'devils'. Looking down on the bristling throng as the light changes with the scudding clouds, the colours shift and seem to flicker, like infernal firelight.

YOU SHOULD KNOW:
The most colourful of the folk tales about the Devil's Town concerns a wedding party making its way to church. God, wishing to prevent extreme wickedness of some sort – the precise details vary from jealous rivalry and violence to incest – turned them all to stone.

Krka National Park

The Dinaric Alps extend down the Adriatic coast from Slovenia to Albania. Rugged parallel ranges of porous karstic limestone, broken and riddled by ravines, underground rivers and caverns, form most of mainland Croatia, while its myriad islands are the summits of a long-submerged western chain. The mountains are scattered with ruined fortresses – the daunting peaks have been a stronghold against invaders from early times – but the landscape is sparsely populated. The geology and wildlife of several areas are now protected as national parks.

The Krka River rises in the mountains near Knin and Mount Dinara and descends, through a typical karstic landscape of gorges, lakes and cascades of 'steps' built up from tufa to the fine old city of Sibenik, and the sea. The riverside scenery of the Krka National Park is diverse and dramatic – cliffs and caves, woods and marshes – with a remarkable range of plants and wildlife and some interesting architectural features. Entry to the park is from either side of the river, at Skradin or Lozovac. It can be explored on foot by paths and walkways, or by boat. Deserted watermills stand by the waterfalls, the Orthodox Krka Monastery at the head of the valley and the Franciscan Samostan Visovac is picturesquely sited on an island. This wonderful patchwork of natural habitats is particularly important for birds. Resident and migratory species range from raptors, including osprey and eagle owls, to tiny, brilliant bee-eaters. The river flows swiftly all year and there are two very dramatic cascades – Roski Slap, at the end of a deep canyon and Skradinski Buk, a flight of 17 ever-widening steps, with fierce torrents gushing around rocks and surging down into the large lower lake.

The picturesque cascades of the Krka waterfalls

Hills reflected in Cerknica Lake

Cerknica Lake

In the beautiful, unspoilt countryside south of Ljubljana, wooded hills, upland and valley farms, streams and isolated villages seem scarcely touched by the modern world. Between the Bloke Plateau and the Rakov Škocjan Regional Park lies an area which on some maps appears as an expanse of water, on others as wetland. This is Lake Cerknica, famous from ancient times for its mystifying periodic disappearances. Full, it measures about 10 x 5 km (6 x 3 mi) and is Slovenia's largest lake; empty, it is a low-lying area of lush hayfields. In 1689, the Slovenian scholar Valvasor proposed an explanation which so impressed the Royal Society that he was made an honorary member. The limestone of this region is perforated by caves and channels and when autumn rains swell streams above and below ground, water bubbles up into a depression which rapidly – often in a few days – becomes a lake. When the subterranean waters eventually recede, the lake empties through karstic sinkholes over a period of several weeks. This intermittent lake has always been a valuable natural resource for farmers and fishermen and, although misguided 19th-century attempts to regulate the flow endangered its ecological balance, the area is now fully protected.

Activities on the lake include boating, windsurfing and skating as well as fishing. Its reed beds, an important habitat for huge numbers of nesting and migrating birds, including storks, reed warblers, corncrakes and lapwings, are a great draw for birdwatchers. The area's other attractions are grouped around the lake. There are good hikes into the hills (the views from the top of Velika Slivnica are superb); picturesque villages, including Otok which is, seasonally, Slovenia's only inhabited island; and, to the east, the little visited Krizna Water Cave, a remarkable network of tunnels and caverns, rivers and lakes.

HOW TO GET THERE:
Regular buses run from Ljubljana to Cerknica; local buses are sporadic. Bicycles can be hired.

WHEN TO GO:
The lake usually fills in October and starts to empty in late May.

DON'T MISS:
The Museum of Lake Cerknica, in a café-bar in Dolenje Jezero, is a family museum. Its displays include objects connected with life by the lake and a slide show, but the star attraction is the owner's working scale model of the area, which demonstrates how the lake fills and empties, with background sounds of locally recorded bird song.

YOU SHOULD KNOW:
The museum only opens on Saturday afternoons, although group visits can be arranged. At Sneznik Castle, south of the lake, there is a Dormouse Hunting Museum. Dormice are considered a great delicacy here and the castle hosts an annual Dormouse Hunting Night to celebrate the start of the season.

A view of Logarska Dolina and the Kamnik-Savinja Alps

Kamnik-Savinja Alps

HOW TO GET THERE:
Regular train and bus service from Ljubljana to Kamnik and buses north from Kamnik. In summer, one bus a day runs from Kamnik to the Logar Valley.
WHEN TO GO:
May to September for walking and climbing, December to March for winter sports.
DON'T MISS:
The Logar Valley is accessible to vehicles and can be overrun by organized tours, but for visitors with plenty of time it is a real joy. There are caves and waterfalls, quiet walks through lovely beech woods, a

The Kamnik-Savinja Alps are part of the long chain of the Southern Alps. Although relatively low by alpine standards, they are dramatically steep and rugged and their sheer north faces are very challenging – mountaineering skills are essential. The gentler southern slopes, though, can be climbed by energetic hikers with good boots, maps and common sense. One group of peaks, which includes 2,558-m (8,392-ft) Grintovec, the highest in the range, can be reached from Jezersko, an alpine resort near the Austrian border. Winter activities – cross-country skiing and waterfall ice climbing – also take place in this area.

Pretty Kamniska Bistrika, deep in a wooded river valley north of the pleasant old town of Kamnik, is the starting place for several walks – long tough hikes up into the mountains and more leisurely rambles around forest, ravines and waterfalls. About 10 km (6 mi) from Kamnik, a combination of cable car and chairlift runs to the top of the high limestone plateau, Velika Planina. In winter, this is a popular skiing and snowboarding area, while in summer its rolling pastures are home to herdsmen and their cattle, and walkers. Hikes up to the plateau and around its scattered settlements, over a gloriously open landscape with views north to the jagged peaks, make a wonderfully gentle introduction to alpine walking.

At the eastern end of the range, the Logar Valley is a favourite with visitors. Here, at the famous Rinka Falls, the river plunges (except in high summer) 80 m (262 ft) from the craggy heights to a beautiful green valley.

profusion of flora and fauna – from rare orchids to golden eagles – and longer hikes into the *cirque* of high mountains around the Rinka Falls or to peaceful, road-less alpine valleys.

YOU SHOULD KNOW:
Some of the narrower, circular trails from Kamniska Bistrika are one way. Sleepy Kamnik was once an important town and has some fine monastic buildings and two ruined castles. One of these was home to the legendary Countess Veronika (half woman, half snake) and her jealously guarded hoard of treasure.

Pohorje

Lying west of Slovenia's second city, Maribor, the Pohorje massif is geologically part of the Central Eastern Alps. There are no towering peaks, but this is Slovenia's favourite winter sports location and home to the annual Golden Fox World Cup women's skiing competition. From the outskirts of the town, a cable car whizzes skiers and snowboarders up to Maribor Pohorje for miles of uncrowded cross-country ski tracks and *pistes* (mostly easy or moderate) and an exhilarating downhill night run. At the western end of the massif, built around the highest peak, Rogla is another popular ski centre.

Pohorje is a year-round destination and when the snow melts, ski tracks become routes for hikers and cyclists. This is a lovely 'big sky' area of rolling, undemanding terrain – thickly forested hills, high moorland and marsh, lakes and waterfalls. It is dotted with isolated farms and tiny churches and criss-crossed by long and short walks over unmade roads and forest tracks from both resorts. A particularly enjoyable hike from Rogla meanders through ancient forest to the Lovrenc Marsh Lakes, where walkers should be careful not to disturb the pools – the resident goblin brings bad weather if angered.

Trails from Maribor start at the Bolfenk cable car terminus. Several of the longer routes pass through Areh; a popular walk continues along a high path with stunning views to the Sunik waterfalls, deep in one of Europe's few tracts of virgin forest.

Maribor is a relaxed and interesting old town and a very good base. South of Rogla are the spa town, Zrece, and the delightful 'City of Flowers and Wine', Slovenske Konjice.

HOW TO GET THERE:
There are good bus and rail links to Maribor.

WHEN TO GO:
May to October for walking, December to March for skiing.

DON'T MISS:
The pretty little church of St Areh stands high in a clearing; inside, a stone monument to St Henry (whose name became Areh) was brought here from the Carthusian monastery in Zice. Outside, the spring is thought to have healing properties and the nearby lodge provides welcome sustenance for walkers.

YOU SHOULD KNOW:
Maribor is a wine-producing region and the vine which grows on one of the medieval houses is, at 400, the world's oldest. It still produces a few bottles of wine from grapes picked, with great ceremony, every October.

Val Grande National Park

HOW TO GET THERE:
By car or train from Milan or Turin
WHEN TO GO:
From March to October, otherwise snow makes the higher paths inaccessible.
DON'T MISS:
The Villa Cigogna Mozzoni, near Varese, a lovely example of Lombardy's Renaissance architecture.
YOU SHOULD KNOW:
For treks of several days' duration, contact the park authorities in advance. You'll need sleeping bags and food, but there are unattended huts with wood burners for cooking and heating.

At 120 sq km (46 sq mi), Val Grande National Park is the largest wild area in Italy and lies 100 km (62 mi) north of Milan, in the Italian Alps. The heart-shaped park, which is surrounded by mountains, is centred on two valleys: Val Pogallo and Val Grande. Until the mid 20th century it contained a number of alpine villages, but war and poverty drove the inhabitants out, leaving nature to take its course. Val Grande was made a National Park in 1992, when it was realized that it had become a wilderness.

Trekking here is exacting and hikers are advised to take extreme care as there are many precipitous ravines. The best plan is to use an official guide because while the major routes through the park have been kept up, there are many others that can be attempted. For those with limited time, Monte Faié is accessible all year round. With an altitude of 1,352 m (4,436 ft), the spectacular view from the top includes the Pedum peaks, Lake Mergozzo and the valley itself.

The valley floor and lower slopes are largely pasture and stands of birch, linden, willow and, most importantly, chestnut. Higher up are ancient beech woods as well as firs that segue into green alder, ferns and moss, then rhododendron and bilberry and, finally, alpine meadows and wild flowers such as gentian, columbine and arnica. The ravines are full of maple, lime, yew and alder.

Many small mammals live here as well as chamois, roe deer, foxes, stone martens and badgers. Bullhead and brown trout thrive in the many streams and rivers, and birds include black grouse, woodpeckers, owls, hawks and eagles.

This is a remarkable place, its remote, silent grandeur the more extraordinary given its proximity to one of Italy's most visited areas: Lake Maggiore.

A view of the lush Val Grande National Park

Maremma Regional Park

Located in the southwestern corner of Tuscany, Maremma Regional Park extends from the mouth of the Ombrone River to Talamone, a 25-km (15-mi) stretch bordered inland by the Aurelia highway. Founded in 1975, the park has a typically southern Tuscan landscape and is dominated by the Uccellina Hills. Softly rounded and covered by dense, shrubby Mediterranean vegetation, the lower slopes consist mainly of pasture and olive groves.

The woods within Maremma are dominated by huge holm oaks, maples and myrtle, and both aromatic and flowering plants such as lavender, rosemary, juniper, clematis and broom bring bright splashes of colour. In spring, several species of orchid can be found. It is this mixture of habitats that prompted the protection of the area.

The park descends gently from the hills across the marshes and dunes close to the estuary, through farmland and pasture to the coastline. To the south, steep cliffs are evidence of coastal erosion. Sandy beaches, protected by indigenous Italian pine forests, are perfect for looking for shells and swimming.

The Ombrone estuary offers splendid birdwatching opportunities; waders, ducks and herons are common. Inland, woodpeckers, finches, bunting, owls, buzzards and kestrels may be seen. Mammals include wild boar, skunks, stone martens, foxes, deer, and many smaller species such as rabbits and hedgehogs. The luxuriant pastures support both horses and the renowned, long-horned Maremma cattle, watched over by *butteri* – Italian cowboys. They not only work with the animals, but also present shows from time to time.

The park offers several trails to follow and organized cycling or horse-riding tours are available. Hire a canoe and follow the Ombrone down to its estuary, it's a bewitching journey.

The coastal landscape of the Maremma Regional Park

HOW TO GET THERE:
By car, train to Grosseto and Alberese stations, or bus to Grosseto on weekdays only

WHEN TO GO:
All year round. From March 23 to September 30 Maremma is open from 08.00 until 17.00. The rest of the year the park is open from 08.30 to 13.30.

DON'T MISS:
The scuba diving at Argentario and the islands of Giglio and Giannutri.

YOU SHOULD KNOW:
There are important Etruscan sites at Roselle, Saturnia, and Pitigliano and modern thermal spas at the base of Monte Amiata. In Talamone, the remains of a Roman villa may be seen.

363

Gran Sasso e Monti della Laga National Park

HOW TO GET THERE:
By train, car or bus
WHEN TO GO:
At any time of year, depending on your particular interest
DON'T MISS:
The fabulous local food available in all the villages and towns in the area, including regional specialities such as *virtù teramane* (a sort of hotpot), scamorze (a type of cheese), truffles, and much more.
YOU SHOULD KNOW:
The Calderone glacier is the southernmost glacier in Europe. Glaciologists believe that it may completely disappear by 2020, due to climate change.

Encompassing three mountain groups, the Gran Sasso and Monti della Laga National Park is one of the largest protected areas in Europe. Formed in 1991 and part of the Appenines, the park includes both their highest peak, Corno Grande, at 2,912 m (9,554 ft), as well their only glacier, the Calderone. Within its territory are hundreds of villages and 44 towns.

The protected area is so vast and covers such diverse landscape and habitat that it is rich with rare flora and fauna, some of which is unique. Over 2,000 different species of plant is found here and mammals include the Abruzzo chamois, red and roe deer, wild cats, wild boar, foxes, polecats, martens, porcupines, small packs of Appenine wolves and many smaller species.

Birdwatchers often make for the Forca di Penne and Campotosto Lake where thousands of migrating birds rest by the shore, although birds can be seen throughout the area. At lower levels, where there are fields and pasture, Ortolan buntings, crested larks and red-backed shrikes may be found. At higher altitudes there are snowfinches, pipits, alpine accentors and choughs. This is also great country for raptors; golden eagles, lanners, goshawks and peregrine falcons are all at home here.

There are many activities to enjoy in the park and wonderful opportunities exist for exploring on foot, horseback, mountain-bike or by canoe. Rivers and streams rush down into the valleys and there are some spectacular waterfalls which, in winter, form an extraordinary sight when they sometimes freeze. Campo Imperatore, a high plateau, is one of Italy's oldest and most popular ski resorts. With guaranteed snow during winter, the park is a magnet for advanced skiers, with off-piste descents attracting free-riders from across Europe. Cross-country skiing is also popular, as is mountaineering and ice-cascade climbing.

Ausoni and Aurunci Mountains

The Ausoni and Aurunci Mountains, located in central Italy, run from the Appenines to the promontory of Gaeta on the Mediterranean coast. Part of the Antiappenini, and also sometimes known as the Volsci, derived from their Roman name, there is no official dividing line between them. The highest peak in the range, Monte Petrella, stands at 1,533 m (5,030 ft).

In 1997, the Monti Aurunci Natural Park was created. If time is limited, this offers an excellent overview of these mountain ranges, from the plain to the top of Monte Petrella with its glorious vistas across the mountains to the sea. Magnificent beech trees cloak the northern slopes, and there are oaks, maples, hornbeams and chestnuts, too. In spring wild flowers such as hellebores, snowdrops, cyclamen, violets, anemones and saffron are abundant. Meadows cover the valley, where brooms, Judas trees and 50 species of orchid thrive. The southern sector is on the route of many migratory birds, but there are also owls, nightjars and nightingales to be seen. Raptors are found at higher levels, where mammals such as wild boar, wildcats, foxes, martens and hares make their homes in the dense woodland.

The rainfall in the mountains, which have typical karst topography, sinks through the limestone to reappear as springs and vernal pools on the lower slopes. This is good habitat for amphibians, and four types of salamander as well as four types of frog can be seen here.

A network of trails for both hikers and mountain-bikes runs throughout the park, and both inside and outside its boundaries the mountains are criss-crossed with small roads linking little medieval villages. Many of the inhabitants still raise cattle and work on the land and in the forests. The villages, with their ancient squares, cobbled streets, archways and churches, are well worth visiting.

HOW TO GET THERE:
By car or train
WHEN TO GO:
Any time of year, but the spring and early summer are best for wild flowers.
DON'T MISS:
The historic town of Fondi with its castle, palazzo, cathedral and medieval churches
YOU SHOULD KNOW:
The Abbey of Montecassino, located just the other side of the Rome to Naples motorway, was founded by St Benedict in AD 529. In February 1944 it was destroyed during fighting between the Allied and German forces. Paid for by the Italian government, reconstruction took ten years. The Polish War Cemetery can be seen from the Abbey.

The Aurunci Mountains

Pollino National Park

HOW TO GET THERE:
Having a car will enable you to explore the entire region.
WHEN TO GO:
Any time of year, but spring and early summer are probably the best times.
DON'T MISS:
The Valle del Mercuri, a beautiful, pristine, natural site
YOU SHOULD KNOW:
The Raganello Gorge, one of the deepest in Europe, can be walked, clambered and swum through with the assistance of a guide.

One of the largest national parks in Italy, Pollino National Park straddles the boundary of Basilicata and Calabria in southern Italy. Its highest peak, Monte Pollino, rises to 2,267 m (7,438 ft). Founded in 1992 to protect the palebark pine, the park's symbol, this is one of the last remaining areas in Italy where it is found.

This vast area of 1,820 sq km (703 sq mi) is fascinating, including as it does many interesting towns as well as archaeological sites and glorious wilderness. It is a region best savoured at length, thus a walking holiday is ideal. Serra Dolcedorme is a major attraction, but there are other lovely ranges, too, including Serra di Crispo where the palebark pine grows right to the peaks – all twisted trunks and branches shaped by the wind. From higher altitudes a view of both coasts may be enjoyed and, with luck, a golden eagle might be soaring through the blue sky above.

As well as mountains there are never-ending upland plains dotted with peacefully grazing sheep, rolling hills and lush valleys, and a profusion of flowering plants and bushes, particularly during spring. Many protected creatures inhabit the region, from wolves, roe deer, hares and black squirrels, to snakes, otters, salamanders and the yellow-bellied toad. Birds include peregrine falcons, red kites, lanners and buzzards as well as numerous smaller species, such as woodpecker and chough.

Rivers and streams are plentiful, plunging through gorges that have been gouged from the rock over millennia. Cave systems, too, are numerous and rich in both prehistoric sites, such as the Romito Caves, and archaeological sites. Castles and monasteries, ancient villages where the older inhabitants still wear traditional dress, ethnic Albanians who maintain their traditional culture and speak their own dialect – all this can be discovered in Pollino National Park.

The primeval Calabrian, or palebark pine, in Pollino National Park

Gargano National Park

The Gargano Peninsula sticks out into the Adriatic Sea like a spur above the heel of the Italian boot. This mountainous massif, comprising several peaks, is situated in the province of Foggia. Almost all of it is part of the Gargano National Park, formed in 1995, which also has lower-lying wetlands and flatlands.

The heart of the park is the wonderful Umbra Forest. Once covering the entire peninsula, the 15 per cent that remains is glorious – broad-leafed trees such as beech, maple, hornbeam, oak and chestnut grow to enormous heights and, beneath them, anemones, violets and cyclamen grow in profusion. Some 35 per cent of all species of flora found in Italy are here, including an extraordinary number of orchids: 61 varieties and still counting.

A natural limestone arch in Gargano National Park

Mammals include about 100 rare roe deer, martens, badgers, wildcats and numerous smaller species, while forest birds include raptors and four types of woodpecker – again, very rare in Italy. Another reason the area is protected is because of its wetlands. There are lagoons, marshes, lakes, vernal pools and springs, as well as the sea. These provide habitat for numerous amphibians and water birds, some of which arrive during their migration to and from Africa and central and eastern Europe.

Between the forest and the sea are large stands of Aleppo pines, olive trees, and typical Mediterranean shrubland. On the coast itself the sea and wind have sculpted wonderful shapes into the limestone cliffs, creating a jagged coastline with many small beaches of sand or stones, often only accessible by boat. There are 128 known caves on the peninsula, 52 of which were used by prehistoric man. Several of the caves can be visited by boat, including the spectacular 47-m (154-ft) high, bell-shaped Grotta Campana.

HOW TO GET THERE:
The best way to explore Gargano is by car, although there are local buses from Foggia.
WHEN TO GO:
Best between April and September.
DON'T MISS:
The Sanctuary of Monte Sat'Angelo sul Gargano. Dedicated to Archangel Michael, this is the oldest shrine in Europe and has been a place of pilgrimage since the 6th century.
YOU SHOULD KNOW:
12 km (7 mi) off the coast are the Tremiti Islands, also part of Gargano National Park. Take a boat trip around the islands to enjoy the beaches and ancient ruins, or scuba dive in the clean, clear waters.

Supramonte Plateau

HOW TO GET THERE:
From Nuoro or Oliena by car
WHEN TO GO:
April to June, September and October
DON'T MISS:
The prehistoric village of Tiscali,
which is built inside a huge cave in
Monte Corrasi.
YOU SHOULD KNOW:
The village of Orgosolo lies at the
bottom of the mountains and has
become famous for its political and
social wall murals, depicting the
struggle between the traditional life
and culture of the local inhabitants
and the views of the State.

Found inland from the Gulf of Orosei, eastern Sardinia, close to Orgosolo, is the high plateau of Supramonte in a mountain range of the same name. Reminiscent of the Dolomites, this limestone massif is covered with forest and is a wonderful region for walking and trekking.

The plateau itself ends abruptly with drops of 1,000 m (3,280 ft) down to the Oliena Plain and its north faces are well known for their difficult and lengthy climbing routes. There are, however, two short routes to the plateau for straightforward hikers. The plateau is weird and wonderful, its typical karst formation laced with drainage gullies and virtually no trails other than the route up Monte Corrasi. This is the highest peak in the area at 1,391 m (4,564 ft). The terrain is bleak, stony and harshly beautiful, with long views across the plateau to the Barumini Mountains. Isolated groups of red peonies appear to live in stone. Beneath the barren summit, gullies shelter many wild plants such as rosemary, cyclamen and lilies.

Visit the region of the Flumineddu River, which is surrounded by a thick forest of holm oak, yew, juniper, holly and oleander. Here the Flumineddu has cut the mountain in two and formed the Gorropu Gorge – one of Sardinia's most impressive natural sites. It is possible for experienced canyoneers to negotiate it with the correct equipment, but part of it is accessible anyway via a pretty path from the valley. There's even the opportunity to enjoy a quick dip along the way.

The mountains are home to mouflon sheep, notable for their curved horns, as well as wild boar, wildcats and pine marten and several smaller species. The great slabs of rock walls provide perfect nesting spots for several raptors, including golden eagles, goshawks and sparrow hawks.

Cies Islands

The Cies is a group of three granite islands off the northwest coast of Galicia, northern Spain. They have been a nature reserve since 1980 and, with six other islands and archipelagos, in the year 2000 they were declared part of the National Land-Marine Park of the Atlantic Islands of Galicia. Once mountains, their cliffs on the Atlantic Ocean side rear sharply from the water and are riddled with caves formed by the action of wind and waves. The eastern aspect is far less severe; here trees and shrubs abound and rare plants grow in the sand dunes.

Although inhabited for centuries, the Cies suffered so many invasions that by 1700 they were deserted and re-populated only when a lighthouse was built on the island in the 19th century. Today, Las Islas Cies are best known for Playa de Rodas, a superb beach of fine, white sand that links Isla de Monte Agudo to Isla do Faro. At high tide the sea covers the area nearest the rocky shoreline, forming a lagoon but leaving a curved sand 'road' linking the two islands.

Many visitors head for the beach, but exploring further is worthwhile. There are marked trails, the toughest of which makes for the lighthouse at the highest point of Monte Agudo, where the views are superb. For those who prefer a gentler climb there is a delightful short hike through woods. Damaged by climate and human activity, one quarter of the woodland has had to be reforested with pine and eucalyptus.

Birdwatching is another delight. There are important colonies of seabirds here, the largest being some 22,000 breeding pairs of yellowfoot gull. Green cormorants and Caspian gulls also breed here and the noise can sometimes be deafening. The Cies Islands are a resting point during the migration of many other birds.

HOW TO GET THERE:
From June to September, travel by boat from Vigo, Baiona or Cangas to Monte Agudo, or join a tourist cruise.

WHEN TO GO:
Between June and September, unless you have your own boat

DON'T MISS:
The three lighthouses on the islands and the two observatories

YOU SHOULD KNOW:
It is possible to camp in the Cies, but permits have to be obtained from the port at Vigo. There is a supermarket and a restaurant but visitors have to take their rubbish away with them as there are no litter bins.

San Martino Island as seen from Monte Agudo

Picos de Europa

HOW TO GET THERE:
The easiest way to see the Picos de Europa is by car, from Oviedo or Santander.

WHEN TO GO:
All year round, but spring, summer or autumn are probably best.

DON'T MISS:
The village of Bulnes. Until 2000 it was only accessible by mule track, but the building of a funicular railway has made it easier to visit and encounter its hardy, independent inhabitants, whose way of life is so completely different from most Europeans.

YOU SHOULD KNOW:
Since 1983 the Vuelta a España, one of Europe's elite road bicycle races, has often used the road from Covadonga up to the lakes. The toughest section is the final 7 km (4 mi), which includes an average 15 per cent gradient for 800 m (2,625 ft).

Extending across three regions and part of the Cantabrian Mountains, Picos de Europa is situated some 20 km (12 mi) from Spain's northern coast, halfway between Oviedo and Santander. Formed of limestone, the impressive karst landscape consists of the Western, Central and Eastern massifs, the first two divided by the spectacular 1.5-km (1-mi) deep Cares Gorge. Spain's first national park was formed here in 1918 and in 1995 the designated area was almost quadrupled. In 2003, it became a UNESCO Biosphere Reserve.

Climbers and hikers are drawn to these mountains and the refuge huts are well used. The highest peak, Torre de Cerredo, reaches 2,648 m (8,688 ft) and many more are almost as high. It is also popular with cavers, as some of the country's deepest caves are found here. Its proximity to the sea means there is often snow, regardless of the season.

Each massif has different characteristics. The western massif boasts the Lakes of Covadonga – two perfect glacial lakes. Covadonga is accessible by car and there is an easy and beautiful hike round the shores of both lakes, winding through beech woods and across swathes of green pasture where shepherds guard flocks of sheep and goats, and delicious cheeses are produced.

The flora and fauna of the Picos de Europa is exciting: Cantabrian brown bears, Iberian lynx, wolves, wild boar, wild horses, roe deer, chamois and ibex are all found here, and birds include buzzards, vultures, golden and short-toed eagles, capercailles and hundreds of smaller species.

It is possible to ride, fish and white-water raft, but simply hiking through the spectacular scenery of mixed forests of oak, beech, walnut, chestnut and maple, and lush valleys filled with wild flowers and butterflies cut with sparkling crystal-clear streams, is both peaceful and healing.

Hikers walk along a trail in Cares Gorge.

Cap de Creus

Situated at the northern end of the Costa Brava, close to the border with France, the Cap de Creus juts out into the Mediterranean. A nature reserve since 1998, protecting both land and sea, the peninsula is the largest uninhabited area of the Spanish Mediterranean. Although the region's holm oak and cork forests were badly damaged from frequent forest fires and over-grazing, thousands of cork oaks have been re-planted.

The coastline rises stark and rugged from the deep-blue sea, indented with tiny bays and rocky islets, many of which are only accessible by boat. The rocks, scoured by centuries of high winds and waves, are notable for their bizarre shapes, some of which resemble birds and animals – for example, the eagle of Tudela.

This is prime birdwatching territory, partly because, as the easternmost point of the Iberian peninsula, it is a magnet for migratory birds. From the highest point at Sant Salvador, several types of swift, black-eared wheatear, rock thrush and crag martins can been seen during summer. Thekla lark, blue rock thrush and black wheatear are permanent inhabitants. Peregrine falcons breed here and Bonelli's eagles hover overhead.

Different species, such as Dartford and Sardinian warblers, inhabit the shrub land that forms most of the landscape – mainly cistus, broom, lavender, gorse and several Mediterranean herbs. Lupins and orchids also thrive, but the most interesting flora, including several endemic species, cling to the narrow coastal strip.

In spring and autumn both Cory's and Mediterranean shearwater fly past, and kittiwakes, skuas, razorbills and gulls arrive for the winter. The clear, unpolluted sea contains a mass of fauna, including precious red coral, as well as spiny lobsters, scorpion fish and sunfish, among others. Certain areas are out of bounds for fishing and scuba diving, but a fascinating underwater world waits for divers.

The rugged coastline of Cap de Creus

HOW TO GET THERE:
By car from Roses, or take an excursion by boat from Roses to Cadaqués.
WHEN TO GO:
April to October unless you are a particularly keen ornithologist. Strong northerly winds are a feature of Cap de Creus during winter.
DON'T MISS:
The lighthouse, with its remarkable views over the Mediterranean. Its old administrative building is now a pleasant bar/restaurant.
YOU SHOULD KNOW:
Salvador Dali, the artist, visited Cadaqués many times from childhood onward and in later life had a house nearby. The extraordinary rock formations along the coast greatly influenced his art. The mayor of Cadaqués donated a rock from the area that will form part of the new headquarters of the Dali Museum in Florida.

*The Sierra de Gredos near the
village of Puerte de Piornal*

Sierra de Gredos

The Sierra de Gredos, part of Spain's central mountain range, is
within reach of Toledo, Ávila, Cáceres and Madrid. Popular with
climbers, it also offers great opportunities for hiking, walking, horse
riding, mountain-biking and paragliding. A Special Bird Protection
Zone, this regional park is home to a wealth of flora and fauna,
including over 20 species of raptor.

The highest peak in the largely snow-capped Sierra de Gredos is
Pico Almanzor. At 2,592 m (8,504 ft), it is also the highest peak in
central Spain. Below the mountain's north face is the Laguna de
Gredos, a glacial lake with paths to five other lakes. The scenery is
glorious, changing from Mediterranean to alpine – depending on
elevation. At lower levels, on the southern side, walk beside clear,
sparkling rivers and along old Roman roads or stop to relish a picnic
in valleys full of wild flowers, lemon and almond trees, and olive
groves. Oak, pine, mountain ash, poplar and birch trees grow in
quantity and, in autumn, a great variety of fungi can be found.
Thyme, rosemary and oregano scent the air. Experts should look

HOW TO GET THERE:
By bus from Madrid to Arenas de San
Pedro, or by car from the north or
south. There are guided hikes and
birdwatching excursions available
from Madrid.
WHEN TO GO:
Spring, summer or autumn
DON'T MISS:
The traditional villages, monasteries,
and fortresses that can be found
within the mountains or the Neolithic
cave paintings called El Collado
Braguillas, close to El Raso.
YOU SHOULD KNOW:
The Sierra is snow-covered during
winter, and cross-country skiing,
mountain skiing (including extreme
descents) and snowshoeing are all
possible activities.

out for endemic species of sedum, saxifrage and antirrhinum.

Higher up, the landscape changes to alpine meadows with swathes of yellow broom and, finally, bare rock face decorated with lichen. Mammals in these mountains include elusive wild cats and beech martens, but Gredos ibex may be seen and otters slip and slide in the many rivers; there are also several endemic amphibians to be spotted. Raptors include golden eagles and several other eagle species, as well as kites, hobbies sparrowhawks and vultures. Altogether, including migratory visitors, over 120 types of bird may be seen in these mountains.

Sierra de Guadarrama

Within easy striking distance of Madrid and Segovia, the Sierra de Guadarrama offers a great escape from the stress of city living. A continuation of the central mountain chain that runs from Spain to Portugal, this range is somewhat lower and gentler than the Sierra de Gredos, its principal peak, Peñalara, reaching 2,428 m (7,966 ft). Running from southwest to northeast, Guadarrama contains many interesting features, including the Peñalara Natural Park and the unusual granite range of La Pedriza.

Many rivers have their source in this region, noted for its high annual rainfall, and there are many small dams in the mountains. The natural park, on the southern slope of Peñalara mountain, contains many small glacial lakes which, during spring, produce small waterfalls and streams from meltwater. At the highest elevations, rock roses, lavender, juniper and ferns abound. Below 2,000 m (6,562 ft) are, firstly, pine forests – in autumn bursting with delicious fungi such as morels and chanterelles; and, secondly, Pyrenean oak – a protected species. A certain amount of logging is permitted here each year to provide the mountain villages with supplies of firewood.

La Pedriza, on the southern slopes of the Sierra de Guadarrama, is one of the largest granite ranges in Europe. Its peaks and cliffs are intersected with valleys and rivers as well as great boulders – some smoothly rounded, others weirdly eroded – which look as though giants have been playing bowls. There must be a thousand different routes for rock climbers, some easy enough for children – although not tots – to manage. Much of the rock is bare, but there are areas of scrub. Raptors are numerous, including over 100 pairs of griffon vultures. The river flows through the valley, cascading into several delightful pools in which to cool off after hiking in the heat.

HOW TO GET THERE:
By train, bus or car from Madrid
WHEN TO GO:
All year round, if you don't mind the snow and ice between December and February
DON'T MISS:
The Royal Monastery of San Lorenzo de El Escorial. Full of world-class art and ancient manuscripts, it is a UNESCO World Heritage Site.
YOU SHOULD KNOW:
Because of its proximity to Madrid, the Sierra de Guadarrama is criss-crossed by road passes and railway routes and caters well for tourists. It can get busy during the summer months but, even so, it is relatively easy to find a peaceful and beautiful spot in which to relax.

Sierra de Espuna National Park

HOW TO GET THERE:
Sierra de Espuna is about 90 minutes' drive from Alicante airport and is easily reached by road from Alhama de Murcia, Totana and Lorca; but try to start from the visitor centre.
WHEN TO GO:
All year round, but May to October or November is probably best.
DON'T MISS:
The 'badlands', known as Los Barrancos de Gebas, in the eastern part of the Sierra de Espuna, and the Walls of Layva – an area of limestone walls that attracts climbers.
YOU SHOULD KNOW:
On December 8, 9 and 10 each year, a barefooted pilgrimage takes place. Starting from Totana, the statue of Saint Eulalia is carried from the ornate Sanctuary of Santa Eulalia to San Roque, where she remains until January 7.

Situated about 40 km (25 mi) from the coast, between Mucia and Lorca, is the National Park of Sierra de Espuna. A forested area rising to 1,585 m (5,200 ft), the park is a pleasant retreat in which to enjoy both hiking and numerous other outdoor activities. In summer it is cooler and offers more shade than the rest of this flat, dry region.

While there are no rivers in the park, there are many springs and streams, enabling it to remain verdant throughout the year. The highest peak, El Morron de Espuna, reaches 1,583 m (5,194 ft) and is often snow-covered during the winter. Pines are plentiful, although oak, cottonwood, elm, poplar and maple also grow on these hills. Forest footpaths and well-maintained tracks make for pleasant walking, horse riding and mountain-biking. On the slopes, hawthorn, juniper and shrubs such as thyme, rock rose and honeysuckle thrive.

Towards the summit of El Morron is a group of 26 curious, circular domed wells called the Las Pozos de Nieve. The remains of snow pits, they were used from the 16th century until the 1920s when new refrigeration techniques took over. During winter, snow was collected and packed into these wells, to be cut into ice blocks and sold to businesses and individuals in nearby towns during the rest of the year.

Wild boar, Barbary sheep, genet, wild cats, foxes, red squirrels, rabbits and hares enjoy this habitat, along with many species of birds – including raptors such as golden eagles, goshawks, sparrowhawks and owls. It is worth spending a night or two camping or staying in a rural refuge to get the most from a visit. For the more adventurous, hang-gliding and paragliding are both available and one of the longest caves in Murcia – which can be found in Pliego village – is waiting to be explored.

Cabo de Gata-Nijar Natural Park

The first terrestrial and maritime Protected Area in Andalusia is located east of Almeria, in southeastern Spain. A UNESCO Biosphere Reserve since 1997, the park is Europe's driest area and contains a wide variety of habitats, including semi-desert steppe, saltmarsh, beaches, dunes, cliffs and a large marine area. Volcanic by origin, ancient calderas, volcanic domes and lava flows are centred around the headland of Cabo de Gata.

This is a wild and rugged landscape. The mountains are craggy and ochre coloured, white sand beaches and secret coves are backed by steep, 100 m (328 ft) cliffs, and lookout towers along the coast are testament to a history of incursions by Berber pirates seeking safety in this inaccessible corner of Spain. The terrestrial area of the natural park is home to low-growing vegetation that has adapted to drought conditions, such as cacti, dwarf fan palms and jujube, or red date. There are several endemic species, including the pink snapdragon. Scrub land consists of wild herbs, Kermes oaks and olives.

Most of the 1,100 species of fauna here are birds, although genets, wild boar and weasels can be seen. The Salinas de Cabo de Gata, a saltwater lagoon separated from the beach by a wide sandbar, is home to many resident birds such as flamingoes, herons, cranes and storks as well as thousands of migratory birds that rest here during their lengthy, biannual journeys. Seabirds include terns, shearwaters, shags and gulls, and the quantity of prey attracts raptors such as ospreys and peregrine falcons.

The pristine waters of the marine reserve cover vast swathes of Posidonia, a seagrass endemic to the Mediterranean. This provides shelter for a mass of marine life such as sponges, corals, sea urchins, anemones, sea stars and diverse fish such as halibut, cardinal fish and sea bream – they all make diving and snorkelling a delight.

HOW TO GET THERE:
By car. The visitor centre is between Retamar and San Miguel de Cabo de Gata.
WHEN TO GO:
Any time of year, but it is probably best between May and October.
DON'T MISS:
The local handicrafts – particularly the rugs and blankets of Nijar.
YOU SHOULD KNOW:
Spanish dramatist Frederico Lorca set his famous tragedy *Blood Wedding*, in the harsh, arid, sparsely inhabited inland area here and Monsul Beach, one of the most stunning coves in Gata-Nijar Natural Park, was where Steven Spielberg filmed the scene in *Indiana Jones and the Last Crusade* when Sean Connery, playing Indiana's father, brings down a German plane by scaring a flock of birds into the propellers.

Sierra de Grazalema Natural Park

HOW TO GET THERE:
The easiest way to visit is by car, as several roads run through the Sierra.
WHEN TO GO:
April to October
DON'T MISS:
The Virgen del Carmen fiesta in Grazalema, held annually in mid July, which culminates with a bull running through the streets of the town.
YOU SHOULD KNOW:
The area is historically significant and has a wealth of remains from the Romans, Moors and Christians, all of whom passed this way. There is even prehistoric cave art in the caves of La Pileta, as well as Bronze Age megaliths.

A UNESCO Biosphere Reserve since 1977, the Sierra de Grazalema is a magnificent area of karst landscape in which cliffs, gorges, caverns and valleys spread across the province of Cadiz and part of the province of Malaga, in southern Spain.

Its 517 sq km (200 sq mi) is scenically spectacular, bursting with flora and fauna, and encompasses 13 pretty white towns and villages, or *pueblos blancos*, within its boundaries. Grazalema itself is one of the most attractive villages and lies between two mountain peaks. Notoriously, the region receives the most rain in Spain, but the upside of this is that 1,300-plus species of plant, including endemics, thrive here. Part of the park is a special reserve area within which grows the best-preserved forests of Spanish fir in the country. Native to southern Spain, this species is very rare, despite having been in existence since the Tertiary Era (1.6–65 million years BC). Other species that grow well are juniper, maple, Portuguese oak and ash, while willows and poplars flourish alongside the streams and rivers.

Fauna include mountain goats, deer, genets, foxes and mongoose, and naturally there is a wealth of birds – including many raptors. The most renowned bird in the Sierra de Grazalema is the griffon vulture. The cliffs in the special reserve host Europe's largest colony.

The Sierra is a superb place to hike through, with many routes of varying degrees of difficulty to be explored. Other activities include exploring the Hundidero-Gato – Andalucia's largest cave system – which can be tackled by experienced cavers with a permit from the local tourist office, plus mountain-biking, horse riding, climbing and canoeing. And for those who love adventure, there are also some excellent spots within the park for hang-gliding.

Sierra de Grazalema

Sierra de Tramuntana

The island of Mallorca, off Spain's eastern coast, is usually thought of as a holiday destination catering for mass tourism. While this is partially true, life inland is calmer and the scenery a delight. The Sierra de Tramuntana is a mountain range in the northwest, stretching from Andratx to the Formentor Peninsula.

Many ancient trails and cobbled pilgrims' routes weave through the mountains, connecting the little medieval villages of the interior. Here, too, are Mallorca's highest peaks: Puig Major, at 1,445 m (4,741 ft) and Massanella, at 1,352 m (4,436 ft). The former is decorated with military installations, but Massanella is a beautiful hike of some three hours, ending with a superb view over the entire island, with Menorca in the distance on a good day.

Walk through the almond groves and gnarled olive trees of this timeless landscape; wild rosemary and other herbs scent the air and the hillsides glow with clumps of yellow broom – during January, February and March, almond and citrus blossom is an added bonus. Higher up, the vegetation changes to Spanish oak forest, carob and pine. Goats and sheep graze the hillsides, while black vultures hang in the sky above, keeping watch for a potential meal. Along the coastal trails, the visitor is blessed with wide, dramatic vistas from high cliffs, interrupted by small, secluded bays. Ospreys and sea eagles can be seen lazily skimming the water in search of food.

The more adventurous may visit the Torrent de Pareis, a gorge that is accessible only to walkers. One of the most spectacular walks on the island, it begins at Sa Calobra, and offers about five hours of scrambling over rocks through fabulous limestone scenery, along a dry river bed.

A flower meadow adds vibrant colour to the Sierra de Tramuntana.

HOW TO GET THERE:
Hire a car or book a taxi to drop you off and pick you up later at a designated meeting place. You can also travel by bus from Palma.
WHEN TO GO:
To avoid crowds, go during the winter months. During summer the region is busier, but the area is cooler and fresher than staying by the coast.
DON'T MISS:
Sa Seu, Palma's 14th-century cathedral, or Bellver Castle, located above the city.
YOU SHOULD KNOW:
The writer, Robert Graves and the artist Joan Miró both lived in Deia, a charming village in the Sierra de Tramuntana.

Garajonay National Park

HOW TO GET THERE:
By air or sea from Tenerife or
Gran Canaria
WHEN TO GO:
Any time of year
DON'T MISS:
The Juego de Bolas Information
Centre, at the park boundary or the
old centre of La Calera – a lovely
white town perched precariously on
a mountainside, its steep steps and
narrow lanes clear of cars.
YOU SHOULD KNOW:
The park and its peak are named
after Gara and Jonay, a local myth of
two unfortunate lovers who were
forced to kill themselves rather than
face separation. Wooden statues of
them can be seen at Garajonay.

The Canary Islands, part of Spain but situated close to Morocco, is a group of seven islands, five of which are popular holiday destinations. Enjoying constant sunshine and very little rain, they are all that remain of a volcanic mountain range. La Gomera, the least heavily populated island, is relatively untouched by tourism; it is also blessed with a unique UNESCO World Heritage Site: the Garajonay National Park.

During the Tertiary period, humid, subtropical forests covered much of the Mediterranean region, but most of them disappeared during the Ice Age. Located in the centre of the island, the 40 sq km (15 sq mi) of Garajonay is one of the best-preserved laurel forests still in existence. Made up of several species of non-deciduous hardwood laurels and laurel-type species, the largest variety reaches up to 40 m (130 ft).

The park is usually wreathed in cloud and mist and the many small

streams and springs ensure extraordinarily lush vegetation, in
complete contrast to the aridity of La Gomera's coastal area and that of
the other Canary Islands. The place has a magical air about it, as
though it has stepped from the pages of Tolkein's fantasy,
The Lord of the Rings. Huge rocks lie scattered about and trees grow
in bizarre, twisted shapes. Large ferns form dripping clumps, and the
forest floor is rich with undergrowth providing cover for birds,
invertebrates and bats. Two endemic pigeons can be found here, as
well as the Gomeran lizard and the Gomeran skink.

The Garajonay National Park comprises mountains and valleys,
cliffs and ravines, and there are several routes through and across this
unusual landscape. Make for the highest point on the island – 1,487 m
(4,880 ft) – which is the summit of the eponymous peak, and enjoy the
panoramic view.

*Looking over the forests of
Garajonay National Park*

Alvão Natural Park

HOW TO GET THERE:
It takes about an hour by car from Porto.
WHEN TO GO:
Spring, summer or autumn is when it is at its best.
DON'T MISS:
The traditional villages, such as Lamas d'Ôlo.
YOU SHOULD KNOW:
BTCV, the international volunteering organization, began its International Working Holidays in Alvão Natural Park in 1994. Since then, volunteers have helped with clearing new invasive species, re-creating traditional meadow management, dry-stone walling and enhancing the health of the various ecosystems.

Located northeast of Porto, Alvão Natural Park spreads across 70 sq km (27 sq mi) of the ridge and western slopes of the Alvão mountains. Formed in 1983, Portugal's smallest Natural Park reaches the height of 1,330 m (4,364 ft) and the Nature Conservation Institute works hard to promote conservation of species as well as the traditional culture of the small villages within its boundaries.

The park bestrides the transition area between the humid coast and the arid interior, and thus falls naturally into two separate components. At its highest altitude, in a rugged, rock-strewn region, the source of the River Ôlo springs from a large granite basin; at its lowest, the river runs through narrow valleys. The geology here – granite and schist – has produced great drops, and probably the most sought-after 'sight' in Alvão is the Fisgas de Ermelo waterfall. This waterfall cascades down a 300 m (935 ft) slope above the picturesque village of Ermelo.

Much of the park consists of green, leafy, mixed species forest that includes black and English oak, silver birch, hazel, holly, bay, chestnut and wild pear. The heathland is mainly covered in heather, gorse, broom and bilberry. Some of the valleys are terraced and planted with rye or with vines, and fruit and olive trees are also grown. There are still wild-flower-rich meadows in which cattle and goats graze. This mixed environment is home to diverse species of fauna; amphibians and reptiles thrive here, and it is a perfect habitat for bats.

Mammals are mainly small – field mice, rabbits, wild goats, wildcats and, very occasionally, wolves. Several types of raptor can be seen, including round-winged eagles and peregrine falcons, as well as many smaller species such as choughs, bullfinches, flycatchers and water pipits.

Cape St Vincent National Park

Cape St Vincent National Park runs for 150 km (93 mi) down the Atlantic coast to the southwestern tip of Portugal, from Porto Covo in Alentejo to Burgau in the Algarve. Truly a national treasure, the park has been protected since 1995 and could not be more different from the popular tourist destinations of the Algarve, being possibly the last genuinely wild coastal area in Europe.

Varying in width from 2–20 km (1.2–12.4 mi), the park is sparsely populated, but rich in flora and fauna – including rare and endangered species. Because of its location and long months of sunshine and very little rain, the flora is mostly formed of thorny shrubs and bushes, bulbs and annuals. Including seaweeds, there are at least 750 species here, 12 of which are unique to the area. *Silene rothmaleri*, a charming little white flower that was believed extinct since 1984, was re-discovered at Cape St Vincent in 2000.

The Cape itself is the most southwesterly point of Europe. The cliffs here rise almost vertically from the ocean, on the edge of which stands a lighthouse, built in the 1840s on the ruins of a 16th-century Franciscan monastery. A myriad of birds nest along this coast, many building precariously perched nests on the rocky cliffs. There are kites, peregrine falcons and Bonelli's eagles, as well as rock thrushes and pigeons. This is the only place in the world where white storks nest on rocks. Another unlikely creature to be found is the otter – rarely found in a marine habitat.

This is a coastline of towering – often ochre – cliffs, small, rocky coves and pristine beaches, backed by rolling hills, pine forests and almond groves. The best way to see it is slowly: walk, cycle or travel on horseback to truly appreciate the area.

HOW TO GET THERE:
Rent a car from Faro or Lisbon.
WHEN TO GO:
Any time of year, but in spring or autumn you will catch the annual migratory birds.
DON'T MISS:
The utterly delicious fish and seafood that can be sampled up and down the coast, or the excellent surfing.
YOU SHOULD KNOW:
Cape St Vincent, sacred since Neolithic times, is where Henry the Navigator built the first great research and training school for navigators, sailors and astronomers. After the famous sea battle of the same name in 1797, when the British defeated the much larger Portuguese fleet, Nelson was knighted and made Rear-Admiral for his efforts.

Cliffs, rocky coves and pristine beaches near Cape St Vincent

The Montesinho Mountains cloaked in heather.

Montesinho Mountains Natural Park

One of the least visited and wildest regions in Portugal, Montesinho Mountains Natural Park was formed not only to protect the rare fauna that survives there, but also the unusually traditional way of life still led by its approximately 9,000 inhabitants. Found in the far northeast of Portugal, its north and eastern edges form the border with Spain.

The villages, such as Montesinho and Franca, have cobbled streets and stone houses that are traditional to the region. Scattered across the slopes are *pombal* – round, medieval dovecotes with horseshoe-shaped roofs. These were built for rearing doves to be eaten, their droppings used as fertilizer.

This is a region of curved mountains separated by valleys, some of which are very steep, others gently sloped. The altitude ranges from 438 m (1,437 ft) at the Mente River to 1,481 m (4,859 ft) at the peak of Montesinho. The eastern section is the most easily accessible, but paths run throughout the park, enabling the visitor to explore the more remote and lush western section.

Along the edges of the streams and rivers running through the park are ash, alder, black poplar, wild cherry trees, willow and hazel,

HOW TO GET THERE:
By car or bus from Braganca to Montesinho or Rio de Onor
WHEN TO GO:
From May to September – winters are long and hard here.
DON'T MISS:
The summer festivals, or saint's feast days, when many of those who have left to work overseas or elsewhere in Portugal return home for a summer break.
YOU SHOULD KNOW:
The villages Miranda do Douro and Rio de Onor have both been the source of anthropological studies. The people of this region speak a curious dialect of mixed Spanish and Portuguese. Some ancient Celtic traditions still exist, too – for example, the traditional music requires the playing of bagpipes.

mixed with herbs such as apple mint, and honeysuckle, jasmine and peonies. Meadows are bursting with scented herbs and wild flowers, including orchids and several endemic species. Chestnuts are an important source of local income and in agricultural areas great stands of sweet chestnut trees can be found.

Higher regions are cloaked in oaks, then heathers and, finally, outcrops of granite. The varied habitat is home to wolves, wild boar, foxes, wild cats and deer, as well as 150 species of bird, including three types of eagle and other raptors. The rivers teem with fish and are a playground for otters.

Serra da Malcata Nature Reserve

The Serra da Malcata lies on the Spanish border at the eastern edge of central Portugal and was created in 1981 in order to preserve the critically endangered Iberian lynx. Their preferred habitat consists of Mediterranean scrub with open forest that includes old trees and dense thickets, as well as meadows in which to hunt.

The nature reserve is perfect country for wildlife of all sorts. Rising to just 1,078 m (3,537 ft), the rolling hills are covered with heather and there is plenty of old oak forest with chestnut and wild cherry trees. At higher levels rare strawberry trees can be seen and, during spring, white and yellow broom provides brilliant splashes of colour. Some of the land just within the reserve's boundaries is used for agriculture, including fruit orchards that look beautiful when in full blossom. Rivers and streams run through the area, beside which grow stands of willow, ash and alder. Small, riverside beaches provide opportunities for paddling, swimming or canoeing.

The Serra da Malcata Nature Reserve is an important region for breeding pairs of various birds of prey, including short-toed and booted eagles and Montagu's harrier. Black vultures also nest here. Mammals include foxes, wildcats, wild boars, badgers, genets, as well as smaller creatures such as hares and rabbits. Otters hunt and play in the rivers, which are full of fish, and every species of amphibian in mainland Portugal has a presence here. It is thought that the Iberian lynx may have become extinct in the reserve, but as they are extremely hard to see, and hunt at night, this is a matter of debate. To be on the safe side, a captive breeding programme is being run across the border in Spain and in due course some of these animals will be introduced to Serra da Malcata.

HOW TO GET THERE:
By road from Castello Branco. The main information office is in Penemacor.
WHEN TO GO:
Between April and October
DON'T MISS:
If you are in central Portugal, don't miss the opportunity of visiting the historic city of Coimbra.
YOU SHOULD KNOW:
The Iberian lynx is about twice the size of a domestic cat, but it has longer legs, a bobtail and pointed ears topped with black tufts. The main reason for its drastic decline is because of a shortage of rabbits – its favourite food.

383

EASTERN MEDITERRANEAN & MIDDLE EAST

Akamas Peninsula

HOW TO GET THERE:
By 4x4, or take a bus from Paphos to Polis.
WHEN TO GO:
From February to November, but between early March and the end of April for the marvellous show of wild flowers, including orchids. Take plenty of water with you if you are there during the height of summer.
DON'T MISS:
Kykkos monastery, a Byzantine marvel founded in 1100; Kourion, a superb archaeological site and the painted churches in the Troodos Mountains.
YOU SHOULD KNOW:
There is an on-going battle over the future of the Akamas Peninsula between the forces of conservation, such as Greenpeace and the European Environment Agency, and the government and developers. Some illegal hotels have already been built, including one overlooking turtle nesting sites.

Jutting into the sea at the northwestern tip of Cyprus is the Akamas Peninsula, named after one of the sons of Theseus and his second wife, Phaedra. The third largest island in the Mediterranean, Cyprus has Turkey lying just 75 km (47 mi) to the north and Syria and Lebanon roughly 106 km (66 mi) to the east.

Covering about 230 sq km (90 sq mi), the Akamas Peninsula is the island's most wildly beautiful area. During the 1980s and 1990s, the British used Akamas for military exercises which, ironically, kept it free of the kind of development that was occurring elsewhere on Cyprus. Thus it remains a superb place in which to walk, mountain-bike, or even explore in a 4x4.

On this mountainous peninsula discover perfect, sandy bays, deep gorges, and forested heights. Thanks to its physical location between Europe, Asia and Africa, an unusually high number of plant species thrive here – 530, of which 33 are endemic – as well as 168 bird, 20 reptile, 16 butterfly and 12 mammal species. The headland is forested with pine, juniper, oak, laurel and myrtle and there are large areas of Mediterranean scrubland, gorges, cliffs and dunes, thus providing several diverse habitats. The most important natural site on Akamas is Lara Bay, where both endangered green and vulnerable loggerhead turtles come to lay their eggs in peace.

Trails snake around the peninsula – one of the loveliest is named after the goddess Aphrodite, who emerged from the sea just off the Cyprus coast and is the island's patron. Starting from the Baths of Aphrodite, it ascends to her sanctuary, noted for a resplendent oak tree that is over 800 years old. Climb higher still to reach a flat, rocky area from which the view is magnificent.

The Akamas Peninsula

Karpas Peninsula

The Karpas Peninsula, otherwise known as 'the Panhandle', lies in the northeast of Cyprus, stretching from close to Famagusta to the far northeastern tip of the country. It is an area of small villages, where the inhabitants either farm in the traditional style, or fish for their living, and the countryside is unpolluted by towns or industry.

The hills, which reach 1,000 m (3,280 ft), are blanketed with pine, cypress and the trees of the Mediterranean scrubland. The beaches, some sandy, some rocky, are not only glorious but also remarkably empty and include Golden Sands Beach. This 6 km (4 mi) stretch of sand and dunes is thought to be the best beach on the entire island, and is a nesting site for rare green and loggerhead sea turtles. Offshore, Mediterranean dolphins are frequently seen dashing and leaping through the sea.

The rare Andouin's gull can be spotted here, too. These fish eaters nest on the Klidhes Isles, just off the tip of the peninsula. Cyprus is good for birdwatching. It lies on the north/south migratory route, which is used by some 300 species of bird. Griffon vultures with their great 2.4 m (8 ft) wingspan overwinter and breed here, and one can also see the endemic Cyprus pied wheatear, the golden oriole, the Cyprus warbler, bee-eaters and rollers.

The Karpas Peninsula is also rich in wildflowers and from February until June the region is bursting with hundreds of brightly coloured species, including yellow crowfoot, purple iris and exquisite pink rock roses. While there are no rivers running through the peninsula, there are 15 springs and many underground reservoirs that enable fruit trees, olives and tobacco to be farmed. Hundreds of wild donkeys roam the peninsula – set adrift after the Turkish invasion of 1974, they have lived and bred here quite happily.

HOW TO GET THERE:
Access is by car only, via Famagusta.
WHEN TO GO:
Arrive in spring for wild flowers and migratory birds, autumn also for the latter, and summer for making the most of the beaches.
DON'T MISS:
The Apostolos Andreas Monastery, a major place of pilgrimage for the Orthodox Church of Cyprus, or the ancient ruins of Salamis.
YOU SHOULD KNOW:
Reptiles wake from their hibernation in May and, although most of them are harmless, the blunt-nosed viper can be deadly.

Golden Sands Beach on the Karpas peninsula

*Gobekli Lake in the
Salacur Valley*

Kackar Mountains

HOW TO GET THERE:
Occasional *dolmuses* (shared taxis) climb the rough road to Barhal from Yusufeli, which is well connected with Erzurum. A summer service runs between Trabzon and Ayder, and from Ayder to Camlihemsin, which has a regular,
year-round service to Pazar on the coast.

WHEN TO GO:
Late May to late September for walking, July and August for climbing the peaks. By September, the longer nights are cold. In summer, it is almost impossible to find accommodation in Ayder at weekends.

The Kackar range, whose densely clustered peaks soar dramatically above the Black Sea coast, is increasingly popular with walkers. It lies outside the troubled Kurdish regions, is relatively straightforward to reach and is remarkable for its beauty and for the Hemsin people – summer inhabitants of the high pastures.

On the southern foothills, villages amid cherry orchards cling to a deeply fissured, wildly rocky landscape, famous for white-water rafting. The walking here is tough, but the weather is excellent. The northern slopes are extravagantly lush. Above the Black Sea tea plantations, where rivers rush and cascade through dense forests, the beautiful, remote Hemsin Valleys are home, in winter, to the pastoralists. This is the wettest place in Turkey.

Experienced climbers head for the Kackar's precipitous alpine peaks but the network of fine walking tracks attracts most visitors. From villages in the lower highlands, long and short treks – with or without guides – make use of the paths which link the *yaylas*, the stone-and-wood summer settlements. Each belongs to a valley village and several can provide meals, even rooms, for hikers. The walking is glorious: the views are breathtaking, the steep meadows are brilliant with flowers and butterflies, the hundreds of glacial lakes reflect the immense, blue, light-filled sky. Grazing cattle, often pompom-bedecked, may be accompanied by Hemsin women, splendid in traditional black-and-orange headdresses. Trekking across the range is very rewarding. From Barhal in the south, the route climbs over the scree slopes of Mount Kackar, Turkey's fourth highest mountain – 3,932 m (12,900 ft) – and down to the alpine village, Ayder. Here, hot springs ease the strains of two or three days' walking before the descent to the coast.

DON'T MISS:
The Hemsins. At the end of May, after days of celebration, all the families take their livestock up to the *yaylas* where the women make butter, yoghurt and cheese. At weekends, Hemsins from cities and overseas rejoin their families for the festivities. Organized treks introduce visitors to the work, culture and merry-making of these remarkable people, thus sharing with them Turkey's tourist income and helping to safeguard their ancient way of life.

YOU SHOULD KNOW:
Weather is unpredictable in the Kackars – even in summer, Ayder can be completely fogged in for days – and hikers should never set out without a guide, local information, or a good map. Kate Clow has produced an excellent walking guide to the mountains.

Kaz Daglari

Kaz Daglari (Goose Mountain), or Mount Ida of Greek classical antiquity, is a conglomeration of peaks above the northern shore of the Gulf of Edremit, southeast of Troy. Its modern name refers to a Turkish folk tale. The summits are windswept and bare. The highest, Kirklar – 1,774 m (5,820 ft) – is a fairly easy climb and the views in all directions are superb. The thickly forested slopes are home to a remarkable abundance of indigenous flora and a recent study of the biodiversity included interviews with plant gatherers and recorded the local names and traditional uses of the herbs and medicinal plants for which Mount Ida is famous.

A number of pleasant villages in the fertile northern foothills are linked by narrow roads and tracks. Attractions for visitors include treks, rides, plane-shaded riverside restaurants and some excellent local produce, including herbal teas, cheeses and tobacco. Higher slopes are thickly clad with pine and beech, threaded by streams, dotted with lakes and waterfalls and criss-crossed by paths.

Above the coast, precipitous southern hillsides are fractured by cliffs and canyons. These are challenging hikes and experience and specialized equipment are essential. Walks from Gure and Zeytinli, pretty little towns at the eastern end of the gulf, are delightful. Good tracks lead through the woods to an impressive waterfall, to some hot springs and up into the hills. In spring, streams race and flowers cover the meadows; in autumn the mountains are clothed in gold and scarlet and visitors gather chestnuts alongside the locals. To walk along quiet trails, away from popular villages and picnic areas, is to experience a landscape rich in ancient legend and traditional rural life.

HOW TO GET THERE:
The north of the range can be approached from Bayramic or Kalkym, the south of the range from the Assos to Edremit coast road. Buses or *dolmuses* (shared taxis) run to all these places.

WHEN TO GO:
May, June, September, or October. Avoid weekends, when Turkish town-dwellers visit and accommodation can be scarce.

DON'T MISS:
In the delightfully named Village of the Wooden Birds (Tahtakuslar Koyu), near Akcay, is Turkey's first private ethnographical museum. As well as a fascinating collection of objects from the nomadic Turkic people – carpets, tents, bridal costumes and so on – it displays contemporary arts and crafts and information on the many legends of Mount Ida and its medicinal plants.

YOU SHOULD KNOW:
The most famous story set on Mount Ida is the *Judgement of Paris*. Paris of Troy was asked to decide who was the fairest goddess: Aphrodite, Hera or Artemis. He chose Aphrodite because she promised him the most beautiful woman in the world – Helen. He sailed for Sparta, abducted Helen, and the Trojan War began. An annual beauty contest now commemorates his fateful decision.

Koprulu Canyon

The sandy coast east of Antalya is strung with beach resorts, but much of the mountainous hinterland is wild and empty, sliced by rivers which race to the Mediterranean. The Koprulu National Park covers a large area of rugged, forested mountains through which the Kupru Irmagi (Bridge River) flows between the towering cliffs of the Koprulu Canyon, below the remains of the ancient city of Selge.

The journey from the coast is lovely; the road meanders through wooded hills and past isolated settlements, becoming increasingly steep and serpentine, with views of distant misty peaks and the silvery river. After Beskonak, a track leads to a narrow Roman bridge, still used to cross the river to an area offering refreshment at waterside restaurants, plus activities on land and water and tracks to the park's other attractions. Near a second bridge (an elegant Ottoman structure) the river forms still, blue pools; upstream, for about 14 km (8.5 mi), it flows deep and calm between tree-clad cliffs, or white and turbulent through narrow, towering ravines. The forest around the gorge comprises huge swathes of dark cypress and mixed woodlands and is home to wild animals which include deer, wolves and wild boar.

The beautiful 12 km (7.5 mi) trail to Selge climbs through thickets of olive, maple and carob trees, past eroded rock formations and the precipitous gullies which once provided an impregnable defence for the Roman city, reputedly home to 20,000 people. The ruins are scattered in tumbled heaps among the stone cottages of present-day residents. The remoteness of this site has hindered archaeological work, but its situation – on a high plateau surrounded by the fields and orchards of Altinkaya and backed by the jagged Kuyucuk mountains – is wonderfully picturesque.

HOW TO GET THERE:
Tours from Antalya, Side and other resorts visit the canyon. The track from Beskonak can be driven with care almost as far as Selge. A daily minibus runs from Antalya to Altinkaya and back.
WHEN TO GO:
Late April to June, September or October
DON'T MISS:
Ancient Aspendos is very close to the route to Koprulu. Extensive remains lie on the hill behind what is, although extensively restored (notably by Ataturk), one of the world's finest Roman theatres. The acoustics are still perfect.
YOU SHOULD KNOW:
Activities in the canyon include rafting, kayaking and hikes into the mountains. Selge, at 900 m (2,950 ft) is noticeably cooler than the lower areas. A bright-green shrub seen growing among the dark trees is *Styrax officinalis*, whose aromatic gum was highly prized for medicinal use and is still used in perfumery. The people of Selge valued the plant so greatly it appeared on their coins.

Rafting in Koprulu Canyon

as at Big Lagoon, the sea has broken through into the claypans to form a shallow inland bay.

Shark Bay itself is a protected marine park and its shallow, clear waters are rich in marine life. The cliff tops of the Peron Peninsula provide good viewpoints for spotting dolphins, turtles and manta rays; even the threatened dugong, a gentle giant of a sea creature, can sometimes be seen grazing in these waters. With fabulous coral reefs to entice divers the bay also boasts the largest number of seagrass species ever recorded in one place anywhere in the world (12, since you're wondering). But the most remarkable feature of all is what thrives in the shallow waters of Hamelin Pool on the eastern side of the peninsula: colonies of sediment-trapping algae, known as stromatolites, which are direct descendants of the earth's earliest life forms, dating back over three billion years.

YOU SHOULD KNOW:
The national park is part of Project Eden, a state government initiative to re-establish native wildlife species by eradicating feral and imported animals such as cats and foxes.

Tyre tracks in the red sand of a road which cuts through the flat scrubland of the Peron Peninsula.

Kalbarri National Park

HOW TO GET THERE:
Kalbarri town, the main base for the park, is 100 km (62 mi) north of Geraldton and 66 km (41 mi) off the main highway running up the west coast.
WHEN TO GO:
August to November
DON'T MISS:
The astonishing displays of colour when the wild flowers of the heathlands and sandplains burst into bloom in the spring.
YOU SHOULD KNOW:
You should carry your own drinking water with you at all times as none is available inside the park.

Rock formations and colours are the main attractions of Kalbarri National Park which lies on Australia's west coast some 600 km (375 mi) north of Perth. The striking landscapes are the result of geological processes over millions of years, during which the terrain has been shaped by deposits of deep, horizontal bands of multi-coloured sands. The centrepiece of the park is the Murchison River which flows out into the Indian Ocean where the small coastal resort of Kalbarri is now located. The spectacular red-and-white banded gorges which the river has carved out of the rock as it winds its serpentine way to the sea are definitely not to be missed. They are best seen from two sites on the upper Murchison, reached by a turning off the Ajana road east of Kalbarri. The cliff top of Z Bend offers the most dramatic viewpoint where you can gaze down to the river far below; you can also walk around the Loop, a wide horseshoe bend in the river, in two to three hours, depending on how many times you are tempted by swimming spots (best to do the walk in the early morning). On the way you will come across a natural rock arch known as Nature's Window.

Still within the park, there are similarly spectacular cliffs along the coast south of Kalbarri town. Tidal inlets and creeks have created a series of coastal gorges which you can enjoy at sites with evocative names like Rainbow Valley, Mushroom Rock and Red Bluff. The view out to the ocean from the cliffs above the Natural Bridge will make you feel very small. A demanding but rewarding coastal trail connects Natural Bridge with Eagle Gorge, 8 km (5 mi) away.

Rugged cliffs along the Indian Ocean south of Kalbarri.

Spangled emperor fish

Ningaloo Reef

For those in the know, Ningaloo Reef on Australia's northwestern coast surpasses the Great Barrier Reef itself. It cannot, of course, compete in terms of sheer scale and variety but Ningaloo has so far managed to escape the worst effects of mass tourism and the other commercial pressures which bedevil its renowned eastern counterpart. The country's largest fringing coral reef, Ningaloo harbours a marine environment of global importance; its entire 300-km (186-mi) length is now protected as a marine park. Proximity to the continental shelf is what gives the reef its stunning diversity of marine life. With some 250 different types of coral and over 500 species of fish recorded, the reef is a diver's paradise, although it also provides exceptional scope for ordinary snorkellers owing to the fact that, in contrast to the Barrier Reef, it lies so close to the coast. Indeed, Ningaloo is the world's only large reef found so close to a continental land mass. Never more than 7 km (4 mi) from the coastline, in some places it is barely 100 m (330 ft) offshore; from the beach at Coral Bay, for example, you can clearly see the white swell breaking over the reef.

If you can tear yourself away from the enchanting world beneath the waves, the North West Cape headland affords a suitably stark contrast. An elevated range with weathered limestone plateaus forms the spine of the peninsula, extending all the way to North West Cape from where there are fine views of the Muiron Islands. The Cape Range National Park covers 506 sq km (195 sq mi) in the northwest of the peninsula. Its arid, exposed terrain is criss-crossed by deep rocky gorges, such as those at Mandu Mandu and Yardie Creek, where you should look out for rock wallabies.

HOW TO GET THERE:
Coral Bay is 227 km (140 mi) north of Carnarvon by road. Exmouth, the main town on the peninsula and the principal base for boat tours to the reef, is a further 129 km (80 mi).
WHEN TO GO:
April to September
DON'T MISS:
In April and May many people come to Ningaloo for the awesome experience of swimming with the world's largest fish, the whale shark. It is a justly popular activity and you should be prepared to pay for the privilege.
YOU SHOULD KNOW:
If you have a 4x4 and the tides are in your favour it is possible to drive the entire way south along the beach from Cape Range National Park to Coral Bay.

A rock formation at sunrise in Purnululu National Park

Purnululu National Park

One of the most extraordinary natural sights in a region full of scenic wonders, Purnululu National Park is much better known as the Bungle Bungles. This mighty sandstone massif (*purnululu* means sandstone in the local tribal language) burst on to the world stage as recently as the early 1980s; until then, its remote location had ensured it was known only to the nomadic Aboriginal peoples whose ancestral land this was and to the odd cattle drover and pilots of the outback. Nowadays this landscape of hundreds of weather-beaten rock domes is a standard feature of Australian tourist brochures, as iconic an image of the country as Uluru.

The terrain is the result of millions of years of erosion and uplift, in the course of which the soft sandstone has worn away to form these curious beehive shapes. But it is not only the shapes that are unusual; the colouring of the rocks is equally remarkable. It is now thought that sediments from two different sources were deposited in alternating strata to create the orange-and-black banding which is such a distinctive feature of the domes. The colouration is caused by the different minerals present: iron and manganese in the case of the orange, while the darker bands are composed of more permeable material where water has supported algal growth.

Spectacular as the stripes appear, they are in fact a fragile crust over a soft and powdery interior that is all too easily eroded. The best way to appreciate the contours of this exceptional landscape is from the air. If you want to reduce your carbon footprint (although probably not by much), the alternative is to take a 4x4 into the park to explore stunning features like Echidna Chasm and Cathedral Gorge.

HOW TO GET THERE:
The ranger station at Three Ways is 53 km (33 mi) east of the Great Northern Highway on a dirt road (4x4s only). The driving time is four hours from Halls Creek to the south and five hours from Kununurra to the north.

WHEN TO GO:
April to December (but note that it is always hot here).

DON'T MISS:
The awe-inspiring walk along Cathedral Gorge with its ever-narrowing ravine and sheer, towering cliffs.

YOU SHOULD KNOW:
There is some dispute over the origin of the name Bungle Bungles; it derives either from the corruption of an Aboriginal name for the area or from a misspelling of one of the grasses commonly found here, bundle bundle grass.

Watarrka National Park

Deep in the Red Centre of Australia the Watarrka National Park is as rugged and isolated a location as you could wish for from the Outback. It comes as a surprise, then, to discover just what a range of environments the park encompasses; as well as the expected desert plains and rocky spurs, you also find plateaus, gorges, red sandhills covered with desert oaks and spinifex, and hidden springs with delicate ferns and cycads growing in profusion around them. It is a surprise, too, to learn that the park is home to more than 600 different types of plant; its name, indeed, refers to the unmistakable umbrella bush which is a common feature of the area.

Watarrka National Park includes the western end of the George Gill Range, itself an extension of the MacDonnell Ranges that frame Alice Springs. At its heart lies Kings Canyon, the natural feature that most people come to Watarrka to see. The sight of the canyon's sheer sandstone walls, rising to 100 m (330 ft) in places, is breathtaking, especially in the early morning sunlight. This is definitely the best time to undertake the 6-km (3.75-mi) walk around the canyon rim, before the day's temperatures become too punishing. The route takes you through a curious maze of little sandstone domes – miniature Bungles – and past a lookout offering a fine view of the imposing southern wall. At the head of the canyon, and roughly halfway along the walk, a surprise awaits you: a sheltered chasm filled with palms and ferns. This haven of greenery is known as the Garden of Eden and it comes complete with a shady pool where you can take a refreshing dip.

HOW TO GET THERE:
Watarrka is 450 km (280 mi) southwest of Alice Springs on sealed roads, so it is accessible in a conventional vehicle.
WHEN TO GO:
April to September
DON'T MISS:
The play of early morning sunlight on the red rocks and cliff faces.
YOU SHOULD KNOW:
Bernadette achieved her ambition of standing on the rim of Kings Canyon in all her finery for the closing scene of the cult film *The Adventures of Priscilla, Queen of the Desert.*

The magnificent Kings Canyon

Cobourg Peninsula

Places don't come much more remote than the Cobourg Peninsula on Australia's northern coast, which juts out into the Arafura Sea northeast of Darwin. Although it is possible to fly in or to reach it by boat (two days sailing from Darwin), the biggest adventure is certainly the overland one which involves an epic 4x4 journey across Kakadu and Arnhem Land. Arnhem Land is a huge wilderness that has remained in Aboriginal hands; access by non-indigenous visitors is carefully managed. A limited number of vehicles is permitted to cross Aboriginal land and no overnight stops are allowed. Camping is possible, however, within the bounds of the Garig Gunak Barlu National Park which covers the entire peninsula. The land area of 2,200 sq km (850 sq mi) is more than doubled by the surrounding waters of Van Diemen Gulf and the Arafura Sea, along with neighbouring islands, which form a marine reserve; extensive coral reefs and seagrass meadows support a rich array of marine life.

The Cobourg Peninsula is a wild and beautiful mosaic of coastal grasslands, dunes, beaches, mangrove swamps, lagoons and patches of rainforest. The ranger station on Smith Point is the base for a visit to the park, although since there aren't any tracks other than the main access route you might as well relax and make the most of the magnificent white sand beaches. There are good birdwatching opportunities, too, as this is an important habitat for waterfowl and migratory birds. If you absolutely have to go on an expedition, then the ruins of Victoria Settlement, a failed attempt in the 1840s to establish a British colony and trading post, await exploration; as they lie on the other side of the Port Essington inlet, however, you need a boat to reach them.

Surf washes onto a rocky beach along the Cobourg Peninsula.

Elsey National Park

The Roper River is one of the principal rivers of the area around Darwin, popularly known as the Top End. Flowing into the Gulf of Carpentaria to the east, the river is a green lung in the arid plains and grasslands south of Katherine. Its upper reaches are protected within the Elsey National Park, which also includes a number of springs that feed the river. During the dry season the Roper presents a picture of calm serenity as it courses its gentle way through large waterholes and over rocks and tufa dams. In the wet season, however, it is an entirely different proposition and you would be hard pushed to believe the raging torrent before you was the same river.

The Roper River - a picture of serenity during the dry season

This is a world which encourages a slower, simpler way of life. Fishing and canoeing are popular activities here, as is swimming, although as with anywhere in the Top End you should heed local advice about where it is safe to enter the water. Cruises along the Roper River are the best way of appreciating the scenery, taking you into an extensive area of freshwater wetlands like the beautiful Red Lily Lagoon. If you prefer to stay on dry land, however, there are numerous trails – including an 8-km (5-mi) return walk beside the river to the Mataranka Falls where you can cool off in the gentle rapids.

A different bathing experience is offered by the thermal pool at the western end of the park. The natural springs at Rainbow Spring pump crystal-clear water into a large pool at a constant 34°C (93.2°F). Fringed by shady palms and set within a patch of rainforest, it is a great place to unwind after a day on the road.

HOW TO GET THERE:
The turn-off to Elsey National Park is a short distance south of Mataranka on the Stuart Highway. Mataranka is 103 km (64 mi) south of Katherine.
WHEN TO GO:
April to October (during the dry season)
DON'T MISS:
An old wartime Aboriginal army camp is an intriguing historical relic within the park.
YOU SHOULD KNOW:
This area was the setting for a famous Australian book, *We of the Never Never*, Jeanie Gunn's classic 1908 tale of the spirit of the pioneering outback.

Kakadu is Australia's greatest national park.

Kakadu

HOW TO GET THERE:
The western boundary of Kakadu National Park is 150 km (93 mi) east of Darwin. From there it is a further 100 km (62 mi) to the park headquarters at Jabiru. You can also enter Kakadu from the south by turning off the Stuart Highway at Pine Creek.

WHEN TO GO:
Any time of year. Most visitors arrive during the dry season months of May to August when the temperatures are at their most tolerable; but connoisseurs reckon the true spirit of the place is revealed only in the wet season, when nature bursts forth in all its verdant profusion.

DON'T MISS:
A boat trip on the Yellow Water billabong, preferably in the early morning or late afternoon. These wetlands provide exceptional opportunities for spotting wildlife.

YOU SHOULD KNOW:
After a period when they were abolished to counteract a decline in visitor numbers, entrance fees for the park have now been re-introduced. A pass gives you access for 14 days.

Everything about Kakadu draws you to superlatives. The facts about Australia's greatest national park are staggering for a start: an area the size of Wales – nearly 20,000 sq km (7,720 sq mi); more different reptile species than are found in the whole of Europe; five out of the world's seven types of turtle; one third of the entire bird species of Australia; over 5,000 rock-art sites. It can all seem rather overwhelming on a first visit, and you wonder whether it is possible ever to get the full measure of the park. The truth is, the most you can hope for is a flavour of this extraordinary place, but what a flavour it is! A huge variety of land forms and habitats are featured in Kakadu, an area large enough to encompass the entire catchment area of a river. As the South Alligator River flows north into Van Diemen Gulf, the landscape changes from sandstone plateaus and heathlands in the south through savannah woodlands and paperbark swamps to the coastal belt, which is made up of tidal wetlands and mangrove forests. Presiding over all is the imposing Arnhem escarpment running down the eastern side of the park.

Kakadu is jointly managed by the Australian government and the local Aboriginal groups who still live in the park and are the traditional owners of the land, much of which remains sacred to them and is consequently inaccessible to the casual visitor. Other sites are only for serious off-road types; at certain times of the year they are not even reached by 4x4s. Places which everyone can get to on sealed roads include the incredible sites at Ubirr and Nourlangie, outdoor galleries of rock art depicting animals, birds, humans and ancestral spirits in paintings, some of which are 20,000 years old.

Kata Tjuta

The stunning assemblage of giant sandstone rocks known as Kata Tjuta in central Australia would be a major destination in its own right were it not for the fact of its world-famous neighbour down the road, mighty Uluru. As it is, the Olgas, as they were formerly known by early European explorers, seem happy enough to cede star billing to the monolith that has become for many people the defining image of the country. But it would be a pity if, having made it all this way to visit 'the Rock', you didn't also allow yourself the time to explore the Olgas as well.

The two natural wonders are just 50 km (31 mi) apart and are both contained within the same national park, which is managed jointly by the local Aboriginal community, who own the land, and the federal government. *Kata tjuta* means 'many heads' in the Aboriginal language, an entirely apt description for this cluster of 36 domed rocks divided by narrow chasms and broader valleys. Whether or not you climb Uluru is a controversial subject these days, but there is no such dilemma here as you are not allowed to climb on the Kata Tjuta rocks. Their smooth, rounded tops may look inviting but the sheer sides of many of the rocks make it an unfeasible prospect. The eastern part of the complex is completely off-limits to visitors since this is a sacred site to the Anangu Aborigines under their men's law. You can still get an outstanding impression of the site, though, by doing the Valley of the Winds walk, a 7-km (4.4-mi) loop trail through a desert landscape of sand hills covered in spinifex and small stands of desert oak.

HOW TO GET THERE:
Uluru-Kata Tjuta National Park is 440 km (275 mi) southwest of Alice Springs.
WHEN TO GO:
May to September (but as this includes the winter months, note that temperatures in the desert can drop significantly at night).
DON'T MISS:
The viewing area on the road to Kata Tjuta from Uluru. The profile of the rocks several kilometres to the north looks stunning, especially at sunrise.
YOU SHOULD KNOW:
Many people are surprised to learn that the largest of the Kata Tjuta rocks, Mount Olga, is actually 200 m (656 ft) higher than Uluru.

The giant sandstone rocks of Kata Tjuta

Litchfield National Park

A couple of hours' drive south from Darwin brings you to the boundary of Litchfield National Park. Less well known – and at 1,500 sq km (580 sq mi) a lot smaller than its neighbour Kakadu – Litchfield is nevertheless many people's preferred option for a taste of a subtropical wilderness. Its scale is more manageable, and the principal sights are more readily accessible than is the case with Kakadu.

The park encloses much of the Tabletop Range, a rugged sandstone plateau with eroded cliffs which drop away to black-soil plains covered in spear grass. The dominant trees of the forest here are the Darwin woollybutt and the stringybark, while sand palms, acacias and banksias proliferate closer to the ground. Litchfield's most famous features are the waterfalls which tumble off the plateau at various points throughout the park. Often set in pockets of dense rainforest, they come with deep plunge pools at their bases, perfect for a refreshing dip following a walk. Wangi Falls are easily the most popular and can get very crowded. Tjaynera Falls are just as attractive and much quieter, as befits their more isolated location. Tolmer Falls are the most impressive, although you can only view them from the cliffs opposite.

The so-called Lost City is a jumble of sandstone pillars and blocks which in places resemble ruined buildings. Genuine man-made ruins are to be found elsewhere in the park in the form of the remains of an old homestead and of a tin mine which operated here in the 1870s. Billabong cruises on the Reynolds River are a good way of seeing Litchfield's abundant and colourful birdlife.

Wangi Falls

Nitmiluk National Park

The Katherine Gorge

The Jawoyn Aboriginal people own Nitmiluk National Park, which is situated near Katherine in the Northern Territory. The visitor centre features informative displays about the park, presented from their perspective. If their many stories and myths can seem a bit bewildering, you should take comfort from the fact that most 'whitefellas' are granted access to only a small part of their Dreamtime cosmology.

The big attraction at Nitmiluk is the Katherine Gorge, where the Katherine River has carved a spectacular 12-km (7.5-mi) course through the Arnhem Land plateau. Although described as 13 separate gorges, which are separated from each other by rapids of varying length (many of which are just rock bars during the dry season), this is really one continuous canyon which turns first this way then that, depending on the prevailing fault lines. The sheer gorge walls may not be especially tall, but when bathed in sunlight their orange hues present a gorgeous spectacle.

The best way to appreciate the gorge is from the water. If you are an intrepid spirit and possess the requisite energy you can explore the gorge under your own power in a canoe. But most visitors take one of the cruises on offer which travel upstream as far as the second, third or sixth gorge, depending on the length of the trip. It's not all plain sailing, though; there are places where you have to disembark for a scramble over rocks in order to board another boat further upriver. Although this sounds like hard work, it actually adds to the sense of adventure and you are given several opportunities to relax with a swim in the mercifully crocodile-free water.

HOW TO GET THERE:
The entrance to Nitmiluk is 30 km (19 mi) northeast of Katherine along a sealed road. There is a shuttle bus from the town to the visitor centre.
WHEN TO GO:
May to September
DON'T MISS:
The cliff-top lookout over the river near the visitor centre. It's a stiff climb but the views are superb.
YOU SHOULD KNOW:
In contrast to its neighbour Kakadu, Nitmiluk National Park actively encourages bushwalkers to tackle its range of marked trails.

Early morning in impressive Ormiston Gorge

Ormiston Gorge

The West MacDonnell Ranges in the heart of Australia boast a number of striking gorges and chasms. The deep shadows cast by their towering walls have made them important refuges for a rich variety of flora and fauna, including several relict plant species surviving from an ancient tropical past. Ormiston Gorge is perhaps the most impressive of all. The presence here of a permanent waterhole, up to 14 m (46 ft) deep, has generated a surprising range of habitats in a relatively confined area: slopes covered in spinifex, mulga woodland, rocky plains and stands of lofty red river gums.

If you come here on a tour from Alice you will probably walk up to the Gum Tree lookout which gives a fantastic view of the 250-m (820-ft) high gorge walls soaring over the pools below. But if this is all you do you will miss much of the magic of this spot; far better to come independently and prepared for a longer trek. The Ormiston Pound circular walk is particularly worthwhile. Starting at the information centre the route traverses rocky slopes before crossing the flat expanse of remote Ormiston Pound and returning down the gorge itself and past the waterhole – perfectly placed for a refreshing dip. The best time to do the walk is in the early morning when the sun lights up the mighty cliffs ahead.

The small campground at Ormiston Gorge is a good base for a longer exploration of the western half of the West MacDonnells. From here it is a good day's walk to Bowmans Gap, or two days to Mount Giles. Spending a night on the mountain is recommended for the stunning view at sunrise over Ormiston Pound to Mount Sonder and its surroundings.

HOW TO GET THERE:
Ormiston Gorge is 135 km (84 mi) west of Alice Springs.
WHEN TO GO:
April to October
DON'T MISS:
The unusual plants you can see here, many with exotic names like Maiden Hair Fern and Glory of the Centre Wedding Bush.
YOU SHOULD KNOW:
Not far from Ormiston is the bed of the Finke River. Dry for most of the year, the Finke is one of the world's most ancient rivers and is thought to have followed much the same course for the past 100 million years.

Simpson Desert

It doesn't come much bleaker than the Simpson Desert, 150,000 sq km (58,000 sq mi) of emptiness straddling the borders of the Northern Territory, South Australia and Queensland. Largely devoid of human activity and as inhospitable as it seems, anyone who has spent serious time in a desert will know that appearances are deceptive and that these environments possess a raw beauty all their own. Habitats you might expect to find, such as gibber plains and mulga scrub, are joined by more surprising ones like gidgee woodland and coolabah plains; these support a fragile but profuse ecosystem of some 800 plant species, 180 types of bird and over 90 different reptiles. If you are fortunate enough to visit immediately after a rare rainstorm you will find the Simpson transformed by carpets of wild flowers which emerge for a brief moment in the sun.

The reason most people come to the Simpson Desert, however, is the sand dunes; rows upon rows of them stretching to the horizon. The Simpson is one of the world's outstanding sand-ridge deserts; the dunes run parallel to one another in a direction dictated by prevailing winds. Crossing the Simpson Desert is one of the outback's great adventures but it is strictly for the experienced and well-equipped 4x4 traveller. The most direct route, the so-called French Line, is also the toughest since it strikes straight across the dunes in a punishing succession of climbs and descents, some as high as 40 m (130 ft).

You do not have to be an adrenalin junkie, though, to get a taste of the Simpson's endless expanses. There are 4x4 day tours from Alice Springs that follow the line of the original Ghan railway, taking you deep into the desert to sights like Rainbow Valley and the mighty sandstone column of Chambers Pillar.

HOW TO GET THERE:
Chambers Pillar, the furthest point of most day tours to the Simpson Desert, is 165 km (103 mi) south of Alice Springs.
WHEN TO GO:
April to September
DON'T MISS:
Don't be too surprised to see camels in the desert. They are the wild descendants of the original beasts brought here by Afghan cameleers before the Ghan railway reached Alice in 1928.
YOU SHOULD KNOW:
Most people crossing the Simpson on one of the long-distance tracks do so from west to east because the dunes' eastern slopes are steeper and therefore a tougher climb.

Sand dunes in Simpson Desert

Mount Remarkable National Park

HOW TO GET THERE:
Drive 45 km (28 mi) north of Port Pirie on Highway 1, then on to park headquarters at Mambray Creek – which is another 5 km (3 mi). The picturesque 13-km (8-mi) drive to Alligator Gorge is from Main Road North, just south of Wilmington. Hiking access to the park is from these two locations and also Melrose at the foot of Mount Remarkable itself.

WHEN TO GO:
Autumn to spring is the preferred time, when vegetation thrives, wildlife is active and the weather is mild. Reflecting this fact, bush camping is permitted from May to October only. Summer visits require serious preparation as the heat can be searing.

DON'T MISS:
The park's beautifully marked yellow-footed wallabies. After being hunted to near extinction for its fur, this delightful rock-hopper is still around – although in nothing like former numbers. They may be seen here because the park runs a conservation programme.

YOU SHOULD KNOW:
There is vehicle-based camping at Mambray Creek with facilities such as a water supply, flushing toilets, solar-heated showers and communal fireplaces (firewood supplied). Bush camping is restricted to 11 designated sites within the park. The Mambray Creek Cabin and lodge at Alligator Gorge must be booked in advance.

In the Southern Flinders Ranges, not far from Adelaide and South Australia's better-populated areas, the opportunity to explore a true wilderness awaits. Mount Remarkable National Park – named after the 960-m (3,150-ft) summit of the same name – offers splendid scenery in diverse terrain that stretches up from coastal plains west of the Flinders Ranges to foothills above the town of Wilmington.

The park is at the intersection of South Australia's two ecosystems – arid north and wetter south – making for interesting combinations of flora and fauna. Native vegetation includes assorted woodland containing trees such as eucalyptus, northern cypress pine, acacia, peppermint box, sugar gum and blue gum. Imposing river red gums line watercourses and there's a brilliant display of wildflowers in springtime. A diversity of wildlife ranges from kangaroos through over 100 bird species to numerous amphibians and reptiles such as the rare carpet python.

The variety of animals and plants adds interest to a rugged landscape that's a star in its own right. The eroded sandstone Mount Remarkable range dominates the park's eastern side. This massive hogsback has impressive outcrops, like Cathedral Rock, with vertical rock faces. To the west, the Alligator Syncline features Mount Cavern and Alligator Gorge. The latter is the top natural attraction in the South Flinders Ranges – a spectacular gorge between ragged quartzite walls, cut over countless millennia by Alligator Creek. The gorge floor is reached by steps and it's possible to go north to the rippled terraces of a fossilized lakeshore or south between red walls along creek banks green with moss gardens.

Mount Remarkable National Park has numerous hiking trails. These escalate from good short walks at Alligator Gorge and Melrose to the challenging long-distance Heysen Trail. Car parks at Mambray Creek and Blue Gum Flat near Alligator Gorge have excellent facilities, including trailheads.

Black Mountain (Kalkajaka) National Park

The name of this interesting national park on Cape York Peninsula in the remote far north of Queensland includes the bracketed Aboriginal name because the area is an important part of the indigenous Kuku Nyungkal people's culture – *kalkajaka* translating

Granite boulders covered in moss, algae and lichen

HOW TO GET THERE:
Start from Cooktown, serviced by two daily flights from Cairns. For old-fashioned outbackers, the park's entrance is 25 km (15 mi) to the south of Cooktown along the primitive but ambitiously named Cooktown Developmental Road. In fact, since 2006, a genuine modern development – the paved Mulligan Highway from Mareeba to Cooktown – has provided easier access.
WHEN TO GO:
Any time. The tropical climate can be hot, wet and humid but the coolest, driest months are June to September.
DON'T MISS:
The James Cook Museum in eponymous Cooktown, where the great explorer arrived as a lieutenant in command of *His Majesty's Bark the Endeavour* in 1770, steering his crippled ship into what became Cooktown Harbour at the mouth of the Endeavour River, to effect repairs after striking a reef. Housed in a grand former convent, it's rated as Australia's finest provincial museum. It has the anchor and cannon of *Endeavour* along with wide-ranging indigenous, pastoral and mining displays – plus a tribute to the Chinese immigrants who played an important role in the development of Cooktown back in Victorian gold-rush days.
YOU SHOULD KNOW:
Serious hikers take note – Cooktown is the northern trailhead for the Bicentennial Heritage Trail. It's as well to make an early start, because the southern terminus is 5,330 km (3,310 mi) away in Healesville, not far from Melbourne. This is the world's longest such trail, running the length of the Great Dividing Range and following old stock routes, wagon roads, river banks and fire trails through Queensland, New South Wales and Victoria. Originally intended for horse riders, it is now tempting hardy walkers and mountain-bikers in whole or part (mostly part!).

as 'spear place'. The prosaic English description is more explicit as the park features an imposing mountain range that appears to be, well, black. In fact, that should read blue-green, because the jumbled pile of massive granite blocks is covered with a film of algae that absorbs light and looks darker than it is from afar. That said, contrasting white patches stand out vividly from their surroundings where boulders have fractured (sometimes explosively) as a result of erosion exacerbated by extreme heat. A few patches of stubborn greenery also intrude on the rocky slopes.

The park is at the top of the UNESCO Wet Tropics of Queensland World Heritage Site in northeastern Queensland's section of the Great Dividing Range, where it meets drier savannah woodlands. The resulting 'Black Mountain' environment has a unique combination of flora and fauna, supporting at least three species – the rock-haunting frog, Black-Mountain gecko and Black-Mountain skink – found nowhere else in Australia. Other interesting creatures include ghost bats and Godman's rock wallabies.

There are excellent observation points for those who simply want to stroll and look (binoculars essential), but anyone getting in among the park's intriguing landscape of monolithic boulders – many the size of houses and stacked in a way that apparently defies gravity – should take sensible backcountry precautions. There are age-old Aboriginal legends and a number of sacred sites, but white incomers soon added their own tales of horses, cattle and even prospectors who entered the Black Mountains in the 19th century . . . never to be seen again.

Carnarvon Gorge

HOW TO GET THERE:
Drive from Brisbane to Roma – 400 km (250 mi). Proceed via Injune in the direction of Emerald until reaching the signed Carnarvon Gorge turn-off – another 200 km (125 mi). Then it's another 20 km (12 mi) along an unpaved road to the gorge itself, which may become impassable after heavy rain. Nobody said it was easy!

WHEN TO GO:
Whenever. The coolest months are April to October. The driest months are July, August and September. February is the wettest month but the climate can be unpredictable at any time of year.

DON'T MISS:
The Amphitheatre, behind the ancient rock wall of Carnarvon Gorge. Entered through a narrow vertical crack, this incredible crevice can only be described as awe-inspiring – and anyone who raises their voice will find that it has the most amazing acoustics, too.

YOU SHOULD KNOW:
Visitors are forbidden to feed the birds, although many ignore this regulation. As a result, bold and opportunistic species such as the laughing kookaburra and pied currawong have become proficient scroungers and developed unnaturally large populations at the expense of less brazen birds, also consuming more than their fair share of natural food resources. Resist their determined advances!

Carnarvon Gorge

In southern-central Queensland, Carnarvon Gorge is the centrepiece of the national park that bears its name. Hidden in rugged uplands of the Great Dividing Range, this 2,900-sq-km (1,120-sq-mi) preserve not only encompasses the mountains but also the inaccessible and heavily vegetated Consuelo Tableland. This is a place where truly awesome landscape vistas roll away in every direction, although most visitors hurry to the enclosed world of Carnarvon Gorge – and what a wonderful world it is for those sufficiently determined to get there. This requires effort (see left) but around 65,000 people make the pilgrimage every year and are well rewarded.

The gorge is 30 km (19 mi) long and 600 m (2,000 ft) deep at the mouth, carved into sandstone by the passage of water and time. Most visitors get no further than the first 10 km (6 mi), as this stretch offers a wonderful variety of natural and cultural features that would require weeks of extended travel and exploration to experience anywhere else in the state, if they could be found at all. The main trail follows the limpid creek where platypus may be seen diving into pools, while an extensive network of graded side trails perambulates through tall eucalyptus trees and lush greenery that includes palms and giant ferns. Side gorges and waterfalls abound, offering exciting voyages of discovery. More remote tracks, including Devil's Signpost and Battleship Spur, are for experienced hikers only.

Carnarvon Gorge is alive with birds – 180 species from the tiny weebill to the mighty wedge-tailed eagle – and home to a fascinating range of animals. To the natural sights and sounds may be added appreciation of the spiritual ambiance of the gorge, as expressed in sacred places such as Cathedral Cave and Art Gallery, where Aboriginal rock art may be seen.

Great Barrier Reef

Great Barrier Reef, Queensland

It's a UNESCO World Heritage Site and has been voted one of the seven natural wonders of the world. Queensland's Great Barrier Reef in the appropriately named Coral Sea is in fact a conglomeration of nearly 3,000 individual reefs and 900 islands stretching for more than 2,600 km (1,600 mi), covering an area of around 345,000 sq km (133,200 sq mi). Bramble Cay, at the top end of the reef in the Torres Straits, is the northernmost point of land in Australia. The reef's southern extremity is Lady Elliot Island, off the city of Bundaberg, around halfway down Australia's east coast.

This vast natural treasure house supports a huge variety of life, too numerous to list in detail but including headliners like whales, dolphins, porpoises, dugongs, sea turtles, sharks, stingrays, seahorses and over 1,500 fish species, plus 200 types of bird that visit or breed on the reef's islands. The majority of the reef is protected by the Great Barrier Reef Marine Park, which seeks to ensure that human intrusion becomes neither excessive nor damaging. Even so, tourism is of major importance to the local economy, with a large number of visitors drawn to the Queensland coast by the opportunity to experience a little piece of this magical marine masterpiece.

Many of them holiday at eco-resorts on reef islands – around 30 cays now have such facilities – while others come simply to look and marvel. The ways of so doing are many and varied, ranging from boat trips in regular or glass-bottomed boats to helicopter overflights, day trips or longer cruises. There are even underwater observatories. But the most popular activity by far is getting up close and personal by snorkelling or scuba diving, often from live-aboard dive boats. Although tourism is economically vital, it is carefully policed to protect the reef for posterity.

HOW TO GET THERE:
Bundaberg rejoices in the title 'Gateway to the Great Barrier Reef' and is an excellent base for offshore exploration. The Whitsunday Islands are another major tourist centre, as is Cairns in Far North Queensland.

WHEN TO GO:
The reef is an all-season destination, with winter seeing the most visitors. June to September are the driest months, October to March the hottest.

DON'T MISS:
The Mon Repos Conservation Park on the mainland near Bundaberg, which has the largest concentration of nesting marine turtles in eastern Australia, including the most important nesting population of loggerheads. Laying season is November to March, but the best period to observe nesting turtles on the beach is from mid November to February. Hatchlings emerge and head for the sea between mid January and late March.

YOU SHOULD KNOW:
It's not only man-made climate change and pollution that is threatening the Great Barrier Reef – nature poses a threat too, as periodic upsurges in the population of crown-of-thorns starfish pose a constant threat to the reef's wellbeing. These spiny sea stars prey on the coral polyps that form the living reef and a single starfish can destroy 6 sq m (65 sq ft) of coral in a year.

Kanangra-Boyd National Park

The extensive Blue Mountains Wilderness is west of Sydney. Some of the most inaccessible terrain in this wilderness – and New South Wales – can be found in Kanangra-Boyd National Park. The scenic park provides almost limitless potential for those self-reliant souls who love solitude to indulge their passion for lonesome wild places.

It has two sections. The gently undulating Boyd Plateau is relatively accessible, has stunning views and offers everything from gentle strolls to stimulating day hikes. An unmade road leads to a campsite at Boyd River and on to the Kanangra Walls area. These are ideal bases for bushwalking or simply enjoying stunning distant views from the rim of the plateau. Some of those views roll away across the labyrinthine Kanangra wilderness area, a broken jumble of thickly vegetated valleys, overgrown streams and sandstone cliffs that stretches for 60 km (37 mi). This empty backcountry should be tackled only by the most experienced and self-reliant of bushwalkers – ideally those also possessing climbing skills.

The park's best-known features are Kanangra Walls –
spectacular orange-and-grey sandstone cliffs that tower above the
shadowed Kanangra Creek Gorge below – and the 225-m (740-ft)
Kanangra Falls, a scenic cascade that spills down an angled rock
face. The car park at Kanangra Walls is the starting point for most
of the park's established walks, including the wheelchair-friendly
path to the first lookout or a stroll down to the nearby falls. The
established Plateau Walk is longer, delivering awesome views of
Kanangra Walls, Falls and surrounding cliffs. Longer hikes lead out
along the Gangerang Range to Mount Cloudmaker and on as far as
Kaloomba, or south to the Gingra Range and thence to the
Kowmung River. It's all wild and wonderful, and the views alone are
worth the effort needed to reach this remote place.

*A lookout point offers
spectacular views over
Kanangra-Boyd National Park.*

*Washpool's rainforest is both
varied and original.*

Washpool National Park

This is the destination *par excellence* for wilderness walkers who like hugging trees, serving as a happy reminder that the interior of Australia may be relatively empty but it's definitely not all arid desert. Washpool National Park in Australia's New England protects some of the most varied and original rainforest in New South Wales, including now-rare Australian red cedars and (wait for it!) the world's largest stand of coachwood trees.

The park was established in 1983 and is an important part of the UNESCO Gondwana Rainforests of Australia World Heritage Site, which underlines the ecological importance of this unique area with its lush flora and interesting fauna. A dramatic landscape of steep gorges, broad ridges, pristine waters and forested escarpments is a haven for threatened animals like the koala, parma wallaby and spotted-tailed quoll, a beautiful cat-like marsupial. It is also a rich habitat for birds, with nearly 150 different species recorded in this unspoilt 650-sq-km (250-sq-mi) reserve.

Washpool National Park offers walking trails to suit every level of fitness and ability, including some limited wheelchair access on short sections of surfaced tracks from the car parks. But the park's true beauty can only be appreciated fully by those willing to venture away from the immediate environs of the highway. The four-hour Washpool Walk regularly features towards the top of lists nominating this wild-at-heart continent's best short wilderness hikes. This inspiring trek takes visitors along twisting paths beside

HOW TO GET THERE:
Washpool is 75 km (47 mi) northeast of Glen Innes and 90 km (56 mi) west of Grafton. It is 500 km (310 mi) north of Sydney. Access is from the Gwydir Highway, taking Coachwood Drive via Gibraltar Range National Park, itself a distracting alternative.

WHEN TO GO:
Whenever – there is no worst time.

DON'T MISS:
The Coombadjha Nature Stroll, linking the picnic areas and campsite of the same name (see below). The track along Coombadjha Creek has signs that provide an informative introduction to the park's features – and there's a delightful shallow pool where swimming is allowed.

rushing boulder-filled streams and through awesome rainforest beneath canopies of tree ferns, accompanied by the distinctive call of bellbirds. For the serious backpacker, the Gibraltar-Washpool World Heritage Walk encompasses an 80-km (50-mi) network of hiking tracks that can occupy up to five days of rewarding exploration in rugged mountain country above the Clarence River Valley on the edge of the Northern Tablelands. Despite difficult terrain – ridges, tors, dry and wet forest, streams and wild rivers, waterfalls and swamps – this walk can be tackled by anyone who is reasonably fit.

YOU SHOULD KNOW:
Two campgrounds serve as basecamps for those undertaking extensive exploration. They are at Coombadjha and Bellbird. The former is at the end of the aforementioned Coachwood Drive and features the beautiful Washpool Walk, a signed 8-km (5-mi) round trip through rainforest. Bellbird is on Coombadjha Road off the Gwydir Highway. Both have basic facilities, including bring-your-own-firewood barbecues.

Yengo Wilderness

As part of the Greater Blue Mountains World Heritage Site, the newly established Yengo National Park stretches for over 70 km (45 mi) from Wisemans Ferry to the Hunter Valley, much of it remote wilderness characterized by predominantly sandstone gorges and rocky ridges. The park is rich in cultural heritage and Mount Yengo, in particular, is sacred to local Aboriginal communities who co-manage the park. The area is still criss-crossed with their traditional routes, established over thousands of years. The Finchley Cultural Walk from Finchley campgrounds leads to an Aboriginal engraving site and has explanatory signs.

The habitat is mainly eucalypt forest – dry on ridge tops and northern slopes, wet in gullies and on southern slopes. There are smaller areas of wet and dry rainforest and some open woodland. Wildlife to watch out for includes koalas, wombats, gliding possums, geckoes and endangered brush-tailed rock-wallabies. A disparate assortment of over 150 bird species has been recorded, including wedge-tailed eagles, masked owls, rare regent honeyeaters, lyre birds and black cockatoos.

Numerous opportunities for short walks exist and there are overnight hiking routes for experienced walkers. Scenic car tours for those disinclined to go afoot, such as the Finchley-Yango-Boree loop that starts near Laguna and gives an excellent overview of the dry sandstone terrain, are well worthwhile. Another scenic drive goes from St Albans via Mogo Creek Road to Bucketty, taking in extensive wetlands and historic Deans Quarry, plus the pleasant must-stop-for-lunch Mogo Creek Picnic Area. Tough types can do the 4x4/trailbike/mountain-bike Big Yango Loop Trail that circles Mount Yengo, with great views over the wilderness area, or tackle the Howes-Yango Trail across the northern section of the park – a five-hour return trip driving a sturdy 4x4. A number of the park's unmade roads are open to vehicle traffic.

HOW TO GET THERE:
From Sydney drive via Wisemans Ferry and the historic township of St Albans to Mogo Campground and Bucketty. For the Big Yango/Finchley area use the F3, take the Peats Ridge exit and go through Central Mangrove and Bucketty to find Yango Creek Road. From Newcastle drive via Cessnock to Bucketty and Mogo Campground, or for the Big Yango/Finchley area take the Wollombi Road from Cessnock.

WHEN TO GO:
Take your pick – summers are very hot, winters are cooler. The heaviest rainfall occurs between December and January.

DON'T MISS:
The awesome vista to Mount Yengo across an expanse of eucalypt dry forest from Finchley Lookout, which has information boards explaining surrounding landforms and much more besides. The lookout is reached from Yango Creek Road, off George Downs Drive near Laguna township.

YOU SHOULD KNOW:
The historic Old Great North Road is a hugely impressive example of 19th-century convict road building that follows the park's southeastern boundary. Note, especially, the sturdy stone remains of the historic Circuit Flat Bridge dating from 1831, which remained in use until the 1930s but has now lost its timber roadway. Ironically, conservation work was done on the bridge in the 1990s by a prison crew from St Heliers Correctional Centre in the Hunter Valley.

Murray-Sunset National Park

HOW TO GET THERE:
Those starting from Melbourne or Adelaide are in for a long drive. Once in northwest Victoria the park can be approached from Red Cliffs, Mildura and Renmark in the north or Murrayville and Ouyen in the south. The Sturt Highway passes through the park's northern section but the remainder is remote wilderness bounded to the south by the Mallee Highway and to the west by the Calder Highway.
WHEN TO GO:
Summer temperatures are very high and anyone bold enough to think of going during the scorching months may find the park has been closed for safety reasons, should a Code Red (Catastrophic) Fire Danger Rating be in force.

Close to South Australia and New South Wales in northwestern Victoria is the state's second-largest national park. This protects one of the last semi-arid regions in Australia that has almost (but not entirely) escaped human interference – there was once a salt production industry and residual evidence of gypsum mining remains. But that's a pinprick set against Murray-Sunset National Park's impressive 6,300-sq-km (2,430-sq-mi) expanse of untouched wilderness. The flattish landscape is filled with grasslands, mallee eucalypts, porcupine grass, saltbush and buloke, broken by stands of native cypress-pine and belah woodlands. River red gums line creeks and black boxwoods surround flood plains. The park has four salt lakes – the Pink Lakes, so called because of their colour in late summer when they've dried out to leave a crust of carotene-tinted salt.

The Pink Lakes - so named due to their colour in late summer when they dry out to leave a crust of carotene-tinted salt.

There are first-class walking trails in the Pink Lakes area, but Murray-Sunset National Park deserves a longer stay. The campground on the shore of Lake Crosbie has good facilities, including a supply of scarce-in-the-park clean drinking water. There are alternative campgrounds at Rocket Lake, Lake Becking, Mount Crozier and Mopoke Hut. Accommodation can also be booked at an old shearer's hut. There are remote campsites with primitive facilities in the wilderness. Those are the very best places to truly appreciate the park's vast isolation and enjoy its wide-open landscapes, incredible sunsets and brilliantly lit starry night skies.

Although vehicles are prohibited in the park's remoter areas and wilderness zones, a number of unmade roads are suitable for road cars – notably the Pink Lakes Track from Linga, Settlement Track along the northern boundary and access roads to Lindsay Island or the Murray River. Beyond that there are numerous routes suitable for exploration with the help of a 4x4. But all tracks are liable to become impassable during or after adverse weather conditions.

DON'T MISS:
Red kangaroos. The park is one of the few areas in Victoria where these iconic creatures can be seen in anything like their original numbers.

YOU SHOULD KNOW:
Campers should not pitch tents or rest up beneath or near river red gum trees, tempting though the cooling shade they cast along creek banks may be. These mighty trees grow to 45 m (150 ft) in height but they can and do quite often drop heavy branches without warning.

Wilsons Promontory

HOW TO GET THERE:
Wilsons Promontory is 200 km (125 mi) from Melbourne, using the South Gippsland Highway. After turning south at Meeniyan for Fish Creek (or going on to Foster before turning right) the destination is Yanakie, just outside the national park and the last place to stock up on essentials (the general store at Tidal River offers only the most basic of supplies). Tidal River is 30 km (19 mi) inside the park boundary. There are weekend and public holiday bus services to and from Tidal River, departing from Foster and going via Fish Creek.

WHEN TO GO:
Outside the prime summer high season is favourite, to avoid the uncertainty of entering the lottery for accommodation (see below) and the period when the park's at its busiest.

DON'T MISS:
The view from the top of Mount Oberon for a wonderful panoramic outlook over Tidal River, rugged coastline and the green interior with its rainforest, woodlands and heathlands. Happily, the uphill hike isn't too hard.

YOU SHOULD KNOW:
So popular is Wilsons Promontory – and so determined are park authorities that it should never be overrun with tourists – that accommodation in self-catering cabins, group lodges and campgrounds at Tidal River during prime summer weeks from Christmas to the end of January is subject to an online ballot held the previous June. However, this does not apply to the park's tented wilderness retreats (luxurious safari camping without the need to bring equipment) or primitive backcountry campsites. Outside the ballot period all accommodation can and should be booked in advance to avoid disappointment. However, that may still happen – the park has a high fire risk and may be closed at short notice if an ominous Code Red (Catastrophic) Fire Danger Rating comes into force.

Perhaps appropriately for such a vast and relatively empty continent, the southernmost point on the Australian mainland is the largest remaining coastal wilderness in the state of Victoria. Colloquially known as 'The Prom' by Victorians, Wilsons Promontory is an unspoiled peninsula jutting into the Bass Strait that boasts a stunning 130-km (80-mi) girdle of inspiring coastline consisting of bold granite headlands, tumbled boulders, sheltered coves, intertidal mudflats, dunes, swamps . . . and beautiful beaches. It has been protected since the late 19th century and is now a national park.

One Tidal River is just what the name suggests, swelling with each tide as it discharges into Norman Bay. The river water has a strange purple-yellow colour as a result of tannin emanating from the large number of tea trees in the area. The other Tidal River is the immediately adjacent settlement that serves as a focal point for visitors, not least because it has one of the park's finest sandy beaches. Also, the drive from Yanakie to Tidal River is super-scenic (don't hurry, abundant local wildlife that includes assorted marsupials, kangaroos, wallabies, koalas and emus is liable to stray onto the road).

The park's information centre at Tidal River has a wealth of information on the park's history – from Aboriginal occupation going back at least 6,500 years to the activities of rough-and-ready sealers in the early 19th century – plus general displays on the park's geology, flora and fauna. This is also the place to learn about disabled access to nearby sites such as Squeaky Beach (named for the sound made when tramping the fine white quartz sand) and the Lilly Pilly nature walk. For those adventurers who wish to look beyond Tidal Bay's siren attractions, there are stimulating wilderness hiking trails that require overnight camping.

The beautiful coastal wilderness of Wilsons Promontory

Bay of Fires

The wild and wonderful coastline known as the Bay of Fires offers fascinating opportunities to explore an unspoilt wilderness coastline and experience the rich diversity of backing woodlands. The bay is on Tasmania's northeastern coast, extending from Eddystone Point to Binalong Bay. Some falls within Mount William National Park while the rest is a conservation area. This is a place of white beaches that shimmer in the sun, intense blue water and orange-splashed granite (the colour coming from lichen).

The northern section is from Eddystone Point to the Ansons Bay outlet, which cannot be crossed. This is in the national park and can be accessed from Eddystone Road, just before the lighthouse. There's a brisk walk across dunes to the shore and visitors should take all necessary supplies, especially drinking water. This is for day use only but Deep Creek campground is close to Eddystone Point.

The middle section encompasses Ansons Bay and is the destination of choice for those who want to spend time communing with nature. The primitive Policemans Points campground offers numerous sites scattered among the trees, many with direct beach access, but happy campers will become unhappy unless they bring everything necessary for their stay, including a portable loo – there are no on-site toilets, no water nor firewood, no rubbish collection. The southern section stretches from The Gardens to Binalong Bay and has several campsites, but again they offer no facilities other than pitches.

This is an outdoor paradise with activities to match – messing about on beaches, swimming, snorkelling, surfing, fishing, boating, camping, birdwatching and walking. These pleasurable pastimes may be possible in many places, but in the case of the breathtaking Bay of Fires it is not what but where – it's the environment that counts and, for those who crave it, the blessing of solitude is guaranteed.

Orange lichen gives the rocks their striking colour along the coastline of the Bay of Fires.

HOW TO GET THERE:
Travel north on minor roads (some paved, some not) from St Helens, which is on the A3 Tasman Way between Scottsdale and St Marys.

WHEN TO GO:
Tasmania's weather is unpredictable and the climate not only varies in different parts of the island but also from day to day. Winters (May to August) can be quite cool and summers are pleasantly warm with long twilit evenings.

DON'T MISS:
The opportunity while on this light-pollution-free island to observe the magnificent *Aurora Australis*, the Southern Lights. It's one of the wonders of the cosmos and, short of travelling to Antarctica, Tasmania is one of the best places in the world from which to view this extraordinary light show. Prime months are April and October but the lights can switch on at any time.

YOU SHOULD KNOW:
The Bay of Fires was so named in 1773 by one Tobias Furneaux, a Royal Navy officer who was part of Captain Cook's second expedition and became the first man to circumnavigate the world in both directions. He was also first to chart much of Tasmania and decided to pen 'Bay of Fires' onto his embryonic chart upon observing a large number of Aboriginal fires burning along the shoreline. Aboriginal middens (shell and bone deposits) are found in the dunes and should not be disturbed.

Ninety Mile Beach

HOW TO GET THERE:
Follow State Highway 1 north to Kaitaia and on up the Aupori Peninsula. Pretty much every left turn thereafter would lead to Ninety Mile Beach – if there were any. But there is beach access at Ahipara in the south, from Waipapakauri in the middle and along the Te Paki stream bed in the north.

WHEN TO GO:
Any time, although winter (June, July and August) occasionally sees the main road closed owing to floods or landslips.

DON'T MISS:
Notable landmarks during the beach drive from south to north are an impressive outcrop of lignite embedded in sand near the mouth of the Waihai Stream (which should be crossed with care!); a pack track across the dunes at Hukatere; and the Bluff – ellipsoidal lava flows with bands of quartz connected to the mainland at low tide via a sand causeway.

YOU SHOULD KNOW:
Oops – it turns out that Ninety Mile Beach is only 55 mi (88 km) long after all. The culprits responsible for the misnomer are thought to be early missionaries who counted a day's journey on horseback as 30 mi (48 km). It took three days to get along the beach so they made it 90 miles, failing to take account of the slower progress of horses plodding through sand.

Forget the perennial problem of finding somewhere to lay down that fleecy towel without treading on another sunbather – as the name suggests, Ninety Mile Beach has room for just about everyone in New Zealand, then some. This extraordinary beach is located on the west coast of the North Island's far north Northland, which still makes it quite far south by international standards. A stunning expanse of white sand arches along Aupori Peninsula from just west of Kaitaia, terminating at the rocky headland of Scott Point near Cape Reinga at the northernmost tip of New Zealand.

Ninety Mile Beach faces the Tasman Sea and is backed by dunes up to 6.5 km (4 mi) wide and up to 140 m (460 ft) tall. They are higher at the northern end, where they resemble nothing so much as the Sahara Desert when approached from the landward side. The dunes steadily decrease in height towards the south where they are stabilized by marram grass and lupins, but elsewhere they are bare but for occasional patches of scrub and constantly being reshaped by the wind. This austere 260-sq-km (100-mi-sq) sea of sand is a lonely wilderness that may soon become pine forests.

There are beachside campgrounds and motels at the southern end, but as a whole Ninety Mile Beach is a wild and lonely natural wonder. Getting onto the beach isn't actually that easy, with few access roads. The best way to see it is to drive. Warning signs suggest that Ninety Mile Beach is a potentially hazardous place for anything with four wheels, particularly for a couple of hours either side of high tide, but it was used as a runway for early airmail flights in the 1930s and with reasonable care provides a perfectly usable scenic highway and a wonderful outdoor adventure.

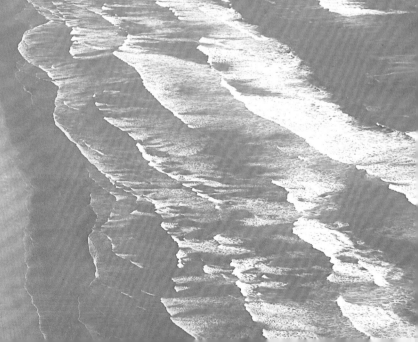

Ninety Mile Beach

Bay of Islands

Close to the northern tip of New Zealand's North Island, in the appropriately named Northland Region, lies the beautiful natural feature that seduced the first European settlers to arrive in the country. Captain Cook named the Bay of Islands after coming upon this natural harbour in 1769. Whalers soon followed, whose profane ways attracted missionaries. The first European child to be born in New Zealand was delivered there in 1815 and the towns around the bay are rich in national heritage sites.

The bay area is as attractive to people today as it was then. This irregular inlet on the northeastern coast is 16 km (10 mi) wide with several arms that extend inland. It is a special destination and its pristine environment attracts plenty of visitors all year round, drawn by wonderful coastal scenery and the opportunity to enjoy a variety of activities from simply romping on white sand beaches to cruising, boating, sailing, sea kayaking, swimming with dolphins and whale-watching. Other popular possibilities are paragliding, jet boating, big-game fishing, scuba diving, snorkelling, cycling, bushwalking, horseback trekking and camping.

But despite the plethora of recreational temptations, the Bay of Islands Marine Park has 144 islands that remain a natural wonderland of native forests, secluded bays and subtropical beaches. This ensures that there are always lonely corners to be found, where those who value solitude can escape the tourist zone. This is particularly true for anyone who goes afloat, exploring the islands until finding a suitably remote spot to land, like an early pioneer stepping ashore for the first time.

In addition to abundant natural charms, the bay is something of a cultural centre, with pleasant towns like Paihia, Russell, Opua, Kerikeri and Waitangi offering craft galleries, museums and heritage trails. There are numerous opportunities to explore Maori culture, too.

Moturua Island, Bay of Islands

HOW TO GET THERE:
The bay is around 60 km (37 mi) northwest of Whangarei. Take State Highway 1 to Kawakawa and turn right for Russell. There are daily flights into Bay of Islands Airport at Kerikeri from all major centres in New Zealand.

WHEN TO GO:
The bay area often experiences fairly heavy summer rainfall in December. It's best to avoid mid December to early February anyway, as school holidays see a serious influx of camper vans, tourists and noisy children. The winter months (June, July and August) are much quieter and a good bet for those who don't like sharing wild places with too many others.

DON'T MISS:
The Mission House (also known as Kemp House) in Kerikeri. This weather-boarded structure with a wraparound veranda is New Zealand's oldest standing building, dating back to 1822.

YOU SHOULD KNOW:
The Bay of Islands has the second-bluest sky in the world, second only to the intense dome above the Brazil's Rio de Janeiro, and that's official. This ensures that the bay's waters, too, are a brilliant blue.

Waipoua Forest

Early navigators soon discovered that New Zealand had one priceless asset – kauri trees. These magnificent straight-growing conifers were ideal for the replacement of masts and spars and also – having great rot-resistant properties – hulls and decking. It didn't take long for emergency ship repairs to be replaced by small-scale commercial logging, which became large-scale commercial logging as the new British colony developed during the 19th century. If the forests weren't logged, they were burned by Maoris and settlers to clear land for farming. Serious logging continued right up to the scandalous decision to clear-fell Warawara state forest in the 1960s. Result? Almost all native kauri forests have been lost to the saw or fire, with only around four per cent of the original stock of these noble trees remaining, mostly in small pockets.

Kauri trees are not necessarily the most abundant species in the forests that bear their name but that merely encourages the huge variety of flora that flourishes beneath spreading crowns. The best opportunity to roam original kauri woodlands with their lush undergrowth – and appreciate what so much of New Zealand was once like – is at Waipoua Forest, although happily around three quarters of Warawara to the north survived after logging was stopped in 1972 following a huge public outcry. Together with neighbouring Waima and Mataraua Forests, Waipoua is the largest remaining tract of native forest in the Northland and home to a large population of nocturnal brown kiwi.

A road through the forest passes impressive kauri stands and provides a wonderful feel for the place. Beyond that, there are plenty of established walks and tramping tracks, ranging from short scenic strolls to long hikes that require overnight bush camping. Full details of these may be obtained at the information centre in Dargaville, where the Waipoua Forest Visitor Centre is also located. The Hokianga Visitor Centre in Omapere is also worth a visit.

Tree ferns grow among the largest remaining stand of mature Kauri forest.

HOW TO GET THERE:
State Highway 12 passes through the middle of Waipoua Forest. It lies to the north of Dargaville and south of Omapere.

WHEN TO GO:
This is a relaxing all-season destination.

DON'T MISS:
The super bonus of the Kauri Coast. The forest touches the sea but its trees give their name to a much longer stretch of headlands, wild beaches with pounding surf, sculpted sand dunes and imposing stands of kauri trees. It should be explored!

YOU SHOULD KNOW:
The country's most famous kauri trees are a major attraction in Waipoua Forest and easily reached from the main road. Tane Mahuta, named after a Maori forest god, is the biggest living kauri. This magnificent tree soars to over 50 m (165 ft) and has a massive girth of nearly 14 m (46 ft). Te Matua Ngahere (Father of the forest) is shorter but fatter, with a girth of 16.5 m (54 ft). A kauri with a circumference of 22 m (72 ft) was felled at Mercury Bay in 1870, ending around 1,500 years of life.

Coromandel Peninsula

Not far from New Zealand's largest city in distance – but a world apart in terms of both ambiance and population – the happy-go-lucky Coromandel Peninsula is separated from the bustling North-Island metropolis of Auckland by Hauraki Gulf. This sparsely populated spur offers awesome scenery, extending for more than 80 km (50 mi) from its starting point at the Karangahake Gorge, a deep fissure at the southern end of the peninsula's mountainous spine, the Coromandel range.

A world apart, when just 55 km (35 mi) of water separates the two? You bet. Coromandel's inhabitants are concentrated in relatively small settlements, with only Thames having a population of more than 5,000. What's more, these historic communities are clustered along the southwestern and southeastern coasts, with population density decreasing rapidly towards the northern tip of the peninsula. The hilly interior is almost completely undeveloped, with steep slopes largely covered in rainforest. Much of the Coromandel range is protected as a lush forest park, providing a challenging opportunity for adventurous bushwalking. But those who prefer to be beside the sea will be gratified to discover long stretches of dramatic coastline where rocky headlands punctuate deserted beaches, with the added bonus of many scenic offshore islands. One highlight should be digging (and relaxing in) a natural spa bath on aptly named Hot Water Beach.

Either way, ecotourism is the local buzz phrase, and many former residents of Auckland have relocated to the southern end of the Coromandel Peninsula in search of the good life and now commute. Residents and visitors alike revel in open-air activities such as surfing, swimming, diving, fishing, kayaking, boating, windsurfing and horse riding – not to mention enjoying the laid-back café society for which towns like Coromandel have become famous.

HOW TO GET THERE:
A good starting point for exploring the peninsula is Thames, which has good road links with Auckland to the north and Tauranga to the south. Thereafter the only roads on offer are State Highways 25 and 25A that loop around the peninsula's shoreline, plus a few minor dead ends and a network of lanes (many unsealed) in the far north. The roads can get busy in summer.

WHEN TO GO:
An all-season destination, but lovers of wild places should note that the Coromandel Peninsula gets very busy during long Christmas holidays (to the end of January) when many active Aucklanders take summer vacations in small towns like Whangamata, Whitianga, Pauanui and Matarangi. But even in high season it's not hard to chase solitude on the peninsula.

DON'T MISS:
The Cathedral Cove recreational reserve with its famous rock arch (now closed – health and safety rules even in New Zealand). Never mind, this loop walk from the end of Grange Road in Hahei still gives access to Gemstone Bay, Stingray Bay and Cathedral Cove's beautiful sand beach. Here is some of the most spectacular coastal scenery on the North Island.

YOU SHOULD KNOW:
The quirky Driving Creek Railway near Coromandel Town in the northwest offers an amazing one-hour return journey through kauri forest via two spirals, three short tunnels and five reversing points up to a mountain-top terminus called – with typical New Zealand humour – the Eyefull Tower. The panoramic view of forested valleys and mountains, coupled with a great outlook over island-studded Hauraki Gulf is pretty special.

Beautiful Cathedral Cove on the Coromandel Peninsula

Waimangu Volcanic Valley

Stand by to be wowed by another world superlative – the globe's youngest geothermal system, the Waimangu Volcanic Valley to the south of Rotorua. As a bonus, the world's largest hot-water spring also awaits (the sizzling Frying Pan) beside the ominously titled Inferno Crater. This protected scenic reserve and wildlife refuge is set in pristine bush country. An extraordinary new landscape was shaped by the eruption of Mount Tarawera in 1886 and the valley now consists of seven craters. Tarawera split in half, opening up a 16-km (10-mi) rift valley and reshaping the landscape into a weird and colourful volcanic wonderland soon to be colonized by verdant vegetation and wildlife, notably wallabies and black swans normally found only in Australia, introduced with help from 19th-century governor and premier of New Zealand, Sir George Grey.

This geothermal masterpiece was named for the Waimangu Geyser, first seen in 1900. It was another top dog, namely the world's most powerful geyser. But four years later it stopped as suddenly as it had started, although not before claiming the lives of two over-curious couples who wanted a closer look and thought they knew better than their guide. It's perfectly possible to make unassisted visits to Waimangu, but local companies offer assorted guided tours for those who prefer not to go it alone.

A paid-for outing usually includes a fascinating cruise on Lake Rotomahana, notable for exotic birdlife and smoking geothermal features of its own. The lake consists of 15 interlinked craters and is the deepest on the North Island. Serious hikers should take the Mount Hazard Trail from the Inferno Crater. This elevated route offers fabulous views down onto the valley floor and across a wider landscape that includes Rainbow Mountain, Mount Tarawera and Lake Rotomahana.

The steaming Waimangu Volcanic Valley

Kahurangi National Park

Beach at Kohaihai River Mouth

It's wild, it's new, it's big, it's exciting – it's New Zealand's latest national park, occupying most of the northwestern corner of the South Island. Kahurangi National Park extends to 4,500 sq km (1,740 sq mi) – a vast wilderness area offering a huge variety of landscapes from rocky coastline to wild rivers, glaciated mountains to deep valley floors, plateaus to alpine meadows. Many spectacular landforms include areas of marble and granite sculpted into tortured shapes, arches and caves by the relentless action of water.

Wonderfully diverse terrain provides an ideal habitat for more than half of New Zealand's 2,400 native plant species. Palms on the coast impart a tropical look, while the vegetation changes from podocarp forest with lush undergrowth in the west to beech forest in the east. There's a thriving bird population that includes iconic species such as the great-spotted kiwi and blue duck. Among the less appealing wildlife are giant cave spiders and carnivorous giant snails that luckily prefer worms to people. A number of programmes will initially protect and hopefully enhance threatened flora and fauna in various areas of the park.

Kahurangi National Park is definitely a destination for two types of visitor, who may actually be one and the same. For this is a place where those who revel in outdoor recreational activities will be well served, as will self-sufficiency types who have the opportunity to heft a backpack into the Tasman Wilderness Area and get away from the stresses and strains of modern life. Demanding caving, kayaking and rafting are popular, while the Karamea River is renowned for trout fishing. A network of walking and hiking trails begins with short strolls from roadends through half- and full-day walks to week-long expeditions. The park has many backcountry huts and several campsites.

HOW TO GET THERE:
State Route 6 runs along the south of the park, while the coastal State Route 60 runs up beside the park to its northern extremity (both from Nelson). A road up the water from Westport (indeed to the west of the park) goes to Karamea and on to a dead end at Oparara. There are no roads but some unsealed vehicle tracks in the park itself. The gateway towns are Motueka, Takaka, Karamea, Tapawera and Murchison.

WHEN TO GO:
Any time. The weather is very changeable. Heavy snowfalls occur in winter and after heavy rain many rivers become impassable.

DON'T MISS:
A guided tour of the splendid limestone Honeycomb Hill Caves at Karamea, world famous for their collection of bones from moa and other extinct bird species. It's also worth doing the kayak trip to the impressive Honeycomb Hill Arch.

YOU SHOULD KNOW:
The long-established 80-km (50-mi) Heaphy Track crosses the park from west to east, taking in stunning coastline, lush forests and extensive downs. It offers ever-changing views. There are huts and campsites along the track (advance booking required), but even on this established trail hikers should have proper clothing, food and backcountry experience. Those making any trip into the interior of Kahurangi National Park should be sure to notify someone of their plans as a sensible precaution (or take a satellite phone!).

*Maud Island in the beautiful
Marlborough Sounds*

Marlborough Sounds

HOW TO GET THERE:
Picton is a transport hub and an
obvious starting point. It's possible to
fly in or ferry across from Wellington
on the North Island or drive up State
Route 1 from the south. A road along
the southern shores of Marlborough
Sounds links Picton with Havelock and
Nelson on State Route 6 to the west.
WHEN TO GO:
The local climate is benign, as befits a
wine-producing region. Summer days
are long and sunny, while winter
weather is mild with frosty nights.
There is quite a lot of tourist activity
in high summer, so those who like
solitude should choose the
off-seasons.
DON'T MISS:
Ship Cove, one of New Zealand's most
historic sites. It was here that Captain
Cook made his base in the 1770s,
proclaiming British sovereignty over
the South Island and (perhaps equally
importantly to him) discovering that a
local plant cured the mariner's curse
and promptly naming it Cook's scurvy
grass. This small bay on the western
shore of Queen Charlotte Sound has a
monument to the great explorer who
used the cove five times during his
two Pacific voyages.
YOU SHOULD KNOW:
The Marlborough Sounds are generally
calm and safe, but first-timers should
acquaint themselves with the few
dangerous spots before taking to
the water.

Although the Marlborough Sounds occupy no more than the
northeastern tip of the South Island, this jumbled assembly of
sea-drowned valleys between Tasman and Cloudy Bays accounts for
one fifth of New Zealand's entire coastline. The DOC (Department
of Conservation) manages over 50 reserves in the area, indicating
how important this marine marvel is in ecological terms. That
awareness notwithstanding, there have been spirited battles
between conservationists and commercial interests like ferry
companies and scallop dredgers.

The port of Picton at the head of Queen Charlotte Sound is the
busy terminus for South Island's road and rail networks – and ferry
traffic to and from the North Island – but the hauntingly beautiful
Marlborough Sounds remain a sparsely populated jigsaw of winding
sounds, craggy islands, peninsulas, quiet bays and steep wooded
hills where many small and isolated communities or individual
homesteads can only be reached by boat. This makes exploration
difficult, but transport may be hired in the form of launches, yachts,
motor boats and sea kayaks. Although some visitors go afloat simply
to explore, sailing and sea kayaking are popular pastimes in their
own right. There are, of course, numerous passenger boats offering
cruises for those who like their scenery to come with minimal effort
and all the trimmings, while water taxis ply from Picton and
Havelock at the head of Pelorus Sound to D'Urville Island.

Serious hikers should essay the Queen Charlotte Track (at least
in part). This super-scenic route follows paths established by the
original Maori inhabitants of the area or early settlers who mined
and farmed hereabouts. The 71-km (44-mi) ridge tramp offers
fantastic views over Queen Charlotte Sound, with numerous
intriguing side paths down to the water. Those in a hurry can
mountain-bike the whole thing in a strenuous day.

Paparoa National Park

Just over 300 sq km (115 sq mi) of prime South Island coastal real estate was lost to developers when Paparoa National Park was established. As it happens, they probably wouldn't want it, for this is wild land described thus in the proposal that led to the park's classification in 1987: 'It contains scenery of distinctive quality, ecosystems of outstanding scientific interest and beautiful and unique natural features. These result from an unusual combination of natural history, geological history and climate which has created an area which has no parallel in New Zealand and perhaps worldwide.' Motion carried, obviously!

Today's visitors may not have a dedicated interest in every then-lauded aspect of Paparoa, but simply enjoying its contrasting landscapes is enough for most. The park covers an area on or near the coast of the northern Westland and rises up to the top of the Paparoa Ranges. A separate section to the north surrounds Ananui Creek. There are many geological variations in the park but the most important is karst landscape – the only lowland karst in New Zealand with undisturbed forest cover, featuring gorges, caves and streams that mysteriously vanish or reappear.

Much of the park is covered in contiguous lowland and montane forest with diversity unmatched anywhere else in the country – wonderful habitat that supports an abundant bird population. It is a vital refuge for the endangered great-spotted kiwi and supports the only known breeding colony of black Westland petrel. The park is also perfect for dedicated backcountry trampers. There are pleasing possibilities for anything from short strolls to day walks and one longer route – the Inland Pack Track cut through the forest in the 1860s to bypass coastal cliffs – but beyond that it's a lonely wilderness crying out to be explored. Other outdoor activities include caving and kayaking.

HOW TO GET THERE:
With great satisfaction, after driving one of the most spectacular coastal roads in New Zealand – State Highway 6 between Westport and Greymouth. The gateway to Paparoa National Park is the township of Punakaiki, which offers shops, accommodation, camping and various organized activities such as canoeing, horse riding, guided caving and scenic tours.

WHEN TO GO:
Winter temperatures average a cool 9°C (48°F) so most visitors prefer the other three seasons – especially summer, with its acceptable average of 17°C (63°F). Take waterproof clothing as the area has a high average rainfall and a reputation for unleashing torrential rain.

DON'T MISS:
The famous Pancake Rocks near Punakaiki. This awesome maze of blow holes and eroded rock formations named for their layered appearance may be viewed from a high-grade walkway that circles the sea cliffs on a promontory south of the Pororari River.

YOU SHOULD KNOW:
The park was the site of the infamous Cave Creek disaster in 1995 when the collapse of a badly constructed scenic overlook resulted in the deaths of 14 people – and the resignation of New Zealand's Minister of Conservation.

Pancake Rocks in Paparoa National Park

Arthur's Pass National Park

Waimakariri River Flats, Arthur's Pass National Park

In the heart of Ka Tiritiri o te Moana – or the Southern Alps as non-Maori speakers sometimes guiltily call them – lies Arthur's Pass National Park. It consists of high country that features tall mountains, extensive scree slopes, plunging gorges and wide rivers. A historic railway and road 'pass' through the middle *en route* from Canterbury to the West Coast. The small community of Arthur's Pass offers a welcoming base from which to explore the park and has a good visitor centre offering general park information and interpretative displays. There are basic campsites at most of the park's entry points and many backcountry huts connected by a considerable network of walking tracks and tramping trails.

The pass sits on the South Island's backbone and there is a marked difference between western and eastern slopes. To the west, luxuriant podocarp rainforest and red-flowering *rata* boasts a lush understorey of shrubs, ferns and mosses. To the east is dry beech and tawhai forest. Snow tussock and alpine meadows may be seen (and visited) from the summit of Arthur's Pass itself. Birdwatching is a popular pastime, with many species to be found in and around Arthur's Pass village. Good 'twitches' include kea, blue duck, rock wren, South Island robin, bellbird and fantail. The endangered great-spotted kiwi may be heard whistling away at night, but will rarely be seen.

More demanding activities include mountaineering (Mount Rollaston is a popular target), mountain-biking (formed tracks only) and 4x4 driving (approved roads only). But this is really a place in which to walk, walk, walk. Gentle strolls from the road allow sedentary types to enjoy champagne mountain air with great views. For more serious hikers there are numerous established half- and all-day hikes, plus more than a dozen overnight routes, including the demanding two-day Mingha/Deception Track over Goat Pass – a classic east-west traverse.

Rangitata River

A liquid rollercoaster drains the eastern side of the Southern Alps between the Lyell and Godley Glaciers and rushes 120 km (75 mi) to the sea near Temuka. The Rangitata River is formed by the confluence of two major tributaries and its most spectacular stretch is in the mountains. Once on the fertile Canterbury Plains it becomes a typical-for-these-parts braided river – a network of small, shifting channels divided by sand bars – before splitting and forming a large island delta, then discharging into the Pacific.

But the gentle pastoral beauty of the Canterbury Plains is not what attracts adventurous types to the swift Rangitata River. Jet boats whizz hither and thither, fishermen exercise their skills (it has some of the best salmon fishing in New Zealand), kayakers test their abilities. If that isn't enough, white-water rafting on the upper river is surely the most exciting way to view the stunning mountain scenery, with various companies offering three-hour white-water, white-knuckle rides that are nonetheless suitable for beginners, with a period of relative calm for safety instruction and familiarization before finally hitting fearsome Grade 5 rapids swirling between monster boulders – the infamous 'Pinch' in the rocky Rangitata Gorge that conducts the racing river out of the mountains.

Those interested in savouring the stunning scenery of the Upper Rangitata Valley as opposed to running the river can drive up either side of the gorge from Arundel, past Mount Peel and on to Erewhon sheep station (right bank) where the Clyde and Havelock rivers merge to form the Rangitata. This was named by Samuel Butler, the first white settler to own nearby Mesopotamia station and author of a famous satire on Victorian life also called *Erewhon*, which almost but not quite spells 'nowhere' backwards. That's how Butler intended it to be read and the name seems entirely appropriate in these back-of-beyond mountains.

HOW TO GET THERE:
Arundel is just past Coopers Creek, off State Highway 79 north of Geraldine. Rafting trips often include transport from Christchurch.

WHEN TO GO:
Any time, although winter with its Antarctic blasts is not for everyone. The weather in the Southern Alps is bracing from June to August, but at least the snow line remains at around 900 m (3,000 ft) and that white mountain topping makes for even more spectacular sightseeing. The Rangitata rafting season runs from September to the end of May.

DON'T MISS:
Rafters can enjoy the sheer thrill of white-water swimming and a daring leap into the river from the famous Jump Rock halfway down Rangitata Gorge. It's the four-metre rock for wimps and the ten-metre rock for anyone more afraid of looking like a wimp than of taking the fearful plunge.

YOU SHOULD KNOW:
The Rangitata Valley in the centre of the Southern Alps was the setting for filming important sequences in *The Lord of the Rings: The Two Towers* and *The Return of the King*. The landscape around Mount Sunday became J R R Tolkien's Kingdom of Rohan in Middle-earth and the Edoras hill-fort set was built there.

A hiker on Cascade Saddle Route in Mount Aspiring National Park

Mount Aspiring National Park

HOW TO GET THERE:
State Highway 6 – the South Island's wonderfully scenic road down the West Coast – cuts through the eastern end of the park from Haast Beach through Haast Pass to Lakes Wanaka and Hawea. The nearest town to Mount Aspiring itself is Wanaka. The park's access points are at the townships of Makarora, Haast and Glenorchy.

WHEN TO GO:
The perfect time to explore the park is summer and early autumn (November to March), especially if the intention is to cross scenic passes between valleys. Off-season is best left to experienced wilderness trekkers and snow-sports enthusiasts who can't resist the heli-skiing. That said, the Matukituki Valley can be walked safely at any time of year.

DON'T MISS:
The Upper Wilkin Valley – one of the most picturesque in the whole of New Zealand, which is saying something. It's a long-weekend trek starting from Makarora and going via the Kerin Forks Hut on the Gillespie Pass Circuit.

YOU SHOULD KNOW:
The Red Hills mineral belt in the southwest of the park is a visual surprise. The high concentration of minerals in the soil accounts for the rusty-red colour and ensures that only the hardiest of plants can survive there.

Nothing beckons lovers of remote places more seductively than Mount Aspiring National Park. A huge wilderness in the South Island's wild west guarantees a soaring sense of freedom, for this vast area is an unspoilt land of stunning views, mountains, glaciers, alpine lakes, valleys and white-water rivers. Beech forests predominate below the bush line, while higher up the vegetation consists of snow-tussock grassland and herb fields bright with wild flowers in spring and early summer.

It's easy to get lost – the park extends to an impressive 3,500 sq km (1,350 sq mi), straddling the end of the Southern Alps and stretching from the Haast River in the north to the Humboldt Mountains in the south. But the awesome spike of Mount Aspiring is a great reference point, proving an irresistible challenge to experienced alpinists. However, the main activity in the park is walking. As ever, there are countless short walks – mostly from the main highway, access roads or local towns – for those content to soak up the awesome scenery without straying too far from folding chairs and picnic lunch.

But serious visitors head for one of the long-distance hiking routes that lead into the interior and often link to adjacent areas. These include the Greenstone and Caples tracks (two fabulous valleys, moderate five-day round trip), Rees-Dart Track (a four-day circuit taking in two rivers and some of the park's best scenery) and the ever-popular three-day Routeburn Track (linking Mount Aspiring and Fiordland National Parks). There are campgrounds and numerous huts within the park (pre-booking advisable in summer), plus plenty of primitive campsites along the various tracks. Peace and quiet are not absolutely guaranteed. This being New Zealand, the sound of jet boats may be heard in the vicinity of the park's larger rivers.

Haleakala National Park

In the southeast of Maui, Haleakala National Park is a wilderness of two halves stretching from brooding volcanic heights at Mount Haleakala down through the clouds (often literally) to verdant coastline at Kipahulu. The island's highest peak often delivers dramatic views across a sea of clouds and this island in the sky is a starkly sculpted landscape of contrasting colours unlike any other.

Haleakala's slopes and the surrounding wilderness offer backcountry hiking against a magnificent backdrop, with access to rare endemic plants and birdlife. It's one of the few accessible places in Hawaii where native species thrive in abundance. This dramatic area on top of the world offers many contrasts, from the dry, cold air of the mountain with its towering cindercones to moist cloud forest rich in ferns at lower altitudes. The wilderness can be accessed from two trailheads near the summit, Halemauu at 2,440 m (8,000 ft) and Keoneheehee (Sliding Sands) at 2,970 m (9,750 ft). The trails eventually merge and lead down to the park's coastal zone. Along the way there are primitive campgrounds and historic cabins that can be booked in advance by overnighters, although the wilderness is also suitable for anything from short strolls to day hikes.

The coastal part of the park is reached by road from Hanu along Maui's spectacular northeastern coast. There is a campground but this area is remote and there is no piped water supply. Ocean swimming can be dangerous but there are plunge pools on the stream that runs down the Oheo Gulch, where the short Pipiwai Trail is popular with day hikers enjoying verdant tropical greenery. Whales, dolphins and turtles can sometimes be spotted offshore.

Cinder cones in Haleakala Crater

HOW TO GET THERE:
There is no public transport to the park. Road access from Kahului to park headquarters and Haleakala's summit is from Routes 37, 377 and 378 (90 minutes). The coastal section may be reached from Kahului in three hours via Routes 36, 360 and 31.

WHEN TO GO:
All year round (but park authorities warn that sensible precautions are needed in this remote area where the weather may be 'hot, dry, wet or cold in any part of the park at any time'). Temperatures range from a high of 27°C (80.6°F) on the coast to a low of −1°C (30°F) atop the mountain.

DON'T MISS:
Seeing stars from the summit of Mount Haleakala on a clear night. Hawaii is one of the best places on earth for astral viewing and Mount Haleakala is one of the best places in Hawaii. The intensity of the Milky Way has to be seen to be believed.

YOU SHOULD KNOW:
There is a park visitor centre at Kipahulu on the coast, one at park headquarters and another near the summit of Haleakala Naturalists are on hand to answer questions and the centres all have cultural and natural history displays.

Kealakekua Bay

The Kona (leeward) Coast of the Big Island of Hawaii is an area of historic settlement with many heritage sites and stern natural beauty. One of the highlights is Kealakekua Bay, 19 km (12 mi) south of Kailu-Kona, the main town in West Hawaii. Horseshoe-shaped Kealakekua is the largest sheltered bay on the island, measuring 2.5 km (1.5 mi) in length and 1.5 km (1 mi) in width. Access is to the south end, where a road winds down to a wharf and Napoopoo Beach.

This is no remote wilderness – just a beautifully unspoilt stretch of rugged coastline with volcanic cliffs rising above an inviting expanse of blue water. The bay offers some of the best snorkelling and scuba diving in the Hawaiian Islands. It's a Marine Life Conservation District and an extensive coral reef protects the bay, creating a calm haven where visibility can be as much as 30 m (100 ft) in water that is invitingly warm. The corals are stunning and host colourful arrays of tropical fish. A pod of Hawaiian spinner dolphins frequents the bay and turtles are frequently sighted. Those who wish to explore the shore must be prepared to do some serious scrambling down steep terrain and brave dense vegetation that crowds the water on gentler slopes.

Kealakekua Bay is famous as the spot where Captain James Cook was killed by indigenous Hawaiians in 1779, having estimated upon arrival that there were two thousand people living in two villages on the bay. A sheer cliff face was the burial site for Hawaiian kings and there were royal residences nearby, but by the early 20th century the once-thriving community had declined to the point where the bay was returned to nature's tender embrace, with abandoned village sites quickly invaded by kiawe trees.

Spinner dolphins frequent Kealakekua Bay.

Molokai

In the geographical centre of the Hawaiian Islands is Molokai, one of the least developed and most interesting parts of the USA's 50th state. The island lies on a west-east axis between Oahu and Maui, measuring 60 km (37 mi) by 16 km (10 mi). The few thousand inhabitants have fiercely resisted efforts to turn Molokai into a non-floating tourist barge. That said, the locals – with a higher percentage of native Hawaiians than any other island – are extremely friendly and their principled stand has preserved much of Molokai's natural beauty for the benefit of

Towering cliffs on the north shore of Molokai

visitors more interested in wild places than lying on white sand beaches (although there are plenty of those, including Papohaku, Hawaii's longest and widest).

The arid western end of the island with its scrubby grazing land and pineapple plantations is less interesting than the eastern half, although both northern and southern shores have some of the most remote and beautiful beaches in all Hawaii. Molokai was formed from two volcanoes. East Molokai's volcano split in half 1.5 million years ago, collapsing into the Pacific Ocean and leaving the world's highest sea cliffs behind (as featured in the movie *Jurassic Park III*). This is an area of breathtaking tropical landscape – a high plateau rising to 1,500 m (4,920 ft) at Kamakou's impressive peak with lush forests that form an extremely diverse ecosystem.

In addition to those awesome cliffs, there are numerous waterfalls – including the pounding 530-m (1,740-ft) Kahiwa Falls – deep gorges and rugged coastline. This is not tourist central – much of this marvellous terrain can only be reached by hard hiking, after access roads suitable only for 4x4 vehicles run out well short of the best sights, including those famous sea cliffs. In fact, the best way to appreciate their soaring grandeur is to take a sight-seeing helicopter ride from Maui.

HOW TO GET THERE:
Fly to Molokai airport, which is served by Hawaii's network of internal flights. Vehicles can be rented at the airport.
WHEN TO GO:
Any time (but the weather in February can be volatile and unpredictable).
DON'T MISS:
The coastal dunes at Mo'omomi, in northwestern Molokai. The western end of the island has been degraded owing to poor land management and over-grazing by goats. Mo'omomi is a Nature Conservancy preserve that protects a lonely area of sand dunes that contain some of the last intact coastal shrublands in Hawaii.
YOU SHOULD KNOW:
Molokai is famous for the work of the now-canonized Father Damien de Veuster, a Catholic priest who cared for leprosy sufferers at a colony on the island in the 19th century before himself dying of the disease aged 49. Ironically, that once-forbidden enclave on the Kalaupapa Peninsula is now one of the easier places to reach on Molokai's rugged north coast, by air or down a tortuous mule path. It is populated by (leprosy-free!) descendents of the original sufferers.

Palmyra Atoll is a tiny National Wildlife Refuge.

Palmyra Atoll

Halfway between Hawaii and American Samoa the true adventurer will (with a little help) find Palmyra Atoll, a tiny speck in the vast North Pacific administered by the USA that extends to 12 sq km (4.5 sq mi). The 14 km (9 mi) of coastline has just one safe anchorage, West Lagoon. An extensive reef system protects two shallow lagoons and 54 sandbars and reef-rock islets that are almost all connected. The largest of these – and the site of Palmyra's airstrip – is Cooper Island. Palmyra's islets are heavily vegetated, with species like stands of rare pisonia beach forest, coconut palms, ferns and shrubs that thrive as a result of heavy equatorial rainfall.

The atoll is a tiny National Wildlife Refuge, protecting both land and marine environments. Palmyra provides the only nesting site for seabirds in a huge expanse of ocean and attracts over one million birds in the breeding season. Resident species include red-footed boobies, brown boobies, masked boobies, white and sooty terns. The atoll is a haven for the endangered green turtle, while the surrounding reef and lagoons are populated by an extraordinary diversity of hard corals – 125 different types, which is three times more than Hawaii or the whole Caribbean can boast. The reef fish are as brightly coloured as the corals they patrol and include various sharks. Whales are frequent visitors.

Palmyra is a stunning marine wilderness and has no indigenous population, although scientists have a base on Cooper Island from which to study the corals. The previous residents were US Navy flyers, for Palmyra was a naval air station in World War II. The crumbling and overgrown remains of this era are still visible, serving as a reminder that everything in paradise is not always idyllic.

HOW TO GET THERE:
With great difficulty. It's possible to fly in to the airstrip maintained by the Nature Conservancy for visiting scientists, but the cost of a private charter is prohibitive. The few visitors privileged to see this magical atoll (and dive on its stunning reef) tend to arrive in cruising yachts.

WHEN TO GO:
Any time – the temperature is a more-than-balmy 29°C (84°F) all year round.

DON'T MISS:
The world's largest land invertebrate, the rare coconut crab. Watch one husk and crack a fallen nut and be mightily impressed.

YOU SHOULD KNOW:
Palmyra Atoll was specifically excluded when Hawaii became the 50th state in 1959, thus becoming the only privately owned overseas territory administered by the USA. Everything but two islets was sold by the then owners to America's Nature Conservancy in 2000, an organization that will preserve Palmyra's unique attributes for future generations.

Western Highlands

The outside world didn't know about the place until 1933, when an aerial survey of the highlands in Papua New Guinea (PNG) found the large, well-populated Wahgi Valley in the Western Highlands. That discovery of a thriving but hitherto unknown culture provides a sobering comment on how far the world has shrunk in 80 years, leaving no stone unturned nor corner unphotographed (if only from space). That initial discovery was followed by a traditional footslogging expedition that built an airstrip close to the Mount Hagen volcano and a virgin site now occupied by the town of Mount Hagen, Papua New Guinea's third largest.

Even so, the vast majority of PNG's population still practises a traditional rural way of life and Papua New Guinea – occupying the eastern half of the island of New Guinea – remains one of the world's least-developed nations. It is also one of the most fascinating destinations for lovers of faraway places, as it is one of the globe's least explored places. That's culturally – with over 800 indigenous languages and tribes – and geographically – with many undiscovered plants and animals said to lurk in the undocumented interior. Only recently has access become possible for tourists, as opposed to the most determined of serious travellers.

The Western Highlands are typical of PNG. This is a dramatic landscape of rainforested mountains, fertile valleys, rushing streams, rivers and swamps in the Lower Jimi Valley. Mount Hagen is an excellent base for exploration of habitats that range from lowland forest to alpine grasslands, dotted with coffee plantations that produce the local cash crop. There are a few hotels and tourist lodges, but this remains a primitive destination not for the faint-hearted. The Wahgi Valley remains a lush green oasis that is intensely cultivated, but Mount Hagen is the gateway to the wild and undeveloped areas further west.

HOW TO GET THERE:
Mount Hagan Airport at Kagamuga is served by private flights for mine personnel and an irregular public service from Cairns in Queensland and local centres including Moro and Port Moresby. Road access is via the Highland Highway from the coastal cities of Madang.

WHEN TO GO:
Any time. The climate is tropical but the uplands are cooler than the coast. Rainwear is essential in the monsoon season from December to March.

DON'T MISS:
The annual Mount Hagen Cultural Show in August, when national, regional and local tribal groups get together at Kagamuga to celebrate their heritage. This vibrant sing-sing sees representatives of the various tribes don wildly differing traditional costumes, paint themselves up and peacefully share common ethnicity through dance and music. Up to 50 tribal ensembles perform enthusiastically before up to 50,000 spectators.

YOU SHOULD KNOW:
Travellers on the Highland Highway face more than the landslips and potholes that bedevil this largely single-track road. The stretch in the Hagan Highlands is notorious for hold-ups and robberies committed by armed bandits rather underwhelmingly known as 'rascals'.

The Baiyer River Sanctuary

Ofu Island

It doesn't represent much of a Pacific empire, but since quitting the Philippines American Samoa is as good as it gets for the USA – and very good indeed for get-away-from-it-allers. This alluring tropical destination is not as high on the must-visit-islands list as it deserves to be. First impressions are not favourable – the capital of Pago Pago on the main island of Tutuila is tattily commercialized – but that's just a visual glitch. The rest of the island is a natural paradise. Towering peaks surround the town's harbour, lonely roads crowded by dense forest switchback over isolated mountain passes and stunning palm-fringed beaches more than match up to the picture-postcard Pacific white-sand/turquoise-sea standard.

The most discerning travellers head for American Samoa's Manu'a Island group in general and Ofu Island in particular. This volcanic isle is completely uncommercial and unspoilt, while Ofu beach on the west coast must be one of the world's finest. This 3 km (2 mi) stretch

of pink coral sand is stunningly beautiful, with a backdrop of swaying palm trees, jagged volcanic peaks and lush greenery. This is a place to swim and walk, often in complete solitude – enjoying the sun, sea and scenery of this dreamy hideaway. Snorkelling off the beach is first-rate, offering wonderful coral formations and vivid underwater life, but it's essential to take the necessary kit. Ofu is not a place where equipment can be rented.

The National Park of American Samoa encompasses 42 sq km (16 sq mi) of land and water on Manu'a islands of Tutuila, Ofu, its twin Olosega and Ta'u, protecting their wild locations from unseemly development. This hopefully precludes the sort of tourist pressure that often overwhelms unspoilt beauty that attracted visitors in the first place. American Samoa remains a dream destination for those willing to make the effort needed to plan a visit.

A beautiful deserted beach

Namenalala Island

Sometimes, getting away from it all requires a fat wallet and a little help from those who cater for those who can afford to get away from it all in singular style. A visit to the privately owned Fijian island of Namenalala offers just such an experience and the ultimate escape. Until the 1980s this 45-ha (110-ac) islet 25 km (15 mi) off the coast of Vanua Levu was uninhabited. From the air the island has an uncanny resemblance to an elongated dragon rising from the azure Koro Sea and might still be uninhabited, but in fact dense vegetation conceals a very exclusive eco-resort.

Just six hexagonal *bures* (Polynesian-style houses on stilts made from timber and woven bamboo) have been built among tall native trees on the dragon's tail, accommodating no more than a dozen guests at any one time, who are treated to the ultimate in desert-island living. Each *bure* overlooks beaches, reefs and a great sweep of sea from a vantage point on the cliff top, while the food is based around fresh produce grown on the island or caught from the surrounding ocean. This is not the sort of resort where pampering is the norm – there is no electricity in the widely spaced *bures* so this is one for those who hanker for a return to nature.

The rest of the island is completely undeveloped and provides the opportunity to explore a manageable stretch of original tropical rainforest. But for most visitors the main attraction will be snorkelling or scuba diving along the 30 km (18.5 mi) of Namenalala's pristine barrier reef, with its brilliant assortment of corals and tropical fish. Other possibilities include sport fishing outside the reef, canoeing, windsurfing, birdwatching . . . or simply relaxing in this secluded paradise.

HOW TO GET THERE:
By boat or seaplane from V

WHEN TO GO:
Any time, although the dry season from May to October is cool, with lower humidity than at other times.

DON'T MISS:
The evidence of Namenalala's mysterious past – the intriguing remains of an ancient ring fortification at the island's highest point, dating back for at least two millennia.

YOU SHOULD KNOW:
There is a generator that runs periodically to recharge batteries for guests' equipment. It is wise to take a selection of basic medications and toiletries as stocks on the island are extremely limited. Stout walking shoes are adequate for the forest trails and an old pair of trainers is useful for exploring tidal pools in rocky sections of the shoreline.

Namenalala Island – the perfect escape

Taveuni

HOW TO GET THERE:
Fly in to Matei Airport from Nadi via Savusavu, or direct from Suva. The ferry from Savusavu takes around seven hours, or there is a small passenger ferry from Buca Bay on the east coast of Vanua Levu.

WHEN TO GO:
Any time – but it has to be October to December to see the fabulous Tagimaucia flowers at their very best.

DON'T MISS:
The extraordinary orange dove, a superstar of Taveuni's vibrant bird population. The male has green-speckled plumage that turns to fluorescent orange in the breeding season.

YOU SHOULD KNOW:
The island's most imposing edifice is the Wairiki Mission, a fine example of colonial Romanesque architecture, noted for the superb singing at Sunday morning mass (visitors welcome). It overlooks the site where local warriors defeated a large number of Tongan invaders in a canoe battle fought just off the beach. The victors celebrated by cooking and eating the vanquished.

The beach at Lavena Point on Taveuni

Cigar-shaped Taveuni is Fiji's third-largest island after Vanua Levu and Viti Levu, extending to 435 sq km (170 sq mi). Taveuni is the tip of a massive shield volcano that rises from the floor of the Pacific. The island is dotted with volcanic cones and has suffered less from land clearance than Fiji's other islands. Consequently, it has an abundance of lush foliage and is known as 'The Garden Island of Fiji'. With a number of small resorts, it is becoming a popular tourist destination but remains a largely unspoilt destination. Many visitors ignore the interior in favour of diving on the island's famed coral reefs but those who prefer to remain ashore will find plenty of wild country to explore, featuring mountains, lakes, rainforests, breathtaking ocean views, mangroves and beaches.

One of Taveuni's most spectacular natural attractions is Lake Tagimaucia, a crater lake at a height of 800 m (2,625 ft), nestling beneath the impressive Des Voeux peak. This is the place to see Fiji's national flower, the red-and-white Tagimaucia that grows nowhere else. See this woody vine high in the forest canopy on the approaches to the lake, which is covered with floating vegetation. It's a healthy all-day hike to Lake Tagimaucia, but non-trampers can get most of the way there using a 4x4 vehicle and view this scenic gem from afar.

Other major attractions on the island are the plunging Bouma Falls and the picturesque Lavena Village with its pristine beach and nature walk. The international dateline used to bisect Taveuni, until some spoilsport rerouted it to stop people hopping from yesterday to tomorrow and back. There is a marker indicating a spot where this once happened, but that's as near to time travel as it's now possible to get.

Barrier Reef

The French overseas collectivity of New Caledonia in the southwest Pacific Ocean has one indisputable claim to fame, which also happens to be a natural wonder that will appeal mightily to lovers of unspoilt places. New Caledonia's Barrier Reef is the world's second longest at 1,500 km (930 mi), surrounding the main island of Grand Terre and various smaller isles. The coral reef encloses an amazing lagoon that extends to 24,000 sq km (9,300 sq mi), recently listed as a UNESCO World Heritage Site.

Despite damage to the reef's eastern section as a result of nickel mining effluent, this unique eco-region remains in rude good health and provides safe haven for a great variety of life, including endangered dugongs (sea cows) and green turtles. Such is the diversity of species that new fish and invertebrates are regularly discovered. So far, 1,000 types of fish, 5,000 different crustaceans, 5,500 molluscs, 600 sponges and 23 species of breeding bird, including the charming red-footed booby, have been recorded.

Coral formations are outstanding and can provide the experience of a lifetime for scuba divers and snorkellers who boat out to the reef, although non-water-babes can get a feel for the place by taking to glass-bottomed craft or indulging in numerous water sports, from kayaking to windsurfing. The lagoon is large enough to ensure that a wonderful sense of lonely adventure is possible, and sub-aqua sights have to be seen to be believed. Grand Terre itself has much to offer. Most tourists focus on New Caledonia's capital of Noumea, a sophisticated colonial town known as 'The Paris of the East'. But the rugged interior and verdant northeastern coast where torturous rivers and jagged peaks tumble into the lagoon are wild places, while trips to the outlying islands reveal a local culture hardly touched by 150 years of colonial influence.

An aerial view of New Caledonia's stunning coral reef

HOW TO GET THERE:
On a cruising yacht (Noumea is the only official point of entry) or by air using long-haul flights to regional centres like Fiji and onward flights using Aircalin. Be aware that visitors without return air tickets are always refused entry. Local Air Calédonie flights serve the outlying Loyalty Islands and the Isle of Pines, as does the fast catamaran *Betico* (at half the price).

WHEN TO GO:
Any time. Bastille Day (July 14) is the excuse for an uninhibited celebration that includes an impressive military parade and fly past. Other notable events are Noumea's August jazz festival and agricultural fairs featuring rodeo and the like in Koné (April) and Bourail (mid August).

DON'T MISS:
The Isle of Pines, where the Kuto/Kanuméra area is a picture-perfect tropical paradise with pristine Pacific beaches backed by stands of towering pine trees.

YOU SHOULD KNOW:
The striking Jean-Marie Tjibaou Cultural Centre in Noumea was designed by the famous Italian architect Renzo Piano and completed in 1998 at a cost of $50 million. This extraordinary collection of ten 'unfinished' hut-like structures was created in celebration of vernacular Canaque buildings and named for an assassinated Canaque leader.

Antarctic Peninsula

HOW TO GET THERE:
Qualify as a climate scientist and wangle a posting to one of the research stations on the peninsula, together employing around 1,500 people. Alternatively, save up and book one of the many cruises that visit Antarctica. Trips to the Antarctic Peninsula usually start from Ushuaia in Argentina or Puerto Williams in Chile. The latest innovation is fly-cruise trips that cut out the lengthy sea crossing to Antarctica and take passengers straight there to meet up with their ships.

It's the end of the book, and the end of the world. Antarctica underlies the South Pole and is the sixth continent. Technically a desert with virtually no rainfall, the coldest place on earth is experiencing rapid global warming that threatens to alter its icy face for ever. The planet's last great uninhabited wilderness is covered by ice that averages 1.5 km (1 mi) in thickness and, if it all melted, sea levels around the world would rise by nearly 20 m (66 ft). No need to panic just yet . . . but it is happening. During the summer's 24 hours of daylight constant solar radiation punctures holes in a protective ozone layer weakened by greenhouse gases.

Nowhere is the big thaw more obvious than in one of the most accessible (a relative term!) areas. The Antarctic Peninsula is the northernmost part of the mainland. Its coasts have the mildest (another relative term!) climate in the continent and are snow-free in summer months. The peninsula is characterized by offshore

islands connected to the mainland by ice and stand-alone ice shelves – many of the latter retreating or disintegrating at an alarming rate. Even so, the wildlife (penguins, seabirds, seals and whales), seascapes and mountainous interior remain spectacular. It's one of the most awe-inspiring places on earth.

Antarctic cruises cater for various tastes. Ships are small, rarely carrying more than 150 passengers and often fewer. Expedition ships offer varying levels of luxury, while some with ice-strengthened hulls go where intrepid passengers can enjoy activities like sea kayaking and mainland camping. At the sharp end (literally) are icebreakers that go where no other ship can venture. Zodiac transfers for scenic shore outings are commonplace, helicopter shuttles and overflights less so. Cruises invariably employ experts who lecture on subjects such as wildlife, geology, oceanography, glaciology and the history of Antarctic exploration.

WHEN TO GO:
The polar summer (a couple of months either side of Christmas).
DON'T MISS:
One or more of Antarctica's unique climatic spectacles – the glowing *Aurora Australis* (southern lights) in the night sky, diamond dust (a low-level cloud made up of tiny ice crystals) or the sun dog (a spot of bright light beside the real thing).
YOU SHOULD KNOW:
Further south, huts on Ross Island in Erebus Bay (named for the island's active volcano) were used as home bases by polar heroes Captain Robert Falcon Scott and Ernest Shackleton. They have been preserved as historic monuments just as they were left by the departing expeditions.

Adelie penguins resting on a piece of glacial ice in the Antarctic Peninsula.

COUNTRIES AND REGIONS

automotive
101

THE CAR INDUSTRY *exposed*

16.4.19

Automotive 101
The Car Industry Exposed

Artwork by Effusion Creative Solutions
Chandler, Arizona

Printed in the United States of America

"An unrectified case of injustice has a terrible way of lingering, restlessly, in the social atmosphere like an unfinished equation."

— Mary McCarthy

I would like to thank my beautiful wife, Kasia Michaels, for her loving support and constant encouragement in both my career and in this book. There are not enough words in the world to describe how inspired I am by just the mere sight of her.

I would also like to thank my two sons, Jake and Dean, for giving me a reason to carry on in the face of adversity. It is their future that motivates me to do all I can to continually push the wheel of progress.

Finally, I would like to thank all the talented attorneys and incredible staff at MLG Attorneys at Law for their hard work and dedication. They embody the concept of individual commitment to group effort.

TABLE OF CONTENTS

7

BY JONATHAN MICHAELS

Have you ever stopped to consider that the automotive industry is one of the largest industries in the world? If you take all the people in the U.S. employed by car manufacturers, parts suppliers and car dealers, as well as those whose businesses are reliant on the distribution channel, over seven million people – or about one in 45 Americans – earn their living in the industry. On an economic basis, if the automotive industry were a nation, it would be the sixth largest country in the world. In the U.S. alone, it is responsible for 3.5 percent of the GDP.

For an industry so significant, surprisingly little is publicly known. For instance, many would be surprised to learn that Kia and Hyundai vehicles have a defect rate of 115 percent. That is, on average every single Kia and Hyundai vehicle that comes off the assembly line has *more than* one defect – and a defect so material that it is sufficient to mandate a federal recall of the vehicle.

Other areas are just as provoking. Electric cars, for instance, are all the rage. Yet, few have an understanding that the lithium necessary to power electric vehicles is a precious Earth metal that has limited supply. Lithium can only be found in four countries in commercial quantities: Chile, Argentina, Australia and China. So, our race to rid ourselves of reliance on the 12 OPEC oil-producing countries has placed us in a position of becoming beholden to an oligopoly of four. A replacement for lithium as a power source for electric cars will undoubtedly be found – it has to be – but the point remains that little is known about an industry that impacts us so greatly.

In 2010, I began a journalistic undertaking that would be eight years in the making. That year, I began authoring a collection of articles on the automotive industry that provoked thought, stirred the conscience and asked questions that insiders didn't want asked. The result of the effort was 101 published articles, exposing the secret nuisances of one of the most powerful industries in the world. This book chronicles those articles.

CHAPTER 1

Sudden
Impact

M A Y   2 0 1 0

Is Toyota's widely-publicized gas pedal recall the appropriate remedy that everyone has been waiting for, or is this merely a quick-fix approach to cover up a deeper-rooted problem with its runaway cars? One thing is sure: With sales of eight models halted, and its pristine image for quality heavily dented, the manufacturer is desperate to get out of the death spiral that could shake its very core.

Good cause exists to question the manufacturer's actions. Reports indicate that since 1999, Toyota and Lexus vehicles have been involved in 815 accidents related to sudden acceleration, resulting in 19 deaths – more than all other vehicle manufacturers *combined*. As the problem mounted, Toyota initially blamed the problem on poorly-designed floor mats, resulting in a recall of 5.5 million vehicles. Then, as the problem seemed to continue, Toyota changed its position and blamed a faulty gas pedal design for the problem, resulting in a recall of another 2.3 million vehicles and the suspension of sales for eight of its vehicles altogether.

But, CTS Corp., the supplier who has manufactured the gas pedals since 2005 and who is the primary recipient of Toyota's blame, casts serious doubt on whether its products are to blame. As CTS points out, the sudden-acceleration problem dates back to 1999, years before CTS began supplying the gas pedal. It is also of note that CTS has been honored three times by Toyota since 2005 for exceeding quality expectations.

More doubt is cast on Toyota's gas pedal fix by reviewing the U.S. vehicle safety records of the runaway vehicles. As reported by the *Los Angeles Times*, of the 2,000-plus complaints of sudden acceleration in Toyota and Lexus vehicles from motorists, only 5% cited a sticking gas pedal as the source of the problem. The *Los Angeles Times* further reports that the National Highway Traffic Safety Administration (NHTSA), the U.S. agency that governs federal vehicle safety, has conducted eight investigations into sudden-acceleration problems with Toyota vehicles over the past seven years, and found that none of the incidents were caused by a sticking gas pedal.

So, what is the problem? Some automotive safety experts fear that it is a latent defect in the vehicles' electronic throttle system. And, this would explain why the problem is identified by vehicle owners as sudden *acceleration*, as opposed to the vehicle remaining at a constant speed when the gas pedal is no longer depressed. If a vehicle was traveling 65 miles per hour and the gas pedal stuck at that position, the car would continue traveling at that same rate of speed after the driver's foot was removed from the gas pedal. A problem to be sure, but not the main issue complained of by motorists. Case in point is the August 2009 incident where off-duty California Highway Patrol officer, Mark Saylor's, 2009 Lexus ES 300 *accelerated* to 120 miles per hour before smashing into the back of a SUV and bursting into flames, killing four occupants of the vehicle. One more important fact: The Lexus ES 300 is not one of the vehicles that are subject to the Toyota stop-sale.

If the actual problem is, in fact, a latent defect in the electronic throttle system, this could prove to be a much more costly and lengthy fix than simply adding a metal shim to the back of a gas pedal. Could Toyota be taking a course of action that puts economics ahead of human life? It would not be the first time a manufacturer has taken such a tact.

In the early 1970's, Ford Motor Company was accused of knowingly allowing a dangerous gas tank design to be released on its popular Ford Pinto. After several Pintos exploded when struck from behind, resulting in numerous fatalities, Ford came under attack for not issuing a recall. However, concern turned to anger when it was alleged that Ford was said to have conducted a cost-benefit analysis, weighing the cost to repair the known faulty vehicles versus the cost of paying out the damage claims that were expected to arise. Nearly forty years later, the incident is still often referred to as an "episode of great corporate malfeasance."

So, what of Toyota's decision to lay blame at the doorstep of the floor mat and gas pedal? Well, it's highly questionable. While this may address the situation, much of the evidence points to a contrary – and potentially much more costly – problem. The question remains whether this is really a genuine effort to correct the problem, or whether it is an effort to show some kind of wide-scale solution that will enable the company to start selling cars again. This would certainly not be the first time Toyota has distorted the facts in favor of economic gain.

Whatever the case with the gas pedal fix, one thing is certain: If Toyota gets it wrong, it could very well turn a significant problem into a catastrophic one. One can only hope that all the evidence pointing to this being an inappropriate wrong fix is wrong, and that this dark episode in consumer safety will be closed forever.

CHAPTER 2

Big Brother
is Looming

JUNE 2010

In some of the most sweeping legislation to hit Capital Hill in years, Senate Financial Reform Bill "S. 3217" is about to change the financial industry's landscape for good. And, that's not welcome news for everybody.

Acting in response to the 2008 financial market meltdown, the Senate is set to begin voting this week on S. 3217, which would create the "Bureau of Consumer Financial Protection" – an agency to be charged with overseeing virtually all consumer-related financial products. The new agency, or the BCFP as it will likely become known, will be given total oversight to stomp out "unfair, deceptive or abusive" lending practices, and will apply to industries far and wide. As President Barack Obama proclaimed, he will block all efforts to exclude from the new agency "banks, credit card companies or nonbank firms such as debt collectors, credit bureaus, payday lenders or auto dealers."

If the intent was to create an 800-pound gorilla in the financial markets, the bill succeeds. In addition to having unfettered oversight to halt any practice the agency determines to be unfair, deceptive or abusive, the BCFP will be required to "conduct examinations" of persons it considers to be "larger participants" of a market. For auto dealers who fall into this category (the BCFP will be left to define what a "market" is, and who is a "larger participant" of that market), they would have to register with the government, and their principles, officers, directors and key personnel may have to undergo background checks by the government.

The intent of the proposed legislation appears to be pure: provide important oversight to the financial industry to prevent a repeat of the 2008 debacle. But, in the haste to prevent this situation from ever reoccurring, one has to wonder whether the current legislation is being driven by reason or by fear. History is replete with hastily-made decisions that appear appropriate when made, only to later cause us to cringe when reminded that we ever engaged in such rash conduct. If there is any doubt on this, just ask any of the 110,000 Japanese Americans who were whisked away into internment camps during World War II.

With the auto industry employing, in one form or another, one out of every six persons in the United States, the question of whether the legislation should apply to the nation's 17,000 auto dealers should not be taken lightly. This is particularly true at a time when the auto industry sold 300,000 fewer vehicles in the United States in 2009 than in 1965 (10.6 million in 2009 versus 10.9 million in 1965), and when goliaths such as General Motors and Chrysler – once thought impenetrable – are toppling under the weight of insurmountable debt. A misstep with this industry could have a dramatic impact on our nation's ability to climb out of our economic freefall.

While the proposed legislation may be appropriate, or even necessary, for the mammoth institutions of Wall Street, the same cannot be said for the auto dealers of Main Street. Auto dealers are already one of the most heavily regulated segments, governed by the Federal Trade Commission, the Federal Reserve Board, the Fair Credit Reporting Act, the Truth in Lending Act, the Federal Consumer Leasing Act, and the Gramm Leach Bliley Act. Adding yet another layer of oversight, such as the BCFP, to an already over-burdened process would only serve to require further infrastructure in dealerships and result in higher prices for consumers.

The legislation would also undoubtedly spawn further consumer litigation against dealers, the cost of which also gets passed on to the consumer. Whether it is a violation of Business and Professions Code Section 17200, the Consumer Legal Remedies Act (Civil Code Section 1780), or the "single document rule" (a requirement that all terms of a loan be contained in a single document), dealers are uniquely positioned to receive attacks from consumers for what are often times hyper technical applications of law. Readers may recall the event in the early 2000s where a southern California law firm filed more than 2,000 lawsuits against auto dealers and repair shops in California for trivial violations, such as abbreviating the words "on approved credit" (O.A.C.) in a print advertisement.

As the bill has been making its way through Congress, at least one Senator has recognized the chilling effect that S. 3217 will have on the auto industry. After the Senate offices received floods of letters and visits from concerned dealers, Senator Sam Brownback (R., Kan.) drafted an amendment to S. 3217 that would exempt nearly all the nation's dealers from the new consumer protection law. This carve out – what has become known as the "Brownback Amendment" – is set to be voted on by the Senate in the upcoming days. If the Amendment passes, auto dealers will escape the grip of a frightened Congress, and be permitted to rebuild their industry without the added weight of additional governmental oversight. As the vote takes place, one can only hope sound judgment will prevail.

CHAPTER 3

The Tesla
Business Model

JULY 2010

Last week marked an epic event in the automotive industry when Tesla Motors launched its ambitious effort to raise $185 million through a public offering of 11.1 million shares of stock. The IPO was historic in that Tesla is now among the ranks of only a small handful of U.S. auto manufacturers to have ever had a public offering (General Motors, Chrysler and Ford, to name a few); the offering was notable in that this is the first time an all-electric car company has ever graced the annals of Wall Street. But the event was remarkable for a much more subtle, and much more important, reason. Tesla's launch signifies the first time in U.S. history that an auto manufacturer of any significant scale has rejected the much-embraced franchised dealer sales system, in favor of company owned stores.

Although some may not recognize it, or perhaps have just never given it much consideration, the neighborhood Ford dealer down the block is not a "Ford" store at all; it is a separately owned business that enjoys a dealer agreement with the manufacturer. This franchise system is as old as the manufacturers who use it, dating back to the early 1900s when Ford and General Motors forged partnerships with budding entrepreneurs who were able to penetrate the local communities in ways that the manufacturers couldn't. Throughout this time, the franchise system gained strength as the accepted way to sell and service automobiles, and to occasionally address other social issues such as the "minority dealer development" programs, where the manufactures assist minority groups in becoming dealers.

Now, some 100 years later, the franchise system is taken for granted as the way cars are sold in the U.S. –until now.

Tesla's attempt to reinvent the way cars are sold is bold, pioneering and stimulating – and for Tesla, potentially problematic. As the franchise system evolved in the U.S., state legislatures began to recognize significant disparities in the bargaining power between large auto manufacturers and independently owned dealerships. These concerns grew as manufacturers were at times put in the position of having to take back independently owned dealerships (for instance, when a dealer was terminated or gave back the franchise), or when manufacturers just tried to open up competing "factory-owned" dealerships altogether. Because of this uneven playing field, several states developed bodies of law intended to protect dealers from unfair competition from their manufacturers. For instance, California prohibits manufacturers from owning dealerships if there is another franchised dealer within 10 miles; New York prohibits factory owned stores if there is another franchised dealer within the state; and Colorado bans manufacturers from owning more than one dealership altogether.

While the dealer laws originated to even the playing field between manufacturers and franchised dealers, it is not difficult to imagine that legislatures might have an interest in expanding the statutory schemes to protect the sanctity of the franchise system. For instance, in March 2010 Colorado passed House Bill 10-1049, which expanded the state's statutory dealer laws to prohibit manufacturers from owning multiple dealerships in the state. Hence, an attempt by Tesla to open two dealerships in Colorado would be deemed unlawful.

With the inroads that the dealer bodies have had with the legislatures, it is not difficult to imagine that a widespread factory-owned dealer system, such as the one being implemented by Tesla, would be deemed unlawful. Arguments could be made that such a system would enable unfair competition with dealers of other line-makes who were not as well-capitalized, or that the system would be against the public interest because dealerships would not be as plentiful, resulting in a diminished ability of the factory-owned dealers to handle maintenance, warranty and recall issues. And, then of course, there is the erosion of the minority dealer development program, which would likely invoke a response from the National Association of Minority Auto Dealers.

Such arguments sound crazy? Think again. In the early 1970s petroleum producers, such as Exxon and Shell, began shedding their historic franchise system in favor of company-owned retail stations. The movement was met with resistance, with dealers claiming that the company-owned stations were unfairly competing with the dealers and that the existence of the stores was against public policy. The Maryland Legislature agreed, and in 1974 Maryland enacted a statute prohibiting any producer or refiner of petroleum products from owning and operating a retail station in the state. Exxon, Shell, Gulf Oil and Ashland Oil challenged the law as an unlawful restraint on trade and a violation of the due process, resulting in U.S. Supreme Court review. In [*Exxon Corp. v. Governor of Maryland*], 437 U.S. 117 (1978), the Supreme Court upheld the law, stating that the law bore a reasonable relation to the state's legitimate purpose in controlling the gasoline retail market; that the statute did not impermissibly burden interstate commerce; and the fact that the statute might have anticompetitive effects was not in itself a sufficient reason to invalidate the law.

Would a state's attempt to regulate the automotive industry lead to a similar result? Probably. Consider the 1978 U.S. Supreme Court case of [*New Motor Vehicle Board v. Orrin Fox Co.*], 439 U.S. 96 (1978), where California's dealer protection laws were upheld as constitutional. The Court held that the California Legislature was constitutionally empowered to enact a general scheme of business regulation that imposed reasonable restriction upon the exercise of the right, stating "the due process clause is not to be so broadly construed that the Congress and state legislature are put in a strait jacket when they attempt to suppress business and industrial conditions which they regard as offensive to the public welfare."

So, what will become of the Tesla business plan? Tesla describes one of its strengths as the fact that it "operates in a fundamentally different manner and structure than traditional automobile manufacturers." Judging by the response to the IPO, where the stock price nearly doubled in the first few days, Wall Street seems poised to embrace the plan. One can only wonder if the legislature will be so kind.

CHAPTER 4

Somebody Tell Them
the Party's Over

AUGUST 2010

For a nation founded on innovation and deeply rooted in the entrepreneurial spirit, one has to wonder how they got it so wrong for so long. The Big 3 that is, now recognized by their new name, the Detroit 3. It is an odd paradox in a way, but just mentioning the names GM, Ford and Chrysler conjure a vast array of thoughts and emotions. Is it Henry Ford's invention of the assembly line? Is it the enormous pride that one exhumed in the 1950s when the family got its first Cadillac? Or is it the long, slow slide the Detroit 3 have endured over the past several decades from world domination to accepted irrelevance?

Looking at the Detroit 3 today, it is hard to imagine that when Bruce Jenner carried the United States to victory in the 1976 Olympics, 86 percent of all new cars sold in the United States were from the Detroit 3. Today, that number has been cut in half, replaced by companies that are leaner, better able to adapt, and better managed. Natural selection has taken over, leaving the once impenetrable stumbling toward extinction.

What is more disturbing than the situation they are in is how they got there. As the Detroit 3 were slipping into the abyss, those in command were celebrating glory days gone by, giving each other "attaboys" on a job well-done and passing out undeserved paychecks. Consider this. In 2008 – the year before the Detroit 3 flew to Washington D.C. in their private jets, looking for handouts – GM paid its CEO Rick Wagoner $14.9 million in compensation. His accomplishment? Presiding over a company who had just posted a three-year loss of $82 billion and whose market share had dwindled to a mere 19 percent.

Now, the country has given GM and Chrysler over $85 billion of taxpayer money to help them escape their self-created mess. For those wanting to keep score, that is $52 billion to GM, $15.5 billion to the privately-owned Chrysler, $15 million to GMAC and Chrysler Financial, and $5 billion to GM and Chrysler suppliers. So, the future of these companies has turned from an issue of national pride to one of genuine concern, as one wonders whether the United States will ever see a return on this enormous outlay of capital.

The answer to this question, and to a large extent the question of whether Ford can also be saved, hinges on whether the Detroit 3 will wake up from their decades-long slumber and begin to actually compete in the new marketplace. To be sure, the Detroit 3 have turnaround plans. But, this is nothing new, and no one should be fooled or surprised when Turnaround Plan 2.0 is just as unsuccessful as the many plans that have come before it.

Some of the prior "sure-fire" turnaround plans that have been laid to rest: In 1979, Chrysler took a $1.5 billion handout from the government under the Chrysler Corporation Loan Guarantee Act. It was seeking to salvage its market share that had declined to a mere 11 percent. Yet, after implementation of the plan, its market share continued to decline, and today is only 8 percent. In 1985, GM rolled out its "Customer Satisfaction" turnaround plan that was sure to save it from continued market erosion. GM's market share at the time, 40 percent. Its market share today, 19 percent.

Even as recently as five years ago, the Detroit 3 had "new" turnaround plans that were sure to fix the damaged brands. In 2005, Ford rolled out the "Way Forward Plan," in what it called "a historic moment for the company," where it committed itself to reinventing the Mercury brand and building cars that people wanted to buy. Five years later, Ford announced that it was eliminating Mercury and that its market share was down to 15 percent. In 2005, GM introduced its plan, called the Four Point Turnaround Plan, where it committed to strengthening its current brands and aggressively targeting key markets. Five years later, GM terminated three of its brands, Hummer, Saturn and Pontiac, and was surpassed by Toyota as the world's largest manufacturer – a title it held for nearly a century.

So, can the Detroit 3 escape the morass and return to world domination...or at least remain viable? Not likely if it is business as usual. At GM, Rick Wagoner was replaced by Ed Whitacre who has been making a variety of cuts. But, are those changes enough? Not according to one GM market executive who had the following to say: "The removal of managers and executives so far has been mainly at lower levels, thinning ranks and taking out layers. It's not replacing people who made the mess and created the culture."

Similar problems can be seen with how the Detroit 3 are approaching their product lineup and distribution systems. Take the following example: Lexus, a brand that was only introduced during the first George Bush presidency, outsells Cadillac by a margin of 2 to 1. But, what's even more surprising is the way it does it. Cadillac sells through a dealer network of 1,316 dealers; Lexus does it with 230.

Upon exiting bankruptcy last year, GM announced that part of its turnaround plan was to have Cadillac emulate the Lexus model, stating that it was looking to close 922 Cadillac showrooms and build a new sales and service network centered around urban coastal regions. However, only months into the plan, GM abandoned the effort, agreeing to keep the same Cadillac network that we have come to know.

If the Cadillac situation appears bad, GM's other brands are actually worse. Take Buick for instance, which has a dealer network of 2,369 showrooms, and which considers itself a competitor to Honda. The average Honda dealer in the United States sells 1,013 new Hondas a year. The average Buick dealer sells only 41. That is 41 new Buicks [per year].

GM is not alone in its brand struggles. Ford, whose CEO Alan Mulally was famously quoted as saying that his Lexus LS430 was the "finest car in the world," is in an equally precarious position. Ford claims that the elimination of the Mercury brand will enable it to focus more clearly on its older sibling, Lincoln. Yet, one must question whether the Lincoln dealers can survive without Mercury. Until now, most of the 1,221 Lincoln dealers have been paired with Mercury franchises, and Mercurys have been responsible for about half of the dealers' sales. Now, with that sales volume gone, the dealers will have to meet their same debt burden, yet with a substantially reduced revenue base – and these are dealers who were barely viable with the Mercury franchises.

As bad as it sounds, all hope is not lost, as the Ford, Chevrolet and Dodge nameplates still enjoy healthy sales. The United States buys about 1.4 million Fords every year, 1.3 million Chevrolets and 500,000 Dodges. These are very respectable numbers, considering that Toyota, the U.S. market leader, sells 1.5 million units. The problem is not that the Detroit 3 cannot build cars; it's that they can no longer support the multi-branded lineup that they enjoyed in years past. A Chevrolet-Cadillac-GMC-Buick lineup diverts precious resources away from what is viable and contributes them to endeavors that are not.

As one who spends a significant amount of time representing dealers in manufacturer-related litigation, it is painful to suggest that the Detroit 3 need to do considerably more to remain viable. But, this is a situation that has been 30 years in the making, and one which is now inescapable. If drastic measures are not taken now, there may not be another opportunity. As Albert Einstein said, "We can't solve problems by using the same kind of thinking we use when we created them."

CHAPTER 5

Electric Shock!

SEPTEMBER 2010

Last Wednesday, the latest entrant to the burgeoning electric car market went on sale, the cleverly-named Nissan Leaf. Rallying around claims of saving the environment and helping the nation rid itself of its dependence on foreign oil, consumers lined up in droves to buy the new commuter car. In fact, it seems like just about every car manufacturer is coming out with a hybrid or electric car. Toyota has the Prius, GM has the Volt, and Tesla has the...well, the Tesla.

So what's behind this movement toward electric cars? Good corporate responsibility? Auto manufacturers responding to consumer demands? Well, sort of. The truth is that in 2007 President George W. Bush signed into law a comprehensive overhaul to the U.S. energy policy, which sets forth new fuel economy standards that auto manufacturers must meet over the next decade or face stiff penalties. The new fuel economy standards will be enforced through the Corporate Average Fuel Economy, or CAFE regulations, enacted in the mid-1970s. This has auto manufacturers jumping.

For those old enough to remember, in 1973 the United States was shocked to its core when the OPEC (Organization of the Petroleum Exporting Countries) nations responded to U.S. involvement in the Israeli-Arab War by imposing an oil embargo against the United States. The embargo resulted in an immediate shortage of oil, and in an instant, a nation that had become accustomed to having all the oil it could consume started to panic. As the price of oil quadrupled overnight, consumers were limited to the days on which they could buy gas and how much they could buy, and oil-dependent businesses scrambled for alternative sources of energy. Even Santa Claus was forced to stay home, as states banned residential Christmas lights and just about every other type of non-essential use of energy.

Recognizing that dependency on foreign oil made the United States vulnerable to oil rich countries, Congress sought to reduce the nation's oil consumption by regulating fuel economy standards in the automotive industry. In 1975, Congress enacted the CAFE regulations, which set forth minimum fuel economy standards that manufacturers had to meet or pay a gas-guzzler tax to the U.S. government. In 1978, the year the law went into effect, all manufactures had to meet an average of no less than 18 miles per gallon. This minimum was increased each year until 1985, when it was set at 27.5 mpg.

While the initial implementation of the CAFE regulations was aggressive, by the mid-1980s the sting from the oil crisis had begun to fade. Fears of OPEC had been replaced by new concerns, and the once stringent CAFE regulations stagnated. From 1985 through the late 2000s the minimum fuel economy remained at 27.5 mpg, despite quantum developments in automotive technology. What's more, auto manufacturers began to exploit the distinction the CAFE regulations made between passenger cars and light trucks, leading to the development of the minivan and the SUV, both of which fell in the more lenient light truck category.

All of this changed on Dec. 19, 2007, however, when President Bush signed into law the Energy Independence and Security Act of 2007. Under this Act, the CAFE regulations received their first major update in nearly 25 years. The law requires fuel economy standards to begin increasing again, starting in 2011 with a standard of 30.2 mpg, through 2020, where it will be set at 35 mpg. Those who fail to comply will be hit with harsh penalties.

With this, the car of the future became the car of today, as auto manufacturers made a concerted effort to steer consumers toward fuel efficient hybrid and electric cars that would increase manufacturers' average fuel economy. But, is this necessarily a good thing? On the surface, it would seem that this is an obvious yes, as hybrid and electric cars consume less fossil fuel and emit fewer pollutants than traditional combustion engines. But, does the analysis end there? Perhaps not.

Hybrid and electric cars are powered by one of two battery technologies, either lithium ion or nickel metal hydride. GM's Volt uses lithium ion technology, while the Toyota Prius uses nickel metal hydride. If the names assigned to the batteries sound more like a Chemistry class and less like Autoshop, it is because battery technologies in general are derived from either rare earth elements or trace metals that are pulled straight from the Periodic Table of Elements, and the batteries being used to power hybrid and electric cars are no exception. Lithium ion batteries use the trace metal, lithium carbonate, and nickel metal hydride batteries use the rare earth element, lanthanide. Both elements are found in the earth's crust, but where and in what quantities?

Geologists estimate that the world has about 6.2 million metric tons of usable lithium carbonate, the valuable trace metal used to produce lithium ion batteries. Currently, the world consumes about 80,000 metric tons per year, the majority of which goes to consumer products such as laptops and cell phones, with consumer demand increasing about 25 percent per year. If consumption were to remain static at today's rate (which it likely would not), the world's known resources would be depleted in about 75 years.

What happens when hybrid and electric cars are factored in? Initially not a lot, but given that the battery for an electric car weights about 400 pounds, this changes quite dramatically as more hybrid and electric cars are produced. The world currently produces about 60 million vehicles each year, a very small portion of which are hybrid or electric. If each of these vehicles were to use lithium ion batteries, this would increase the annual consumption of lithium carbonate to about 550,000 metric tons per year. At this rate, the world's known resources of 6.2 million metric tons would be depleted in just a little over 10 years.

But, there are larger problems. Unlike oil, which is generally subterranean, usable lithium carbonate is located almost exclusively in salt flats, and its extraction involves an invasive strip-mining process that is neither politically nor ecologically sound. Then, there is the matter of its location. Nearly 80 percent of the world's lithium carbonate is located in the South American countries of Argentina, Bolivia and Chile, whose governments would enjoy an oligopoly over the rest of the world in a manner far greater than that of the OPEC countries.

The other battery technology used by hybrid and electric cars, nickel metal hydride, is perhaps more concerning. Its rare earth element, lanthanide, is more plentiful than lithium carbonate, but it also comes with significant drawbacks.

Because lanthanide is found mostly in massive rock formations, the procedure to extract it is costly and destructive. Then, as with lithium carbonate, there is the matter of its location. Ninety-seven percent of the world's supply of lanthanide is produced by one country: China. This is a fact that has not escaped China's attention. As former Communist Party leader Deng Xiaoping has stated, "There is oil in the Middle East, there is rare earth in China."

Despite these concerns, manufacturers are presenting hybrid and electric cars as the definitive solution to the fossil fuel problem. Could it be that it was easier, and hence less expensive, for auto manufacturers to expand upon established battery technology that has been in existence for years, rather than develop new alternative fuel technologies that were less mature? Whatever the answer, one thing is likely to be certain: if consumers begin adopting hybrid and electric cars, it will not be long before a nation-wide infrastructure of charging stations begins to develop; and at this point, any hope of other alternative fuel technologies will likely be lost – at least until it becomes time to repeat this process all over again.

CHAPTER 6

The Ghost in
the Machine

OCTOBER 2010

It's fascinating when you think about it, but the day has actually arrived where the average commuter car has more software code in it than existed in the Apollo 11 spacecraft that put the first man on the moon. Just how far have we progressed? The Apollo 11 Lunar Module of 40 years ago was run by "top-secret" IBM punch cards that were mated to binary mainframe computers. Today, the average Kia has some 100 million lines of software code running through 70 on-board microprocessors, operating everything from intermittent windshield wipers to regenerative braking systems. And, we've not seen anything yet.

Thus far, automotive software applications have mostly been related to either replacing mechanical systems, such as throttle cables and ignition systems, or adding features of obvious convenience, such as entertainment systems and integrated controls. But get ready, because Car 2.0 is coming. Ford has recently announced its partnership with Microsoft to develop the "Hohm Energy Management Application" – a cloud-based system that will seamlessly transfer information between your home and your Ford vehicle. You like syncing between your mobile phone and your desktop? Try syncing between your daily driver and your house. One can imagine the possibilities. Transfer the movies from your home entertainment system to the video screens in the backs of the headrests for the kids; or how about transferring [*energy*] between your home and your car? It is not that far off.

Tesla has perhaps one of the most intriguing products soon to hit the market. Its touted Model S completely dispenses with traditional controls, dials, knobs and instrument clusters altogether. In their place is a touch screen computer monitor that can not only sync with every mobile application you can think of, but can also be upgraded or reprogrammed remotely. Want to offer consumers the next version of the coolest electronic gadget? Just send out a download for the reprogram. Have a recall notice that you need to get to consumers? No problem, simply send out a message that will display on every on-board monitor until addressed.

We have certainly traveled quite a way since the first on-board computer that was introduced on the 1978 Cadillac to display fuel economy. But, with progress can come challenge, and nowhere is that more apparent than with software applications in automobiles. The world held its breath as engineers peered into Toyota's maligned runaway car problem, wondering if it could possibly be that the problem was actually caused by a software glitch. The concern had less to do with Toyota, and more to do with the realization that we could have spent the last several years creating technology that we now may not be able to control.

The results for Toyota appear to be inconclusive, and therein lies much of the problem. With software becoming more complex by the minute, detecting problems can prove to be a near impossible task. Consumers may think that the problem is mitigated by requiring automotive manufacturers to adhere to stringent regulations before unleashing their ground-breaking software developments on the public; but they would be wrong.

You may be surprised to learn that the National Highway Traffic Safety Administration (NHTSA), the regulatory agency responsible for ensuring motor vehicle safety, does not require the software systems contained in vehicles to meet any specific safety level. It is even more concerning when it is understood that for a current production automobile, about 45 percent of the manufacturing cost is devoted to electronics – systems that are independently made by different subcontractors that are expected to perform properly when combined in a single automobile.

One may think that the reason the NHTSA does not regulate electronics is because it is unable to do so. But, this too would be incorrect. Other industries have long regulated the development and implementation of software and electronics to ensure that the systems are safe and reliable.

Consider aviation, and the approach taken by the Federal Aviation Administration (FAA). The FAA applies a rigid set of standards to software applications, officially called DO-178B "Software Considerations in Airborne Systems and Equipment Certification." DO-178B was developed by the Radio Technical Commission for Aeronautics and the European Organization for Civil Aviation Equipment and has been adopted by the FAA as a guiding document to evaluate software reliability. Part of the program is a safety assessment process and hazard analysis, which examines the effects of a failure condition in the system. If a system fails, what impact will this have on the aircraft; is it simply a matter of consumer inconvenience, or will it threaten the integrity of the aircraft? Before certifying the software for use, the FAA satisfies itself that the software is reliable, and it understands that if there is a malfunction, what the resulting impact will be.

In fairness, one could say that the automobile industry is not an exacting comparison with aviation. After all, Boeing and Airbus aren't exactly rushing to come out with the newest version of a Facebook application that will integrate with the cockpit. But, the point remains that some type of minimum standards is necessary to prevent a catastrophic event.

In the wake of the Toyota scare, Congress began to vet an auto safety bill that would require brake override systems for all vehicles and provide more funding for NHTSA. However, as the Toyota situation began to fade from recent memory, the urgency of the legislation quelled and the bill is now an item that Congress plans on addressing at a later time. In the interim, one can only hope that the urgency of the legislation is not something that is reignited by yet another catastrophic event.

CHAPTER 7

The Killing Fields

NOVEMBER 2010

At the stroke of midnight on Oct. 31, 2010, the landscape of the automotive industry in the United States forever changed. With the final tick of the second hand, dealer agreements for some 500 General Motors dealers expired, ending generations of businesses across the country. This, it was held, was the way the "New GM" would move forward.

While the fate of these dealerships may now be certain, the way that we arrived here is unsettling. The trouble began in 2008, when leaders from GM, Chrysler and Ford responded to the deep economic downturn by traveling to Congress in private jets, asking for bailout relief. As they arrived in ostentatious fashion, the corporate executives claimed that their companies would not remain viable without immediate taxpayer dollars. With the possibility of a collapsed automotive industry being too much to risk, the Treasury agreed to provide $80.7 billion in grants and loans to Chrysler and GM. However, before the funds were committed, President Barack Obama created the "Presidential Task Force on the Auto Industry" and the "Treasury Auto Team," two agencies sanctioned to review Chrysler and GM's restructuring plans. This is where the problems began.

In February 2009, both Chrysler and GM submitted restructuring plans that included a gradual reduction of their dealer network that, they claimed, would allow them to become "more competitive" with foreign competition. This move was generally consistent with the automaker's plans of consolidating franchises in smaller markets and discontinuing the Plymouth and Oldsmobile brands that had been in place since the 1970s. However, the Treasury Auto Team – lead by two non-industry executives (investment banker Ron Bloom and private equity group founder Steven Rattner) – rejected the two plans, giving the automakers 60 days to submit a "more aggressive plan" for dealership terminations, stating that it would be "a waste of tax payers' money" to not take this opportunity to significantly reduce their dealership networks. The Treasury Auto Team was looking to emulate the "Toyota Model," which suggested that smaller dealership networks would reduce competition among dealers and increase sales volume for the remaining dealers, which in turn, would allow dealerships to invest more in their facilities, and improve brand equity.

Chrysler and GM responded to the request by submitting aggressive plans, which set out to swiftly shutter scores of dealers. In June 2009, the same month that Chrysler and GM filed for bankruptcy protection, Chrysler notified 789 dealerships that they would be terminated in 22 days, and GM notified 1,454 dealers that they would no longer be able to order new vehicles and that they must wind down all operations by Oct. 31, 2010. The Bankruptcy Court then ratified these termination procedures – a critical fact, given that state franchise laws generally [*forbid*] auto manufacturers from terminating dealers without good cause. With that, America was set to have its new dealership network.

However, while the Treasury Auto Team pushed for a drastic, and immediate, reformatting of the Chrysler and GM dealer networks, public sentiment did not follow. With the average dealership employing 50 people, and generating $15 million in annual sales, the termination of these businesses would result in the unemployment of 115,000 individuals, and the loss of $35 billion in annual sales to local economies –

many of which rely on these dollars to generate precious tax revenue. Hence, in late 2009 President Obama signed into law the Consolidation Appropriations Act of 2010, which enabled the terminated dealers to have their dealer agreements reinstated through an arbitration process. For Chrysler dealers, who had already been terminated six months earlier, the decision to arbitrate was challenging, as many of them had already ceased operations. For GM dealers, who were still operating until October 2010, however, the law breathed new life into their fateful situation. Of the 1,454 terminated dealers, 1,169 pursued arbitration.

The arbitration procedures have now concluded, and it has been determined that 500 GM dealers will lose their livelihoods. But with the businesses that will be lost and the lives that will be forever changed, an important, if not critical, question lingers: Is this justice served? Have we, as a society, appropriately thinned the ranks of the dealer networks, and set up the domestic manufacturers to better compete; or have lives been permanently altered without proper consideration?

Following the billions of dollars that were given to Chrysler and GM, many members of Congress had been asking the same question, prompting a full audit of the situation by the Office of the Special Inspector General for the Troubled Asset Relief Program (SIGTARP). In its 41-page report, SIGTARP made public several startling findings. First, while the auto executives told Congress that the elimination of its dealers would result in substantial costs savings to the manufacturers, neither Chrysler nor GM gave [any] consideration to these cost savings when making their termination decisions. Moreover, the amounts purportedly saved by the manufacturers varied greatly between Chrysler and GM – Chrysler estimated cost savings of $45,500 per dealer, while GM estimated savings of $1.1 million per dealer – calling into serious doubt the credibility of the claims.

But, more troubling were SIGTARP's findings relating to the reasoning behind GM's decision to close its 1,454 dealers. GM officials stated that the termination decisions were based on an objective criterion: dealers who either failed to have a dealer performance score of at least 70 (which measures customer satisfaction, etc.) or sold fewer than 50 cars in 2008 were selected for termination. However, the SIGTARP audit found that GM did not uniformly apply the criteria to the entire network; that GM terminated dealers who did not qualify for termination, while retaining others who did; and that GM retained little to no documentation on its decision-making process, making outside review nearly impossible. So troubling were the findings, that SIGTARP has opened an investigation into possible illegal activity surrounding the terminations, which could result in prosecution by the Department of Justice.

Upon learning of SIGTARP's findings, members of Congress urged President Obama to issue an administrative mandate, halting the Oct. 31, 2010 termination date for the GM dealers until a full investigation could be completed. As Steven LaTourette (R-Ohio) and John Boehner (R-Ohio) wrote in an official letter to the Oval Office just days before the looming date, "there is too much at stake to proceed in an atmosphere where dealers were denied so much crucial information in a process rife with secrecy."

The calls by lawmakers to save the dealers from termination went unanswered, leaving their dealer agreements to expire on Oc. 31, and closing another chapter on justice unserved. So, the automakers will continue on their way, SIGTARP will move forward with its investigation, and the entrepreneurs who served the automakers, in many cases for generations, will join the expanding ranks of the unemployed.

CHAPTER 8

The Dirty Little Secret

DECEMBER 2010

In just one month's time, the long-anticipated overhaul to the Corporate Average Fuel Economy (CAFE) regulations will take effect, marking the first increase in the U.S. fuel economy standard since the start of Ronald Regan's second term. The CAFE regulations, enacted in response to the 1973 Oil Crisis, establish the minimum standards auto manufacturers must meet across all vehicle lines, or pay substantial penalties. The standard has remained at 27.5 miles per gallon for the last 25 years; yet all of this is set to change in January, when the standard begins its march from 30.2 miles per gallon in 2011 to 35 in 2020. This, it was held, would move the United States toward greater energy independence, increase the production of clean renewable fuels, and reduce our impact on the environment.

Car makers have responded to the legislation by making more fuel-efficient internal combustion engines and, more publicly, by racing to the market with hybrid and electric vehicles. GM states it is proud to be "a leader on a path to energy independence;" Nissan claims that its focus is "innovation for the planet." Public support has never been stronger for eco-friendly products, and manufacturers are happy to supply fleets of new vehicles that cater to the emotion of doing something good for the environment. Yet, amidst the rush to produce, and consume, the next best thing that will save the planet, what is the truth behind the environmental sensitivity of hybrid and electric vehicles? You might not like the answer you are about to hear.

To assess a vehicle's impact on the environment, it is necessary to consider the entire life cycle of the vehicle, from inception to destruction. While fuel consumption is the most obvious factor, it is but one factor among many to be considered. Also included in the analysis are design and engineering, raw material sourcing, manufacturing, transportation, distribution and marketing, recycling and disposal. Hybrid and electric vehicles certainly excel in fossil fuel consumption, but the analysis is not so one dimensional.

As famous as hybrid and electric vehicles have become for their fuel savings, they are beginning to develop an infamy for the pollutants they create in the manufacturing process. With nearly 400 pounds of battery packs on board the average electric vehicle, the complexity of the manufacturing process has skyrocketed, which requires more energy and creates more emissions. As a recent study undertaken by Toyota found, the Prius was the worst in its class for emissions created during the manufacturing process. Another study found that it takes 113 million BTUs of energy to manufacture a Prius, which is the functional equivalent of about 1,000 gallons of gasoline consumed before the vehicle ever hits the showroom floor.

And, then there is the matter of the raw materials. Hybrids and electrics are powered by one of two battery technologies: nickel-metal hydride and lithium ion. The rare earth elements used to produce these batteries (lanthanide and lithium) are strip-mined from solid rock, refined into their core elements, transported from their country of origin to the place where they will be manufactured into usable battery packs (usually China or Japan), and then transported again to the auto manufacturer assembly plant, where they finally make their way into the environmentally-friendly vehicle.

But, what is perhaps most surprising about the hybrid and electric vehicle is the impact consumer use has on the environment, as this is the area where the hybrids and electrics are seemingly impenetrable. While hybrids and electrics certainly have a far less direct use of fossil fuel than their internal combustion counterparts, they also have an indirect use that is quite staggering.

Every hybrid and electric vehicle draws its energy by plugging into the electric grid, and this drawdown of energy itself results in pollution to the environment. But, just how much? The answer to that question depends largely on where you live, and more specifically, how much electricity your country generates from dirty sources such as coal and oil. In Germany, 49 percent of all energy is derived from fossil fuels; in the United States, it is 55 percent. So, how much pollution is emitted by plugging an electric vehicle into an electric grid that derives 55 percent of its energy from dirty sources?

"Pollution" is actually broken down into five separate chemical compounds: carbon monoxide, carbon dioxide, hydrocarbons, nitrogen oxide and sulfur oxide. In a report published by the U.S. General Accounting Office, the impact of an electric vehicle plugged into the electric grid was compared with the tailpipe emissions of an internal combustion vehicle, with startling results. Carbon monoxide and hydrocarbons were virtually nonexistent with the electric vehicle; carbon dioxide and nitrogen oxide were at the same level in both vehicles; and the electric vehicle emitted *12 times* more sulfur oxide than the internal combustion vehicle. Sulfur oxide is a precursor to acid rain and atmospheric particulates, and is associated with increased respiratory symptoms and disease, difficulty in breathing, and premature death.

At least one study has attempted to quantify the impact hybrid and electric vehicles have had on the environment, as compared to internal combustion vehicles. In a study entitled *"Dust to Dust"* by CNW Marketing Research Inc., 312 production vehicles were ranked on an "energy cost per mile" basis. The report found that in many cases hybrid vehicles had higher energy costs than conventional cars. For instance, the Honda Accord hybrid had an energy cost of $3.29 per mile, while the conventional Honda Accord was $2.18, meaning that the Accord hybrid will consume about 50 percent more energy than the non-hybrid version.

While car makers should be applauded for the efforts to find a solution that will eliminate dependence on foreign oil and reduce harmful effects to the environment, all that glitters is not gold in the hybrid and electric vehicle market – at least not yet. Perhaps as technology improves and further alternative fuel sources are explored, we will get much closer to the answer we are looking for. But, in the meantime, we shouldn't be fooled into thinking that we are helping the environment by plugging in that new electric car.

CHAPTER 9

Ethanol
Still Ablaze

JANUARY 2011

The dawn of a new year brings with it many familiar events: cool evenings in front of a crackling fire, the sweet smell of pumpkin pie, and, of course, old acquaintances not being forgotten. But, with the turn of the calendar also come more practical traditions, the most notable of which is new legislation taking effect. On Dec. 17, 2010, President Barack Obama signed into law the Tax Cuts and Unemployment Extension Bill, which extends unemployment benefits and tax cuts for many through the end of 2011.

Officially called the "Middle Class Tax Relief Act of 2010," HR4853 is sweeping legislation that contains many features of which you may be aware, and a few that you may not. For instance, one such aspect of the legislation that will end up impacting us all is the provision that extends the Volumetric Ethanol Excise Tax Credit to Dec. 31, 2011. The Ethanol Tax Credit provides a credit to gasoline blenders of 45 cents for every gallon of ethanol blended into gasoline, as well as imposing a tariff on imports of ethanol of 54 cents per gallon.

While providing tax credits and tariffs on ethanol may seem innocent enough, when the country is still reeling from the $700 billion bank bailout and states are teetering on the brink of financial collapse, one has to question whether we can afford the tax relief. And, a larger question looms: even if we could afford it, should we?

The Volumetric Ethanol Excise Tax Credit was enacted in 2004 to incentivize refineries to deploy resources to developing ethanol as a mainstream alternative to fossil fuel. Since that time, ethanol has begun to chip away as a mainstream fuel source, with auto manufacturers beginning to produce cars that are capable of consuming mostly ethanol. Known as "E85," or fuel that is 85 percent ethanol, some 2,000 filling stations across America have gone green, catering to the new "flex fuel" vehicles.

While the need to reduce our dependency on foreign oil is paramount, is ethanol the solution to get us there? Given that we are providing what will likely be hundreds of millions of dollars in ethanol tax credits, the answer is not to be under-valued.

Derived from sugar cane, potatoes, and most notably corn, ethanol is actually the same type of alcohol found in ordinary alcoholic beverages. While it can be distilled from a variety of organic sources, corn appears to be the best suited donor – or at least the one that has become most widely adopted. And, that is where the controversy begins.

While perhaps seldom considered by those outside of the "corn-belt," corn is a highly consumed commodity around the world. Aside from the obvious application as a direct consumable, corn is used in everything from soft drinks to baby food, and it is milled into countless industrial products, such as plastics, adhesives, paint and insulation. However, the largest use of corn is livestock feed, where cattle, poultry and hogs rely on it for daily consumption.

Because of the widespread use of corn, any change in the supply or demand of the commodity has a powerful impact on the prices of corn-derived products. When the price of corn rises, so does the price of processed foods, meat and poultry, and a variety of industrial products. What impact does the use of corn in ethanol have on all of this? It is difficult to measure with absolute certainty, but fundamentals of economics teach that increased demand necessarily increases price. This could be the case with corn, where the price per bushel (which is a little less than 10 gallons) has soared from $210 in 2004 (when the Volumetric Ethanol Excise Tax Credit was first enacted) to its current rate of $620 – an increase of about 300 percent.

Balanced against this is the benefit realized by ethanol use in fuel. After all, many would tolerate increased consumer prices if it resulted in a viable solution to the fuel consumption dilemma. With ethanol, however, it appears that this may not be the case. Ethanol as a fuel contains about 35 percent *less* energy per unit than ordinary gasoline, meaning that E85 will produce lower mileage than gasoline and will require more frequent refueling. Coupled with this is a significant limitation in capacity. If all corn grown in the U.S. were used for ethanol fuel, it would only displace about 12 percent of the current U.S. gasoline consumption, making ethanol, at best, a marginal clean energy solution.

And, then there is the matter of production. To convert corn into usable ethanol, the stock goes through a lengthy distillery process, where it is dried, fermented and burned, and then blended into ordinary gasoline to make E85. Each of these processes consume energy, and perhaps more importantly, emit greenhouse gases. To put this into perspective, *National Geographic Magazine* reports that it takes one unit of fossil fuel to produce 1.3 units of corn-based ethanol – certainly not a quantum leap in terms of energy conservation.

When the lower energy per unit of ethanol is considered, it is questionable whether corn ethanol provides any net benefit on energy consumption. While it may, many clean energy advocates are voicing concerns over the continued subsidy of corn ethanol, calling it an ineffective technology that will not reduce dependence on oil. Given this, and given ethanol's impact on consumer prices, is it now time to stop subsidizing the ethanol industry, and instead allow market forces to dictate? Whatever your position, recognize that the stakes are high in this ever-changing game of trying to find the next viable clean fuel solution.

CHAPTER 10

Do It for
the Kids

FEBRUARY 2011

Few things in life are more tragic than the loss of an innocent young life. There is just something about the playful innocence, the insatiable curiosity, and yes, the mischief and trouble that causes our society to go to great lengths to protect our young. It is because of this that we have the AMBER Alert (America's Missing Broadcast Emergency Response) and Megan's Law (which grants the public access to California's 63,000 registered sex offenders), and that list is about to expand.

To be completely correct, it actually already has, yet few are likely aware of it. In 2007, President George W. Bush signed into law the "Cameron Gulbransen Kids Transportation Safety Act," which aims to change the way cars are designed and manufactured to provide better protection for children. However, because the law deferred its impact until 2011, the bill went largely unnoticed; but, all of that is about to change as the law requires the U.S. Department of Transportation to propose new rulemaking no later than Feb. 28, 2011.

It is expected that in three weeks, Transportation Secretary Ray LaHood will announce a major revision to Federal Motor Vehicle Safety Standard No. 111 – the standard that regulates rear view mirrors. LaHood has indicated that he is looking to require that all new cars be equipped with backup cameras to guard against what has become (or perhaps, what has always been) a serious problem with blind spots when cars are in reverse. The regulation is being phased in September 2012 and will take full effect by 2014.

Blind spot injuries have become somewhat of an epidemic in the nation, particularly with the proliferation of larger multi-purpose vehicles. According to figures maintained by the National Highway Traffic Safety Administration (NHTSA), on average 292 people are killed every year from being inadvertently backed over, with another 17,000 injured – 3,000 of whom suffer incapacitating injuries.

The part of the problem that is particularly troubling is that children under five, who are difficult to see and who like to hide, account for 44 percent of all backup deaths and injuries. To make matters worse, the vast majority of accidents involving children are committed by the child's own parent, as was the case of little Cameron Gulbransen, the namesake of the federal legislation. In 2002, while backing out of his driveway, Dr. Greg Gulbransen accidently backed over and killed his 2-year-old son, Cameron.

Secretary LaHood has suggested that backup cameras will cut the casualty rate in half, and looks to have all passenger cars, pickup trucks, minivans, buses and low-speed vehicles with a gross vehicle weight rating of up to 10,000 pounds equipped with backup cameras by 2014. And, this has the industry in knots.

By itself, the cost per vehicle to add the backup camera does not seem like much. For vehicles that already have video screens, the cost is about $58 to $88; if the vehicle does not have a screen, it is about $159 to $203. But all of this changes when 16.6 million new cars are factored in (the number of new cars the Dept. of Transportation believes will be sold in 2014), with the total cost reaching an estimated $1.9 to $2.7 billion annually.

50

Lobbyists for automakers are resisting the proposal, calling the rulemaking overreaching – and they may have a legitimate argument. Under Executive Order 12866, the Dept. of Transportation is required to establish the "economic value of a statistical life" for the purposes of analyzing safety measures. The Dept. of Transportation's current valuation of a statistical life is $6 million – and that is where the problem comes in.

With a cost of $1.9 to $2.7 billion annually, the backup camera proposal results in a cost of $11.8 to $19.7 million per life saved, or about 2 to 3 times over the Dept. of Transportation's standard – and the standard of virtually every other federal agency. For instance, the Food and Drug Administration uses a statistical value of $6.5 million; the Environmental Protection Agency uses $7 million. Hence, with the department greatly exceeding its own statistical standard – and the standard of all other agencies – this proposal may be ripe for judicial or congressional challenge as an administrative act beyond the agency's authority. Mercedes, Honda, Nissan and GM have already voiced their concerns over the proposal, and they may be willing to take their fight even farther.

LaHood appears to be undaunted by the tremors of a challenge to come, and for that he should be applauded. Is the proposed rule in excess of the department's guidelines? Perhaps. Is the mandate, as a whole, going to be expensive for the industry? Undoubtedly. But, sometimes good sense and common decency have to prevail over a cold statistical analysis. As LaHood recently noted, "There is no more tragic accident than for a parent or caregiver to back out of a garage or driveway and kill or injure an undetected child playing behind the vehicle." With the cost of this proposal being less than the average cost of a stereo upgrade, it is time that we as a society take responsibility for protecting our leaders of tomorrow.

CHAPTER 11

How Many More Have to Die?

MARCH 2011

It's interesting how our mindset on vehicle safety has shifted so dramatically over the last several decades. Many of us grew up in an era where seatbelts were seldom thought of, and even more rarely used; and other safety measures, such as mandatory child-seats, were not even a consideration. And, while it is hard to imagine it today, it was not that long ago that some states had no laws against drinking and driving; and for those that did, the blood alcohol limit was often set at 0.15 – or about twice today's legal limit.

But as technology advanced, and awareness improved, we began not only to accept the importance of these measures, but embrace them. Seatbelts are a part of our daily routine; children are secured in their four-point harness car seats; and those convicted of drinking and driving face serious penalties. And for this, countless lives have been spared.

Now, welcome to the new millennium, and the newest public enemy number one: cell phone texting. We all have done it at some point or another. Glancing at our phone while driving down the freeway to see who is texting us; and at times, sending a quick response. We are not acting irresponsibly when doing this, or so we think, for it only takes a moment of our attention. And, therein lies the problem.

While there is something sinister about knowingly getting behind the wheel while intoxicated that justifiably invokes scorn from society, reading a quick text while driving seems innocent enough, and certainly not on the same level as drinking and driving. And, it is because of this that the problem is compounded. While most of us recognize the danger of drinking and driving, and go to lengths to avoid doing it, we fail to recognize that texting and driving can be just as deadly – or according to some, even more so.

In 2009, *Car and Driver* magazine conducted an experiment on the impact of texting while driving, as compared to drinking and driving, with staggering results. The magazine took its editors to a deserted air strip and compared reaction times while sober, with a blood content of 0.08 (the legal limit), and while texting. To establish a baseline, the magazine determined that while driving 70 miles per hour, it took editor Eddie Alterman 0.54 seconds to respond to a car suddenly braking in front of him. A car traveling 70 miles per hour covers 103 feet per second, meaning that Alterman traveled 56 feet before reacting. When Alterman had a blood alcohol content of 0.08, this added four feet to his reaction time, for a total of 60 feet. What was shocking, however, was the distance added when texting. When Alterman was reading a text, his reaction time was increased by 36 feet, for a total of 92 feet; and when responding to a text, his reaction time was increased by 70 feet, for a total of 126 feet traveled before reacting – or two and one-half times over his baseline, and more than double his reaction time when legally drunk.

This test is not an anomaly. In 2009, the Virginia Tech Transportation Institute released the results of an 18-month study that involved placing cameras inside the cabs of more than 100 long-haul trucks. The cameras recorded the drivers over a combined driving distance of three million miles, and concluded that when the drivers were texting, their risk of crashing was 23 times greater than when not texting. The study also found that drivers typically take their eyes off the forward road for an average of 4.6 seconds when sending and receiving texts – or for a vehicle driving 70 miles per hour, about 475 feet.

To put the magnitude of the problem into perspective, in 2009 there were 33,808 fatal vehicle accidents in the United States, 10,839 of which were alcohol-related. The National Highway Safety Traffic Administration (NHTSA) *estimates* that of the total fatalities, 5,500 were caused by "distracted drivers," but it readily admits that it does know for certain how many deaths are actually caused by texting because, unlike alcohol-related accidents (where alcohol content can be measured and confirmed), there is really no way to confirm whether a death was caused by cell phone use. As Department of Transportation Secretary Ray LaHood recently commented, "We believe that this data represents only the tip of the iceberg because police reports in many places do not routinely document whether distraction was a factor in vehicle crashes."

If it seems that the problem is bad now, it appears to be getting worse, particularly among younger drivers. In a recent study conducted by Nielson, the company found that the average teenager sends 3,339 texts per month – or more than 100 per *day*, and up 8 percent from a year ago. And, as you may expect, many of these teenagers are texting while driving. In an investigation undertaken by Nationwide Insurance, the company found that 37 percent of people between the ages of 18 to 27 readily admit to texting while driving. In fact, the problem has become such an epidemic that it has engendered its own acronym – DTW, or "driving while texting."

Yet, in the face of this, many legislatures have been slow to respond to the growing problem. So far, only 30 states have banned texting while driving (California being one of them). But, even with legislation, the problem will likely persist, as it often seems innocent enough to read a quick text, and the

55

problem is extremely difficult to police. And, unlike being arrested for drinking and driving, which carries with it severe consequences, the penalty for texting and driving in California is a $20 ticket for first time offenders, and a $50 ticket for repeat offenders.

There is a solution to all of this. Although not widely known, several companies are introducing devices that can be installed in cars that will block text messaging while the car is in use. Currently, the devices are primarily being marketed as a way for parents to ensure that their teenage sons and daughters are not texting while driving, but the potential for wider-spread use is evident.

Should these devices be required for all new car sales? Perhaps. It all depends on your stance on the liberty given to personal freedoms; and the point at which the convenience afforded by cell phone usage is outweighed by the loss of life. Is cell phone use while driving an important liberty? Undoubtedly. But, how many more people have to die before we truly recognize the seriousness of the problem, and take action that is designed to actually mitigate against it?

CHAPTER 12

Will Oil Become Extinct?

APRIL 2011

Twenty-one million barrels. Crude oil, that is; or more specifically, the amount of crude oil the United States consumes on a daily basis. What is surprising about this is not that most of our supply comes from foreign sources – that is a fact adopted by all but the most extreme skeptics; what is surprising is that the United States outstrips every other country's consumption by an order of magnitude practically unimaginable. While the United States consumes 21 million barrels a day, the next highest single consumer is China, with its 1.3 billion people, who consume seven million barrels per day.

Think this disparity is because China has yet to fully realize its industrial revolution? Consider the fact that the United Kingdom consumes two million barrels a day, and the *entire* European Union (consisting of 27 member countries) consumes 14 million barrels.

America's disparate consumption of oil creates two obvious, ever-present problems: oil supplies are not infinite, and reliance on foreign oil subjects us to the whims of others. Just when will oil supplies expire? No one really knows for certain, in part because oil exploration is an inexact science, and in part because oil rich countries tend to frequently "update" their stated oil reserves, perhaps in an effort to raise their international relevance.

In 1980, Saudi Arabia reported that it had reserves of 168 billion barrels of oil. By 2008, that number had *increased* to 264 billion barrels, despite a continuous drain on reserves through daily use. Other neighboring countries have followed suit. In 1980, Iran claimed a reserve of 58 billion barrels, by 2008 that figure had risen to 138 billion. That same year, the United Arab Emirates claimed 30 billion in reserves, but by 2008 the number had grown to 98 billion. Regardless of which reports one wants to believe, under all circumstances, it appears that we will burn through the world reserves within the next 100 years, which means that we are only a generation or two away from facing a brand-new frontier.

And, even if oil supplies were limitless, continued unrest in the Middle East only serves to underscore the problem created by relying on OPEC (Organization of the Petroleum Exporting Countries) for our oil supply. Anyone old enough to recall the 1973 Arab oil embargo will understand just how quickly life can change when unlimited access to oil suddenly terminates.

Bipartisan thoughts aside, the current presidential administration has done much to begin the long haul to rectify this problem. Last Wednesday, President Barack Obama delivered a major policy speech at Georgetown University, entitled "Blueprint for a Secure Energy Future," wherein he announced a broad push to cut America's reliance on foreign oil by one-third by 2025. As part of the plan, by 2015 all new cars and trucks bought by the federal government will be alternative-fuel vehicles – a number that currently totals 663,000 vehicles according to the U.S. General Services Administration. In addition, the administration plans to form "partnerships" with private companies that want to upgrade their large fleets with alternative-fuel vehicles, handing out attractive financial incentives to companies who make the switch.

However, perhaps the biggest push is President Obama's plan for the private sector, where he is considering increasing the CAFE (Corporate Average Fuel Economy) regulations – the minimum fuel economy standards that auto manufacturers must meet across all vehicle lines – from its current level of 30.2 miles per gallon to an average of *62 mpg* by 2025. To understand just how drastic a move this is, consider that in 1978, when the CAFE rules took effect, the standard was 18 mpg, and from 1989 to 2009, the level stagnated at 27.5 mpg.

Consistent with this, the U.S. Department of Transportation and the U.S. Environmental Protection Agency have released a "Notice of Intent to Improve Fuel Economy and Reduce Greenhouse Gas Emissions for 2017-2025," which considers decreasing greenhouse gas emissions by six percent a year for the years in question, with the net result being 62 mpg by 2025. The agencies are also considering three, four and five percent decreases, with a three percent decrease resulting in a 47 mpg level by 2025. As President Obama stated, "We cannot keep going from shock to trance on the issue of energy security, rushing to propose action when gas prices rise, then hitting the snooze button when they fall again."

The U.S. Department of Defense is also getting involved, experimenting with alternative fuel sources for military operations. Just two weeks ago, an F-22 Raptor flew a maiden test flight at Mach 1.5 on a 50-50 fuel blend of conventional petroleum-based jet fuel and a biofuel derived from camelina, a weed-like plant not used for food. Noting "no noticeable differences" from traditional jet fuel, the test will perhaps pave the way further for exploration of alternative fuel sources in commercial and military aviation.

Will hybrid and electric vehicles, and alternative fuel aircraft be the solution? Perhaps. Or, perhaps other technologies will be invented, or reinvented, that will pave the way for a substantial reduction in our oil consumption.

Whatever the outcome, one constant remains: Until a solution is found, we are only a misstep away from being foisted into another energy crisis that could substantially alter life as we know it. And, this is an outcome we simply cannot afford.

CHAPTER 13

How Soon
We Forget

MAY 2011

On the one-year anniversary of the $16 million fine imposed against Toyota – the largest fine ever levied by the National Highway Traffic and Safety Administration (NHTSA) against an automobile manufacturer – little has been done to change the system that allowed the problem to exist in the first place. Students of history will recall that the Toyota calamity was notable for two significant reasons: NHTSA's $16 million fine was the largest in the agency's 24-year history; and the fine represented a mere fraction of Toyota's $1.2 billion profit it earned in just the first *quarter* of 2010.

Initiated in 1966 under what has become known as the National Traffic and Motor Vehicle Safety Act, NHTSA is the agency responsible for policing vehicle safety in the United States. And, while NHTSA has countless regulations on vehicle safety, its ability to penalize those who fail to comply has become largely symbolic.

To put the issue in perspective, consider that a modern automobile has some 10,000 moving parts, and more electronics and microprocessors than were present on the shuttle that embarked on the first lunar mission. Now consider that automobile manufacturers place about 15 million of these vehicles in the hands of U.S. consumers each year, and that an average automobile will remain on U.S. highways for about 12 years.

Despite everyone's best efforts, things will go wrong. The modern-day automobile has become far too complex for anyone to believe that parts won't fail, and that manufacturing processes won't be flawed. This increase in complexity is reflected in the steady rise of vehicle recalls year-over-year. For instance, when the vehicle recall system was instituted in 1966, NHTSA processed less than 100 recalls per year. The current automobile, however, generates about 800 recalls in the United States annually, and there is no indicating that this number will not continue to grow.

Under our current vehicle recall system, the responsibility for initiating and administrating recalls is left largely to the automobile manufacturers. Pursuant to 49 U.S.C. Section 30118, manufacturers must report a safety defect to NHTSA within five working days of discovery, even if the cause of the defect is unknown. The problem comes in when manufacturers fail to comply, as NHTSA is limited in its policing authority.

It would be naïve to believe that manufacturers do not consider the economic impact of issuing a recall before acting, and some may say that the direction they take is largely governed by the strength of their moral compass. We have seen what happens when manufacturers put economics ahead of the loss of life. The Toyota gas pedal recall is the most recent example, but it is far from the only one. Those who were present in the 1970s will recall Ford's decision to not recall the Pinto, despite knowing that its gas tank was prone to exploding upon rear impact.

It often times takes national events to expose the misgivings of those in command. For Toyota, it was the horrid 911 call by the CHP officer who was in the run-away Lexus, made just moments before he and his family were killed. For Ford, it was the internal memo to its upper management, demonstrating that it would be more cost effective to deal with the litigation arising out of Pinto-related deaths than to issue a recall.

While these companies ultimately paid the price – in the poll of public opinion, if nothing else – the fact that they were able to take this direction in the first place is troubling. Driven by the allure of the almighty dollar, and enjoying the practical reality of corporate immunity, the executives determined that they would be better off to allow a dangerous instrumentality to remain on the highways than to correct the known problem.

Legislation was introduced last year that would have changed all this. Under HR 5381, coined the Motor Vehicle Safety Act of 2010, the nation's vehicle recall program would have undergone a much-needed overhaul. Under the bill, the cap on civil penalties for manufacturers who fail to report, or who provide false, misleading or incomplete information to NHTSA, would have increased from $16 million for each instance to $300 million. But, perhaps the most important aspect of the proposed legislation is the impact it would have had on manufacturer executives.

Under Section 307 of the bill, the principal officer of a manufacturer would be required to certify that all information supplied to NHTSA is accurate and does not omit a material fact. Those who fail to comply would be subjected to stiff civil and criminal penalties. The bill would have also required all vehicles to contain a data recorder starting in 2015, set a standard on start-stop buttons so that consumers would have a consistent method of turning off a vehicle, and protected whistle-blowers from manufacturer retaliation.

In the early 2000s, our nation witnessed countless individuals lose their personal fortunes when the Enron and WorldCom scandals revealed that the company executives had knowingly misstated financial information in their reporting to the Security and Exchange Commission. We responded by enacting the Sarbanes–Oxley Act of 2002, which required certification by top level executives as to the accuracy of their reporting.

Corresponding legislation in the automotive industry, as it relates to vehicle recalls, is not only appropriate, it is necessary. The proposed HR 5381 did not pass, but it needs to. We have witnessed too many acts of self-interest to believe that the situation will not reoccur. As George Santayana famously said, "Those who do not learn from history are doomed to repeat it."

CHAPTER 14

Winning at All Costs

JUNE 2011

There once was a time when U.S. automakers enjoyed global dominance, quelling all would-be competitors with thoughts of an impenetrable market share. At a time when life was far simpler, and "what was good for GM was good for America," the Big 3 controlled an astounding 90 percent of the domestic market, cementing their place in history as one of Karl Marx's great oligopolies.

But with fame and fortune, so often comes complacency and comfort, and perhaps most importantly, the loss of the sense of urgency that helped create the empire in the first place. Today, the land of milk and honey has long past for the Big 3, having been humbled by insolvency and a slide into continued irrelevance that was decades in the making. Competitors have been quicker and leaner, resulting in a paradigm shift among consumers who once would not have considered buying a foreign car. Through years of neglect, Ford, GM and Chrysler's domestic market share has been reduced to 44 percent, making them a minority in the very industry they helped create.

The Detroit 3, as they are now known, have each responded to the crisis in differing ways. Ford has restructured its balance sheet; GM has had a public execution of its most senior executives; and Chrysler has surrendered control to Fiat. Yet, with change comes challenge, and nowhere is that more apparent than at Chrysler, where the manufacturer has embarked on an unusual – and highly suspect – path to redemption.

For all manufacturers, California is the cornerstone of market relevance. With its 30 million people and optimal weather, manufacturers view the sunshine state as critical to gaining, or regaining, national recognition; and the fight for market share is fierce. California has been particularly challenging for Chrysler, where the automaker has been diminished to controlling just 5 percent of the market.

Chrysler has put itself back in the hunt by creating a flagship sales presence in the heart of the southland that will redefine how new cars are displayed and sold. In January 2011, Chrysler opened Motor Village of Los Angeles, a $30 million dealership facility that sprawls four floors and 189,000 square feet. As Chrysler boasts in the press, this company-owned dealership serves as the "grand showplace" for Chrysler, Jeep, Dodge and Fiat brands.

While at first blush the creation of the Chrysler superstore may seem like a welcomed attempt at Chrysler's return to glory, the discussion is more involved than it may at first appear. Like most states, California has a statutory scheme on how dealerships may be operated within the state – an effort to protect both dealers and consumers, alike. Recognizing that new car dealers make up a substantial portion of the state's overall economy, and that privately-owned dealerships are not on equal footing with the massive financial resources of auto manufacturers, the Legislature has placed stringent restrictions on when automakers may become involved in retail distribution.

Under California Vehicle Code Section 11713.3, auto manufacturers may only hold an ownership interest in a dealership that is within 10 miles of another dealership of the same line-make under two limited circumstances: First, when the subject dealership is part of a minority dealer development program (where a minority dealer operator buys out the manufacturer over time); and second, a manufacturer may temporarily hold an ownership interest in a dealership for a period of no more than one year (when, for instance, a private dealership is sold back to the factory, and the factory is looking for a new buyer).

Chrysler's Motor Village superstore is within 10 miles of several privately-held Chrysler dealerships, and neither of the limited ownership exceptions apply, raising serious concerns about the legitimacy of the manufacturer's actions.

Chrysler's involvement in the subject dealership dates back to mid-2008, when it bought the franchise from then-operator Maurice Claff. Chrysler then moved the dealership across town to the Motor Village location – a location about five miles away – and reopened the dealership in 2011 as its flagship company-owned store.

During this process, Chrysler submitted several statutory notices to the California New Motor Vehicle Board, attesting that the relocation of the dealership was less than one mile (which precludes neighboring dealers from being able to "protest" the relocation) and that its ownership of the dealership was part of a bona fide dealer development program (which would have allowed it to have an ownership interest in the store).

Both statements were blatantly untrue, which has invoked the ire of the dealer community, and now the New Motor Vehicle Board itself, who voted unanimously last month to have the Department of Motor Vehicles conduct a formal investigation into the matter. If Chrysler is found to have knowingly violated the statutory scheme, the DMV has the authority to impose civil penalties against the automaker, or worse, suspend Chrysler's manufacturer license – an act that would ban its sale of new cars in the state.

The agencies entrusted to look after the well-being of the dealer community take this matter seriously, and so too should Chrysler. The Vehicle Codes at issue are long-standing and well-understood in the automotive industry, and there can be no justifiable excuse for Chrysler's actions. Yes, times are difficult, and yes, Chrysler needs to regain market share; but employing acts of deception to circumvent the law is simply not acceptable. Chrysler had full awareness of the severity of its actions, and for this it must be held accountable.

CHAPTER 15

Will the Real Team Lotus Please Stand Up

JULY 2011

Throughout time, man has been fascinated with festivals of speed. There is just something in our DNA that compels us to see who can run harder and faster than ever before; and who will suffer the agony of defeat. For all the changes that humanity has experienced, the quest for competition has remained constant, as if it is the one thing that keeps us tethered to our sense of being.

Days of old saw chariot racing as the highest level of sport, with Greeks and Romans cheering as man and horse raced through mud-pounded streets. Modern-day technology has enabled us to push the limits of physics further than ever imagined, but the nature of the game has remained the same. We all want to know who will push through pain and exhaustion, and take themselves to the brink of impossible, all for the love of speed.

Today, Formula 1 racing is the sport of kings, where gladiators climb into carbon fiber supercars capable of reaching 230 miles per hour and cornering with a lateral g-force of 5Gs – or five times a person's body weight. Make no mistake about it, Formula 1 is the world's most popular sport, with an unprecedented following.

Just how big is Formula 1? The Superbowl, with its 100 million viewers, is lauded as being the largest single viewing event; and that it is. But a Formula 1 season, which makes its way through 20 different countries, commands an annual viewership of 527 million people – or nearly 10% of the world population. With races held in front of the King of Bahrain and the people of Brazil, and nearly everywhere in between, Formula 1 has established itself as big money business.

Perhaps not surprisingly, Formula 1 teams pay remarkable sums to dance on this world stage. As an example, Ferrari routinely budgets $450 million for a *single* Formula 1 season – a price that entitles it to enter a mere two cars and two drivers in the 20-race season. Sponsorship and naming rights can be nearly as extraordinary, with companies vying for just a sliver of Formula 1's world-wide recognition. As Bloomberg recently noted, energy drink maker Red Bull spent an astonishing $675 million in Formula 1 over the past five years.

Given this backdrop, it is no surprise that when things go wrong in Formula 1, they go really wrong, with the potential for financial devastation and global humiliation. The sting of the big stage was recently experienced by Group Lotus, the maker of Lotus road cars, when they began a tussle over rights associated with the Lotus name – a dispute that brought forth decades of history.

Founded in the 1950s by automotive legend Colin Chapman, Lotus had an illustrious career in Formula 1 that is nearly as old as the sport itself. Dating back to 1958, Lotus has amassed seven Formula 1 constructors' titles and six drivers' championships, making it one of the most successful marquees in the sport.

In an effort to shield itself from liability that could flow from racing accidents, when Lotus first entered Formula 1, it did so through a separate entity called "Team Lotus," leaving its road-going cars under "Group Lotus." Through the years, and while the company was controlled by founder Colin

Chapman, this all appeared to work well, with the two groups generally having common ownership and common goals.

Yet in 1994, following the death of Chapman and the onslaught of a global recession, Lotus abandoned its Formula 1 racing efforts, allowing Team Lotus to fall into bankruptcy. The British Administer (the equivalent of a Bankruptcy Trustee) then sold off Team Lotus' assets in a liquidation sale, and the Lotus moniker vanished from Formula 1 forever; or so we thought.

Enter the new millennium, and business mogul Tony Fernandes, the Malaysian entrepreneur who founded AirAsia and Tune Hotels. In 2010, Fernandes licensed the right to use the "Lotus" name in Formula 1 from car manufacturer Group Lotus, organizing a team under the name Lotus Racing. The union was short lived, however, as Fernandes and Group Lotus soon began feuding, culminating in Group Lotus cancelling the license agreement and revoking Fernandes' right to use the Lotus name.

Yet, Fernandes discovered another way to achieve his end: Buy the Lotus Formula 1 trademark rights from the person who purchased the Team Lotus assets from the 1994 bankruptcy estate, and change the name of team from Lotus Racing to "Team Lotus." The plan worked, and Fernandes entered the 2011 season with as Team Lotus.

However, as this was occurring, Group Lotus began to grow concerned that Fernandes was attempting to launch a hostile takeover of the car company. Hence, Group Lotus responded in 2011 by launching its own Lotus Formula 1 team, resulting in two teams laying claim to the same name. Such a move is akin to two teams calling themselves the Los Angeles Dodgers, with both using the same logos and trade dress.

With mass confusion created by the dueling Lotus teams, it was not long before litigation ensued, with both parties claiming that the other was infringing on their valuable Lotus trademark. The dispute was ultimately heard last month before Justice Peter Smith of the High Court of Justice in England and Wales, who ruled on Group Lotus' summary judgment.

In a rather bewildering opinion, Justice Smith ruled that *both* parties were entitled to use their "Lotus" Formula 1 team name. Fernandes, Smith held, had properly licensed the "Team Lotus" trademark following the 1994 bankruptcy, entitling him to field a "Team Lotus" Formula 1 team; and Group Lotus was the owner of the "Lotus" trademark worldwide, entitling it to use "Lotus" to its liking.

To make matters more confusing, Smith also held that Group Lotus had the right to use the black and gold color scheme that has been historically associated with Team Lotus. As a result, Fernandes is racing "Team Lotus" with the car manufacturer's current color scheme of green and yellow, and car manufacturer Group Lotus is fielding a "Lotus" team with Team Lotus' traditional black and gold livery.

As both teams ready themselves for an appeal, one cannot help but wonder what the future will hold for these feuding camps. Will one of the teams capitulate under the mounting public pressure, or will we all wait, amid the confusion, for team "Lotus" to win the next Formula 1 race? Whatever the result, it will likely be an exciting turn to the highly-charged, emotional battle.

CHAPTER 16

The $1 Million
Question

AUGUST 2011

The automobile dealer network is one of the oldest and most established franchise systems in our nation's history, dating back to the dawn of the 20th century when businessmen with a pioneering spirit saw a future that others did not. Through the use of the sprawling dealer network, local entrepreneurs like Louis Chevrolet and Henry Ford became captains of industry, building larger-than-life empires that would forever change the world.

With this, the fortunes of manufacturers and dealers became forever intertwined, as one would not exist without the other, and the demise of one would have a lasting impact on the future of the other. Yet, while their existence is co-dependent, the risk is not necessarily equal. With a manufacturer's risk being diversified over hundreds, if not thousands of individual dealerships, automakers are insulated from the business failures of single point stores. However, the inverse is not necessarily true: The fall of a brand will frequently result in the single point dealer's certain death.

With so much uncertainty in the marketplace of late, brand strength and manufacturer viability is a worrisome topic for nearly every dealer. The past 15 years have seen the demise of Oldsmobile, Hummer, Saturn, Pontiac, Plymouth, and now Mercury – and the list may not yet be complete. Students of recent history will recall GM executive Bob Lutz infamously referring to Pontiac and Buick as "damaged brands" – a statement that preceded Pontiac's shutdown, ending its 84-year history. Buick survived the cut, but is on its fifth tagline in twice as many years, demonstrating anything but stability and suggesting that the story may yet be unfinished.

This discussion is all too real for dealers of marginal brands, such as Lincoln dealers who were recently told by Ford that they had to invest $1 million in their dealership facilities or face termination. With Mercury now on its way out, Ford (who owns Mercury and Lincoln) has announced its renewed interest in the Lincoln brand, and it is now demanding that its dealers make substantial facility improvements to support the cause. This, Ford claims, will help the brand compete against the likes of BMW and Mercedes.

The challenge for the dealers is that Lincoln sales may not be sufficient to support the increased investment. Just how off is the brand? According to *Automotive News*, BMW sells about 290,000 vehicles in the United States annually, Mercedes is at 240,000, and Lincoln trails dramatically at 51,000.

Even more concerning is that there is no certainty that Ford won't later decide to shutter Lincoln after all. It was just a few short years ago that Ford announced its renewed enthusiasm for the Mercury brand, calling it a "niche marque" that would "put stylish design within the reach of the middle-class sophisticates."

Believing that they would be supported by the Mercury brand, many dealers recently agreed to build new facilities at staggering costs. Renee Chirico spent $7.7 million on his new Lincoln-Mercury facility in Clifton, New Jersey, and Pete Adcock invested $5.5 million on his dealership expansion in Frederick, Maryland – only to find out that Ford would later abandon its interest in the Mercury brand in 2009.

Ford has offered the terminated Mercury dealers compensation for the loss of their investment, the amount of which varies depending on the dollars invested. Renee Chirico, who invested $7.7 million in his new facility, was offered $733,575; and Pete Adcock, who spent $5.5 million on his dealership expansion, was offered $181,026. Many dealers have rejected Ford's offers and elected instead to pursue civil lawsuits or administrative hearings before their state's motor vehicle departments.

So, what does the Lincoln dealer do who is presented with the $1 million Hobson's choice? Interestingly, it is not altogether clear that the automaker has the authority to even make such a demand – at least in the state of California, which just may be home to more Lincoln stores than any other state.

California Vehicle Code Section 11713.3 makes it unlawful for any manufacturer to terminate, or refuse to renew, a franchised dealership without demonstrating "good cause" under Vehicle Code Sections 3060 and 3070. Sections 3060 and 3070 define good cause as the amount of business transacted by the dealer, the permanency of the investment, whether the dealer is rendering adequate services to the public, and the like. Importantly, refusing to comply with the manufacturer's demand to build a $1 million facility does not constitute "good cause," such that an otherwise performing dealer could be terminated.

So, what leverage does Ford have over the dealer who refuses to invest? Truly not much – which raises the question of why the manufacturer would make such a demand, and whether the act of making the demand under the threat of termination is itself unlawful.

The analysis undertaken by the subject dealers should be whether, in this economic climate, a further investment into their dealership facility would enable them to sell more cars, and have an ultimate economic gain. If the answer is yes, then it is most certainly the correct decision. But, if the reason for making the investment is anything other, that decision may be one that needs to be seriously reconsidered.

CHAPTER 17

Troubles with the New Fuel Regulations

SEPTEMBER 2011

Last month, President Barack Obama announced his ambitious overhaul to the Corporate Average Fuel Economy, or the CAFE standards, for consumer cars and trucks – a move that will dramatically change the landscape of the automobile industry for decades to come. With as much fanfare as could be generated from a political event, President Obama declared this undertaking "the single most important step we've ever taken as a nation to reduce our dependence on foreign oil."

The proposed new CAFE regulations fly past the 18 mile per gallon standard set by Congress when the bill was enacted in 1975, setting a high watermark of 54.5 miles per gallon by 2025. Under President Obama's new plan, stringent increases would be phased in beginning with 2017 and steadily increasing through 2025. But, tethered to an array of incentives and credits, the touted 54.5 mpg standard actually results in an average of closer to 40 mpg. And, that's where the math starts to get fuzzy.

Under its current architecture, electric vehicles would count as having "0 emissions" (even though their use of the electrical grid makes them far from emission free), and each electric vehicle sold by the automakers in 2017 would count as two vehicles, with the multiple reducing to 1.5 in 2021. Similarly, each hybrid vehicle sold in 2017 would count as 1.6 vehicles sold, phasing out to 1.3 vehicles in 2021, with hybrid trucks having eligibility for credits during the entire 2017-

2025 program. All of this means, of course, that automakers can get credit for meeting the CAFE standards without actually doing so.

While the program is not as advertised, what's most troubling about the proposed standard is its early endorsement on a technology yet to be proven. By incentivizing early introduction and adoption of electric and hybrid vehicles, the plan forces manufacturers to invest billions of dollars in a technology that is still in its infancy stages, and which may not be the best method of achieving a goal that is still some 14 years off. To put this into perspective, consider how the iPhone, introduced in 2007, has revolutionized the world, and how inconceivable that technology would have been in 1993.

The strength of America has always been its diversity, its curiosity and, most importantly, its ability to innovate. Yet, with the forced adaptation of a particular technology, market forces and natural selection fall away, leaving an unfortunate wake of unexplored ideas.

President Obama's plan will also bring to bear Adam Smith's "law of unintended consequences," as manufacturers exploit the regulation every way imaginable. We witnessed this with the first enactment of the CAFE regulations in 1975, which, in its attempt to squeeze consumer transportation, resulted in the death of the station wagon and the birth of the gas-guzzling SUV – a "truck-based" vehicle that fell outside the stringent CAFE standard, and which now represents nearly 20 percent of the vehicles on road. Ironically, the initial CAFE regulations created the very thing they were designed to quash.

So what is the unintended consequence that will result from the new onslaught of legislation? The answer is actually not all that difficult to see, which makes the proposed standard all the more vexing. A short lesson in physics will show that one of the easiest ways to increase fuel economy is a reduction in weight, and it is natural to expect that the first, and least expensive, place that manufacturers will turn is weight trimming.

This seems innocent enough, but it is not the entire story, as the proposed regulation does not treat all passenger vehicles equal. In an effort to curry favor with the Detroit 3, President Obama exempted the large truck market from the brunt of the fuel saving standards, giving them until 2020 to begin their phase-in, and even then, at lower levels. The result of all of this? A widening disparity in the size of passenger car and trucks.

The consequence of big trucks and small cars on the road is obvious, but we need not rely on pure logic, as several studies have been conducted on the danger this creates. A report by the National Highway Traffic and Safety Administration, or NHTSA, found that a reduction of a car's weight by 100 pounds has an increase in the occupant fatality rate by as much as 5 percent. As the report stated, "When two vehicles collide, the laws of physics favor the occupants of the heavier vehicle...heavy vehicles were in most cases longer, wider and less fragile than light vehicles." A study by the Harvard Center for Risk Analysis found that CAFE standards resulted in 2,200 to 3,900 additional motorist fatalities per year. The National Academy of Sciences reached similar results, concluding CAFE regulations to be responsible for 2,600 highway deaths per year.

The disparity between passenger cars and light trucks was duly noted by Volkswagen in its harsh criticism of the proposed regulation: "Volkswagen does not endorse the proposal under discussion. It places an unfairly high burden on passenger cars, while allowing special compliance flexibility for heavier light trucks.... The proposal encourages manufacturers and customers to shift toward larger, less efficient vehicles, defeating the goal of reduced greenhouse gas emissions."

If the Obama administration sought to reduce our dependence on foreign oil – an important goal to be sure – a higher gasoline tax would have been the way to do it. Such a tax would have the natural result of altering the demand curve for fuel inefficient vehicles, and market forces would have responded with innovation, the likes of which we have never seen. Yet, as Congressman John Dingell noted, gas taxes are a smart and sound policy, but it is one that "kills you with the voters." President Obama avoided a run-in with voters over an unpopular gas tax, and instead took a hero's welcome with the 54.5 mpg standard. Perhaps not that curious of a move, considering that the race for the White House has entered its unofficial beginning.

CHAPTER 18

The Pain Is
Far from Over

OCTOBER 2011

There are certain moments in a nation's history that define generations and forge the creed by which we live. The scars left by the Great Depression are still clearly visible. Those present in the 1960s can likely recall where they were when they learned that President John F. Kennedy had been shot. The current generation is left with the hurt of Sept. 11, and more recently, the financial meltdown that threatened to collapse a nation.

This week marks the third anniversary of the extraordinary relief that was required to stall, or at least slow, the 2008 global financial crisis that was born out of Wall Street greed. As our economy splintered and century-old companies failed, the elected few worked through the triage to prevent the collapse of it all. The solution was the Emergency Economic Stabilization Act of 2008, a sweeping bill that was signed into law by President George W. Bush on Oct. 3, 2008 and which established the $700 billion "Troubled Asset Relief Program" – a program that enabled the administration to dole out billions of dollars to teetering companies with the stroke of a pen.

To say that the legislation was of epic proportions is to only state the obvious. Students of history will likely look at these acts in the same way we reflect back on the Great Depression, by asking: How could such a thing have ever happened? And, while the initial shock of the calamity has subsided, our economy still sputters through the recovery, as if to tell us that the wounds are much deeper than we wanted to believe.

Any optimism has been quelled by the harsh reality that things are just not looking better, despite the passage of time. Standard & Poor's downgraded the United States' AAA debt-rating for the first time in the agency's 70-year history, putting our country's default risk below that of Australia, Denmark and Finland; and *Economist* magazine puts the risk of the U.S. moving backwards into another recession at 1 in 2.

Through this, U.S. automakers have been bludgeoned by shakeups, bankruptcies and sell-offs, and have lost market-share that was decades in the making. Chrysler executives are now eating pasta and GM is eating crow, while Henry Ford's kingdom has been whittled down to a fraction of the goliath it once was. To see just how bad it is, consider that in 2006 U.S. vehicle sales were at 17 million units, with many industry experts predicting that the magical 20-million-unit mark would soon be surpassed. Yet, by 2010 U.S. sales had retreated to 11 million units – the same number of vehicles sold in 1968, when our population was just a tick over 200 million.

While new vehicle sales have plummeted, there is an untold story about the collateral impact this creates. One of the major supply chains for used vehicle inventory is lease returns, and the 2008 slowdown is now beginning to have a heavy impact. As automotive research firm R.L. Polk & Co. noted, between June and November 2008 new car leases fell 58 percent, creating an industry-wide shortage of late-model used vehicles. The result? Used car prices are about to drastically increase.

If this sounds bad, the problem will be exacerbated as consumers begin to realize that their leased vehicles have a residual value that is far less than the price of a comparable vehicle. The natural result of this will be that more consumers will purchase their cars at the expiration of their lease, further shortening the supply of available inventory.

Just how bad can it get? Manheim Auctions, the world's largest wholesale auction provider, has been tracking used vehicle prices since 1995, and notes that used vehicle prices have already begun to soar. Using 1995 as a baseline with a score of 100, Manheim maintains a used car price index that measures prices month-over-month, adjusted for the time value of money. In May 2011, the index hit a record-high 127.8, meaning that – as of May – the cost of buying used was approaching the cost of buying new. As we get deeper into 2011, this outlook promises to worsen.

While this spells trouble for consumers, it is particularly worrisome for automotive dealers, who are already struggling to remain viable with sunken new car sales. And, what's bad for dealers is bad for the economy, as new car dealers make up 7 percent of California's retail economy and provide for $5.3 billion in annual payroll. This does not take into consideration the thousands of independent automotive dealers who depend exclusively on used car sales for their business, and who will be greatly impacted by the lack of supply.

Kelly Blue Book and Edmunds.com have been reacting to the shortage by steadily adjusting their used car pricing guides up, with Edmunds noting that nearly 70 used cars models are nearing the price of new. As Edmunds.com analyst Joe Spina stated, "I don't expect any dramatic decreases in used prices for at least 18 months." Other industry analysts are less optimistic, such as the National Automotive Dealers Association who opines that it could be as late as 2017 before used car prices return to their prior levels.

For an industry that sells some 30 million used cars each year, higher transaction prices will have a chilling effect on the growth of our economy. Given the size of the sector, and the direct impact it has on jobs, finance and state tax revenue, this is a problem that will impact us all.

CHAPTER 19

Basking in the Ferrari Sun

NOVEMBER 2011

At some point, things have to get better – at least that is what we keep telling ourselves, as if repetition will change our harsh reality. Wishful thinking aside, the world is as mixed-up as it has ever been, and there is little reason to believe that salvation is near. President Obama's $447 billion jobs bill failed in the Democratic-controlled Senate last month, and that should come as no great surprise. A recent New York Times / CBS News poll found that Americans' distrust of government is at an all-time high, with 89 percent of pollsters believing that our elected leaders will not "do the right thing" – a knock against Democrats and Republicans, alike.

The global financial crisis has destroyed our confidence in all things once perfectly understood. In October, the Consumer Confidence Index retreated to the dreadful level of 39.8 – just a point off the low-water mark of 38.8 during the October 2008 meltdown, and a universe away from the dizzying 144.7 in January 2000. And, if there is no belief that the government can pull us from the doldrums, don't look for the private sector to carry the day. The Conference Board's "Measure of CEO Confidence" reported last month that chief executive confidence declined substantially in the last two quarters, pinning it at its lowest level in over two years.

For those fortunate enough to have a degree of wealth – or, in these times, at least a steady job – an important question arises about where to invest in a time of crisis? Tough times or not, savers still need a safe haven for their money, and the choices are becoming less plentiful. According to the Federal Deposit Insurance Corporation (FDIC), 427 banks have failed since 2008, and while the FDIC does provide a backstop, its insurance is limited to $250,000 and it only applies to insured banks. Gold bullion has been a refuge to some, but with its price nearing $2,000 a troy ounce, the risk of devaluation is significant to those who have been late to invest.

With traditional markets closed to logical investors, alternative asset classes have suddenly become more attractive, and nowhere is this more prevalent than the burgeoning classic car market. If recent history is an indicator of things to come, the developing classic car auction industry is quickly becoming the most unlikely of heroes, exploding under the enthusiasm of contrarian thinkers.

This past August, five auction companies gathered in Pebble Beach for the annual Concours d'Elegance motorcar gathering, with staggering results. In the four-day event, 919 classic cars were sold for an astonishing $198,399,797 – passing the 2007 banner year by an incredible $64 million. At a time when economists world-over have been searching for a monetary sanctuary, the Pebble Beach auctions were smashing records at a magnificent clip.

RM Auctions set the record for the highest grossing sales day in auction history at $60.5 million – that's $60.5 million of cars sold in a *single day* – and Gooding & Company sold a company best $78 million in its two-day event. In all, the Pebble Beach auctions witnessed 31 sales in excess of $1 million, and two over $10 million; but it was a 1957 Ferrari 250 Testa Rosa that stole the show, selling for an auction record of $16.4 million. Yet, the sale of the Ferrari is as notable for the story behind the story, as it is for its recorded-setting price.

Originally, built by the Ferrari factory as a "test mule" for future Testa Rosa models, the 1957 Ferrari 250 was raced extensively in the 1950s and 1960s by some of the best drivers of the day. When it was deemed no longer competitive, the car was sold several times over, until it was doused with gasoline and set on fire by its then-owner, in an attempt to collect insurance proceeds. The burnt-out car was then sold in 1970 to Charles Betz and Fred Peters, two Southern California college professors, as a "project car" for a mere $2,500. The professors then spent the next 18 years restoring the car to show-quality standards, and the rest, as they say, is history.

If the classic car market is begging to catch fire, it is Ferrari that is blazing the way. *Sports Car Market* reported last month that Ferrari prices at the Pebble Beach auctions rose 35% over last year, with most of the $1 million-plus sales belonging to the Italian car maker. And, this makes sense, given the strength of the Ferrari brand. *Businessweek* ranks Ferrari as one of the top 100 most recognizable brands in the world, and Fiat (who owns Ferrari) places the trademark value at $7.3 billion. In fact, the 64-year-old company's name has become so strong that its merchandising and licensing division actually outstrips its car sales, with the division garnering $1.5 billion in annual sales.

But, it is not just Ferraris that investors are flocking to. In the same Pebble Beach auctions, a 1931 Duesenberg sold for $10.3 million, the highest price ever paid for an American car, and several other nameplates held or increased in value.

Still not convinced? Consider that last year, a 1935 Bugatti T57 sold in a private party transaction for *$37 million* – the highest price ever paid for a car. And yet what is perhaps more surprising is that, as with the 1957 Ferrari 250, the car had been purchased years earlier for a mere $60,000, before being restored to award-winning perfection.

And, the market is continuing to evolve. As collectors redefine what is considered "art," unrestored barn-yard finds are all the rage. Take the 1925 Bugatti Brescia that was purchased last year at Bonhams for $364,700, and is now on display at the Mullin Automotive Museum. The catch? The car had been on the bottom of Lake Maggiore in Switzerland for the past 70 years, until discovered by recreational scuba divers. And, as the market continues to evolve, the $364,700 paid for the Bugatti will probably prove to be cheap money.

Non-traditional times call for non-traditional thinking, and it is those who embrace change that will succeed. As Albert Einstein has famously said, "We can't solve problems by using the same kind of thinking we used when we created them." Be bold. Think different.

CHAPTER 20

Spend It Like You Got It

DECEMBER 2011

A wise man once said, "You can't spend your way to success." But don't tell that to the automotive manufacturers who are dead set on spending big – particularly when it's not their money being spent.

As manufacturers become increasingly brand-oriented, they are dedicating considerable effort toward designing, and in many cases re-designing, dealership facility programs. The initiatives require franchised dealers to conform to a specific "brand" architecture, and dictate every aspect of facility design, from awnings and fascia to floor tiles and furnishings. And, when the next manufacturer comes out with a shinier plan, the one-upmanship games begin, with manufacturers recasting their design concepts to include brighter floors and bigger windows.

The point of all of this is to create a uniform look among a sprawling dealer base and give their product brand identity. In years past, manufacturers only required dealers to use conforming trademarks and proper signage, but those days are long gone. Automakers now have complete design plans and regulate which architects and vendors must be used and what type of furniture may be bought. To give but a few examples, General Motors has its "Essential Brand Elements," Toyota has the "Image USA II," and Mercedes-Benz just calls its program "Autohaus."

In their rush to beat out the competition, manufacturers are cajoling, inducing, and strong-arming dealers to tear down their existing facilities and build to the hilt – even if it means tearing down a facility that was just erected under the manufacturer's outgoing program. The industry has seen more than an occasional case where a dealer has been required to restart construction because the design program changed during the renovation process.

Consider the case of Mercedes-Benz dealer Keenan Motor Group of Doylestown, Pa. who is about to build a new facility under the freshly minted Autohaus program. The project will replace a dealership that was built just six years ago at a cost of $20 million, but is no longer factory compliant.

As independent businesses, the cost of construction is borne almost entirely by the dealers – and the costs are staggering. Under the Autohaus program, 88 percent of U.S. dealers have renovated their facilities at a cost of $1.4 billion. Asbury Automotive Group, a publicly traded dealership conglomerate with 80 retail stores, plans to spend $100 million in facility improvements between now and 2013.

To be fair, manufacturers do contribute to the cost of construction by providing incentives to dealers who participate in the programs. Mercedes pays its Autohaus dealers $400 per car sold over a three-year period. General Motors makes quarterly payments to its Essential Brand Elements dealers in amounts that are dependent on the size of the project.

But, the cost of real estate and construction is at risk money fronted by the dealers, who can only hope to recover the investment, assuming the brand remains viable. In just the last 10 years or so, Pontiac, Hummer, Saturn, Oldsmobile, Daewoo, Mercury and Plymouth have been laid to rest, leaving a wake of empty dealership facilities and countless dealers who are still paying the construction debt.

Because of this, many dealers are resistant to facility design programs. And, while manufacturers cannot force an existing dealer to participate in their program, many are using every ounce of political and coercive power to get facility upgrades. One method that has been particularly popular is conditioning manufacturer approval for the sale of a franchise on a new facility being built. Yet, such tactics are of questionable validity, as franchise agreements require manufacturer approval to not be unreasonably withheld.

The issue appears to be coming to an ahead, as automotive juggernaut and Fortune 500 company Sonic Automotive is challenging the practice. Sonic has sued Mercedes in North Carolina, complaining that the automaker is illegally tying approval of a buy-sell to renovations at four other Mercedes stores owned by Sonic. And, the controversy is not limited to Mercedes. Sonic has also charged Toyota with blocking its attempt to sell four of its Toyota stores by tying approval to upgrades under the Image USA II program.

State legislatures have begun to take notice of the issue, with the National Automobile Dealers Association reporting that legislation is under review in 15 states, and that others have already signed bills. Colorado, for instance, enacted HB 1049, which requires a manufacturer to reimburse a dealer for facility upgrades made within five years, if the dealer is terminated for anything other than fraud. A Florida law requires that manufacturers pay 80 percent of their vehicle incentives to dealers who do not participate in manufacturer programs. And, Virginia passed a bill this year deeming dealers who have made improvements to their stores within the last 10 years to be in compliance with an automaker's current program.

California has also acted. In 2009, Gov. Arnold Schwarzenegger signed into law SB 424, now codified as California Vehicle Code Section 11713.13, which prevents a manufacturer from requiring a facility upgrade unless it is "reasonable" to do so. Yet, what is reasonable is not defined, leaving much debate about whether manufacturers can require upgrades for California dealers.

The California legislation is a good first step toward leveling the playing field, but stops well short of what is necessary to fully address the issue. So long as it is the dealers' capital at risk, they need to be provided with more protection from having to construct, and re-construct, dealership facilities that meet the pleasure of the manufacturer. Any other result leaves too great a power with the party who has everything to gain and very little to lose.

CHAPTER 21

Up in
Smoke

JANUARY 2012

The plan was seemingly perfect. Put all of America's might behind the emerging electric car industry and help the U.S. automakers reclaim their place as global leaders. GM was positioned to be first to market with its Chevrolet Volt – the car would pave the way for the company's future – and the Obama administration was in full support. In his 2011 State of the Union Address, President Barack Obama told the nation that he wanted the U.S. to be "the first country to have one million electric vehicles on the road by 2015."

GM had just completed its public stock offering at $33 per share, and it sought to boost public enthusiasm by proclaiming that it would sell 10,000 Volts by the end of 2011. The Department of Treasury was bullish on the outcome. In April 2011, the Treasury announced that it would sell off its 25 percent ownership in GM in late 2011, and recover its multi-billion investment in the automaker. But needing a price of $53 per share to break even, everything needed to go right – and it seemingly was.

In mid-2011, President Obama announced that the 2025 Corporate Average Fuel Economy (CAFE) regulations would carry a standard of 54.5 miles per gallon, and that special credits would be provided to manufacturers of electric cars. The announcement cemented electric cars as the technology of the future, leaving market forces to reward companies that embraced the concept.

And with this, the stage was perfectly set: The U.S. would recapture its investment in GM, the country would reduce its dependence on foreign oil, and the domestic automakers would start their march toward global relevance. So, when a routine crash test involving a Chevrolet Volt took place on May 12, 2011 in the Burlington, Wis. – a town of 11,000 – few took notice.

The test was supposed to be a standard rating test administered by the National Highway Traffic Safety Administration (NHTSA) – and at first it was. The Volt showed impressive structural integrity, receiving a five-star rating by the agency. However, three weeks following the test, while parked in the neighboring NHTSA storage facility, the Volt's 288 lithium ion batteries began to ignite, engulfing the vehicle and three others in flames.

The Volt fire was remarkable for the manner in which the event's aftermath was handled, as for the event itself. Following the fire, NHTSA officials discussed the event with GM executives, but failed to disclose the matter to the public or conduct further testing on the Volt's battery. Of particular concern was the fact that the Regulatory Affairs Subcommittee held Congressional hearings on Oct. 12, 2011 into whether the new CAFE regulations would impact vehicle safety – and NHTSA said nothing of the Volt fire.

It wasn't until Bloomberg News broke the story on Nov. 11, 2011 that the public was finally informed. The following week, NHTSA conducted simulated crash tests on three additional Volt batteries, with one of the battery packs emitting sparks and another catching fire. NHTSA then announced that it was opening a safety investigation into the Volt battery system.

After the story broke, the Treasury Department reversed its decision to sell off its GM stock, and indicated that it was now expecting a $24 billion loss on its GM investment. The prognosis may not even be that good, as the company's stock has sunk to $20 per share and is trending downward.

The failure of NHTSA to come forward about the Volt fire has some members of Congress brewing. In December, three U.S. House members sent a letter to NHTSA Administrator David Strickland, accusing the agency of "deliberately suppressing" known safety risks of the Volt. And former NHTSA Administrator, Joan Claybrook, appears to agree. In a recent statement, Claybrook said that the failure to disclose "makes no sense" and that in her view the event was delayed "because of the fragility of [Volt] sales." Last month, GM publicly announced that it was far from reaching its sales goal of 10,000 Volts by the end of 2011.

U.S. Transportation Secretary Ray LaHood denies allegations that NHTSA withheld information about the Volt, but members of Congress remain unconvinced. The Regulatory Affairs Subcommittee has announced that it will be holding Congressional hearings later this month about whether NHTSA intentionally failed to disclose the fire in an effort to support the Obama administration's push for electric cars. Expect the hearings to garner attention from GM's top brass, as the subcommittee has also demanded an explanation from GM CEO Dan Akerson.

Pundits might say that the Obama administration was trying to ride into an election year with a turnaround of the slumping auto industry and a recovery of the billions handed out to automakers during the global financial crisis. Certainly, had GM's Volt been the darling the company had expected, and its stock price risen precipitously, the administration would have received resounding applause for the miraculous turnaround.

But, that didn't happen, and now the administration and the automaker are caught in a public relations nightmare. What is at issue is not whether the Volt's battery design is faulty, but whether information was timely disseminated in an unvarnished manner. It would be offensive for an automaker to withhold safety information about one of its vehicles; it is unforgivable for a governmental agency that is charged with policing automakers to do so. Recall that not long-ago NHTSA extolled a maximum $16.4 million fine from Toyota for hiding safety defects related to sudden acceleration – an event that cost the company countless sums in lost sales, product recalls and damaged goodwill.

With a 25 percent ownership in a company that distributes products around the world, we cannot afford even an appearance of favoritism. Whether real or perceived, a governmental cover-up of safety defects can cost us dearly, both in terms of domestic confidence and global credibility. In such fragile times, this is a cost far too great to endure.

CHAPTER 22

The Billion Dollar Blunder

FEBRUARY 2012

How could everything go so wrong when all was supposed to be so right? The year was 2008, and legendary sports car manufacturer Porsche was in its zone. The iconic 911 was more popular than ever, and with the addition of a sports utility vehicle and a soon-to-be-released sports sedan, the company had successfully transitioned from role of specialty niche manufacturer to fully developed global powerhouse.

And, the carmaker was far from done. With architecture being drawn for the 918 Spyder and the 911 GT3 R Hybrid, Porsche sought to bring hybrid technology to the supercar world – something that would forever change the landscape of the sports car market. Porsche hoped that the "halo" effect of these two products would propel the company to record sales figures, stating that its goal was to double its annual output to 200,000 units. For a company that had never sold more than 97,000 cars, a mighty goal indeed.

As Porsche's success continued, its confidence beamed, leading to out of this world ambition. In 2008, with a recent track of remarkable achievement, the company embarked upon an undertaking so enormous that any misstep could result in the company's demise. That year, Porsche sought to execute a hostile takeover of automotive juggernaut Volkswagen – a company 16 times larger than Porsche and well-placed in German politics.

With $151 billion in annual sales and 9 marquee brands, the Volkswagen group was Europe's largest carmaker and prized jewel of the German government. Once owned entirely by the government, the German state of Lower Saxony retained a 20 percent ownership of the company, and enacted a law specific to Volkswagen which gave it unlimited veto power over any proposed corporate action.

Porsche began the takeover by secretly buying up hoards of Volkswagen stock. As Volkswagen shares began to thin, speculation swirled on who was behind the raid – and Porsche denied any involvement. Yet, on October 26, 2008 Porsche revealed that it had acquired 75% of Volkswagen's stock – leaving a mere 5% available for the public market – resulting in a "short squeeze" of historic proportions.

With speculators around the world betting that the price of Volkswagen stock would decline, the sudden news of the Porsche takeover caused the stock price to soar, and investors who had shorted the stock (or bet on its decline) scrambled to cover their positions. As few shares were available for the surging demand, the price of Volkswagen's stock *quadrupled* within days to over €1,000 ($1,300) per share – making Volkswagen the world's most valuable company virtually overnight.

Yet, Porsche's quest to overtake Volkswagen was marred with miscalculation. Porsche had spent some €14 billion ($18 billion) in cash buying Volkswagen stock, and when its cash reserves ran dry it took on €10 billion ($13 billion) in debt to finish the acquisition. Porsche had counted on being able to access Volkswagen's massive cash reserves to repay the debt, yet when the credit markets seized up the banks began demanding immediate repayment. The situation turned into a full-scale crisis when the German state of Lower Saxony vetoed Porsche's access to the stockpile of cash, leaving the company with billions in debt.

With Porsche unable to service its debt, Volkswagen saw this as an opportunity to turn the tables on the would-be raider and add Porsche as a tenth brand to its automotive group, which already included Audi, Bentley, Bugatti and Lamborghini. Hence, in August 2009 Volkswagen paid €3.9 billion ($5 billion) for 49.9 percent of Porsche's auto-making business, and an option to purchase the rest, with the final merger decisions to be made by the end of 2011.

As the deadline for merger decisions neared, claims against Porsche of stock manipulation began to mount – causing Volkswagen to slow its enthusiasm for a fully-integrated merger of Porsche's global operations. Then on December 31, 2011, a pair of lawsuits brought by institutional investors were filed in Germany, seeking €4.8 billion ($6.2 billion) from Porsche for stock manipulation. And, the claims may have merit. Previously, German prosecutors had raided Porsche's headquarters in Stuttgart, Germany, seeking information related to market manipulation of Volkswagen shares.

Institutional investors have also filed suit against German President Christian Wulff for €1.8 billion euros ($2.3 billion) for his role in the events. Prior to his election in June 2010, Wulff served as the premier of state for Lower Saxony and on Volkswagen's board of directors. As a key decision maker for the company, investors are alleging that Wulff knew of Porsche's stock manipulation and failed to protect their interests.

Amidst the swirling legal issues, Volkswagen chief executive Martin Winterkorm said last month that a fully-integrated merger with Porsche now "isn't possible," suggesting instead that Volkswagen may simply buy the remaining 50.1 percent interest in the car-making unit, and roll it into its global operations. Without such a deal, it is not clear just how long Porsche can survive – or at least continue to flourish.

In a world of consolidated rollups, it is sad to see one of the few remaining great independents topple into amalgamation. Ferrari is now owned by Fiat; Rolls Royce is owned by BMW – and it appears that Porsche will soon follow suit. But with each rollup, a piece of what made the company great inevitably dies. Lamborghinis now use Audi engines and Maseratis now use Chrysler parts, and with that they sacrifice an indispensable part of their heritage and soul.

For many, Porsche is the embodiment of all that is right in the sports car world. A car that never should have made it, and yet refuses to quit. It is the standard against which all competitors are judged, and is as much loved for its quirkiness as it is for its perfection. The key is in the wrong place, the engine is at the wrong end, yet it is the car's eccentricity that causes grown men to swoon and little boys to dream. One can only hope that with the pending rollup into the Volkswagen conglomerate, the company can retain a piece of its DNA.

CHAPTER 23

Progress
Interrupted

MARCH 2012

There are few things in life more challenging than bringing a new vehicle to market. Beyond the obvious need to have a vehicle that satisfies market demand, there are countless regulatory requirements in the United States and abroad that throw engineering, design and feasibility into a steady state of conflict and strife. Sovereign nations issue differing standards on everything from bumper height to airbag deployment, only serving to further complicate an already overly complicated process.

Then there is the matter of cost. Manufacturers frequently spend billions to bring a car to market, with no assurance of market acceptance. For example, in 1986 Ford spent $6 billion to develop the Ford Contour – a car it thought would become an instant hit – only to find that consumers were lukewarm on the product. More recently, Jaguar spent $1 billion developing aluminum-bodied cars, only to abandon the technology and retreat to steel-bodied cars.

So, when famed car designer Henrik Fisker – the man responsible for designing the Aston Martin DB9 and the BMW Z8 – set out to start a new electric car company, he was not short on ambition. As a startup company, Fisker lacked infrastructure, a dealer base and, most importantly, brand recognition. And, as an electric car company, Fisker was forging its path into market acceptance with undeveloped technology.

To succeed, Fisker would need enormous financial support – a quest that was greatly enhanced in 2009 when the U.S. Department of Energy agreed to lend the company $529 million of taxpayer money. The loan, under the Advanced Technology Vehicles Manufacturing Loan program, came at a time when the U.S. auto industry was teetering on the brink of extinction, and the Treasury was doling out millions to save existing companies and build new ones.

The Department of Energy loan to Fisker has been a lightening-rod for criticism from the beginning. Pundits were incensed that after Fisker received the loan, the company began manufacturing its first car, the $103,000 Karma, overseas in Finland. Critics were also disturbed that Fisker would only be building a few thousand Karmas each year – a negligible amount by industry standards. Fisker maintained that the majority of the Department of Energy loan was earmarked for its second car, code-named Project Nina, which was to be built in a 3.2 million-square-foot manufacturing facility that Fisker purchased from GM in Delaware.

It now appears doubtful that Fisker will be receiving the loan proceeds at all. The loan payout schedule was based on Fisker achieving certain milestones with the Karma rollout, which it failed to do. The Karma has been delayed by cash flow troubles, regulatory holdups, and a battery recall – delays that the Department of Energy says disqualify the company from receiving the remaining $336 million in loan proceeds. As a result, Fisker has halted work at the Delaware plant and started laying-off employees.

The election-year decision to pull the loan from Fisker has wide-spread implications for Fisker and the industry. When the $336 million was taken off the table, Fisker went back to its investors and pressed them hard for further contributions, under the threat of serious dilution. This caused one California shareholder to sue the company last month in the Orange County Superior Court for fraud, breach of fiduciary duty, and violation of California's securities laws. In the complaint, Plaintiff Daniel Wray claims that he was given nine days to make a capital investment of 40 percent of his earlier investment, or lose rights associated with his preferred stock.

The turmoil at Fisker has resulted in notable change. Last Tuesday, Henrik Fisker was replaced as CEO of the company by Tom LaSorta, the former chief executive of Chrysler from 2005-07. Henrik Fisker is now the company's executive chairman and design chief officer, and has been divested of the day-to-day decision making over the company that bears his name.

Outside Fisker, parts suppliers who were preparing for the Project Nina contracts have had to idle workers. Most notably, battery supplier A123 – also a recipient of a Department of Energy loan – has laid off 300 workers in the last eight months and cut its sales forecast by 20 percent upon news of the loan freeze. As a result, A123 has seen its stock fall from nearly $6 per share to under $2.

It is likely that Fisker believed that the Karma delays were not material to the Department of Energy loan, and that the financing could be renegotiated once the Karmas began being delivered. Even if that was the case, all of that changed last October when a scandal erupted over the Department of Energy's $535 million loan to startup Solyndra, the California solar panel manufacturer.

The problems for Solyndra began in late 2010, when it defaulted on its government loan, yet still continued to receive the remaining $95 million loan balance. Then, in 2011, when the company was out of cash, the government allowed

Solyndra to borrow an additional $75 million from its private investors, and it agreed to subordinate the taxpayer loan to the new money. In October 2011, the company laid off all 1,100 workers and filed bankruptcy, leaving the government in a junior position to the recent investors.

The Solyndra scandal has resulted in Congressional hearings, accusations of political cronyism, and a virtual certainty that the Obama administration will not be renegotiating the Fisker loan during this pivotal political climate. But the happenings at Solyndra and Fisker underscore a larger question of whether the government should be playing the role of venture capital investor for startup endeavors in the first place.

Yes, we need to support emerging industries, and yes, we need to create jobs. But, is placing bets on startup companies, who have yet to prove they have an ability to succeed, the proper way to steward taxpayer money? Startups face immeasurable risk, particularly in emerging industries. While we would like to see their efforts succeed, the reality, however harsh, is that many will not. Using taxpayer funds as high risk investment capital is not an appropriate deployment of government revenue. Although some companies may succeed, and perhaps Fisker will be one of them, the risk is far too great to tolerate.

CHAPTER 24

The Love of All Things Ferrari

APRIL 2012

When one of the most rare and beloved cars on the planet gets wrapped around a tree, the automotive community weeps. When the accident is caused by a Special Agent of the Federal Bureau of Investigations and an Assistant United States Attorney, the world takes notice.

Introduced in 1995 to celebrate Ferrari's 50th anniversary, the Ferrari F50 is one of the most important automobiles of the modern era. With just 349 built – one less than Ferrari thought the market would accept – the car is a treasure to see and euphoria to drive. The street-legal racecar will top 203 mph in the blink of an eye, and do so in a way that is unmistakably Ferrari. And, at a cost of $750,000, this is a pleasure that very few will experience.

Whether overcome by greed, or having surrendered to temptation, airline pilot Tom Baker was not about to be denied this ride of a lifetime. In 2003, Baker walked into a Ferrari dealership in Rosemont, Pennsylvania and stated that he was looking to buy a Ferrari F50. Baker had concocted a story that he was the CEO of a California tech firm who had just flown in from Atlanta to see the car, and with a limousine waiting outside the story seemed to fit. Baker just wanted to take a quick test drive before he committed.

When the salesman handed Baker the keys to the supercar, it would be the last time he would ever see Baker, or the dealership's famous Ferrari. Baker hopped into the car and sped off, never to return, leaving the confused salesman behind and igniting a tale of urban legend. Baker then transported the car to his home in Kentucky, where he parked it next to a Ferrari 328 GTS he had stolen from a North Carolina dealer and a Ferrari Testarossa he stole from a dealer in Long Island.

Baker then took the F50 to car shows in Kentucky and treated it as his own, before selling it to an emergency room doctor in 2008. When the doctor called the Ferrari factory to confirm the car's vehicle identification number, he learned that the car had been stolen and he reported it to the local law enforcement. Because the car had been transported across state line, the matter was referred to the FBI. The FBI confiscated the car and notified Motor Insurance Corp., the insurance company who had reimbursed the dealership for the $750,000 loss, that the car had been recovered. The FBI then requested that the insurance company allow it to maintain possession of the car while it investigated the crime. And, this is where the story gets interesting.

In May 2009, while the car was being held by the FBI, Special Agent Frederick Kingston and Assistant U.S. Attorney Hamilton Thompson took the Ferrari out of the Lexington, Kentucky storage facility for an "undisclosed" reason. With Special Agent Kingston behind the wheel, the two drove the Ferrari down the country roads before losing control of the car and slamming it into a tree. With a bent frame and the driver's side of the car caved in, the Ferrari – officially number 29 of the 349 built – was a total loss.

After the accident, Motor Insurance Corp. submitted a claim to the FBI and the Department of Justice for the $750,000 that it had paid to the Ferrari dealer for the loss. However, the agencies rejected the claim on the ground that the Ferrari was being "detained" by the FBI at the time of the incident, and that they were not responsible for the claim. The insurance company then tried to get documents relating to the crash under the Freedom of Information Act, but the government refused this request as well.

After trying to resolve this matter informally for nearly two years, and getting nowhere, in March 2011 Motor Insurance Corp. filed a lawsuit against the United States in the District Court for the Eastern District of Michigan. The insurance company brought claims for negligence and conversion, and importantly, for the turnover of the documents it originally sought under the Freedom of Information Act. The United States moved to dismiss.

The question raised was an interesting one, since sovereign immunity prevents lawsuits against the U.S. unless the U.S. has specifically allowed the claim for relief. Fortunately for Motor Insurance Corp., the U.S. had enacted the Federal Tort Claims Act, codified as 28 U.S.C. § 1346(b), which allows claims against the U.S. for negligent acts of federal employees while acting within the course and scope of their employment. Yet, there are exceptions.

The U.S. claimed that the "detention of goods exception" precluded Motor Insurance Corp.'s claim. Under 28 U.S.C. § 2680(c), the U.S. is immune from claims arising out of "the detention of any goods, merchandise or other property by any officer of customs or excise of any other law enforcement officer." Thus, the U.S. argued, because the vehicle was damaged while being detained by the FBI – even if it was being taken out for a joyride – it had no responsibility for the $750,000 loss.

Motor Insurance Corp. argued that because it had voluntarily consented to the FBI's storage of the Ferrari, the vehicle was not being "detained" at all. Motor Insurance Corp. presented the District Court with federal authority that defined a detention as the "deprivation of control and a right of dominion over the property," not a voluntarily entrustment. Hence, because the insurance company voluntarily agreed to the FBI's request that it be allowed to keep the car, the car was not being detailed and the exception did not apply.

The District Court disagreed with Motor Insurance Corp., stating that its argument had "no merit." The court reasoned that the FBI had the right to detain the vehicle regardless of Motor Insurance Corp.'s consent, and then speculated that had the insurance company not consented, the FBI "would have taken the vehicle into its custody" anyway. The court also rejected Motor Insurance Corp.'s request for documents under the Freedom of Information Act as unnecessary. As the court held: "A plaintiff is not entitled to discovery where the court needs no further information to decide a motion to dismiss."

The District Court then dismissed Motor Insurance Corp.'s case, and with that a bit of the integrity of the judicial system. Sometimes things just need to make sense, and immunizing the government from the FBI's act of irresponsibility is both politically and legally unsound. Motor Insurance Corp.'s only crime was cooperating with the authorities, and for this it got stoned-walled for two years and recovered nothing on its $750,000 claim.

This is a poor result, particularly given that it was shrouded in requests for documents under the Freedom of Information Act. That the decision was based on the District Court's pure speculation that the FBI would have confiscated the car had Motor Insurance Corp. not consented makes it all the more troubling. Whether Motor Insurance Corp.'s claims would have ultimately prevailed remains an open question, but its claim for damages should have been allowed to reach a jury of its peers. The summary dismissal of its claims, without allowing the company access to any of the information it sought, is an offensive distribution of justice.

CHAPTER 25

An Industry Lost

MAY 2012

If anything, America's greatest asset is its ability to innovate. Our nation's fabric is woven from unconventional thinking and the courage to dream. From this, we have introduced to the world everything from motion pictures to commercial aviation to hip-hop; and often times before the dust settles we are at it again, rethinking the industry we just created. Alexander Graham Bell spurred an industry with the invention of the telephone, and some 100 years later, Steven Jobs took the industry into the fourth dimension with the introduction of the iPhone.

Our inventors have made us yearn for products we didn't even know we wanted, keeping our economy at the forefront of the race for supremacy. The automotive industry was transformed by Henry Ford from a small-town cottage industry into one of the most influential trades in the world, with the introduction of the assembly line and the Model T. And, what Ford started, General Motors and Chrysler finished, building empires of unimaginable significance.

In their day, the Big Three controlled 85% of the world's auto production. Yet, decades of complacency have toppled the once mighty, and well-intended regulatory measures have precluded new entrants from achieving success. It is the latter issue that has proven troublesome, as it has chilled innovation and driven away the entrepreneurial spirit.

There once was a time when automotive safety was given little consideration. Whether driven by cost or genuine concern of market rejection, automakers for years resisted even the most basic precautions. Yet, this all changed in the 1960s when the National Academies of Sciences released a watershed report that highlighted the danger of the automobile and the industry's reluctance for safety measures. The report noted that in 1965 auto accidents killed 107,000 Americans and permanently disabled another 400,000 – calling the problem an "epidemic of modern society" that is the nation's most important environmental health problem.

Congress' response to what had become a national debate was to enact the 1966 Highway Safety Act and to create the Department of Transportation. At the time of signing the law, President Lyndon B. Johnston is quoted as saying, "[W]e have tolerated a raging epidemic of highway death ... which has killed more of our youth than all other diseases combined. Through the Highway Safety Act, we are going to find out more about highway disease – and we aim to cure it."

The 1960s legislation also led to the creation of the National Highway Traffic and Safety Administration (NHTSA), which has since then assumed full responsibility for vehicle safety. NHTSA has promulgating numerous Federal Motor Vehicle Safety Standards, which regulate items you would expect, such as child seats and airbags, to the truly remote, such as windshield glazing and pneumatic tires. And, while the first safety standard was the requirement for seat belts, much has changed over the last 40 years. Today, the Federal Motor Vehicle Safety Standards are a labyrinth of regulations that are deep, complex and unforgiving.

To meet these stringent requirements, automakers are required to put their cars through a battery of front, side and rear crash tests – at costs that run into the hundreds of millions. On average, U.S. automakers crash 60 to 100 cars before they are certified for consumer duty, an endeavor that is both costly and time consuming. Given this, it is no surprise that carmakers typically spend over a billion dollars and several years bringing a car to market, with no guarantee of consumer acceptance.

While all of this is good for consumer safety, it is troubling for the entrepreneur trying to enter the market. Over the past several years, countless U.S. companies have tried to break into the industry, with little success. Fisker and Tesla are the newest to attempt the journey, and they too are showing signs of stress. Fisker's financial troubles have been the subject of national attention, and Tesla is one of the most frequently shorted stocks on the exchange. It is an open question of whether they will make the cut, but the smart money is against them.

The last domestic car company to enter the U.S. market and achieve sustainability was Chrysler, who undertook the challenge in 1925. Given the nearly insurmountable costs associated with bringing a car to market, it is a serious question of whether any ground-up company can accomplish the task. And, this is a fact that should concern us all, as we are on the cusp of losing an industry we helped to create.

A solution to the problem has been posed, and it is one worth considerable note. In October 2011, Congressman John Campbell introduced H.R. 3274, known as the "Low Volume Motor Vehicle Manufacturer's Act," which would exempt vehicle manufacturers from NHTSA compliance while they were in their ramp-up phases. Limited to manufacturers who produce less than 1,000 vehicles per year, the Act would enable entrepreneurial companies to achieve a level of success before having to encounter the type of capital outlay that is associated with full NHTSA compliance.

While the bill's enactment would be mean that certain vehicles would be on the road that have not achieved NHTSA compliance, is this necessarily an intolerable result? Many Americans drive cars that were built years ago, and long before crumple zones and airbags had even been considered. On balance, are we not willing to tolerate a low volume manufacturer's car on the road, in exchange for a heightened likelihood of the manufacturer's success?

Congress appears to think not. The bill is currently being reviewed by the House Committee on Energy and Commerce, but its prognosis looks dim. According to Civic Impulse, LLC, the entity that tracks activities in the U.S. Congress, the bill has a 3% chance of being passed, and this is a travesty in the making. There cannot be a more appropriate time to save our stake-hold in one of the most important trades, and enable our inventors to redefine the industry in ways we could never imagine.

CHAPTER 26

Injustice
Defined

JUNE 2012

The last four years have laid witness to some of the most extraordinary events in our nation's history. The 110-year-old Lehman Brothers toppled in an instant, Merrill Lynch was sold over a weekend, and our government began doling out billions in an effort to save it all. Sweeping measures of enormous degree were taken on a moment's notice, as policy makers contemplated financial devastation if immediate action was not taken.

The domestic automotive industry was at the epicenter of the crisis, suffering from decades of complacency and neglect. Foreign automakers were quicker, leaner and more competitive, leaving the domestics laboring under the weight of billions in debt. And when the credit markets froze, the manufacturers' continued viability was called into doubt.

Chrysler and GM responded to the crisis by making deep cuts in their employee base, closing factories and eliminating slow moving vehicle lines. They also sought to thin their franchised dealers over the course of several years. In its plea to Washington for financial relief, GM said that it would eliminate 1,650 dealers over the six years, and Chrysler claimed to have similar plans although it was less specific about the details.

In February 2009, President Barack Obama created the Presidential Task Force on the Auto Industry, whose purpose was to review the Chrysler and GM restructuring plans. The Auto Task Force reviewed the manufacturers' plans, and rejected them claiming that they were not fast enough in their dealer closures. The automakers were then given 60 days to submit a "more aggressive plan." As the Auto Task Force noted, it wanted the manufacturers to emulate the "Toyota model" of having fewer dealers, with higher sales per dealer.

Chrysler and GM revised their plans to call for the immediate termination of a combined 2,243 dealers through a pre-packaged bankruptcy process. Under this new plan, rather than a slow wind down of the dealers, Chrysler and GM would terminate the dealerships right away, using the bankruptcy powers to cut off all liability. The Obama administration then approved the plan, and Chrysler and GM received $81 billion in financial support as they exited bankruptcy.

While the dealership closures were said to be a cost savings measure, many pundits believe that terminating independently owned franchises was of marginal benefit to the manufacturers. In fact, two of the members Auto Task Force publicly admitted that cost saving measures were not a factor in requesting the immediate dealership closures. Rather, it appears that the Auto Task Force was focused on melding the manufacturers into the Toyota mold, even though Chrysler executives stated that such a model would "never work" for Chrysler.

Because of the financial devastation to the 2,243 terminated dealers and the public outcry that followed the Obama administration's decision to support the plan, in 2009 Congress began holding hearings to determine whether law should be passed to reinstate terminated dealers. The hearings resulted in the passage of the Consolidate Appropriations Act of 2010, which enabled terminated dealers to file for arbitration requesting reinstatement.

The legislation was predicated on the idea that the Chrysler and GM closures were arbitrary and capricious, and the act sought to impose a standardized criterion for termination. If the dealers were found to be "under performing" using objective criteria, then termination would be authorized; otherwise, the dealers would be reinstated in the dealer network. Of the 789 Chrysler dealers that were terminated, 418 filed for arbitration. Of this number, several were voluntarily reinstated or otherwise informally resolved, and 108 went to a decision, with 32 prevailing.

Following the conclusion of the arbitrations, questions arose as to exactly what was meant by the word "reinstatement." The dealers naturally took the position that reinstatement meant just that; that they were entitled to resume their position in the dealer network at their prior location. After all, most of the dealers still held the real estate, which in many cases was not being utilized but was still subject to a mortgage. Yet, Chrysler took the position that reinstatement only entitled the dealers to a "letter of intent" to be reinstated at a future date and at an undetermined place.

In 2010, litigation ensued against Chrysler, with the terminated dealers seeking to enforce their arbitration awards. In the much-anticipated ruling, Judge Sean Cox of the U.S. District Court for the Eastern District of Michigan, held that the terminated Chrysler dealers who were successful in arbitration were entitled to no more than "a customary and usual letter of intent to enter into a sales and service agreement" with Chrysler.

The court further held that the letter of intent did not necessarily need to reinstate the dealer in the same location, only that the dealer generally be permitted to rejoin the

Chrysler network. Thus, it would be perfectly acceptable for Chrysler to take a dealer who had been in business for 30 years, as was the case with Village Automotive Center in Royal Oak, Mich., and provide the dealer a letter of intent for a franchise in an entirely different part of the state.

While there are obvious differences between reinstatement and a letter of intent for reinstatement, the most important distinction is one that may not be very well known. Under most state dealer laws, a letter of intent for a franchise gives neighboring dealers a right to protest the proposed new dealership. In California, for instance, Vehicle Code Section 3062 states that a dealer within 10 miles of a proposed new franchise may file a protest with the California New Motor Vehicle Board to block the new dealership from being established. Once a protest is filed, a trial on the merits is required to determine whether good cause exists to establish the new franchise.

For the 32 terminated Chrysler dealers that prevailed in arbitration, the court's ruling means that their win was not a win at all, but rather the start of another arduous path of litigation and appeals. For dealers who have already been out of business for three years, the prospect of further litigation over the next several years is all but certain death. For those who have already suffered so much – and who have proven that they never should have been terminated – such a result is a manifest case of injustice.

CHAPTER 27

Theft, Hiding
and Restitution

JULY 2012

Some 67 years ago, the last of the great world wars drew to an end, and with that we briefly closed a chapter on crimes against humanity, failures of diplomacy, and tyrant dictators seeking to rule it all. With laws of morality no longer in place, soldiers pillaged with unnatural frequency and nations took without due process – all with the expectation that the details would be lost in the chaos of it all.

And for many years they were mostly right. Families lost prized possessions and museums were robbed of historical artifacts, without any real hope of recovery or compensation. Yet, recent court decisions are shedding light on the rights of those who were victimized nearly seven decades ago.

Last month, a court in Hamburg, Germany ruled that the heirs of Hans Prym had the right to the return of one of the most important Mercedes-Benz cars in existence. The 1935 Mercedes-Benz 500 K Roadster – one of 29 built – was the centerpiece of the Mercedes-Benz display at the Berlin Motor Show before being sold to German industrialist Hans Prym later that year. Hans Prym is best known for having invented the clothing snap, and the Prym family business is considered to be the oldest family business in Germany, dating back 14 generations.

The vehicle had been stored at the Prym family estate near the border of Belgium during World War II when U.S. troops took over the property and set up a military outpost. Prym had been imprisoned by Allied forces, and U.S. troops confiscated the Mercedes-Benz. The vehicle was then shipped to the U.S. where it was sold on the collector car market, trading hands several times over.

The vehicle publicly resurfaced in 2011 when Southern California resident General William Lyon sold it at the Pebble Beach classic car auction for $3.8 million. General Lyon, whose car collection is worth an estimated $200 million, sold the car at RM Auctions with two other classic Mercedes-Benz vehicles. It is likely that as the car changed hands over the years, its origin became less perfectly understood. In selling the car, RM reported that the vehicle's complete history was "unknown at this time."

Dutch car collector Frans van Haren bought the car and then shipped it to Essen, Germany for the Techno Classica collector car event. When the vehicle arrived at the event, the Prym heirs were waiting with German police who impounded the car, pending court resolution.

In June, the Hamburg Regional Court ruled that the heirs were entitled to the car, noting that the German statute of limitations for conversion is tolled while the property is out of the country. And with this, a firestorm of litigation is sure to ignite, as each purchaser of the vehicle attempts to reclaim their purchase money from the prior owner. This, in itself, creates a host of interesting issues, as various statutes of limitation will likely come into play, with varying rules on tolling and discovery.

In a similar decision, U.S. District Judge Thomas Griesa of the Southern District of New York ruled that a book collector was required to return a 16th century book worth $600,000 to a museum in Stuttgart, more than six decades after it was stolen by a U.S. Army Captain. Likewise, the U.S. Immigration and Customs Enforcement Office recently reported that it is requiring the return of a porcelain centrepiece valued at over $1 million to a museum in Stuttgart. The artifact had been stolen from a castle where it was hidden by a German museum during World War II.

Yet, one of the most significant legal challenges to a war taking is the one brought by the seven grandchildren of Louis Renault, who have sued the French government for reparations after the French government took the entire Renault auto-making business from the family following World War II.

During the Nazi occupation of France, Renault had fallen under German control and was producing tanks and vehicles for the Third Reich. The company's founder, Louis Renault, claimed to be opposed to the German occupation, but members of the French resistance believed he was collaborating with the Germans.

Three weeks after France was liberated in 1944, Louis Renault was arrested on unspecified charges. Renault died one month after imprisonment. Four months later, General Charles de Gaulle's provisional government nationalized the automaker, even though Renault had never been tried or convicted. The other two French major automakers, Citroen and Peugeot, were also under German control, but neither were nationalized after the war.

The grandchildren of Louis Renault have sued the government under a groundbreaking law enacted in March 2010 that allows citizens to challenge the conformity of legislation with the French constitution. The heirs say their family received no compensation from the French government at the time, and that the move was unfair punishment for Louis Renault's attitude during the war. Because Renault had not been convicted of a crime, and no compensation was paid, the family argues that the confiscation was unconstitutional. If successful, the heirs stand to receive $143 million.

It is unknown how the Renault legal battle with turn out, but it is certainly interesting – and encouraging – to see that significant moves are being made to return war-taken property to their rightful owner. It is enough to have suffered through the travesty of war; they should not have the added burden of shouldering a financial loss that was unjustly administered.

CHAPTER 28

The Grand
Ole Plan

AUGUST 2012

Ford did it. Chrysler and GM did too. Now Land Rover is joining the party to eliminate its franchised automobile dealers across the United States – all for the purpose of establishing grand showplaces in strategic locations throughout the nation.

The truth be told, geography is largely to blame. Well, that and greed.

Long before the advent of instant messaging and super highways, our country was quilted by independent townships, separated by a fort night's travel. Today, a trip from Los Angeles to Riverside is inconvenienced by construction and traffic, but not long ago the trip was a tough day's travel. Poor highways – or worse, dirt roads – were the norm, dividing our country into a multitude of towns, each with their local hardware store, market, and yes, dealership.

Yet, much has changed over the years, and the need for a franchised dealer in every bedroom community no longer remains. Residents of Riverside are perfectly capable of driving to the neighboring city of San Bernardino buy a car, and their conduct demonstrates that they are willing to do so.

As a result, the number of new dealers has dropped precipitously over the years. In 1950, for instance, the U.S. laid home to some 47,000 franchised dealerships. Today, despite our population having more than doubled, the number is 17,500. And now, what has not been eliminated through natural selection, is being subjected to manufacturer desires.

Many dealers throughout the nation are economically viable, but not part of the automakers' plan to continue representing the brand. And therein lies the struggle. Dealers often times have years, if not decades, of established goodwill in their business, yet the look, size and location of the dealership no longer fits within the manufacturer's plan.

The problem is only exacerbated when new entrants come to the marketplace without the legacy of a historical dealer base. For instance, in 2008, the year before GM filed for bankruptcy, Cadillac (which was established in 1902) sold 161,159 vehicles through 1,422 franchised dealers. That same year, newcomer Lexus sold 260,087 vehicles through 226 dealers. Put another way, in 2008 the average Cadillac dealer sold 113 vehicles; the average Lexus dealer, 1,150.

It is no surprise then that when the domestics sought to shudder many of their dealers in the 2009 bankruptcies, they told President Obama's Auto Task Force that they wanted to emulate the "Toyota dealership model" – sell more vehicles through fewer consolidated dealerships. And what Chrysler and GM accomplished through the bankruptcy courts, Ford, Range Rover and others are attempting to accomplish on their own.

After eliminating the Mercury brand, and pledging to stand behind the remaining Lincoln dealers, Ford announced that it was seeking to reduce it Lincoln's dealer network by more than 25 percent. Now, Range Rover has joined the fray, seeking to consolidate its Jaguar and Land Rover dealerships into single locations, reducing its dealer network by 20 percent.

The thought behind fewer, consolidated dealerships is that more resources can be put into grand showplaces, which will serve to highlight the brands. If there is any doubt over this consider that Chrysler recently opened up a 200,000 square foot, four-story megastore in downtown Los Angeles for all of its brands. Mercedes-Benz has done likewise, opening a $220 million, five-story, 330,000-square-foot dealership in the heart of Manhattan.

To some, this may be seen as progress; to others it is capricious. Range Rover, for instance, is pushing its new program because it wants to be able to sell luxury cars and sports utility vehicles under the same roof. As Andy Goss, CEO of Jaguar Land Rover North America, recently stated, "We know the recipe for success, particularly in the luxury market, is to look at what BMW and Mercedes-Benz have done. Forty-five percent of people who own a Jaguar also own an SUV. It is the same customer base. It would be foolish not to try and get those customers."

Yet, while trying this new approach may result in more sales for Range Rover, the cost for the experiment will be borne almost entirely by the dealers. To the dealer community that built the automotive marketplace, manufacturers should not be able to force closures and consolidations because of a new marketing agenda. Legislatures tend to agree.

Most states, like California, have enacted statutes which protect franchised dealers from predatory trade practices, and make it illegal for a manufacturer to terminate a dealer without establishing "good cause." Good cause is typically seen as fraud, failing to remain open, or transferring the dealership without the manufacturer's consent.

Yet, while this protects dealers from outright termination, it does nothing to prevent coercive tactics designed at accomplishing the same result. For instance, Chrysler is making the new, and lucrative, Dodge Viper only available to dealerships that comply with certain facility guidelines. GM offers financial incentives to dealers who comply with its "Essential Brand Elements" facility program. And Range Rover is having a "sit down meeting" with its dealers to explain the benefits of consolidation.

While the customer may have a better buying experience at a consolidated megastore, this needs to be balanced against the dealers' economic interest. Dealerships are big business, employing countless members of the community and generating millions in local tax revenue. This, of course, is to say nothing of the years of hard work and dedication from the dealer principals themselves, as well as their at-risk capital. Failing to recognize these attributes in the implementation of a new marketing plan retards capitalism and chills investment. While the automakers may not want to hear it, sometimes you have to dance with the one that brung ya.

CHAPTER 29

Market Forces Challenge Electric Car Industry

SEPTEMBER 2012

In his January 2011 State of the Union address, President Barack Obama announced to the world that the U.S. would lead the charge to replace the internal combustion engine that has been powering cars for the last 100 years. "We can replace our dependence on oil with biofuels and become the first country to have a million electric vehicles on the road by 2015," President Obama said. "The future is ours to win."

To fulfill this mission, President Obama deployed $2.4 billion into electric car technology and revamped the Corporate Average Fuel Economy (CAFE) standards to provide for special credits for manufacturers of electric cars. The CAFE standards, which were established by Congress in 1975 in response to the 1973 Arab Oil Embargo, dictate the average fuel economy that automakers must meet, or face gas-guzzler penalties.

For 2011, the CAFE standard was 30.2 mpg. In July 2011, however, President Obama radically revamped the CAFE standard to reach an average of 54.5 mpg by 2025. To get to that number, President Obama provided an array of special rules that apply only to manufacturers of electric cars.

Electric vehicles will count as having "0 emissions" (even though their use of the electrical grid has an impact on emissions), and each electric vehicle sold in 2017 would count as two vehicles. As a result, the actual real-world gains from the new CAFE standards are closer to 40 mpg, not the advertised 54.5 mpg. Nevertheless, the point remains that President Obama has thrown all of his resources behind the electric car industry.

If the story ended there, all would be right in the automotive world – at least in this segment of it. Yet, market forces have proven more dominate than political might, as the electric car industry has stumbled in its infancy phases. CBS News released a report this summer which indicated that the U.S. will fall "well short" of having one million electric vehicles on the road by 2015.

According to CBS News, many of the electric car manufacturers the Obama administration was counting on have either scaled back their estimates or gone out of business altogether. As a result, CBS News believes that the achievable number is closer to 300,000 electric vehicles by 2015 – and that is assuming that companies like Fisker, who is teetering on the brink of insolvency, remain viable. If more companies fail, the actual number could be much lower.

"I think these forecasts were very unrealistic, and history is showing that scaling an automobile company is much more difficult than many of these people thought," said Craig Carlson, managing director of Carlson Group, Electric Vehicles. And Carlson is not alone.

Last month the National Petroleum Council completed a two-year study that was requested by Secretary of Energy Stephen Chu, culminating in the report Advancing Technology for America's Transportation Future. The study involved more than 300 participants from the private sector, universities and government, and included the likes of Toyota, BMW, Duke, MIT, National Academies and the Department of Transportation.

The study found that "internal combustion engine technologies are likely to be the dominant propulsion systems for decades to come, with liquid fuel blends continuing to play a significant, but reduced role." Alternatives were possible, but speculative: "Profound changes are possible with disruptive, yet highly uncertain, innovations such as ultra-light-weight vehicle materials; new electric vehicle battery technologies; low-cost, low-pressure storage for natural gas or hydrogen; or breakthroughs yielding lower cost, low carbon transportation fuel."

Interestingly, the study found that "vehicles fueled with compressed natural gas – not electric batteries – will emerge as the biggest competitor to the combustion engine."

"There is a great deal of uncertainty regarding which individual fuel-vehicle systems will overcome technology hurdles to become economically and environmentally attractive by 2050. Therefore, government policies should be technology neutral while market dynamics drive commercialization." Instead of endorsing any particular technology, the report concluded, "the federal government should take a leadership role in convening state, local, private sector, and public interest groups to design and advocate measures to streamline the permitting and regulatory process in order to accelerate deployment of infrastructure."

Notwithstanding these findings, President Obama has doubled-down on his commitment to the electric vehicle sector, announcing that he will commit an additional $4.7 billion of tax dollars to electric vehicle. Of this, $3.7 billion will be tax credits for buyers of electric vehicles, and $1 billion will be used to bring advanced-technology vehicles to 15 cities.

The deployment of these additional funds brings the president's electric vehicle tab to $7.1 billion – a steep amount given the uncertainty of the technology. What could $7.1 billion have bought? How about 417 new high schools, 788 new prisons, or the salary of 13,564 elementary school teachers for 10 years.

In truth, President's Obama's proclamation to put one million electric vehicles on the road by 2015 was little more than political fodder that had more to do with polling than sound economic policy. Shed of its glitz and fanfare, it was a fallacious statement at the time that has proven itself out in the manner expected.

And for his part, Mitt Romney's proclamations are no better. At the Republican National Convention last week, Romney promised to make North America "energy independent" by 2020 – as if publicly saying it would somehow make it come true.

On a subject as large as consumer transportation, government policy simply cannot outstrip prevailing market forces, and any attempt to do so will only result in the spoilable of efforts. Perhaps Mark Twain said it best: "Never try to teach a pig to sing. It wastes time and annoys the pig."

CHAPTER 30

Could GM Be at It Again?

OCTOBER 2012

In the world of automotive juggernauts, market share is everything. Perhaps this is true in every industry, but it is a particularly important topic among the Detroit 3, who have seen their global dominance wither away to market irrelevance over the past several decades.

There once was a time when many believed, "What's good for General Motors is good for the country." But those days are long past, replaced by contempt for taking billions from the federal government, or perhaps worse, genuine indifference for its product offerings.

Through decades of complacency, GM managed to give up acres of market share to newcomers who many thought did not have a fighting chance. In 1965 - the year that Toyota sold its first car in the U.S. - GM controlled 49 percent of the U.S. market. Today, GM's market share has dwindled to 19 percent and Toyota has become the largest automotive manufacturer in the world.

If it sounds as though the building was ablaze without anyone taking notice, all was not lost on GM's executive brass. In the 1990s GM hatched a plan to regain its market share by rolling up private capital dealerships into consolidated factory owned stores. This, GM reasoned, would allow the manufacturer to put financial strength into operating the dealerships and enable it to steal back its market share from the competition.

From the surface, factory owned stores might sound like a fine idea. However, most states, including California, have enacted strict legislation prohibiting automakers from owning dealerships under most circumstances. The policy behind the rule is that private dealerships, which have significant investment capital at risk, would not have a chance of competing against the factories, which have billions at their disposal and could manipulate product allocation.

California's approach to the issue is to prohibit manufacturers from owing a dealership within 10 miles of a privately held dealership of the same line-make, with two limited exceptions. First, a manufacturer may temporarily hold a dealership for less than a year, such as when a dealer surrenders the franchise back to the manufacturer. Second, a manufacturer may own a dealership as part of a bona fide "dealer development program" - a program designed to enable those who lack the capital or experience to become part of the dealer network.

Under California's dealer development program, the manufacturer owns the vast majority of the dealership business, with the dealer development candidate making an initial investment and then buying out the manufacturer over time. As the Legislature stated, "A dealer development program has the sole purpose of making franchises available to persons who lack the capital, training, business experience, or other qualities required of prospective franchisees and who have no other method of acquiring the franchise."

In its 1990s effort to recapture its lost market share, GM sought to roll up several private dealers in the San Fernando Valley into consolidated factory owned stores. To avoid California's prohibition against company dealerships, GM officially held the stores as part of a bona fide dealer development program.

Specifically, in the late 1990s GM enlisted the support of mega-dealer Wes Rydell, who was to play the part of the inexperienced dealer development candidate that could not break into the industry. However, Rydell was anything but, having built a chain of 30 dealerships in the Midwest. GM then purchased nine dealerships in the San Fernando Valley, closed four of them and consolidated the remaining five with its partner Wes Rydell - with GM investing $18 million for a 90 percent share of the enterprise.

GM's actions set off a firestorm of trouble, with dealers objecting, the Department of Motor Vehicles launching an investigating and the California Senate Judiciary Committee conducting hearings. GM admitted to the Judiciary Committee that its ownership of the dealerships did not involve a dealer development situation, but claimed that its actions were necessary to recapture market share.

The Legislature blasted GM for its actions, amending the law to prevent a manufacturer from ever being able to abuse the system again. In what has become known as the "GM Amendment," the Legislature took the exceptional act of codifying its Legislative intent by stating that the law should never be used for "any improper purpose, including the consolidation of privately-owned dealership by a sophisticated investor or operator posing as a dealer development candidate."

If the story ended there, this could perhaps be chalked up to an incredible act of indiscretion, spurred by fear of falling market share. But recent activities with GM dealerships in the San Francisco East Bay market have many wondering whether GM is making another attempt at consolidating a vital market.

In an industry where it frequently takes years, if not decades, to establish oneself in a dealer network, Inder Dosanjh has built a GM empire in the San Francisco East Bay virtually overnight. From 2008 to 2011, Dosanjh acquired nine East Bay GM dealerships, closed four and is operating the remaining five - a pattern strikingly similar to that of Rydell's in the San Fernando Valley. Adding to the twist, in 2010 long-time GM employee Jim Gentry reportedly left the automaker to become Dosanjh's chief financial officer.

Dosanjh's instant empire has raised objections from many and resulted in at least one dealer suing GM for conspiring to steal their dealership. The lawsuit alleges that GM is covertly using Dosanjh as another front man to consolidate dealerships in another important market. Other dealers in the area are promising to similarly file claims of conspiracy and fraud.

Time will only tell whether Dosanjh's miraculous story is a repeat of GM's insidious plot to gain market share at all costs, or whether it is just that - a miraculous story of individual success that is fortuitously tied to strikingly similar events of a decade gone by. For the sake of GM, the dealers involved and the integrity of the legislative process, we should all hope that this is nothing more than an eerie coincidence, and that GM is not up to its tricks again.

CHAPTER 31

Obama and the Automotive Industry

NOVEMBER 2012

Every presidential election presents the country with a unique opportunity to fundamentally alter the course of history. The decision we make this November will lay the foundation for economic, environmental and foreign policies for the next four years, or possibly the next eight, and in many respects, for generations to come.

To put the gravity of the decision into perspective, consider the impact that Franklin D. Roosevelt had on our society with his creation of Social Security, the Securities and Exchange Commission and federally insured banks. Or think about the fateful decision made by Harry S. Truman to drop an atomic bomb on Japan, killing a quarter of a million Japanese civilians. No one can know what challenges will confront the winner of this election; we can only hope that he will have the fortitude, wisdom and courage to make good decisions in the face of adversity.

In his quest to win over voters and glide to a second term, President Barack Obama has made several sweeping statements about his first term accomplishments. To be fair, both candidates have stretched the truth about as far as the imagination can travel. Governor Mitt Romney would just about have us believe that his accomplishments include ending world hunger, freeing the human spirit, and turning water into wine – if he was allowed to drink the stuff.

But there is one claim that President Obama has made that has many pundits brewing: "Obama saved the auto industry." The claim has been central to his candidacy, and for good reason. Not only does it show that his efforts prevented a financial calamity for the nation, but it is a particularly important topic for the swing states of Ohio and Wisconsin, which surround Michigan and are acutely impacted by the automotive industry. And it is not lost on the President that no Republican has ever been elected to office without winning Ohio.

To be sure, had Chrysler and General Motors ceased as a going concern, the fallout would have been tremendous. But, what is less certain is whether the concern would have materialized absent billions in government handouts. It cannot be ignored that Ford, who had similarly seen its market share erode over the years, did not take the free money, and it remains viable. And there is little to suggest that market forces could not have adequately handled the situation.

But there was a bailout, and the Obama campaign has ridden the high horse into our living rooms with claims of salvation. But, are they true? Like most things in politics, the answer depends on how you spin the statistics.

In Bill Clinton's opening remarks at the Democratic National Convention, he stated, "Now there are 250,000 more people working in the auto industry than the day the companies were restructured. Governor Romney opposed the plan to save GM and Chrysler. So here's another jobs score: Obama two hundred and fifty thousand, Romney, zero." Is there truth to the statement?

The Bureau of Labor Statistics shows that in June 2009, when GM and Chrysler filed bankruptcy, auto manufacturers and dealers located in the U.S. employed 1,634,100 workers; today that number is 1,870,700 – a net gain of 236,600

(Clinton's 250,000). But, here's the catch. The number represents jobs for the *entire* auto industry, both domestic and foreign-owned. So, Obama is taking credit, for instance, for the increase of jobs at the BMW plant in South Carolina, and the Nissan plant in Tennessee.

The numbers for GM and Chrysler, the actual benefactors of Obama's efforts, are much different. According to GM's annual report, in June of 2009 GM North America employed 70,000 workers in the United States. Today that number stands at 74,500, a net gain of 4,500 jobs. The increase in jobs at the smaller Chrysler (which is private and does not publish its numbers) is unknown, but industry analysts opine that it is likely in line with GM's. And then there is a deeper, untold story that weighs heavily in the analysis.

As part of the $61 billion given to GM and Chrysler, President Obama required the manufacturers to come up with an aggressive plan to thin ranks of their dealer networks. When the automakers proposed a gradual closure of hundreds of dealerships over a five-year span, the administration rejected the plan as too shallow and too slow.

The Treasury Auto Team that had been established by President Obama theorized that GM and Chrysler needed to follow the "Toyota model," which suggested that a smaller dealership network would reduce competition and increase sales for the remaining dealerships. This, in turn, would enable the dealerships to invest more in their facilities, thus improving brand equity.

GM and Chrysler returned with a new plan for drastic cuts in their dealer base: GM proposed to terminate 1,454 dealers within 16 months, and Chrysler suggested cutting 789 dealers in just 22 days. The plan was approved, and through the power of a pre-packaged bankruptcy proceeding, scores of family-owned businesses died in an instant.

With the average dealership employing 52 Americans, the total job loss from the 2,243 dealership closures was expected to be 116,636. Public outrage resulted in Congress passing the Consolidated Appropriations Act of 2010, which allowed targeted dealers to challenge the termination. But for many who went dark after being told they were terminated; the congressional act could not revive the business that had been allowed to go cold.

The President's actions also lead to a formal investigation by the Special Inspector General for the Troubled Asset Relief Program (SIGTARP). In its July 2010 report, SIGTARP found that the Treasury Auto Team, which advised the President on the viability of the GM and Chrysler plans, consisted of 17 individuals – none of whom had any experience or expertise in the auto industry. The report also found that, while the purpose of the TARP program was to "preserve and promote jobs of American workers," job loss was not a significant factor in the Auto Team's review of the manufacturers' plans.

The SIGTARP investigation also found that since the terminated dealerships were privately owned, it was debatable whether their closure would result in any significant cost savings for the manufacturers; but even if savings were to be had, this was not a significant factor for the Auto Team in determining the need for dealership closures. Instead, SIGTARP found that the Auto Team was driven by the "theory" that GM and Chrysler should emulate the Toyota model of fewer dealerships.

The report concluded, "[A]t a time when the country was experiencing the worst economic downturn in generations and the Government was asking its taxpayers to support a $787 billion stimulus package designed primarily to preserve jobs, [the] Treasury made a series of decisions that may have substantially contributed to the accelerated shuttering of thousands of small business and thereby potentially adding tens of thousands of workers to the already lengthy unemployment rolls – all based on a theory and without sufficient consideration of the decisions' broader economic impact."

For the thousands of dealers who lost their family businesses, many of which had been owned for generations, it certainly does not feel as though President Obama "saved" the auto industry. Consider that even as of today, some three years later, many of these dealers are still paying back the millions in debt their business incurred, without the benefit of a business, income or future hope. For these dealers, who are left to weather the harsh consequences of this life-altering decision, the permanency of their situation can only be relieved by the hope that after this November, they will never again have to hear that President Obama "saved" the auto industry.

CHAPTER 32

Oh, What a Tangled Web We Weave

DECEMBER 2012

You would think that billion-dollar companies that grace the halls of the New York Stock Exchange, the *Wall Street Journal* and the Fortune 500 would have the good sense to govern themselves with principles of honesty and integrity. If they don't do it because it's the right thing to do, you would expect that they would at least do it protect the reputation they worked so hard to build.

Yet, pursuit of the almighty dollar is a temptation too great to resist for some, resulting in company-wide scandals that harm the innocent and cost shareholders millions. With committees overseeing nearly every act of corporate governance, and teams of lawyers there to monitor it all, it is hard to imagine that any act of malfeasance could make its way through without incident. But, at times the pressure to perform outstrips the mandate to play by the rules, causing industry-wide calamities that stir a nation and shake consumer confidence.

If there is any doubt about it, consider that the U.S. Environmental Protection Agency (EPA) recently concluded its investigation into claims that Hyundai and Kia misrepresented the gas mileage claims for their vehicles. After receiving numerous complaints from consumers, the EPA launched an investigation that revealed that Hyundai and Kia overstated fuel efficiency numbers on 900,000 of their vehicles by as much as 6 miles per gallon.

The findings implicated eight Hyundai models (Elantra, Sonata, Accent, Azera, Tucson, Veloster, Santa Fe and Genesis) built between 2011 and 2013, and five models of its subsidiary Kia (Optima, Rio, Sorento, Soul and Sportage) built during the same time period.

Hyundai initially denied any wrongdoing, issuing a statement that "this case has no merit, as our advertising is accurate and in full compliance with applicable laws and regulations." Yet, when the EPA's data indisputably showed that the company's fuel economy claims were false, Hyundai finally came clean. As the company stated, "Given the importance of fuel efficiency to all of us, we're extremely sorry about these errors."

The company blamed "procedural errors" at testing operations in Korea for the problem. But, given that Hyundai Motor Group is the fourth largest automaker in the world (after Toyota, General Motors and Volkswagen), it is hard to believe procedural errors are to blame. This is particularly true given that Hyundai recently launched a marketing campaign centered on its fuel economy claims.

In 2011 (the same year the false claims began), Hyundai launched the "Save the Asterisks" campaign, which stated that most of Hyundai's models achieved 40 mpg; unlike its competitors who only offered 40 mpg on specialized, low-volume models. As the EPA discovered, however, *none* of Hyundai's models actually achieved 40 mpg.

Yet, the marketing campaign worked. As reported by *Automotive News*, Hyundai's sales in 2011 were up 20 percent, and Kia's sales (its subsidiary) were up 36 percent. But, with 900,000 misrepresented vehicles now in consumer hands, the companies are left to manage a public relations crisis.

Just how bad is it? Consider that the average American drives 13,476 miles per year, and keeps their car for an average of 5.95 years. Taking the Kia Soul as an example, which was represented as being capable of 35 mpg, but actually gets 29 mpg, a consumer would spend $2,057 more on gas over the life of the car than expected. Now, consider that there are 900,000 consumers who are similarly situated – all of whom are entitled to compensation for the misrepresentation. Factor in that many state statutes have attorneys' fees clauses for consumer fraud claims, and it is easy to see how the claims could run into the billions.

Financial pundits have shared concern about the loss the companies will incur. In the days following the companies' admission that they lied to consumers about their cars' fuel economy standards, Hyundai's stock fell seven percent, causing a $3.1 billion loss in market value. And Moody's reports that "the impact on the companies' brand recognition and sales performance in North America could be more material, given that high fuel efficiency has been one of their key selling points and the region is the group's largest market."

Surprisingly, this is not the first time Hyundai and Kia have come under fire for misrepresenting their vehicles to consumers. In 2001, the Korean Ministry of Construction and Transportation discovered that Hyundai and Kia misrepresented their vehicles' horsepower ratings by as much as 10 percent. The misrepresentation resulted in a class action lawsuit that was settled for $125 million. The fuel economy scandal looks to be more far reaching, and costly.

While the profit-driven misdeeds of Hyundai and Kia are troubling, the two Korean manufacturers are far from the only ones putting profit before morality. Earlier this year, three executives of the Japanese auto parts company, Furukawa Electric Company, pled guilty to conspiring with other automotive companies to price-fix the cost of their components. The company paid a $200 million fine to the U.S. Department of Justice (DOJ).

The Furukawa criminal convictions led to an industry-wide investigation by the DOJ that sprawled over four continents, including Asia, Europe and Australia. So far, nine companies have paid multi-million-dollar fines, and eleven executives have pled guilty to criminal charges. Another eleven companies are still being investigated by the DOJ, which has issued several search warrants and conducted numerous raids.

Wall Street's fictional character Gordon Gekko famously said, "Greed is good. Greed is right. Greed works." Well, greed also kills. Greed destroys reputation, and inflicts untold damage on the innocent, all of whom deserve it the least. For Hyundai and Kia, it is the consumers who were sold goods that were not as advertised; it is the dealers who will struggle to maintain a shrinking market share; and it is the shareholders who will watch their values diminish overnight.

It is a shame how little some have learned in the two hundred years since Sir Walter Scott first imparted his words of wisdom upon us. But, perhaps it is the struggle of good versus evil that makes life so interesting, dynamic and, yes, unpredictable.

CHAPTER 33

Chrysler Dealers Sue U.S. for Violating Fifth Amendment

JANUARY 2013

To be sure, September 2008 was a pure financial mess. Toxic credit default swaps and irresponsible subprime lending created an unsustainable housing market that served as the underpinnings of the day's economy, and when it all collapsed – as it had to – Wall Street's biggest and brightest were caught drowning under the weight of their overstated balance sheets. The nation gasped as the 150-year-old Lehman Brothers tumbled into bankruptcy, and panic set in as we began to realize that many more could follow.

Lawmakers responded to the crisis by enacting the 2008 Troubled Asset Relief Program (TARP) – a $700 billion fund used by the Treasury to bailout companies that were considered to be an indispensable part of the economy. TARP was implemented immediately, which is as much of its downfall as it is its salvation. Companies like AIG and Citibank needed billions immediately, and so billions were handed out without considerable thought given to the consequences that might develop.

Part of the economic bailout was aimed at the domestic automotive industry, where the Treasury committed $80.7 billion to Chrysler and General Motors, and their respective financing arms. In exchange Chrysler and General Motors were required to present President Barack Obama's Auto Task Force with "aggressive" restructuring plans that included a reduction of 25 percent of their dealer networks.

For Chrysler, this meant terminating 789 dealers; for GM it was 1,454.

The manner in which Chrysler and GM went about terminating their dealers was distinctly different, although both were done through the bankruptcy court. GM gave its dealers wind-down agreements where they were phased out over a 16-month period and then paid a termination fee, in exchange for a release of all claims. Chrysler, on the other hand, gave its 789 dealers a mere 22 days to cease all business operations, and then paid them nothing for their franchises and years of service.

Because of the enormous financial investment dealers are required to put into their franchises, nearly all states have laws that only allow manufacturers to terminate dealers for "good cause." Dealers routinely invest millions into facilities, parts, equipment and goodwill, and are required to obtain substantial credit lines for the vehicle inventory they carry. To put into perspective the magnitude of just how important dealerships are to the economy, consider that the average dealership in California generates $50 million in annual sales, employs 85 people, and pays $4.5 million in federal, state and local taxes.

So, when Chrysler informed 789 of its dealers that they were going to be terminated in just 22 days, and that it was all going to be insulated from attack in a pre-packaged bankruptcy filing, shockwaves were felt throughout the dealer community. Now, however, the dealers are fighting back.

In three companion lawsuits filed in the Federal Court of Claims in Washington D.C. (*Spitzer Motor City v. U.S., et al.*), several hundred former Chrysler dealers have filed claims against the United States for violating the Fifth Amendment of the U.S. Constitution. Under their theory, the U.S. orchestrated Chrysler's termination of their franchises when it provided the automaker with billions in public TARP funds, resulting in a "taking" of their property without just compensation. Their argument is garnering considerable support.

In his recent book *Overhaul*, Steven Rattner, the head of the Auto Task Force, acknowledged that the Task Force specifically sought to terminate the Chrysler dealers through the bankruptcy court so that it didn't "run afoul of the takings clause of the U.S. Constitution." In a report to Congress by the Special Inspector General for TARP, the Inspector General found that the U.S. purposefully utilized the bankruptcy code "in a quick and surgical way" to terminate the dealer networks.

However, the Government's attempt at insulating its actions through the bankruptcy court is now falling short. In two of the takings cases filed by the former Chrysler dealers, the trial judge has rejected the notion that the U.S. cannot be held liable for violating the Fifth Amendment because the takings were sanctioned by the bankruptcy court: "[T]he Chrysler bankruptcy was an irrelevant and complicating event. Bankruptcy court rulings should not be used by [the U.S.] to prevent plaintiffs from pursuing their takings claims in this court."

In denying the Government's motion to dismiss, Judge Robert Hodges stated that the dealers presented "unusual allegations that nevertheless create the prima facie feel of a takings case warranting just compensation." Unusual because, under current U.S. Supreme Court authority, categorical takings have thus far only involved real property. But, as Judge Hodges noted, the Supreme Court has stressed the importance of considering takings in the context of surrounding events, anticipating that unique cases would arise. As a result, the Supreme Court refused to develop a set formula for determining when a taking occurs, but instead requires courts to perform an ad hoc, factual inquiry.

In response to the assertion that the termination of the franchises was done by Chrysler, not the U.S., Judge Hodges noted that "when separate corporate entities act for the U.S., the U.S. is liable for their takings." The court also stated that the dealers were entitled to demonstrate that the loss of their franchises was the direct, natural and probable result of the Government's actions.

The *Spitzer Motor City v. U.S.* takings cases are the first to challenge the Treasury's disbursement of TARP funds; and if right, they will expand current U.S. Supreme Court case law on the interpretation of the Fifth Amendment, and result in billions being paid to the dealers who lost everything. For the dealers who lost franchises that had been in their family for generations, or those who are still paying back the debt they incurred when purchasing what they thought was a solid investment, such a day will finally bring resolution to the nightmare of it all. As Mary McCarthy stated in *My Confession*: "An unrectified case of injustice has a terrible way of lingering, restlessly, in the social atmosphere like an unfinished question."

CHAPTER 34

The Electric Car Myth

FEBRUARY 2013

In truth, it never really had the potential many had hoped for. Supporters were hoping that the electric car would be the regeneration of an industry, but boundless enthusiasm could not replace the state of technology and sound economic principles.

Until recently, profit seekers were throwing money at anything electric; much the same way that profiteers had forked over millions to early dot com companies at dizzying speed. Lack of a proven track record – and in some cases, lack of a business altogether – were of little deterrent as investors sought to latch onto the next big thing.

The electric car will most definitely be a part of our future, just not in the way many had envisioned. The industry needs time to explore, develop and fail in all-natural ways, and the technology that survives this natural selection process will be the one that reigns.

The problem that we have is that we are attempting to force an industry down a path it is not ready to forge. Advances in technology introduced us to the electric car, and had it been able to chase consumer demand, all would have been right in the automotive world.

But, our desire to rid ourselves of foreign oil dependency caused us to leap to a platform that was unable to sustain the weight of the jump. The U.S. Executive Office, both under

President George W. Bush and Barack Obama, made commitments to back an industry that was too young for the job. Both Presidents committed hundreds of millions to companies that had never manufactured anything, and were woefully underequipped to make the kind of technological advances that were being expected of them.

And if President Bush's second term was aimed at U.S. energy independence, President Obama bet the farm on the electric car industry. In his January 2011 State of the Union address, President Obama promised that the U.S. would be "the first country to have a million electric vehicles on the road by 2015." This was followed by an overhaul of the Corporate Average Fuel Economy (CAFE) standards, where manufacturers will be required to reach a fleet average of 54.5 mpg by 2025. That number had been hovering around 27.5 mpg for the last 25 years.

The problem with all of this is that we are now forced to endorse a technology that is not ready for the challenge. Industry experts generally agree that a fleet average of 54.5 mpg is not achievable without the electrification of some of their fleet. But, because the cost of production is so high, and consumer demand has been razor thin, automakers will likely slash electric car prices to move units, and spread the losses among the remaining fleet. This, of course, will result in higher car prices for the majority of car buyers who still opt for internal combustion vehicles.

If there is any doubt on this, consider that the Secretary of Energy Stephen Chu recently published the results of a two-year study that found that "internal combustion engine technologies are likely to be the dominant propulsion systems for decades to come, with liquid fuel blends continuing to play a significant, but reduced role." Even more interestingly, the study found that "vehicles fueled with compressed natural gas

– not electric batteries – will emerge as the biggest competitor to the combustion engine."

The truth about electric cars is that consumers find them interesting, but not nearly compelling enough to buy. At least not yet. When the Chevy Volt and Nissan Leaf were introduced, the automakers trumpeted predictions of immediate success. However, the products have been anything but, with sales that were a fraction of what was expected.

And now even the dealers are showing signs of product fatigue. *Automotive News* reported last month that some Chevrolet dealers are refusing the carry the Volt because of the special tools they have to buy to service the vehicles. For instance, Volt dealers are required to purchase a $4,735 battery depowering tool to drain the car's 435-pound battery pack for repair. This has some dealers saying that the math just doesn't pencil.

Consumers are showing that they tend to agree. While President Obama promised to have the U.S. be the first country with one million electric vehicles on the road by 2015, we will not come close to reaching this mark. CBS News recently released a report that shows that the achievable number is closer to 300,000.

The result of all of this is that we have a mixed-up industry that is in the middle of an unsolvable riddle. Consider the case of Fisker, the Orange County electric car startup. After taking in $1.2 billion in cash, and incurring years of production delays, the company produced a mere 2,000 cars worldwide. It is now out of cash, out of production, and hoping that it will receive a stay of the inevitable bankruptcy execution.

And Fisker is still one of the bright spots. Many others, such as A123 Systems and Ener1, have already fallen to dominant market forces, dragging millions in taxpayer dollars down with them. To add insult to the discussion, last week the U.S. Bankruptcy Court approved a sell of the remains of A123 Systems to China's largest auto parts maker; meaning that we unintentionally used $249 million in government funding to enrich China's electrical car development. Not exactly the result that everyone was hoping for.

In the sober aftermath of the frenzy, none of this should be all that surprising. Industries need time to develop and technologies need time to mature. Forcing a fixed solution to a variable problem will only serve to stunt growth. As Bob Lutz, the one-time Vice Chairman of GM, famously said, forcing car manufacturers to adhere to CAFE regulations is "like forcing a clothing maker to sell smaller shirts to get people to lose weight."

CHAPTER 35

Chasing the
Seven Percent

MARCH 2013

Saint Bernard of Clairvaux, the 12th century Catholic Church leader, is frequently credited with saying that "the road to hell is paved with good intentions." A timeless axiom that rings as true today as it did 1,000 years ago, the saying has befallen scores of men who have created chaos in the wake of well-intended order.

To be sure, President Barack Obama's legacy will be stamped with the success - or failure - of his sweeping healthcare reform, the Patient Protection and Affordable Care Act. Signed into law on March 23, 2010, "Obamacare," as it has become known, aims to provide health insurance for the many who are currently without.

The law has withstood U.S. Supreme Court review and endured public scrutiny in a hotly-contested 2012 presidential election, but can it survive actual implementation? This is the question that has many business owners stirring.

According to the Congressional Budget Office (CBO), there are currently 53 million uninsured persons in the U.S., 11 million of which are illegal aliens. The CBO estimates that after the legislation has been fully implemented in 2019, that 30 million people will remain uninsured - a reduction of about 7 percent. What remains unknown, however, is how businesses both small and large will respond to the legislation.

In broad strokes, starting in January 2014 all citizens will be required to have health insurance, or pay a penalty of $95 per year (which will increase to $695 by 2016). Insurance companies will be required to issue policies regardless of a person's medical condition, and all applicants of the same age and geographical location must be given the same premium, regardless of pre-existing condition. Businesses of 50 employees or more will be required to provide insurance to all full-time employees, or pay a penalty of $2,000 per employee (exempting the first 30).

To see what might happen, it is necessary to understand the current state of affairs. According to the Kaiser Family Foundation, in 2012 the average health premium was $5,615 per year for an individual. The U.S. Bureau of Labor Statistics reports that businesses with fewer than 50 employees provided health benefits to 39 percent of their workforce, and businesses with 50 or more (who will now be required to offer insurance) provided the benefit to 59 percent of their employees.

Economists far and near are hypothesizing how business owners will respond to the new law, with varying conclusions - a result likely driven by the person's political affiliation. But politics aside, human behavior is driven, in large part, by a scarcity of resources and a desire to prosper.

Employees of small businesses (defined as fewer than 50 employees) will likely experience two behavior modifications. Currently, 61 percent of these employees are not provided insurance by their employer. Under the Affordable Care Act, all of these individuals will be required to obtain insurance, and this is where things get interesting.

Many insurance analysts expect that premiums will radically increase when the act takes effect in January 2014. Because insurance will be a "guaranty issue" (it must be provided irrespective of the person's pre-existing conditions), it is expected that many will choose to pay the $95 fine and forego the insurance until they get sick. The result will be insurance pools that are smaller and sicker, and therefore more expensive. As Mark Bertolini, the CEO of Aetna, recently stated: "We're going to see some markets go up by as much as 100 [percent]."

For the small business employee who is not provided insurance through the workplace, the increase in premiums may prove too great to bear. They may simply pay the $95 penalty and get the guaranteed insurance when they need it. It is also reasonable to believe that employees who currently obtain their own policy may remove themselves from the insurance pool, saving the premiums, and similarly get insurance when they need it.

For small businesses that do currently provided insurance, this too may change. Consider a business that employs 25 people. If the increase in premiums is just 50 percent of current rates (and it could be more), the employer's annual expense will increase by $70,000 virtually overnight. This too could result in a price tag that may prove too great to bear, leading to a reduction of small businesses that offer the benefit. Given that insurance is typically the third largest expense (behind rent and payroll), don't be surprised if this is the result.

But the real problem will be experienced with businesses of 50 or more, which will now be required to provide insurance to all full-time employees or pay a fine of $2,000 per employee. For owners of these businesses, life is about to dramatically change.

Take a business that employs 100 people and currently does not provide insurance. For this business owner, starting in 2014 the businesses will have an added annual expense of

$561,500 (based on today's average of $5,615) to over $1 million if the prediction of 100 percent premium increases holds true. Given the enormity of this cost, many will opt to pay the $140,000 fine ($2,000 for each employee over 30 employees) and avoid the problem altogether.

Of the 59 percent of large businesses who do offer insurance, this too could change. If the increase in premiums is anywhere near the 100 percent mark, many employers may elect to pay a fine of $2,000 per employee, as opposed to an $11,230 insurance premium. The larger the business, the larger the incentive to not provide insurance.

The law strikes a particular nerve for certain industries that trend right around the 50-employee mark. New car dealerships, for instance, employ an average 53 employees, putting them squarely in the sights of the mandate. For the 17,450 new car dealers across the U.S. that employ nearly 1 million, this is an issue that has not gone unnoticed.

Because of the high cost of penalties and increased premiums, the legislation likely will lead to significant underemployment. Not only will businesses cram-down their workforce to under 50, but many will reclassify employees as "part time." Because the law only requires insurance for full time employees (30 hours per week or more), many will hold their employees to 29 hours per week, and then make up the lost labor by adding more part time employees. This is particularly true in industries that do not historically have 9-to-5 jobs, such as retail, education and hospitality.

If there is any doubt that employers will game the system, consider that the state of Virginia will be requiring all part-time state to employees work no more than 29 hours per week, so that they will not qualify for the mandatory insurance. Others will do the math and surely follow. As a natural result of all of this, a substantial portion of the workforce will become underemployed, and yet still be required to obtain coverage. Only now they will have fewer paycheck dollars to obtain the expensive insurance.

President Obama was certainly well-intentioned in trying to provide affordable health care, but perhaps this falls under the category of "no good deed goes unpunished." This law will squeeze many individuals out of the insurance market, under-employ many at a time when we can least afford it, and increase the cost of consumer goods, as businesses try to recoup the cost of penalties they incur. This is a cost that will be borne by us all, solely for the purpose of chasing the seven percent.

CHAPTER 36

The Root of
All Evil

APRIL 2013

When the heads of the Detroit automakers made their famous trip to Washington DC in 2008, arriving in private jets and asking to be bailed out from their financial woes, the world was shocked at their level of disconnect. Did they really just tell Congress that they were broke and about to go under, while their $50 million jets waited on the tarmac? Many Americans would relish the opportunity to be so unfortunate.

The arrogance of the event typified everything wrong with the system, and at the same time was rather predictable. Executive pay for Fortune 500 companies had been out of whack for years, with top brass reeling in rich compensation packages that had little to do company performance. And executive pay untethered to company results, officers had little reason to dwell on the risks associated with the deals they were making.

Consider the case of Kenneth Lewis, the former CEO of Bank of America, who raked in $140 million in compensation from 2001 to 2009, while his company slid into the financial abyss. Under Lewis' watch, Bank of America was brought to near extinction, requiring a $45 billion U.S. bailout – the largest of any bank under the emergency program. Under mounting criticism, Lewis left in 2009, triggering an automatic severance payment. The amount: $135 million.

Economists have long agreed that executive compensation should be linked to both long term company performance and the average pay for the standard worker. Peter Drucker, one of the most influential modern-day thinkers on corporate governance, opined that CEO pay should be more than 20 times that of the average worker. The Economic Policy Institute noted that for most of the past century, CEO pay was directly in line with this, earning CEOs roughly 20 times as much as the average employee.

Yet according to a Businessweek study, in 2008 the average public company CEO received pay that was 400 times that of the average employee. What's worse, much of the pay did not fall into the category of long-term, incentive-based compensation. Quick cash was the name of the game.

If the public was shocked in 2008 to learn just how out-of-line executive pay had become, it was downright outraged when bailout recipients continued to give their executives outlandish pay. In late 2008, for instance, Merrill Lynch paid out $3.6 billion in bonuses to its employees, even though Merrill's performance would have put the firm out of business had it not been for the bailout. In the last three months of 2008 alone, the company reported losses of $21 billion.

To reign in executive pay for companies that received Troubled Asset Relief Program (TARP) funds, Congress placed strict limitations on executive compensation for TARP recipients. The Treasury Department created the Office of the Special Master for TARP Executive Compensation, which was charged with establishing pay packages for the 25 highest paid employees at companies whose receipt of TARP funds was considered "exceptional."

In a Feb. 4, 2009, address to the nation, President Barack Obama brought clarity to what would be permitted: "Top executives at firms receiving extraordinary help from U.S. taxpayers will have their compensation capped at $500,000 – a fraction of the salaries that have been reported recently. And if these executives receive any additional compensation, it will come in the form of stock that can't be paid up until taxpayers are paid back for their assistance."

Initially, the Special Master was responsible for the executive pay at seven companies. However, after five of the companies repaid their TARP debt, today the number stands at just two: General Motors and its sister company, Ally Financial (formerly General Motors Acceptance Corporation). So, are the salaries of the GM and Ally executives in line with the president's promised salary cap? Not even close.

In a 2013 report released by the Special Inspector General for the Troubled Asset Relief Program (SIGTARP), the Inspector General found that the Special Master "did not establish meaningful criteria" for determining executive pay at its covered companies, and that it "could not effectively rein in excessive compensation." The report blasted the Special Master for the lack of oversight, and lead to hearings before the U.S. House Oversight and Government Reform Committee.

Just how bad is it? Get ready to be sick. In 2012, nine of the 22 highest paid GM executives received cash pay that violated the president's $500,000 pay cap, and all 22 executives received stock that vested immediately, not after the TARP funds are repaid. With the cash and stock combined, the GM salaries ranged from a low of $1,236,250 to a high of $9,000,000.

Ally's 2012 pay plan was just as offensive. Six of its 21 highest paid executives received cash pay over $500,000, and as with GM, all 21 executives received stock that vested immediately. Ally's salaries ranged from $1,934,667 to $9,500,000. Under the guiding economic principle that a CEO's pay should be no more than 20 times that of the average worker, this would mean that the average Ally employee should be taking home $475,000 per year, which certainly is not the case.

It is unforgivable that the Special Master approved the same type of outlandish salaries that created the financial crisis in the first place, and it is shameful that GM and Ally requested them. As President Obama stated in his February 2009 address, our nation needs to stomp out this type of reckless behavior. "This is the height of irresponsibility. It's shameful. And that's exactly the kind of disregard of the costs and consequences of their actions that brought about this crisis."

GM and Ally should take a page out of Warren Buffett's playbook. Buffett, the self-made billionaire who built Berkshire Hathaway into one of the most profitable companies of our day, received an annual salary in 2008 (when other CEOs' pay plans were skyrocketing) of $100,000 and a bonus of $75,000.

Buffet did allow himself one perk. In 1989, he purchased a corporate jet that he appropriately called "The Indefensible." But in true Buffett style, he managed to turn even this into a success, parlaying the transaction into the purchase of NetJets – a company that has now become the largest private jet provider in the world.

Perhaps Saint Paul was right. The love of money is a root of all kinds of evil. We can only hope that corporate executives' love of the quick buck won't put us right back into a place of wondering how it all got so bad so quickly.

CHAPTER 37

The Fallen Angel

MAY 2013

If the National Football League glimmers in the U.S. media spotlight, Formula One racing downright dominates the rest of the world. Set on a global stage, where races dance from continent to continent, the motorsports gala has become the sport of kings. In its 19-race season, the circuit traverses through Asia, the Americas, Europe and the Middle East, playing to sold-out arenas twice the size of the Super Bowl.

The economics of the sport are massive. Each race is broadcast to over 200 countries, attracting an average of 336 million television viewers per event. To put the number into perspective, the 2012 NFL regular season reached 200 million viewers for the *entire* season. The yield generated Formula One's popularity is also enormous. Consider that Ferrari team driver Fernando Alonso – a name that many will not recognize – has an annual salary that exceeds that of Tiger Woods, LeBron James and Phil Mickelson *combined*.

The man who has stood atop of this empire for nearly 30 years is 82-year-old billionaire Bernie Ecclestone. If you don't recognize him as being the fourth richest person in the U.K., you may recall that it was his 22-year-old daughter Petra Ecclestone who purchased Aaron Spelling's Los Angeles mansion in 2011 for $85 million in cash. At the time it was listed, the 56,000 square foot manor was the highest-price house in the U.S. Certainly, something every debutante needs.

Bernie Ecclestone has done yeoman's duty in commercializing a sport that was once reserved for hard-core motorsports enthusiasts, and for this he has earned the nickname "F1 Supremo." Ecclestone has been particularly canny about using the sport to commercialize emerging markets, bringing races to the likes of Abu Dhabi, New Delhi, Budapest, Kuala Lumpur and Bahrain. And for this, he has gained the reputation as being either the most innovative thinker in the history of the sport, or the toughest negotiator imaginable, extracting millions in race fees from host cities.

Ecclestone's official role in Formula One is that of commercial rights holder. Ownership of the series has long been vested in a conglomerate of three banks that have permitted Ecclestone to serve as the face man and chief negotiator for the series. Yet a mid-2000s attempt by a New York hedge fund to purchase the series set in motion a chain of events that threatens to take down the man who built it all.

In 2005, Bluewaters Communications approached German-owned bank, BayernLB, about purchasing its 46.7 percent interest in Formula One. On Oct. 4, 2005, after months of negotiation, Bluewaters offered to buy BayernLB's shares for $1 billion in cash. Bluewaters also offered to beat any bona fide competing offer by 10 percent.

Bluewaters thought the deal was all but done, but they underestimated kingpin Bernie Ecclestone. On Nov. 25, 2005, London-based CVC Capital Partners issued an unexpected press release, announcing that it had purchased BayernLB's shares in Formula One for $831 million. The other two banks, J.P. Morgan and Lehman Commercial, sold their interest to CVC two weeks later for $419 million, giving CVC complete ownership of the series. CVC agreed to keep Ecclestone on as the front man of the sport.

For the next five years, CVC enjoyed rich profits from the series. In 2007, it declared a $1 billion dividend, and in 2012 a second $1 billion was paid. That same year, CVC sold a 5 percent interest in the series to another bank consortium for $500 million, placing a valuation of Formula One at $9.1 billion.

The decision to sell the interest in Formula One to CVC for less money than had been offered by Bluewaters was more than curious to German officials – particularly given that the transaction was entered into by a German-owned bank. In January 2011, German authorities arrested Gerhard Gribkowsky, the chief risk officer at BayernLB in charge of selling the bank's Formula One shares. The charge: accepting a $44 million bribe from Bernie Ecclestone to have the sale consummated with CVC, not Bluewaters.

And there's more to it. The money trail shows that Ecclestone actually received the bribe money from BayernLB itself. Ecclestone claims that the payment to him from the bank was a finder's fee for brokering the deal, but others believe that the finder's fee agreement was simply drawn up by Ecclestone and Gribkowsky to enable them to use the bank's money to fund the deal.

Whatever the case, the following is certain: At trial, Gribkowsky admitted to accepting the bribe, Ecclestone admitted paying the money, and Presiding Judge Peter Noll described Ecclestone as the "driving force" behind the payments. Gribkowsky is now serving an 8½-year sentence in a German prison, and officials are determining whether to charge Ecclestone.

The conviction has created a firestorm of litigation across the continents. Bluewaters has filed a civil complaint in New York against Ecclestone and Gribkowsky for fraud and tortious interference, seeking $650 million and punitive damages. BayernLB sent a formal demand to Ecclestone for $400 million it claims it lost as a result of the bribery scheme. And Dieter Hahn, an individual who had an agreement with BayernLB that was to pay him 10 percent for any sale over $1 billion, has filed a lawsuit against Gribkowsky and Ecclestone in the London High Court seeking $171 million in damages.

The situation at hand could be the beginning of Ecclestone's long slide from quasi-royalty to fallen angel. Even for a man of wealth, the legal battles that lie ahead for Ecclestone are nearly immeasurable – saying nothing of the problems he will face if criminal charges are pursued. As has happened with many a man who has been seduced by the greed of power and money, this may be the last we see of our good friend Bernie.

CHAPTER 38

Eliminating
All Doubt

JUNE 2013

Few things in life can be more daunting than the launching of a new car company. The automobile is by far the most complex – and dangerous – piece of machinery ever to be placed in the hands of a consumer. Consider that the modern-day automobile has some 10,000 moving parts and 100 million lines of software code running through dozens of on-board microprocessors. This symphony of parts not only needs to work, but to keep working through years of consumer use. The wrong part fails at the wrong time, and the result is catastrophic.

If the complexity of the automobile doesn't deter would be entrants from making a run at the market, federal regulation just might. To help protect the public from all sorts of vehicle-related disaster, the federal government has created an enormous web of vehicle safety standards that govern everything from bumper height to airbag deployment. Get one wrong and you will never get out of the gate. Equally onerous are the regulations that govern fuel economy and vehicle pollutants. To be sure, automakers have felt the blunt impact of our government's attempt at being environmentally responsible.

For those able to overcome the barriers of actually producing a compliant automobile, they are left only to realize that they are now in a marketplace that has been dominated by billion-dollar giants for generations. GM was founded in 1908, and Toyota has been at it since 1937. Their years in the marketplace have not just resulted competitive wisdom, but billions in annual sales. The top four auto groups – GM, Volkswagen, Toyota and Hyundai – are responsible for a combined $700 billion in annual sales.

So when the South African immigrant Elon Musk set out to start a new car company in 2003 at the age of 31, few gave him much of a chance. If it wasn't for the fact that he sold PayPal – a company he founded when he was 28 – the year before to eBay for $1.5 billion, and committed substantial personal funds to the new car company, it may never have had any chance at all.

Named after the 19th century electrical engineer and inventor Nikola Tesla, Tesla Motors has taken the world by storm. At a time when established car companies typically spend over a billion dollars to bring a car to market, Tesla has managed to engineer and develop two cars on an entirely new electric vehicle platform for a fraction of the cost. The challenges involved in mass producing any vehicle are manifest; doing it with an emerging technology is near impossible.

If the fact that Tesla has been able to successfully produce consumer cars on new technology sounds impressive, consider that during the entire time that Elon Musk has been ramping up Tesla, he has been splitting his time with SpaceX, a rocket company he founded in 2002 for the purpose of enabling human exploration and settlement of Mars. In 2012, SpaceX became the world's first private company to send a cargo payload to the International Space Station.

What is perhaps most surprising is that Tesla's main vehicle, the Model S, doesn't just work; it excels, wildly. Consumer Reports, which has been objectively reviewing consumer products since 1936, stated that the Model S performed better, or just as well overall, as any other vehicle of any kind that the company had ever tested. Motor Trend agreed, making the Model S the 2013 Car of the Year – marking the first time in the company's 64-year history that the award had not gone to internal combustion vehicle.

Consumer acceptance has been equally glowing. The California New Car Dealers Association recently reported that the Model S was the third best-selling luxury car in California for the first quarter of 2013, beating out Audi and Lexus. The automaker has managed to garner a 12.7 percent market share for a vehicle that began to ship less than a year ago.

It perhaps should not have been a surprise when Tesla's stock closed at over $100 per share last week. Yet the math is still nearly unimaginable, given that the company has been in business for only 10 years, and public for less than three. To put it into context, Tesla as a company is worth more today than Fiat – a company that owns Ferrari, Alfa Romeo, Maserati and 20 percent of Chrysler. Tesla's stock has risen from its initial offering price of $17 to a high of $110 – a 650 percent increase. And with this, the company has been able to repay the $465 million loan it received in 2010 from the Department of Energy, nine years early.

Elon Musk has been a maverick not only in his vision, but in his eagerness to challenge conventional wisdom. Perhaps nowhere is this more evident than with Tesla's vehicle distribution system. Traditional thinking is that vehicles are sold through independently-owned franchised dealers. Yet Musk thwarted that system in favor of a labyrinth of factory-owned stores throughout the U.S.

The move has invoked a firestorm of pushback from powerful dealer groups, who contend that state franchise laws preclude, or should preclude, Tesla from bucking the franchise system. And the states are taking notice. In April, the Virginia Dept. of Motor Vehicles denied Tesla a dealership license, and the North Carolina legislature is voting on a bill that would make it illegal to for any manufacturer to sell a vehicle directly to a consumer.

The attacks on Tesla raise serious questions as to the constitutionality of the laws at issue. Certainly states have a right to protect the interests of their citizens, but such interests need to be squared with the Commerce Clause and preventing a restraint on trade. Musk is showing no signs of backing down, so the challenge that awaits could be one for the ages – and perhaps one that reshapes the fabric of our nation's dealership system.

CHAPTER 39

So, You Think You're Safe?

JULY 2013

It is astonishing, when you think about it. On a near-daily basis, most of us step into some form of automotive transportation without giving a single thought to the integrity of the vehicle. We go to great lengths to ensure that we are protected and secured in the vehicle, but give little thought, if any, to the question of whether the vehicle itself is sound. With almost blanket immunity, we assume that the vehicle will just work, and keep working for as many years as we maintain ownership.

Yet the number of things that can go wrong with a vehicle is infinite. The modern-day automobile has some 10,000 moving parts, manufactured by hundreds of different suppliers, all of which need to perform as intended through years of use. The failure of some parts is mere inconvenience; the failure of others is widespread catastrophe.

The announcement last week by the National Highway Traffic Safety Administration that it is launching a nationwide investigation into braking failures of the Honda Odyssey minivan underscores the severity of the issue. The charge is that 2007 and 2008 Honda Odysseys are suddenly braking without the driver applying the brakes, a defect that is believed to be derived from the vehicle's stability management system.

Enacted in 1966, the National Traffic and Motor Vehicle Safety Act gives the Department of Transportation's National

Highway Traffic Safety Administration (NHTSA) the authority to require manufacturers to recall vehicles that have safety-related defects. Since then, NHTSA has overseen the recall of 502 million vehicles, tires and child safety seats. And as vehicles become increasingly complex, recalls are becoming more frequent.

In its first year of existence, NHTSA issued 58 recalls, affecting 982,823 vehicles. Last year, that number grew to 664 recalls – or nearly three every day the agency was open – impacting 17.8 million U.S. vehicles. Considering that there were 14.4 million sold in the U.S. in 2012, we have officially reached the era where more vehicles are recalled each year than are actually sold.

While many of the recalls are for non-life-threatening issues, such as a windshield wiper malfunction, an increasingly large number of recalls are for matters that can lead to consumer fatality. And the number is on the rise.

From 1970 to 2000, the industry saw relatively few recalls that lead to immediate consumer uproar. The most famous recalls of the era were the Ford Pinto recall, which affected 1971 to 1976 Ford Pintos that were prone to exploding on rear impact; the Audi 5000 recall, which recalled 1978 to 1983 Audi 5000s because of runaway acceleration; and the Ford Explorer recall, which impacted 1991 to 2000 Ford Explorers equipped with Firestone tires that were prone to rollover.

In the last 10 years, however, the number of recalls that relate to life-threatening issues has risen precipitously. In 2009, Toyota recalled 4.3 million vehicles due to the now-famous unintended acceleration problem; yet that was just the beginning of a series of critical recalls that would soon follow. In 2012, both Toyota and Honda issued recalls of over one million vehicles each for risk of spontaneous fire. In fact, in 2012, Honda and Toyota accounted for a combined 8.7

million recalled vehicles in the US, through 28 separate recall campaigns.

While the numbers are staggering, the results should not be overly shocking. Manufacturers are attempting to squeeze more efficiency and advancement from cars that ever before. And while it has always been the case that manufacturers have been seeking vehicle advancement, they have never before attempted to do it with such a level of vehicle autonomy. It used to be that fuel injection and cruise control were the height of vehicle advancement. Today, it is start-stop technology, vehicle stability management and regenerative braking.

It is this overlay of moving parts and software code that creates a perfect host environment for vehicle malfeasance. Consider that the average vehicle contains 100 million lines of software code running through dozens of on-board microprocessors. By way of comparison, the Apollo 11 spacecraft that put the first man on the moon was run by "top-secret" IBM punch cards that were mated to binary mainframe computers.

It is proving near impossible for manufacturers to keep software code and machined part in a steady state of intended harmony for any kind of extended period. Honda and Toyota, while owning the title of having issued the largest recalls, are far from alone in their inability to keep their products safe. GM, Ford and Chrysler combined for 6.2 million recalled U.S. vehicles in 2012, having issued 54 separate recall campaigns.

To be sure, the automobile is the most complicated product to ever be placed in the hands of a consumer. It is heavy and powerful, and capable of propelling consumers to speeds well over 100 mph in a matter of seconds. Recent developments, such as airbags, ABS braking and vehicle stability control, have enabled the automobile to become infinitely safer. Yet, ironically, the complexity of these very systems creates conflict in the ability of manufacturers to deliver a vehicle that is defect free.

Anyone who has seen their desktop computer suddenly crash without explanation can appreciate the sensitive nature of non-mechanical machinery. As manufacturers further pursue the unison of machine and computer, no one should be surprised at the unintended consequences that will naturally follow.

CHAPTER 40

The Deadliest Weapon

AUGUST 2013

On average, 14 people die in the U.S. every day as a result of distracted driving, with scores more seriously injured and sentenced to a life term of debilitating injuries. Think for a moment about the tens of thousands of people who are living their life confined to a wheelchair, or the legions of people who have had to burry a loved one because of distracted driving, and then try to pretend that it is not an epidemic of national proportion.

Initially, the problem was cell phone use – a problem that many states tried to remedy with bans on hand-held devices. Today, 39 states have outlawed hand-held devices (California being one of them), but in truth this does little to rectify the problem. The general consensus among the scientific community is that there is a negligible difference between talking on a cell phone with and without a hands-free device; it is just plain dangerous no matter how it is used.

This should be a concern to all. The National Safety Council, a non-profit organization that was chartered by Congress in 1913, estimates that at any given moment, 9 percent of drivers on U.S. highways are talking on their cell phones. This, the agency estimates, results in 1.1 million crashes every year.

Now, overlay the issue of cell phone use with texting and driving. The U.S. has seen an enormous increase in text messaging over the past five years. For the calendar year

2007, there were 363 billion text messages sent in the U.S.; by 2012, that number had grown to 2.2 trillion. It would be naïve to think that this increase has not made its way into the automobile, and that the problem will not further escalate.

It is no surprise that the biggest users of text messaging are the younger generation – but what's concerning is that this generation drives, and that they don't stay young forever. You may be surprised, or even downright shocked, to learn just how prolific texting has become for Generation Y. In a study performed by Experian Marketing Services, a person between the ages of 18 and 24 sends and receives an average of 3,853 texts per month.

As these drivers age, and bring their technology habits with them, we will become a driving population that is more accustomed to living life with the smart phone in one hand, and everything else in the other. Given this, it should not be overly surprising to learn that the National Safety Council estimates that at any given time, 1.3 percent of the driving public is texting while driving.

Yet, amazingly, some states still don't get it. There are nine states that have do not have a ban on texting while driving, and there are six states – New Mexico, Montana, South Dakota, Oklahoma, Missouri and South Carolina – that have no limitation whatsoever on what drivers can do with their cell phone behind the wheel. This means that in these states, it is perfectly acceptable for a school bus driver to be texting while driving, or a truck driver to be surfing the web while speeding down the highway.

So serious is the problem that in December 2011, the U.S. National Transportation Safety Board (NTSB) has issued a recommendation that all 50 states ban any form of cell phone use while driving, even with a hands-free device. The recommendation also urges states to implement harsh penalties for violation of the law. However, because the ability to regulate driver behavior is left to the states, we are left with a quilt-work of legislation – and so far every state has ignored the NTSB recommendation to ban cell phones altogether.

The automotive industry's response to the crisis has been to create a platform of advanced technology designed to take the cell phone out of the hand. Drivers can now talk on their cell phone through a car's Bluetooth device, text friends through speech-to-text technology, and post messages on Facebook through voice recognition. Automakers say that the systems not only address safety concerns, but also cater to consumers who want to stay connected while driving.

Yet a June 2013 study by David Strayer, a neuroscientist at the University of Utah, found that infotainment and voice recognition systems actually exacerbate the distracted driver problem, and are far more dangerous than the devices they are trying to replace. While a hand-held cell phone will take a driver's hand off the wheel, voice-activated systems take a driver's mind off the road.

The study found that voice recognition and speech-to-text systems require substantial cognitive output. Unlike talking with a person, who can interrupt and ask for clarification, use of voice recognition systems require the driver to layout and think through the command. While the task by itself is not overly difficult, the human brain is not able to engage in the function without experiencing a deficit in the attention needed for driving.

According to David Strayer's study, the impairment created by voice recognition and speech-to-text systems is far more severe than that of having a 0.08 blood-alcohol level, the legal standard for intoxication across the country. Yet, automakers are far from slowing their advancement of these systems. Electronics consulting firm IMS Research reports that by 2019, more than half of all new cars will integrate some type of voice recognition into their systems.

What's worse, the infotainment systems themselves are becoming increasingly complex. To name but a few, Audi's premium "Connect" service provides drivers with a Google Earth navigation experience, while Tesla allows its drivers to surf the web on the car's beautiful 17-inch touchscreen monitor *while driving*.

The U.S. Department of Transportation has urged automakers to voluntarily limit the technology applications in their vehicles, but the arms race has already begun. Manufacturers are feverishly packing their cars with all the cutting-edge technology they can muster, all in the hope of luring consumers to their showrooms and moving more iron. Unfortunately, we will likely have to experience a national tragedy that will sober us all, before we take the responsible and necessary step of focusing more on driver safety and less on driver entertainment.

CHAPTER 41

Pop the Champagne

SEPTEMBER 2013

If the U.S. economy has been suffering through a great recession the last five years, the automotive industry has been in a downright depression. In the mid-2000s, U.S. auto sales were bristling at 17 million new car sales per year – a pace that put us on track for a historic 20 million sales by 2013.

Yet in 2008, we learned just how fragile an economy can be, as we watched the 110-year-old Lehman Brothers topple into bankruptcy, taking with it the fortunes of many. The year following the Lehman collapse, the automobile industry slid into the abyss, with U.S. sales plummeting to 10 million – the same number of vehicles sold in 1968, when our population was just a tick over 200 million. All that had been taken for granted for generations was suddenly lost, as manufacturers once thought invincible confessed to the world that they were now insolvent.

The health of the auto industry is a concern to all, as it serves not only as a leading indicator of things to come, but our economy could not rebound without it. One out of every ten people in the workforce is employed by the automotive industry, making the sector the most significant contributor to the nation's welfare. The industry supports everyone from factory workers and parts manufacturers to dealerships and classic car restorers. Consider that in California alone, new car dealers generate just shy of $100 billion in annual sales, and they are responsible for 9 percent of the state's sales tax.

As bleak as the last five years have been, economists are finally beginning to celebrate the industry's recovery.

While we have yet to return to pre-recession numbers, light vehicle sales are expected to surpass 15 million units this year, with predictions of 17.5 million by 2016. And the companies who made it through the fog of the last five years have emerged healthier and stronger than ever. The Detroit Three have returned to profitability, and the shakeup has made room for new entrants, such as electric car manufacturer Tesla whose stock recently surged past $170 per share.

While the rebounding sales numbers are impressive, it is increased consumer confidence that is the greatest achievement to report. Public dealer groups, such as AutoNation and Sonic, are again on buying sprees, competing with each other as they acquire private dealerships, and retail buyers are feeling bullish about being able to support the payments that are attached to a new vehicle purchase.

AutoNation, the largest dealership group in the nation, reported that its 2013 first-quarter revenue rose 12 percent to $4.1 billion. Michael Jackson, the company's CEO, stated that he expects business to remain strong, driven by accelerated product launches, continued replacement demand and robust availability of consumer credit. "We are at the beginning of a broad-based recovery for the economy and auto retail," Jackson said.

And if the retail side of the industry has seen a return of confident buyers, the classic car industry has just exploded with enthusiasm. Classic car sales reveal much about the state of the economy and the direction it is heading. With their million-dollar price tags, classic cars attract financial moguls who tend to be smart with their dollars; few people who have had the wherewithal to accumulate a fortune are willing to risk it in uncertain times.

So it was quite a thing last month, when the annual gathering of collector car auctions at Pebble Beach reported that they sold a $307 million of collector cars in the three-day event. The highlight of the show was a 1967 Ferrari 275 GTB that sold at the RM auction for $27.5 million, wildly surpassing predictions of what the car would bring.

Yet the 1967 Ferrari is as famous for what it is not, as for what it is. As crazy as it is, the $27.5 million car is not the most expensive car ever sold – that distinction goes to a 1962 Ferrari 250 GTO that sold 3 months ago for $35 million in a private transaction; nor is it the most expensive car ever sold at an auction – that would be a 1954 Mercedes Benz Formula One racecar that sold in July for $29.6 million.

According to Hagerty, the collectible-car insurer and valuation firm, the average price of collectible Ferraris has increased 70 percent since 2010, with the average price at $2.6 million. And the values appear to be increasing. Last month, an owner of another 1962 Ferrari 250 GTO turned down an all cash offer to sell the car for $45 million, speculating that the price for the famed Ferrari will soon reach $50 million. Not bad for a car that had an original price of $6,000.

What is most rousing about the activity in the classic car market is that the only thing that is actually being traded is confidence. In truth, the assets themselves are little more than used cars with little value other than their rarity and pedigree. The only reason to throw crazy money at the cars is the confidence that another smart, wealthy person will find it wise to risk even more of their fortune for the same asset.

Case in point, the 1962 Ferrari 250 GTO that was recently sold for $35 million was purchased at auction a decade ago for $9 million; and it is this very car that industry experts are now thinking will broach the $50 million barrier. And it is this that speaks volumes about the state of our economy and times that are yet to come.

For a nation that has seen the toughest times in generations, the recovery of the automotive sector is a relief to all. Plants will soon be buzzing at capacity and dealerships will see a return of flush times – and we will all rejoice the good fortune that will befall our shattered economy. For a nation that has been through a nuclear winter, it just may be time to pop the champagne and finally have something to celebrate.

CHAPTER 42

Head
Rush

OCTOBER 2013

The release last week of Ron Howard's "Rush" has served to highlight the intense love affair that the international sporting world has with Formula One racing. The film chronicles the 1976 racing season, highlighting the rivalry between racing legends James Hunt and Niki Lauda. But it is the exposure of the sport to the U.S. masses that is the film's true hallmark of success.

Formula One has long been considered the world's most dominant sport, consistently playing to sold-out arenas twice the size of the Super Bowl. The series not only challenges the manufacturer-owned race teams to ruthlessly innovate, but its ability to complete a 20-race season is itself an engineering masterpiece.

Each Formula One race is held in a different country — sprawling through Europe, North America, South America, Asia and the Middle East — necessitating the immediate and constant transfer of tons of precision equipment and scores of engineers across international borders. With each race team employing about 100 traveling personnel, all of whom are from differing countries of origin, the immigration issues alone are mind-blowing.

As an example of the complexity, consider that on Oct. 6 the teams race in South Korea, and then have to be ready to race the following Sunday in Suzuka City, Japan. This is followed by races in India, Abu Dhabi and the U.S., before concluding the season on Nov. 24 in Sao Paulo, Brazil.

Given this, it is no surprise that the top Formula One team (Ferrari) has an annual budget of $470 million and that it employs 525 people. By way of comparison, top Indy car teams (which travel throughout the U.S.) have annual budgets of about $15 million and employ an average of 20 people.

The payoff is equally substantial. Each race is broadcast in some 200 countries, attracting an average of 336 million television viewers per event. To put this into perspective, the 2012 NFL regular season reached 200 million viewers for the *entire* season. In fact, the marketing advantage of Formula One was so strong, that in 2005 energy drink giant Red Bull bought a Formula One race car and outfitted it with Red Bull logos. According to Formula One's industry publication, Formula Money, Red Bull's "advertising value equivalent" — the price it would have had to pay to buy a similar amount of on-screen exposure — was $415 million in 2011.

In part because the stakes are so incredibly high, and in part because of the nature of the sport, Formula One fosters an environment that thrives on risk. In a setting where winners and losers are defined by hundredths of a second, teams are encouraged — if not compelled — to bet it all on the hope of success. The result: teams push each other harder than everyone imagined. Pit-stop times hover around 2.4 seconds, and cars redline at 20,000 RPM, subjecting their drivers to lateral G-forces of 5.4G.

If Formula One teams are the primary risk-takers, then the man who stands on top of it all —— Formula One boss Bernie Ecclestone — adds an exclamation point to the discussion. The fourth wealthiest person in the U.K. (recall that it was Ecclestone's 22-year-old daughter, Petra Ecclestone, who bought Aaron Spelling's Los Angeles mansion in 2011 for

$85 million in cash), 82-year-old Ecclestone has been the Formula One kingpin for nearly 30 years.

Ecclestone's official role in Formula One is "commercial rights holder"; ownership of the series has long belonged to three banks that have permitted Ecclestone to serve as the face man for the series. Yet a mid-2000s attempt by a New York hedge fund to purchase the series set in motion a chain of events that is changing it all.

In 2005, Bluewaters Communications offered to buy out the largest stakeholder in the series, German bank BayernLB, which held a 46.7 interest, for $1 billion in cash. The offer was the culmination of months of negotiations, but just to make certain that it would not be outbid, Bluewaters also offered to beat any competing offer by 10 percent.

Bluewaters thought the deal was all but done. However, just six weeks after the offer was made, the German bank announced that it was selling its interest to CVC Capital Partners for $831 million. Two weeks later, the remaining banks (JP Morgan and Lehman Commercial) sold their interest to CVC for $419 million.

The sale resulted in a windfall for CVC. Not only did it pay considerably less than what Bluewaters was willing to pay, but it picked up an asset that was worth considerably more than the $1.25 billion it paid. For instance, in 2007 CVC declared a $1 billion dividend from the series, and in 2012 a second $1 billion dividend was paid. The series has a current valuation of $9.1 billion.

The other benefactor of the transaction: Ecclestone. As part of the transaction, the London-based CVC agreed to keep Ecclestone on as the front man of the sport — something that appeared doubtful under the Bluewaters deal.

The decision to sell the series for hundreds of millions of dollars less than it would have otherwise received caught the attention of the German officials, who launched an investigation into the internal affairs of the bank. The investigation revealed that Gerhard Gribkowsky, the bank's chief risk officer and the person in charge of selling the bank's Formula One interest, had secretly received a $44 million payment from Ecclestone right before the series was sold. Gribkowsky admitted to the authorities that the payment was a bribe from Ecclestone to have the sale consummated with CVC, not Bluewaters, and he is now serving an 8½-year sentence in a German prison.

The mischief has resulted in a melee of litigation between Bluewaters, CVC, the German bank, Gribkowsky and Ecclestone, for damages in the hundreds of millions of dollars. Actions are now pending in U.S. District Court in New York and the London High Court, but the real question was whether German officials would dare touch Ecclestone, with his quasi-royalty status in the sport.

This summer, Munich prosecutors answered that question with a resounding "yes," when they indicted Ecclestone on charges of bribery and incitement to breach of trust. If convicted, Ecclestone could face 10 years in a German prison.

For the man who once said, "In Formula One, everyone cheats; the trick is not to get caught," this indeed may prove to be one trick too many for the famed Ecclestone. At 82, his time was limited anyway, but it is a shame his exodus from the sport will forever be linked to scandal, disgrace and perhaps prison. As Shakespeare wrote of his figure Julius Ceasar, "The evil that men do is remembered after their deaths, but the good is often buried with them." For Ecclestone, his alleged attempt at maintaining control over the series he helped build may be eternally branded in the memories of all concerned.

CHAPTER 43

Dodging a Bullet

NOVEMBER 2013

Few words can describe the unmitigated disaster that nearly befell our country last month when a New York bankruptcy judge was set to rule on one of the most explosive cases before the judiciary. The ruling could have inflicted untold damage on our fragile economy, sending scores of citizens into the financial abyss, and disrupting business relationships central to our continued viability. Yet, by the narrowest of chances, the matter settled on Oct. 21 after several failed mediation attempts and a hotly contested trial.

What was at issue was whether General Motors had fraudulently diverted hundreds of millions of dollars away from the bankruptcy court in an effort to shield assets from the insolvency process and give a group of the company's important creditors preferential treatment. The trial centered around whether GM secretly made a deal with a collection of hedge funds who owned $1.3 billion in bonds after the bankruptcy proceedings were initiated, and then backdated the agreement to before the date of the bankruptcy filing.

The mischief was discovered by a trust representing GM's unsecured creditors in 2012, who filed a lawsuit in the bankruptcy court where GM's insolvency proceedings were initiated. The matter was assigned to Judge Robert Gerber, the same judge who presided over GM restructuring proceedings and who ultimately approved the pre-packaged bankruptcy that enabled the automaker to shed billions in debt.

The case, formally known as *Motors Liquidation Company CUG Trust v. Appaloosa Investment Ltd, et al.*, sought to set aside the deal with the hedge funds and claw back the $450 million in cash that was transferred away from bankrupt the company as part of the transaction. Yet, the real question was whether the alleged act of dishonesty would give the bankruptcy court cause to set aside the entire bankruptcy proceeding — an event that would have catastrophic implications.

GM's 2009 Chapter 11 filing was the fourth largest in U.S. history, behind Lehman Brothers, Washington Mutual and WorldCom, and sought to rid the company of billions in debt. At the time of filing, GM stated that it had $82 billion in assets and $173 billion in debt. The pre-packaged bankruptcy filing allowed the company to sell off its best assets to "new" GM, leaving the remainder of the old company to be liquidated for the benefit of creditors.

Setting aside the bankruptcy would saddle new GM with billions in debt, and reinstate obligations long considered to be voided — events that would cast long shadows over our current recovery. Not only would GM immediately become financially strapped, but uncertainty would shudder throughout the economy. For instance, legitimate questions would surface about whether the 1,200 GM dealers who were terminated in the bankruptcy proceeding would be automatically reinstated, or whether the tens of thousands of GM retirees would have their retirement benefits returned.

To be sure, the threat of collapse was acutely understood. As Judge Gerber stated upon learning of the hedge fund deal: "When I heard about that, it wasn't just a surprise, it was a shock ... The bottom line is, is that this matter is huge ... There was a lack of disclosure to the court on the matter with the potential to injure [GM] creditors to the extent of hundreds of millions, if not billions of dollars."

What caused the hedge fund deal to be cut in the first place is actually quite interesting. In 2006, believing that GM was headed toward bankruptcy, Fortress Investment Group began buying bonds at a steep discount that were issued by GM Nova Scotia Finance Co., a subsidiary of GM Canada. Other hedge funds soon joined in, and by June 2009 four hedge funds owned $1.3 billion in the Canadian company's bonds.

As GM began preparing its restructuring package, it realized that the hedge funds were in a position to force GM Canada into bankruptcy, an event that would greatly impact GM's planned bankruptcy in the U.S. If the Canadian unit was forced into bankruptcy in Canada, the chances of GM having an expedited bankruptcy in the U.S. would evaporate.

On Friday, May 29, 2009 — three days before the June 1 deadline given to GM by the U.S. Treasury — representatives from GM and the hedge funds met in New York at the offices of GM's lawyers to negotiate a deal that would keep GM Canada out of bankruptcy. GM needed the hedge funds to waive the $1.3 billion owed to them under the Canadian bonds, and the bond holders used every ounce of leverage they had.

After negotiating through the weekend, a deal was finally struck: The hedge funds would waive the $1.3 billion owed, and GM would transfer $450 million to GM Canada, of which $367 million would be given to the bond holders, and the hedge funds would be entitled to submit a claim to the U.S. bankruptcy court in the amount of $2.67 billion.

The problem, however, was that the deal was allegedly consummated after the actual bankruptcy filing. The lawsuit by the creditors trust claims that the bankruptcy was filed on June 1, 2009, at 7:57 a.m., but that the hedge fund deal was not completed until later that morning. The creditors claim that metadata shows that the agreement was not finalized until

10:37 a.m. — two hours and 40 minutes after the bankruptcy filing — making it a post-petition transaction that would require bankruptcy court approval. The failure to obtain the approval would vitiate the agreement, and could reopen the entire bankruptcy proceeding.

GM appeared to be concerned about the claim. While it stated that it considered the lawsuit to be meritless, at the same time it filed documents with U.S. Securities and Exchange Commission that its exposure to the lawsuit could be as much as $918 million. Some believe that number to be woefully understated.

After the case proceeded to trial, and while the parties were awaiting Judge Gerber's decision, a settlement was reached that avoided the tremendous uncertainty associated with a court ruling. Under the terms of the deal, new GM will pay the hedge funds $50 million cash, and the funds will reduce their claims in the bankruptcy court from $2.67 billion to $1.55 billion.

The settlement appears to be a windfall to the bondholders. They bought $1.3 billion in bonds at a steep discount, and received $367 million in June 2009, with an additional $50 million to be paid now. In addition, they will be entitled to make a claim in the bankruptcy court for $1.55 billion, which is reported to be paid out in stock in new GM.

While the deal with the bondholders is indeed rich, it avoids a calamity of epic proportions. Reopening the bankruptcy — a very possible outcome — would have threatened the viability of the reconstituted GM, and initiated a firestorm of litigation throughout the nation. For all concerned, we can rest easy knowing that this is one disaster that was thankfully averted.

CHAPTER 44

Life,
Interrupted

DECEMBER 2013

Few things in life are more tragic than an early, unexpected loss. While we understand that the belief is unsustainable, we nevertheless cling to the idea that death will only visit us at the end of a long and illustrious life. When it arrives early we feel cheated, as if an indiscernible right has been wrongfully taken from us.

This last week, our belief in all that is right was tested when actor Paul Walker was killed in a tragic car accident near Valencia, leaving behind a 15-year-old daughter. The 40-year-old actor is best known for his role in the "Fast and Furious" films — a series of films that ironically focused on the underground culture of illegal street racing.

The details of the event have become fairly well-known: Walker was hosting a fundraiser for his charity, Reach Out Worldwide, when his friend and business partner, Roger Rodas, asked him to go for a ride in his Porsche Carrera GT. Walker, a big car enthusiast, was ever so happy to oblige.

The trip should have been very ordinary. Both Walker and Rodas were racecar drivers, and they co-owned a high-performance automotive business, Always Evolving, that built cars for speed. Walker's daytime job was that of a Hollywood actor, and Rodas was a financial advisor at Merrill Lynch, but their passions intersected in the boyish world of high-performance cars. In an interview conducted this past May, Walker reported that one of his biggest frustrations in life was that he had not broken the 200 mile per hour barrier yet. He had only made it to 197.

While the results from the police investigation will not be available for some time, it appears that Rodas lost control of the Carrera GT on a sweeping 45 mile per hour turn and slid into a light pole, causing the car to all but disintegrate and burst into flames. The accident happened just blocks from the charity event, drawing horrified party-goers to the scene. In one of the most heart-breaking moments, Rodas' 8-year-old son was reported as trying to rescue his father from the burning wreckage.

Officials will only say that "speed was a factor," but this is likely a monumental understatement. The accident occurred on Hercules Street in Santa Clarita, a street that runs through an isolated business park and forms a 1-mile loop. The California Highway Patrol reports that the area is a known hot spot for street racing, and the Los Angeles County Sheriff's Department acknowledged that this was not the area's first speed-related crash. Locals refer to the area as "Hercules curve."

One theory is that that Rodas was "drifting" the car around the corner when he lost control, as the back end of the car slid out. The $450,000 Carrera GT, with its 612 horsepower, is widely known as being difficult to control. According to Autoweek, the Carrera GT is "a difficult car to drive for even professionals."

Whatever the cause, the event is likely to ignite a firestorm of litigation. The loss of any life is undeniably tragic, but the loss of a high wage earner like Walker creates a special set of considerations.

If Rodas was indeed speeding, a claim by Walker's estate will surely follow. Rodas will likely have an automobile policy, and perhaps even an umbrella policy, but the limits of insurance will likely be grossly insufficient to cover the value of Walker's claim. Walker is reported to have earned $39 million from his role in the "Fast and Furious" films, and at the age of 40 his estate will likely attempt to recover a long stream of the celebrity's future earnings.

Then there's the city of Santa Clarita, who could find itself the recipient of a claim for knowing that the area is used for illegal street racing, and failing to take reasonable steps to prevent it. If the city truly understood that the loop was a commonly used for weekend racing (when the surrounding businesses were closed), it could have a serious problem — even with the limitations of governmental immunity.

But perhaps the biggest target is Porsche itself. While high performance cars are meant to be just that, this does not absolve the manufacturer of responsibility for creating cars that are reasonably safe. And there are serious questions about whether the Carrera GT meets this standard.

To the surprise of many, this would not be the first time that Porsche has had to answer for deaths caused by its Carrera GT. In 2005, two individuals were killed in a Carrera GT while racing at the Fontana Speedway in Southern California. The driver was traveling at 145 miles per hour when he swerved to avoid a slower moving car; the back end of the car slid out and the Porsche hit a wall, killing both occupants.

Porsche was sued (along with the other driver and the race track) under the theory that the Carrera GT was too difficult a car to handle even for professional drivers. In particular, the plaintiff claimed that Porsche's failure to equip the car with electronic stability control, or what Porsche calls PSM, was a design defect. After two Porsche engineers provided conflicting testimony as to why the car did not come with stability control (one testified that the chassis could not handle it, the other testified that customers did not want it), Porsche participated in a $4.5 million global settlement.

And that was not the first time that Porsche had been held accountable for building a dangerous high-performance car. In 1983, a jury awarded an estate $2.5 million when a father was killed in a Porsche 911 turbo, under the theory that the car's turbo-lag and oversteer made it too difficult for the average driver to handle.

As racecar drivers, Walker and Rodas tested the limits of physics and engineering; now their estates will likely test the limits of tort liability in an effort to recover for their enormous loss. Whatever the outcome, financial recovery will never be enough to cover the loss suffered by the minor children left behind. They would surely give it all back for just one more day of being able to play ball, or one more school performance the fathers could attend. As for Walker? Well, his terribly ironic quote says it all: "If one day the speed kills me, do not cry because I was smiling."

CHAPTER 45

Success, Redefined

JANUARY 2014

On Dec. 9, 2013, the U.S. Treasury sold its last share of General Motors stock, concluding its four-year investment into the automaker that stirred considerable debate. At the high-water mark, the U.S. owned 61 percent of GM, placing itself squarely in the midst of private competition, and forcing it to compete against those it was charged with protecting.

The total investment in GM reached $49.5 billion — an amount according to RSMeans Data, a leading supplier of U.S. construction costing, sufficient to build 9,000 new elementary schools. But GM was too big to fail, or at least that's how it was billed, causing legitimate concern to rip through the nation about what would happen if nothing was done. Lehman Brothers had just failed — a 158-year-old company that had withstood two world wars and the Great Depression — and panic replaced dispassionate reasoning among America's elite thinkers.

In fairness, time for decision-making was unimaginably short, creating snap decisions of enormous consequence. Merrill Lynch was sold in a weekend; AIG was rescued with an $85 billion loan on a Tuesday night. One can only imagine the pressure the decision-makers were under to not let the economy fail in an instant.

Adding to the panic was a November 2008 report by the Center for Automotive Research (CAR), a Detroit-based consulting firm, stressing the importance of bailing out the

Detroit automakers. The CAR report opined that 3 million jobs would be lost among the automakers and their supply chains if a bailout of the Detroit Three was not immediately implemented.

The CAR report anticipated the worst-case scenario: a complete liquidation of GM, Ford and Chrysler. In truth, however, the loss would have likely been far less severe. Ford passed on the opportunity to take a bailout, and it was fine; and GM and Chrysler would have likely been sold off in parts to competitive buyers through a Chapter 11 reorganization.

A complete shut-down of the Detroit Three and their supply chains was highly unlikely, leaving open the question of what would have happed had the U.S. not intervened. Followers of Adam Smith — the economist long credited with creating the capitalist theory — would argue that GM and Chrysler should have fallen to market forces. The multitude of new companies that would have emerged would have been leaner, stronger and more capable of participating in a competitive landscape.

The harsh truth is that the bailout was only necessary because the companies had been complacent for decades, leading to billions in losses. If there is any doubt on this point, consider that in 1969, GM enjoyed 46 percent of the U.S. market share; in 2009, its share was 19 percent. For the thousands of companies that were not bailed out during the economic cleansing, on an intellectual level it is difficult to understand why they were allowed to fail, when the automakers who were equally deserving of failure were not.

But the threat of widespread unemployment was too great to risk, and the time to decide was too short to contemplate, leading to the decision to not let GM and Chrysler fail. And the decision may have been the right one, but it was not without cost or consequence.

After the Treasury's sale of the last share of GM stock last month, the investment in GM resulted in a net loss to taxpayers of $10.5 billion. The investment in Chrysler was also bad, but not nearly as costly: The U.S. only lost $1.3 billion on that investment.

Critics and supporters alike can participate in the debate about whether saving the automotive industry was the right thing to do. The White House has put its usual spin on the $11.8 billion loss, stating that "GM has now repaid every taxpayer dollar my administration committed to its rescue, plus billions invested by the previous administration," and that "Chrysler has repaid every dime and more of what it owes American taxpayers for their support during my presidency."

Of course, these are only half-truths; the statements fail to account for moneys lent at the end of George W. Bush's administration, and in the case of GM, it fails to account for the investment that was converted to stock and sold at a $10.5 billion loss. But the point remains that the Treasury considers its parlay into the private sector to be an overwhelming success.

Yet like statistics, success can be defined by the person manipulating it. To be sure, the Detroit automakers are doing far better now, but that does not answer the question of whether we are better off following the Treasury's intervention into the private market. And there is an important companion to this question: what of the Treasury's role of venture capital investor in automotive startups.

Consider that in November 2013, Fisker Automotive filed for bankruptcy, handing the Treasury a $139 million loss on its at-risk investment. What's worse, the remains of Fisker are being fought over by two Chinese companies, Hybrid Tech Holdings and Wanxiang Group. One way of looking at this is that the U.S. paid $139 million to enrich the Chinese with electric car technology.

In another example, battery maker A123 filed bankruptcy after receiving $263 million from the Treasury, with its parts also being sold off in bankruptcy court to the Chinese-based Wanxiang. Certainly not the result President Barack Obama envisioned when he made the statement, "I don't want those jobs taking root in places like China, I want those jobs taking root in places like [Colorado]."

While the decision to intervene in the Detroit failure, and to play venture capital investor into automotive startups may have been proper, it is a decision that should be challenged every step of the way. A thin line exists between a government that tries to save for the better of the whole, and one that imposes its will for the better of the people. As Mark Twain once said, "The mania for giving the Government power to meddle with the private affairs of cities or citizens is likely to cause endless trouble."

CHAPTER 46

Rock
Bottom

FEBRUARY 2014

It's absolutely incredible when you think about it. How something so majestic, so profitable, could have fallen so far. At a point in time, it represented all that was right with America — all of the hope and opportunity that served as the foundation for the American Dream. Yet now, it is a shell of that existence, rife with lost ambition and viral despair.

Detroit once stood as the city with the highest per-capita income in the nation, stamping out products that continued to surprise and innovate. In the city that forever forged "made in the U.S.A." into our minds, Detroit represented America's pride, honor and dignity. Now, it is a symbol for all the world to see, of what happens when creativity and competitiveness are replaced with complacency and entitlement.

On July 18, 2013, Detroit filed for Chapter 9 bankruptcy protection, earning the title of being the largest municipal bankruptcy in U.S. history. The city owes $18.5 billion to over 100,000 creditors, many of whom are counting on payment for shear survival.

In fairness to city management, Detroit's troubles were not self-inflicted. A city is only as strong as its industries, and Detroit has long been captive to an automotive industry that refused to reinvent. For decades, the "Detroit 3" rested on the success of terrific products that came generations before, thinking that their stature could never be challenged. When it was, the automakers were far too slow to react, allowing substantial market share — and Detroit's future — to slip into the abyss.

Now, Detroit is hemorrhaging in every way imaginable. The city has some 78,000 abandoned homes, 40 percent of the street lights don't work, and if you need the police to come in a hurry, it could be a problem: The average emergency response time is 58 minutes.

And it is likely to get worse before it gets better. Detroit has had a steady line of the city's brightest leaving for better opportunities — or any opportunity — for quite some time. Consider that in 1960, Detroit was the fourth largest city in the U.S. with 1.8 million people. Today its population is at 700,000, making Detroit the only city in the U.S. to have *ever* passed the 1-million-person mark, and then retreat under it. In fact, between 2000 and 2010 Detroit's population fell by 25 percent; of those remaining, 60 percent are "functionally illiterate," meaning they have difficulty reading, writing and speaking.

Even if the city is able to shed its debt through the bankruptcy process, no one seems to have an answer to the question of how it will avoid an immediate return to insolvency. In 2012, Detroit's annual revenue was $2.3 billion. Its annual expenditures: $2.6 billion. If expenses are not cut — expenses that are already insufficient to run the city — in a mere decade, the city will be in the hole another $3 billion.

And if these problems were not enough, in the midst of its financial turmoil, a rather unexpected, and serious, conversation has arisen. As the court and the creditors began trying to make sense of it all, it became apparent that the city has one very valuable asset that could provide major financial relief: its art.

The Detroit Institute of Arts is one of the largest, and most important, art collections in the U.S., with 100 galleries of classic art from around the world. Harkening back to the city's heyday, when "what was good for GM was good for America," Detroit began amassing a world-class collection of exquisite art that rivals the collections of nearly every U.S. city. In its 700,000 square-foot Italian Renaissance facility — a white marble fortress large enough to house 12 football fields — the museum owns some 65,000 pieces of classic art. And therein lies the controversy.

Creditors, who have long been suffering, are clamoring to have the art sold to help pay for the $18.5 billion in debts. But should it?

Bending to mounting pressure, Detroit's city manager recently had Christie's auction house appraise the museum's art to see how much it might fetch; the result will shock you. In its December 2013 report, Christie's opined that the works could bring as much as $867 million — and here is the part that is shocking — for just 5 percent of the museum's art.

Now, a debate has ripped through the city about what it should do — or should be required to do — with opposing questions that are deep and philosophical. Can a city justifiably cling to its exquisite antiquities, when its citizens are struggling for daily survival? Would forcing the city to sell off its art tear out its soul, and do long term damage from which it might never recover?

To be sure, putting the art on the block will cause many of the works to be lost to the world forever, and this is a result we should all mourn. Billionaire collectors will grab what they can for their private compendia; Steve Wynn owns works by Pablo Picasso, Claude Monet, Andy Warhol and Vincent van Gogh, and record mogul David Geffen owns $1.1 billion worth of art.

197

In truth, the question is as difficult as any ever posed. Selling the art will result in quick cash — cash that is so desperately needed by so many — but the damage will be deep, severe and lasting. The city will forever lose a critical part of its genetic makeup, like the blinding of a man who once stood on the sands to watch the tide roll in.

And then there is the economics. It cannot be forgotten that museums are revenue generators of all sorts. In a 2012 report by Americans for the Arts, the study found that the arts stimulate $135.2 billion of economic activity and create 4.13 million full-time jobs.

But, of course, the real loss is the art's intrinsic societal value; the loss of creativity, imagination, exploration and all that is abstract. As Paul Allen, co-founder of Microsoft stated: "In my own philanthropy and business endeavors, I have seen the critical role that the arts play in stimulating creativity and in developing vital communities.... [T]he arts have a crucial impact on our economy and are an important catalyst for learning, discovery, and achievement in our country." For Detroit, one can only hope that all will not be lost.

CHAPTER 47

The Evil
That Men Do

MARCH 2014

Sometimes people engage in acts so vile, they begin to erode our belief in all that is right and just. Acts of corporate irresponsibility are nothing new; wayward executives have long put profitability and success ahead of moral correctness. But some decisions are just so reckless, it is impossible to understand how they ever met with boardroom approval.

On Feb. 13, General Motors issued a recall of 778,000 Chevrolet Cobalt and Pontiac G5 vehicles for "ignition key failure" — a situation where the vehicle unexpectedly turns off while driving, disabling the car's power steering and power brakes, shutting off the vehicle's airbag system, and cutting off acceleration.

The defect is about as serious as they come. Imagine driving on a windy mountain road, or through a busy city intersection, and having your vehicle suddenly shut off — cutting off the power steering, power breaking and acceleration. Or worse, imagine it happening to your teenage daughter, as was the case in 2006 when 18-year-old Natasha Weigel and her 15-year-old friend, Amy Rademaker, suddenly lost control of their Chevy Cobalt and slammed into a tree, killing them both.

In making the unprecedented recall, GM issued a statement that it was "deeply sorry" for the catastrophic events, and that it was "working to address the issue as quickly as [it] can." GM North America President Alan Batey stated, "Ensuring our customers' safety is our first order of business."

On its surface, GM's public statement suggests that the company is acting with full corporate responsibility: As soon as it learned of the problem, it acted swiftly to correct it. In truth, however, the Detroit automaker had known of the defect for a decade, only issuing the recall when it got caught actively concealing it.

The genesis for the recall was a recent lawsuit brought by the estate of Brooke Melton, a pediatric nurse killed on her 29th birthday when her Chevy Cobalt lost power while driving on the highway. Depositions in the case revealed that GM engineers had experienced the defect in 2004, while testing the Cobalt at the time of the vehicle's launch. In further testing, the engineers were able to replicate the problem, leading to the opening of an internal investigation on the issue. However, as GM stated in a Feb. 24 letter to the National Highway Traffic Safety Administration (NHTSA), "After consideration of the lead time required, cost, and effectiveness of each of these solutions, the [investigation] was closed with no action."

In 2005, after the Cobalt was launched, GM received new field reports of vehicles suddenly losing engine power, leading to yet another internal investigation. A GM engineer redesigned the ignition key to solve the issue, but after an initial approval, the redesign was canceled. Instead, the company elected to issue a "service bulletin" to dealers to install a snap-on key cover for customers who complained of the problem. However, as GM engineer Gary Altman testified in his deposition, the cover was an "improvement, it was not a fix to the issue."

In September 2005, the GM legal department began opening files on fatalities caused by the ignition key failure, and by 2007 GM had tracked ten crashes related to the defect. In October 2006, the service bulletin was updated to include the four other GM vehicles that used the same ignition system: the Chevrolet HH, the Pontiac Solstice, the Saturn Ion, and the Saturn Sky.

In 2009, GM opened yet another investigation into the ignition problem, and concluded that the ignition system needed to be redesigned — the same conclusion it reached years before. However, this time GM did not cancel the redesign, and the change was made for the 2010 model year cars. However, nothing was done to recall the 2005 to 2009 defective vehicles that were in the hands of consumers.

After the lawyers in the Brooke Melton lawsuit discovered that GM had been concealing the ignition key defect since 2004, GM had no choice but to act. In mid-February, the company recalled 778,000 Chevrolet Cobalt and Pontiac G5 vehicles. On Feb. 24, it sent a formal letter to NHTSA, explaining that the defect had caused 22 front-impact crashes and six deaths, and admitting that it had known of the defect since 2004, but had failed to act. GM did not explain, however, why it had not issued a recall for the four other vehicles that used the same defective part.

Under mounting pressure, on Feb. 27 — just three days after GM had supposedly come clean to NHTSA — GM increased its recall to include another 842,0000 vehicles that also use the defective part, and now stated that it knew of 31 crashes and 13 deaths. The veracity of this statement, however, is also suspect, as GM is only counting fatalities from "front-impact" crashes, when it knows that the defect caused deaths in other types of accidents. Case-in-point: The crash involving Brooke Melton — the one who started it all — was a side impact crash, meaning that GM does not include her in its fatality count

GM's conduct in concealing the ignition key defect is going to lead to legal problems that are vast and deep. NHTSA requires that automakers report all known safety defects to the agency within five day of learning of the defect, and has the authority to issue fines of up to $35 million. As former NHTSA head, Joan Claybrook, stated, "This is an immoral act by General Motors to cover up this defect, not tell people and then the result was inevitable, that people were going to die and be injured and that to me is unconscionable."

But its troubles with NHTSA will pale in comparison to the problems it will face with congressional hearings that will undoubtedly follow, and the civil liability that it will face, as juries around the country impose what will likely be hundreds of millions of dollars in punitive damages. Students of history will recall that in the 1970s, Ford similarly concealed a gas tank defect in its Ford Pintos, going so far as to conduct a mathematical analysis that it would be more cost effective to not fix the problem. As Ford reasoned, it would cost $137 million to fix the vehicles ($11 per car), compared to paying an estimated $49.5 million to the families of the 180 people it expected to be killed by the defect. When the jury learned of this, it imposed $125 million in punitive damages — and that was 35 years ago.

Tragedy is certainly nothing new. From the dawn of the Roman Empire to the 16th century Julius Caesar, people have been enduring the evil the men do. Last month, GM stated that "[t]oday's GM is committed to doing business differently and better." In truth, this statement only applies when today's GM has been caught, for just a few months ago it was perfectly content to continue the cover up. For a bludgeoned automaker that was on the rebound, having been caught with this act of dishonesty was the worst possible thing that could have happened. For today's GM, the ides of March have come.

CHAPTER 48

GM'S Day of Reckoning

APRIL 2014

This week, General Motors CEO Mary Barra will appear before an angry panel of examiners in the House and the Senate, where she has been summoned to testify about how and why the Detroit automaker concealed known safety defects in more than 1 million vehicles for over a decade.

The hearings signify a remarkable change of events in the leader's short tenure. Just two months ago, Barra was christened as the first female to ever assume to role of chief executive of a major auto manufacturer. For a male dominated industry, the move appeared to be bold, innovative and in many ways, brilliant.

At the time, all appeared to be going so right for the automaker: The government had sold off the last of its shares in GM stock, public support for the company was beginning to return, and the company was back to writing financial statements in black ink. The "new GM" that emerged from the 2009 bankruptcy promised to be all things different.

Now, Barra is at the helm of a company that is in an unmitigated free-fall: GM has admitted that it knowingly concealed a defect with its vehicles' ignition switch that caused consumers to die.

While the public is brewing over the company's level of deception, what is most upsetting is the lack of intellectual honesty the company has displayed in managing the crisis.

In an attempt to quell the outrage, GM is making statements like "[t]oday's GM is committed to doing business differently and better," inferring that it is voluntarily issuing the recall and rectifying the problem. The truth, however, is that the only reason that GM came clean is because a pair of its engineers testified in June 2013 depositions about the defect. One engineer testified that GM had known of the vehicle defect since the mid-2000s and made a "business decision" to not fix it; the other read more than 80 customer complaints into the record that were filed with GM beginning in 2005 about the safety defect.

The depositions were in a wrongful death lawsuit brought by the estate of pediatric nurse Brooke Melton, who was killed on her 29th birthday in a Chevy Cobalt, and were the beginning of a cascade of information about how the company had been concealing the safety defect for over a decade. GM settled the lawsuit on Sept. 13, 2013, and launched what has been reported as its *eighth* internal study of the ignition switch.

While GM knew in the middle of 2013 that it was exposed, it would wait another eight months, until Feb. 13, 2014, to issue a recall. Federal law requires all manufacturers issue a report to the National Highway Traffic Safety Administration (NHTSA) within five days of learning of the defect, or face a fine of up to $35 million.

When it issued the recall, GM stated that was "working to address the issue as quickly as [it] can." However, at the time of the recall GM knew that it was only recalling half of the vehicles that had the deadly switch. The Feb. 13 recall was only for the Chevrolet Cobalt and Pontiac G5; it inexplicably did not include the Chevrolet HHR, the Pontiac Solstice or the Saturn Ion and Sky, all of which used the same lethal part. Years before, GM had issued a service bulletin to dealers informing them that all of the aforementioned vehicles had a defective ignition switch. It wasn't until the public began questioning why GM was not recalling the other vehicles that used the same part that the second recall was issued, enlarging the U.S. recall to 1.4 million.

At the time of making the February recalls, GM stated in a report to NHTSA that it learned of the defect "in 2004." Now, it turns out, this is untrue. On March 12, GM filed another report with NHTSA admitting that the company actually knew of the in 2001 — three years earlier than it first maintained, and 13 years before it took any action to protect the public.

What's even more incredulous, during the 13-year time period the company told scores of consumers who complained about the issue that it didn't have enough evidence of a defect. According to an in-depth report by the New York Times, when surviving family members contacted the company about the problem, they were either told that they didn't have a case or were met with unreturned phone calls. In one instance, GM told a family of an accident victim that it would come after the family for legal fees if the family's lawsuit wasn't dismissed.

And it's getting worse. Friday, nearly six weeks after the first recall, GM issued a third ignition switch recall, expanding the U.S. recall to 2.2 million vehicles. That same day, GM issued a "stop order" to its dealers to stop selling Chevrolet Cruze vehicles equipped with the 1.4-liter turbo engine. The Cruze is GM's number one selling U.S. car. While stop orders are not terribly uncommon, they are virtually always accompanied by a reason for the directive; this order was remarkable in that it gave no reason, leading to questions about what else the company is hiding.

Now, lawyers in a Texas class action have filed an "emergency motion," asking the judge to order GM to inform owners of the recalled cars that they should immediately park them. The so called "park it now" motion will be heard Friday of this week, and if granted will potentially sideline more than 2 million consumers. The motion should be taken very seriously. GM has admitted that its cars are dangerous, and states on its website that it is "*very* important" that consumers remove all items from their key ring when driving the vehicles. Given that most consumers will not heed the warning, the motion may have merit.

GM admits that its vehicles are responsible for 13 deaths, and that its legal department opened a file on the first one in 2005. Yet, even GM's death count is wrong, as it is only counting "front impact" crashes in the tally. If a recalled vehicle caused a consumer to die because it rolled over, or was in a side impact, GM chooses to not count it. Case in point: Brooke Melton, the pediatric nurse who started it all, is not included in GM's death count because her Cobalt killed her in a side impact crash.

GM's conduct should be seen for what it is: A company that went to great lengths to hide a lethal defect in millions of cars, all in pursuit of financial gain. The company claims that "customer safety is [its] first order of business," and that it is "providing full and complete responses to NHTSA." But the statements are little more than PR wizardry. Until it got caught, GM was perfectly content to allow consumers to die; and now that its deceit has been exposed, GM is only telling NHTSA what it thinks it has to. With a firestorm of litigation across the nation, a criminal investigation underway, and relentless congressional interrogation into the bowels of the company, all that GM knows — and is not telling — will be exposed. This, history will show, will be GM's day of reckoning.

CHAPTER 49

Tesla's Federal Showdown

MAY 2014

For thousands of automotive dealers across the United States, the dealer franchise system is as sacred as they come. Established at the turn of the 20th century as the mechanism for automakers to distribute their products to the masses, U.S. dealers have served as the blueprint for how cars are sold worldwide. Tesla is now threatening to disrupt it all.

For generations, the model has been the same: A manufacturer enters into a franchise agreement with an entrepreneur to sell the manufacturer's cars; the entrepreneur invests time and capital to build a dealership and service the local community; the automaker sells the cars to the dealer, who in turn, sells the cars to the public, and offers financing, registration, warranty and repair work.

This arrangement resulted in early conflict, which has since been evened with state legislation. Knowing that dealers had a tremendous sunk cost in supporting a brand, early manufacturers were in a position to exert control over the dealer under the threat of a whole host of consequences, such as terminating the franchise, refusing to provide product, or underwriting a competing dealer. So, for instance, if the manufacturer wanted to sell slow moving product to a certain dealer, there was little that could be done.

Recognizing the disparity in bargaining power, in the 1930s states began to enact dealer franchise laws that regulated items such as when a dealer could be terminated, how inventory was to be allocated, when a manufacturer could require the dealer to make (and pay for) a facilities upgrade, and whether a manufacturer could own a dealership.

The franchise law framework proved worthwhile. Dealers and manufacturers had occasional flare-ups, but for the most part the laws kept peace the dealer-manufacturer world. Then came along Tesla.

Founded by the 42-year-old billionaire Elon Musk, the same person who revolutionized online merchant services with his company PayPal, Tesla is disrupting everything familiar in the automotive world. Its sales are astounding. Consider that in 2013, Tesla sold 18,000 Model S vehicles to 23,000 Chevrolet Volts — and it did so with a car that starts at $70,000 (the Volt starts at $34,000). Consumer Reports called the Model S the "best car it has ever tested," and so it is perhaps not surprising that Tesla's shares are trading at $207, while Ford is struggling to break $15.

Then there are the dealers. Taking a page out of Apple's "Think Different" campaign, Tesla has decided to forgo the traditional dealer network route, opting instead to open a series of company-owned stores. Like the Apple stores, the Tesla stores are placed in high-end shopping malls, where they offer an entirely different buying experience. Customers schedule a test drive with a Tesla employee and then are directed to the company's website (called the "Design Studio") to outfit the car with features and make the purchase. This has franchised dealers and state regulators stirring.

The Tesla business model is deeply criticized for oversimplifying the car buying process and the dealer-consumer relationship. Unlike disposable consumer goods, vehicle purchases are mired in complexity. Substantial disclosures have to be made, the vehicles have to be properly registered and insured, and vehicle financing is an animal all its own.

Then there is the matter of warranty, service and recalls. Unlike traditional dealers, who have service bays to meet the demands of consumers, the Tesla stores offer no such amenities. Tesla addresses the issue by dispatching service vans to consumers' homes, but this solution is short lived, at best. A service van can never match the abilities of a full-scale service center, and Tesla's ability to service its customers will necessarily wane as the units in operation age and become more plentiful. It is one thing to send service vans out when the company has 20,000 new cars in the hands of consumers, and quite another when there are 250,000 aged units on the road.

Pundits also point out that franchised dealers are much more likely to advocate a covered warranty repair than a manufacturer (the repairs are paid for by the manufacturer, resulting in profit to the dealer), leading to fewer warranty repairs being allowed. They also note that the franchised dealer system necessarily drives price down, as same line-make dealers are required to compete against one another for market share. Because Tesla will own all of its stores, price elasticity would be less at play.

All of this had led to a nation divided, and a flurry of legislation throughout the states. So far, five states have banned Tesla from selling cars (New Jersey, Arizona, Texas, Virginia and Maryland), two states allow sales but with significant restrictions (Colorado and Georgia), and two others have pending legislation (New York and Ohio). If the legislation in New York and Ohio go through, Tesla will be prevented from, or significantly restricted from, selling cars to just about 100 million people — or one-third of the U.S.

This rush of activity has caught the attention of the Federal Trade Commission, leading to an inevitable showdown in the federal arena. Last month, three high-ranking FTC officials came out against what they called the "protectionist" network of laws in the U.S. that govern automotive dealers. As they stated: "The legal protections expanded until in many states they included outright bans on the sale of new cars by anyone other than a dealer-specifically, an auto manufacturer. Instead of 'protecting,' these state laws became 'protectionist,' perpetuating one way of selling cars-the independent car dealer."

The question raised by the Tesla business model is fundamental to how we see ourselves, how we respond to new and innovative ideas, and ultimately, how we choose to govern a capitalistic market. Is it un-American to disallow an entrepreneur, who builds a better mousetrap, to simply sell its product to qualified consenting adults who are desirous of buying it? Or, are the states within their rights to protect the franchised dealer, and ultimately consumers, from what they believe to be an unacceptable erosion of the long-standing vehicle sales model? To be sure, both are entrenched in their views, and with so much at stake, the debate with not end without federal intervention.

CHAPTER 50

Moments of Atrocity

JUNE 2014

Sometimes, good can only rise from depths of pure evil. We are safer today with air travel because of the atrocity of September 11. We were casual with our security screening, and innocent lives were stolen from their families because of it. Nothing can be done to unwind these horrific events, but the families can take a small degree of solace knowing that the event served as a catalyst for substantial change.

As much as our security systems failed us on September 11, our vehicle recall system fails us today. GM's recall scandal of 2014 – while certainly not on the level of an act of terrorism – arises from a similar maligned intent to deceive those it was charged with protecting. Publicly, GM boasted its "safety first" campaign. Yet secretly the company knew its products were gravely defective, and that scores of innocent people would either die or be seriously injured because of it. The company succeeded in achieving both.

To understand just how bad the situation was, appreciate that GM engineers knew in 2001 that the ignition switch for the Saturn Ion was prone to failure, and that this would lead to mass fatalities. Yet because the fix would have set the company back an extra $0.57 per unit – an amount it considered to be an "unacceptable business case" – GM knowingly built the Ion with the defective part. It then built another five vehicles with the same ignition switch (the Chevrolet Cobalt and HHR, the Pontiac G5 and Solstice, and the Saturn Sky), and then engaged in a company-wide cover-up to conceal it all.

The vehicles that GM was making were so defective that in 2008 it held a learning seminar to educate its employees on which words they needed to avoid when referring to GM cars in written reports. The list of the 69 banned words included "catastrophic," "decapitating," "inferno" and "mutilating," as well as such mocking phrases as "Kevorkianesque," "rolling sarcophagus" and "you're toast." GM marked the presentation as "Confidential," thinking it would never leave hallowed grounds of the Detroit Renaissance Center, yet the presentation was subpoenaed by the National Highway Traffic Safety Administration (NHTSA) earlier this year.

Of course, GM told none of this to its consumers who called the company to report vehicle defects. It didn't tell them that it had known of the defects since 2001, and it didn't tell them that it held a seminar on how to avoid creating damning reports. Instead, it disavowed any responsibility for its defective cars, telling family members of the dead and injured that their claims had no merit. The *New York Times* reports that in certain instances, GM even threatened to go after families for attorneys' fees if they pursued their claims.

Initially it was thought that GM had only concealed from the public the fact that it had known of the defect for years. Now, however, it has also come to light that GM failed to inform a family who reported a fatality in 2010 that the car contained an Event Data Recorder – a black box of sorts – that would have captured evidence of the ignition switch position at the point of impact. In a federal lawsuit filed in Central District of California last month, the family of 20-year-old Ben Hair, who was killed in his 2007 Pontiac G5, alleges that GM intentionally withheld this information from them, so that they would be unaware of the vehicle's ignition switch defect.

All of this has resulted in a cataclysmic year for the automaker. In the first five months of 2014, GM issued 29 recalls covering some 13.8 million cars. To put this into perspective, this is more cars than the company sold in the last five years combined, and nearly as many cars as were sold in the U.S. by every car manufacturer in 2013.

GM's blatant disregard of the federal recall laws shows just how badly the recall system has failed us. Federal regulations require automakers like GM to notify NHTSA within five days of learning of a safety defect in its vehicles. This would have required GM to provide notice of the defect to NHTSA during the first year of first George W. Bush's first presidential administration.

The failure of the recall system lies in its inability to penalize companies like GM for their failure to comply. The maximum fine for disobedience is $35 million. Last month GM was fined this maximum amount, but for a company like GM that had $155.4 billion in sales in 2013, this represents about 0.02% of its annual revenue. GM was aware of this and took full advantage of the system, tossing aside all regard for human life. Its management had no integrity in how they dealt with consumers, and NHTSA wasn't there to provide it for them.

A $35 million fine will never command the type of compliance needed. As an interesting comparison on fines, consider that in 2007 the Federation Internationale de l'Autromobile (FIA), the governing body for Formula One racing, caught the McLaren Mercedes race team spying on its competitor Ferrari. The FIA fined McLaren Mercedes $100 million for the act of malfeasance – and this was just for gaining an advantage in a race.

NHTSA's recall system is seriously broken, and Congress needs to take this opportunity to dismantle it. It doesn't need to be fixed, it needs to be smashed with an anvil and then rebuilt with purpose. How a company like GM could conceal a defect for 13 years, knowing that people were dying, is beyond all comprehension, and it is unacceptable.

Many a Congressman have trumpeted their plans to introduce legislation to raise the fines that NHTSA can levy. Yet we don't need theatrical grandstanding; we need a visceral response to this abominable situation that is designed to stomp out this type of fraudulent conduct forever.

If an individual takes the premeditated act of recklessly endangering the lives of others, and people are killed, the individual would be tried for murder. GM's reckless disregard for human life should be treated no differently. The penalties for fraudulent conduct like this need to threaten the very existence of the infringing company, and subject its top management to criminal prosecution.

The tragedy of September 11 resulted in a reconstituted screening process that, while invasive, helps protect us all. The Enron and WoldCom calamities of the early 2000s resulted in the creation of the Sarbanes-Oxley Act, a federal law that provides severe civil and criminal penalties for accounting mischief. Congress needs to take this opportunity to enact the GM Fraudulent Recall Act of 2014, to ensure that an automaker is never again allowed to engage in this type of fraud and deceit. Anything short of this will deprive the families who have lost it all of any sense of justice.

CHAPTER 51

The Company Without a Soul

JULY 2014

Last week, General Motors announced the establishment of its "victim compensation fund" — a pool of money that it will offer to the scores of people it killed and maimed over the past 10 years with its defective products. The underpinnings of the plan rest on GM's company-wide cover up of an ignition switch defect that exists in millions of its vehicles. When the ignition switch is jarred, it cuts off all power to vehicle, disabling the engine, power brakes, power steering and airbags.

The defect had been known by GM engineers as far back as 2001, when the vehicles that contained the switch were designed. GM engineers experienced the shutoff firsthand during testing, but shrugged it off as a "customer convenience" issue — as if having a 4,000-pound car suddenly shut off while driving was a matter of mere convenience. Since GM had no concern about having satisfied customers, it chose to leave the switch in place.

What started out as incompetence changed to pure malice as GM began to receive reports from consumers about the death and injury the ignition switch defect was causing. Federal law requires GM to notify the National Highway Traffic Safety Administration (NHTSA) within five days of learning of the defect. Yet, GM chose to conceal the issue, and actually held company seminars on how to write reports so that the defect not be discovered. GM then shamelessly told injured consumers that it had no responsibility for the damage it had caused.

All of this became public because GM refused to resolve a 2013 lawsuit brought by the family of Brooke Melton, a pediatric nurse who was killed in a Cobalt on her 29th birthday. Although Melton's family would likely have been satisfied with a quick and inexpensive settlement, GM would have none of it. As a result, Melton's lawyers pressed on, and discovered that GM had been concealing the defect for years. Melton's family went public, and now GM is faced with a crisis of epic proportions.

After the concealed ignition switch defect became public in February, GM had to come clean on all of the defects in its vehicle line up. As a result, GM has recalled 28 million cars so far this year — as many cars as it has made in the last seven years — revealing that the company had been concealing defects in its vehicles for years. All told, the refusal to resolve Melton's lawsuit will likely cost the company over $10 billion. The price of arrogance is astonishing.

GM responded to the crisis by first hiring Anton Valukas, a former U.S. attorney for the Northern District of Illinois, to conduct an internal investigation, and then hiring Kenneth Feinberg, best known for his work on the BP oil spill and 9/11 victim's compensation fund, to set up a fund for this case.

Valukas completed his investigation last month, and placed virtually all the blame for the ignition switch cover-up on a low-level engineer, Ray DiGorgio. In what has been called the "the best report money can buy," Valukas scapegoats DiGorgio, and clears GM management of involvement. GM then railroaded DiGorgio out of town, and claimed that it had been cleansed of its evil.

Valukas accomplished what GM paid him to do: He cleared its top management of any wrongdoing. Yet in doing so, Valukas irresponsibly marred DiGorgio as a rogue employee who acted alone in concealing the defect. This was a known fallacy.

In documents subpoenaed by the Department of Justice two weeks ago, it was revealed that Doug Parks, a high-ranking GM officer, knew about the defect in 2005 and participated in discussions on whether the company should fix it. Parks is now one of the top lieutenants in CEO Mary Barra's new regime, belying Barra's public statements that she is leading a changed company.

GM's second plan of attack was to roll out the Feinberg-backed victim compensation fund. GM's media blitz touts the plan as having no monetary cap, implying that the company will give away as much money as necessary to compensate those it spent the last decade injuring. In truth, however, the plan will do little to provide compensation to those who deserve it.

To receive payment, applicants will be required to prove that the ignition switch defect "was the proximate cause of the accident causing death or physical injury." For applicants who will be unrepresented by counsel and who will not benefit from the rights of discovery, this will prove to be an impossible feat.

Because GM concealed the ignition switch defect for so many years, none of the accident victims knew to look for evidence of ignition switch failure, and therein lies the problem. Many of the wrecked vehicles have been long ago crushed, taking along with them evidence that links the crash to ignition switch failure. For many people, all that is known is that they their vehicle shut off and they lost the ability to control it. The problem becomes more serious for drivers that were killed, as the person who witnessed the defect is now dead. While experienced counsel could reconstruct the accident scene, requiring laypersons to do so will prove to be an impossibility.

To make matters worse, because there are millions of vehicles that are affected by the ignition switch recall, and the submission process is quick and easy (all that is required is that a form be mailed to the administrator), it is likely that just about anyone who has ever been involved in an accident in a qualifying vehicle will submit a claim. With the system flooded with tens of thousands of claims, it will be difficult, if not impossible, to determine who should properly receive compensation.

Had GM seriously wanted to compensate ignition switch victims, there were many ways it could have done so. As just one example, it could have set up an expedited arbitration process, where it pays for the claimant's attorney fees if they are successful, and provides the claimants with a rebuttable presumption that the accident was caused by the ignition switch defect if there were no skid marks present (one of the hallmarks of the defect).

Yet, GM has no interest in compensating victims with the Feinberg plan, or in exposing the truth with the Valukas investigation. These are nothing more than media-backed exhibitions, designed to save the company from much-deserved extinction. If GM was sincere about answering for its sins, it would stop trying to have claims barred by the bankruptcy court, and enter a plea of guilty in the court of public opinion. But it would never do so, because such an act would be embossed in honesty and character, traits that have been absent from the company for all too long.

CHAPTER 52

There's No Honor
in the System

AUGUST 2014

Fuel economy is a funny thing. While it is always a consideration for some consumers, its presence on the central stage for others frequently follows world energy politics. In 1973, when the price of crude oil quadrupled in six months during the OPEC oil embargo, fuel economy consideration was at an all-time high. The same was true in 1979, when oil supplies were cut off in the wake of the Iranian Revolution. Those old enough to have lived through it will cringe at the memory of hour-long gas lines, and the introduction of green, yellow and red flags at gas stations around the nation.

The oil crises of 1973 and 1979 shifted consumer thinking, and automakers behavior soon followed. The events paved the way for what were, at the time, obscure foreign brands like Honda, Datsun (the former name of Nissan) and Toyota. Without the panic of the times, those brands likely would not have been able to nose their way into the massive market share that had long been dominated by the likes of General Motors, Ford and Chrysler.

In the 30 years that followed, however, much had been forgotten about the sting on the 1970s, and how quickly comfort — if not life — can turn. Carmakers returned to building just about anything they wanted, and consumers seldom objected to moving fuel economy far down the list.

All of this changed at the onset of the 2008 Great Recession, when the most recent energy crisis erupted. By

July 2008, gas had risen to $4.50 per gallon — a 100 percent increase over the year before. With this came changing consumer attitudes; gas guzzling Hummers were out, and fuel-efficient Priuses were in.

Gas prices have fallen to $3.45 per gallon, but the adjustment has not been enough to alter consumer behavior. Consumer Reports indicates that fuel economy is the most important factor in buying a car, and this is not just a matter of economic savings. Unlike prior years, when economic principles were largely at play, today's discussion is more complex, involving factors such as the impact on the environment.

What is constant, however, is the opening for new entrants into the market. This energy crisis has laid fertile ground for the likes of Tesla, Fisker and others; and while they will not all make it, they were all given an opportunity that was otherwise nonexistent.

Now, other manufacturers are running to catch up, recognizing that the game is all about fuel economy. The word of the day is "40" — as in build a car that generates 40 miles per gallon, and you are in the money. For those just an inch under the bar, the pain is too much to take, leading to all sorts of mischief.

The buying decision all comes down to a sticker. The official title is the "Monroney sticker" (named after Mike Monroney, the Oklahoma senator who sponsored the Automobile Information Disclosure Act of 1958), but most people know it as the window sticker — the all-important sticker that provides the vehicle's fuel economy.

The U.S. Environmental Protection Agency governs the portion of the window sticker that addresses fuel economy, and here is where things get interesting. While the EPA requires that manufacturers disclose fuel economy standards, there is no requirement that the manufacturers be *truthful*.

The EPA imposes no fines on manufacturers who overstate their fuel economy standards; it provides no licensing censure; and until two years ago, it never even checked to see if the numbers were accurate. Now, the EPA conducts an audit of about 15 percent of new vehicles, but even this is based mostly on consumer complaints. By far and large, the EPA relies on the honor system for manufacturers to get it right, with no penalty for failing to do so. This has led to disastrous results.

In 2012, Hyundai and its subsidiary Kia were sued in a series of consumer class actions for under-reporting the fuel economy of its U.S. vehicles. The companies had just launched the "Save the Asterisks" campaign — a campaign that boasted 40 mpg on most Hyundai models, unlike its competitors, who only offered 40 mpg on specialized, low-volume models. As the EPA discovered, however, *none* of Hyundai's models actually achieved 40 mpg.

Hyundai and Kia are not alone. In 2013, Ford was also sued by consumers for overstating the fuel economy standards on its Ford Fiesta, Fusion and C-Max, and its Lincoln MKZ. All three automakers have now admitted that they misrepresented their vehicles' fuel economy standards, but claimed, rather predictably, that it was the result of a "procedural error."

To make matters worse, even if the EPA did actually monitor manufacturers' fuel economy claims, it would likely have little meaning to the average consumer. Many would be surprised to learn that the procedure used by manufacturers to calculate gas mileage doesn't involve driving a single mile on an actual road. Instead, the EPA requires that manufacturers "simulate" driving conditions to measure fuel economy. The

EPA is currently considering regulations that would require manufactures to check their simulated fuel economy results against actual driving results.

The EPA's system is about as flawed as one can imagine. It does not need a system that checks simulated results against real-world results; it needs to toss the simulated test out on its ear and replace it with a system that is both accurate and meaningful. Moreover, the EPA should not rely on consumers to police and catch manufacturer malfeasance; the agency should levy harsh fines on automakers who don't get it right, for whatever reason.

Thousands of consumers make vehicle buying decisions every day, thinking that they are purchasing a vehicle that has certain characteristics, which it may not. To some, the difference of a few miles per gallon may be marginal, but to others the economic impact is significant. Over the lifetime of the car, the difference in fuel consumption can be thousands of dollars, and for many, that is substantial. Manufacturers should not be allowed to cheat, consumers should not be misled — and everyone should consider the issue to be substantial, for we are nothing without our intellectual integrity.

CHAPTER 53

The Shocking Truth

SEPTEMBER 2014

On July 9, 2010, an Alameda County jury returned a verdict of $15 million against Enterprise Rent-A-Car for the tragic death of Raechel and Jacqueline Houck, two sisters in their early 20s who had rented a defective car from the company. The Chrysler PT Cruiser they were driving experienced a power steering fluid leak, which caught fire and caused them to lose control, hitting a semi-truck head on.

The untimely death of the girls was sorrowful, as is the case with any life interrupted, but the true tragedy of the event stems from the fact that Enterprise had received a recall notice from Chrysler about the very defect that caused their death, and knowingly rented the vehicle anyway. As the Enterprise Northern California manager testified, the company's policy was "you've got to keep booking," even if that meant putting consumers in unsafe, recalled cars. As he stated, "It was a given. The whole company did it."

The passing of Raechel and Jacqueline Houck, while undeniably tragic, served to expose an issue that had been lurking in the shadows of commerce for years: Rental car companies are under no obligation to fix a car that has been recalled before renting or selling it, and they are under no obligation to notify consumers that the car they are renting has been recalled.

In the public outrage that followed the Enterprise wrongful death trial, the National Highway Traffic and Safety

Admiration (NHTSA) launched an investigation into how rental car companies were handling recall notices. In 2011, the U.S. Government Accountability Office released a report which detailed the manner in which recalls were addressed.

The report found that rental car companies had generally developed a two-tier system for recalls: Recalls that were determined to be serious safety issues were sidelined from operation, and all other recalled vehicles were kept in service, with the recall being addressed at the convenience of the company, if at all. However, there was no standard calculus used to determine what constituted a safety defect serious enough to take car out of operation — and out of the company's profits.

Cally Houck, the mother of Raechel and Jacqueline Houck, sought to change all this by pushing for legislative change that would standardize the industry; in July 2012, the Raechel and Jacqueline Houck Safe Rental Car Act of 2012 (H.R. 6094) was introduced to Congress. The premise of the bill was simple: Rental car companies would be required to conduct recall repairs before they could rent or sell a car, and if the car was already in the hands of a consumer when the recall notice was received, they would be required to notify the user.

Yet, the rental car industry is big business, and profitable companies like to keep their profits. Hertz alone had $10.8 billion in revenue in 2013, with $663 million in profit. So, the consortium of companies (Hertz, Enterprise, Avis, National, Advantage, Alamo and Budget) defeated the legislation, and put in its place a "pledge" among themselves to not rent vehicles that have been recalled for a "safety" defect.

In truth, the only evolution in the rental car companies' approach is that is now has a label attached to it, worthy of a PR campaign. The companies are still self-prescribing what is needed to take the vehicles out of operation, with no regulatory oversight.

Given what has occurred this year with manufacturer recalls, the issue has never been larger. As of August 2014, manufacturers had recalled 44 million U.S. vehicles — far more than any other *full* year in history, and with numbers continuing to rise. With many of these vehicles being owned by rental car companies, the problem is far from solving itself. Hertz, for instance, owns 490,000 vehicles in the U.S., most of which are General Motors products. If Hertz were to sideline all of its recalled vehicles, it may just go dark.

And there is little reason for optimism. GM continues to issue recalls at an astonishing clip, and it has little ability to fix the vehicles it calls defective. GM has recalled 30 million U.S. vehicles this year (by way of comparison, it sells about 2.7 million vehicles in the U.S. annually), and the company does not have nearly enough parts to service the recalls. The process for addressing the issue is arduous and lengthy. It must ramp up the supply chain, source and manufacturer the parts, ship the parts, train the dealer personnel on how to install them, and then repeat this process for each of the 66 recalls it has issued.

To show just how cumbersome it is, of the 2.6 million vehicles impacted by the February 2014 ignition switch recall, only *7 percent* have been repaired to date. Add another 28 million recalled vehicles to the mix, and continue to issue further recall campaigns, and it is uncertain if all of the cars will ever be fixed.

To complicate matters, as an accommodation to consumers with recalled vehicles, GM has offered to provide consumers with loaner vehicles while they wait for their vehicle to be fixed. This exposes a whole other issue about who pays for the insurance, maintenance and repair on the vehicle while being used for months on end, but the more immediate issue is that the "loaner" vehicles are actually rental cars themselves. GM is pulling its loaner vehicles form Avis, Hertz and Enterprise — calling into question whether the consumers are really any better off.

The financial impact on rental car companies of legislation to fix the problem would undoubtedly be great. Avis is estimating that its loss this year from voluntarily pulling cars to be "an eight figure number." And it is probably right. But the rental car companies were free to negotiate financial claw-backs in their large purchases of inventory from manufacturers in the event of recalls. Consumers, on the other hand, don't have a chance at fairness, when they are put into a defective vehicle with no advance warning, all in the name of profit. This is simply a cost that our society cannot bear.

CHAPTER 54

Twenty Years
Out

OCTOBER 2014

In its quest to be the first manufacturer to develop an autonomous car, General Motors designed the "Highways & Horizons" pavilion — a public display of its self-driving cars that would change the way we think of private transportation. The showing represented "almost every type of terrain in America and illustrating how a motorway system may be laid down over the entire country — across mountains, over rivers and lakes, through cities and past towns — never deviating from a direct course and always adhering to the four basic principles of highway design: safety, comfort, speed and economy."

The year was 1939, and the pavilion — dubbed "General Motors Futurama" — was presented at the New York World Fair. Experts of the day predicted that automated cars would be common place by 1960, forever displacing traditional motoring.

We think of the concept of autonomous cars as a recent convention, brought on by the power of the microchip, cloud-based computing and the Internet, but in truth carmakers have been waxing on about self-driving automobiles for the past 80 years with the same conclusion: They are about 20 years out.

At the 1962 Seattle World Fair, GM introduced the Firebird III concept car that had an "electronic guide system [that] can rush it over an automatic highway while the driver relaxes." Today, the carmaker is working on its Super Cruise

Cadillac, which would allow drivers to take their hands of the wheel, as the car travels in its lane, automatically slowing down or speeding up depending on traffic. Its engineers believe that self-driving cars will become available by the end of the next decade — the same prediction made back in 1962.

Much legislative ink has been consumed on the issue as well, as nations also rush to be the first to develop the driverless car. In 1991, Congress enacted the Intermodal Surface Transportation Efficiency Act, which instructed the U.S. Department of Transportation to "demonstrate an automated vehicle and highway system by 1997." The program was followed by the Transportation Equity Act for the 21st Century in 1998, the Safe, Accountable, Flexible, Efficient Transportation Equity Act in 2005, and the Moving Ahead for Progress in the 21st Century Act in 2012. Yet despite the expenditure of billions in public revenue, none of these acts succeeded in achieving the goal set out by GM in 1939 of creating an automated highway system.

The goal of having autonomous cars is undeniably pure: They would allow the young or infirm to travel with independence, they would eliminate human error and help avoid accidents, and they would greatly reduce traffic congestion. But is this an achievable goal? More to the point, can machine ever duplicate the delicate finesse involved in exercising judgment, or interpret the social cues required in responsible driving?

Interestingly, in 2012, Stanford University undertook an all-out effort to build an autonomous racecar, with the thought being that a self-driven car should be designed to achieve the limits of physics and mathematics, and then scaled back for daily commuting. The university's efforts resulted in an autonomous racecar capable of achieving 150 mph and, driven by algorithmic formulas, capable of theoretically achieving the fastest line on the track a car could take. When they pitted the racecar against professional drivers, however, they were unable to beat the drivers, even though it was mathematically impossible to outperform the university's car.

What's even more interesting are the results from the studies the university conducted on the brain waves of the professional drivers. The studies revealed that the professional drivers emitted very few theta brainwaves (used for heavy cognitive thinking), and displayed almost all alpha brainwaves (emitted when the brain is at rest), even though they were taking the racecar to the outer limits of physics. The conclusion the study reached was that even at the highest level of performance, the human exercise of judgment in driving was a reflex activity, and that perhaps the goal of autonomous driving should be to assist drivers, rather than replacing them.

Nevertheless, innovators and lawmakers are still pressing ahead to develop the self-driving car. Perhaps most famously, Google is in the process of developing its autonomous car, powered by software called Google Chauffeur. Following substantial lobbying efforts by Google, on June 29, 2011 Nevada passed a law permitting the operation of autonomous cars within the state. In May 2012, the Nevada Department of Motor Vehicles issued the first license for an autonomous car to a Toyota Prius modified with Google's experimental driverless technology. Since then, three additional states (California, Florida and Michigan) and the District of Columbia have passed laws allowing driverless cars.

Still, pundits have concerns about the safety of driverless cars. Recall that not so long-ago Toyota was required to pay a $1.2 billion fine for covering up the unintended acceleration in certain models of its vehicles. The official verdict is that the root of the problem was never found, but many industry experts believe that it was a software glitch. Whatever the cause of the Toyota safety issue, the event underscores how glitchy software can be. Consider the trillions of dollars that have been invested in the personal computing industry, and still we deal with computers freezing and software crashing on an all too frequent basis.

At a 2014 symposium on automated vehicles in San Francisco, 500 industry experts were asked about the viability of autonomous cars. Asked when they would trust a fully robotic car to take their children to school, more than half said 2030 at the very earliest. A fifth said not until 2040, and roughly one in 10 said "never."

It is undeniable that automated cars, if they ever actually become a reality, will reduce human error in daily driving. A computer simply won't fall asleep at the wheel, or drive home from a party when it shouldn't. But can a computer ever out perform a human in judgment-related tasks, or successfully interpret the facial cues of a nearby motorist? And when an accident occurs with the self-driving car — and it will occur — is it not more difficult to understand and reconcile the computer-generated mistake, than that of our human counterparts?

We have the ability to land a commercial airliner with an automated system. It is really a function of physics, with little that can go wrong. Yet, at the point when it matters, we make a conscious decision to turn off the autopilot and return the controls to a person who can reason, judge and exercise discretion. We need to employ that same methodology in daily driving. Fortunately for all drivers on the road, the automated car is, and always will be, 20 years out.

CHAPTER 55

A Failed
System

NOVEMBER 2014

The sad truth is that automakers face little deterrent from U.S. authorities to correctly represent their vehicles' fuel economy standards. The Environmental Protection Agency has long required manufacturers to state a vehicle's fuel economy on the window sticker (officially called the Monroney sticker), but there is no regulatory penal system in place for manufacturers who fail report correct numbers. The main source of deterrent has been private class actions.

Last week, the EPA took a large step toward changing all of this when it imposed a historic $350 million fine against Korean automaker Hyundai and its subsidiary Kia for overstating fuel economy standards on 900,000 vehicles sold in the U.S. The fine ended a two-year investigation by the EPA into the automakers' vehicles, and is the largest ever imposed against a manufacturer for overstating fuel economy ratings.

The penalty is being touted by the EPA as a strong movement toward stomping out fuel economy misrepresentation. As Attorney General Eric Holder stated, "This unprecedented resolution with Hyundai and Kia underscores the Justice Department's firm commitment to safeguarding American consumers, ensuring fairness in every marketplace, protecting the environment, and relentlessly pursuing companies that make misrepresentations and violate the law."

However, the event underscores just how broken the system is at protecting the public from unscrupulous manufacturers. The fine was levied under the federal Clean Air Act, a law designed to protect the ozone layer from toxic pollutants. The EPA could not impose a fine for making a material misstatement on the vehicle Monroney sticker — because no such statutory scheme exists. Instead, the EPA had to shoehorn the fine into the Clean Air Act by claiming that Hyundai and Kia understated their vehicles' greenhouse gas emissions by 4.75 million metric tons. This violation enabled the agency to impose a fine.

The $350 million fine was really a combination of $100 million in cash, $50 million to establish an independent fuel economy certification group, and the forfeiture of greenhouse gas emission credits claimed to be worth $200 million dollars. The case is "historic" because at $350 million it is the largest of its kind — and really because it is the only of its kind. Virtually every other EPA enforcement case under the Clean Air Act in the last five years involved the unlawful emission of refrigerants into the environment. The classic case is the retailer who has leaky refrigerators, such as Costco recently fined for having faulty refrigerators in half of its stores.

Using the Clean Air Act to address fuel economy misrepresentations is a novel and positive concept. Still, the fine imposed by the U.S. government falls short of the financial impact the class action lawyers could extract from Hyundai and Kia in their private claims. That amount was $395 million, which raises the question of why are private citizens more capable of policing fuel economy fraud than the federal government.

If there was ever a time when a punitive system was needed, now is it. In today's ecofriendly world, the fight for fuel-efficient supremacy has become fierce, with 40 mpg serving as the benchmark of success. Produce a car that achieves over 40 mpg, and you are in the money; fall short and you lose market relevance.

In 2011, Hyundai and Kia (collectively the fourth largest automaker in the world, after Toyota, General Motors and Volkswagen) launched the "Save the Asterisks" campaign, which touted its vehicles as achieving 40 mpg; unlike their competitors who only offered 40 mpg on specialized, low-volume models.

The marketing campaign worked. As reported by Automotive News, Hyundai's sales in 2011 were up 20 percent, and Kia's sales (its subsidiary) were up 36 percent. However, after receiving numerous complaints from consumers, the EPA launched an investigation that revealed that Hyundai and Kia had overstated their fuel efficiency numbers by as much as six miles per gallon.

Hyundai and Kia initially denied any wrongdoing, issuing a statement that "this case has no merit, as our advertising is accurate and in full compliance with applicable laws and regulations." Later, however, the automakers admitted to misstating the fuel economy on 13 of their nameplates.

The financial impact on American consumers is not insignificant. Consider that the average American drives 13,476 miles per year, and keeps their car for an average of 5.95 years. At a national average of $3 for a gallon of regular gasoline, the misrepresentation of six miles per gallon results in a consumer spending spend $1,061 more on gas over the life of the car than expected.

Nor are Hyundai and Kia alone in making misrepresentations. In 2013, Ford admitted that the fuel economy rating on the 2013 C-Max Hybrid was overstated by four miles per gallon. In June 2014, it admitted that six of its cars had overstated fuel economy standards, including the Lincoln MKZ hybrid which was overstated by seven miles per gallon. Ford has been sued in class actions, but not fined by the U.S. government.

Now Mercedes-Benz has joined the fray. Last month, the German automaker was caught by the EPA in a spot-check audit as having overstated the fuel economy standards on the 2013-14 C300 4-matic models. The "C" class is the manufacturer's most popular model.

The EPA has the gumption to prosecute these types of claims. As Holder stated, "This type of conduct quite simply will not be tolerated. And the Justice Department will never rest or waver in our determination to take action against any company that engages in such activities — whenever and wherever they are uncovered." The problem rests in the agency's inability to penalize those it regulates. Until Congress changes this, and gives the EPA the real ability to impose substantial fines for fuel economy misrepresentation, we will continue to see manufacturers abusing the system, and getting away with it all.

Year of
the Snake

DECEMBER 2014

To be sure, 2014 will be remembered as a year the world changed — the year that honest disclosure gave way to raw deception; the year that automakers challenged our belief in all that is right and just.

The crisis began with General Motors' admission on Feb. 7 that it had been concealing an ignition switch defect in its vehicles for 13 years. GM has now admitted that it killed 33 citizens; but for years, it callously sat back and denied any knowledge of a defect with its vehicles. The truth, of course, is that GM had been receiving notices from the families of the dead that its vehicles contained a fatal defect, but it continued to build the cars anyway.

What makes the matter so much worse is the unabridged cover-up — the willingness to lie about it all without a scintilla of remorse. When GM "came clean" about the 13-year concealment, it stated that it made a decision to issue a recall on Jan. 31, a week before the public announcement. However, this has also been proven to be untrue.

In a series of emails discovered by lawyers in the class action against GM, it is revealed that GM placed an "urgent" order for 500,000 replacement ignition switches on Dec. 18, six weeks before the date testified to by GM chief executive Mary Barra in the congressional hearings.

The emails demonstrate that GM sought to carefully plan its public relation spin, putting reputation ahead of public safety. The delay was not without consequence. One lawyer who has filed a wrongful death claim against the company indicated that that the death of his client occurred between the Dec. 18 purchase order date and the Feb. 7 recall.

It is also of interest that the independent report, commissioned and paid for by GM, found none of these implicating emails. The 315-page report prepared by former U.S. Attorney Anton Valukas — heralded by Barra as "extremely thorough" — cleared GM's top brass of any wrongdoing.

To understand the magnitude of the human destruction caused by GM, consider the case of Candice Anderson, the 25-year-old Texas woman who in 2004 lost control of her Saturn Ion and hit a tree, killing her fiancé. Anderson, who was also seriously injured, was indicted by a grand jury for vehicular manslaughter, and plead guilty to the lesser charge of negligent homicide, receiving a five-year sentence. Last month, Anderson was acquitted of the charge, after the court was shown evidence that the accident was caused by GM's ignition switch defect.

If it were only GM that had engaged in the deception, some level of understanding could be applied. But we soon learned that still waters run deep, as other manufacturers began to confess atrocities of their own.

Earlier this year, 10 manufacturers issued recalls for vehicles that contain airbags manufactured by Japanese parts supplier Takata. The recall, which covers some 7.8 million vehicles, claims that the airbags are prone to shoot shrapnel into the driver's face upon deployment. The company, which is now subject to a Department of Justice criminal probe, has reportedly known about the defect since 2004, but did not initiate a recall. *The New York Times* reports that beginning in 2004 Takata began pulling airbags out of vehicles at junk yards and tested them after work, on weekends and during holidays, to keep it a secret.

So serious is the situation that the National Highway Traffic Safety Administration (NHTSA) has taken the unusual step of issuing a consumer advisory, urging vehicle owners with defective airbags to take immediate action. As the agency stated, "NHTSA urges owners of certain Toyota, Honda, Mazda, BMW, Nissan, Mitsubishi, Subaru, Chrysler, Ford and General Motors vehicles to act immediately on recall notices to replace defective Takata airbags."

And the problem continues to grow. Last week, Honda filed a report with NHTSA indicating that it had failed to report 1,729 death and injury claims to federal regulators between 2003 and 2014. The underreporting is a serious violation of federal law, which requires that manufacturers report safety defects to NHTSA within five days of learning of the claim. Honda, who will likely receive the maximum $35 million fine, blames the failure to report on a computer error and a misreading of the federal law.

Manufacturer malfeasance is also not limited to issues of safety. This year, Ford and Mercedes admitted that they misrepresented fuel economy standards for their vehicles. The admissions follow a finding that Hyundai engaged in the same type of fraudulent conduct, leading to a $395 million federal fine.

This, in itself, demonstrates just how broken the system is. Lie about your vehicles' fuel economy, receive a $395 million fine. Conceal a safety defect for over a decade, killing people along the way, pay $35 million.

Changes are underway, but they cannot come soon enough. Arizona is the first state to sue GM for the concealment of the ignition switch defect, but it will not be the last. The lawsuit subjects the automaker to $3 billion in civil penalties for violating Arizona consumer protection statutes. Other states will surely look to their own statutes for similar financial penalties.

Sen. John Thune, R-S.D., has said that "this year should be a wake-up call," saying that "we can do a better job of addressing safety issues as they arise and holding automakers, their suppliers, and NHTSA accountable." Thune's proclamation is about a pound short of scornful indignation.

We don't need to do a better job of holding manufacturers accountable, we need a completely revamped statutory scheme that governs them. We need fines that significantly impact the multi-billion-dollar corporations they are assessed against, and criminal penalties imposed against the executives who lead them. If the automakers are untethered to a sense of ethics, we need stiff monetary fines and jail time that will help them find it.

CHAPTER 57

An Uber Mess

JANUARY 2015

By now, most consumers have likely heard of, or used, Uber — the ride-sharing app that is doing its best to reform the taxi industry. In what has become known as a "peer-to-peer economy," Uber connects ride-seeking consumers with drivers who provide transportation in their private cars. The convenience is manifest: Riders can hail and track the location of their upcoming car simply by clicking a button on their smartphones, and then pay for the service through a credit card they have on file.

Launched in San Francisco in June 2010, Uber has burgeoned into a world-wide phenomenon now in 53 countries and 252 cities. And with its size has come wealth. Last month, Uber completed a $1.2 billion capital raise at a valuation of $41.2 billion — making the company more valuable than Xerox, Staples and Rite Aid *combined.*

Uber's simplistic business model has been the foundation of its success; however, the same simplicity has regulators — and the taxicab industry — stirring. Unlike the heavily regulated taxi industry, Uber skirts onerous regulatory requirements by insisting it is a technology company, not a transportation service provider.

And there is reason to care. Common carrier regulations protect the public by insuring that ride-share vehicles are properly maintained, that drivers' backgrounds are thoroughly checked, and that proper insurance is in place. Stepping into a private individual's car changes all of that — and there are consequences.

Uber drivers have been accused of dangerous mischief at alarming rates. Last month, an Uber driver in Boston was arrested for raping, kidnapping and assaulting a female passenger; he is being held without bail. The same month, an Uber driver in New Delhi, India, was arrested for raping a female passenger; he had been arrested for rape on two prior occasions before becoming a driver for Uber. In September, an Uber driver in San Francisco was arrested for hitting a passenger in the head with a clawed hammer, fracturing his skull; the passenger lived, but it is unclear whether he will regain vision in his left eye.

The danger created by the lack of regulation has led to several governments around the world banning the ride-share company. So far, Uber has been banned in Nevada, Portland, Germany, France, New Delhi, the Netherlands, Thailand, Brussels, Toronto and Spain. Several other jurisdictions, including California, are similarly considering a ban.

Uber claims it has the "safest rides on the road," stating that its background checks are "often more rigorous than what is required to become a taxi driver." There seems to be little truth to this, however, leading to a December lawsuit filed against the company by the Los Angeles and San Francisco district attorneys for unlawful business practices. The lawsuit seeks redress for Uber's misleading claim that it conducts "industry-leading" background checks.

The gold standard for background checks is Live Scan, an electronic fingerprinting process that searches databases maintained by the Department of Justice and the FBI for prior criminal activity. The Live Scan process also automatically updates when subsequent activity occurs, such as if a driver was arrested for drunk driving or rape. Uber's background checks do not use the Live Scan process, but a less expensive online service that requires no fingerprinting.

To understand the disparity in what it takes to become an Uber driver versus becoming a taxicab driver, consider the following. In San Francisco, a taxicab applicant must attend a seven-hour class, take and pass an exam administered by the San Francisco Municipal Transportation Agency (SFMTA), personally appear for an interview by the SFMTA, submit to a Live Scan examination, and submit a 10-year printout of the applicant's DMV driving record that is current within 30 days.

To become an Uber driver, the applicant must have a 2004 or newer car, an auto insurance policy, a driver's license, submit to the online background check, and then watch a short video on how to use the Uber app. If drivers want more training, they must pay as much as $65 for a four-hour class.

And then there is the matter of liability. Whereas most taxicab drivers are employees of the company, subjecting the company to vicarious liability for the tortious acts of its employees, Uber specifically classifies its drivers as independent contractors. The classification is being challenged by a class action filed in Boston, which claims that Uber drivers are not properly paid overtime, but if it holds, riders and other motorists could be left without recourse in the event of driver misconduct.

Insurance will not likely bridge this gap. Uber requires its drivers to click a box indicating that they "plan" to drive a commercially insurance insured vehicle, but it is unlikely that drivers are doing so. The issue is significant.

242

Personal automobile policies will not cover intentional torts committed by a driver against a passenger. Even for ordinary acts of negligence, such as where a driver gets into an accident, the passenger may still be without coverage. Much like homeowners' policies that have exclusions for business operations out of the home, it should be expected that insurance companies will deny claims made by Uber passengers, citing to the commercial nature of the relationship.

This all leaves Uber consumers in the unenviable dilemma of whether to utilize Uber's enormous convenience, while accepting the risk of rides with dangerous drivers and limited recovery if things go wrong. There does not appear to be another alternative.

Travis Kalanick, Uber's founder and chief executive, ought to be applauded for the genius involved in creating the ride-share company. Its fault lies not in its concept, but in its execution. Common carrier regulations, while onerous, serve an important purpose in protecting citizens from rogue drivers, unmaintained vehicles and uninsured claims. Until Uber recognizes that it cannot sidestep this integral part of the transportation system, its passengers will continue to be the subject of brutal attack, and Uber will continue to rack-up bans throughout.

CHAPTER 58

Swimming in a Sea of Oil

FEBRUARY 2015

Last year the U.S. achieved a goal long considered unapproachable: It surpassed Saudi Arabia and Russia to become the world's largest producer of oil. At 12.5 million barrels per day, the U.S. now extracts more oil than any of the OPEC countries, and more than Iran, Iraq, Kuwait and Qatar combined.

It wasn't always this way. In 2006, the U.S. produced 8.3 million barrels, and before that one must go back to the 1960s to see production anywhere near 2014 levels. But crude oil prices of $140 per barrel in the late 2000s brought in a bevy of pioneering oil explorers, hoping to ride the wave of demand and profitability.

Oil production from shale rock formations, and in particular hydraulic "fracking," enabled exploration into areas once thought impenetrable. The controversial method of fracking is where rock is fractured by hydraulically pressurized liquid made of sand, water and chemicals, allowing oil to flow through the fractured rock horizontally. U.S. Energy Information Administration estimates about 29 percent of U.S. oil production comes from tight oil formations. The process has drawn criticism from those concerned about ground water contamination and stimulation of seismic activity.

The combination of reaching oil in tight places and the settling of global politics has resulted in crude oil trading at

$45 per barrel — some 70 percent off the high-water mark of 2009. The question is, how long will it last? The last time oil was in a free-fall was in the mid-1980s, when the oil market saw a drop of 80 percent. It took 25 years for the market to rebound to pre-disruption levels.

While it is unlikely the recovery (if, in fact, we are at the bottom) will take that long, there is reason to believe that soaring prices may not be on the horizon. At the November 2014 meeting of the OPEC nations (Algeria, Angola, Ecuador, Iran, Iraq, Kuwait, Libya, Nigeria, Qatar, Saudi Arabia, the United Arab Emirates and Venezuela), the consortium decided to not respond to falling prices by reducing supply to meet demand. Saudi Arabia responded to the 1980s oil crash by doing just that, only to find that prices kept falling, causing it to lose valuable market share. It was not about to make the same mistake.

The net result for Americans is good, unless you are in an oil rich state like Texas or North Dakota. While high crude oil attracted scores of profit-seeking explorers to the oil patches, the opposite is true when oil is trading for a fraction of 2009 prices. With profitability gone, miners are seeking to scale back spending on everything that is not critical, which is being felt by the townships that surround them.

But for the rest of us the result is euphoria, with significant market impact. For every $20 decline in the price of a barrel of oil, consumers should expect to see a $0.50 decline in the price of gas at the pump. The national price of gas is hovering at $2 per gallon, and the Energy Information Administration estimates that the average U.S. household will save about $750 per year because of the lower gas prices. As Goldman Sachs chief commodity analyst Jeff Currie stated, the oil crash is the most "startling and far-reaching market development" since the financial crisis.

And there's more. Americans will likely see a dip in the cost of air transportation this year. American Airlines, the world's largest carrier, is estimating a savings of $1.3 billion in 2015 because of depressed fuel costs. And the goods we buy and consume that are trucked in from ports and assembly lines will likely cost less.

There is reason to believe this could go on for a while. The U.S. has 30.5 billion barrels of proven oil reserves (defined as being 90 percent likely to be recoverable under existing economic and political conditions, with existing technology), and the Energy Information Administration estimates we have another 198 billion barrels that are technically recoverable, yet undiscovered. The U.S. has also for the first time surrendered the title of being the world's largest importer of oil, passing the mantle to China, who consumes 11 million barrels a day and only produces 4.4 million barrels.

Americans have assuredly changed their diet over the past decade, weaning itself off their severe oil dependency. In the early 2000s, Hummers and Escalades were the way to be seen; today, Hollywood's elite roll in Teslas and Priuses. But, will this too change?

To a large extent, the rush to alternative fuel vehicles was in response to surging oil prices; now that the sting at the pump has softened, will the industry for electric vehicles cool? The Corporate Average Fuel Economy (CAFE) regulations put in place in by President Barack Obama in 2011, which require automakers to increase fuel economy to 54.5 miles per gallon by 2025, will in many ways prevent a full retreat, but consumers may be less willing to switch to new technology now that they don't have to.

Electric vehicles have been newsworthy, but their sales figures demonstrate slow market acceptance; and $2 gas could stunt further adoption. From 2010 to date, Chevrolet has only sold 72,000 Volts in the U.S. (compared to a prediction of 45,000 units per year), and the much-hyped Tesla has only sold 50,000 vehicles. To put those numbers into perspective, consider that Ford sells about 750,000 F-150 trucks in the U.S. *each year.*

And it is the traditional internal combustion vehicles that are highly profitable — not the new technology vehicles. Each Volt, which sells for $39,000, costs General Motors about $88,000 to produce, resulting in $49,000 loss per vehicle. For an industry still recovering from the great recession, high profit vehicles are a must.

Low oil prices are here to stay — at least for a long fortnight — and markets will bustle with stimulation. Prices will dip and consumers will have more to spend, creating elation for all — other than those at the epicenter of the oil production. And as for the auto industry, no one should be surprised to see manufacturers pushing the profit-rich vehicles they have been building for decades. Until the next surge, the good times are here again.

CHAPTER 59

Getting It
Right

MARCH 2015

Last week, a senate committee passed legislation that promises to revolutionize automotive safety. The bill gives whistleblowers who report automotive safety issues to the federal government 30 percent of all fines paid by the automaker that exceed $1 million.

The Motor Vehicle Safety Whistleblower Act (S.304) was introduced by U.S. Sens. John Thune, R-S.D., and Bill Nelson, D-Fla., late last year in response to the General Motors ignition switch scandal that shocked the nation. In February 2014, GM admitted that it had been concealing a safety defect in its cars for 13 years, knowing that the defect was killing consumers. Under federal law, manufacturers have just five days to report safety defects to the National Highway Traffic Safety Administration (NHTSA) or face a fine of up to $35 million.

In response to public backlash, GM set up a victim compensation fund with Kenneth Feinberg, best known for administering claims in the 9/11 terrorist attacks and the BP gulf oil spill. While GM claimed that only 12 deaths were linked to the ignition switch defect, Feinberg has pinned 57 deaths on the manufacturer, with many more still under consideration. A total of 479 death claims have been submitted.

The GM scandal revealed that the company fostered a culture of cover-up, where low-raking and high-ranking

248

officials alike were complicit in concealing the safety defect. The Motor Vehicle Safety Whistleblower Act is designed to disrupt corporate culture, and incentivize employees to come forward with information that could prevent death or serious injury.

As Thune stated, "By encouraging employees in the auto sector to speak up about auto safety problems, we can help prevent injuries and even deaths for American drivers." "This legislation will be a powerful tool to help ensure that problems regarding known safety defects are promptly reported."

The bill grants whistleblower status to employees and contractors of motor vehicle manufacturers, parts suppliers and dealerships who report the issue. The whistleblowers are also given anonymity when coming forward. If the report results in monetary penalties imposed by the U.S. Department of Transportation or Department of Justice that exceed $1 million, the whistleblower receives 30 percent of the penalty.

There has never been a greater need for automotive safety reform; the last five years have been atrocious for the industry. The current decade began with Toyota failing to recall its cars that had sticky gas pedals, and has become increasingly worse. In 2014 alone, NHTSA imposed more fines on automakers than during its entire 43-year history *combined*.

The issue seems to come down to defiance and complete disregard for consumer safety. In January 2015, for instance, NHTSA imposed two $35 million fines on Honda for failing to report deaths and injuries to federal regulators — a flagrant violation of the laws well known to every vehicle manufacturer.

Now NHTSA is investigating claims that Japanese airbag manufacturer Takata did not recall 15 million airbags, where the inflators have been shown to shoot shrapnel throughout the interior of the vehicle upon deployment. On Feb. 20,

NHTSA issued a fine of $14,000 per day against Takata for failing to cooperate in the agency's investigation. When NHTSA requested documents related to the defect, Takata dumped 2.4 million pages of documents on the agency without any guide to or explanation of the content. The faulty airbags have been linked to six deaths.

With its anonymity and high financial incentives, the Motor Vehicle Safety Whistleblower Act could seriously change the way the manufacturers hold back information. The maximum fine that NHTSA can issue is currently $35 million, but there is talk of this increasing substantially. Transportation Secretary Anthony Foxx has requested that the maximum penalty be increased to $300 million.

Penalties can also get stiffer when the Department of Justice files criminal charges against an automaker. In March 2014, the DOJ settled its criminal case with Toyota, which was born out of the 2010 unintended acceleration cover-up, for an astonishing $1.2 billion. Had the case been reported under the Motor Vehicle Safety Whistleblower Act, the tipster would have anonymously walked away with $360 million. Many pundits expect the DOJ to similarly file criminal charges against GM for the ignition switch cover-up.

History shows that few manufacturers are immune from wrongdoing. Since 1999, when NHTSA began making notice of the fines public, penalties for failure to issue recalls have been assessed against Hyundai, GM (four times), Volvo, Ford (three times), BMW, Honda, Isuzu, Toyota (four times) and Chrysler.

The legislation passed the Senate Commerce, Science and Transportation Committee with bipartisan support, and is now being sent to the full Senate for a vote. If the bill passes the Senate and the House, it will be presented to President Barack Obama to be signed into law.

Sadly, the odds of the bill's passage are placed at 36 percent. If the bill fails to become law, it will be because of competing egos — not because of a lack of genuine merit. The industry's safety problems have motivated many a politician to craft legislation that addresses the issue, while at the same time elevating themselves to legendary status. Politicians are looking to revamp the automotive industry in the way that the Sarbanes-Oxley Act revolutionized public finance — all while giving themselves the same type of fame that came to U.S. Sen. Paul Sarbanes, D-Md., and U.S. Rep. Michael G. Oxley, R-Ohio.

Our elected leaders must deliver on their campaign promises of being the voice of the people, and forget being credited with the one responsible for drafting the legislation. The Motor Vehicle Safety Whistleblower Act must pass. It is simple and straightforward, and it provides the right incentive to expose a cancer that has been eating away at the ethics of an industry.

CHAPTER 60

Paul Walker, Concluded

APRIL 2015

On Nov. 30, 2013, 40-year-old Hollywood sensation Paul Walker died tragically, when the Porsche Carrera GT his friend was driving crashed in horrific fashion on the public-street racecourse they had created. Walker is best remembered for his leading role in "The Fast & Furious" franchise — a series of hit movies that began in 2001 and, ironically, center around the subculture of illegal street racing.

At the time of his death, Walker was in the middle of filming the seventh installment in the franchise, "Furious 7," and questions immediately surfaced about whether the movie could continue in his absence. The issue was sensitive, and one not easily balanced, as family, friends and fans were grieving from the loss, while Universal Pictures, the studio that owns the franchise, was in the throws of full production. And to complicate it, few could understand how the accident happened, and who should be held responsible for causing it.

The loop in the industrial park where Walker crashed his car was called "Hercules cure," named by the Santa Clarita locals who raced the illegal circuit on weekends, when most of the neighboring businesses were closed. Walker owned a high-performance automobile business in the park with his long-time friend Roger Rodas, called Always Evolving. On the day in question, Walker and Rodas were hosting a fundraiser for Walker's charity, Reach Out Worldwide.

Walker and Rodas were both experienced racecar drivers, and were intimately familiar with the loop, so nothing should have gone wrong. Yet life sometimes cheats even the best performers. Rodas had asked Walker to go for a ride in his 2005 Porsche Carrera GT — a $450,000 supercar with 612 horsepower that Porsche describes as being "as close to a racecar as we will ever get." Walker, who had publicly said that one of his biggest frustrations in life was not crossing the 200-mile-per-hour barrier (he had only made it to 197), was happy to oblige.

Shortly after Walker and Rodas left, the fundraiser was interrupted by an explosion that was heard around the world. Rodas had lost control of the Carrera GT on a sweeping turn and crashed into a light pole, causing the car to burst into flames and all but disintegrate. Horrified partygoers rushed to the scene, and tragically, Rodas' 8-year-old son tried to rescue his father from the burning wreckage. Walker is survived by a 15-year-old daughter. No child should ever have to endure such travesty.

The investigation by the Los Angeles County Sheriff's Department concluded that Porsche was traveling up to 94 mph in a 45-mph zone when Rodas lost control. And with this, a firestorm of litigation ensued. Kristine Rodas, widow of Rodas, filed a lawsuit against Porsche North America, claiming that the vehicle's defective suspension caused the accident, and that the race-ready vehicle should have had a crash cage and fuel cell, both of which would have mitigated against death in the crash.

Porsche has been sued before for high-speed death claims relating to its Carrera GT supercar, the most famous of which occurred when a driver lost control of the car at 145 mph on a Southern California racetrack. In that case, Porsche participated in the $4.5 million global settlement.

Separately, Walker's family sued Rodas' estate for its refusal to return the actor's vehicles. According to the lawsuit filed in the Los Angeles County Superior Court, Rodas was in possession of 17 cars that were owned fully or partially by Walker, and that Rodas' family is refusing to give up the vehicles.

The largest question, however, centered on what would become of "The Fast & Furious" franchise, and more specifically, the production of "Furious 7," which was left with half of a film shot and no leading actor. And the question was not of idle significance. As of the time of Walker's death, the franchise had grossed $2.5 billion worldwide, making it Universal's largest franchise of all time — eclipsing the studio's greats like "Jurassic Park," "Jaws" and "E.T."

With production delays averaging about $250,000 per day, the cost of suspending the film promised to become astronomical. Ultimately, after considerable rewrites, Universal used Walker's younger brothers, Cody (26) and Caleb (37), as stand-ins to complete his remaining scenes. After a four-month break and $50 million in production delays, filming resumed in April 2014 and concluded three months later. With its original production budget of $200 million and the $50 million delay, "Furious 7" has become the sixth most expensive movie of all time.

Most movie studios purchase film production insurance, policies that are designed to cover unforeseen production problems, such as the death or injury to an actor, and Universal was no exception. Fireman's Fund placed the policy for "Furious 7," and will likely be required to pay the entire $50 million production delay — making it the most expensive insurance claim in Hollywood history. The prior high was $20 million when John Candy died during the filming of "Wagons East!" in 1994.

The work done to salvage the film paid off in spades. "Furious 7" opened this past weekend, exceeding all expectations. Industry analysts expected a robust opening of $115 million, but no one could have anticipated the record-breaking $143.6 million the movie grossed, making it the highest-grossing debut for a film in the month of April of all time. Combined with the $240.4 million the film grossed overseas, "Furious 7" brought in a total $384 million in just *three days*.

The movie's record-setting debut is life's poetic response to tragedy realized. It would have been stunning to have the film completed with any degree of success; record-setting numbers are just beyond words. Tragedy strikes in the most unexpected ways, whether self-inflicted or random accident, often taking with it those who we could never imagine living without. We have wept the loss of James Dean, Kurt Cobain, John Lennon and many more whose talents and charisma have resonated in our souls.

Now Paul Walker is added to the list. But if we mourn, let it be for ourselves and not for him, as he was living his passion until the very end. As he famously said before his untimely death, "If one day the speed kills me, do not cry because I was smiling." Rest in peace Paul Walker.

CHAPTER 61

The Tragedy of Progress

MAY 2015

When Steve Jobs stood on the stage Jan. 9, 2007, at the Macworld Conference and Expo to introduce the iPhone, he could have hardly known that he was about to change the way the world thinks, works and communicates. Mobile phones had been around for years, but the iPhone challenged society to think in abstract dimensions. In an instant, flip phones were replaced with an endless world of apps; every consumer became an expert photographer; and all the wonders of the Internet were obtainable in an instant.

To be sure, the iPhone has changed all those who subscribe to modern advancement. If you don't own one, you likely have a replica made by one of the many competitors who scrambled to catch up. And this is to say nothing of the myriad of iPads and tablets that have blurred the line between personal computing and personal lifestyle.

Jobs could also never have known the devastation the iPhone would unleash on the world with texting and driving. For those who truly don't care, it takes place at speed — driving on the freeway with preoccupied intentions. For the rest, the start of it is innocent enough. At just about any red light, drivers can be seen texting — or worse, scrolling through Facebook — while waiting for the light. Then the light changes, but the conversation has started, and now another motorist is added to the statistical count of being a distracted driver.

The problem is significant enough to label it a full-blown crisis. Just how serious is it? According to studies conducted by the National Highway Traffic Safety Administration (NHTSA), 17 percent of all traffic accidents involve texting and driving. Put in terms a little more relevant, by the end of the day another 16 Americans will have lost their lives to it.

The physics of it are disturbing. NHTSA reports that that sending or receiving a text takes a driver's eyes from the road for an average of 4.6 seconds, the equivalent — when traveling at 80 mph — of driving 539 feet, or almost two football fields, blindfolded. The federal agency has determined that texting and driving is *six times* more dangerous than drinking and driving.

Society has thrown its full force at stomping out drinking and driving. In California, offenders are penalized with suspended drivers' licenses, fines of up to $3,600, alcohol school, skyrocketing insurance, and up to six months' imprisonment. Yet texting and driving in California will get you a fine of just $20.

And that's the good news. Some states don't see it as a problem at all. Mississippi, Oklahoma, Missouri and Texas only ban texting and driving under limited situations, such as in school crossing zones, and two states — Montana and Arizona — have no law against it whatsoever.

The only state that has appropriately addressed the situation is Alaska, who imposes a fine of $10,000. After that it is a steep falloff, with nearly every state ignoring the seriousness of the issue. Kentucky's fine is $25, Florida's is $30, and Colorado's is $50.

And the problem is getting substantially worse. Smartphone use has proliferated in the most viral fashion. In 2008, there were 238 million smartphones worldwide; today there are 1.9 billion, an *800 percent increase* — meaning that a quarter of the world's population has them. Given the number of people that live in undeveloped or underdeveloped countries, the statistic is astounding.

But what is most surprising — and troubling — is that little is done to curb the problem smartphones bring with them. NHTSA establishes the Federal Motor Vehicle Safety Standards, which regulate every aspect of vehicle safety, from bumper height to side view mirrors. Many of the safety standards address true items of driver safety, like the requirement for seatbelts and airbags. Yet the safety standards are silent on the biggest killer of all, texting.

One might expect that the lack of regulation may be because little can be done to prevent it. But that is not the case. A host of companies have emerged that prevent drivers from texting and driving, such as the Louisiana company CellControl. CellControl has developed, and is currently selling, a solar-powered device that is placed on a vehicle's windshield, and which creates a "driver-zone" where texting, emailing, browsing and apps are disabled, but which leave the remaining passengers in the car free to use the full function of their phones.

And CellControl is not alone. Apple has filed a patent application for a device called "lock-out," which also promises to prevent drivers from using similar functions on their smartphones. The company is looking to incorporate the technology into its soon-to-be-released infotainment system, CarPlay.

While texting drivers are 23 times more likely to get into an accident than non-texting drivers, another NHTSA statistic, it is hard to understand why regulators have not rushed to address the issue. Lawmakers could easily match the penalty to the gravity of the problem, as Alaska has done, or better — enact a Federal Motor Vehicle Safety Standard that requires disabling technology for all new vehicles. NHTSA requires rear view cameras, child lock doors, and a host of other safety features — all in the name of making driving safer — but ignores what has become public enemy number one.

If text-blocking laws are enacted a year from now, it will be a year too late. In that time period, 5,800 more citizens will be dead, and another 330,000 will be injured. Let that number sink in for a moment. In the September 11 terrorist attack — the tragedy of all tragedies — we lost 3,000 American lives. Here we are losing people double that rate every year, and we are responding with a $20 citation.

For the first 50 years of automobile transportation, drinking and driving was similarly treated as an academic problem, not worthy of significant attention. It wasn't until 1969, when Teddy Kennedy drove his car off Dike Bridge, killing his passenger, that public outrage set in. We need to recognize that we are on the cusp of another — larger — societal harm, and address it before it becomes an inferno. As George Santayana famously said, "Those who fail to learn from history are doomed to repeat it."

CHAPTER 62

War
Crimes

JUNE 2015

The Porsche brand is about as iconic as they come. Built on decades of precise German engineering, the brand is the pinnacle of automotive excellence. They have raced in everything from the 24 Hours of Le Mans to Formula One, and have danced in minds of millions who have dreamed of owning one. To drive one, they say, is to steal a page from the innocent days of youth.

The company was founded in 1948 by Ferdinand Porsche, the Czech-born engineering marvel who was one of the greatest contributors to early 20th century automotive development. Few are likely aware that Ferdinand Porsche invented the first gasoline-electric hybrid automobile, the Lohner-Porsche "Semper Vivus" (translated as "Always Alive"), which in 1901 was capable of reaching 35 mph. Few are also likely aware that he designed the Volkswagen Beetle, and was instrumental in founding the Volkswagen automotive juggernaut.

Yet for all of his contributions, there is one distinction that Ferdinand Porsche will never escape: war criminal.

At the 1933 Berlin Motor Show, German leader Adolf Hitler announced his intention to motorize the nation by ensuring that every citizen could own either a car or a tractor. In June 1934, the Nazi-controlled German Reich Automobile Industry Association awarded Ferdinand Porsche a contract to produce a series of prototypes for a high-volume, low-cost automobile called the "KdF-Wagen" (standing for Kraft durch Freude, or "Strength through Joy"). Porsche later convinced Hitler to change the name to Volkswagen, or the "people's car."

Following receipt of the Volkswagen contract, Porsche developed deep ties with the Nazi regime. At Hitler's urging, Porsche denounced his Czechoslovakian citizenship and became a member of the Nazi party, as well as Hitler's much-feared military organization the Schutzstaffel, or the "SS." With funding from the Third Reich, in 1938 Porsche oversaw the development of the first Volkswagen factory in Wolfsburg, Germany, and at the Berlin Motor Show in 1939 he introduced the first production-ready Beetle.

When Germany invaded Poland in September 1939, starting World War II, Porsche's plant was converted to a German military operation, staffed largely with prisoners-of-war. During these years, Ferdinand Porsche served as head of the German Tank Commission, where he oversaw production of the Tiger I, Tiger II, Elefant, and Panzer VIII Maus. For his efforts, Porsche was awarded SS-Ehrenring (the "SS Honor Ring") and the War Merit Cross, the successor to the German Iron Cross.

It is reported that at the war's end in 1944, 90 percent of Volkswagen's workforce was non-German. Today, the Volkswagen Group, which is still based in Wolfsburg, Germany, is the second largest car manufacturer in the world, selling over 10 million cars annually.

On December 15, 1945, French authorities arrested Ferdinand Porsche on charges of being a war criminal. Porsche was imprisoned for 22 months before his son, Ferry Porsche, was able to buy his freedom. In 1948, Ferdinand and his son Ferry formed the Porsche automobile company we know today, called Porsche AG.

What is perhaps most surprising about Ferdinand Porsche's story is that it is not necessarily unique. The French car company Renault, started in 1899 by French industrialist Louis Renault, lived a similar past.

In May 1940, when Germany invaded France, the Renault car company fell to the control of Nazi Germany. Over a period of four years, Renault produced 34,232 vehicles for the German army, and is rumored to have been paid $120 million, the equivalent of $1.6 billion in 2015 dollars

On September 22, 1944, Louis Renault was arrested by the French authorities as a war criminal for collaborating with Nazi Germany. He died just four weeks later, with his family claiming that he was severely beaten. An x-ray taken after his death confirmed that he had a broken neck vertebra.

On January 1, 1945, just three months after he died, France seized and nationalized the Renault car company by order of General Charles de Gaulle. Louis Renault, who was never tried, was posthumously charged with "guilty enrichment obtained by those who worked for the enemy." At the time the company was nationalized, Renault's wife Christiane and her son Jean-Louis owned 95 percent of the company stock, and had received nothing for their shares.

Renault's heirs have twice attempted to challenge France's nationalization of the car company. In 1954, Renault's wife and son were told by a French court that they could not challenge the order by the de Gaulle government. In March 2010, France enacted a law allowing citizens to challenge the challenging the nationalization. In 2011, seven of Renault's heirs attempted to use this law to overturn the nationalization, but the court ruled that it did not have jurisdiction of consider the matter.

The Renault car company, which now owns a 43 percent controlling stake in Nissan, has built a Renault-Nissan alliance that puts it at the fourth largest automaker in the world. Put another way, one out of every 10 cars sold in the world is manufactured by the Renault-Nissan alliance. The Renault estate has never received any form of compensation for what the forward-thinking industrialist created.

We shall soon not forget the devastation created by the Second Great War, or the history of those who participated in it. The war claimed an astonishing 60 million lives — some 3 percent of the world's then-population — and shattered the lives of countless more for the loss of friends, family and countrymen. Time moves on, but let us never forget our past.

CHAPTER 63

Uber's Worst Nightmare

JULY 2015

It's hard to imagine that things could have gotten worse. Earlier this year, ride-share giant Uber Technologies was hit with a bevy of class actions over claims that the company was fraudulently advertising its cars as the "safest rides on the road." Citing to a string of rapes and assaults by Uber drivers, the lawsuits allege that the company's drivers have virtually no training, are not fingerprinted and checked against the Department of Justice criminal database, and are put through a minimal screening process.

Now, Uber has been dealt an even more significant blow — and one that goes to the core of its business model. Last month, the California labor commissioner issued a ruling that an Uber driver should have been classified as an Uber "employee," not an independent contractor.

The case was never intended to be significant. In September 2014, Barbara Berwick filed a claim with the labor commissioner's office, seeking reimbursement of expenses for the two months she had worked as a San Francisco Uber driver. Berwick didn't have an attorney, and no one was expecting much from the claim.

All of that changed, however, when hearing officer Stephanie Barrett issued a 12-page opinion, citing substantive case law and Labor Code statutes, and concluded that under California law Uber drivers should be classified as employees, not independent contractors. The labor commissioner then found that Uber owed Berwick $4,152.20 in expenses, mileage reimbursements, toll charges, and interest for her two months of employment.

A blanket classification of "employee" for its drivers would be the death knell for Uber. Not only would the company be required to pay substantial payroll taxes, which it would not have to pay for independent contractors, but the expense reimbursement could be unfathomable. Consider that Berwick was awarded slightly over $4,000 in unpaid expenses for just two months of work. Now consider that Uber has 22,000 in San Francisco alone, and another 140,000 throughout the rest of the U.S.

As a relevant comparison, and a hint at what could be in store for Uber, last month Fed Ex paid $228 million to settle a lawsuit regarding the misclassification of 2,300 Fed Ex Ground drivers. With 160,000 U.S. drivers at issue, the financial impact could be catastrophic — even for a company with billions in cash.

But the direct financial impact is just the beginning. Classification as employees would also give drivers substantive legal rights that they so far have not been able to enjoy, such as workman's compensation insurance, unemployment insurance, overtime benefits, and health care benefits. It would also expose the company to an array of claims for wrongful termination, unlawful discrimination, failure to make reasonable accommodations, and unsafe work environment.

And there's still more. Classification as employees also makes the company legally responsible for the actions of its drivers that are performed within the scope of their employment. Up until now, Uber had taken a hardline position that its drivers are independent contractors, shielding the company from their drivers' malfeasance. This position, however, would be eviscerated with an employee classification, opening the company up to an onslaught of lawsuits for acts undertaken by its drivers. This would not only apply to heinous acts lie rape and assault, but also to virtually every car accident its drivers negligently caused.

For consumers, an employee classification would likely be seen as a tremendous victory, as it would likely force the company to take more care in hiring and training its drivers, and it would give consumers a party who could shoulder financial responsibility for the acts of the drivers.

Uber is appealing the decision to the San Francisco County Superior Court, but that may just make things worse. Currently, the labor commissioner's decision is limited to Barbara Berwick and her entitlement to $4,000. At the labor commissioner level, the opinion does not have precedential effect. But, if the decision is affirmed through the California court system, it would become binding on the company and all of its driver-employees, at least in California. The question would then become whether other states would look to the California ruling, and reach similar findings.

There is reason to believe they might. In May, the Florida Department of Economic Opportunity (an agency similar to the California labor commissioner) ruled that Uber driver Darrin McGillis was also misclassified as an independent contractor. As with the labor commissioner's ruling, the Florida decision only relates to McGillis. But Uber is also appealing that decision, which if unsuccessful would also make the ruling applicable to all Florida Uber drivers.

All of this comes at a time when Uber is under attack in other parts of the world. Last month, thousands of French taxi cab drivers took to the streets in protest against UberPOP, the European equivalent of UberX. The French cab drivers are required to pay government taxes for the services they offer;

because UberPop drivers are not licensed, they do not pay the taxes.

France has banned the UberPOP ride-sharing app, but Uber has generally ignored the ban. In June, cab drivers organized a protest, blocking roads to Charles-De-Gaulle and Orly airports, and causing a near standstill for air travelers. The protests turned violent, as cab drivers began attacking Uber drivers and burning their cars.

In the days after the riots, French police sweep Uber France's headquarters, arresting two Uber managers. The managers have been indicted on charges of engaging in deceptive commercial practices and instigating an illegal taxi-driving service. Other countries that have banned Uber include Germany, Thailand, Netherlands, Belgium, India and Taiwan.

There is much to be determined in the new sharing economy, and those who are forging the market will be fighting battles for time to come. For Uber this labor issue is moment-defining. If Uber comes down on the wrong side of it, the billions it has amassed may quickly evaporate, replaced with an army of unwanted employees who will truly be wagging the dog.

CHAPTER 64

Chrysler's Fine
Not Nearly Enough

AUGUST 2015

On July 2, after years of abuse and defiance, Chrysler finally answered for its actions at a public hearing before the National Highway Traffic Safety Administration in Washington D.C. At issue was whether Chrysler had met its obligation of protecting consumer safety in recalling millions of defective vehicles.

The result of the hearing was the imposition of a $105 million fine — the largest ever in the history of the automotive industry — as well as the requirement that Chrysler buy back 600,000 vehicles from consumers and give another 1.5 million consumers compensation in the form of gift cards and trade-in allowances.

But the fine only tells part of the story; it glosses over the cascade of recall abuses the manufacturer engaged in for years leading up to it.

Congress engineered the U.S. recall system, codified in the National Traffic and Motor Vehicle Safety Act, to be remarkably simple. Once a manufacturer learns of a safety defect, it is required to initiate a recall and notify NHTSA within five days. It is then required to notify consumers of the recall within 60 days, and repair the vehicle within 60 days of a costumer's request for a fix. If the manufacturer fails to make the repair within this proscribed period, it is required to buy back the vehicle at the original purchase price, less depreciation.

Then there are obligations to supply NHTSA with copies of the notices sent to consumers and dealers about the recall, and to work with NHTSA throughout the recall process in a manner designed to promote consumer safety.

At the hearing last month, NHTSA investigated 23 recent Chrysler recalls, covering some 11 million vehicles, and found that Chrysler violated the Safety Act in "every one of the 23 recalls." The agency found that Chrysler repeatedly failed to notify owners about recalls in a timely manner, provided the agency with false and misleading information, failed to timely repair defective vehicles, and obstructed the agency's statutory oversight.

The recalls at issue are as serious as they come. They include ignition switch failure (1.6 million vehicles), rear axle lock-up (550,000 vehicles), loss of power brakes (650,000 vehicles), fuel tank rupturing (1.6 million vehicles), loss of steering control (1 million vehicles), vehicle stalling (300,000 vehicles), and airbag deployment problems (3.9 million vehicles).

To show just how egregious this situation has become, Chrysler's fuel tank recall is particularly enlightening. Students of history will recall the exploding Ford Pinto case from the early 1970s, where Ford had determined that it was more cost effective to payout the anticipated 180 wrongful death claims than repair the defective vehicle. The defect with the Pinto was that the gas tank was located behind the rear axle, which could become impaled and explode in a rear collision.

Following the Pinto scandal, virtually every manufacturer moved the fuel tank to a safety zone ahead of the rear axle, with one notable exception — Chrysler, which manufactured the 1993 to 1998 Jeep Grand Cherokee and the 2002 to 2007 Jeep Liberty vehicles with the fuel tank behind the rear axle.

In 2009, NHTSA began investigating the Chrysler fuel tank issue. Noting that the fuel tank had been responsible for 51 deaths, NHTSA took the unusual step of requesting that Chrysler recall the subject vehicles. Chrysler initially refused, but ultimately issued a recall in June 2013.

Here is where things get interesting.

Under the Safety Act, Chrysler was required to notify consumers of the recall by August 2013 (within 60 days of initiating the recall) and fix the vehicles with 60 days of being requested by consumers. NHTSA discovered, however, that Chrysler did not even place a purchase order with its supplier for the replacement part until January 2014 — seven months after the start of the recall. The result? Consumers were told that their vehicles were at risk of catching fire in a rear end collision, but that no parts were available for them to be fixed. Even today, *two years* after the recall, Chrysler has fixed only 6 percent of the Jeep Grand Cherokee and 30 percent of the Jeep Liberty vehicles.

If it is any sign that the public has had enough, earlier this year a Georgia jury issued a $150 million verdict against Chrysler for the death of a 4-year-old boy who was riding in a Jeep Grand Cherokee that was hit from behind, causing it to burst into flames.

Consumers who own Grand Cherokee and Liberty vehicles are far from alone in having to wait months and years for automakers to fix their defective cars. Scores of Chrysler owners are frequently being told by dealers that they have no idea when, or if, the parts will arrive, and that the recalled vehicles cannot be fixed without the parts. As a result, consumers are put in the position of having a Hobson's choice: either sideline the car that may be their only means of transportation, or continue to drive it and subject themselves to possible death or serious injury.

What makes Chrysler's conduct so egregious is that it has all the resources to address the defects; it just chooses not to do so. If this were 2009, when manufacturers were fighting for daily survival, some level of understanding for the malfeasance might be possible. But this is a company that reported $1.4 billion in pretax profit for the second quarter of 2015 alone, and is predicting a pretax profit for the year of $4.9 billion.

And what's worse is that the $105 million fine — a mere *2 percent* of Chrysler's 2015 profit — will do little to correct the conduct of Chrysler or other automakers. The truth is, our regulatory system is far from where it needs to be to control these international conglomerates. So long as NHTSA is doling out justice one teaspoon at a time, our cars will only be as safe as manufacturers want them to be.

CHAPTER 65

Gold Rush

SEPTEMBER 2015

When the pope's Ferrari sells for over $6 million, you know the weekend is going to be special — though no one could have predicted just how much.

Last month marked the 65th annual Concours d' Elegance — a gathering of the world's most important collector cars on the famed Pebble Beach golf links. The weekend is dotted with champagne parties at spectacular seaside mansions, put on by Rolls Royce, Aston Martin and the likes for their special clientele; but the stars of the weekend are the elite collector car auctions that attract collectors — and investors — from around the world.

The auctions are a sight to see, attracting a sub-culture of pedigreed car collectors who most were unaware even existed. Registered bidders come from some 30 different countries, with the intent of buying, selling or closely watching some of the rarest cars in the world. And the prices are staggering.

By now, six years removed from the chill of the frozen economy, things are beginning to return to normal. Analysts predict new car sales to hit 17 million this year, a level not seen since 2000, and U.S. housing starts are at a robust 1.2 million per month and steadily climbing. Yet sales of classic cars have just gone off the charts, setting — and then breaking — records at an astonishing clip.

The Pebble Beach weekend saw over $400 million of collector cars sold in just three days, marking one of the most explosive microcosms the world has ever seen. The weekend is dominated by two auction houses, RM Sotheby's and Gooding & Company, both of which had record-breaking sales results, selling some 62 cars over the $1 million mark, and seven over $10 million.

These are not anomalies. Hagerty's Blue Chip Index, a study of collector cars prices over a 10-year period, shows just how valuable these cars have become. On average, collector cars have demonstrated a 500 percent increase in value over the last 10 years, with certain makes far outstripping even this pace. Ferraris, without a doubt, are the crown jewel.

Several Ferraris make up the highest end of the market, such as the 1958 Ferrari 250 GT California, a cult classic among followers. Non-enthusiasts will best remember the Ferrari 250 GT as the Ferris Bueller car that suffered a fateful ending, after a spirited ride by the local valet. In April 2005, the average price of a Ferrari 250 GT was $1.5 million. By April 2015, 10 years later, the average price had climbed to $14 million, an 850 percent increase — and this is *through* the recession.

What is more amazing is that the prices have continued since then. Last month, four months following the latest report by the Hagerty's Blue Chip Index, a Ferrari 250 GT sold at Gooding & Company for $16.8 million ($2.8 million over the April 2015 Index value); and that was a car, as insiders say, that was "well-bought." No one should be surprised to see this car return to Pebble Beach in a few years, crossing the block for over $20 million.

As dizzying as those prices are, they are far from the top of the market. Last year at Pebble Beach, a 1962 Ferrari 250 GTO sold for $38 million, setting the highest price ever paid for a car at an auction. Now consider that the auction houses fetch 10 percent of the transaction price from the buyer *and* the seller — $7 million in this instance — and you start to get an understanding of the economics at play.

While the $38 million record price is substantial, most 250 GTO owners are unwilling to sell for less than $50 million. But the market will likely get there, quickly.

What is interesting to consider is strength of the market through a beaten economic time. To be sure, the market got hammered during the recession, but the speed at which it has rebounded is nothing short of dramatic. It will now be interesting to see what happens with the market, as the collectors become flusher with cash. While $20 million cars are out of the reach of most, it is the entry level collecting at the $300,000 mark that will make a difference. As more dollars vie for attainable cars, it will elevate their prices, pushing up the prices of the truly collectibles above it.

And it is not just collectors who are in the game. The steady increase in the market has driven many to consider collector cars as solid alternative investments, and for good reason. A car well-bought will yield more passive income to the buyer than most workers in the advanced-world will make in years of full-time employment.

Of course, it takes money to get in the game, and an uneducated buy can kill you, which is why professionally managed investment funds — a mutual fund of sorts for the collector car market — are becoming attractive investments. With the Dow Jones 10-year return at 62 percent, and the collector car market 10-year return at 500 percent, it is understandable that astute money managers have put together professionally led funds aimed at acquiring automotive investments.

In fact, the S&P has developed the Dow Jones Investment-Car Index, pitting its returns against the 30 companies that make up the Dow — and the Industrial Average is not winning, not by a long shot.

At some point, the market will fall; markets always do. Investors will scamper, and pundits will snicker, as prices fall to unthinkable levels; but when the market corrects, collectors will be left with ultra-rare assets that have important historical attributes that touch people in a way that most other investments don't.

Car collectors are driven by a passion to hold that piece of history that was important to them as a child, or to control a car that symbolizes a significant moment in time. As long as passion is involved, there will be people abound who are willing to make illogical decisions to satisfy their inner need, and this is why the collector car market will always be fertile ground for solid investment.

CHAPTER 66

When Will
They Stop?

OCTOBER 2015

In 2009, Volkswagen Group sat as the third-largest automaker in the world, trailing behind long-time leaders Toyota and General Motors in the heated race for automotive supremacy. The company had come a long way from its ominous beginning in 1937, when it created the "people's car" under the governmental control of the Third Reich.

The fact that Volkswagen was even that large is a statement about the automotive industry itself. There once existed a time when the manufacturers themselves conceived and nurtured all of the automakers. General Motors, for instance, created Buick, Cadillac, Pontiac, GMC and Chevrolet in the early 1900s; and Ford likewise cultivated the Ford, Lincoln and Mercury brands over the ages.

But the 1990s saw a revolution of sorts, with automakers consolidating scores of smaller brands under larger controlling groups. Volkswagen officially became "Volkswagen Group," and since then has gone on to acquire Audi, Bentley, Bugatti, Lamborghini, Porsche and Ducati, as well as other non-US brands.

By 2009, Volkswagen was selling 6.3 million vehicles worldwide annually, and was on track to catch and eventually eclipse Toyota and GM. It was that year that Volkswagen made the decision to outfit its 2.0-liter TDI diesel cars with a complex software code that would enable vehicles to detect when they were being subjected to emissions testing.

Taking inputs from steering position and pedal movements, this "defeat device" detected when the car underwent emissions tests and manipulated the amount of nitrous oxide the vehicle emitted. In test mode, the vehicles were shown to be compliant; in real world driving conditions, however, the cars emitted as much as 40 times more pollutants.

The TDI diesel was Volkswagen's answer to the hybrid craze. Without significant inroads into the hybrid lineup, Volkswagen branded its diesel as cars "clean diesel" vehicles that were an attractive alternative to hybrid technology. From 2009 to 2015, Volkswagen sold some 500,000 Audi and Volkswagen branded vehicles in the U.S. that were pre-loaded with the emissions detecting software. This same software was embedded in another 10.5 million cars worldwide.

Volkswagen was successful in gaining substantial market share. By 2015, the company had succeeded in becoming the largest automaker in the world, boasting 600,000 employees, $270 billion in annual revenue, and sales of over 10 million new cars per year. The company that had given us common transportation and eternal free love was now the most powerful force in the automotive industry.

Volkswagen's decision to outfit its cars with test-defeating software has caused immeasurable harm to consumers and dealers alike. The automaker has issued a "stop order" to all U.S. dealers, precluding the sale of all new 2.0 TDI diesel vehicles, leaving dealers with the heavy burden of having to pay for the inventory finance charge on cars they cannot sell.

Consumers who now have cars that are not emissions compliant have it worse. Not only are the cars publicly seen as damaged goods, eliminating any legitimate resale value, but in the United Kingdom motorists are taxed on the amount of emissions their cars generate. So serious is the situation that the German Federal Motor Vehicle Office told Volkswagen that if it does not present the government with a "binding" plan of how the cars will be fixed by Wednesday, the government will bar the cars from operating on German highways.

Stateside, the scandal will cost the manufacturer greatly. Under the Clean Air Act, the U.S. government has the ability to fine Volkswagen $37,500 for each of the 500,000 noncompliant vehicles, or $18 billion. This is in addition to the actual costs of the repairs and a bevy of class actions alleging fraud. (Disclosure: My firm filed one such action.)

What is most disappointing about the situation is that Volkswagen officials felt comfortable enough to cheat in the first place. While our system does not necessarily encourage cheating, it does little to prevent it. In July, the Department of Transportation fined Chrysler $105 million for failing to inform the National Highway Traffic Safety Administration of safety defects and providing the agency with false information. In September, the DOT fined GM $900 million for concealing a deadly defect with its ignition switch for 13 years.

The fines against Chrysler and GM demonstrate everything that is wrong with the system. In both situations, vehicle defects led to tragic consumer deaths. And in both situations, the companies were allowed to rectify the situation by writing a check out of their massive profits, living free to cheat another day. No executives were jailed, and other than a few obligatory scapegoats, no careers were disrupted.

The situation with Volkswagen should be more of an expectation than a surprise. The expected fallout from the debacle will be a few billion dollars in fines and class action settlements, along with a few billion dollars to repair the vehicles. While these numbers are sizeable, they become less so when it is considered that the company recorded a profit of $12.3 billion over last year. Now consider that from 2009, when the scandal began, through the first half of 2015, Volkswagen generated $97.1 billion in profit. Even fines and recall costs of $10 billion are a mere 10 percent of the period's profit.

Until personal culpability becomes a part of the equation, we will never have a system free of deceit. The temptation to win at all costs is just too great, and the system gives the decision-makers all but complete immunity from severe forms of punishment — even though the harm they bring to others is life altering.

The Enron WorldCom financial scandals of the early 2000s resulted in the creation of the Sarbanes-Oxley Act of 2002. Under the act, senior executives take individual responsibility for the accuracy and completeness of corporate financial reports: Misstate a publicly reported financial statement, cause people to lose money, and you go to jail. Under the current automotive format, however, misstate the nature of your vehicle systems, cause people great harm including death, and face no personal responsibility.

To put a stop to the never-ending cycle of manufacturer abuse, we need to hold senior executives accountable for their stewardship over the massive companies they control. If prison terms, not percentages of profits, were a consequence of concealment and deceit, we would foster a culture where we would be surprised by the company that strayed into darkness. Right now, it is only a matter of time until we get the next public apology for having put the allure of profit above human life.

CHAPTER 67

Generation Forward

NOVEMBER 2015

There once existed a time when automobiles were the embodiment of society's love of freedom. Cars represented more than ordinary utility. For many, they were the fundamental expression of personal choice, where personality reveled in the freedom to pick up and go. Few can forget James Dean's love of Porsches or Elvis Presley's collection of Cadillacs, making the cars nearly as famous as the celebrities who drove them.

We used to be a society where little boys daydreamed about what kind of car they wanted to own, igniting neighborhood arguments about which car was the coolest. At the time, budding teenagers waited with angst for the day they could get their driver's license, transgressing through their first true rite of passage.

But those days have given way to a new generation of drivers who are increasingly indifferent about what the automobile has to offer. With instant access to so much data, gaming and communication, teenagers have found freedom in their smartphones, leaving little room for excitement about daily transportation.

The automobile's place in society has dramatically changed. To be sure, the automobile is still a necessity and has many passionate enthusiasts, but the attitude toward cars has experienced a fundamental shift. Schoolyard debates over whose car is fastest have given way to exchanges over whose phone is coolest. And gone are the days when the family car was ritualistically handed down to the first born — no one keeps a car for that long anymore. Now, cars are becoming short-term holds, thanks in large part to the modern-day automobile lease, with cars increasingly being kept for only two or three years. With 28 percent of all new cars being leased, frictionless car ownership has never been higher.

Confounding the issue is the proliferation of a new breed of cars that converse in a language many have never considered. Electric, hybrid and hydrogen technology have gained on market share once controlled exclusively by the internal combustion engine.

All of this raises the question of what is the future of the automobile? Many pundits opine that autonomous vehicles are the wave of the future. But considering the state of the technology, the regulatory framework that would need to be erected, and the dotted network of self-driving and consumer-driven vehicles, it may be optimistic to believe that autonomous vehicles are right around the corner. It is also worthwhile to note that manufacturers have been talking about self-driving cars since General Motors first introduced the concept at the 1939 World's Fair, with the conclusion always being the same: They're about 20 years out.

The car of our future is much more likely to be the "connected car" — a natural and fluid extension of the personal data devices to which we've become accustomed. Apple chief executive Tim Cook recently noted that the automotive industry is in for a "massive change," and he could not have been more right. The industry is at an infliction point, where discussions of horsepower are being replaced with discussions of connectivity.

Apple is currently launching CarPlay, a system that connects iPhones to car interfaces, but expect this to be the beginning of the conversation. As consumers experience seamless transition between their computers, their phones and their televisions with more and more frequency, we should expect manufacturers to cater to this demand in a way that Adam Smith never could have imagined when he advanced the theory of the invisible hand.

In truth, improvements in technology have diminished the relative benefits of car ownership. We have seen this with the firestorm Uber has created, as consumers clamor for rideshare benefits, maximizing the use of vehicles in operation, while at the same time reducing the need for individual car ownership. We are advancing toward a world where car ownership is a choice — not a requirement.

Manufacturers can only combat this by introducing cars that are as advanced in terms of their connectivity as their drivability. Syncing your phone with your car will become passé, as cars begin to offer a host of new features such as real-time vehicle tracking, active window displays, remote vehicle shutdown and active health monitoring.

Consider a car that gives you the ability to track your teenager's whereabouts at all times, or a car that can be shut down in the event of a theft or a high-speed police pursuit. Or consider a vehicle that can monitor your health and call the paramedics in the event of a heart attack or seizure, while at the same time slowing you to a stop. Imagine the benefits for fatigued driving alone. The National Sleep Foundation reports that 4 percent of all drivers have had an accident because of fatigue, resulting in 1,550 annual deaths and $12.5 billion in monetary losses.

In a joint study conducted by the University of Michigan and the U.S. Department of Transportation, vehicle-to-vehicle communications systems are being tested. These "V2V" systems emit a short-range safety signal 10 times per second, and detect signals from other vehicles to determine when a potential accident is imminent. Federal transportation officials estimate that V2V technology could prevent 76 percent of the crashes on U.S. roads, saving some 25,000 lives per year.

As manufacturers begin to roll out this new breed of automobiles, enthusiasm will return to the marketplace for this new embodiment of freedom. Luxury, fuel economy, safety and performance by themselves are no longer enough. Consumers have come to expect that of the modern-day automobile —— a statement in itself about how well manufacturers have addressed consumer demand. But the game has now changed, with the market shifting toward keeping the consumer connected with all that is familiar.

Privacy rights over user data will undoubtedly be a concern, as automakers and telecommunication providers will have access to an unprecedented amount of valuable information. In this regard, federal legislation is certain to become hotly debated, with consumers ultimately winning out — as the connected car will change the way we approach daily life in the years to come.

CHAPTER 68

The Harder
They Fall

DECEMBER 2015

By now, the world understands exactly how dastardly Volkswagen has been: It engineered a device whose sole purpose was to defeat emissions testing, and then outfitted 11 million diesel vehicles with the devise, claiming that they had created the world's first "clean diesel."

In its quest to become the largest automotive manufacturer in the world, and without a competitive hybrid product in its lineup, Volkswagen unleashed its diesel vehicles on an unsuspecting public, accepting award after award for its revolutionary product. It is inconceivable that a company as large as Volkswagen would even try such a move — particularly given how regulated the industry is, and the likelihood of getting caught — but as a wise man once commented, the love of money is the root of all kinds of evil.

Now caught in a freefall of its own making, the question becomes how extensive will the carnage be, and whether regulators will finally administer a punishment that fits the crime?

The propensity to lie, cheat and steal is unfortunately nothing new to the automotive industry. General Motors proved this last year when it was revealed that it had been concealing a deadly ignition switch in millions of its vehicles for 13 years; and Chrysler eroded any remaining faith we had in the industry this past July when it admitted that it had been providing the National Highway Traffic Safety

Administration with false and misleading information about defects in its vehicles for years.

The government's response to both scenarios was pitiful: GM was fined $900 million and Chrysler was forced to hand over $105 million, but not one managing officer was jailed or even charged with a crime, even though scores of consumers innocently — and unnecessarily — died. Instead, the companies purged their sins by writing checks from their massive stockpile of profits they derived from the very defective cars that were at issue.

Now the Department of Justice has an opportunity to restore the public's faith in our government's ability to control those it is charged with managing by handing down a real fine against the company that made $97.1 billion in profits over the last six years, and jailing all U.S. nationals who were involved in the scam.

This, however, presents a dilemma of epic proportions that cannot be ignored: GM and Chrysler, two American born companies, were given extreme leniency for killing people, and now Volkswagen may get wholly shellacked for adding a little more pollution to the environment. No one should forget that Volkswagen has long stood as Germany's crown jewel.

While Germany is certainly upset about this episode — or at least embarrassed — recognize that Volkswagen is the country's largest company, employing some 600,000 people. Diplomatic relations with Germany have been good for years, but the country who served as our arch enemy a mere half-a-century ago may not view an uneven attack on its beloved manufacturer with complete acceptance. With Russian jets being shot down by terrorist missiles and bombs being detonated in Paris sporting arenas, the world's political environment isn't exactly stable, and unleashing a deserving attack on Volkswagen may cause our foreign relations to become a little more out of round.

Aside from the criminal and political implications, one has to wonder whether Volkswagen has the financial resources to survive the scandal. The Environmental Protection Agency has the ability to levy fines of up to $37,500 per vehicle for Clean Air Act violations, exposing the company to as much as $19 billion in fines. And that is in the U.S. alone, which only has 500,000 of the 11 million defective cars worldwide. If every country imposes the maximum fine, no company in the world could withstand such a front.

Then there is the matter of the cars themselves. It remains to be seen what the fix will be; whether it will be a mere software update, or whether it will so invasive that buying back the cars is the only viable remedy. Whichever the case, it will either be expensive, or really expensive, and this assumes that the list of gamed cars does not continue to grow. Volkswagen has admitted to cheating on 11 million 2.0-liter diesel engines, but the EPA recently informed the automaker that it believes that the company's 3.0-liter diesel engines were part of the scam, too. Volkswagen has disputed this, but then again it disputed any wrongdoing with its 2.0-liter engines initially as well.

If it seems like that things could not get worse, consider that the European Investment Bank is deciding whether to recall $5.2 billion in loans (of which $2 billion is still outstanding) it made to Volkswagen for the development of lower emissions engines. The bank is reportedly seething, as it is required to fulfil certain climate targets with its loans, and now risks being out of compliance.

Volkswagen has substantial assets, but will are they deep enough to cover all the implications of what is at hand? The company's 2014 annual report reflects a net equity position of

$95.6 billion, which includes cash of $20.3 billion. Volkswagen has set aside $7.3 billion to cover the scandal, but informed thinkers believe that this is not nearly enough. Credit Suisse, the Zurich-based financial service holding company, has predicted a best-case-scenario for Volkswagen of $26 billion, and a worst-case-scenario of $86 billion. It is no surprise then that earlier this month the company applied for short term loans of $21.5 billion, and announced that it will be slashing $12.8 billion in expenses next year.

If the company survives — and it is still an *if* — it may have to shed a part of its 12-brand empire that it spent the last two decades building. This means that iconic brands such as Lamborghini, Ducati, Bugatti and Bentley, brands which are nice to have, but do not add to overall company profit, may soon be put on the block.

Of course the real losers in the equation are the consuming public and the stockholders of Volkswagen, neither of whom did anything to deserve any of this. While consumers have seen their cars devalued, investors have seen fortunes evaporate as Volkswagen stock has plummeted since the news of the scandal broke. In May, Volkswagen stock was trading on the Frankfurt exchange at $250 a share, yielding a market cap of $126 billion. Those same shares have now seen a low price of $102, and a market cap of $56 billion — a market loss for investors of $70 billion.

In many ways, the more things change, the more they stay the same. The scandal is new, but the element of greed is not. History is replete with bad actors who have impaled themselves with mortal, financially driven wounds, exposing themselves to all kind of grief. Volkswagen now joins the long list of social outcasts who have proven, time and time again, that greed is an element of human nature that we will never escape.

CHAPTER 69

What Will Become of Us?

JANUARY 2016

On Dec. 31, 2015, at 7:03 p.m., a Toyota Yaris careened out of control on the Interstate 10 freeway, accelerating uncontrollably through the Los Angeles metro. Unable to stop or slow the vehicle, the driver hurled off the freeway, striking another car and killing all of its four occupants, as well as a 7-year-old boy travelling in the Yaris.

All of this concerns a car that has a notorious reputation for being plagued with problems. In a study analyzing cars from 2009 to 2011, the Highway Loss Data Institute found that the Toyota Yaris had the "highest frequency" of injuries among all cars on U.S. roads, by a margin of 2-to-1 over the national average.

What's concerning about the New Year's Eve accident is that it is a near identical rerun of the August 2009 episode where a CHP officer and his family were trapped inside a Lexus (made by Toyota) with an accelerator that stuck. The horrific events were burned into the memories of many, as the CHP officer called 911 in a plea for help. The officer and his family of three were killed moments later when their Lexus slammed into the back of another vehicle, launching the Lexus 100 feet into the air, then down an embankment.

Memorialized in the chilling 911 call, the 2009 accident ignited a firestorm of litigation against Toyota for cases of "unintended acceleration" of its vehicles. At issue was Toyota's electronic throttle control system, a mechanism where the engine throttle is controlled by an electronic signal sent from the gas pedal to the engine throttle, as opposed a mechanical linkage connecting the two, as was traditionally done.

The unintended acceleration melee ended in 2014, when Toyota agreed to pay $1.6 billion to consumers in the class action settlement, and another $1.2 billion to the U.S. Treasury in settlement of the Justice Department's criminal complaint. Or so we thought.

The New Year's Eve crash has renewed questions about vehicle safety, and in particular whether Toyota has completely resolved the problem. Shockingly, when Toyota issued a recall of its U.S. vehicles for the unintended acceleration, the Yaris was not among them. And yet, the Yaris contained the same electronic throttle control system that was at the heart of the dispute. What's more, although Toyota did not recall the Yaris in the U.S., it did recall the car in Europe.

In fact, in a Consumer Reports study of 450 complaints made to the National Highway Traffic Safety Administration about vehicle unintended acceleration, the company found that 130 cases involved Toyota vehicles that were not recalled by the automaker. This included the 4Runner, FJ Cruiser, Land Cruiser, Sienna, Yaris and Scion.

Toyota will undoubtedly be sued for wrongful death for the fatalities caused by the New Year's Eve crash, but that glosses over the larger, more fundamental issue that is at center of this debate. For years, manufacturers have responded to critical defects in their vehicles only when forced to do so. Toyota recalled (some of) its vehicles only after a blood-curdling 911 call was aired to the public. General Motors recalled (again, some of) its vehicles for an ignition switch defect after one of its engineers mistakenly testified in a deposition about knowing of the defect for over a decade. And Volkswagen recalled (yes, some of) its vehicles for emissions tampering only after a small West Virginia university published a study, exposing the fraud.

In each of the instances, the manufacturers were content to allow the public to be deceived, and reap monster profits from the very vehicles that were causing the harm. The Department of Justice filed criminal complaints against Toyota and General Motors, ultimately resulting in the transfer of some that profit to the U.S. coffers. Yet, in neither instance were any high-ranking company officials criminally prosecuted or jailed.

In a filing on Monday, the Department of Justice brought charges against Volkswagen for its part in the fraudulent scheme. Notably, none of the company's executives have been named.

There are serious measures that could be employed, which would impact the way manufacturers behave, and ultimately prevent the kind of tragedy that befell the families of the Toyota Yaris incident. In April 2015, the U.S. Senate passed the Motor Vehicle Safety Whistleblower Act, a bill that gives whistleblowers to employees and contractors of motor vehicle manufacturers, parts suppliers and dealerships who report vehicle defects. The whistleblowers are given anonymity when coming forward, as well as 30 percent of all fines paid by the automaker that exceed $1 million.

The bill has been sent to the House for consideration, and as a sign that the public is fed up with automakers' continuing misdeeds, the bill is predicted to have a 44 percent likelihood of success, up from 36 percent in April.

The Motor Vehicle Safety Whistleblower Act will go a long way toward shattering the glass culture of secrecy that has manifested in the automotive society for decades. But, it needs to be coupled with individual accountability by high ranking company officials, charged with overseeing the design, manufacture and recall of their vehicles.

The Sarbanes-Oxley Act of 2002 got it right, and Congress ought to take a page out of its rulebook and apply it to the automotive sector. On the heels of the Enron scandal of 2001, the Sarbanes-Oxley Act requires that senior executives take individual responsibility for the accuracy and completeness of corporate financial reports, under the threat of prison. No one could seriously dispute that consumer safety is not at least as important as financial well-being.

Absent major reform, we should not only tolerate, but expect, those in command to lie, cheat and steal about the products their companies manufacture and distribute. Perhaps it's the love of profit, or maybe it's just the love of being the biggest, intertwined with loads of ego, that have created a culture of deceit. Whatever the case, Congress needs to wield its power in a proper and measured form, designed to cut the head off the snake once and for all.

CHAPTER 70

Oil's New Economy

FEBRUARY 2016

There are few commodities in the world that affect daily life like oil. It's just everywhere. The easy application is gasoline, but the list beyond that is mind-numbing. Oil is used to make plastic, cosmetics, detergent, nylon and a host of other non-obvious consumer goods we use on a daily basis. So when the price of oil drops, its impact ricochets throughout the economy.

Oil didn't kill the economy in 2008, but it made every effort to snuff out its last breath. At the time, the U.S. was consuming a world-leading 20 million barrels a day, while producing a mere 5 million barrels. The delta of 15 million barrels we imported on a daily basis traded at $145 per barrel, yielding a net loss to our local economy of $800 billion per year. For an economy that was down, the blow was near fatal.

But the world's oil market has changed dramatically in the past decade, driven largely by new U.S. oil exploration techniques that allow us to extract oil once thought unrecoverable. The technique is called hydraulic fracturing, aka "fracking," a process where rock is fractured by hydraulically pressurized liquid made of sand, water and chemicals, allowing oil to flow through the fractured rock horizontally.

Thanks to fracking, the U.S. has become the world leader in oil production — surpassing historical giants Saudi Arabia and Russia — churning out a massive 14 million barrels per day. Because of a refusal to change our usage habits (we still consume 19 million barrels daily), the U.S. still has a deficit of 5 million barrels per day. But the gap is closing considerably.

U.S. oil production has also been chiefly responsible for driving down the world's price oil to its current rate of $30 per barrel. The impact on U.S. consumers has been dramatic. The national average for gasoline is hovering at $1.79 per gallon, the lowest in years, and a far cry from the U.S. historical high of $4.41 in 2008.

The low price of gasoline has helped the U.S. auto industry rocket to a historical high of 17.5 million vehicles sold in 2015, besting the prior high of 17.4 million in 2000. The auto industry, which employs some 8 million Americans, has been a major contributing factor to our bright economy.

And it is likely to get better. The International Energy Agency estimates that 2016 will experience an oversupply of oil to the tune of 1.5 million barrels per day, and industry experts close to the situation expect oil to drop to $20 a barrel, further stripping down costs across all sectors. Some are even more bullish, such as the Royal Bank of Scotland, who predicts a price of $16 per barrel — a price not seen since 1946. Such levels would rip through consumer prices like nothing in recent memory.

The historical low price of oil leaves a lingering question of why it is being allowed to exist. Those old enough to have witnessed the 1970s will remember with great angst how beholden we were to the 12 OPEC nations (Algeria, Angola, Ecuador, Iran, Iraq, Kuwait, Libya, Nigeria, Qatar, Saudi Arabia, the United Arab Emirates and Venezuela), as embargos were put in place against the U.S. in 1973.

Responding to U.S. involvement in the 1973 Yom Kippur War, the oil-rich OPEC countries cut supply to the U.S., raising prices by 400 percent virtually overnight. The dramatic reduction in supply caused the U.S. economy to immediately seize, leading to the 1973 stock market crash — the first slap-down to the U.S. economy since the Great Depression.

For Saudi Arabia, the current downturn in oil prices is starving out its economy. Located in a wasteland desert where no man should live, Saudi Arabia is a one-trick pony whose economy rises and falls with the price of oil. Despite its efforts at diversification, oil remains accountable for 80 percent of the country's revenue.

With 270 billion barrels in proven reserves, compared to the U.S.'s 25 billion, Saudi Arabia leads the world in political clout and has the ability to trim supply all the way up the demand curve. So, given that its economy is tethered to the price of oil, why in the world would it not do so?

The answer appears to lie in the Saudis' efforts to break the back of the American oil industry, by keeping prices low in the hope of driving out U.S. oil pioneers. It is ironic, but it was oil prices that brought in a bevy of new petroleum explores; now it is the prices that are driving them out.

When oil was trading at $145 per barrel in 2008, extracting it from hard to reach places began to make a lot of sense, and the fracking industry exploded in the oil rich states of North Dakota and Texas. But fracking is terribly expensive. For every barrel produced by Saudi Arabia, U.S. shale drillers spend 10 to 15 times as much to extract the same amount. Saudi Arabia is willing to endure the pain, betting that it will break the new-found U.S. oil industry.

The Federal Reserve estimates that the nation has lost 70,000 oil production jobs in the last three months, and it will likely not get better for the oil states anytime soon. Industry experts say that prices need to stay at least $60 per barrel for fracking to remain viable. Current prices of $30 per barrel, and worse, predictions of $20 or lower, are killing the local industry.

If Saudi Arabia is right, taking the pain now will produce long term benefits for the Arab nation, as it and the other OPEC nations will again control the world's supply of oil, and ultimately its price — that is, until new technologies make shale drilling more affordable.

As our rebound from the 2008 economic crisis begins to cool, the question of what will happen with the price of oil is one that should concern us all. With U.S. consumption far outstripping any other nation, our economic outlook will, to a large degree, be tied to the price of oil and our ability to become self-reliant. We have made tremendous strides, but much is yet to be done. As William Shakespeare famously said, "It is not in the stars to hold our destiny, but in ourselves."

CHAPTER 71

EPA Slams the Door on High Performance

MARCH 2016

If the Volkswagen emissions scandal has done anything, it has highlighted the enormous rule-making ability the Environmental Protection Agency possesses. The continued viability Volkswagen is threatened — if not brought into serious doubt — by the company's attempt at sidestepping the EPA's powerful mandate: build clean cars, or don't sell in the U.S.

Now that the dust on the Volkswagen scandal is beginning to settle, the EPA has set its sights on a new target: the high-performance industry. The EPA recently proposed new legislation that promises to have a stinging impact on the performance seeking after-market industry.

At issue is a new set of proposed standards currently pending before Congress that would make it a crime to modify a certified motor vehicle for purposes of competition.

In generic terms, the racing industry is made up of two distinct subsets: Vehicles that began life as a race car and are used solely for that purposes — those vehicles are left untouched by the proposed legislation — and the huge segment of vehicles that started out as an ordinary sports car and were modified for performance gains.

The EPA's proposed legislation would impose a fine of up to $3,750 for any person who manufactures, sells or installs a device that "bypasses, impairs, defeats or disables" an emissions control on a certified motor vehicle. The fine goes up considerably for dealers or manufacturers who tamper with or remove an emissions control devise; those infringers would be subject to a fine of $37,500 per vehicle.

In simple terms, the proposed bill would all but kill the cottage industry of high-performance manufacturers. All sorts of high-performance parts that make up the $86 billion industry would be instantly outlawed, and the world (or at least the Western part of it) would be ridded of virtually any type of system that attempted increase a car's horsepower. Gone would be turbo chargers, exhaust upgrades, manifold modifications, and the like.

For those not wedded to the high-performance industry, such a change might not sound all that troubling. However, for the 6,383 companies who are members of the 55-year-old Specialty Equipment Manufacturer Association, such a law would result in instant death for their businesses, as well as the thousands of installation and sales facilities located throughout the U.S. The shuttering of these businesses would result in the loss of hundreds of thousands of jobs, as well as billions in tax revenue for the municipalities where the products and services are sold.

Also gone would be the semi-professional motors sports industry, and the scores of historic races that surrounds them, such as the 24 Hours of Daytona, the 12 Hours of Sebring, and the like. This, of course, would also result in the loss of race and fan revenue, and the likely closure of many of the stadiums themselves, such as the Daytona International Speedway whose renovation was just completed in January at a cost of $400 million.

What is interesting is that most of the high-performance industry caters to automotive enthusiasts, who want nothing more than to try to get 10 more horsepower out of the cars, for nothing but water-cooler bragging rights. The impact on the environment from such activity is minimal, if it exists at all, as the cars still have to pass strict smog certification requirements.

Meanwhile, it is perfectly legal to have a gas-powered leaf blower that decimates the environment at every turn. In 2011, the car experts at Edmunds measured the pollutants that a consumer-grade leaf blower emits, as compared to a 6,200-pound Ford F-150 SVT Raptor, one of the biggest vehicle offenders to the environment. The study found that the leaf blowers, which are being used daily throughout neighborhoods, emitted 299 times more hydrocarbons than the large Ford truck.

In fact, the list of unregulated, heavy polluters is quite long. Consider that chainsaws, lawnmowers, off-road motorcycles, snowmobiles and jet skis emit more pollution that just about any car the EPA is trying to regulate with its new proposal. Now consider how many lawns are mowed every day, or how large the U.S. timber industry is, and the magnitude of the unregulated industry becomes perfectly clear.

The EPA is claiming that the new legislation simply seeks to "clarify" it prior rule making ability. However, in its 46-year history, the EPA has never sought to regulate — or criminalize — those who simply attempted to modify a consumer vehicle for performance gains. The new legislation is a sweeping departure.

What is ironic is that the proposed changes seek to regulate the half of the motorsports industry that is the least offensive. A new Corvette with a $1,500 exhaust modification still drives and performs much like a stock vehicle, with just slightly more oomph that its stock brethren. But they both have to comply with all Federal Motor Vehicle Safety

Standards, and both have to pass EPA-mandated smog certifications.

The pure racing industry, on the other hand, is not nearly as benign. Consider that NASCAR, whose vehicles are devoid of mufflers, catalytic converters or other emissions control devices, burn dirty fuel at the rate of about two miles per gallon. With the dozens of cars participating in each race, and scores of races each year, the impact on the environment monumentally trumps modified pedestrian cars.

And, of course, there are many more sanctioned racing bodies than just NASCAR; there are also Indy Car and Formula One, to name just a few. To be sure, these leagues are all doing their part to have their cars become greener, but point remains that the EPA is criminalizing the wrong party. Yes, we all need to do what we can to protect the environment, and we need to be responsible for our lasting carbon footprint. But taking a shotgun to the high-performance industry will not solve the enduring problem we have with global warming; it will only serve to bankrupt thousands of businesses, and leave scores of Americans unemployed, if not unemployable altogether.

CHAPTER 72

Autonomous Cars
Have Finally Arrived

APRIL 2016

It is fascinating when you think about it – the day of the autonomous car has finally arrived. Google has jumped to the lead in the race, logging some 1.5 million miles in its fleet of Toyota, Audi and Lexus self-driving cars. But by no stretch is Google alone in this quest. Apple, Ford, Mercedes and some 22 other companies are busy developing autonomous vehicles they hope will take the market by storm.

In many ways, this is a day few historians thought would ever come. Car companies have been talking about the self-driving car for generations, with few successes along the way. General Motors started the conversation in 1939 with its "Futurama" concept car it presented at the New York World Fair. At that time experts predicted automated cars would be commonplace by 1960, forever displacing traditional motoring.

Then at the 1962 Seattle World Fair, GM introduced the Firebird III, a concept car that had an "electronic guide system [that] can rush it over an automatic highway while the driver relaxes." Experts of the day opined the autonomous car was about "20 years out."

Much legislative ink has been consumed on the issue as well, as nations also rush to be the first to develop the driverless car. In 1991, Congress enacted the Intermodal Surface Transportation Efficiency Act, which instructed the U.S. Department of Transportation to "demonstrate an automated vehicle and highway system by 1997." The program was later followed in 1998 by the Transportation Equity Act for the 21st Century, the Safe, Accountable, Flexible, Efficient Transportation Equity Act in 2005, and the Moving Ahead for Progress in the 21st Century Act in 2012. Yet despite the expenditure of billions in public revenue, none of these acts succeeded in achieving the goal of creating an automated highway system set out by GM in 1939 – that is, until now.

With the advent of amazingly-powerful microchips, pinpoint GPS tracking and real-time cloud computing, the autonomous car has migrated from mythical legend to modern day reality. And with it come a host of ethical and legislative issues that are crisscrossing the nation.

Until now, motor vehicles had to be operated by licensed drivers who are required to pass a regimented licensing test to qualify for membership. Anyone who has received a speeding ticket has heard the adage that "a driver's license is a privilege, not a right." Now, however, the line is become increasingly blurred in determining who – or what – is allowed to operate a motor vehicle on public roads.

And the conversation is necessary. For all their attributes, autonomous vehicles are not without flaws. On February 14, 2016, one Google car famously crashed when it changed lanes and put itself in the path of an oncoming bus.

This incident is not isolated. According to the University of Michigan Transportation Research Institute, self-driving cars being tested in real-world traffic have a crash rate of more than double that of conventional vehicles. On average, conventional vehicles are involved in 4.1 crashes per one million miles driven. Autonomous vehicles are more than double this, averaging 9.1 crashes per one million miles driven.

One reason for the higher crash rate is that autonomous cars follow the rules of the road to a fault, providing no consideration for real-world driving conditions, such as other motorists who often drive with the flow of traffic, even if it is over the posted speed limit. Having a car that obeys every rule often surprises other drivers, who are expecting more of an ebb and flow in driving patterns.

And then there is the matter of fault, and who exactly is the responsible party for an accident caused by an autonomous vehicle. Is it the registered owner of the car, the person who was in the car, the manufacturer of the car, the service who is providing computing data, or a combination of all? No one seems to have much of an answer.

Currently, there are seven states (California, Nevada, Michigan, Tennessee, North Dakota, Florida and Washington DC) that have enacted legislation regulating autonomous cars. Since 2015, 22 states have introduced legislation to address the issue.

And therein lies part of the problem. As states rush to legislate autonomous cars, our nation will be left with a quilted regulatory framework on what will be required to place an autonomous vehicle on the roadway, and who is responsible for its misgivings. Complicating the issue is the fact that, by their nature, the cars travel, resulting in a potential for conflicting state laws, where, for instance, a car that is domiciled in one state gets into an accident in a neighboring jurisdiction.

Last month, leaders of self-driving car companies testified before the U.S. Senate Committee on Commerce about the need to have Congress regulate the industry to avoid a patchwork of state laws. Testifying were executives of Google, General Motors, auto parts supplier Delphi and ride-sharing service Lyft. As Google executive Chris Urmson stated, "If every state is left to go its own way without a unified approach, operating self-driving cars across state boundaries would be an unworkable situation and one that will significantly hinder safety innovation, interstate commerce, national competitiveness and the eventual deployment of autonomous vehicles."

With every advancement of technology comes unforeseen setbacks, and frequent strife. Calculators of the 1960s allowed for blistering mathematics, but also created a culture of lazy thinkers. Cell phones gave us enormous freedom, but also brought on texting and driving. The autonomous car will undoubtedly provide societal benefits; just think about all the disabled and elderly people who will now be free to travel. But exactly how it will work itself out is, at this point, still a matter of great debate.

CHAPTER 73

NY's Response to Texting and Driving

MAY 2016

Would you believe that after all the fatalities, all the media attention and all the pain suffered by scores of families, four states still find it perfectly acceptable for motorists to text and drive? Arizona, Montana, Texas and Missouri have yet to come to the realization that distracted driving is the biggest killer of them all.

Drinking and driving is public enemy number one, but the truth is that texting and driving is infinitely more deadly. The National Highway Traffic Safety Administration (NHTSA) reports that drivers take their eyes off the road for an average of 4.6 seconds when sending or receiving a text. Put in terms of physics, at 80 miles per hour that is the equivalent of driving 539 feet, or nearly two football fields — blindfolded.

The epidemic, and yes it is an epidemic, is as serious as they come. NHTSA studies reveal that 17 percent of all traffic accidents involve texting and driving. Said another way, by the end of the day another 16 Americans will tragically, and unnecessarily, lose their lives to it. The federal agency has determined that texting and driving is six times more dangerous than drinking and driving.

Yet in spite of these rather alarming statistics, few states have enacted any measures designed to stomp out the problem. Save Alaska, which imposes a $10,000 fine for texting and driving, no state has given the problem the attention it deserves. In California, for instance, the fine for texting while driving is $20. The statistically less dangerous offense of drinking and driving, on the other hand, slaps offenders with suspended drivers' licenses, fines of up to $3,600, alcohol school, skyrocketing insurance and up to six months' imprisonment.

In recent proposed legislation, however, New York is taking a serious stab at cracking down on the problem — with questionable constitutionality. New York state assembly bill A08613, if passed, would allow police officers to search cellphones of motorists involved in automobile accidents, without a warrant, to see if they were using their phones around the time of the crash. Motorists who refuse to surrender their phones would face a revocation of their drivers' licenses for up to one year and a $500 fine.

Referred to as Evan's Law, a respect to the 19-year-old who was killed by a distracted driver, the bill does not specify exactly how the cellphones will be searched. The New York Legislature stated, however, that technology is being developed by the Israeli company Cellebrite which would allow police officers to scan cellphones to determine the traffic on the phone, without actually viewing any of the user's personal content.

While certainly relevant to the consideration of traffic accidents, the proposed legislation is sure to ignite a firestorm of controversy. In 2014, the U.S. Supreme Court handed down the seminal case of Riley v. California, where the court unanimously ruled that police may not search the cellphones of criminal suspects upon arrest without a warrant, finding that any such search violates the Constitution's Fourth Amendment prohibiting unreasonable searches and seizures.

Under the Supreme Court's current interpretation of the Fourth Amendment, police officers may search a criminal suspect's personal items that are incident to the arrest, such as wallet or briefcase, if they have probable cause to believe that a crime has been committed, the officers' safety is at issue and it will prevent the destruction of evidence.

Cellphones, however, are manifestly different. As Chief Justice John Roberts wrote, "Cell phones differ in both a quantitative and qualitative sense from other objects that might be kept on arrestee's person ... Many of these devices are in fact minicomputers" that "could just as easily be called cameras, video players, rolodexes, calendars, tape recorders, libraries, diaries, albums, televisions, maps, or newspapers."

Central to the court's opinion was the consideration that "the sum of an individual's private life can be reconstructed" by searching through their cellphone. The New York legislation, however, which only authorizes the scanning of cellphones to determine traffic — not content — may be seen as different.

Proponents of the legislation claim that the accessing of traffic, not content, avoids the concerns and potential legal challenges based on privacy rights or claims of unlawful search and seizures. The strength of that argument remains to be seen. There are no assurances, for instance, that once in possession of the driver's cell phone, the police officer won't access the legions of photographs, videos, emails and text messages on the phone, all of which are personal to the user.

And, what's worse, the Supreme Court's tolerance for warrantless searches extends only to suspected criminal conduct. The New York legislation applies to all motorists involved in traffic accidents, regardless of who was at fault, and regardless of whether any criminal conduct is suspected.

Absent drastic action, there is no easy answer to the riddle of how to curb texting and driving. It is a crisis of national proportions that is getting worse by the day – and with no end in sight. The current system of powder-puffing drivers with meaningless $20 fines is a having no affect at all. Although it dances on the edges of what is constitutionally acceptable, New York's proposed legislation at least makes an effort at holding people responsible for the troubling conduct.

In truth, Congress should take the drastic action of requiring that all cell phones sold in the U.S. be equipped with text disabling devices. The technology exists to disallow texting and emailing while on the highway; the decision to impose it is a matter of desire, not ability. There is just no other solution that will arrest the problem, and rid our highways of this reckless conduct.

CHAPTER 74

Airbag Recall Understood

JUNE 2016

By now, most understand that our nation faces an epidemic of automotive recalls, igniting both fear and confusion in the hearts and minds of consumers. Spurred on by General Motors' shocking admission that it had known of a deadly ignition switch defect in its vehicles for 13 years, but failed to issue a recall, all sorts of automaker misdeeds have come to light, leading manufacturers to issue recalls at alarming rates.

Gone are the days of the occasional repair, replaced by confessions of highly compensated executives who sat idly by as scores of consumers lost their lives. In all too many instances, top brass knew of the devastation their products were creating, but chose profit over human life as their navigating light.

If GM's ignition switch fraud started the calamity, Japanese airbag supplier Takata is perfecting it. The tier one supplier who was once best known for building the world's first crash-test plant for testing seat-belts under real world conditions, has had its reputation hammed under the scandalous admission that it knew about deadly defects with its airbags, but did nothing to recall them.

At issue is the metal airbag inflator, which has been prone to rupture during airbag deployment, sending metal shrapnel into the occupant's face. The problem has been traced to the use of an ammonium nitrate-based propellant without a chemical drying agent. When the airbags are exposed to environmental moisture and high temperatures, the propellant can become so explosive that it bursts through the metal inflator. To date, Takata airbags are responsible for 10 deaths and 139 injuries.

Takata began installing the ammonium nitrate airbags in vehicles in 2002, and according to one whistleblower, the company knew of the defect back in the 1990s, when the airbags were being designed. It was not until April 2013, however, that the first recall was issued; and it would be another 18 months before it became publicly known that Takata had been concealing its knowledge of the defect.

Takata's refusal to disclose critical information cost it dearly. In February 2015, the National Highway Traffic Safety Administration (NHTSA) fined Takata $14,000 per day for not cooperating with its airbag investigation, and in November 2015 it imposed a $200 million fine against the airbag manufacturer — the largest in the governmental agency's 46-year history.

The faulty inflator resulted in a recall of 28.8 million airbags, dubbed by NHTSA as "the largest and most complex safety recall in U.S. history." And until last month, we thought the nightmare ended there. In May, however, NHTSA stated that it was requiring more than doubling the size of the Takata recall, to include an additional 40 million airbags.

The recall of nearly 70 million airbags has created all sorts of logistical problems for regulators. To begin, Takata does not have nearly enough airbags to service the recall. As a result, NHTSA is conducting a "rolling" recall of airbags to be replaced through 2019. So while consumers are being told that their vehicles may contain a deadly defect, they are being provided with little relief in terms of real-world solutions.

Some manufacturers are offering to disengage passenger airbags (driver airbags are a federal requirement, even if they contain a defect), and are issuing "do not sit" warnings for seating positions where disengagement is not possible, such as the driver's seat.

What's worse, according to the U.S. Senate Committee on Commerce, Science and Transportation,

four manufacturers — Toyota, Fiat Chrysler, Volkswagen and Mitsubishi — are still selling new vehicles with defective airbags that will eventually need to be replaced. Because NHTSA is issuing a rolling recall, the vehicles are legal to sell, even if they could subject the purchaser to death or disfigurement.

Perhaps most concerning is that NHTSA's plan to replace these 70 million airbags is contingent on the tenuous notion that Takata actually remain in business. Takata, who is battling a bevy of class actions and a Department of Justice investigation (which could result in billions in fines), puts its worst-case scenario at a whopping $24 billion.

Does Takata have the armor to withstand that kind of blast? Not even close. The company, whose shares are traded on the Tokyo Stock Exchange, has taken a beating since the scandal broke. Once touted as the godfather of automotive safety, Takata currently has a market cap (the aggregate value of all outstanding shares) of $308 million.

Its balance sheet is better, reflecting a book value of $1.2 billion, but is still concerning given the gravity of the situation at hand. And there is little reason to believe the company will have much earning power in the future. All but shunned from the automotive industry, when the company is done building replacement airbags, it will be required to reinvent itself in a manner few have ever done.

It appears that the market agrees. Since the scandal broke, Takata shares have lost 87 percent of their value, leaving investors who have ridden the stock down wondering when they should jump ship. In terms of U.S dollar comparisons, Takata stock is trading at 434 yen, or about $4 per share. While it has yet to become a penny stock, the forecast is not promising.

It is reported that there are some 120 million Takata airbag containing ammonium nitrate installed in U.S. vehicles (many vehicles contain multiple airbags), leaving open the question of whether the recalls will stop at the current 70 million, or if the calamity will continue to grow. For consumers who are left with the Hobson's choice of abandoning their vehicles or continue to drive them, one can only hope that the end is near — and that Takata will remain viable long enough to do something about it.

CHAPTER 75

Britain's Exit and the Auto Industry

JULY 2016

The sanctity of the European Union – a sovereign pack architected in the 1950s to prevent another flare-up of extreme nationalism that led to two World Wars – was called into serious question last month, when Britain voted to secede from the Union.

Frustrated by a perceived imbalance in immigration and economic regulation, Britain opted to go it alone, leaving the remaining 28 members wondering if an exodus is the right solution. The 2015 Greece debt crisis tested everyone's faith in the entire European experiment, and now that Britain has voted to leave, other powerhouses like France and Germany are white-boarding the same.

Even if the EU is not teetering on the verge of collapse, Britain's exit has proven it to be a brittle system, dotted with criticisms from nearly all sovereign members. While some may think the system is too big to fail, most held the same opinion of the Soviet Union before it toppled in 1991, proving that no political sisterhood is immune from collapse.

Regardless of whether the EU will fall, Britain's exit is certain to have a cascading effect on economies and industries around the globe. Perhaps hardest hit will be the automotive sector, which will suffer mightily under the weight of the falling pound and new European tariffs that are sure to be imposed.

The British pound closed out last week at a U.S. dollar exchange rate of $1.28 – a 30-year low – and most economists in the know are forecasting financial parity with the dollar by the end of the year, or early 2017 at the latest. A weak pound means falling profits for manufactures who sell in Britain, and for dealer groups, such as Penske Automotive Group and Group 1 Automotive, who have retail stores there. Penske, who has 94 dealerships in Britain, witnessed a 20 percent stock beating since news of the exodus broke.

Of even greater concern is the near-certainty of new tariffs to be imposed by the EU on cars exported from Britain. The United Kingdom, Europe's second largest car market, produces 1.7 million cars annually, with 58 percent of them being shipped to EU nations, resulting in an annual export of some 27 billion pounds. European Union nations, a status that Britain no longer maintains, enjoy friction-free trading among members in the automotive industry.

The flow of cars in the opposite direction is even more drastic. Of Britain's 2.6 million new cars sold annually, 2.2 million are imported, and mostly from EU countries. A retaliatory British-imposed tariff against EU nations would dramatically impact consumer prices and automaker profits.

Most expect the EU to impose a 10 percent tariff on Britain's automotive exports, and that Britain will do the same against EU member countries, resulting in an automotive market that will be out-of-round for years to come.

The impact of Britain's exit will hardly be contained to the land of right-handed vehicles, with carmakers around the globe feeling the impact. While many consider traditional British vehicles to be just that – British – the truth is that most U.K. automakers have been rolled up into other automotive juggernauts. Mini and Rolls-Royce are owned by BMW, Jaguar and Land Rover are owned by India's Tata Motors, and

Bentley is owned by Volkswagen. The result of this, of course, is that these manufacturers will take a double hit has they are taxed on importing and exporting their own cars across Britain's borders.

Tata Motors, who owns Jaguar and Land Rover, sustained a 12 percent drop in the price of its stock the day after the Brexit news was announced – its biggest fall since 2012, wiping out $2.5 billion in the company's market capitalization in just 24 hours. And it gets worse for the Indian company's two luxury car makers.

Prior to leaving the Union, Britain had negotiated a deal with the European Parliament whereby Jaguar and Land Rover vehicles were subjected to a much less onerous fuel economy target by 2020. With Britain leaving, that deal is now in jeopardy, leaving open the question of whether the two carmakers will need to modify their vehicle lineup (at great expense), or face stiff financial penalties for not complying with the standardized fuel economy targets.

And it is not just traditional British line-makes that will be hit. Nissan is the country's second-largest auto producer, with a production run of 475,000 units, followed by Toyota, who builds 190,000 in the U.K. annually. Honda and GM also have production facilities in England, with GM's facility the most likely to be shut down given the uncertainty swarming the nation. It remains to be seen who will leave, but currently all four automakers export the majority of their English-made vehicles to the EU, subjecting them to the hefty new EU tariffs that are certain to come.

German carmakers will also be hard hit. According to the German Association of the Auto Industry, the U.K. is the biggest single export market for German automakers, and about half of England's new car registrations are German name-plates. So BMW, Volkswagen, Audi and Mercedes should be in a panic over what will become of their profits.

Britain's departure from the EU will sting for a while, but the real question is whether the EU will remain a sustainable unit moving forward. The quick answer is that the song will remain the same, but deep thinkers are not so quick to agree. German Chancellor Angela Merkel recently issued a statement of concern that Britain could be just the first of several nations to pull out of the alliance, citing rank dissatisfaction among members over migration and economic disparity.

The centralization of a common economic unit, the euro, which is subscribed to by 19 of the remaining 28 member countries, certainly makes the conversation more dynamic – particularly with certain countries lagging behind the economic engines of Germany and France. Regardless of what happens with the rest of the EU, the global economy will have to travel down a long and windy road in dealing with Britain's recent decision, with much uncertainty and economic fallout sure to come.

CHAPTER 76

The Brazilian Nightmare

AUGUST 2016

This week will mark an Olympic first on many levels: the first time Brazil has hosted the Olympics; the first time the summer Olympics have been held in a South American city; and the first time the games have been held in a Portuguese-speaking country. Now another first can be added to the list: the first Olympics to be embroiled in such a deep malaise of controversy and scandal.

Brazil, a country that is rich in beauty and natural resources, is suffering the worst recession in more than 100 years. While recessions are generally defined as a fall in GDP for two successive quarters, Brazil has had falling GDP in eight of its last 10 quarters, leaving its citizens with a jobless rate of 11.3 percent — a number that is undoubtedly underreported because it does not include those who are underemployed, or those who have given up looking for work altogether.

Amidst its economic tatters, the country is doubling down on its bet that spending big on a world stage will rescue it from financial disaster. In 2014, Brazil spent $11 billion of taxpayer money to build soccer stadiums and infrastructure for the World Cup. The hope was that lasting tourism would develop, bringing riches to its local economy. But two years later, the stadiums have fallen into disuse — and worse — have become a financial liability to the cities that are required to maintain them. And for this, Brazil's tourism showed no significant increase from recent years.

Now Brazil is betting big again, this time spending $12 billion on the 2016 Olympic games, a two-week event hosted in poverty-stricken Rio de Janeiro. Yet if the expenditure on the World Cup was imprudent, the outlay for the Olympics is proving to be downright dreadful.

Thus far, the attention Brazil has garnered has done more to highlight the country's failures than its successes. As but one example, the country's new light rail system, which was built to transport athletes and tourists to and from the Olympic venues, is eight months delayed, pitting the train's opening right up against the start date of the games. Brazil is hopeful that the train will work as planned, but has had no time to test any of its systems. What's more, the $3 billion train system (which came in at twice the amount budgeted) unexplainably ends eight miles short of the Olympic venues, forcing travelers to take busses for the remainder of the trip. Not exactly the engineering marvel Brazil had hoped to showcase.

The financial pressure on the city is taking its toll. In June — just two months before the start of the games — the governor of Rio de Janeiro declared the host city to be in a "state of financial emergency." With the world ready to descend onto the city, the governor's cry of financial calamity should be a concern for all.

If Brazil's financial affairs are concerning, the very real health crisis created by the Zika virus is downright frightening. The outbreak of the Zika virus, an infection generally transmitted by infected mosquitos, began in Brazil in 2015, and is as serious as they come. The disease has been shown to cause birth defects in pregnant women and debilitating neurological problems in adults. And these are not statements of puffery. A recent study conducted in Rio showed that of women infected with the Zika virus during pregnancy, a full 29 percent developed fetal abnormalities. Now consider that Rio currently has 26,000 cases of the Zika virus.

So serious is the problem that Harvard Public Health Review is demanding — indeed, insisting — that the summer games be immediately postponed, or moved to a different country altogether. The respected publication argues that the mass migration of 500,000 tourists into the epicenter of the crisis will result in an exponential advancement of the virus, as infected travelers unwittingly bring the disease back home from the games with them.

The health concern has also reached competing athletes, some of whom are refusing to travel to Brazil to participate in the summer games. Equally concerned are media personnel who are scheduled to travel to the country to cover the games. While covering the Olympics is ordinarily a career-defining moment, a contingency of NBC employees is nonetheless refusing to travel to Rio to work on the network's Olympic broadcast.

And if it seemed as though things could not possibly get worse, two weeks ago they managed to when Bernie Ecclestone's mother-in-law was kidnapped at her home in Sao Paulo, Brazil. Bernie Ecclestone, who will turn 86 in October, is the celebrated head of Formula One, and the fourth wealthiest person in the United Kingdom. Recall that it was Bernie Ecclestone's 22-year-old daughter, Petra Ecclestone, who bought Aaron Spelling's Los Angeles mansion in 2011 for $85 million in cash.

Bernie Ecclestone recently married 38-year-old Fabiana Flosi, a Brazilian national. On July 22, Fabiana Flosi's 67-year-old mother, Aparecida Schunck, was abducted and held for $37 million ransom. The kidnappers were arrested over the weekend, and the mother-in-law was freed from her capture, but not before news of the abduction sent shockwaves throughout the international community. Formula One is the world's most popular sport, with some 500 million television viewers annually (the NFL, by contrast, has 200 million), creating a wide avenue for mass dissemination of the Brazilian abduction.

The kidnapping of a family member of Formula One's elder statesman only served to underscore yet another problem Brazil faces: crime. With 51,000 murders in 2014 alone (the U.S., which is significantly larger, had 12,000), Brazil has the highest homicide count of any country in the world. Broken down on a population basis, Brazil logs 24 homicides for every 100,000 residents, cementing a very real security concern for the Olympic games.

Demands for postponement aside, it appears that the games will go forward as scheduled, yet with an assumption of risk that is far greater than ever bargained for. The games are truly treasures of society, bringing international unity and advancement of sport in a way that nothing else can. Yet when they serve to further impoverish an already hard-hit country, and subject tourists to infectious disease and alarming crime, rational thinking needs to settle in. Let us not forget that the stated goal of the Olympics "is to contribute to building a peaceful and better world." This is one instance where the arrow is far off the mark.

CHAPTER 77

The Exporting Enigma

SEPTEMBER 2016

The number is staggering, really: $438 billion. That is the amount the federal government spent in excess of revenue it collected in 2015. Pundits will tussle over who is responsible for the deficit — particularly in an election year — with Republicans and Democrats alike apportioning blame to one another with adolescent fervor. But the larger question is how can a nation that is capable of so much, fall so short in balancing a federal budget, year after year.

Run like a business, the country would seek to maximize its revenues and trim its expenses, all in an effort to yield a sustainable profit. But the country is not a business, of course, saddled with scores of societal expenditures that are necessary for the good of the country. It is the question of which expenditures should be made, and where the revenue should come from, that stirs national debate.

Regardless of whether a particular public spending gains popular attraction, all can agree that government spending is to be made by the people, for the people. Given this, and considering the enormous federal deficit our country faces, many would be surprised to learn that the federal government has committed substantial resources to addressing an issue that has little, if anything, to do with protecting public welfare.

At issue is the practice of exporting new luxury vehicles out of the country. Auto manufactures who sell in the U.S. have had a long-standing policy prohibiting new car dealers from exporting new cars to foreign countries. The policy makes sense to a degree, or at least to the automakers, as manufacturers price cars differently in different countries.

To understand the price differential, consider the BMW X6 that has a starting price of $61,900 in U.S. dealerships. In China, that MSRP is $171,000. Part of the difference in pricing is tariffs imposed by the foreign country, but much of it is just automakers exploiting market forces in differing lands. That gain, manufacturers argue, should be reserved for the automakers themselves who have chosen to maximize the capitalistic model.

Given the significant price disparity in many countries, a cottage industry has emerged where profit seekers buy cars in the U.S., and export them to foreign lands, paying the local tariffs and realizing the substantial profits above them. While dealers are prohibited by their manufacturers from engaging in such conduct, ordinary citizens are not shackled by such contractual restrictions.

Manufacturers hate the practice, because it cuts into the profits they would prefer to keep for themselves, but in truth there is little they can do about it. Or at least, that has been the case until now.

Recently, the federal government has elected to weigh in on the conversation, seeking to stomp out the practice of ordinary citizens exporting cars for profit. Using public funds to fuel their cause, the government has begun a practice of seizing cars and freezing bank accounts of individuals and businesses attempting to export luxury cars out of the U.S. Such was the case with Efans Trading Corp., who is said to have exported 2,000 high-end vehicles to China, valued at some $80 million. In 2013, the government seized $7 million in cash and 47 vehicles from Efans, and then sued them in U.S. district court for forfeiture.

The government claims that such conduct is "contrary to law," yet it has not been able to articulate which law it is contrary to. Vaguely, the government has stated that the practice constitutes wire fraud — a law designed to prevent artifices to defraud — but who is being defrauded remains a mystery. And at least one federal judge agrees.

In 2013, the Secret Service seized vehicles and money belonging to Automotive Consultants of Hollywood, and then sued the company for forfeiture, also claiming that the company's actions were contrary to law and tantamount to wire fraud.

In ruling on a motion to dismiss, the U.S. district court noted that the government does not allege that the company engaged in an illegal export scheme, or that it was smuggling automobiles out of the country. Rather, the government rested its case on the premise that "luxury vehicle manufacturers do not want their dealerships to sell new vehicles to a purchaser who intends to export the car."

The court noted that all of the company's dealings when buying the cars — which were fully paid for — were with the dealer, not the manufacturer. Because the company never made any statements to the manufacturer, the court reasoned that it could not have engaged in an artifice to defraud it.

Resting on these "significant due process concerns," and noting that the U.S. had failed to demonstrate that the company had broken any laws, the court ordered that the vehicles and funds be immediately returned to the company. As Judge Sandra Bechwith wrote, "it appears to the court that the primary concern of the manufacturers is guarding their foreign market profits from competition."

The practice of exporting cars to foreign lands is undoubtedly frustrating to manufacturers. It is estimated that 35,000 new luxury vehicles are purchased in the U.S. and shipped out of the country each year, costing the automakers millions. An economist hired by BMW estimates the losses for that manufacturer alone are over $200 million per year.

Automakers argue that there are legitimate reasons for prohibiting practice, such as difficulty issuing recalls on cars that are exported abroad. But the truth is that manufacturers are merely seeking to protect their profit from competitive erosion. Such a goal is perfectly defensible, but when public resources are used to protect that goal, the line has been crossed. Government effort should not — and cannot — be used to preserve private sector profits, when no law is being broken and no citizen is put at risk. Should Congress choose to regulate the practice, so be it. But until the time, this public market should be free of unwarranted intrusion.

CHAPTER 78

Formula One's $8 Billion Deal

OCTOBER 2016

At 5 feet 3 inches tall, 85-year-old Bernie Eccelstone has stood supreme over the Formula One enterprise for nearly half of a century, transforming the race series from a unique event for purists to the most popular sport in the world. Now his empire is being sold in an $8 billion deal between Liberty Media (buyer) and CVC Capital Partners (seller). The transaction is said to net Eccelstone a cool $1 billion, adding to his already massive financial empire.

Formula One has lagged in popularity in the U.S., but expect that to change with the acquisition by Liberty Media, the U.S. media company founded by business mogul John Malone. Liberty Media controls much of what America sees, boasting an asset list that is nothing short of amazing. To name but a few, Liberty Media owns Paramount Pictures, Time Warner, Sirius XM, MTV, Live Nation and Time Inc. Progressive thinkers should expect Liberty Media to use these deep anchors in social and traditional media to indoctrinate the U.S. market into a sport that has so dominated the rest of the world.

Intellectually, Formula One is a fascinating study. While the open wheel cars may look similar to Indy cars, the comparison ends there. For the Indy car series, each team purchases a pre-fabricated chassis and engine that are for all intents equal to one another. The teams then travel among cities in the U.S. and compete in events such as the

Indianapolis 500, a Memorial Day tradition in the Midwest. Indy car teams have annual budgets of about $15 million and employ an average of 20 people.

If the Indy series is an exercise in algebra, Formula One pushes the limits of quantum physics. Where Indy teams compete on driver alone, each Formula One team is required to construct its own vehicle from the ground up, under a web of technical regulations that change year-to-year. The efforts that go into it are staggering.

Mercedes' Formula One team, for instance, has an annual budget of $467 million, and employs 700 full time people in its new a 15-acre Formula One compound, located just north of London. In staggered shifts, the employees work 24 hours a day, 7 days a week, designing and constructing two cars that will be raced in the current Formula One season. To put an exclamation point on the discussion, consider that each year 250,000 working hours are put into designing the vehicles, and 200,000 working hours are put into production. And this is just one team.

These efforts result in not only large publicity for the teams, but also in advancement of technology that is enjoyed by every-day drivers. Commuter cars have disc brakes, independent suspension, superchargers and paddle shifters because of their development and testing on Formula One tracks.

In its 21-race season, the Formula One races sprawl throughout Europe, North America, South America, Asia and the Middle East, playing to sold-out venues twice the size of the super bowl. Each race is held in a different country, necessitating the immediate and constant transfer of tons of precision equipment and scores of engineers across international borders.

Take the last two races of the season, for instance, where the teams compete in Brazil on Nov. 13, and then in Abu Dhabi – some 8,000 miles away – a mere two weeks later. With each race team employing about 100 traveling personnel, many of whom are from differing countries of origin, the immigration issues alone are staggering.

The economics of the sport are equally massive. Each race is broadcast throughout the world, attracting an annual viewership of 500 million. The NLF, by contrast, peaks at 200 million. In fact, the marketing advantage of Formula One was so strong, that in 2005 energy drink giant Red Bull bought a Formula One racecar and outfitted it with Red Bull logos. According to Formula One's industry publication, Formula Money, Red Bull's "advertising value equivalent" — the price it would have had to pay to buy a similar amount of on-screen exposure — is $415 million per year.

The yield generated by Formula One's popularity is also enormous. Consider that Mercedes team driver Lewis Hamilton – a name that many will not recognize – is the fourth highest paid athlete in the world, with an annual salary exceeding that of Serena Williams, LeBron James and Phil Mickelson combined.

Much of Formula One's success can be attributed to Bernie Ecclestone, the British business magnate who commercialized a sport that was once reserved for hard-core enthusiasts. It was Ecclestone who brought Formula One to the likes of New Delhi, Budapest, Kuala Lumpur and Bahrain, creating value where others saw dust.

Ecclestone not only extracted millions in race fees from previously untapped markets, he convinced the countries that it would be economically beneficial to build expensive Formula One tracks, advancing the argument that the added exposure would increase tourism and build credibility alongside other sporting nations. Many countries bit, including Abu Dhabi who in 2009 built a Formula One track in the Yas Marina at a cost of $1 billion – quite a sum for a single-purpose venue. But the capital of the United Arab Emirates isn't complaining, noting that its tourism has increased substantially year-over-year.

And for all his successes, or perhaps because of them, Ecclestone has been a lightning rod for controversy. It was a mere two months ago that the mother of his 38-year-old wife was kidnapped by Brazilian thugs and held for a $37 million ransom. And before that, Ecclestone was charged by the German police with the crime of bribery, accused of giving a German bank official a $44 million bribe to have the bank vote a certain way on an earlier sale of the bank's interest in Formula One.

Liberty Media has agreed to keep Ecclestone on as CEO following the acquisition, but for a man who will turn 86 this month, the question of how much longer he can do it, is legitimate. Irrespective, with Liberty Media's purchase of the franchise, all should expect Formula One to seep into the fabric of American culture, carrying with it an international globalization that will bring us closer, yet again, to a world of blurred borders.

CHAPTER 79

The Next Four Years

NOVEMBER 2016

In a week's time we will have a new leader of the free world, and with it a new era of policy, diplomacy and economy will usher in. The last eight years have laid witness to certain economic growth, pulling our country from near-certain ruin to stable financial health. While the recovery may not have been as bristling as some would have preferred, we are far removed from the days of 10 percent unemployment and eye-popping foreclosures.

With a change in administration, a natural question arises about what type of economy our President will oversee. Seven years of straight economic growth should be worrisome to all, as recessions like to loom in the corner, repeating themselves with frightening regularity. From 1945 to 2008, periods of economic expansion have averaged some 57 months, putting our seven-year recovery squarely at the outer edges of a recessionary cycle.

Superficially, recessions are difficult to understand. As the population grows, so does the need for goods and services, which increases national output, or GDP. The increased economic activity causes businesses to employ more people, giving rise to increased household income. More money to spend only pushes the needle further into economic health, begging the question of why would it ever stop.

The trouble comes in when markets become oversaturated with goods and services, as profiteers rush to capitalize on the increased demand. Consumers can only buy so many new refrigerators, televisions and cars, and when the desire for consumption fills, demand falls. In an effort to remain profitable, employers begin to reduce salaries and lay off workers, and downward the economy begins to go.

It is no surprise then that there have been 49 recessions in our country's history, returning every few years with unwelcomed certainty. Academically, a recession is defined as two consecutive quarters of negative GDP. The National Bureau of Economic Research – the largest economic research team in the U.S., and organization formally charged with announcing the start of a recession – puts a finer point on the discussion. The NBER defines a recession as: "A significant decline in economic activity spread across the economy, lasting more than two quarters which is 6 months, normally visible in real GDP, real income, employment, industrial production, and wholesale-retail sales."

The nation's GDP for the second quarter of 2016 was a stagnated 1.4 percent. While this is far from a negative growth rate, GDP has been on a general decline since mid-2014, when output stood at a high of 5 percent. While not necessarily indicative of what will happen this go-around, it is interesting to note that in the second quarter of 2008 GDP had fallen to 2 percent, before plummeting to negative 8.2 percent later that year.

Equally interesting is consumer behavior in the housing market. The Composite Home Price Index shows that single-family home prices have steadily increased since the end of the last recession, reaching 2005 price levels, and just a tick below the 2006 peak. What is concerning, however, is that the home ownership rate (the percentage of homes that are occupied by the owner) has fallen dramatically to 63 percent, the lowest since the Index began tracking the data in 1965. By way of comparison, in 2006 nearly 70 percent of all U.S. homes were owner-occupied.

Also relevant to the housing market discussion are new home mortgage applications, which were down 6.9 percent in October. Housing starts (the number of new residential construction projects started) also slowed considerably in the third quarter of the year. With housing prices at 2005 levels, and consumer home ownership at an all-time low, it would not be a surprise to see a cooling of the market – particularly when GDP is on the downturn. Stated another way, now is not the time to buy.

Perhaps the biggest worrier of them all is the Consumer Price Index, the price paid by consumers for a basket of goods and services. As of September 2016, the Index measured 241 points – the absolute highest since the start of the Index in 1950 – meaning that we are now paying more for goods and services than at any time since the end of the second World War.

The average price of a new car today is $33,560, an average that has risen year-over-year for generations. In 2016 dollars, a new car in 1980 – the year Ronald Regan took office – cost an average of $21,413, or about 35 percent less than today. Perhaps as a result of increased prices, consumers are holding on to their new car purchases for a record 11.5 years.

In 2009, U.S. auto sales plummeted to 10.4 million, down from 16.4 million in 2006. The industry has come roaring back, hitting a seasonally adjusted annual rate of 17.8 million units this year. Yet, indicators suggest that this number may also begin to cool. Many automakers have experienced a decrease in sales from 2015, leading to large built-up inventories. This year BMW is down 5.2 percent; Ford is down 8.1 percent.

Car dealership profitability appears to be echoing this trend. On average, dealership profitability is down 2.9 percent from the same time period in 2015, and with most dealers carrying higher than normal inventory levels, further profit erosion will likely occur. Decreased profitability is reflected in a slowing of dealership acquisitions. Public company acquisitions of domestic dealerships fell from $1.5 billion in 2014 to $775 million in 2015, a downward trend that continues into 2016. Blue sky multiples are down as well, meaning that dealerships are worth less today, and owners will have a more difficult time trying to sell.

Sadly, the time has come for an economic chill. Too many indicators suggest that the recovery has moved on, and that the nation will soon experience a constricted economy. Fortunately, downturns typically mirror the expansions they follow, and if true, the next recession should be about as mild as the recovery recently experienced. The U.S. is still the undisputed economic leader, making up 29 percent of the world's economy; the time has just come for consumers to retreat, businesses to shutter, and the new regime to steward over it all.

CHAPTER 80

Texting and Driving:
Public Enemy No. 1

DECEMBER 2016

It has migrated from a menacing problem to a full-blown epidemic of national importance: Texting and driving is the single most deadly thing one can do behind the wheel of an automobile. For decades, scores of marchers repudiated drinking and driving, with full community support. Virtually every state has stiff intoxication laws designed to stomp out the practice, and jailing the minority who fail to comply. Yet, texting and driving escapes even base scrutiny, being treated as a mere annoyance, not the cold-blooded killer it is.

The National Highway Traffic Safety Administration classifies texting and driving as six times more dangerous than drinking and driving. In a recent study conducted by the NHTSA, it was concluded that drivers take their eyes off the road for an average of 4.6 seconds when sending or receiving a text. At 80 miles per hour that is the equivalent of driving 539 feet — or nearly two football fields — blindfolded.

The danger presented by texting and driving is certainly comprehensible, but the physics alone do not begin to reveal the magnitude of the problem. All but the biggest of sinners make a concerted effort to avoid driving while drunk, resulting in relatively few intoxicated motorists on the roads at any given time. The same cannot be said for texting.

Society's relationship with the smartphone has far exceeded convenient connectivity. Truth be told, users are increasingly developing a genuine compulsion for their smartphones, texting, Facebooking and gaming at every idle opportunity. A visit to any Starbucks illustrates the point, where consumers are unable to last four minutes without reaching for their phone, to be reunited with their cyberspace community.

The problem is that this relationship does not cease when the user gets back in his car. It is far too easy to check a text while driving, or start a conversation via text while at a red light. The triggers are constant, unleashing the compulsion to reconnect, much in the same way the smell of whisky can cause the sober to stray off path.

Not only is the compulsion present, but our rational ability to avoid the danger is biologically impaired. The University of Kansas recently conducted a study on the subject, and found that drivers have great difficulty resisting the cellphone temptation because the prefrontal cortex, the part of the brain responsible for decision making, is fully engaged by the task of driving.

Now consider the velocity at which cellphone use is occurring. Unlike drinking and driving, which is a danger to be sure, but infrequent in comparison to the number of drivers on the road, the number of drivers using their smartphones while driving is ghastly high. In a 2011 study, the U.S. Department of Transportation concluded that at any given moment 660,000 people — or nine percent of all motorists — are texting and driving on public roads. The number is far greater today, some five years later. In 2011, 93 million Americans owned smartphones. Today that number has rocketed to 207 million, meaning that nearly every driving citizen owns one.

Adding to the problem is the seemingly innocent nature of the practice. While few would make the decision to booze it up and then take the keys to the car, quickly checking or responding to a text seems hardly a sin at all. The net result of all this is that texting is not only six times more deadly than drinking and driving, but occurring at a significantly greater rate. It should be no surprise then, that by the end of the day another sixteen Americans will die at the hands of texting drivers.

And while the focus so far has been on private motorists, we should expect to see texting to bleed into public transportation, where a careless conductor endangers the lives of hundreds. If there is any question of this, consider the horror that ripped through a Tennessee community when a school bus driver killed three elementary school children, and hospitalized 21 more, with his quick reply to a text.

Given its rank danger, it is downright shocking that legislatures across the country attach little importance to the practice. In California, get caught driving in the carpool lane, disadvantaging compliant motorists, and receive a $480 fine. Endanger the lives of drivers everywhere by texting down the highway, and pay a mere $20 fine. In fact, four states — Arizona, Montana, Texas and Missouri — find the practice perfectly acceptable, seeing fit to not outlaw it at all.

In reality, compliance laws will have little effect on driver behavior. It is just too easy to quickly reply to a text, and too difficult to police, for laws to have any significant impact. The only solution is complete abstinence, which will never voluntarily happen in a world of smartphone addiction.

The proper solution is for smartphone companies like Apple, Samsung and Google to program their phones in a manner to prevent the practice from happening in the first place. The technology has been available for a while, begging the question of why the corporate giants haven't exercised a modicum of social responsibility in their quest for greater profit.

The solution is simple: block the cellphone from use (saving, perhaps, phone calls and navigation) when it begins travelling at a slow rate of speed, such as five miles per hour; and then don't let it resume normal use until it has come to rest for a sustained period, such as five minutes. The phones are already outfitted with GPS technology, which tracks rate of travel, and which could easily support the application.

Critics may point out that this unfairly punishes safe phone use in transportation, such as busses or trains. The solution is simple there too: allow users to bypass the lockout by manually typing in a message, such as "I am not driving." While some motorist will undoubtedly abuse the system, the masses, who are innocently sending a quick text, would not.

It is remarkable that phone makers have not already conceived of and implemented this simple fix, and indeed, used it as part of their selling pitch, much in the way breweries run advertisements pleading with party-goers to not drink and drive. Acknowledging the danger, and providing a well-crafted solution, would be a market gainer.

If the profiteers cannot find it within them to change their ways, Congress ought to show them the light by banning the use or distribution of any cellphone that does not contain a lockout system. The continued practice of juggling chainsaws has to stop, now, before more citizens unnecessarily die. The problem has surged; the technology is here; someone needs to take leadership and define the new era of smartphone use.

CHAPTER 81

Automotive Weaponry

JANUARY 2017

War used to be such a simple concept; tragic to be sure, but nevertheless fundamentally simple. A set of opposing troops would march toward one another, firing bullets into the faces of the other, with the last one standing claiming sovereign victory. War was always a matter of international politics — a dictator's attempt at a massive land grab, or an effort to impose the will of a society on the souls of another.

Today, conflict is defined by an entirely new set of rules that greatly complicate the discussion. The Islamic State group thrives on the element of surprise, with loyal followers engaging in suicide missions that kill and maim scores of the innocent. Historically, this meant using suicide bombers to inflict their terror, yet that is changing — and it should concern us all.

Twice last year, we saw attacks on the public were meaningfully different than any others that had come before. In July, a 19-ton cargo truck drove into a crowd of French citizens celebrating Bastille Day in Nice, killing 86 people and injuring 434 more. In December, another cargo truck was driven into a crowded Christmas market in Berlin, killing 12 and injuring 56. The Islamic State claimed responsibility for both attacks, saying that they were targeting "citizens of coalition nations that fight the Islamic State."

On the surface, the pair of events is concerning because it suggests a new, easier way of implementing terror. Driving a

337

truck into a crowd is easier than assembling a menacing bomb that could be detected or deploy improperly. On a deeper level, it is greatly concerning that the terrorist's regimes have stumbled on automobiles as a method of spreading their message.

What has begun as a crude act of driving a vehicle into a crowd can, and likely will, morph into a cyberattack on vehicles on a mass scale. Today's vehicles are more complicated and more advanced than ever before, each carrying an average of 100 million lines of code. As manufacturers make efforts to churn out autonomous or semi-autonomous vehicles, expect that number to jump to 200 to 300 million lines in the near future. As Mary Barra, the CEO of General Motors recently stated, "I fully expect the auto industry to change more in the next five years than it has in the last 50." And this is where the concern lies.

"White hat hackers" — those who work to identify security weaknesses in order to enhance overall security — have already proven that breaking into a car's computer is no difficult task. Those close to the industry will recall the publicized event last year where a group of friendly hackers placed a journalist in a Jeep Grand Cherokee to demonstrate how they could take over controlling the vehicle from a laptop thousands of miles away.

The Islamic State may be at the infancy stages of cyberattacks, but make no mistake about it, they have arrived. In April 2016, the Islamic State targeted 3,000 ordinary New Yorkers in a cyberattack, posting their personal information online and announcing, "We want them dead." The month before, an Islamic State group hacked into the New Jersey Transit Police website and obtained the names, home addresses, phone numbers and working locations of the officers, calling on its supports to carry out lone wolf attacks on the officers.

It is only a matter of time before the Islamic State — or another terrorist regime — begins attacking the interconnectivity of cars, reigning havoc on all. Reckoning back to the Jeep Grand Cherokee incident, imagine the destruction that could be caused if hackers simultaneously caused each Grand Cherokee to fully accelerate, while disabling the steering and brakes. Or consider the resulting damage if terrorists caused the vehicles to start in people's garages in the middle of the night, causing their house to fill with toxic exhaust. These scenarios are not that farfetched.

Mary Barra has recognized the concern: "The threat landscape is continually evolving, and sophisticated attacks are specifically designed to circumvent even the most robust defense systems. Whether it is phishing or spyware, malware or ransomware, the attacks are getting more and more sophisticated every day."

Counter-cyberattack company Security Mentor suggests that the auto manufacturers place "bug bounties" on their cars, offering rewards to anyone who can hack into their systems. The company believes that employing emerging hacking techniques is the only way automakers can guard against malicious intent. So far, manufacturers have been resistant to the idea.

Federal legislation will eventually join the conversation, but don't expect the cavalry to arrive soon. Sens. Edward Markey (D-Mass.) and Richard Blumenthal (D-Conn.), members of the Commerce, Science and Transportation Committee, introduced a bill called the Security and Privacy in Your Car (SPY Car) Act that would direct the National Highway Traffic Safety Administration and the Federal Trade Commission to establish federal standards to secure automobiles and protect drivers' privacy. The bill has languished in committee and died when the 114th Congress ended on Jan. 2.

Heraclitus of Ephesus, the pre-Socratic Greek philosopher, famously said, "If you do not expect the unexpected, you will not find it; for it is hard to be sought." As unfortunate as it is, we are all but a stone's throw away from the catastrophic implementation of a cyberattack on our vehicles of today and tomorrow. We cannot wait to create a defense after the carnage has occurred. We must act now, and expect the unexpected.

CHAPTER 82

The Mexican Standoff

FEBRUARY 2017

During his campaign trail, President Donald Trump blasted the North American Free Trade Agreement (NAFTA), calling it "the single worst trade deal ever approved in this country," and promising to either renegotiate it or break it if he was elected. At the center of his attack was the U.S. automotive industry, which has been sending manufacturing jobs to Mexico since NAFTA's introduction in 1994 at a dizzying rate.

The goal of NAFTA was to eliminate trade tariffs between the U.S., Mexico and Canada, providing for a North American super-pack of sorts, and reducing the price of consumer products by enabling production at the most economically viable location. After 13 years of implementation, the U.S. Department of Commerce indicates that U.S. exports to Mexico have increased by 93 percent, and imports from Mexico have risen by 190 percent. The disparity of even trade has resulted in a U.S. trade deficit with Mexico of $49 billion, causing consternation among some policymakers and many economists.

Trump promises to reverse this trend by leaning on companies to bring jobs back to the U.S., or face a 20 percent important tariff if they do not. Ford recently capitulated to pressure put on it during the 2016 presidential race by scraping its plans to build a $1.6 billion plant in Mexico, opting instead, reluctantly, to construct a $700 million plant in Flat Rock, Mich.

On the surface, the move looks like a win for the American people, and perhaps it will be. But a much larger question looms of whether the U.S. would be better off by having the automotive industry leave Mexico in favor of the U.S.

If we lived in a binary world, where cars were either black or white, the question might be easy to resolve. But in an economy that is confronted with a kaleidoscope of issues, the answer is considerably more muddled.

To begin, Mexico has been a contributor to the automotive industry for about as long as cars have been in existence. GM has been building cars there since 1921, Ford since 1925, and today the country produces cars for GM, Fiat Chrysler, Ford, Nissan, Honda, Toyota, VW, Mazda and Kia, making it the eighth largest automobile producer in the world.

On the most basic level, bringing the automotive industry home would mean closing the factories in Mexico and building new ones in the U.S. The billions it would cost to replicate the plants in the U.S. would be good for builders in the local economies, but consumers would likely experience the brunt of the blow, as the manufacturers pass the costs on through higher retail prices.

And while the sound of bristling activity has a nice ring to it, the Detroit automakers, who shuttered thirteen U.S. plants during the recession, aren't exactly clamoring to open new ones. All indicators are that U.S. car sales are expected to slow, after peaking in 2016 at 17.6 million, putting the billions it would take to transplant the seven Mexican factories at risk. Idling factories rank high as one of automakers' greatest concerns.

If the factories were built, the labor force needed to run them would be substantial. GM, Ford and Chrysler currently employ some 36,000 workers in Mexico at an average cost of $8 per hour. The same labor force in the U.S., controlled by the United Auto Workers Union, demands a wage of $58 per hour, yielding an annual payroll for the three manufacturers of $4.3 billion — or about $3.6 billion more than the $600 million needed to employ the same workforce in Mexico.

While the rust-belt, and to some extent the nation, would be well-served with the influx of $4.3 billion in payroll dollars, it is no small guess where the year-after-year increased payroll obligation will land. And that's the good news.

If automakers buck the system — as Toyota is promising to do — and refuse to withdraw their Mexican operations, a 20 percent tariff on imported vehicles would be disastrous for consumers. Car buyers should expect to pay thousands more for the same product than they previously paid.

But the discussion of a 20 percent import tariff has a finer point, even for cars built in the U.S. Today, factories are more of assembly plants than true manufacturing facilities, where thousands of integral parts — many of which are sourced in Mexico — are homologated into a finished product. The Chevrolet Silverado, built in Fort Wayne, Indiana, has more than 51 percent of its parts made in Mexico, begging the question of whether it is a "made in America" car at all.

Further complicating the matter is the new world order, where the tens of thousands of parts that make up a vehicle often come from multiple producers in different countries, traveling travel back and forth across borders several times. As Steve Arthur, an automotive analyst at RBC Capital Markets stated, "The free flow of components is integral to the supply chain in auto manufacturing." It is not a situation that can be easily or inexpensively reversed.

With parts making up two-thirds of a car's value, a border tax on parts sourced in Mexico would still lead to increased consumer cost, even if the cars are assembled in U.S. factories. Jim Lentz, CEO of Toyota North America, stated that the cost of the Toyota Camry, which is made in Georgetown, Ky., would increase by about $1,000 with a 20 percent border tax.

If a border tax is instituted, there is also risk that automakers will leave Mexico, but not necessarily come to the U.S. Adam Smith, the father of modern-day economics, would argue that automakers will run statistical comparisons, pitting high manufacturing costs of U.S. production against cheap labor, shipping expenses and import tariffs that would be realized by offshore assembly. With a cascade of opportunities in a globalized world, it is not certain that the U.S. would win that competition.

The Center for Automotive Research, a Michigan-based nonprofit, opines that "[a]ny move by the United States to withdraw from NAFTA or to otherwise restrict automotive vehicle parts and components trade within North America will result in higher costs to producers, lower returns for investors, fewer choices for consumers, and a less competitive U.S. automotive and supply industry." Whether that bears true remains to be seen, but one thing is all but certain: we are about to find out.

CHAPTER 83

Drive It Like
You Stole It

MARCH 2017

For some, ownership of a rare automobile is as enjoyable and relevant as possession of historically significant fine art. Though automobiles were conceived as a means of convenient transportation, the last century has laid witness to their migration into vessels of luxury, sport and collection.

Markets have responded accordingly. The most expensive Rembrandt ever sold at auction was "Portrait of a man, half-length, with his arms akimbo" — a stellar masterpiece painted in 1658, which sold to Steve Wynn for a cool $33.2 million. The most expensive Ferrari ever sold at auction was the 1962 Ferrari 250 GTO — one of 39 built, which was hammered at $38.1 million.

The collector car market has burgeoned into a highly specialized and exacting art form of sorts, not unlike the fine art industry, where historically significant assets trade for millions. And like the fine art industry, when lost treasures suddenly resurface, collectors rejoice.

One such event occurred last week, when it was reported that the famed Mustang that Steve McQueen drove in the 1968 movie "Bullitt" had been found, after having gone missing some 49 years earlier. As urban legend goes, Warner Bros. lost track of the car after filming was complete, giving rise to swirling theories of conspiracy.

The car was not insignificant, nor was the movie. The Bullitt Mustang has been one of the most sought-after missing vehicles for decades, eclipsed only by the Porsche 550 Spyder that James Dean was driving when he was killed. For the movie's part, in 2007 the Library of Congress selected "Bullitt" for preservation in the U.S. National Film Registry as being "culturally, historically, or aesthetically significant."

Experts believe that the Bullitt Mustang will sell for over $1 million at auction, which raises a relevant point: To whom will the money belong? The two car restorers who found the Mustang will undoubtedly claim ownership, and proceeds from the sale. Yet Warner Bros., the producer of the movie and the owner of the vehicle at the time of disappearance, will likely do the same. And what if an insurance company paid Warner Bros. for the loss in 1968; would it be entitled to the proceeds? And if it is, would it be the $2,500 it likely paid in 1968 for the value of the car (plus time-value of money), or the seven-figure purse that will undoubtedly be paid by the winning bidder?

A similar scenario was cast in what is considered the largest treasure recovery in U.S. maritime history. In the 1850s, Eastern Seaboard residents flocked to Northern California to capitalize on the nation's gold rush. With air and rail travel yet to be developed, steam ships were used to transport prospectors from New York to San Francisco to harvest the gold, returning them later to the east coast with their new-found treasures.

In September 1857, the SS Central America — one of the major gold rush transportation vessels — was caught off the coast of South Carolina in a category 2 hurricane, sinking the steamer, 500 souls and 30,000 pounds of gold. The sinking kicked off the "Panic of 1857" — the predecessor to the Great Depression and the first worldwide economic crisis.

For 131 years, the SS Central America and its treasure of gold laid 7,200 feet below the surface, at a depth thought to be unrecoverable. Yet in 1988, a team of scientists developed a submersible that could withstand the crushing atmospheric pressure at that depth, recovering the gold that had been considered lost forever.

The recovery was valued at $150 million, and with that a firestorm of litigation ensued. Thirty-nine insurance companies filed suit, claiming that they paid out $1.2 million in claims to the owners of the gold, and that they were entitled to the proceeds. The recovery team claimed that the gold had long been abandoned, that the insurance companies make no efforts to find it, and that they were the rightful owners.

After years of litigation, the U.S. District Court for the Eastern District Virginia ruled that the recovery team was entitled to 90 percent of the proceeds, with the insurance companies splitting the balance. Central to the court's reasoning was the fact that the recovery team spent "three frustrating years" and $10 million scouring the sea floor in search of the gold.

The SS Central America is not alone in determining the rightful owner of lost artifacts. In 2011, General William Lyon sold a 1935 Mercedes-Benz 500 K Roadster at a Pebble Beach collector car auction for $3.8 million. The car was one of 29 built, and was the centerpiece of the Mercedes-Benz display at the 1935 Berlin Motor Show before being sold to German industrialist Hans Prym later that year.

The car also had another important attribute: It had been confiscated by U.S. troops during World War II, and then shipped to the U.S. where it was sold on the collector car market. In 2012, however, a court in Hamburg, Germany, ruled that the heirs of Hans Prym had ownership rights to the seized vehicle. When Dutch car collector Frans van Haren, the

347

person who bought the car from General Lyon in 2011, brought the car to Germany for the Techno Classica collector car event, the Prym heirs were waiting with German police who impounded the car.

The event presents a perfect candidate for yet another bevy of litigation, where generations of buyers will try to unwind their purchase and recoup their loss. Yet with so much time having passed, success is far from certain.

Ownership of lost or stolen assets presents an interesting dilemma, with a trifecta of legitimate claimants vying for possession. And while the Bullitt Mustang has been found, many more are still at large. Quentin Tarantino's Chevy from the movie "Pulp Fiction," Sylvester Stallone's 1950 Mercury, and nine James Bond cars from the film "Spectre" are among those stolen and still missing. When and if the cars are found, many will rejoice and the process of determining to whom the treasure tolls will begin, once again.

CHAPTER 84

Generation Next

APRIL 2017

There once existed a time when our teenage youth dreamt wildly of the car they someday hoped to own, adorning their bedroom walls with posters of European exotics and American muscle. Getting your driver's license was as much of a rite of passage as any, exposing our budding generation to a cornucopia of opportunities, freedom and self-exploration.

The last century has seen a nation routed in cars, whether it be because of the enormous utility they provided or the visceral emotions they invoked. Lost legend James Dean was known as much for the Porsche he drove as the three films he started in, as is true with Elvis and his Cadillac, Steve McQueen and his Ferrari, and a long list of other A-list celebrities.

Yet something has changed over the last decade, as social media has upended America's love affair with the automobile. Millennials (those born between 1981 and 2000) have found a brave new world, hinged on constant connectivity and instant gratification. They don't drive to the mall to shop and socialize, because they buy everything online and connect through an increasingly complex web of social platforms. Talking in person — in fact, talking at all — has been supplanted by texting, messaging and Facebooking; and the fact that "Facebook" (and, for that matter, Google and Uber) has become a verb just about says it all.

Empirical data shows just how far the country has digressed from the automobile. According to the U.S. Department of Transportation, in 1978 50 percent of all Americans obtained their driver's license by the time they were 16; by 2008, that number had dropped to 30 percent. In a recent study conducted by Gartner, one of the world's leading information technology research companies, 46 percent of all those between the ages of 18 to 24 said they would choose internet access over owning a car.

Emerging platforms such as ride-share programs and autonomous cars are only serving to further the gap. To be sure, ride-shares and autonomous cars advance an enormous societal good. Ambulatory citizens and the elderly now have a convenient and inexpensive way to move about the world, and the number of drunk driving deaths that will be avoided will be staggering. Yet, for all their good, the advancements in technology have had a numbing effect on America's passion for the industry.

Of course, none of this means that cars won't be built, or that sales won't take place. As our population continues to grow, so too will our need for cars. Expect, however, that more sales will be made for the purpose of fulfilling the ride-share needs, or for driverless cars altogether.

So prevalent has this become that economists are now conducting modeling called the "mileage crossover point" — a determination of when it makes economic sense to no longer own a car, and rely solely on ride-shares. Data from the Federal Highway Administration shows that Americans take an average 534 trips per year in their cars, and log an average 13,476 miles per year, with an average commute of 25 miles. Using Southern California Uber (non-surge) rates, taking Uber everywhere would cost $18,115 per year.

Weighed against this is the average cost of mid-size car ownership for the same miles traveled, which as measured by the AAA, is $8,876 per year. Car ownership is clearly cheaper than using Uber for everything, but that conclusion begins to change as the miles driven is manipulated — hence the mileage crossover point. For Southern California, the crossover point is 6,500 miles, meaning that if you drive fewer miles per year than this, it is a better economic decision to avoid car ownership. As cars become more autonomous, avoiding car ownership will only become more attractive.

It is no surprise then that last month microchip giant Intel announced its plans to acquire the autonomous vehicle technology firm Mobileye for $15.3 billion — a purchase price that was 60 times Mobileye's earnings. Ford is also jumping in the game, having announced at the 2017 Detroit Auto Show that it will be shipping "level four" autonomous cars by 2021.

SAE International, an engineering professional association, has developed a six-tier scale for automated driving, with level zero being no automation and level five being full automation. Ford CEO Mark Fields compared the automotive industry to the film industry, noting that Kodak missed the opportunity to reinvent itself as a digital film company that would embrace mobility.

It remains to be seen whether Ford will reach its ambitious goal, but it is apparent that autonomous technology is quickly becoming the gold rush of the new millennium. Goldman Sachs has projected that the market for autonomous vehicles will grow from $3 billion in 2015 to $96 billion in 2025 and $290 billion in 2035. Boston Consulting Group predicts that by 2035, 12 million autonomous vehicles will be sold globally.

While most agree that our future will be filled with autonomous vehicles, the road to get there will be complicated and thorny. Last September, the Department of Transportation issued a federal policy that was to provide guidance on the testing and deployment of automated vehicles. Yet, the policy was far from federal law, leaving the states to themselves to regulate the industry.

States have begun exercising this authority, resulting in patchwork legislation throughout the industry, with no clear definable direction. California also passed legislation last fall that allows autonomous vehicle testing if conducted at specified locations and the if vehicle operates at specified speeds. In December, Michigan enacted the Safe Autonomous Vehicle Act, which prohibits any company who is not a vehicle manufacturer (such as Intel) from testing self-driving fleets in the state. In all, eleven states have passed laws regulating autonomous vehicles.

As Generation Z (those born after 2001) begins to age, one has to wonder if their relationship with the automobile will have any resemblance to relationship experienced by the generations who came before, or if they will even care. To be sure, times are changing, and that is not necessarily a bad thing, just different. As aptly stated by Alexander Graham Bell, "When one door closes, another door opens." Our door to the passionate relationship with the automobile is about to close; it remains to be seen what will be behind the next door that opens.

CHAPTER 85

Phantom
Stock

MAY 2017

Tesla, Inc. — the famed electric car company named after Serbian physicist Nikola Tesla — has done what many considered to be the impossible: It has become the most valuable car company in the nation. Last month laid witness to Tesla's stock surge to $314 per share, resulting in a market capitalization of $51.3 billion, and catapulting the company past valuations of both Ford and General Motors.

The accomplishment is no small feat. GM has been selling cars since 1908, and for 77 years it stood as the largest car manufacturer in the world. Ford was never far behind. Established in 1903, and having revolutionized industrial thinking with the invention of the assembly line, there once existed a time when one in every four cars sold in the U.S. was branded with the blue oval.

Yet none of that seems to matter, as Tesla has disrupted an industry that has enormous barriers to entry, and is steeped in tradition. Tesla had its public offering in 2010. The last American car maker to go public before that was Ford, in 1956.

The public financial climb that Tesla has accomplished is nothing short of miraculous. Its shares have rocketed from an initial offering price of $17 per share to eye-popping $314, meaning that an initial investment of $25,000 would have yielded a return of nearly $500,000. If we only knew when to invest.

Comparatively speaking, Tesla's stock price is way out of whack. GM, which is still the third largest car manufacturer in the world, trades for $34; Ford, ranked fifth in world order, sells at $11. To exemplify the point, consider that in 2016, GM sold 10 million cars worldwide. Tesla has sold 211,000 in its entire 14-year existence, making its annual vehicle production somewhat of a rounding error in real-world car making.

Then there is the matter of financial results. GM's operations yielded a 2016 net profit of $9.4 billion. Ford posted a 2016 profit of $4.6 billion. Tesla, which has never experienced a profit, stated in its 2016 annual report that it lost $773 million last year. What is worrisome is that the situation seems to be getting worse. The company's first public reporting indicates that it lost $82 million in 2008, and reporting's since then indicate that its losses have increased year-over-year, with only mild deviations (its best year was a loss of $74 million, and in 2015 it lost $889 million).

If that is not concerning — and it should be — the losses are looking to become markedly worse. Last November, Tesla completed its $2.6 billion acquisition of SolarCity, a California-based solar energy company started in 2006 by Elon Musk's cousins, Peter and Lyndon Rive. Musk claims that the move will create operational synergies with Tesla, but at what cost? Like Tesla, SolarCity has been losing money at an alarming, and increasing, rate. In 2012, the company posted a net loss of $64 million; last year it lost $820 million. Had Tesla and SolarCity been combined for all of 2016, they would have experienced a collective $1.6 billion loss.

Tesla is cognizant that its financial path may be thorny for time to come. In its 2016 annual report, it acknowledged that it had experienced significant manufacture delays, and noted that if it is unable to reduce manufacturing costs of the Model S and Model X, its financial condition "will suffer."

Not long ago, Reuters reported that Tesla loses $4,000 on every car sold, calling into play the age-old colloquial line that "it will make it up in volume." Tesla disputed the report, but publishing financial statements that are flooded with red ink is not confidence-inspiring.

If its financial picture is so bleak, why is it that investors are happy to throw money at it hand-over-fist? Some speculate that the company will become the dominant force in the alternative energy space. The thought is not all that crazy.

As of the close of the first quarter of 2017, Tesla was the second largest global pure electric car manufacturer in the world (after the Renault-Nissan alliance), a position it will not likely surrender. Not only has the company established a stronghold on the segment, but consumers seem to prefer to buy electric cars from industry disrupters, as opposed to established goliaths. This fundamental truism is all too well-known by industry giant Nissan, which put enormous effort into producing an all-electric car, the Nissan Leaf, only to find that it could not eclipse Tesla's sales.

And then there is the matter of the consumer satisfaction. Year-after-year, Tesla has been far outstripping the competition in consumer satisfaction surveys — a fact that is inexplicable, considering the enormous difficulty involved in mass producing a vehicle. In February, Consumer Reports named Tesla as the top American car brand. Its cars are just well made.

Yet, not everyone is bullish on Tesla's future. Last week, Merrill Lynch cut its price forecast on Tesla shares, opining that the manufacturer's "long-term viability" was at risk. Citing the acquisition of SolarCity as a major drag on Tesla's cash reserves, Merrill Lynch analyst John Murphy believes that there are "material risks to the longer-term viability" of the company. Merrill Lynch is recommending that investors avoid the stock, expecting the stock price to be cut in half over the next 12 months.

Other pundits are in accord, noting that because the company has never turned a profit, it isn't capable of having a P/E ratio, or price-earnings ratio, the typical yardstick used for valuing a company that measures its current share price relative to its per-share earnings. Ford has a P/E ratio of 7.5, while GM is 5.6. Using fundamental securities reasoning, GM is a better buy. Because a P/E ratio cannot be calculated for a company that has never turned a profit, Tesla doesn't even rank.

Whether we are witnessing a Tesla bubble — and, indeed, whether Tesla will even remain viable — is yet to be seen, but one thing is for certain: Elon Musk has succeeded in disrupting an industry that prides itself on being impenetrable. His product is well-received, well-made, and well on its way to creating a magnificent case study on how to accomplish the impossible.

CHAPTER 86

Oh, Snap!

JUNE 2017

Snapchat, America's latest internet darling, recently raised $3.4 billion in its public offering, catapulting the company past the high-watermarks previously set by tech giants Google ($1.6 billion) and Twitter ($1.8 billion). The March IPO, with its opening share price of $17, is just the latest billion-dollar stock spin-up of a young company that has yet to earn its first dollar.

The offering set the 5-year-old company's valuation at $24 billion — more than the value of Fannie Mae, AutoNation and Jet Blue combined. Yet while those companies posted a 2016 profit of $13.5 billion, Snapchat continuously drowns in a sea of red.

Under the stewardship of 26-year-old CEO Evan Spiegel, Snap Inc. has posted losses that would make even Tesla shudder. Soon after the close of its public offering, Snapchat posted its financial results for the first quarter of 2017, reporting a three-month loss of $2.2 billion. Wall Street was expecting heavy bleeding, but no one was prepared for this kind of carnage just one month after the company took billions from investors.

In truth, $2 billion of the loss was due to an orgy of stock-based compensation that was passed out to wild-eyed employees immediately after the raise, creating instant millionaires with other people's money, and setting the 20-something-year-old employees up for a lifetime of private aviation. Yet even after deducting the fast cash-grab, the company posted a first quarter loss of $188 million — a remarkable feat considering that the company manufacturers nothing and has only 1,859 employees.

Snap's losses have actually been mounting precipitously for some time. In 2015, it lost $382 million; in 2016, the loss was $515 million. This year, excluding the bundles of cash handed out to its employees, Snapchat is trending to lose a staggering $750 million, begging the question of whether it will ever earn a buck. Much of Snapchat's value proposition was its steady increase of end-users. Yet with each user it adds, it becomes significantly less viable.

And then there is the matter of Facebook. In 2013, Facebook's CEO Mark Zuckerberg made a run to buy Snapchat for $3 billion. Evan Spiegel rejected the offer, telling Zuckerberg in a personal letter that in a few years the company would be "dancing on Facebooks' grave." The response didn't sit well, launching an all-out mission to create a platform that would beat Snapchat at its own game.

In August 2016, Facebook (which owns Instagram) launched "Instagram Stories," an app that mimics Snapchat in several respects, including having pictures and video that disappear after 24 hours. The impact has been manifest. Snapchat closed the first quarter with 166 million users, but its rate of acquisition has begun to materially slow, raising serious concerns from investors who thought they were buying an increasing user base that would never end.

Just how bad is it? Drawing on Facebook's 1.9 billion users, Instagram Stories has become a virtual overnight success, amassing 200 million users in just eight months. And it gets worse. Facebook has also inserted the "Stories" feature into its main Facebook platform, as well as its WhatsApp and

Messenger platforms, leaving some wondering whether Snapchat will be able to withstand the assault.

When Snapchat isn't drawing criticism from Wall Street analysts, it is drawing fire from concerned parents everywhere, who have become gravely concerned about one particular feature of its app: the speed stamp.

Much of Snapchat's novelty has been the user's ability to overlay a picture with a particular filter, such as the time the picture was taken, the altitude where the picture was taken, or the speed the phone was traveling at the time of capture. And it is this last one that has turned deadly.

The majority of Snapchat's users are 18 to 24 years old, and some have begun the challenge of seeing how fast they can drive while taking a selfie, all so they can have the picture stamped with the vehicle's speed, impressing their friends with their wild-like ways. For those familiar with the app, the speed stamp almost invites recklessness.

In one instance, 18-year-old Georgia resident Christal McGee sped her Mercedes to 107 miles per hour so that she could take a selfie in front of her three friends in the car, before losing control and crashing into another driver. The crash-landed McGee in jail on felony charges, and put the other driver, Wentworth Maynard, in intensive care for five weeks with traumatic brain injuries. The event also put Snapchat at the center of a brewing debate about the social — and legal — responsibilities technology companies have with their products.

The Maynard family sued Snapchat, alleging that it knew its users were engaging in reckless driving with the speed filter, and that it was aware of prior accidents because of it. Earlier this year, the Georgia trial court dismissed the lawsuit, stating that Snapchat had immunity under the Communications of Decency Act of 1996.

The Communications of Decency Act was originally enacted in response to concerns about minors' access to online pornography, and has sense been expanded to provide federal immunity to any cause of action that would make an internet service provider liable for information originating with a third-party user.

The obvious application of immunity clause is, for instance, trying to sue Yelp for a negative review. In such instances, Yelp should enjoy immunity for a third-party's positing that it neither endorses nor supports. Failing to protect companies such as Yelp would serve to chill community platforms where information, both positive and negative, is freely exchanged.

Yet the mischief created by Snapchat is of a different cloth. Creating an app directed toward teens which offers — if not encourages — its young users to engage in knowingly reckless conduct is at the heart of irresponsibility. Yes, users need to act with responsibility, but we also need to be cognizant of the realities of youth, and hold companies responsible for creating foreseeable, or more appropriately stated, predictable, dangers to society. As the world enters a new era, the situation will not be getting better.

CHAPTER 87

Selling Cars
in Tomorrowland

JULY 2017

There are certain things that come around every once-in-a-while that change life as we know it. Businesses were never the same after having been introduced to the fax machine, unlocking a world of reviewing and signing documents in an instant. Apple's iPhone engulfed us in a creed of mono-communication, leaving a generation of citizens impervious to in-person social interaction. And now there is Uber.

Heralded for providing the convenience it offers, the full impact of Uber is far from realized – particularly in the automotive industry. At the young age of six, Uber has morphed into an industry-changing juggernaut, operating in 83 countries, and determined to alter humanity's ray of existence. Taking the natural progression of this to its logical conclusion, the impact on automotive makers and distributors will be manifest.

In truth, the automotive industry is currently experiencing a false sense of euphoria. Pundits celebrated last year when the industry recorded 17.4 million new cars sales in the U.S., leaping form the drudges of the Great Recession. The rise was notable. In 2009, the U.S. logged 10.6 million new car sales – or 300,000 fewer cars than were sold in 1965 – making the recovery look herculean.

Yet while we are far removed from the depths of the downturn, we are still short of a robust industry. To put it in perspective, consider that in 2000 the U.S. experienced 17.8

million new car sales. Now consider that, on a smoothed regression analysis, from 1965 to 2000 new car sales generally matched population growth. In 1973, the U.S. sold 14.6 million cars; in 1986, 16.3 million. Sales of 17.4 million in 2016 is not brag-worthy. Adjusted for population growth, the industry should be moving 20 million units a year – an uptick of 15 percent.

The industry could still be climbing back – and 2017 could be a banner year – but there is a larger issue looming of whether, on a long-term basis, the auto industry will ever be the same. While the impact is still in its infancy stages, it is nearly guaranteed that ride-share platforms will change the way the consuming public views car ownership.

Historically, save for densely populated metropolises, the industry relied on a one-car-for-one-person model. Unless there was a planned family outing, most motorists on the road have been sole commuters, driving the car they owned to the destination they chose. With ride-share platforms, however, vehicle ownership is becoming less necessary, as communities aggregate and share their resources.

So prevalent is the concept that economists have coined the term "mileage crossover point" – the point at which economists say one should avoid car ownership. Currently, the crossover point is 6,500 miles per year; drive fewer miles than that and taking Uber is a better deployment of your resources.

The break-even point for car ownership is still fairly low, which is why car sales have not fallen off the cliff; but it is not a far stretch to envision the mileage crossover point rising precipitously as ride-share technologies advance, reducing the costs for all. If, or perhaps when, the mileage crossover point reaches 13,747 miles – the average distance driven, as reported by the U.S. Department of Transportation – consumer buying behaviors will forever change.

Coupled with this is the fact that car prices have outstripped inflation year-over-year for quite some time, leading to serious affordability issues. In 1980, the average price car was $7,574. Adjusted to 2017 dollars, this average price of $22,847 dwarfs the average price currently experienced of $33,300. According to a study conducted by the financial service firm Bankrate, median-income households cannot afford the average price of a new car in 24 of the largest 25 U.S. cities.

This is not to say that car companies or dealerships will cease to exist, but the model will undoubtedly change. On the manufacturing side, expect car makers to invest heavily in autonomous driving and direct relations with consumers. State franchise laws prohibit automakers from simply doing away with franchised dealers, and selling direct to consumers, but as the industry fights for fewer sales, anticipate that manufacturers will maximize fleet sales to companies such as Uber, or attempting to service consumers directly with ride-share platforms of their own.

Dealership platforms will also change. The U.S. currently has 16,700 franchised car dealers, but as fewer cars are sold to fewer consumers, expect this number to change. Yet rather than pure abolition, the dealership model will likely convert to fewer franchises, but with stronger stakeholders and larger dealerships.

The change actually began some twenty years ago, when corporate rollups began buying single-point stores, resulting in large, publicly-traded franchise owners, such as AutoNation and Penske Automotive Group. Expect this trend to continue, as consolidated operations allow owners to combine administrative offices and negotiate better vender contracts.

The dealership models that will prove to be successful, regardless of size, will be those who embrace the change, shed non-value-adding functions and find ways to reinvent. To remain competitive, dealers will need to exude transparency and offer consumers an omni-channel, seamless experience at every pre and post-sale touch point. Redesigned infrastructures that allow for digital experiences with relationship-based sales consultants who focus on building trust relationships will be key.

Equally critical will be recognizing – and exploiting – unique partnership opportunities with emerging technologies that service the transportation industry, which go far beyond the mere sale or service of a vehicle. As consumers become less concerned with vehicle ownership and brand identity, surviving dealers will be those who recognize that customers are becoming utility-based, and will be making consuming decisions based on experience, ease of transaction and cost. Those who cater to this environment will conquer the brave new world.

CHAPTER 88

The Truth About Lithium

AUGUST 2017

Lithium – the natural resource mined from the Earth's crust – is perhaps the best-known commodity that people know the least about. Yet with multiple sovereign states betting their future on an industry bustling with electric vehicles, failure to understand the world's order on the non-renewable element could prove fatal.

Originally discovered in 1817 by Swedish chemist Johann August Arfvedson, and named after the Greek word "lithos" (meaning stone), lithium is a soft and highly-reactive metal, enjoying autonomic number 3 on the Periodic Table (behind helium at 2 and hydrogen at 1), making it the least dense solid element in the world.

Commercial production of lithium began in Germany in 1923, with its initial application in high-temperature grease for aircraft engines, before proving to be the central element in city-leveling hydrogen bombs. During the Cold War era of the 1950's to the 1980's, the U.S. became the world's leading producer of lithium; yet after the fall of the Soviet empire, commercial uses for lithium waned and production efforts plummeted.

As the U.S. Government sold off its stockpiles of lithium, it was believed that the metal's future had been relegated to the mundane application of ceramics, thermoplastics and pharmaceuticals. In 1991, however, Sony invented the lithium-ion battery and in doing so, unintentionally set in motion a series of events that would forever change the world.

Unlike conventional alkaline batteries that are non-rechargeable and limited in capacity, lithium-ion batteries capitalize on the element's highly reactive nature, creating energy storage that can be replenished and has superior holding capacity. Many believe that without the invention of the lithium-ion battery, the freedom created by laptop computers and mobile phones would never have been discovered.

Now, the batteries are serving as the backbone of the electric car industry, and our bridge away from reliance on foreign oil. Yet, while we are quick to lean on lithium-ion batteries as the surefire solution for all our transportation problems, few understand the macroeconomic analysis behind it.

In nature, lithium is never found in isolation (such as the way gold or oil may be); rather it is always combined with other elements that neutralize its reactive properties. As an element, lithium is highly flammable, corrosive to the skin, and reacts readily with air and water. Lithium deposits are generally strip-mined from brine pools and igneous rocks, before being chemically separated from their host elements.

The critical questions, however, are where does it come from, and how much exists? The U.S. Dept. of Interior reports that there are 14 million metric tons (a unit of weight equal to 1,000 kilograms or 2,205 pounds) of lithium in the world, and that it is primarily found in four countries: Chile (7.5 million metric tons), China (3.2 million), Argentina (2 million), and Australia (1.6 million). The U.S., by comparison, only has 32,000 metric tons.

The question then becomes, how much are we using, and how long will it last? In 2016, world lithium consumption was pegged at 37,800 metric tons; but expect that number to change dramatically as the automotive industry pivots from internal combustion engines to electric propulsion.

Tesla, for instance, presents an interesting case study. The budding automaker recently reported that it will need 27,000 metric tons of lithium – or about 70 percent of the world's production – to power its 2018 sales target of 500,000 electric vehicles. The report led company founder Elon Musk to state, "we would basically need to absorb the entire world's lithium-ion production" to meet its sales goal.

As others enter the market, demand for lithium will skyrocket, creating a lithium gold rush of sorts. And a shortfall. UBS Financial estimates that electric cars will account for 9.2 percent of global light vehicle sales by 2025, up from only 1 percent today, resulting in an anticipated annual need of 420,000 metric tons of lithium per year.

As demand-side economics begin to dominate, one should expect prices to surge. Recent history supports this conclusion: in 2012, lithium traded at $4,500 per metric ton; today the price has doubled to $9,100. And we are just getting started.

All of this is only relevant, of course, when compared to the other non-renewable natural resource we are running from: oil – the fossil fuel energy source controlled by the 12 OPEC nations. According to the Institute of Mechanical Engineers, there are 1.3 trillion barrels of proven oil reserve left in the world's major fields. If our use stays static at 35 billion barrels year, one should expect our oil supply to be depleted in 37 years.

Lithium tells a slightly less optimistic story. If we were to remain static at 2025 projected consumption levels of 420,000 metric tons per year – a highly improbably theory – our world lithium supply would deplete in about 33 years. If Bloomberg is correct in its prediction that by 2040 electric vehicles will reach a 30 percent market saturation, we will all be in for a wild ride.

The rush to lithium-energized cars presents an interesting comment on society, and how we respond to perceived crises. As unpopular as the truth may be, to calm the pain associated with our reliance on foreign oil, we traded one natural resource that was controlled by a group of 12, for another controlled by an oligopoly of 4 – and one in which China is a major player – with little thought given to the wild prices we will pay as the Earth's supply quickly diminishes.

This is not to say that electric cars are not the way of the future. They may be. But with each vehicle rolling off the assembly line, we are painting ourselves further into a corner of needing to find a new way of storing and harvesting the energy these vehicles need to operate – something we will undoubtedly do. Yet, the first step in that journey is recognizing that we have not found the magic bullet that will solve all our transportation energy needs. For now, place electric vehicles under the category of "work in progress."

CHAPTER 89

Autonomous Fear

SEPTEMBER 2017

The future is already here in many respects, at least as it relates to autonomous vehicles. While fully autonomous "level 5" vehicles are still some time out, scores of automakers are already introducing level 2 (partial driving automation) and level 3 (conditional driving automations) vehicles to the consuming public.

This year, the redesigned Cadillac CT6 will exhibit GM's new "Super Cruise" technology, a Level 2 autonomous system that will allow the driver to take his hands off the steering wheel in limited highway settings. The system uses a small camera located on the top of the steering column to track driver head position, signaling that driver input is required if the driver has turned attention away from the road ahead for too long.

The top of the hill, however, belongs to Audi, whose new A8 will be the first production vehicle with level 3 autonomy. At speeds of up to 37 miles per hour, the vehicle will accelerate, steer and brake on its own, without requiring the driver to take back control on regular brief intervals; when the vehicle can no longer ensure safe operation, such as in hazardous driving conditions or at higher speeds, the car will signal that the driver will have 10 seconds to take back control.

Audi claims that in 2020, it will introduce a level 4 vehicle, which will offer hands-free driving at posted highway

369

speeds, with the vehicle being capable of executing lane changes and passing cars independently.

On the face of it, the benefits of autonomous technology are tremendous. Aside from allowing multi-tasking and the transportation of ambulatory citizens, Audi claims that automated vehicles will eliminate 94 percent of accidents of all car accidents that are attributable to human error.

Yet the technology is not without incident. Many will recall the May 2016 incident where Joshua Brown, a former Navy SEAL, was killed when his Tesla Model S collided with a semitruck, while the vehicle was being operated in autopilot mode. The National Transportation Safety Board concluded that Brown was at fault, as he ignored seven warnings from the vehicle to retake control. But the incident underscores a manifest problem of consumers misusing — or misunderstanding — the limited nature of an "autopilot" system.

And there is a much larger issue looming. From a macro sense, autonomous cars operate on LIDAR (Light Detection and Ranging) technology, combined with other sensory-receiving devises, such cameras, radar and ultrasonic sensors. Here is where the problem arises.

In a series of white-hat attacks, hackers have demonstrated just how susceptible an autonomous car can be to a variety of attacks. In one of the most shocking incidents, researchers at UC Berkeley figured out how to hack self-driving cars by putting innocent-looking stickers on street signs. By calculating the algorithms used by a vehicle's LIDAR system, the researchers learned that strategically placed stickers on a stop sign tricked the autonomous car into reading the sign as 45-mile-per-hour sign.

What is most troubling about the experiment is the ease at which it was conducted, and the subtle nature of the intrusion. To the human eye, the stickers looked like harmless graffiti, not the LIDAR-jamming algorithms they truly were. And the experiment was not alone.

Other white-hat attacks include sending beams of light to the car's LIDAR system on the same wavelength that the LIDAR uses. With this, the hackers were able to erase stationary objects in the LIDAR's sensory output. In another attack, researchers captured the laser pulse emitted by a LIDAR, added delay, and then sent back a corresponding pulse using their own laser, causing the vehicle to think that objects were in its path when they were not.

Other researchers have shown that the inter-related cameras used by self-driving cars can be blinded by a series of LED lights, causing the vehicle to immediately stop; and still others have tricked LIDAR systems into believing objects are not present by wrapping them in acoustic dampening foam.

While much of the industry has, correctly, focused on the cyber-hacking of autonomous vehicles, crude, physical manipulation of LIDAR systems has gone largely unnoticed. And it is here, where countermeasures are perhaps the most difficult to employ, that the danger is the greatest. With every advancement in LIDAR and radar technology, hackers will try to find algorithmic ways to disrupt the system.

Counter-cyberattack company Security Mentor suggests that the auto manufacturers place "bug bounties" on their cars, offering rewards to anyone who can hack into their systems, with the hope of building more resilient systems. The current wisdom for countermeasures includes outfitting cars with redundant systems and employing random emitting signals.

Whatever the solution, the need is paramount, as terrorists' cells have focused heavily on using automobiles as methods of mass destruction. Few can forget the Bastille Day massacre that occurred in Nice last July, where 86 people were killed and 434 more injured when a 19-ton cargo truck drove into a crowd of celebrating citizens. Or the cargo truck driven into a crowded Christmas market in Berlin last December, killing 12 and injuring 56.

It has been said that technology has advanced more in the last 30 years than in the last two thousand, and perhaps nowhere is this more true than with the advancement of the automobile. The simple, yet reliable concept of an internal combustion engine being used to propel a family of four has morphed into a journey that not long ago would have been considered pure fiction. It is now up to us to prevent this advancement from being our ultimate transportation downfall.

CHAPTER 90

Will They
Ever Learn

OCTOBER 2017

Last week, Nissan added its name to a long list of automotive manufacturers who have been ensnared in public controversy over corporate malfeasance and the cars it sells to the consuming public. In an unprecedented move, Nissan announced that it was recalling every car it sold in Japan between October 2014 and September 2017.

At issue is an allegation that Nissan falsified inspection documents to make it appear as though its vehicles had been inspected by authorized technicians, when in fact they were not. Nissan will now have each recalled vehicle inspected by certified technicians, who will confirm that the vehicles are fit for public consumption.

The recall is the second incident of misconduct for a Japanese car company in as many years. Last year, Mitsubishi admitted that it published falsified fuel economy standards for 620,000 of its Japanese market vehicles.

Nissan's news comes as consumers are all but numb to automakers' admissions of non-truths. The levy first broke in February 2014, when GM admitted that it had been concealing a deadly ignition switch defect in its vehicles for 13 years. Public outrage reached a high-pitch tenor when it was revealed that GM elected to not correct the defect during the manufacturing process because it would have cost an additional $0.57 per unit. Dozens of consumers lost their lives because of the defect.

Since then, an onslaught of automakers have been caught concealing great acts of malfeasance. In 2015, the National Highway Traffic Safety Administration investigated 23 recalls conducted by Chrysler, covering some 11 million vehicles, and found that Chrysler violated the Safety Act in "every one of the 23 recalls." The agency found that Chrysler repeatedly failed to notify owners about recalls in a timely manner, provided the agency with false and misleading information, failed to timely repair defective vehicles, and obstructed the agency's statutory oversight. NHTSA issued a $105 million fine against Chrysler.

That same year, Volkswagen was caught outfitting its diesel cars with a complex software code that enabled the vehicles to detect when they were being subjected to emissions testing. Taking inputs from steering position and pedal movements, this "defeat device" detected when the car underwent emissions tests and manipulated the amount of nitrous oxide the vehicle emitted. In test mode, the vehicles were shown to be compliant; in real world driving conditions, however, the cars emitted as much as 40 times more pollutants. The malfeasance resulted in a $15 billion class action settlement.

2015 also laid witness to the Takata airbag scandal, where Japanese airbag manufacturer Takata admitted that it had known for 11 years that its airbags were prone to shooting shrapnel into occupants' faces upon deployment, but failed to issue a recall. When the recall was finally issued, 70 million airbags had to be replaced, creating "the largest and most complex safety recall in U.S. history." NHTSA responded to the concealment by imposing a $200 million fine against the airbag manufacturer — the largest in the governmental agency's 46-year history.

There are also a host of other less notable, but nonetheless extremely serious, acts of concealment, such as Honda's 2016 admission that it failed to report 1,729 death and injury claims to federal regulators between 2003 and 2014; or the admissions by Ford, Mercedes and Hyundai that they too misrepresented fuel economy standards for their vehicles.

Our recall system is organically simple. Once a manufacturer learns of a safety defect, it is required to initiate a recall and notify NHTSA within five days. It is then required to notify consumers of the recall within 60 days, and repair the vehicle within 60 days of a costumer's request for a fix. If the manufacturer fails to make the repair within this proscribed period, it is required to buy back the vehicle at the original purchase price, less depreciation.

The problem is that the system does not have a penalty for those who violate it. It is telling that in each of the situations referenced above, automaker officials felt comfortable enough to cheat in the first place. While our system does not necessarily encourage cheating, it does little to prevent it.

Until personal culpability becomes a part of the equation, we will never have a system free of deceit. The temptation to win at all costs is just too great, and the system gives the decision-makers all but complete immunity from severe forms of punishment — even though the harm they bring to others is life altering.

The Enron WorldCom financial scandals of the early 2000s resulted in the creation of the Sarbanes-Oxley Act of 2002. Under the act, senior executives take individual responsibility for the accuracy and completeness of corporate financial reports: Misstate a publicly reported financial statement, cause people to lose money, and you go to jail. Under the current automotive format, however, misstate the nature of your vehicle systems, cause people great harm including death, and face no personal responsibility

In 2015, Congress passed the Motor Vehicle Safety Whistleblower Act, bill introduced by Republican Sen. John Thune of South Dakota and Democratic Sen. Bill Nelson of Florida. The act allows employees or contractors of automakers, parts suppliers, or dealerships who report violations of federal vehicle safety laws to get up to 30 percent of any monetary fine over $1 million. Whistleblowers can expose any violation that originated anywhere in the world, as long as the vehicles or their components are sold in the U.S. The act also offers the whistleblowers the ability to act anonymously.

The Motor Vehicle Safety Whistleblower Act is a good start in shattering the glass culture of secrecy that has manifested in the automotive society for decades. But, it needs to be coupled with individual accountability by high ranking company officials, charged with overseeing the design, manufacture and recall of their vehicles.

NHTSA's recall system is seriously broken, and Congress needs to take this opportunity to overhaul it. Many a congressman have trumpeted their plans to introduce legislation to raise the fines that NHTSA can levy. Yet we don't need theatrical grandstanding; we need a visceral response to this abominable situation that is designed to stomp out this type of fraudulent conduct forever.

If an individual takes the premeditated act of recklessly endangering the lives of others, and people are killed, the individual would be tried for murder. This reckless disregard for human life should be treated no differently. The penalties for fraudulent conduct like this need to threaten the very existence of the infringing company, and subject its top management to criminal prosecution. Anything short of that will be injustice delivered.

CHAPTER 91

It's Harder Than It Looks

NOVEMBER 2017

This past summer, Tesla accomplished the unimaginable: It became the most valuable car company in the nation, surpassing both General Motors and Ford in total market value. With a market cap of $66 billion, Tesla stunned an industry that has high barriers to entry and is steeped in rich tradition.

By comparison, the numbers are jaw-dropping. GM, which has been producing cars since 1908 and is the third largest car manufacturer in the world, traded this past July at $35. Ford, which has been selling since 1903 and ranks fifth in world order, traded at $10. Tesla, however, which sold its first car in 2008, rung in the bell at an astonishing $395 per share.

The feat becomes even more miraculous when it is remembered that Tesla rolled out its public offering in 2010 at $17 per share. An investment of $25,000 would have yielded a return of $580,000. If we only knew when to invest.

The fact that Tesla ever became relevant is even a bit of an astonishment. The last American car maker to go public before Tesla was Ford in 1956, and that was only after it had successfully demonstrated sheer market dominance. Recall that there once existed a time when one in every four cars sold in the U.S. was branded with the blue oval.

What makes the matter all the more shocking is the company's lack of fundamentals. In 2016, GM sold 10 million cars and posted a profit of $9.4 billion. Ford raked in $4.6 billion. Tesla, on the other hand, has sold a little over 200,000 cars in its entire existence, and in 2016 posted a loss of $773 million.

So, why then have skilled traders been throwing throngs of investment-dollars at the company? Future prospects, presumably. After the successful launch of the low-volume Model S, Tesla announced its plan to produce a high-volume economy car that would rocket the automaker to respectable levels of legitimacy. And that's when the public went crazy.

At $35,000, the new Model 3 seemed like a sure thing. And if there was any doubt about it, the market put that to rest with consumers lining up to place $1,000 down to secure their place in line to receive one. As of the end of 2016, Tesla had received 664,000 deposits for the range-topping car, yielding $664 million of available cash for the company.

Now they just have to build it. And that's where things get interesting. The Model 3 went into production this summer at the NUMMI manufacturing facility in Fremont, California, with the highest of hopes. Elon Musk publicly stated that Tesla would be churning out 10,000 Model 3's per week by the end of 2017 (GM produces about 200,000 cars per week by comparison), and many pundits pegged Tesla's long-term viability on its ability to meet this goal.

Then reality set in. Musk has found that going from the low-volume Model S to a high-volume economy car is much more difficult than anticipated. How much so? As of the beginning of November, Tesla has only produced 260 cars — a far cry from the predicted 10,000 units per week.

Musk, who describes the situation as "Dante's Inferno," blames the catastrophe on the failure of suppliers to timely deliver parts, and he is probably right. But managing supply chain deliveries is the essence of a manufacturing process. In large part, car manufacturers are assemblers of a myriad of parts produced by a quilt-work of suppliers sprinkled throughout the world. A windshield wiper doesn't show up, and an entire assembly line can be idled for weeks.

The fallout from the calamity is now beginning to surface. Last month, Tesla fired 700 employees, resulting in a complaint being filed by the United Auto Workers. Then it announced its third quarter financial results, which were staggering — even for Tesla.

Historically, Tesla has been financially insolvent. The company's first public reporting indicates that it lost $82 million in 2008, and filings since then show that its losses have increased year-over-year, with only mild deviations. In its best year, Tesla lost $74 million. Last year, it lost $888 million.

Now, Tesla is in a financial freefall of epic proportions. It reported a third quarter loss of $671 million — or about a $7.5 million per day. All of this only adds to the company's shaky balance sheet. Last November, Tesla completed its $2.6 billion acquisition of SolarCity, a California-based solar energy company started in 2006 by Elon Musk's cousins, Peter and Lyndon Rive. Musk claims that the move will create operational synergies with Tesla, but at what cost? Like Tesla, SolarCity has been losing money at an alarming, and increasing, rate. In 2012, the company posted a net loss of $64 million; last year it lost $820 million. Had Tesla and SolarCity been combined for all of 2016, they would have experienced a collective $1.6 billion loss.

The market is now beginning to respond. While the market was bullish on the company when the Model 3 went into production, hiking the stock price to $395 per share, the recent news of production delays, mass firings and enormous financial losses has hit the company hard. As of the close of last week, the stock was trading at $306, resulting in loss in market cap of $15 billion.

There is not great reason for optimism inside the company's headquarters. According to S3 Partners, a financial technology company with $2 trillion in assets under management, Tesla is now the largest equity short in the U.S. and Canada, with short interest totaling $8.27 billion. Gene Munster, a former analyst at Piper Jaffray and now venture capitalist at Loup Ventures, predicts that Tesla will not reach profitability until the third quarter of 2020.

The question is will it make it? Certainly Tesla has been innovative, refreshing and engaging, but how much longer can it withstand quarterly losses that are nearing $1 billion? One thing is for certain, if Musk cannot find a way to get the production delays under control, Tesla will be remembered as that company that once-upon-a-time had a shot at greatness, but fell victim to the realities of moving into mass production. In truth, it's a lot harder than it looks.

CHAPTER 92

Will They Make the Turn?

DECEMBER 2017

There once existed a time when the financial question of the day was whether Tesla's stock would ever fall from its dizzying height of $395 per share. For a car company that only sold its first car nine years ago, and that has never turned a profit, it was a legitimate question.

Now the question has turned, with pundits asking whether the company will make it at all. Last month, Bob Lutz, former vice chairman of General Motors, issued a harsh criticism of Tesla, stating that its fixed costs are out of control, and the company "is going out of business." As the person responsible for development of such products as the Chevrolet Malibu, the Ford Explorer and the Dodge Viper, Lutz is not offering an uneducated opinion.

And there are many reasons to believe he may be right. Tesla's expenses have precipitously increased virtually every quarter over the last decade, ballooning to its present-day expenditure of $1 billion per quarter. Stated another way, Bloomberg recently conducted an analysis that, on average, Tesla has spent $480,000 every hour of the day over the past 12 months. At its current cash burn, Bloomberg predicts that Tesla will be out of cash by August 2018.

Tesla bet its financial future on the newly minted Model 3, the $35,000 consumer car that it expected to produce in great volumes. Demand for the product has been outstanding, with over 600,000 consumers lining up to give the company a deposit of $1,000.

Now, the company just has to make them, and that is where the problem has arisen. As Tesla has discovered, moving from production of the low-volume Model S to the high-volume Model 3 has proved to be substantially harder than expected.

When production of the Model 3 began this past summer, Tesla anticipated building 10,000 units per week by the latter part of this year. Yet, in October the company only built 180 units for the entire month, blaming production delays on suppliers who failed to timely deliver. Whatever the case, the products are not rolling off the assembly line, and without vehicles being delivered, sales revenue will not be coming in.

And for the products that are being built, the vehicles are plagued with quality problems. In a recent interview that Reuters conducted with nine Tesla factory workers, problems ranged from doors not closing, to missing interior trim, to water leaks and the like. Approximately 90 percent of the vehicles that do actually make it off the line are revealed to have quality problems in final inspection. Toyota quotes a defect rate of 10 percent. A report titled "Beyond the Hype" by JD Power opined that the vehicles were "not competitive" in the quality of build, and lacked "precision and attention to detail."

The competitive landscape is also beginning to change. When Tesla first made its splash, a new economy-old economy struggle began to emerge. iPhones were in; conventional thinking was out. Yet while Tesla has been the Cinderella of the party, with seemingly untouchable public support, the titans of the industry are beginning to catch up.

Last week, GM held a media-packed demonstration in San Francisco of its new all-electric autonomous vehicle, the

Chevrolet Bolt. Proving that a goliath like GM can still be entrepreneurial, the automaker unleased a bevy of autonomous Bolt vehicles on the streets of San Francisco, to media delight.

Yet Tesla is no lightweight in product development, to be sure. Last month, amid reports of its production woes, Tesla announced that it was introducing two new vehicles: the Tesla Roadster and the Tesla Semi.

The Roadster is a $200,000 luxury sports car, which Tesla claims will be the fastest production car on the planet. With a 0 to 60 time of 1.9 seconds, the car would set the industry ablaze and be the new benchmark to beat. If they can build it. It is one thing to claim it, but it is quite another to do what storied supercar manufacturers — including Ferrari, Porsche and Lamborghini — could not do.

Tesla's other new product, the Semi, is just as interesting, and equally as ambitious. The company claims that the Semi can accelerate from 0 to 60 in five seconds flat, can carry a load of up to 80,000 pounds, has a range of 500 miles, and can travel up a five percent grade with a max load at 65 mph, compared to a conventional diesel truck that can travel 45 mph. Again, if they can build it.

Tesla boasts that the Semi can be charged in 30 minutes with its new "megacharger." But the devil is in the details. One of Europe's leading energy consultancies, Aurora Energy Research, has analyzed the data released by Tesla, and determined that for the megacharger to work, it would have to provide power that is ten times more powerful than Tesla's current network of "superchargers." To put the mission into context, Aurora Energy Research concludes that this is the equivalent of providing power for 3,000 to 4,000 homes. All through one cord.

The claims sound great, but for a company that is not currently capable of producing a $35,000 car without water leaks, setting the world on fire with this type of earth-shaking technology might be hatched in a den of fiction.

And one has to wonder if the announcements (and claims) have much to do with Tesla's emerging need for gobs of cash. To stand in line for the Roadster, you have to have a $45,000 check in hand, and to lay a deposit for the Semi, you will need to shell out a $20,000 deposit. If nothing else, it makes one wonder if the company is trying to finance its massive expenditures by taking customer deposits. After all, this is the same company that is currently holding over $600 million in customer deposits for the Model 3.

Whether Tesla will turn the corner remains to be seen. One thing is for certain, however; the bloom is beginning to fall off the rose, and Tesla is learning just how difficult it is run with the big dogs, and why many just stay on the porch.

CHAPTER 93

Electrifying!

JANUARY 2018

This week, the 51st rendition of the Consumer Electronics Show will rain down on the desert, Las Vegas style. Originated in 1967 as a small offshoot of the Chicago Music Show, CES has blossomed into the largest convention Las Vegas holds, by a long shot. With 2.4 million square feet of convention floor space that will squeeze in 180,000 attendees in just four days, CES has become the place to be for our technology-rich world.

The show has laid witness to all sorts of firsts. Members of Generation X will remember with a chuckle the Atari Pong game, which debuted at CES in 1975. Then there was the VHS (1977), the camcorder (1981), the CD player (1981), the DVD (1996) and the Xbox (2001).

Today the electronics show has as much to do with modern day transportation as gaming, as car makers traverse convention and explore a new way of thinking automotive. It used to be that car launches were reserved for spotlight national auto shows. Now, automakers are flocking to CES at unprecedented rates, bringing with them a cadre of electric, autonomous and connected vehicles to display.

So large is the electric vehicle presence, that CES has created a "Vehicle Technology" section of the show, with a dedicated 297,000 square feet of exhibit space. This year, automotive exhibitors are up 23 percent over the 2017 show, powered by forward-thinking manufacturers that want to capitalize on the new world order.

The curious proliferation of automotive manufacturers to an "electronics show" only serves to underscore the position non-traditional cars are taking in our society. In 2010, electric vehicles were a rogue experiment, backed by optimism and high hopes. Now they are a proven technology, redefining the way we think and act about transportation — all at an exploding rate.

In 2015, 1 million electric vehicles dawned our national and international highways. A year later that number doubled, challenging anyone to name another industry that experienced a 100 percent market increase in just 365 days.

And, in truth, the veneer has yet to even be scratched. With all of their hype and impressive numbers, electric cars still only make up 0.2 percent of the total passenger light-duty vehicles in worldwide circulation. Experts in the industry predict that electric vehicle registrations will hit 70 million by 2025 — a 3,500 percent increase in market penetration just seven years from now.

Just how high will it go? The International Energy Agency, a coalition of 29 countries established in 1974, predicts that by 2060 the world will have 1.2 billion electric cars in circulation. To be sure, early adopters of the concept will enjoy market advantages much in the same way J. Paul Getty capitalized on oil exploration in Saudi Arabia before the rest of the world caught on. Visionaries frequently eat well.

Much of the segment's success has to do with global policy on improved environmental citizenship. The 2015 Paris Agreement is but one example. Adopted by 172 countries, the Paris Agreement seeks to stop global warming by limiting the increase in the global average temperature to pre-industrial levels. The electrification of transport plays a large role in achieving the reversal of increased world temperature, by decarbonizing our energy system.

The U.S. is demonstrating that it is committed to the cause. In 1974, the U.S. enacted the Corporate Average Fuel Economy (CAFE) standards in response to the 1973 Arab Oil Embargo that nearly choked out our national economy. In an effort to rid ourselves of our dependency on foreign oil, the Department of Transportation required manufacturers of vehicles sold in the U.S. to achieve an average of 18 miles per gallon, across all models sold on domestic land.

The CAFE averages have increased throughout the years, with the current average requirement set at 35.5 miles per gallon. In 2011, however, President Barack Obama doubled-down on alternative fuel transportation, requiring manufacturers to achieve an average of 54.5 miles per gallon across their line-makes by 2025.

It is widely understood that automakers will be unable to achieve the heightened requirement using internal combustion engine technology, all but sealing the fate of having electric cars become an integral part of our transportation architecture. Adding to this was President Obama's 2016 proclamation to accelerate the deployment of electric vehicles and charging-station infrastructure.

In a program backed by $4.5 billion in loan guarantees, the Department of Transportation is establishing a robust network of electric vehicle charging stations on 48 of the nation's 55 interstate highways, covering some 25,000 miles of traveled land. In conjunction with this, 24 state and local governments are committing to procure electric vehicles in the fleet operations.

Given the electric vehicle's position in our automotive ecosystem, it is perhaps no surprise that electric car manufacturer Tesla has become such an overnight sensation, leading to all kinds of surprising riches. At the latest count, Tesla enjoys $56 billion market cap, catapulted by a dizzying stock price of $326 per share. To compare, Ford — the company founded in 1903 that is largely responsible for the modern-day assembly line — sits with a market cap of $52 billion and a sagging stock price of $13.

What exactly has Tesla achieved? Nothing, to be quite blunt about it, other than awaken a society to all that is possible with a different way of thinking. Tesla is pacing to lose about $1 billion per quarter — or about $480,000 every hour of the day — yet investors are throwing money at it in a way that would make a drunken sailor blush.

The success of Tesla, in the face of its financially disastrous performance, only serves to underscore the enormous opportunity that exists for those who think different and challenge convention. With a 0.2 percent market saturation, the electric vehicle segment is bristling with opportunity — and the forward thinkers who are raining down on CES with their think-different vehicle technology will be the ones who take the day.

CHAPTER 94

The Future
of Privacy

FEBRUARY 2018

It all started with Cadillac really. In 1996, General Motors introduced the Cadillac OnStar system — an onboard communication system that linked active drivers with a GM call center — and with that the world of consumer privacy forever be changed. The OnStar system was a road paved with the best of intentions. Drivers could get hands-free, turn-by-turn directions or call for dinner reservations, and in the event the vehicle's airbags deployed, the call center would automatically dispatch emergency units.

Yet with the development of this technology a national debate ensued, which has now been two decades in the making. What started out as seemingly benign has turned into anything but, as analog motoring steps aside in favor of the digital era. Connectivity was initially defined as unobtrusive baseline communication between motorists and call centers. Now, however, connected cars often know more about drivers than their spouses, as every movement, every stop is digitally recorded.

To put the issue in perspective, consider that the first space shuttle contained some 500,000 lines of software code. Today, the average 2018 automobile contains 100 million lines, all of which are working together to transmit information to the automakers who created them. At present, 78 million cars are embedded with a cyber connection. By 2021, technology research firm Gartner estimates that 98 percent of all cars will be connected. Like to stop by Starbucks at 8:15 every morning? Your car will know it — and so will its manufacturer.

And therein lies the issue. To whom does this private information belong? Presently, no U.S. laws govern the ownership, storage or use of data collected on motorists' behavior. In 2014, 19 automakers issued a pledge to the U.S. Department of Transportation, promising self-governance on how private motoring data collected would be used. Under the Privacy Principles for Vehicle Technologies and Services, manufacturers promised to restrain from selling motorist data to third-parties absent consumer consent. What the pledge doesn't reveal, however, is that most manufacturers request and obtain that consumer consent in fine print buried deep in purchase agreements, leading to a real lack of appreciation as to the digital relationship that exists.

If there is any question on how this information is being harvested and used, Israeli startup company Otonomo seems to provide the answer. The self-proclaimed "first connected car data marketplace," Otonomo has been leading the charge to monetize motorist data. Currently, nine car manufacturers give Otonomo access to their raw data, who then analyzes its, packages it and sells it to third parties, sharing the profits with the automakers.

And don't expect this business model to slow. Automotive giant and parts supplier Delphi recently invested $25 million in Otonomo, hoping to capitalize on the wide-open market selling consumer data for substantial profit. To be sure, it is not lost on automakers that selling consumer data is 100 percent margin, while turning new cars is a still single-digit margin game.

Exactly how invasive will the practice be? Motoring data will allow manufacturers to create a behavior fingerprint of sorts on each consumer, giving merchants the ability to market to individual consumers with known behavior. Make a trip to Taco Bell every week? Don't be surprised to see your inbox fill up with advertisements from south of the boarder.

While the peddling of some behavioral data might register as merely annoying, one could imagine a host of scenarios that invade much further. For instance, what of the motorist who secretly makes a trip to the HIV clinic each week, expecting his health concerns to be known only to him? The clinic is bound to secrecy by the federal privacy rule known as HIPAA, but collected motoring data is free to be sold to the highest bidder. Or how about consumer data that could be sold to insurance companies, who will know now exactly how often you speed, how frequently you wear your seatbelt, and how far you drive every day. At best, the leakage of such private information could be galling; at worst, the selling of personal behavioral data could be seriously disruptive, or even life-altering.

And then there is the matter of security. According to the book "Code Complete" by software expert Steve McConnell, the best software companies can push programing errors down to about 0.5 bugs per 1,000 lines of code. If true, this means that the typical new automobile has approximately 50,000 bugs, raising the question of how secure is data, and what happens in the event of a breach? Students of history will remember the 2015 recall of 1.4 million Jeep vehicles, after white-hat hackers demonstrated that they could take over operation of a Jeep Cherokee from a laptop located some distance away.

Privacy concerns in the automotive sector are nothing new, and in fact legislation has been enacted to address other areas of confidentiality. The Driver's Privacy Protection Act of 1994 regulates the disclosure of personal information contained in the records of state motor vehicle departments, while the similarly named Driver Privacy Act of 2015 covers ownership of data recorded by monitoring devices, such as a vehicle's event data recorder.

There is hope that an answer will soon evolve. This past June, the Federal Trade Commission and the National Highway Traffic Safety Administration hosted a workshop on the issues of privacy and security in connected cars. Yet as with most technology issues, the advancement of computing expertise far outstrips the evolution of appropriate legislation.

Without question, the technology present in connected cars is not just convenient, it presents an enormous overall societal good. A 2015 study commissioned by the global management firm Boston Consulting Group revealed that driver assisted technology can help avoid 28 percent of all of today's automobile accidents, preventing approximately 9,000 fatalities per year, and saving $250 billion in societal costs annually.

The answer to the riddle is not to quell automotive advancement, but to harness it in a way that can allow its powerful benefits to be employed, while maintaining a reasonable level of confidentiality in the data harvested. We are close, but until federal regulation controls profiteering manufacturers, we will all be at risk of having our every move monetized on the open market.

CHAPTER 95

A Bit More
Than a Coin

MARCH 2018

There once existed a time when technological advances brought us "amazing" inventions, like the microwave oven or the cordless phone. In the day, it seemed as if life suddenly moved from a gray-scale existence to a two-dimensional kaleidoscope of colorful brilliance, as fax machines, cable TV and portable cassette players dazzled consumers by the millions. Against the backdrop of the horse-drawn carriage, such innovation seemed simply mind-blowing.

Today, the curve of societal advancement is practically vertical, exponentially multiplying itself with every fortnight that passes. Our present-day Generation Z youngsters chuckle at concepts that society used to consider ground-breaking, as they board a well-fueled bullet train into the mysterious future. To be sure, analog thinking will never be revived.

If technology can be compared to a metaphoric speedboat, then bitcoin is madman behind the wheel. A modern form of currency, bitcoin is a snippet of code that represents ownership of a digital concept, allowing consumers to send and receive payments without passing through a central authority. Unlike traditional fiat currency, where governments and central banks can issue as many units as they want, bitcoin is tightly controlled by an underlying algorithm formula that allows a small number of new bitcoins trickle out every hour until a maximum of 21 million units has been reached.

The consuming public is consuming bitcoin in ravenous fashion. When the cryptocurrency was introduced in 2010, it traded at $0.08 per coin. By December 2017, the price had skyrocketed to $19,800 per coin — a 25 million percent increase — before settling down to its current price of $9,500. If we had only known then what we know now; a $40 early investment in bitcoin would have produced a freshly-minted billionaire.

Bitcoin is based on a concept called blockchain technology, an electronic ledger of sorts created in 2008 by a person or group known as Satoshi Nakamoto. A blockchain is a series of electronic records, or blocks, that are securely linked together using a cryptograph method, a mechanism of constructing and analyzing protocols that prevent third parties from reading private messages. Information contained in blockchains cannot be altered in any way, creating a safe haven for all sorts of private data.

Blockchain technology is advancing so fast that in 2014 we migrated to its second-generation application, a remarkable statement given that much of the consuming public was not even aware its first. As reflected in a paper from the Economist, the second-generation blockchain is "a programming language that allows users to write more sophisticated smart contracts, thus creating invoices that pay themselves when a shipment arrives or share certificates which automatically send their owners dividends if profits reach a certain level."

Marveled by its endless applications, the automotive industry has emerged as a front-runner in adopting blockchain technology. In supply chain management, where success or failure lives on the edge of just-in-time delivery, blockchain implications can harmonize individual stages of manufacturing, bringing plant-wide efficiency. Automobile production facilities have traditionally homologated a myriad independent sub-manufacturing processes, culminating in a single finished product. With blockchain technology, these islands can be efficiently managed, maximizing efficiency and reducing waste. Blockchain has the ability to be as revolutionary to the manufacturing process as Henry Ford was to the assembly line.

And Porsche is committed to bringing the technology mainstream. In a pilot program, Porsche is testing blockchain's impact on the interconnectivity of cars and the storage of sensitive consumer behavioral data. Noting that traditional central servers can be hacked, Porsche believes that the security blokchain brings to the discussion is revolutionary.

As a for instance, in its new Mission E full-electric car, Porsche is exploring the possibility of having the vehicle digitally sign a roaming contract to recharge its battery wirelessly, all while handling the subsequent payment itself. Porsche has also developed an app that will allow the consumer to unlock its car in 1.6 seconds — six times faster than current technology that uses a centralized server. There are also other possibilities, such as having the car pay tolls, parking fees and other charges itself.

Idom, one of Japan's largest used car automotive groups, has partnered with the country's largest cryptocurrency exchange Bitflyer to enable bitcoin payments at its dealerships across Japan. So far, 26 dealerships have started accepting bitcoin payments, with another 550 locations to be added.

Equally as far reaching is the global blockchain company Uservice, an automotive service provider aimed at created an ecosystem for the life of a car. Currently, car ownership and service is highly fragmented, with certain ambiguity over whether the car has ever been in an accident, whether the vehicle has deferred maintenance and supplying banking and insuring needs.

Uservice aims to change all of this by optimizing all processes related to the purchasing, operation and maintenance of a car. Combining a large number of dealers, car service providers, insurance companies, financing companies and suppliers of spare parts, Uservice hopes to create one single, secure chain for the life of each vehicle, eliminating questions of vehicle history and streamlining the ownership process.

Auto-sharing is also likely to be affected by blockchain technology. Ernst & Young recently announced that it is launching a blockchain-based system that will enable companies or groups of individuals to more easily share vehicle ownership. Recording vehicle ownership, logging the use of vehicles, and apportioning insurance costs and other transactions among a group of owners could change the way we approach owning a car.

Blockchain technology is about to revolutionize our lives, much in the same way personal computing changed the speed of commerce. There will be some confusion and discomfort for sure, but in the long run crypto technology change the way we interact with the world in which we live, bringing with its secure streamlined processes that centralize acres of independent data.

CHAPTER 96

Development
in Progress

APRIL 2018

Last month, two U.S. citizens lost their lives to autonomous vehicles: Elaine Herzberg, who was struck by a self-driving Uber in Tempe, Arizona and Walter Huang, whose autonomously driven Tesla Model X hit a freeway concrete divider in Mountain View, California. The two incidents ignited a fiery debate on the issue of autonomous vehicles, and their appropriateness for 2018 consumption.

The first autonomous fatality was in May 2016, where Joshua Brown, a former Navy SEAL, was killed when his Tesla Model S collided with a semi-truck, while the vehicle was being operated in Autopilot mode. The two recent fatalities have only served to underscore how far we still have to go.

Officially, the National Highway Traffic Safety Administration has created five categories for self-driving technology: Level 1 (hands on), Level 2 (hands off), Level 3 (eyes off), Level 4 (mind off) and Level 5 (steering wheel optional). Presently, most carmakers that offer autonomous features, such as Tesla's "Autopilot," are Level 2 technology. For instance, the redesigned Cadillac CT6 will introduce GM's new "Super Cruise" technology, a Level 2 system that will allow the driver to take their hands off the steering wheel in limited highway settings.

Audi claims that its new A8 will be the first production vehicle with Level 3 autonomy. At speeds of up to 37 miles per hour, the vehicle will accelerate, steer and brake on its own, without requiring the driver to take back control on regular brief intervals; when the vehicle can no longer ensure safe operation, such as in hazardous driving conditions or at higher speeds, the car will signal that the driver will have 10 seconds to take back control. The company claims that in 2020 it will introduce a Level 4 vehicle, which will offer hands-free driving at highway speeds, with the vehicle being capable of executing lane changes and passing cars independently.

Autonomous technology undoubtedly presents a score of societal goods. Ambulatory and infirm citizens can finally experience freedom in the way that most take for granted. And, in theory, roadways filled with self-driving cars would reduce accidents by removing human error from the equation. Traffic would also be conceivably thinned, as connected cars communicate with one another, eliminating the lag time inherently embedded in traditional motoring.

Yet, advancement comes at a cost. Autonomous driving is far from perfected, and nirvana is quite some time away. Tesla claims that if you are driving a car equipped with Autopilot hardware, you are 3.7 times less likely to be involved in a fatal accident. Yet, this statement appears to be based on fuzzy math.

In this comparison, Tesla compares its Autopilot crash rate to the overall U.S. traffic fatality rate — which includes bicyclists, pedestrians, buses, and semi-trucks. Using a more appropriate apples-to-apples comparison of the fatality rate for passenger cars and light trucks compiled by the Insurance Institute for Highway Safety, the Tesla Autopilot driver fatality rate is almost four times higher than that of a typical passenger vehicle.

The recent Uber fatality in Arizona provides an understanding as to why. Autonomous vehicles generally operate using lidar (light detection and ranging) systems. Using rapid pulses of laser light, and measuring the amount of time it takes for each pulse to bounce back, lidar systems paint a 3-D picture of the world around it. Yet, even the best lidar systems work a bit like the game Battleship; the laser pulses have to land on enough parts of the object to give an understanding of its shape. This can be particularly difficult for if the vehicle is moving at high speed, or if an object is moving perpendicular to the vehicle, as was the case with recent Uber fatality.

When struck by the autonomous Uber vehicle, Elaine Herzberg was walking her bike in a wide-open roadway, perpendicularly to the vehicle that hit her. Video footage from the event shows that the car did not brake or steer away from pedestrian. The fact that the vehicle's lidar system failed so dramatically reveals just how infantile the technology is, despite society's wishes to the contrary. The hard truth is that lidar systems are just far less likely to detect objects that are moving perpendicularly to a vehicle than the average human.

Then there is the matter of driving too perfectly. Until we have a system that is thoroughly homogenous, we will suffer with having motorists with differing intentions: Humans will want to get to their destination as quickly as possible, while being moderately safe, and fully autonomous vehicles will want to be fully compliant with motoring laws. Self-driving cars will make complete stops at all stop signs and drive no faster than the posted speed limit. The problem is that no one else does.

According to information maintained by the California Department of Motor Vehicles, autonomous vehicles have been involved in 66 accidents since 2014, most of which occurred because the vehicles were driving too safely.

Companies involved in developing self-driving cars are trying to determine how to make autonomous cars integrate better with their human-operated counterparts.

Yet, this is a riddle without an answer. Carmakers can never develop an autonomous car that intentionally speeds or roll stop signs. If a citizen were to be killed by an autonomous vehicle that was designed to break the law, the manufacturer could bet its bottom dollar that it would be facing a stiff award of punitive damages. No company with a care of self-preservation would ever put themselves such a compromised position.

Until we have roadways that are all autonomous, we will continue to blend cars operated with human judgment with ones who operate true to their petri dish beginnings. And disaster of various degrees will persist. Autonomous technology is far from perfected, but the end result will benefit generations who have yet to even be conceived. Elaine Herzberg and Walter Huang were unfortunate casualties in the necessary road to technological perfection. And they unfortunately will not be the last, but in the end it will be a road worth traveling.

CHAPTER 97

The Long and the Short of It

MAY 2018

Electric car manufacturer Tesla has been called many things: a newcomer, a disrupter, a game-changer, and among many others, the company that revolutionized an industry not fond of revolution. And while receiving all of these well-deserved accolades, it is equally deserving of another descriptive title: financial catastrophe.

This month, Tesla released its 2018 first quarter financials, with horrid results. In the first three months of the year, Tesla managed to lose another $784 million, drawing question as to how much longer the company can tiptoe through the raindrops before landing squarely in the middle of an ink-red puddle.

In 2017, the carmaker lost $2 billion as it struggled to get its low-cost Model 3 into full production. Tesla bet its financial future on the newly minted Model 3, the $35,000 consumer car that it expected to produce in great volumes. Demand for the product has been outstanding, with over 600,000 consumers lining up to give the company a deposit of $1,000.

Chief executive Elon Musk promised by the end of the year to have the company churning out 5,000 Model 3s per week, but production delays derailed the company greatly. Tesla has now discovered that moving from production of the low-volume Model S to the high-volume Model 3 is substantially harder than expected. Far from humming along at 5,000 units per week, Tesla produced just 1,550 Model 3 vehicles in the entire fourth quarter, goading Musk into making predictions of a brisk 2018 comeback.

The first quarter, however, has been anything but. Musk reduced his Model 3 production target to 2,500 per week, but in the first three months of the year the company is averaging just 750 units per week — off the new mark by 70 percent, and a mere smattering of the original 5,000 weekly unit prediction.

And then there is quality control. In an interview that Reuters conducted with nine Tesla factory workers, problems ranged from doors not closing, to missing interior trim, to water leaks and the like. Approximately 90 percent of the vehicles that do actually make it off the line are revealed to have quality problems in final inspection. Toyota quotes a defect rate of 10 percent. A report titled "Beyond the Hype" by JD Power opined that the vehicles were "not competitive" in the quality of build, and lacked "precision and attention to detail."

All of this, of course, leads to the question of what's next, and will the company make the turn. Financial pundits are beginning to seriously question whether it ever will. The recent quarterly posting brings the company's lifetime losses to $5.7 billion, underscoring the often-overlooked fact that the company has never turned a profit. Add to it the fact that the losses have increased quarter-over-quarter for nearly the company's entire twelve-year existence, and legitimate concern is more than justified.

Presently, Tesla has $2.7 billion of cash on hand, but with quarterly losses nearing the $1 billion mark, the stockpile will evaporate like water on hot Arizona asphalt. Musk has stated that Tesla will achieve full GAAP profitability in Q3 and Q4 of this year, but with so many broken promises the chief executive's predictions are now being taken as salesman-life puffs.

Students of history will recall when Musk famously pronounced that the company would hit profitability by 2016. One has to admire his optimism, but high hopes will never be sufficient to overcome industrialized realities. To put the problem into context, Bloomberg conducted an analysis that in 2017 — the year after Musk promised profitability — the company torched $480,000 every hour of the day during the 12-month period.

In stark contrast to Musk's promise of 2018 profitability, Moody's predicts that the company will have to hit up investors for another $3 billion in cash to stay solvent. Tesla already owes $10 billion in long-term and convertible debt, with required interest payments of $230 million in November and $920 million in March 2019. Add to that lagging Model 3 production, and there is little reason to believe that the company can survive without massive, and perhaps multiple, cash infusions. For its part, Moody's has downgraded the company's debt into junk-bond territory.

Others are equally concerned. In 2017, Tesla stock hit the dizzying price of $390 per share, yielding a market cap that actually exceeded that of goliaths GM and Ford, which in itself is miraculous. The company that has never turned a profit, and struggles to make 750 cars per week, was actually more valuable than a 100-year-old car manufacturer that produces 10 million cars per year.

But with its recent public filings, market support is all but evaporating. Its stock has fallen some 25 percent to its current $300 value, and many believe that is just the beginning. Goldman Sachs predicts that Model 3 production will even out at 1,400 units per week, and is pinning its year-end stock price at $195. Goldman believes that cash calls will be made as soon as the third quarter of the year, and is encouraging its clients to place sell orders.

JPMorgan sees a 40 percent price deterioration, pegging the stock at $180 per share. As JPMorgan analysist Ryan Brinkman stated, "Tesla will face several milestones in 2018 relative to the ramping of production of the Model 3, which we believe will be difficult for the company to meet."

The net of all this is that Tesla has achieved yet another descriptive tag: the most shorted stock in America. According to financial analysists S3 Partners, in April the dollar amount of shares shorted on Tesla increased 28 percent to $10.7 billion.

With the smart money on the street betting against a Tesla comeback, one has to wonder if the bloom has finally been knocked off the rose. And with market confidence at an all-time low, will Musk be able to continue borrowing his way out of trouble? His dance to the horizon has been dotted with broken promises, and this very well may be where the needle gets taken off the record.

CHAPTER 98

Driving to Recessionary Times

JUNE 2018

As a society, we tend to have short memories, or in some cases, no memories at all. It is difficult to imagine, but 2018 will usher in a new class of young millennials who are, for the most part, complete strangers to the Great Recession. 2009 marks the year they first learned of Justin Bieber, not the year they lost their job, their home or their family.

It should be no surprise then that our nation is spending with perceived immunity. Automotive juggernaut Edmunds reports that there are now 1.26 vehicles on the road for every licensed U.S. driver, the highest the nation has ever had. Yet, times are beginning to cool, and with it the economic suffering will come. The U.S. Federal Reserve reports that car loan delinquencies have already grown to $23.3 billion, the highest level since 2008. And it is about to get worse.

In 2016, U.S. auto sales hit an all-time high of 17.5 million units. This number has been on a decline since then, however, with a 2018 prediction of 16.8 million units. Fewer car sales mean that automakers will begin to idle workers and shutter non-essential factories. General Motors dropped shifts at five plants since last autumn, Ford laid off thousands of workers due to shutdowns in May, and Nissan just announced that it is cutting U.S. production by 20 percent.

None of this should come as a surprise, as we have enjoyed nine years of straight economic growth. To be sure, recessions like to loom in the corner, repeating themselves with unwelcome regularity. From 1945 to 2008, periods of economic expansion have lasted an average of 57 months, putting our 108-month recovery far past the outer edges of a recessionary cycle. We are very past due.

Superficially, recessions are difficult to understand. As the population grows, so does the need for goods and services, which increases national output, or GDP. The increased economic activity causes businesses to employ more people, giving rise to increased household income. More money to spend only pushes the needle further into economic health, begging the question of why would it ever end?

The trouble comes in when markets become oversaturated with goods and services, as profiteers rush to capitalize on the increased demand. Consumers can only buy so many new refrigerators, televisions and cars, and when the desire for consumption fills, demand falls. In an effort to remain profitable, employers begin to reduce salaries and lay off workers, and downward the economy begins to go.

It is no surprise then that there have been 49 recessions in our country's history, returning every few years with unwelcomed regularity. Academically, a recession is defined as two consecutive quarters of negative GDP. The National Bureau of Economic Research — the largest economic research team in the U.S., and the organization formally charged with announcing the start of a recession — puts a finer point on the discussion. The NBER defines a recession as: "A significant decline in economic activity spread across the economy, lasting more than two quarters which is 6 months, normally visible in real GDP, real income, employment, industrial production, and wholesale-retail sales."

Currently, the nation's GDP is stagnated at 2.3 percent. While this is far from negative growth, GDP has been on a steady decline since 2014, when output stood at a high of 5 percent. While not necessarily indicative of what will happen this go-around, it is interesting to note that in the second quarter of 2008 GDP had also fallen to 2 percent, before plummeting to negative 8.2 percent later that year.

Equally concerning is the current status of the crude oil market. According to the Federal Reserve, "a big increase in oil prices has preceded nearly every U.S. recession since World War II." In January 2016, crude oil traded at $30.24; today it stands at $64.68 — an increase of 115 percent. To put this into perspective, in January 2007 crude traded at $72.31, and by June 2008 it climbed to $160.95 — an eerily similar increase of 120 percent.

Perhaps the biggest worrier of them all is the Consumer Price Index (CPI), the price paid by consumers for a basket of goods and services. According to the U.S. Department of Labor, the CPI is currently hovering at 251 points — the highest mark since the start of the Index in 1950. This, of course, means that we are paying more for goods and services than at any time since the end of the second World War, including adjustment for inflation.

To give an example, consider that the average price of a new car today is $36,270, a figure that has risen year-over-year for generations. Putting this into perspective, a new car in 1980, after adjusting for inflation, cost an average of $21,372, about 42 percent less than today.

Our housing market has also exploded, albeit not with the vertical trajectory of the 2000s. This expansion has been wearing sneakers, quietly advancing on us without much attention. The Composite Home Price Index shows that single-family home prices, adjusted for inflation, have finally reached dizzying 2007 levels. Said another way, when folks talk about how overheated the housing market was in 2007, the same statement applies to the market today. Housing is at an all-time national high.

The time has come for an economic chill. Too many indicators suggest that the recovery has moved on, and that the nation will soon experience a constricted economy. Fortunately, downturns typically mirror the expansions they follow, and if true, the next recession should be about as mild as the recovery we recently experienced.

For big thinkers, news of a downturn is not all that bad. As Warren Buffet famously said, "be fearful when others are greedy, and greedy when others are fearful." For those positioned correctly, and immune to the panic of it all, the downturn will be a land of opportunity, where fortunes will be made and lost in a New York minute.

CHAPTER 99

Investor's Paradise

JULY 2018

If one were to take a guess as to the strongest asset class for investment, considerations such as fine art, rare wine or blue-chip stocks might come to mind. Investment banking powerhouses across the country have long had client portfolios chocked-full of traditional-based instruments, all confident that the strategies will yield handsome returns. Yet, the starlet of the investment stage is not precious stones, rare coins or even Big Board stocks — it is a heroine of a different breed, and one that might surprise many: classic cars.

Ten years removed from the chill of the frozen economy, investment strategies are beginning to become clear. Rare watches have appreciated 65 percent; fine art has appreciated 130 percent; and precious jewels 147 percent. The Dow Jones has yielded an impressive 215 percent return. However, these returns pale in comparison to the 404 percent return the collector car market has achieved during this same time period.

Classic cars as investments have become so significant that the Dow has created the "Dow Jones Investment-Car Index," a comparison of 50 collector cars and their results over a 10-year period. In fact, German bank Suedwestbank AG is recommending that its high net worth clients add collector cars to their investment portfolio, noting that the investment class has significantly outstripped Germany's main stock index, the DAX.

If there is any question on this point, consider the Ferrari 250 GTO. In 1962, when the car first was first introduced, it had strike price of $6,000. By 2004, GTOs were trading at $10 million, and six years later — at the height of the recession — the Italian machines were crossing the block at $26 million. If that sounds incredulous, consider that by 2014 GTOs had climbed to $38 million, and just last month, a "Gran Turismo Omologata" (the full name of the GTO) sold for an eye-popping $70 million. To put this into context, the highest price ever paid for a Rembrandt was $33 million, paid for the 1658 masterpiece "Portrait of a man, half-length, with his arms akimbo."

If the Ferrari 250 GTO sounds like an anomaly, it is not. In 2013, RM Auctions sold a Ferrari F50 for $800,000. In 2017, the auction house sold essentially the same car for $3.1 million. And if Ferraris have stolen the show, Porsches have taken the whole darn auditorium. In the last 10 years, classic Porsches have increased an astonishing 683 percent. What is particularly significant about this is that, unlike Ferraris which have become stratospheric in their pricing, classic Porches are still relatively affordable.

Endearingly dubbed the "poster effect," children of the 1970s and 1980s who have now hit full earning potential stride are buying the cars they had posters of when they were kids, and the market reflects it. Porsche 911s from the era are becoming scarcer than a sunny day in Seattle, and muscle cars are not far behind. The Dow Jones Investment-Car Index reports that the 1970 Plymouth Hemi 'Cuda has a 10-year increase of 500 percent.

What is particularly interesting is the resiliency the market has had through challenging times.

Take for instance the 1958 Ferrari California, the car made famous as the Ferris Bueller car that suffered a fateful ending.

411

In 2005, the average price was $1.5 million. By 2015, 10 years later, the average price had climbed to $14 million, an 850 percent increase — and this is through the recession. In fact, according to WMG Advisors, collector cars are the only asset class that that actually rose in 2008, when all other assets were in a freefall.

The market is so stimulating that even the Vatican is getting in on the game. In 2015, the sovereign nation sold the Pope's Enzo Ferrari for $6 million, and last year the Supreme Pontiff's Lamborghini Huracan sold for $1 million — the proceeds of which were donated to charity.

Next month will mark the 68th annual Concours d' Elegance — a gathering of the world's most important collector cars on the famed Pebble Beach golf links. The weekend is dotted with champagne parties at spectacular seaside mansions, put on by Rolls Royce, Aston Martin and the likes for their special clientele; but the stars of the weekend are the elite collector car auctions that attract collectors — and investors — from around the world.

The auctions are a sight to see, attracting a sub-culture of pedigreed car collectors who most were unaware even existed. Registered bidders come from some 30 countries, with the intent of buying, selling or closely watching some of the rarest cars in the world. Last year, $328 million of collector cars were sold over the three-day weekend.

With numerous cars crossing the $1 million threshold, the Pebble Beach weekend marks one of the most explosive microcosms the world has ever seen. To put the event into context, consider that the auction houses fetch 10 percent of the transaction price from the buyer and the seller — $65 million for the weekend — and you start to get an understanding of the economics at play.

Last year, the star of the show was a 1956 Aston Martin DBR1 that sold for $22.6 million, followed by a 2016 Le Ferrari that sold for $7 million. The Le Ferrari sale was particularly interesting, given that the car sold new the prior year for $1.4 million, some $5.6 million less than the auction price. And demonstrating the pure mania of the day, another 2016 Le Ferrari sold for $10 million at an RM auction the following month. The market isn't even waiting for them to become classics.

If the retail side of the automotive industry has seen a return of confident buyers, the classic car industry has exploded with enthusiasm. With their million-dollar price tags, classic cars attract financial moguls who tend to be smart with their dollars. For those with the industry specific know-how, fortunes are there to be made in a New York minute in an industry that is bristling with hyperactivity.

CHAPTER 100

All Things
100

A U G U S T   2 0 1 8

On the continuum of life, 100 years is not a terribly large amount of time. In 100 years, a glacier will move 50 meters, a redwood tree will amass its full height of 200 feet, and the big island of Hawaii will grow by seven square miles. Those may seem like significant achievements, until it is remembered that it took 12,000 years to form Niagara Falls, 6 million years to forge the Grand Canyon, and 70 million years for the Indio-Australian and Eurasian plates to collide, creating Mt. Everest.

In the turn of a centurion mark, the Great Pyramid of Giza was erected and the immortal faces of Mount Rushmore were carved, but world evolution only marginally advanced. It simply takes time for monolithic changes to be made. In the language of evolutionary development, 100 years is a mere blip.

Societies are no different. Julius Caesar roamed the land some 2,100 years ago, and notwithstanding sustained periods of famine, conflict and drought, it took until the year 476 for the Roman Empire to collapse. Changes in the imperium created by King Rolumus occurred at a plodding rate. The same can be said of the Ming Dynasty, the Windsor Monarchy and Imperial Japan — they all rose, and fell, at an exceptionally steady pace.

If societal evolution is a concept of linear advancement, it is rather odd then that in the last 100 years, life has progressed at such an exponential clip. It is almost as though civilization advanced one teaspoon at a time, until the last 100 years, when progression came raining down in industrial-sized buckets. For thousands of years, horseback and boating were the only appreciable modes of transportation; today we blast into space with such regularity that it is hardly seen as newsworthy. Times when people marveled at the invention of the locomotive have been replaced with military fighters that transgress the globe at Mach 6 speeds.

Just how far have we advanced in 100 years? In 1918, women couldn't vote, sit on a jury, hold a professional license or even open a bank account in their own name. It wasn't until the following year when the 19th Amendment was passed, that women finally began to have appropriate standing in society, yet even then it was at a dreadful pace. Women could finally vote, but until the Equal Credit Opportunity Act of 1974, it was perfectly legal for banks to refuse to issue credit cards to women solely because of their gender. Incredibly, women could not even gain full admittance to Harvard, Dartmouth, Yale, Columbia, Brown and Princeton until the Jimmy Carter era, when total gender integration finally occurred.

In 1918, lifetime health was anything but expected. Ninety-five percent of all births took place at home, and life expectancy was a mere 39 years — largely believed to be the result of the Great Influenza Pandemic, a plague that ripped through the borders, killing 50 million people globally. Vaccinations, of course, had not been invented, and if parents wanted a family of four, they often saw the wisdom of starting with a family of five.

Even the simplest of things were not offered as given. Our nation did not have minimum wage, only eight percent of homes had phones, there was no Mother's Day or Father's Day, and it was not until March 1918 that Congress passed the

Standard Time Act, the law which established time zones throughout the U.S. Prior to that, 6 a.m. was 6 a.m., everywhere.

1918 also saw the formation of the 18th Amendment, a constitutional ban on the sale, manufacture and transportation of alcoholic beverages. It was still legal to drink it, but get caught selling a glass of wine, and you would be marking off days inside a cell for quite some time. Citizens would have to wait until 1933 before enjoying an adult beverage that wasn't served by lawbreaking moonshiners.

Yet perhaps the most significant aspect of 2018 is that it marks the 100th anniversary of the end of World War I, the war that was sure to "end all wars." The great world conflict claimed 16 million lives (the Gulf War, by comparison, claimed 20,000), and resulted in the freeing of Poland, Estonia, Yugoslavia, Czechoslovakia, Hungry and Yugoslavia. The end of the war also paved the way for the Paris Peace Conference and the Treaty of Versailles, but it also created a void in Eastern European politics that allowed for the formation of the Union of Soviet Socialist Republics, the ironfisted regime that stood firm until December 25, 1991.

On a macro basis, the automotive industry propelled the U.S. to international supremacy without apology. In 1918, there were a mere 8,000 cars on U.S. highways, and a mere 144 miles of paved U.S. roads. But that year General Motors acquired the Chevrolet Motor Company of Delaware, and from that point forward, motoring would never be the same. It its 77-year reign as the largest automotive manufacturer in the world, GM brought us everything from front-wheel drive vehicles, to cars with turn signals, to in-dash AM/FM radios, continually challenging its competitors to innovate.

1918 also saw the creation of General Motors Acceptance Corporation, the automotive financing company that has since been renamed Ally Bank. GMAC was the origination of the consumer auto financing and dealer floorplan financing, both of which revolutionized the industry. Prior to that, consumers left to their own to figure out how to pay for vehicle, and dealers had little assistance in buying cars from the factory.

So, if the last 100 years have caused the development curve to vertically skew, what can we expect over the next 100? Ask 50 people, and you will get 50 different answers, but some public thinkers predict that life expectancy will hit 150 years, colonization on other planets will have begun, we will have one world currency and we will forget how to drive.

For ages, all roads led to Rome. Society progressed one solid step at a time, with inventions occurring at a generational rate. Now, inventions occur faster than a presidential campaign, pushing us into areas that barely seem believable. Not so long ago, sending a written message to China took weeks to complete. Today, a six-year old with a smart phone can accomplish the task in less than a second. It is certainly an interesting time, and one can only wonder, what will the next 100 bring.

CHAPTER 101

Chapter 11,
Here We Come

S E P T E M B E R   2 0 1 8

There's no shame in a bankruptcy filing. The ability to discharge accumulated debt is one of the fundamental underpinnings of America's entrepreneurial system. While no one likes to lose out on repayment of a debt, the safety net provided by the U.S. Bankruptcy Code is what allows individuals to take risk, innovate and explore. Without it, the growth curve of our capitalistic society would suddenly flatten, as new ideas would be too risky to mine.

Some of our country's most notable businesses and statesmen were only able to reach their status through the use of the bankruptcy system. Before starting Disney, in 1923 Walt Disney filed bankruptcy with his first film company; Henry Ford put his first car company into a reorganization in the early 1900s, after it only produced 20 cars; and in 1875 H.J. Heinz filed bankruptcy when his first attempt at starting a condiments company failed to turn a profit. Even Abraham Lincoln was not immune from business failures, as his failed general store pushed him into bankruptcy in 1832.

If market positions persist, Tesla will likely be the next notable figure to use the Bankruptcy Code to save its future — or at least it should be. Seldom has there been a company that has created such an enormous market presence with such a disastrous financial reality. At present, Tesla has a market cap of $45 billion, making it more valuable than the 115-year-old Ford Motor Company that is valued at $37 billion, and just behind General Motors which is worth $48 billion.

The fact that Tesla, which produced 100,000 cars last year, can even be mentioned in the same sentence as Ford and GM is in itself a supernova of a miracle. GM, a company that produces 10 million cars per year, could misplace 100,000 cars and not realize it for six months. The disparity in production is just that large.

But it is Tesla's continual inability to turn a profit that should be worrisome to all. So, what is the face-the-brutal-facts reality? In 15 years of operation, Tesla has never managed to turn a profit — or get even close to it. In 2013, its best year, Tesla lost $74 million; last year, it lost $2 billion. In the first quarter of 2018, it lost $784 million; and in the second quarter, it lost another $520 million. In its lifetime, it has amassed a total of $6 billion in accumulated losses.

Against this backdrop is its debt. As present, Tesla owes $9.4 billion in long-term debt, with required interest payments of $230 million in November and $920 million in March 2019. As of June 30, it had $2.2 billion of cash on hand, but at the present spend rate of $6,500 every minute, the company will burn through this like a young sailor on a weekend furlough. Moody's says the company needs another $2 billion to make it to the end of the year.

Elon Musk is banking on the newly minted Model 3 to salvage the company's future. At a price point of $35,000, the Model 3 was expected to be the high-volume product that would surge the company into profitability. But so far, the Musk's dreams of production lines humming along have been smashed by the anvil of supply chain reality.

Musk had promised that by the end of last year the company would be churning out 5,000 Model 3s per week. The results, however, were far from it, with the company producing just 1,550 Model 3 vehicles in the entire fourth quarter. Musk reduced his 2018 Model 3 production target to 2,500 per week, this too was far off. In the first three months of the year, the company averaged just 750 units per week.

Musk, who described the situation as "Dante's Inferno," blames the catastrophe on the failure of suppliers to timely deliver parts, and he is probably right. But managing supply chain deliveries is the essence of a manufacturing process. In large part, car manufacturers are assemblers of a myriad of parts produced by a patchwork of suppliers sprinkled throughout the world. A windshield wiper doesn't show up, and an entire assembly line can be idled for weeks.

According to Goldman Sacks, if the company continues to miss production schedules, it could need to raise $10.5 billion to make it through 2019. Bob Lutz, the person responsible for development of the Chevrolet Malibu, the Ford Explorer and the Dodge Viper, has been openly critical about Musk's inability to manage the company's costs, noting that he's been keeping Tesla going by returning to the capital markets for funding. "That may work one more time, and then he's going to run out of money again, and then he's cooked," Lutz said. 'At this rate, Chapter 11 is a certainty."

Tesla has been living on a sustained stated of market euphoria, supported in large part because it is the only viable electric car company in existence. But at some point, adrenalized enthusiasm is not enough, and economic fundamentals settle in. As a reality check on the harshness that markets can deliver, Ford — which raked in $7.6 billion profit last year — was recently downgraded by Moody's to a rating of Baa3, one notch above a junk bond rating.

So, what should happen? Tesla has a brand that is worth a thousand golden doubloons and a raving fanbase that is only surpassed by lovers of Apple. It is the right idea at the right time, seizing an opportunity that was missed by so many. But, the realities of supply chain management are too severe for the company to handle. Producing 50,000 Model S vehicles per year one thing; trying to pump out 500,000 Model 3s is a whole new frontier.

Tesla should file for Chapter 11 bankruptcy protection, disavow its heavy debt and emerge with a healthy balance sheet that can give the company a chance at success. In truth, the company needs a strategic partner who can fund its weighty infrastructure and who has large scale production knowledge. While a GM-owned Tesla would certainly take away much of the company's specialness, it would allow the company to remain buoyant, and even give it a chance to flourish.

Francis Ford Coppola managed to turn a $52 million estate into a sea of red ink, and Mike Tyson spent though a $400 million fortune, before they both filed for bankruptcy protection. Tesla's spend was a little more severe, but the protections are there still the same. The company can still save the day — and keep the specialness it created — by swallowing its pride and using the Bankruptcy Code as it was intended to be used: To shed debt and allow innovation to succeed.